Macroeconomics: An Irish and European Perspective

Anthony J. Leddin

and

Brendan M. Walsh

Macroeconomics

An Irish and European Perspective

Anthony J. Leddin
and
Brendan M. Walsh

Gill & Macmillan

Gill & Macmillan
Hume Avenue
Park West
Dublin 12
with associated companies throughout the world
www.gillmacmillan.ie

978 07171 5631 3

Designed by MPS Ltd
Printed by Rotolito Lombarda, Italy
Indexed by Cliff Murphy

The paper used in this book comes from the wood pulp of managed forests.
For every tree felled, at least one tree is planted, thereby renewing natural resources.

A CIP catalogue record is available for this book from the British Library

To
Sofia, Alana and Stephen
A.J.L.

The next generation:
Aoibhinn, Eliza, Sadhbh, Connie, Charlie,
Joey and Ruairi
B.M.W.

Preface

In the late 1980s, we believed there was a need for a book that allowed Irish students to study modern macroeconomic theory and policy based on data and illustrations from the Irish economy. The first edition of the authors' *Macroeconomy of Ireland* appeared in 1990, and our belief was vindicated by the feedback from students and colleagues. In response to popular demand, a second edition was published in 1992, a third in 1995 and a fourth in 1998.

We labeled the fifth edition, published in 2003, the 'EMU edition'. We pointed out that Ireland's entry into EMU and the adoption of the single currency in 1999 radically altered the Irish macroeconomy. Ireland could no longer exercise control over its interest rates and the demise of the Irish pound implied the loss of a separate national exchange rate, while fiscal policy would be constrained by the Growth and Stability Pact.

This new 2013 edition could be referred to as the 'Great Recession' edition. Ireland experienced an unprecedented property and construction bubble from 2002–2007. This was followed by a devastating crash in 2008. The result was a deep and prolonged recession and a return to high unemployment and emigration. As this book is published, the recession is by no means over, but it could be said that the economy has been through the 'eye of the storm'. There are grounds for believing that the worst of the crash is behind us and the prospect now is for a slow, gradual recovery.

Both the theoretical and descriptive content of this new edition have been thoroughly updated. It contains new material on short- and long-run macroeconomic models. These models are used to illustrate the possible adjustment of the Irish economy out of the current recession given the constraints of EMU membership.

A central aim is to provide Irish students with the theory and data they need to understand how the Irish economy functions within the euro area. We hope that our new edition will serve the current generation of Irish economics students just as well as the five previous editions of our book served earlier generations.

This new book contains numerous tables and diagrams, which draw extensively on data provided by the Central Statistics Office and other sources. We are indebted to Michelle Ahern, who worked for us as a research assistant and helped compile the tables and graphs used in this book. We are also indebted to Jennifer Banim of the Central Statistics Office for guidance on the balance of payments methodology.

This book was written during 2012 when one of the authors was visiting the University of Waikato, New Zealand, and the Red McCombs School of Business, University of Texas, USA. We are indebted to Bridget Daldy, Mark Holmes, Dan Marsh, Brian Silverstone and Michael Cameron in Hamilton, New Zealand, and Robert Prentice in Austin, Texas, for their hospitality and the facilities provided.

We would like to thank Marion O'Brien and Catherine Gough at Gill & Macmillan, and Jane Rogers who contributed in no small way to the completion of the transcript. As always, our greatest debt is to successive generations of students in our economic courses in Ireland, New Zealand and the USA who helped us improve the exposition of the theories and policies contained in this book. The authors alone are responsible for the views expressed herein and any remaining errors.

A.J.L., Plassey, Limerick
B.M.W., Dublin
February 2013

Contents

CHAPTER 1

Introduction to Macroeconomics

1.1 Introduction

There are two main branches of economics: *microeconomics* and *macroeconomics*.

Microeconomics is the study of how individuals and societies manage their scarce resources. It is based on the fact that we have unlimited wants and limited resources and we must make choices. Examples of the topics covered in microeconomics include:

- What is the level of output that maximises a firm's profits?
- How would a higher tax on beer affect its consumption?
- What are the economic returns to education?
- What happens to the consumption of oranges when the price of apples falls?

Macroeconomics, on the other hand, is concerned with the study of the economy as a whole. It deals with topics relating to economic growth, unemployment, inflation, international trade and exchange rates. The topics dealt with in macroeconomics seem quite different from those studied by microeconomists. Examples of macroeconomic topics are:

- How long will the current recession last?
- Why is there unemployment?
- Do economies automatically revert to full employment?
- What are the costs of high inflation?
- How can inflation be kept under control?
- What causes interest rates and exchange rates to fluctuate?
- Why are some countries rich and some poor?

Microeconomics and macroeconomics are interrelated. The millions of micro decisions made by households and firms translate into the macro aggregates.

The main goals of macroeconomic policy are:

1. Maintaining the economy close to its 'full employment' or 'potential' output path.
2. Avoiding the boom–bust instability that is a recurrent threat in modern economies.
3. Combining full employment with price stability or a low inflation rate.
4. Adopting policies that promote increased productivity and long-term economic growth.

We will return to these themes throughout this book.

1.2 The Irish Macroeconomy

In Table 1.1 we use the latest available data and estimates to provide a picture of the Irish economy in 2012. The table presents data on many of the key variables that are discussed in detail in later chapters.

TABLE 1.1 The Irish economy in 2012

Population (000s)	4,585.4
GDP at current market prices (€ million)	163,150
GDP per capita (€)	35,580
Real growth rate in 2012 (%)	1.8
GNP at current market prices (€ million)	126,300
GNP per capita (€)	27,544
Real growth rate in 2012 (%)	−0.2
Total labour force (000s)	2,159.1
Total at work (000s)	1,836.2
Agriculture, forestry and fishing (000s)	87.1
Industry (000s)	327.7
Services (000s)	1,421.4
Unemployment (000s)	323.0
Unemployment rate (%)	15.0
Net emigration (000s)	34.4
General government balance (€ million)	−13,305
General government balance (% GDP)	−8.2
General government debt (end-2012) (€ million)	191,900
General government debt (end-2012) (% GDP)	117.7
Balance of payments current account (€ million)	3,049.0
Balance of payments current account (% GDP)	1.9
CPI inflation rate (annual)(%)	1.8
End-year exchange rate: $/€	1.32
End-year exchange rate: £/€	0.82

Sources: Economic and Social Research Institute, Quarterly Economic Commentary, Autumn 2012; Department of Finance, Budget 2013

The concept of gross domestic product (GDP) measures the value of the total output of goods and services produced in the country over a calendar year. The related concept of gross national product (GNP) measures the value of the output accruing to Irish residents. A nation's output as measured by GNP is closely linked to its national income. The more the nation produces, the higher its income. In Chapter 2 we go into some detail to explain the differences between GDP, GNP and national income and why they are particularly important in Ireland.

Dividing by the population of Ireland in 2012 we obtain a figure of €35,580 for GDP per capita (or per person). This is a widely used indicator of the standard of living. GNP per person, on the other hand, was €27,544 – 22.5 per cent lower than GDP per person and this in the Irish context is probably a better indicator. Moreover, while real GDP grew by 1.8 per cent in 2012, real GNP actually fell by 0.2 per cent.

Table 1.1 shows the size and structure of the Irish labour force. It may be seen that while there were over 4.5 million people in the country, the labour force was just over 2.1 million and the number employed just over 1.8 million, so for every 100 persons in employment there were 150 people who were not working. These would include children, homemakers, pensioners and the unemployed. In Chapter 4 we discuss the importance of the ratio of the employed to total population in more detail.

It is a misnomer to call Ireland and other advanced countries 'the industrialised countries'. In Ireland, as in all modern economies, most people work in the service sectors. In 2012 over three-quarters of those in employment worked in services. Fewer than five per cent worked in the agricultural sector and the remaining 15 per cent were in various manufacturing and industrial sectors.

In 2012 in Ireland the unemployment rate was very high. Fifteen per cent of the labour force was classified as 'out of work'. Chapter 4 is devoted to a discussion of how unemployment is measured and the factors that determine the unemployment rate. We point out that the costs of unemployment to individuals and society are very serious. One of the key policy issues facing the Irish economy is how to achieve a substantial reduction in the unemployment rate.

By 2012 emigration from Ireland had once again become significant. It is estimated that in the year to April 2012, 87,100 people left Ireland to take up residence abroad. This was partially offset by an inflow of 52,700 people immigrating to Ireland, so the net outflow was 34,400. The net outflow of people from the country helps to keep the unemployment rate in check, but it is widely regarded as a symbol of economic weakness that so many of our young people have to leave in search of employment.

Ireland's public finances have seldom been out of the headlines since the start of the crisis in 2008. In Table 1.1 we show that there was a 'general government deficit' equal to 8.2 per cent of GDP in 2012. This measures the gap between tax receipts and government spending. (We explore the technical details behind this measure in Chapter 7.) Despite the corrective actions taken in successive budgets since 2008, this deficit is still unsustainably high. The level of borrowing incurred required to bridge the gap between spending and receipts has led to exponential growth in the country's debt in recent years. By the end of 2012 the government debt had reached 118 per cent of GDP, compared with only 25 per cent as recently as 2008. We are committed to bringing the deficit down to three per cent of GDP by 2015. This aim will drive the macroeconomic policy agenda over the next three years.

In Chapter 13 we discuss in some detail the significance of the balance of payments and how it is measured. Table 1.1 shows that the widely quoted current account, which records the balance of trade in goods and services with other countries, recorded a small surplus in 2012. The improvement in this balance since the onset of the recession has been one of the few bright spots in an otherwise gloomy macroeconomic situation.

Maintaining price stability is a goal of macroeconomic policy. The most widely used measure of a country's price level is the Consumer Price Index (CPI) and the rate of change in this index is the most widely used measure of the inflation rate. In 2012 the annual average inflation rate was 1.8 per cent by this measure. In Chapter 3 we go into some detail on how inflation is measured and discuss the costs of high inflation.

Since 1999 Ireland has not had a separate national currency. In that year we 'irrevocably' fixed the exchange rate of the old Irish pound to the newly launched euro. In 2001 the euro was introduced as an actual currency. Since then we have shared it as a common currency with the other members of the euro area. But we still trade heavily with the UK and the USA, which are outside the euro area. The exchange rate between the euro, the dollar and the pound are extremely important influences on the Irish economy. The final entry in Table 1.1 shows that a euro was worth $1.32 and £0.82 at the end of 2012. One prediction that we make with confidence is that by the time the student is reading this book these rates will have changed. However, although we discuss the theory of the foreign exchange market in detail in Chapters 13 and 14, we cannot provide any clues as to whether the euro is likely to grow stronger or weaker against other currencies over the coming year.

1.3 Political Economy

Macroeconomic issues are never far from the front pages of the media. As a consequence the outcome of elections is strongly related to economic performance as the electorate tends to blame the politicians when things go wrong and vote for them when times are good. Table 1.2 shows the

TABLE 1.2 How the macroeconomy affects election outcomes

	Unemployment	Inflation	Comment	Election outcome
1973	5.7%	10.0%	Relatively low U but high π	FF lose, FG + Lab returned
1977	8.8%	16.7%	Increase in both U and π	FG + Lab lose, FF returned
1981	9.9%	21.0%	Increase in both U and π	FF lose, FG + Lab returned
1982 Feb	11.4%	18.9%	Another increase in U and π still high	(Feb): FG + Lab lose, FF returned
1982 Nov	11.4%	18.9%	No change in high U and π	(Nov): FF lose, FG + Lab returned
1987	16.9%	3.4%	U much higher but significant decrease in π	FG + Lab lose, FF returned
1989	15.1%	3.3%	Both U and π slightly lower	FF + PDs win
1992	15.3%	3.0%	Little change in both U and π	FF + Lab win
1994	14.7%	2.4%	U still high and slight decrease in π	FF lose, FG + Lab + DL win
1997	10.3%	1.5%	Improvement in both U and π	FG + Lab + DL lose, FF + PDs win
2002	4.4%	4.6%	Significant improvement in U but increase in π	FF + PD win
2007	4.6%	4.9%	Little change in either U or π	FF + GP + PD win
2008	6.3%	4.1%	Increase in U and little change in π	FF + GP win
2011	13.5%	−0.9%	Significant increase in U and deflation	FF + GP lose, FG + Lab win

unemployment rate (U) and the inflation rate (π) at the time of elections in Ireland from 1973 to 2011. In general, when unemployment and inflation are increasing the incumbent party or coalition does not get re-elected. The one year this was not the case was in 1997 when, despite a fall in both unemployment and inflation, the coalition of Fine Gael, Labour and the Democratic Left lost the election. Once Fianna Fáil retained power in 1997, they rode the favourable economic tide and won each of the following elections up to the crash of 2008. As unemployment soared and inflation turned into deflation in 2009, Fianna Fáil lost the 2011 election. The party managed to retain 20 seats compared to 77 seats in the previous election. There does appear, therefore, to be a strong link between economic performance and election outcomes.

While the electorate are quick to blame politicians for economic outcomes, we should note that the degree of involvement of politicians in the economy varies greatly across countries. At one extreme, in a fully planned economy all productive resources are owned by the state, and the use of all the country's economic resources is centrally planned. North Korea is one of the few remaining examples of an economy run along these lines, but in the past the Soviet Union and People's Republic of China were organised as centrally planned economies.

In a 'mixed economy' productive resources are mainly privately owned and the allocation of resources is mainly left to the price system and the profit motive. Nonetheless, in most modern economies, including Ireland, the state owns many productive assets and raises taxes to provide many key services such as health and education as well as to support the incomes of pensioners and the unemployed. Developed economies differ significantly in the degree of state involvement and state control over resources. At one end of the spectrum are countries like Hong Kong and Singapore, where a *laissez-faire* philosophy prevails and state involvement in the economy is fairly low. At the other end of the spectrum are countries like Norway, Sweden and Denmark, where the state directly or indirectly controls well over half of GDP and there is a very highly developed welfare state. In France the state is very *dirigiste*, guiding and directing the productive sectors of the economy to a degree that would be unacceptable in the USA.

An intense debate rages about the proper role for the state in a modern economy. This was vividly illustrated during the 2012 US presidential election. The Republican Party espoused 'right-wing' anti-state positions, arguing for cuts in taxes and lower public spending, while the Democratic Party argued the case for higher taxes and maintaining public services. The electorate endorsed the Democratic ticket, but the fiscal problems facing the country remained unresolved after the election and these divisions continue to hinder an agreement on how to close the gap between tax receipts and public spending.

1.4 Macroeconomic Constraints

The main objective of macroeconomic policy is to achieve an increase in real (inflation-adjusted) output or GNP, low unemployment and low inflation. As a rough rule of thumb, a soccer formation of four-four-two would not be terribly wide of the mark. An economy growing by four per cent per annum, with unemployment around four per cent and inflation close to two per cent could be said to be performing very satisfactorily. It is difficult to achieve all three objectives simultaneously. Economists draw attention to the existence of trade-offs; that is, the way in which society has to sacrifice one objective to attain another. For example, it is often argued that reducing income inequality entails sacrificing or accepting a low rate of economic growth. Similarly, low unemployment may be bought only at the expense of high inflation. Squeezing high inflation out of the system may require undergoing a period of high unemployment.

It is clear that in 2012, while inflation was at an acceptably low rate (1.8 per cent), the Irish economy was not performing well on the unemployment and growth criteria. An unemployment rate of 15.0 per cent is unacceptably high and the economy is clearly growing too slowly to restore full employment in the near future.

Due to the fiscal crisis besetting many countries, including Ireland, policy-makers are finding it hard to reconcile their desire to win votes by stimulating the economy with the need to balance the books.

From time immemorial sovereigns and governments have found it hard to live within their means. They have always been tempted to run deficits, allowing spending to run ahead of tax revenue. This is particularly true in times of recession when output is stagnant, unemployment rising and tax receipts falling.

We noted that due to Ireland's recent fiscal deficits the general government debt has risen at an unsustainable pace. An increasing share of GDP has to be raised in taxes to pay interest payments on Irish government bonds. With a growing proportion of tax receipts earmarked for debt service, the government's ability to spend in other areas, such as education or job creation, is increasingly constrained. As a result we are now in the unpleasant situation where higher taxes are being imposed on the public not to finance badly needed improvements in our health and education systems, but simply to honour commitments to our creditors.

Ireland faced this dilemma in the 1980s. Tough measures were imposed to restore balance to the public finances but it took several years before growth resumed and unemployment began to fall.

Unfortunately we faced the same scenario again in 2008. By 2010 the fiscal crisis was so acute that the government had to agree to a 'bail-out' by the Troika (European Central Bank (ECB), European Union (EU) and International Monetary Fund (IMF)) and signed up to an austerity programme that postponed the prospect of emerging from recession. The trade-off between restoring balance to the public finances and stimulating growth in income and employment is harsh.

1.5 Globalisation

Modern economic development has been closely linked to the rapid growth of international trade. The opening up of new global trading routes in the fifteenth and sixteenth centuries led to an explosion of trade between Europe, America and Asia. International trade grew even more rapidly with the development of steamships, the installation of a global telegraph network, the removal of tariff barriers to trade and the spread of the Gold Standard, which facilitated international commerce. By the end of the nineteenth century the world economy had become highly integrated and countries round the globe were closely linked through trade. This first great wave of globalisation was interrupted by the growth of protectionism early in the twentieth century and then by World War I and the economic instability of the 1920s, which culminated in the Great Depression of the 1930s.

However, the international financial system was rebuilt after World War II and free trade was gradually re-established. Facilitated by ever-cheaper communications and transport, international trade grew very rapidly between 1950 and the end of the twentieth century. The rise and spread of the Internet, since it was launched in the 1980s, was only the latest in a series of technical advances that have spurred international trade. The emergence of China as a major manufacturing base in the 1990s made us all aware of the new wave of 'globalisation', symbolised by the flood of new consumer products imported to Europe and the USA from formerly poor countries in Asia. The iPhone 5 contains numerous chips for radio frequency, flash memory, audio, camera, orientation, networks and Bluetooth. It is said to be 'made in China' although most of the value added derives from the Californian design and parts manufactured in Britain, Korea and Japan, as well as raw materials sourced in Africa.

High capital mobility is a feature of modern globalisation. Most large companies are now 'multinationals' and the world's financial markets are closely interlinked. Currencies, stocks and shares are traded on a twenty-four-hour basis round the world. Developments in one market are quickly felt at the other side of the world.

The globalisation of financial markets is also evident in the way companies steer their revenues and profits across international boundaries in order to minimise their tax liabilities. This has become a burning issue due to the revelation that, for example, the coffee shop chain Starbucks paid only $13.8 million in corporate income taxes since its establishment in the UK in 1998, despite having made $4.8 billion in sales over that period. This was done by complicated accounting procedures that minimised the profits reported in Britain, transferring them to the lower-tax Dutch location. Ireland benefits from this type of 'tax planning' because our low corporation profit tax rate encourages multinationals to locate here and to attribute a large share of their worldwide profits to their Irish subsidiaries. We discuss the issues raised by these practices in Chapter 13 and elsewhere in the book.

Although there are many barriers to the free movement of people, and anti-immigrant feeling is high in many countries, vast numbers of people move internationally in search of employment and a better life. This is another aspect of globalisation. We in Ireland are very conscious of this due to the exodus of young Irish people to the UK, the USA, Australia and New Zealand. But the flows from Ireland to the rest of the world are small compared, for example, to the vast numbers of Indians working overseas in booming Asian economies or of Latin Americans who work in the USA.

Economists think of modern 'globalisation' as a continuation of trends that have been going on since the late Middle Ages. They generally regard international trade and the specialisation that it promotes as major sources of increased prosperity, both for exporting and importing countries, for countries investing abroad and for those receiving inflows of capital. However, many non-economists fear that globalisation is a crude exercise in unbridled economic power by multinational companies leading to the spread of US economic dominance. These views are not very accurate. International capital flows are not all from the world's rich countries to poor countries. India and China are now major overseas investors. Even a small country like Ireland is home to several multinational companies, such as CRH, the Kerry Group, Glanbia, Paddy Power and Ryanair. On the other hand, brands traditionally associated with Ireland – like Guinness beer and Jameson whiskey – are owned by multinationals whose headquarters are outside Ireland.

The British car industry has been revitalised by inflows of investment by foreign companies. Rolls-Royce is now owned by the German company BMW, cars as symbolically British as Jaguar and Land Rover are now made by the Indian Tata Group, while Nissan is the largest single producer of cars in Britain. These are all examples of how widespread and complex the phenomenon of globalisation has become.

1.6 Macroeconomic Models

Macroeconomic models attempt to summarise how complex economies operate. They focus on interrelationships between key macroeconomic variables such as income, employment and inflation. Irrelevant details are stripped away. The purpose of building such models is to help policy-makers understand how instruments – such as government spending and taxation or interest rates – affect outcomes such as the levels of unemployment and inflation. We describe a number of macroeconomic models in this book.

Macroeconomic models need microeconomic underpinnings. These take the form of assumptions about how markets behave. The most prevalent assumption in economics is some variant of the idea that prices are flexible and quickly adjust to equate supply and demand in all markets. This happens because excess demand causes prices to rise and the market clears, and excess supply causes prices to fall.

From a macroeconomic perspective a key issue is how quickly this process occurs, especially in the labour market. It is recognised that prices and wages tend to be 'sticky' or inflexible in the short and even medium term. They adjust only sluggishly in response to changes in supply or demand. This can be because firms and households have entered into fixed contracts and it takes time to adjust output prices as input prices change. The result is that excess supply is not immediately eliminated in all markets. This helps explain the persistence of high unemployment.

In the course of this book we repeatedly ask how long it takes for wages and prices to adjust to bring the economy back to full employment after the onset of a recession.

However, economists assume that in the long run there is complete flexibility of prices and all markets, including the labour market, clear. When this happens, the economy is producing its 'potential' level of output and unemployment is not a problem. However, one of the most famous sayings in economics is Keynes's dictum that 'in the long run we are all dead'. The question of how long it takes to return to this long run equilibrium after an economic shock remains a burning topic in economics.

Many of the chapters in this book discuss short- or medium-run macroeconomic models, but in Chapters 19 and 20 we summarise a model of the economy in the long run.

George Bernard Shaw noted that 'if all economists were laid end to end, they would not reach a conclusion'. Listening to economists on the airwaves or reading their views in print journalism, it is clear that disagreements and controversies persist. Economics is still a young discipline and each major event – such as the current recession – sheds new light on how economies function. Progress has been made and a measure of agreement has been reached among mainstream economists on certain key macroeconomic issues. The policy response to the crisis of 2008 in the USA was far more enlightened than what occurred after the crash of 1929. Although many European economies are still suffering from high unemployment and falling living standards, and the recovery in America has been anaemic, we have avoided the policy mistakes that led to the disastrous collapse of the world economy in the 1930s. Advances in macroeconomic theory deserve much of the credit for this.

1.7 The Development of Modern Macroeconomics

The roots of modern macroeconomics reach back to the seventeenth century. In the 1660s William Petty, who travelled in Ireland with Oliver Cromwell, laid the foundations for some key macroeconomic and statistical concepts, including national income accounting and the quantity theory of money. A century later, in 1758, François Quesnay published a *Tableau économique* (Economic Table), which outlined a model of the flows of economic activity and the value added by various economic sectors. In 1776 Adam Smith published *The Wealth of Nations,* which is probably the most famous book ever written by an economist. Smith devoted a lot of space to explaining why some nations were growing and becoming prosperous, while others remained poor and backward.

The economic crises of the early nineteenth century spawned a debate about what we would now call the business cycle. Robert Malthus and David Ricardo contributed to this debate and later in the century Karl Marx used some of their ideas to predict that macroeconomic crises would become worse and eventually lead to the collapse of capitalism. Some believed that this prophesy was being fulfilled when the crisis of the 1930s spread across the world.

It is fair to say that the pre-eminent macroeconomist of the twentieth century was John Maynard Keynes (1883–1946). From his early work on the economic consequences of the Paris Peace Treaty (1919) to his major work *The General Theory of Employment, Interest and Money* (1936) he set the agenda for modern macroeconomics. He focused on the causes of the business cycle and especially the near-collapse of the world economy in the 1930s. He argued for policies that would reduce unemployment and avert the deep recessions to which modern economies were prone. The last days of his life were devoted to helping design the 'Bretton Woods System'. This led to the establishment of the IMF and the World Bank and played a significant role in the rebuilding of the international economic system after the war.

In the 1950s the macroeconomic policies that Keynes advocated gained considerable influence, especially in English-speaking countries. The appeal of his theory lay in the way it seemed to show governments how to reduce unemployment without kindling inflation. Academic economists debated the foundations of Keynes's ideas, attempting to elaborate on his models and reconcile them with classical microeconomic theory. Paul Samuelson – the first American Nobel Prize winner in economics – wrote the first modern textbook of economics aimed at university students. He labelled his reconciliation of Keynes's ideas with the older orthodoxy 'the neoclassical synthesis'. This synthesis gained acceptance by the majority of economists.

However, during the 1960s a revisionist school of thought gained ground in economics. This grew from the debate between the Keynesians and the monetarists, whose intellectual leader was Milton Friedman, a professor of economics at the University of Chicago. This debate centred on the effectiveness of fiscal policy, which used government spending and taxation as policy instruments, relative to monetary policy, which used interest rates and exchange rates as instruments. The monetarists cast doubt on the idea that there is a trade-off between inflation and unemployment, which was a key tenet of Keynesianism.

In the 1970s, the classical counter-revolution gained ground. As economies began to experience stagflation (rising inflation and rising unemployment), scepticism increased about the validity of the Keynesian model and in particular the ability of macroeconomic policy to achieve lasting reductions in unemployment even at the price of higher inflation.

New and sophisticated versions of the classical model were being published that re-examined the older models of how expectations were formed by firms and households. The chief exponents of this new theory were the American economists Robert Lucas (who was awarded the Nobel Prize in 1995), Thomas Sargent (awarded the Nobel Prize in 2011) and Robert Barro. The 'new classical' or 'rational expectations' school of macroeconomics argued that there is no long-run trade-off between inflation and unemployment. Moreover, they argued that most of the existing macroeconomic models were of no help in evaluating the likely effect of policy decisions. We discuss various aspects of these debates in the main theoretical chapters of this book.

Although debate will always continue among academic economists, it is probably true to say that a new synthesis has now emerged that incorporates the post-Keynesian ideas of recent decades into the Keynesian framework. The main ideas that Keynes fought to introduce in the 1930s are now part of mainstream economics.

In an appendix to Chapter 3 we list the Nobel Prize winners in economics. The citations will give the reader an indication of the many directions economics has taken. But it is striking how many of these Nobel Prizes have been awarded for work based on Keynesian topics. A rough calculation suggests that about 15 of the 43 awards were made for work in macroeconomics and almost all of this was strongly influenced by Keynesian ideas.

While it is true that macroeconomics is only one of many fields in modern economics, it is probably fair to say that it is the most important one.

1.8 Key Terms and Concepts

In this chapter we outlined:

- the main topics that macroeconomic theory deals with
- the goals of macroeconomics, especially the goals of maintaining a high real growth rate, and keeping the unemployment rate and the rate of inflation low
- the manner in which macroeconomic policy is constrained by the need to maintain fiscal balance; that is, keeping government spending in line with the available tax receipts
- the difference between different types of macroeconomic models
- the development of modern macroeconomics.

Appendix 1.1 Study resources: the Irish economy

A wealth of statistical material and commentary on the Irish economy is readily accessible online. Students are encouraged to consult these sources to update the data contained in this book and to keep abreast of current macroeconomic developments and controversies.

STATISTICAL SOURCES

The starting point for anyone seeking data on the Irish economy is the **Central Statistics Office** (CSO) website: www.cso.ie/en/. The site is very user-friendly and students are encouraged to explore it. Here are some highlights:

- If you go to www.cso.ie/indicators/Maintable.aspx you will find a very useful set of graphs showing how some key economic indicators have been behaving over the past year.
- At 'Releases and Publications' you will find the latest releases for all the main economic and social indicators, grouped under headings such as 'People and Society', 'Labour Market and Earnings', 'Climate and Environment', 'Economy' and 'Business Sectors'.
- The tab 'StatBank (CSO Main Data Dissemination Service)' brings you to a comprehensive database that allows you to download in Excel format time series for hundreds of variables.

For more detailed financial and banking statistics, students should go to the **Central Bank of Ireland**'s website: www.centralbank.ie/Pages/home.aspx. Follow the link to 'Economic Policy and Statistics' and you will find a wealth of data relating to the Irish economy (naturally there is some overlap with series from the CSO site).

The **Department of Finance** makes available a great deal of information about the developing fiscal situation (including the latest exchequer returns) under the heading 'Financial and Economic Information' at www.finance.gov.ie/. This site also publishes summaries of the outcome of the reviews of the IMF/EU Programme.

The **ECB** has a very detailed range of financial and foreign exchange statistics for the whole of the EU on its website: www.ecb.int/stats/html/index.en.html.

Eurostat is the statistical office of the European Union and its website contains data for all member states. The site is a bit tricky to navigate, but it allows the student to download data on a variety of economic and social topics for 27 or more countries. See http://epp.eurostat.ec.europa.eu/portal/page/portal/statistics/search_database and http://ec.europa.eu/economy_finance/publications/european_economy/2011/pdf/2011-05-13-stat-annex_en.pdf.

Two other international sources are worth bearing in mind. The first is the **Organisation for Economic Co-operation and Development** (OECD), which maintains a database for all its member countries at www.oecd.org/document/0,3746,en_2649_201185_46462759_1_1_1_1,00.html.

The **IMF** provides a global database at www.imf.org/external/data.htm.

Finally, explore trends in a range of key variables (including income per capita and life expectancy) from countries all round the world at www.gapminder.org.

COMMENTARIES ON THE IRISH ECONOMY

The **Central Bank**'s commentaries on the Irish economy can be obtained at the site mentioned above: www.centralbank.ie/polstats/econpolicy/Pages/default.aspx.

The **Economic and Social Research Institute** (ESRI) publishes a summary of its Quarterly Economic Commentary at www.esri.ie/irish_economy/. This site also allows you to access its research publications on the Irish economy.

The **IMF** website has a section devoted to material relating to Ireland, including its reviews of the IMF-EU Programme: www.imf.org/external/country/irl/index.htm.

Since its launch in December 2008 the Irish Economy Blog (www.irisheconomy.ie/) has proved popular with a wide range of people interested in the Irish economy. For students it is a very valuable source for recent statistical releases, discussion papers, academic studies, and op-ed pieces.

On a broader playing field, the **VoxEU** site, www.voxeu.org/, provides a forum for 'Research-based policy analysis and commentary from leading economists'. This has been a very valuable source of analysis of the ongoing crisis in the Eurozone.

CHAPTER 2

National Income and Economic Performance

2.1 Introduction

This chapter is concerned with national product and national income, how it is produced and how it is measured. We summarise briefly some basic ideas about how the factors of production are combined to produce the output on which our living standards and income depend. We then move to a more detailed discussion of how national product and income are measured, using 2011 data for Ireland.

2.2 The Aggregate Production Function

A nation's output of goods and services (denoted by the symbol Y) is produced by the factors of production, particularly:

- labour
- physical capital
- human capital
- natural resources.

Physical capital refers to the stock of equipment and structures that are used to produce goods and services. This includes plant and machinery, buildings and so on. Physical capital makes workers more productive. The accumulation of physical capital has been one of the drivers of modern economic growth.

Human capital is the knowledge and skills that workers acquire through education, training and experience. Investment in education and skills has been another driver of modern economic growth.

Natural resources refer to the inputs into the production of goods and services that are provided by nature, such as land, rivers and mineral deposits. These can enrich a country when exploited in a sustainable way.

These inputs are combined together according to the available *technology*: the economy's application of science and know-how to producing goods and services. Better technology allows more to be produced from a given input of labour and capital. Waves of inventions, from the steam engine to modern computers, have been a major source of increased productivity and rising living standards.

The relationship between the factors of production and output is described by the aggregate production function:

$$Y = AF(L, K, H, N) \quad (1)$$

Where:

Y = output or GNP
A = the level of technology

L = labour
K = physical capital
H = human capital
N = natural resources
(all measured in physical units or quantities).

F( ) is a mathematical function (read as 'function of') that shows how the inputs (explanatory variables in brackets) are combined to product output (the dependent variable). As technology improves, high A will shift the whole production function upwards. More will be produced from a given level of inputs.

Returns to scale

A key characteristic of a production function is *returns to scale*. To illustrate what is meant by this concept, let us consider the following production function (we ignore technology and natural resources for simplicity):

$$Y_1 = F(K_1, L_1)$$

Now multiply all the inputs up by the same factor z, so that:

$$K_2 = zK_1 \text{ and } L_2 = zL_1$$

If $z = 1.2$, all inputs are increased by 20 per cent. Returns to scale tells us what happens to output as a result of the increase in the factors of production employed, $Y_2 = F(K_2, L_2)$.

- *Constant returns to scale* occurs if $Y_2 = zY_1$, that is, a 20 per cent increase in the inputs leads to a 20 per cent increase in output.
- *Increasing returns to scale* occurs if $Y_2 > zY_1$, that is if output increases by more than 20 per cent.
- *Decreasing returns to scale* occurs if $Y_2 < zY_1$, that is if output increases by less than 20 per cent.

Increasing returns to scale implies that as an economy grows bigger, output increases more rapidly than the inputs of labour and capital. Many modern industrial processes enjoy increasing returns to scale and this leads to rapid productivity growth as the size of firms increases. Firms serving global markets enjoy economies of scale that could never be achieved by firms confined to local markets.

Production functions with constant returns to scale have an interesting implication. Setting $z = 1/L$,

$$(Y/L) = AF(1, K/L, H/L, N/L)$$

Output per worker (Y/L), or labour productivity, depends on physical capital per worker (K/L), human capital per worker (H/L), and natural resources per worker (N/L), as well as the state of technology, (A).

Productivity

Productivity refers to the amount of output produced for each unit of input. Labour productivity can be measured as the amount of output produced per hour worked. If other inputs, such as capital, are also increasing, we need to measure 'total factor productivity', that is output adjusted for all the inputs that are used to produce it.

Increased productivity explains most of the variation in living standards over time and between poor and rich countries. Countries with high living standards (high output per capita) have higher productivity than countries with lower living standards. Improved technology as well as more capital has been the key to modern economic growth.

2.3 Measuring the Output of Nations

In the previous section we denoted 'output' as Y, without specifying what is contained in Y. In this section and the next we introduce some of technicalities of measuring national output and income in a modern economy.

Gross domestic product (GDP) is probably the most familiar concept in macroeconomics. (The relationship between GDP and GNP is explained below.) It is widely referred to in commentaries on how countries are performing. GDP is a measure of the total output of goods and services produced in the country over a period of time, usually a calendar year or quarter. The Irish Central Statistics Office (CSO) estimates that GDP in Ireland in 2011 was €159 billion. The population of Ireland was 4,588,3000 at the 2011 census, so in 2011 Irish GDP per person was equal to €34,652. This is the statistic that is almost universally used in international comparisons of living standards and economic performance. However, as we shall see later, it needs to be used with caution because it suffers from many limitations, and some of these apply with particular force to the Irish data.

NOTE: The source for most of the data in this chapter is the *National Income and Expenditure Accounts* (NIE) published by the CSO and available at www.cso.ie/en/media/csoie/releasespublications/documents/economy/current/nie.pdf.

The value of a nation's output is closely linked to the value of its income. If a person works harder at his or her job and produces more goods and services that are sold in the market place, their income should rise accordingly. The same is true at the national level: the more goods and services a nation produces, the more income it generates. GDP is therefore closely related to *gross national income* (GNI). The exact relationship between them is explained below.

The variation in GNI per person between countries is huge. However, care must be taken in making such international comparisons. Each country measures its national income in its own currency. Ireland uses the euro, the UK the pound sterling, the USA the dollar, India the rupee and so on. To obtain international comparability, the easiest approach would be to convert each country's national income to a common currency, usually the US dollar. But this suffers from the major drawback that the purchasing power of a currency within a country is often not accurately reflected in its exchange rate.

For example, the exchange rate between the Thai baht and the US dollar is about 31:1, but an American tourist in Thailand finds that 310 baht will buy a lot more *local* goods and services than $10 would in the USA. An evening meal, for example, would cost much less in Thailand than in the USA.

The poorest countries in the world are not as poor as is suggested by comparing their national income per person at market exchange rates. To get a truer picture of relative standards of living round the world it is common to use an artificial currency such as the purchasing power parity (PPP) dollar to adjust for differences in purchasing power. (We discuss the concept of PPP in detail in Chapter 15.) This is the measure we use in Table 2.1.

Table 2.1 shows GNI per person in international dollars for a selection of countries in 2011; the countries on the left are among the richest in the world and the countries on the right a mixture of middle income and very poor countries.

NOTE: The methodology behind measuring living standards in 'PPP dollars' was devised by the Irish statistician R. C. Geary (1896–1983), who in 1949 became the first Director of our CSO and went on to become head of the National Accounts Branch of the United Nations (UN) in New York (1957–1960) and founding director of the Economic and Social Research Institute (ESRI) in 1960.

TABLE 2.1 Gross national income (GNI) per capita (2011) in PPP terms

Country	GNI	Country	GNI
Norway	47,557	Brazil	10,162
USA	43,017	South Africa	9,469
Switzerland	39,924	Albania	7,803
Canada	35,166	China	7,476
Germany	34,854	India	3,468
Australia	34,431	Gambia	1,282
UK	33,296	Haiti	1,121
New Zealand	23,737	Congo, Dem. Rep	280

Note: This measures national income in 'constant 2005 PPP dollars'

Source: UN Human Development Index 2011 Ranking: http://hdr.undp.org/en/statistics/

It is clear that even when allowance is made for the differences in purchasing power within countries, there are enormous international differences in national income per person. Norway, the USA, Switzerland, Canada, Germany and Australia are among the richest countries in the world, and Ireland too belongs in the rich countries' club. In contrast, some of the poorest countries are to be found in Africa – Gambia, Congo, Kenya, and Ethiopia, for example – while Haiti and several countries in the Caribbean and Latin America are also very poor. Countries like Brazil, South Africa, India and China could be labelled fast-growing emerging economies.

Table 2.1 suggests that the average Norwegian is 170 times better off than the average resident of the Congo and 14 times better off than the average Indian. However, as we discuss in the appendix to this chapter ('Beyond GDP'), there are many reasons for treating these comparisons with some scepticism. They tend to exaggerate the true differences in economic well-being between countries. Nonetheless, the gap between the standard of living in the world's poorest and richest countries is huge.

It is important to emphasise that the national income per person measure (so widely used in international comparisons) is an average. Even in the poorest countries of the world there are wealthy families. For example, while average income in India is very low, it is estimated that it is home to more than 150,000 millionaires. For this reason, statisticians pay attention to the distribution of income, as well as to its average level, when comparing well-being across countries.

One measure of poverty is income of as little as a dollar a day. While this monetary value may have a bearing in the developed world, it can mean little in a less developed country where people are constantly seeking the basic needs of food and water from one day to the next. Statistics are never going to reflect the gap in welfare or the standard of living between today's rich and poor countries.

2.4 The National Income Accounts

In this section we give some details of the methodology that lies behind the measurement of domestic and national product. There are three basic approaches to measuring the nation's economic activity:

- adding up the expenditure on domestically produced goods and services
- adding up the income earned by the factors of production, principally capital and labour
- adding up all the output produced by the country's factors of production.

FIGURE 2.1 The circular flow of income

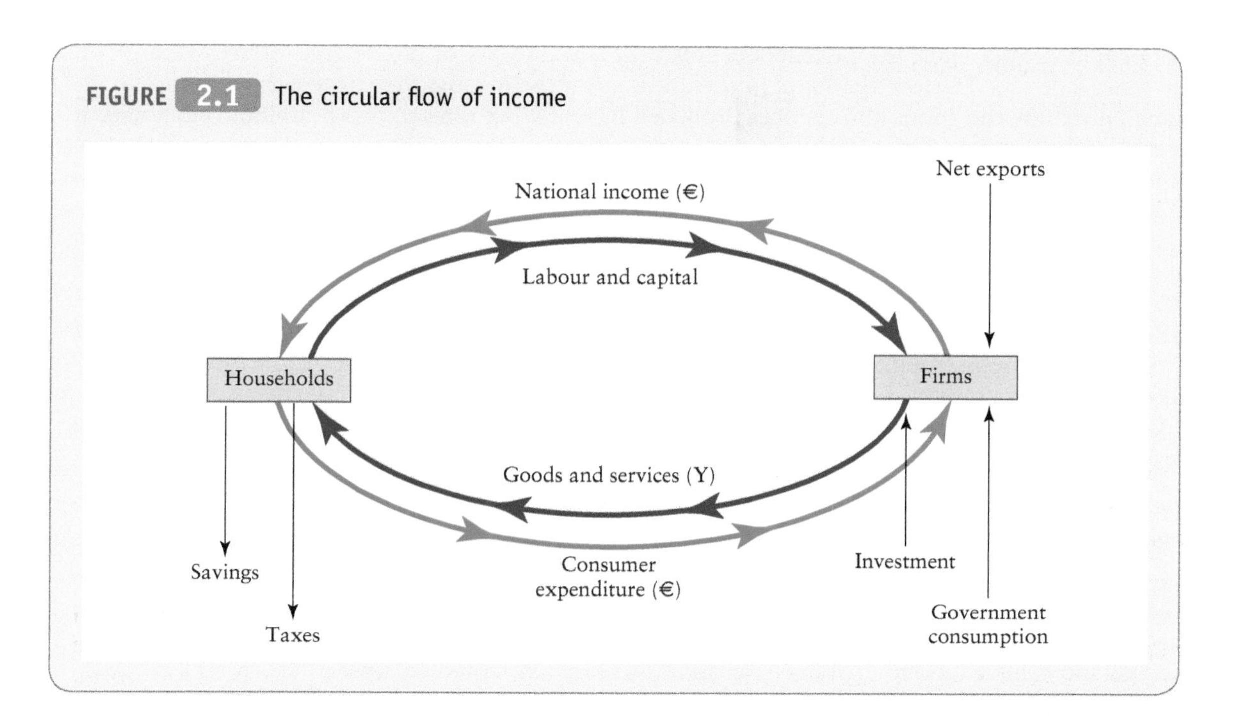

These approaches should yield the same total because every euro spent by a person or firm on Irish goods and services becomes income to an Irish resident. Put another way, national output is the source of national income.

We start by looking at the income and expenditure approaches. Figure 2.1 presents a simplified model of the economy as a circular flow of income. This model can be traced back to a court physician to Louis XV, François Quesnay (1694–1774). The modern version owes much to the work of John Maynard Keynes in the 1930s.

Initially, we assume that there is no government and foreign trade sector. We also assume that the price level is fixed or constant. These simplifying assumptions will be dropped later and the model elaborated to correspond more closely to the real world.

Due to these simplifying assumptions, there are only two kinds of economic agent in the economy: households and firms. Households own the factors of production: land, labour and capital (which includes not just physical capital such as machinery, buildings and natural resources but also human capital in the form of know-how, technology and institutional structures, e.g. the legal system). The diagram shows the flows between the sectors as two loops.

The factors of production – land, labour and capital – are made available to firms in return for payments of rent, wages, interest and profit. Wages are paid for the use of labour, rent for the use of land, interest for the use of capital, and the owners of firms receive profits. The sum of rent, wages, interest and profit equals national income.

NOTE: If we ignore rent, interest and profits, the two loops on the top of the diagram simply represent people going to work and receiving a salary or wage for their labour, which produces output that is sold to consumers.

Consider the two loops on the bottom of the diagram. Firms combine the factors of production to produce goods and services (GDP, denoted by the symbol Y). We just assume that inputs of land, labour and capital enter the production function, and outputs of goods and services emerge on the other side (Y). To close the loop, households, using the income they have earned (national income), purchase the goods and services produced by firms. We refer to this household expenditure as personal consumer expenditure (C). Given that the two loops on the bottom are equal, that is, expenditure equals output, it follows that:

$$Y \equiv C \tag{1}$$

where the symbol ≡ denotes an identity or something that is true as an accounting definition or identity. Personal consumption (C) is the value of all goods and services bought by households. It includes durable goods (goods that last a long time, e.g. cars and TVs), non-durable goods that have a short lifespan (food, clothing) and services (work done for consumers, e.g. dental and medical treatment, car repairs, restaurant meals).

Going a stage further, since all the money received by firms is passed on to households in the form of wages, rent, interest, and profit, total expenditure equals national income (NI). Hence:

$$NI \equiv Y \equiv C \tag{2}$$

The essential message of the simplified circular flow diagram given in Figure 2.1 is that, in the aggregate, we consume what we produce, and we spend what we earn. People go to work and get paid, and spend their income purchasing the goods and services produced by the firms for which they work. If there were a general strike, people would not go to work, they would not receive any income and firms would not produce output. The economy would collapse.

Saving and investment

We can now add two additional flows showing saving (S) and investment (I) to the diagram. Households do not spend all their income; they save some of it. This represents a leakage from the circular flow and is shown as the line pointing away from Households labelled Savings. Now given that people must either spend or save their income, it follows that the sum of consumer expenditure and saving equals NI. That is:

$$NI \equiv C + S \tag{3}$$

In the modern economy, household savings are channelled through the financial system (banks and building societies). This system is discussed in detail in Chapter 9. Firms borrow from the financial institutions in order to finance investment (I). Investment refers to firms' expenditure on new machinery and buildings. This implies that households do not buy all of the goods and services produced by firms; firms purchase goods and services from other firms. This is shown as the line labelled Investment pointing towards Firms.

Investment (I) is spending on capital goods that will be used to produce other goods – or provide a flow of services – in the future. It includes spending on plant and equipment (machinery), spending by households and landlords on housing units and offices, and inventory investment (or changes in stocks).

NOTE: Investment is the output of new capital in the course of a year. It is a flow. Suppose at the start of a year the Irish economy had €1,000 billion worth of capital and during the year investment goods worth €10 billion are produced: by the end of the year the capital stock of the economy will have grown to €1,010 billion (ignoring the depreciation of capital in the course of the year). The stock of capital at the end of year has increased by the new investment. The distinction between stocks and flows is very important. A *stock* is a quantity measured at a point in time. A *flow* is the quantity produced over a time period. A person's wealth is a stock, but a person's annual income is a flow. The level of debt is a stock, but the level of borrowing is a flow.

In this expanded model, total expenditure now equals consumer expenditure plus investment (there are two forms of expenditure). Substituting into (2), above, we obtain:

$$NI \equiv Y = \text{Total expenditure} \equiv C + I \quad (4)$$

This relationship states that NI equals Y, which in turn equals total expenditure. Total expenditure, in turn, is divided into households' consumer expenditure and firms' investment expenditure.

NOTE: Two components of 'investment' are listed in the NIE. The main one is 'gross domestic fixed capital formation'. It includes both private and government investment. The word 'fixed' tells us that changes in stocks are not included. A much smaller component of 'investment' consists of changes in the level of stocks. When firms run down their inventories or stocks to meet demand, this is like negative investment, whereas accumulating stocks is like positive investment. The NIE lists the 'value of physical changes in stocks' separately. The significance of 'gross' is that no allowance has been made for depreciation or 'capital consumption'. 'Domestic' investment takes place in the country. It excludes investment undertaken by Irish firms abroad.

The government sector

We now expand the circular flow of income model to include a government sector. The government affects the circular flow of income and expenditure because it levies taxes on households and firms and makes transfer payments to them under various social welfare schemes such as the state pension and the Jobseeker's Allowance. (Transfer payments are not made in return for any goods or services supplied. They are sometimes called benefits or entitlements.)

We denote the difference between taxes and transfer payments as net taxes (NT), which measures the net flow from households to government. Net taxes represent another leakage from the circular flow, shown in Figure 2.1 as the line pointing towards Taxes.

The government uses its net tax revenue to pay the people who work in the public sector and to purchase goods and services from private sector firms. These purchases are known as government current expenditure or public consumption, G. This is shown in Figure 2.1 as the line labelled Government expenditure pointing towards Firms.

At this point we have three types of expenditure on goods and services: consumer spending (C); investment (I); and government spending (G):

$$NI \equiv Y = \text{Total expenditure} \equiv C + G + I \quad (5)$$

NOTE: In the NIE accounts, government consumption (G) is called 'net expenditure by public authorities on current goods and services'. It does not include social welfare payments, national debt interest paid to Irish residents, grants to farmers and firms – which are transfer payments – or government investment spending, which is included in investment (I). Government consumption expenditure (G) amounted to 40 per cent of total government spending in the last decade, the remaining 60 per cent being transfer payments.

The foreign sector

Let us now consider the relationships between the rest of the world and the domestic economy. The output of Irish firms sold to non-residents is known as exports of goods and services (X). This is an additional source of income and stream of spending that must be included in the circular flow of income and expenditure. On the other hand, purchases by Irish households and firms from abroad constitute imports of goods and services (M) and must be deducted as a leakage from the circular flow.

So now we have four types of spending on Irish produced goods and services: personal consumption expenditure (C); government consumption expenditure (G); investment (I); and exports (X). However, the C, G, and I measures include spending on imported goods and services. If you buy a book imported from the UK it is included in C. Much of the capital equipment purchased by firms is imported from abroad. We need to deduct imports (M) from total spending to arrive at spending on Irish-produced goods and services.

If we subtract imports from exports we arrive at net exports, NX = X − M. This NX is the net demand for Irish-produced goods and services occurring in the 'foreign sector' of the economy. It is shown in Figure 2.1 as the line pointing towards Firms.

By adding up C, G, I and NX we obtain a measure of the total expenditure on the nation's output of goods and services. This is GDP, denoted by the symbol Y.

$$Y \equiv C + I + G + X - M$$

or:

$$Y \equiv C + I + G + NX \tag{6}$$

In Table 2.2 we present the estimates of gross domestic product (Y) for 2011 published in mid-2012. (These estimates are preliminary and will be revised over time.) It may be seen that the shares of private consumption (C), government consumption (G) and investment (I) in GDP are respectively 51 per cent, 16 per cent and 10 per cent of the total, which are all close to the corresponding EU averages. However, exports (X) and imports (M) amount to 105 per cent and 83 per cent of GDP respectively, which are among the highest in the world. The net exports figure, (X − M), is also exceptionally large relative to GDP, amounting to 22 per cent of GDP.

The output or value added approach

The output approach to measuring the value of domestic production concentrates on the value added at each stage of production. Value added is the difference between the value of a firm's output and the cost of the inputs it uses. We can illustrate this approach using a very simple example. Assume that only one good – a book – is produced in the economy. A sawmill produces timber, which it sells to a paper mill for €4. The value added at this stage is €4 (4 – 0). The paper mill uses

TABLE 2.2 Expenditure on GDP at current market prices, 2011

Symbol	Full description	€ million	As a % of total expenditure
C	Personal consumption of goods and services	81,308	51%
+ I	Gross domestic capital formation	16,112	10%
+ G	Net expenditure by public authorities on current goods and services	25,410	16%
	Physical change in stocks	227	
+ X	Exports of goods and services	166,791	105%
− M	Imports of goods and services	−131,875	−83%
	Statistical discrepancy	1,020	
equals GDP (Y)	GDP at current market prices	158,993	100%

Source: CSO, National Income and Expenditure Annual Results for 2011 (July 2012), Table 5

the timber to produce €7 worth of paper, which is sold to the publisher. The value added at this stage is €3 (7 – 4). The authors produce a manuscript (using no inputs except their own labour) and sell it to the publisher for €10. The value added by the authors is €10 (10 – 0). Finally, the publisher combines the paper and the manuscript and produces a book that is sold in the bookshops for €30. The value added by the publisher and distributors is €13 = (30 – [10 + 4 + 3]).

By summing the value added at each stage in the production process we obtain domestic output, which in this case is €4 + €3 + €10 + €13 = €30. Only one final product – a book – is produced and its value is €30.

The expenditure and income or value added approaches to estimating GDP in principle yield the same figure and could be used to cross-check the statistical accuracy of the estimates. In reality the information available does not allow both approaches to be completed independently and there are limitations to the accuracy with which the components of these flows are measured.

Gross national product (GNP)

GDP (denoted by the symbol Y) is a measure of the value of the total output of final goods and services produced in the country and the income to which it gives rise. However, not all of the income generated in producing this output actually stays in the country or accrues to people resident here. In Ireland a substantial outflow of money occurs because of the repatriation of profits by multinational firms operating here and the interest on externally held Irish national debt. The difference between inflows and outflows of this type is referred to as 'net factor income from the rest of the world' (F). When these are added to GDP we obtain GNP.

In Ireland in 2011, F amounted to a net outflow of €31,977 million. It therefore has to be entered as a *negative* number:

$$\text{GDP} + \text{F} = \text{GNP}$$

$$€159{,}000 - €31{,}977 = €127{,}023$$

In most countries the ratio of GNP to GDP is close to 100. It is 102 in the UK, 99.3 in the euro area and 100.7 in France. For this reason, GDP is often used and GNP ignored in international comparisons of living standards. But this is misleading for Ireland, where the GNP/GDP ratio is 80. GDP overstates by a significant margin the income actually accruing to Irish residents as a result of the output produced in Ireland. For this reason, it is preferable to use Ireland's GNP per person in international comparisons even when GDP per person is used for other countries.

If we divide Ireland's GNP by the population we obtain a figure of €27,683 for Ireland in 2011. This is a better measure of Ireland's standard of living than the GDP per person figure quoted earlier.

2.5 From National Product to National Income

National income measures the net value added by the factors of production. Traditionally these payments are classified as wages and salaries (payments to labour), rent (payments for the use of land and property), interest (payment for the use of capital), and profits, which can be thought of as a residual payment to entrepreneurs who take risks.

However, the data are not classified in exactly this manner in any table in the Irish NIE accounts. Instead income is broken down into two broad categories: agricultural income and non-agricultural income. The latter is then broken down into wages and salaries ('remuneration of employees'), profits and into several sub-categories.

These magnitudes are measured at 'factor cost' and not at 'market prices' as in the previous section. To give an example of the difference between factor cost and market prices, consider the example of a pint of beer. The market price of a pint of beer may be €4.00 in a pub, but indirect taxes (VAT and excises) account for about €2.00 of this. Only €2.00 goes to pay for the production and distribution of the beer. This €2 is paid to factors of production and enters into national income at factor cost. Hence the difference between market price and factor cost is the indirect taxes.

Only payments that actually go to the factors of production are included in national income at factor cost. Indirect taxes, T_i, like VAT and excise taxes levied on expenditure, are stripped out, while subsidies (S_u) that lower the price of goods and services below what they would otherwise be are added back in.

Table 2.3 shows how the CSO presents Irish national income. First, the sum of agricultural and non-agricultural income equals net value added at factor cost, NVA_{fc}. The fact that agriculture accounts for only three per cent of national income may come as a surprise. It is a long time since Ireland could have been characterised as an 'agricultural country'.

When net factor income from the rest of the world, F, is added to NVA_{fc} we obtain net national product at factor cost, NNP_{fc}:

$$NVA_{fc} + F = NNP_{fc}$$

To move from NNP_{fc} to NNP_{mp} we must add indirect taxes (T_i) and subtract subsidies (S_u).

$$NNP_{fc} + T_i - S_u = NNP_{mp}$$

TABLE 2.3 Irish net national income, 2011

		€ million	% of NNI_{fc}
	Income from agriculture, forestry, fishing	3,248	3
	Non-agricultural income of which:	125,201	
	Wages and salaries	62,450	65
	Profits	46,598	49
	Employers' contribution to social service	5,315	6
	Adjustment for stock appreciation	−620	
	Statistical discrepancy	−1,020	
NVA_{fc}	Net value added at factor cost	127,429	
F	Net factor income from rest of the world	−31,976	
NNP_{fc}	Net national product at factor cost	95,453	100
T_i	National indirect taxes	17,678	
S_u	National subsidies	640	
NNI_{mp}	Net national income at market prices	112,491	
GDP_{mp}	Gross domestic product at market prices	158,993	
D	Provision for depreciation	15,809	
NDP_{mp}	Net domestic product at market prices	143,184	
F	Net factor income from rest of world	−31,977	
NNP_{mp}	Net national product at market prices	111,207	
EU	EU subsidies less taxes	1,284	
NNI_{mp}	Net national income at market prices	112,491	

Source: CSO, National Income and Expenditure, Annual Results for 2011, Tables 1 and 7

This is usually referred to as net national income at market prices or just net national income (NNI):

$$NNI_{mp} = NNP_{mp}$$

Table 2.3 also shows the distribution in 2011 of national income at factor cost between the various categories. Sixty-five per cent of national income accrued to labour and another six per cent was paid as social insurance contributions, bringing the total to 71 per cent. This is very much in line with international experience. In the United States, labour's share in national income has been approximately constant close to 70 per cent over the post-war period.

At the end of Table 2.3 we travel back in the other direction and show how GDP is related to national income. If we start from GDP measured at market prices, we can derive NNI by first subtracting the allowance for depreciation (D) and then adding net factor income from the rest of the world (F) and EU subsidies less taxes. The identity is:

$$GDP_{mp} - D + F + EU = NNI_{mp}$$

It can be seen that NNI_{mp} amounts to only 71 per cent of $GDP_{mp,}$ due to the outflow of income abroad due to debt service and profit repatriation and the allowance for depreciation. NNP_{fc} equals only 60 per cent of GDP_{mp}. We emphasise yet again that these gaps are unusually large in Ireland due, in particular, to the size of the net outflow of factor payments to the rest of the world.

When estimating national income, the CSO starts by estimating agricultural income from data on crop production, etc. Non-agricultural income (wages and salaries, the income of the self-employed, profits, interest payments and rents) is estimated from data supplied by the Revenue Commissioners and other sources. These estimates of income form the basis of the GDP estimate. The expenditure figure is then reconciled with the income figure by treating personal consumer expenditure (C) as a residual. This may seem somewhat unsatisfactory as it means that errors in the measurement of other parts of GDP accumulate in C.

National disposable income

Deriving gross national disposable income (GNDI) follows much the same route as was followed in deriving NNI, but we do not subtract out depreciation. Table 2.4 starts with GDP_{mp}. As in Table 2.3, net factor income from the rest of the world, F, is added to obtain GNP_{mp} and then EU subsidies less taxes (EU) are added to obtain gross national income at market prices (GNI_{mp}). Finally, other transfers to and from the rest of the world (TR_{rw}) are added to obtain GDNI:

$$GDP_{mp} + F = GNP_{mp}$$

$$GNP_{mp} + EU = GNI_{mp}$$

$$GNI_{mp} + TR_{rw} = GNDI$$

We are now in a position to show how savings (S) fits into the NIE accounts. Household income is either spent or saved. Similarly, gross national disposable income (GNDI) is either consumed or saved.

$$GNDI = Consumption + Savings$$

Total consumption can be divided into two categories: personal consumption (C); and public or government consumption (G). Hence:

$$GNDI = C + G + S$$

Table 2.4 shows that personal consumption accounts for almost 65 per cent of GNDI, government consumption for another 20 per cent, leaving only 15 per cent for gross national savings.

TABLE 2.4 Gross national disposable income and its uses, 2011

		€ million	
GDP_{mp}	GDP at market prices	158,993	
plus F	Net factor income from rest of world	−31,977	
equals GNP_{mp}	GNP at market prices	127,016	
plus EU	EU subsidies less taxes	1,285	
equals GNI_{mp}	Gross national income at market prices	128,301	
plus TR_{rw}	Net current transfers from rest of world	−2,443	
equals GNDI	Gross national disposable income	125,858	
Uses of GNDI = C + S	**Consumption + Savings**		% of GNDI
C	Personal consumption of goods and services	81,308	65
G	Government consumption	25,410	20
GNS	Gross national savings	19,140	15
D	Provision for depreciation	15,809	13
NNS	Net national savings	3,331	3

Source: NIE, Annual Results for 2011, Table 7

Box 2.1 EU taxes and subsidies and transfers from the rest of the world

In the past, EU subsidies were relatively large because of the importance of the support to farm prices and other current subsidies received from the EU, but they have declined sharply in recent years while our tax contribution to the EU has increased.

Current transfers from the rest of the world include a variety of flows. Remittances to Ireland from emigrants living abroad were relatively large in the past, but nowadays there may be a net outflow under this heading as immigrants to Ireland send some of their savings back to their home countries. Money is also transferred from Ireland to the rest of the world in the form of overseas development assistance. This figure amounts to approximately 0.5 per cent of GDP.

When an allowance is made for depreciation, we see that net national savings accounts for only three per cent of GNDI. The savings rate is among the most important determinants of growth in the long run. The present Irish savings rate is very low, due in particular to the high level of borrowing in the public sector.

2.6 Adjusting for Inflation

Earlier in this chapter we briefly discussed some issues that arise when comparisons are made on the level of national income between countries. Somewhat different issues arise when we compare national income or GDP within a country over time. We discuss the measurement of inflation in some detail in Chapter 3, but here we present a brief account of how it has affected comparisons of GDP or GNP over time.

As GDP changes from year to year, it is important to distinguish between changes in nominal and real GDP. *Nominal GDP* is measured using the current year's prices. It could be thought of as the volume of output (hundreds of bicycles, millions of computer chips, thousands of opera performances and so on) multiplied by the current price level.

$$\text{Nominal GDP} = \text{real GDP} \times \text{current price level}$$

Nominal GDP can increase just because the price level rises, even if there is no increase in the volume of output. An increase in *real GDP*, on the other hand, means that a larger quantity of goods and services has been produced (more bicycles, computer chips, operas). In terms of improving the country's standard of living, it is the change in volume GDP or real GDP that matters. Changes in real GDP are also what drive the level of employment in a country.

Put another way, people are not better off because the price level has risen. If they were, Robert Mugabe's Zimbabwe, with its one million inflation rate in 2007, would be one of the richest countries in the world.

If we calculate GDP at a given price level, that is by holding the price level constant, we obtain a measure of real output called GDP at constant market prices, to distinguish it from GDP at *current* market prices. The price index used to calculate GDP at constant market prices is known as the GDP deflator. In the next section we use data for real GNP to show how the Irish economy has performed over the decades.

As an example, consider the hypothetical data in Table 2.5. There are only two goods: A and B. The prices and quantities of each good are given for three years. Given this data, we wish to compute nominal and real GDP in each year using 2011 as the base year (the year from which prices are frozen). Nominal GDP is calculated by multiplying the Ps and Qs for each year:

$$2011\text{: €}25{,}860 = \text{€}22 \times 900 + \text{€}30 \times 202$$

$$2012\text{: €}27{,}200 = \text{€}24 \times 950 + \text{€}32 \times 210$$

$$2013\text{: €}33{,}310 = \text{€}26 \times 1000 + \text{€}34 \times 215$$

Real GDP is calculated by multiplying each year's Qs by the 2011 P.

$$2011\text{: €}25{,}860 = \text{€}22 \times 900 + \text{€}30 \times 202$$

$$2012\text{: €}27{,}200 = \text{€}22 \times 950 + \text{€}30 \times 210$$

$$2013\text{: €}28{,}450 = \text{€}22 \times 1000 + \text{€}30 \times 215$$

It can be seen that once prices are held constant, over the period there is a much smaller increase in real GDP (€28,450) compared to nominal GDP (€33,310). The percentage change in real GDP from one year to the next is known as the *real growth rate*. This is a particularly important variable in macroeconomics and receives a great deal of media attention when the figure is published. Using the hypothetical data in Table 2.5, in 2012 the real growth rate was 5.18 per cent:

$$5.18 = \left(\frac{27{,}200 - 25{,}860}{25{,}860}\right) \times 100$$

TABLE 2.5 Real and nominal GDP (hypothetical)

	2011 P	2011 QTY	2012 P	2012 Q	2013 P	2013 Q
Good A	22	900	24	950	26	1000
Good B	30	202	32	210	34	215

TABLE 2.6 Gross national product at constant market prices

Year	GNP € millions	% change	Population	GNP per capita €	% change
2006	137,145		4,239,800	32,347	
2007	142,848	4.2%	4,307,314	33,164	2.5%
2008	140,316	−1.8%	4,375,801	32,066	−3.3%
2009	128,988	−8.1%	4,445,376	29,016	−9.5%
2010	130,202	0.9%	4,516,057	28,831	−0.6%
2011	126,983	−2.5%	4,588,300	27,675	−4.0%

Note: Chain-linked volume measures, with prices referenced to 2010

Source: CSO, National Income and Expenditure Annual Results for 2011 (July 2012), Table A

In 2013, the hypothetical real growth rate was 4.6 per cent.

$$4.6 = \left(\frac{28{,}450 - 27{,}200}{27{,}200}\right) \times 100$$

NOTE: When calculating real GDP, it would appear that prices are held constant. That is, prices never change from their base year values. However, relative prices are changing all the time. In Table 2.5, for example, over time the price of good A may fall and the price of good B may rise. If you change these relative prices, the corresponding real growth rates will change as well. (Experiment with the prices in Table 2.5 to see this.)

To keep the base up to date, every few years a new base year is chosen. Prices are again held fixed and real GDP calculated. Recently the CSO moved to a new chain-weighted method. In this case, the base year prices change continuously over time. Average prices in 2011 and 2012 are used to compute real GDP in 2012, and average prices in 2012 and 2013 are used to compute 2013 real GDP. The year-to-year growth rates are then put together to form a 'chain'. This technique ensures that prices used to compute real GDP are never far out of date and hence it is a more accurate measurement.

Table 2.6 shows GNP at constant market prices for the Irish economy from 2006 to 2011. (Note that we now switch to GNP, as opposed to GDP, as this is the most relevant measure for the Irish economy.) This is the output of the Irish economy over time, but holding prices constant. It can be seen that real output increased significantly in 2006 but fell dramatically in 2009. A graph of the real growth rates over time is referred to as the *business cycle*.

In Table 2.6 we also show the population numbers and derive GNP per capita. This data again highlights the dramatic fall in the real growth rate in 2009.

2.7 The Business Cycle

The holy grail of macroeconomic policy is to keep the economy close to what may be called its potential real growth rate, avoiding inflation on one side, and unemployment on the other. We can think of potential real growth rate as the economy's sustainable growth path. Associated with this potential growth rate is the natural rate of unemployment. This is not zero unemployment as it is never possible to have no unemployment (see Chapter 4).

NOTE: In New Zealand it is said that there were four people unemployed in the early 1960s and that the Minister for Labour knew both their names and their addresses. Times have changed and in 2012, the unemployment rate in New Zealand is seven per cent.

Potential output is also associated with full utilisation of the country's capital equipment and other resources. If the economy grows faster than potential it will overheat, generating inflationary pressures. If it grows more slowly, the unemployment rate will rise and spare capacity will emerge. We discuss this issue in greater detail in Chapter 4.

NOTE: As explained at the outset of this chapter, the rate of growth is determined by the economy's factors of production (the labour force and capital stock) and technological improvements. The potential growth rate is the rate consistent with full employment and low inflation. In an Irish context it is hard to define what this sustainable growth rate is. During the boom years of the last decade we experienced a huge inflow of immigrants to our labour force. In a sense this raised our potential growth rate. Our sustainable growth rate is also affected by inflows of high-tech foreign direct investment that augment our productive capacity. The sustainable growth rate can also be high during a period of 'catching up', as the economy moves from low-productivity activities (such as traditional farming) to high-productivity activities (such as software development). It is difficult at this point in time to gauge what is the relevant figure for our long-run potential growth rate in the years ahead, but it is certainly lower than it was between 1994 and 2007.

In reality, modern economies do not grow at a steady, constant rate, year in, year out. Instead the growth rate is quite erratic. There are booms, when the growth rate is above its sustainable level, followed by busts, when the growth rate falls below this level. These fluctuations constitute the business cycle. During the 1990s and early part of the present century, many economies experienced a long period of steady growth with low unemployment and low inflation. This was called 'the Great Moderation'. It seemed as if the business cycle had been tamed. But this hope was rudely dashed after 2007, when most of the advanced economies of the world were plunged into a very deep recession.

There is no hard and fast definition of how long a downturn must last to constitute a recession. The convention in the USA is that if a contraction lasts for two or more consecutive calendar quarters, the economy is said to be in a recession. If a recession is prolonged and deep, it may be called a depression, but the distinction is not clear-cut. The present crisis has been the severest many countries have experienced since the 1930s, but hardship is not on the same scale as it was then. As a compromise, it has been labelled the Great Recession.

One thing that has not changed is that the business cycle remains unpredictable. We can be sure that a boom will not last indefinitely, but we cannot predict when the downturn will occur. Hopefully, the present recession will not continue forever, but who can foresee when it will end?

Figure 2.2 shows the real growth rate of the Irish economy for each year from 1950 to 2011. The rate has not been adjusted for population change, so it shows the growth of the whole economy, including the part attributable to the increase in the labour force and population. It is clear from the chart that the performance of the Irish economy has been very erratic, with growth as high as nine per cent in several years in the late 1990s but falling to *minus* eight per cent in 2009. While the long-run growth rate has averaged just over three per cent, there have been very significant fluctuations round this average. This volatility shows that we have not succeeded in stabilising the economy around its potential growth rate. Much the same could be said for many other economies, although the Irish experience has been more volatile than most.

FIGURE 2.2 Real GNP growth rate (%) Ireland, 1951–2011

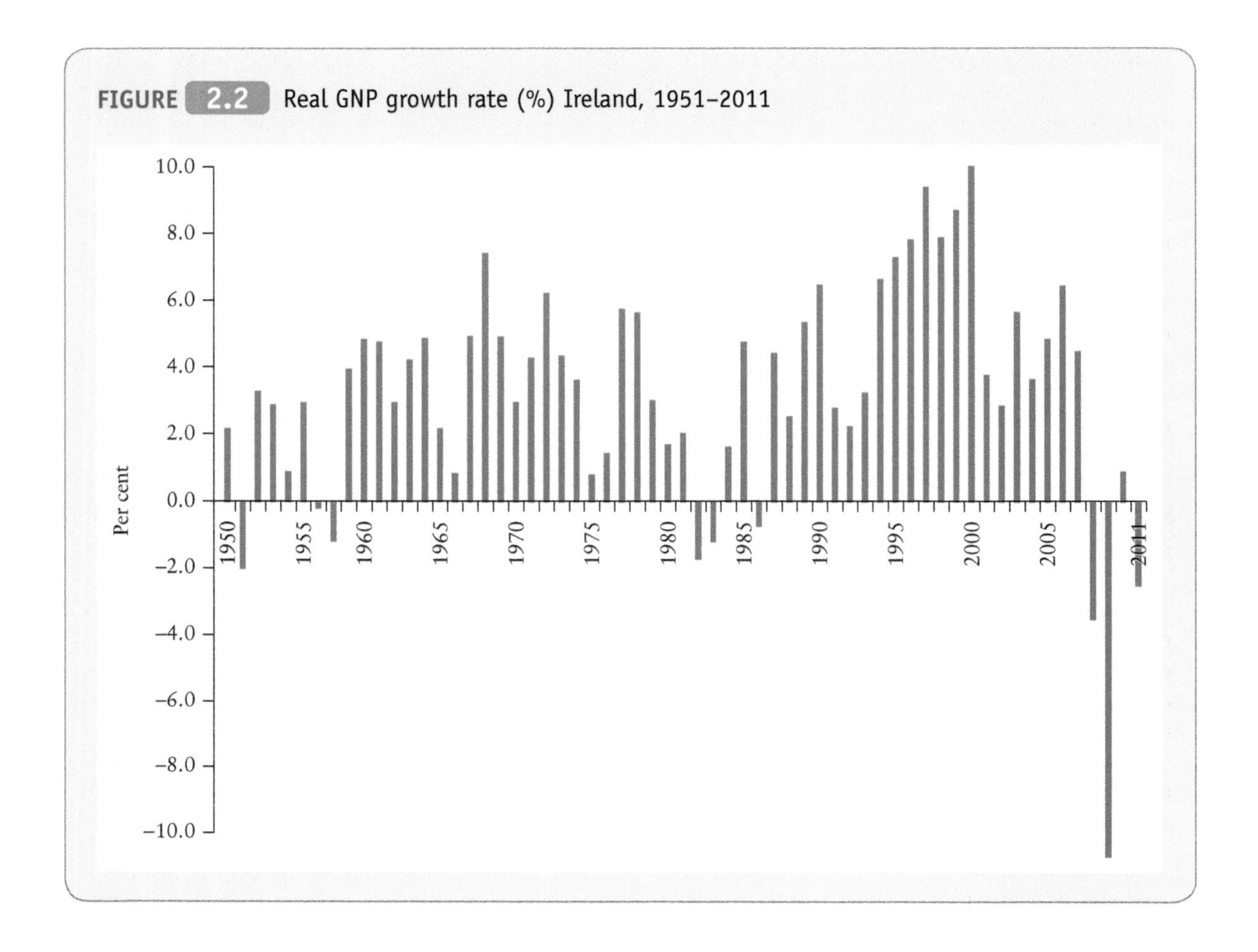

The economy went through a severe recession in the mid-1950s, with negative growth rates recorded in two years. Things picked up during the 1960s, although there was a brief downturn in 1967. The 1970s were marked by some initial growth followed by a severe recession caused by the 1973 global oil crisis. The second energy crisis at the end of the 1970s, combined with poor economic policies, triggered a prolonged recession in the 1980s.

However, the economy finally recovered at the end of the decade and during the 21 years from 1987 to 2007 we experienced an amazing growth spurt. Real GNP grew at an annual average rate of 5.6 per cent, while real GNP per person averaged 4.6 per cent. The size of our real GNP more than trebled over this period and real GNP per person grew to two and a half times its starting level.

The rapid growth of the Irish economy attracted international attention and the label 'Celtic Tiger' was use to describe it by economist Kevin Gardiner in a 1994 report for the stockbrokers Morgan Stanley. Ireland's growth spurt was to last much longer than anyone anticipated in the 1990s, only finally coming to an end with the post-2007 crash. We return to a discussion of the factors that contributed to this exceptional performance in Chapter 22.

In 2007 the Irish property and banking bubble began to collapse and our economy felt the repercussions of the worst global recession in decades. The subsequent downturn was very severe. As shown in Table 2.6, real output increased significantly in 2007 but since then has fallen by a cumulative total of just over 11 per cent. On a per person basis, the fall has been equal to almost 17 per cent. This is by far the biggest contraction in real output we have suffered since World War II.

Business firms have an enormous interest in gauging the prospects for future growth. If they believe that the markets into which they are selling are going to expand they are likely to hire more workers, employment will rise and unemployment fall. However, if they are gripped by pessimism and believe that sales will fall, they will shed workers and unemployment will rise. Figure 2.2 implies that doing business in Ireland over the last 60 years has been like being on a roller-coaster. During the 1980s and since 2008 firms struggled to survive, whereas in the 1990s and early 2000s firms and businesses prospered and expanded.

Firms are eager to obtain forecasts of economic growth both for Ireland and for the foreign markets into which they sell. These forecasts influence their decisions about hiring and investment. Preparing economic forecasts is now a big industry. Numerous national and international agencies, banks and consulting firms prepare forecasts giving their view of the likely performance of the Irish and other economies one or two years into the future. In Ireland the forecasts prepared by the Central Bank of Ireland, the ESRI, the OECD and the IMF attract headlines every quarter.

Unfortunately, economists' ability to forecast the future is poor. Economics is not like astronomy, which can make very precise predictions of the movements of the planets years into the future. As we pointed out above, the business cycle does not follow a predictable path. The economic system is subject to a high degree of randomness because it is buffeted by 'shocks' – external factors that of their nature cannot be predicted.

The list of shocks is long and includes the impact of wars on oil prices, spells of extreme weather, political upheavals and changes in technology. These are the 'unknown unknowns' that can blow even the most sophisticated forecast off course. If you look back just five years, you will see that few forecasters in Ireland or elsewhere foresaw the severity of the recession that would hit the economy in 2007.

Figure 2.3 shows the business cycle for the United States from 1980 to 2011 using GDP figures. Again, the volatility is apparent. The fastest spell of economic growth was during the two Clinton

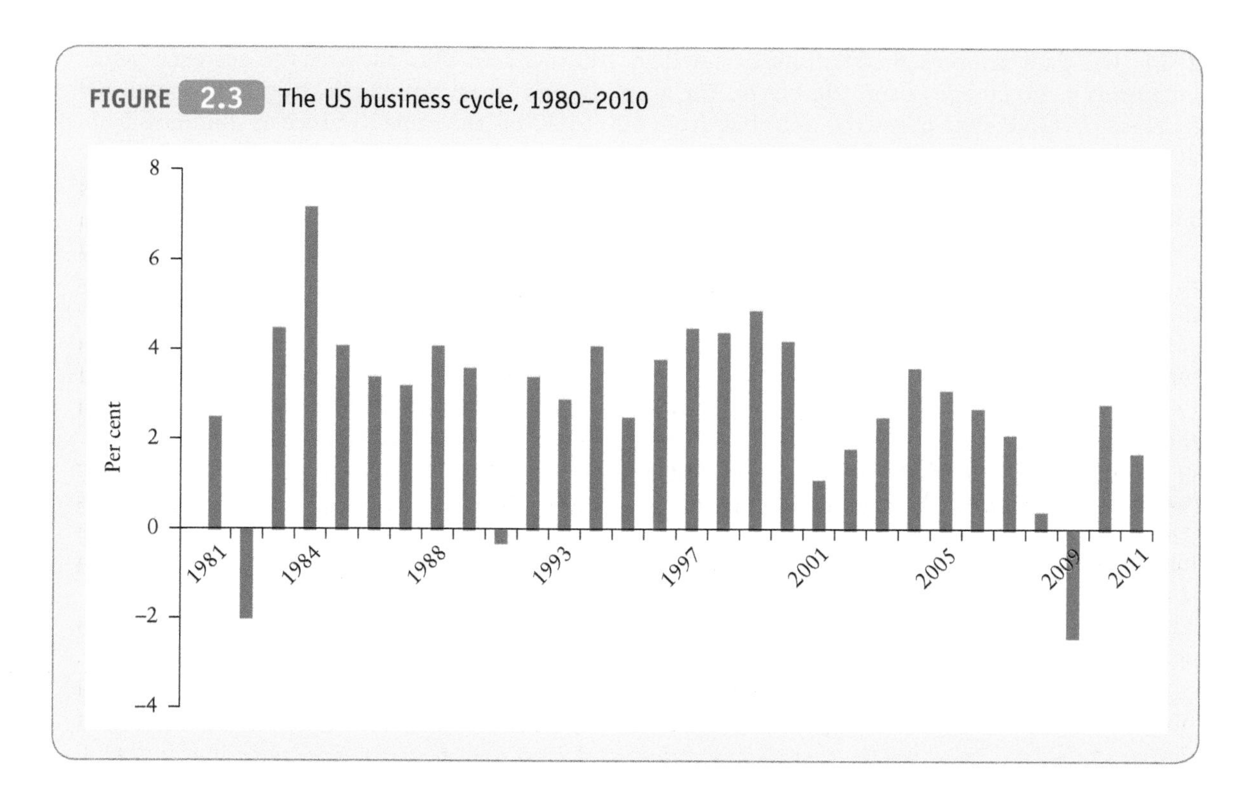

FIGURE 2.3 The US business cycle, 1980–2010

presidencies from January 1993 to December 2000, when growth averaged 3.4 per cent. (Clinton used the slogan 'It's the economy, stupid' during the 1992 presidential campaign to remind voters of the recession.)

If a trend line is fitted to the US real growth rate it is downward sloping, perhaps reflecting the fact that the USA is a mature economy on the frontier of technology. This means that it cannot grow as fast as Ireland did in the 1990s and early in this century, when we were catching up with the advanced economies.

2.8 The Long-run Performance of the Irish Economy

The previous section dealt mainly with the short-run, cyclical performance of the economy. In this section we provide a brief account of the performance of the Irish economy over the long run. We present a more detailed discussion of this topic in Chapter 22.

When looking at the long-run behaviour of the economy, it is important to take account not only of inflation but also of population change. The population of Ireland has fluctuated to an unusual extent. During the 1950s the population declined by over one per cent a year, reaching a low point of 2,818 thousand in 1961. In the 1970s it grew by about 1.5 per cent a year, the highest population growth rate in Europe.

In the late 1980s the population declined due to the resumption of large-scale emigration and the decline in the birth rate. But during the 1990s the population again increased at about 1.5 per cent a year. This was due to the combination of the rise in the Irish birth rate and the unprecedented rate of net immigration to the country.

The 2011 Census of Population revealed that the population had grown to 4,588 thousand – an increase of 63 per cent over the 1961 figure and the highest total recorded in the twenty-six counties since 1861. Our view of the country's economic performance would be distorted if we did not take these population fluctuations into account.

Figure 2.4 shows the trend in Irish GNP and GNP per person at constant prices from 1960 to 2011. The data are presented as indices equal to 100 in 1960. This allows us to see each year's income as a percentage of the 1960 level. The graph is on a logarithmic scale, so that proportional increases in GNP appear equal – doubling from 100 to 200 is the same distance as doubling from 200 to 400. For a given growth rate the slope of the line is constant. So changes in the slope of the lines indicate changes in the growth rate. This brings out the very high growth rates recorded in the 1990s and early in this century.

The data show that between 1960 and 2011 real GNP grew at an annual average rate of 3.7 per cent, while real GNP per person grew at 2.7 per cent. If income grows at 2.7 per cent it will double in just over 26 years. This implies that each generation is twice as well off as its predecessor. Despite the setback after 2007, in 2011 Irish real income per person was almost four times the level recorded in 1950.

However, it is unlikely that Irish income will average this high growth rate in the future – the fast growth recorded in certain periods since World War II contained a large element of 'catch-up' as Ireland moved from being one of the poorest nations in Europe to being up there among the leaders.

People today may not necessarily be 'happier' than they were in the past, but they certainly have more and a greater variety of goods and services at their disposal. Many students now drive their own cars to college, whereas in the past almost all of them cycled, walked or took the bus! Virtually all of them have mobile phones and other electronic gadgets that were unheard of a generation ago.

Real GNP has not risen in all countries over the years. Some countries have had no long-term improvement in living standards and a few have even experienced decline. North Korea is an

FIGURE 2.4 GNP and GNP per capita at constant market prices

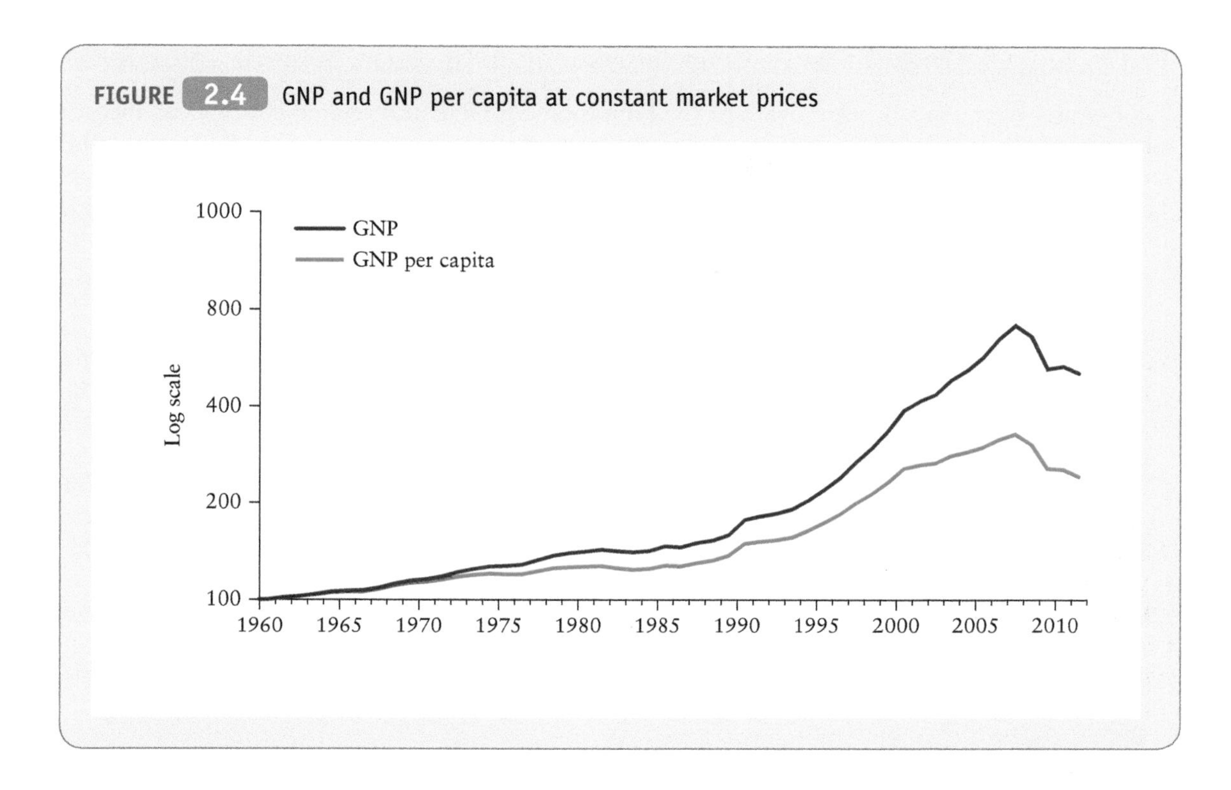

example of a country where there has been little economic progress for decades. Africa contains many 'failed states' that have been torn apart by civil wars, economic mismanagement and natural disasters. However, there are many rapidly growing countries in Africa today, with many formerly extremely poor countries experiencing new prosperity on the back of a boom in commodity prices and better economic policies. Once poorer states begin to grow they can record very high growth rates as they go through the catch-up process that Ireland experienced in the 20 years before 2008.

It is also relevant to look at the level of income and output per person at work. When the participation rate (the proportion of the population in the labour force) is rising, the rate of growth of income per person will be faster than that of output per worker. A rising participation rate, especially among women, was one of the factors behind the rapid rate of growth of income per person in Ireland in the 1990s and the first decade of this century.

2.9 Key Terms and Concepts

In this chapter we:

- outlined the concepts of gross domestic product (GDP), gross national product (GNP) and national income (NI) and the relationships between them
- discussed how to adjust for inflation and derive the real growth rate
- provided data on Ireland's real growth rate over the short run (the business cycle)
- discussed some aspects of Ireland's longer-term economic performance.

Appendix 2.1 Beyond GDP

Economists have always been aware of the limitations of GDP and related concepts as measures of economic well-being. They caution that these measures include only what can be brought under the 'measuring rod of money', as the Cambridge economist Alfred Marshall put it. But despite this caveat, journalists and policy-makers have tended to pay enormous attention to the latest estimates of GDP and little heed to its shortcomings as a standard by which to measure human progress.

This has changed in recent years. The growing interest among policy-makers and academic economists in supplementing the conventional measures of economic welfare with broader indicators of the progress of society was signalled by the publication in 2009 of the *Report of the Commission on the Measurement of Economic Performance and Social Progress*, whose authors included two Nobel Prize-winning economists, Joseph Stiglitz and Amartya Sen, as well as the prominent French economist Jean-Paul Fitoussi.

In 2010 the EU launched the website Beyond GDP (www.beyond-gdp.eu/), and in 2012 the American economist Jeffrey Sachs co-edited the first *World Happiness Report*. In the preface to this report he states:

> *The United States has achieved striking economic and technological progress over the past half century without gains in the self-reported happiness of the citizenry. Instead, uncertainties and anxieties are high, social and economic inequalities have widened considerably, social trust is in decline, and confidence in government is at an all-time low. Perhaps for these reasons, life satisfaction has remained nearly constant during decades of rising Gross Domestic Product (GDP) per person.*

The last point is consistent with the famous Easterlin hypothesis, according to which beyond a certain threshold the average level of subjective well-being is not significantly higher in richer than in poorer countries; and well-being does not increase within countries as their incomes rise over time. This paradox is usually explained in terms of the declining marginal utility of income, the importance of relative rather than absolute income, and the tendency for expectations to rise with increasing affluence (Easterlin 1974).

A recent study of the effects of the Great Recession on the US population concluded that even large macroeconomic shocks to income and unemployment produce only small and hard-to-detect effects on life satisfaction. Although unemployment remained very high, by the end of 2010 measures of subjective well-being had largely recovered from the impact of the recession. Similarly, the Irish evidence suggests that despite soaring unemployment and falling income, most measures of subjective well-being have held up quite well since 2007 (Walsh 2012).

Behind this new emphasis in economics is a broad agreement on the need to take account of data on both objective and subjective quality of life indices to supplement the traditional measures of economic growth and well-being. The CSO has responded to these trends by publishing since 2003 an annual report called *Measuring Ireland's Progress*. This contains not only the standard economic indicators, but also a wealth of information on demographic and educational trends, environmental standards and other indicators of the quality of life.

In addition to these broad and philosophical issues as to what exactly GDP measures, other technical difficulties relating to the measurement of GDP have long been recognised by economists and national income accounting statisticians. These include the following.

DOUBLE COUNTING

Only final goods should be included in GDP, which is based on adding up all the value added in the economy. Intermediate goods that are used to produce final goods should not also be included because this would give rise to double counting and an overestimate of GDP. In this chapter we gave the example of producing a book and emphasised that the value of the paper and other inputs to book production should not be counted on top of the value of the book itself. That seems clear enough, but in reality the dividing line between intermediate and final goods is not always so clear-cut. A lot of what we count as 'final' output is really only needed to help the rest of the economy function – policing and the legal system are important examples. A country does not become richer or happier by recruiting more police officers or locking up more people in jails.

HOUSEHOLD PRODUCTION AND NON-MARKET ACTIVITIES

National income accounting is primarily concerned with activities that are bought and sold: that is, brought under the measuring rod of money. Non-market activities, such as 'do-it-yourself' repairs or cooking and cleaning in the home, are not included in GDP. So, for example, if a parent stays home and looks after his or her children it does not count in the NIE statistics. But if the children are put into a crèche it does, because money is paid for the service.

A related issue is how to value 'leisure'. A person who works 60 hours a week will earn more money than they would if she only worked 40 hours, but they forego a lot of free time for this extra income. Should some value be attached to this loss of leisure time and deducted from the increased GDP that results from the overtime? This is not a trivial issue. In the United States people work notoriously long hours and have relatively few vacations – on average the working year comes to about 1,800 hours, whereas in countries like France, Germany and Denmark it is around 1,400. (The figure for Ireland is 1,500.) In many Western European countries there is a strong emphasis on the importance of free time as a component of well-being, but this is not reflected in the GDP data.

SPILLOVER EFFECTS

Spillover effects or 'externalities' can be either positive or negative. An example of a negative spillover or external diseconomy is the pollution caused by a factory. The environmental damage caused by the sulphur dioxide (SO_2) emissions from the Moneypoint power station in County Clare, equal to about 67,000 tonnes per annum, is a pertinent example. One of the biggest issues facing the world in our century is how to deal with the effects on the world's climate of the carbon emissions from burning fossil fuels. Ideally, the polluter should compensate those affected by the pollution, but in practice the 'polluter pays' principle is difficult to enforce. Various 'emissions trading' systems have been devised in response to the problem of global warming, but these have had limited effect so far.

Important examples of positive spillover effects or external economies are rarer, but they do exist. For example, the grounds of a university campus yield positive benefits to local residents. More importantly, the civilising effect of educating students may benefit not just those students, through their enhanced earning capacity, but also the whole community.

A lot of work is being done to 'green' the national accounts by taking account of the impact of economic activity on the environment. This involves preparing estimates of the damage done to the environment in the production of economic output and subtracting this figure from the conventional measure of GDP.

THE UNDERGROUND OR 'BLACK' ECONOMY

The underground economy consists of unreported, undetected and unmeasured economic activity. There are two main types of unrecorded transaction: illegal transactions, such as drug trafficking and prostitution, which are not reported for obvious reasons; and legal transactions, such as small building jobs and 'nixers', that are kept hidden to avoid paying taxes. It is estimated that the black economy in Ireland could be between three and 10 per cent of GDP. Other countries, such as Italy and Greece, are believed to have even higher levels of unrecorded economic activity.

ISSUES RELATING TO MULTINATIONAL COMPANIES

The activities of multinational companies (MNCs) in Ireland have a major impact on our GDP estimates. Because of Ireland's relatively low corporation tax rate (12.5 per cent) there is an incentive for international companies to engage in 'transfer pricing': selling components and raw materials at artificially low prices to subsidiary companies in Ireland in order to maximise the profits they record in this low tax jurisdiction. This has the effect of artificially boosting the Irish GDP figures. As we saw, in Ireland GNP is about 20 per cent lower than GDP. This is an unusually large gap. To avoid this distortion, it is recommended that Irish GNP be used in international comparisons, even when GDP is used for other countries.

CHAPTER 3

Inflation

3.1 Introduction

The macroeconomic ideal is an economy that combines rising living standards with price stability and full employment. In later chapters we discuss what macroeconomic policy can do to achieve these goals. In this chapter we discuss the measurement of inflation and look at the Irish record. We defer a discussion of the causes of inflation to Chapter 9, where we explain how the money supply is determined in a modern economy and how this influences the rate of inflation.

3.2 Measuring Inflation

Microeconomics is concerned with the relative prices of goods and services. The macroeconomic concept of inflation, on the other hand, refers to the rate of change in the *aggregate* price level. This is measured using a price index, such as the Consumer Price Index (CPI) or the EU's Harmonised Index of Consumer Prices (HICP). These indices track changes in the cost of a basket of goods and services bought by a representative household. They are widely used to track changes in the cost of living and to adjust contracts, rent agreements, pensions and so on.

How price indices are constructed

The most widely used price index in Ireland is the CPI. To construct the CPI, the CSO employs 200 people to collect the prices of a basket of goods and services that includes about 1,000 items. Prices are obtained from a panel of retail and services outlets in 82 towns and cities around the country on the first Tuesday of each month. Information is gathered on sales and special offers as well as regular prices. In all, some 45,000 individual prices are collected each month.

We can use the very simplified hypothetical data in Table 3.1 to illustrate how a price index is constructed. In this example, there are only three goods in the consumer's basket – bananas (kilos), books, and petrol (litres). We show the prices of these goods (per unit) and the quantities purchased by the consumer, in the base year 0 and the current year 1. The object is to calculate the rate of inflation for this basket of goods between these two years.

You can see that the prices of all three items have risen between the two years, but by different percentages. The price of bananas rose by 16.7 per cent, of books by 20.0 per cent, and of petrol by 50.0 per cent. A crude way to measure inflation would be to take the simple average of these increases, which yields an estimate of 28.9 per cent.

This is unsatisfactory, however, because it gives equal weights to each of the commodities. In year 0, the consumer spends more than twice as much on petrol (€24.00) as on bananas (€10.50) and the price of petrol has risen proportionately more than the price of bananas. The logic of constructing prices indices is to give the most weight to the price increases that are most important in the consumer's budget.

Our hypothetical data show that in year 0 the total consumer spending was €54.5 (€10.5 + €20 + €24). Hence she spent 19.3 per cent of her budget on bananas ((€10.5/€54.5) × 100), 36.7 per cent

TABLE 3.1 Measuring inflation for a hypothetical basket of goods

Year	Bananas	Books	Petrol
		Prices (P)	
0	€1.50	€10.00	€1.20
1	€1.75	€12.00	€1.80
		Quantities (Q)	
0	7	2	20
1	8	3	17
		Outlay (PQ)	
0	€10.50	€20.00	€24.00
1	€14.00	€36.00	€30.60
Price increases %	16.7%	20.0%	50.0%
Unweighted average %		28.9%	
Total outlay in year 0 = $\Sigma P_0 Q_0$		€54.50	
Total outlay in year 1 = $\Sigma P_1 Q_1$		€80.60	
Cost of year 0 quantities at year 1 prices = $\Sigma P_1 Q_0$		€72.25	
Laspeyres inflation index = $\Sigma P_1 Q_0 / \Sigma P_0 Q_0$ Year 0 = 100		132.6	
Rate of inflation		32.6%	
Cost of year 1 quantities at year 0 prices = $\Sigma P_0 Q_1$		€62.40	
Paasche inflation index = $\Sigma P_1 Q_1 / \Sigma P_0 Q_1$ Year 0 = 100		129.2	
Rate of inflation		29.2%	

on books and 44.0 per cent on petrol. If we weight each of the price increases by these shares we obtain a weighted increase of 32.6 per cent. That is:

$$32.6 = 0.193 \times 16.7 + 0.367 \times 20.0 + 0.44 \times 50.0$$

This is significantly higher than our first crude estimate of 28.9 per cent. Algebraically, we can summarise the procedure as follows.

For the three goods being considered, $i = 1, 2, 3$:

Q_{i0} = the amount of good i in the CPI basket in the base year, 0 (Q_{10}, Q_{20}, Q_{30})

P_{i0} = the price of good i in the base year, 0 (P_{10}, P_{20}, P_{30})

Q_{i1} = the amount of good i in the CPI basket in year 1

P_{i1} = the price of good i in year 1

$$\Sigma_1^3 Q_{i0} P_{i0} = \text{the cost of the basket in year 0}$$
$$= (Q_{10} \times P_{10}) + (Q_{20} \times P_{20}) + (Q_{30} \times P_{30})$$
$$= (7 \times 1.5) + (2 \times 10) + (20 \times 1.10) = 54.5$$

$$\Sigma_1^3 Q_{i1} P_{i1} = \text{the cost of the basket in year 1}$$
$$= (8 \times 1.75) + (3 \times 12) + (17 \times 1.8) = 80.6$$

The ratio:

$$\frac{\Sigma_1^3 Q_{i1} P_{i1}}{\Sigma_1^3 Q_{i0} P_{i0}} = \frac{80.6}{54.5} = 1.48$$

This tells us the cost of the basket in year 1 relative to its cost in year 0; that is, how much more the consumer spent in year 1 relative to what she spent in year 0. This reflects both the increased cost of the three goods and the changed quantities of the goods purchased, so it is not a measure of inflation.

To obtain a measure of inflation, we need to hold constant the basket of goods being purchased. One way of doing this is to calculate the cost of buying the basket of goods bought in year 0 at the prices prevailing in year 1, that is:

$$\Sigma_1^3 Q_{i0} P_{i1} = (Q_{10} \times P_{11}) + (Q_{20} \times P_{21}) + (Q_{30} \times P_{31})$$

$$= (7 \times 1.75) + (2 \times 12) + (20 \times 1.8) = 72.25$$

We now compare this with the actual cost of this basket in year 0. This gives the following measure of the increase in the price level:

$$\frac{\Sigma_1^3 Q_{i0} P_{i1}}{\Sigma_1^3 Q_{i0} P_{i0}} = \frac{72.25}{54.5} = 1.326$$

This shows that the price index has increased by 32.6 per cent. That is, converting the ratio to a percentage increase gives us the rate of inflation between year 0 and year 1. This is a 'base weighted' price index because the basket of goods purchased in year 0 is the reference point. It is called a Laspeyres index, after the German economist who developed this approach in the nineteenth century.

Table 3.2 shows the level and the rate of change in the Irish CPI since 2005. It can be seen that the inflation rate was four per cent or over in 2006, 2007 and 2008, but fell to *minus* 4.4 per cent in 2009 and *minus* 1.0 per cent in 2010. Over these two years we experienced a cumulative *deflation* of over five per cent. (Deflation is defined as a fall in the price index.) However, in 2011 inflation returned at a rate of 2.6 per cent.

TABLE 3.2 CPI inflation 2006–2011

	CPI Dec 2011 = 100	Inflation rate %
2005	90.3	
2006	93.9	4.0
2007	98.5	4.9
2008	102.4	4.0
2009	97.9	−4.4
2010	96.9	−1.0
2011	99.4	2.6

Source: CSO database

TABLE 3.3 Weights used in Irish CPI, 2011

Commodity group	%
Housing, water, electricity, gas & other fuels	17.5
Restaurants & hotels	14.2
Transport	15.1
Food & non-alcoholic beverages	11.4
Recreation & culture	8.1
Miscellaneous goods & services	9.9
Alcohol & tobacco	4.9
Clothing & footwear	5.2
Furnishings, household equipment & maintenance	3.2
Communications	3.5
Health	4.6
Education	2.5
Total	100.1

Source: CPI Detailed Sub-Indices, December 2011; www.cso.ie/releasespublications/documents/prices/current

The CSO uses the Household Budget Survey to ascertain consumers' expenditure patterns. Based on expenditure patterns in a sample of over seven thousand private households around the country, the CSO calculates the share of total expenditure (the weight) spent on food, drink, clothing, fuel, housing and so on. Table 3.3 shows the commodity groups and the associated weights currently employed by the CSO. It might seem disconcerting that spending on alcohol and tobacco has a higher weight than clothing and footwear or that health and education have relatively low weights. But bear in mind that most health and education services are provided in the public sector and not paid for directly by the consumer.

The CSO also publishes the Harmonised Index of Consumer Prices (HICP). This index is designed by the European Statistical Office, Eurostat, and is used by the ECB to monitor inflation in the EU. The HICP is calculated on the same basis for all EU countries and published monthly. It is based on a sub-set of the data collected for the CPI, excluding approximately eight per cent of total CPI expenditure. Of most significance is the fact that mortgage interest and building materials are excluded. (Housing is regarded as an investment rather than a component of consumer expenditure.) During housing booms and when interest rates are rising, the HICP will indicate a lower rate of inflation than the CPI.

Table 3.4 illustrates the use of a price index to convert nominal, or current-year, data to real, or constant price, data. The table lists the box office receipts (in millions of US dollars) of eight of the highest-grossing movies of all time. It also shows the US CPI in the year of each movies' release relative to the base year 2010. Which is the highest-grossing movie? It would be misleading to answer this on the basis of the current price data because the purchasing power of a dollar back in 1939, when *Gone with the Wind* was released, was considerably higher than in 2008, when *The Dark Knight* was released. In 1939 you might have gone to the movies and had dinner afterwards for less than five dollars. In 2010 five dollars would not have got you into the movie.

TABLE 3.4 Box office receipts for high-grossing films

Movie	Year of release	Receipts in current $ million	CPI 2010 = 100	Real box office receipts in 2010 prices	Rank
Titanic	1997	600.78	75.4	797.1	5
The Dark Knight	2010	533.32	100.0	533.3	6
Star Wars	1977	460.94	27.7	1,663.3	2
E.T.	1982	434.95	44.7	973.7	4
Spider-Man	2002	373.38	83.9	445.1	8
Jurassic Park	1993	356.78	67.6	528.2	7
Gone with the Wind	1939	198.66	6.6	2,995.5	1
The Sound of Music	1965	163.21	14.8	1,104.3	3

We need to deflate the current-price (or nominal) receipts by the CPI in the year of their release and express them all in constant-dollar (2010) dollars. This is done in the fourth and fifth columns of the table. The receipts can now be compared in 'real terms'. For example, *Gone with the Wind* had receipts of $198.66 million at a CPI of 6.6. Converting this to 2010 prices when the CPI index was 100 gives:

$$\frac{198.66}{6.6} \times 100 = \$2,995.5$$

We can see that when inflation is taken into account *Gone with the Wind* was the biggest earner whereas *Spider-Man*, with receipts of $373.38 million, is ranked eighth.

The GDP deflator

A widely used alternative measure of economy-wide inflation is derived from the GDP (or GNP) deflator, which as we saw in Chapter 2 is used to convert current-year GDP to constant-price GDP. The GDP deflator is an index calculated by dividing GDP at current market prices by GDP at constant market prices. The rate of increase in this index is a measure of inflation based on all the goods and services entering GDP. Table 3.5 shows these calculations for the period 2005 to 2011. It may be seen that the inflation estimates based on the GNP deflator differ from those based on the CPI shown in Table 3.2. There are several reasons for this.

First, the prices of domestically produced capital goods are included in the GDP deflator but not in the CPI. Second, the prices of imported consumer goods are included in the CPI but not in the GNP deflator. Finally, the basket of goods is fixed at a base year in the case of the CPI but varies from year to year for the GNP deflator. These two measures of inflation show a similar trend over time. However, in 2008 the inflation rate as shown in the CPI was +4.0 per cent while that derived from the GNP deflator was −3.2 per cent. This unusually large discrepancy was due to special factors operating in that year, including the strength of the euro relative to the pound and the dollar.

Why price indices can overstate inflation

There are three reasons why the CPI can give an overstated measure of inflation. First, there is 'substitution bias'. We saw that the CPI is a Laspeyres index that uses base year weights when averaging price increases. It therefore does not reflect consumers' ability to reduce their consumption

TABLE 3.5 GDP deflator, 2006–2011

Year	GDP at current prices € million (a)	GDP at constant prices € million (b)	GNP deflator, 2010 = 100	
			level (a)/(b)	% change
2005	163,462	155,975	104.8	
2006	177,729	161,590	110.0	4.9
2007	188,729	170,389	110.8	0.7
2008	178,882	166,796	107.2	−3.2
2009	161,275	157,695	102.3	−4.6
2010	156,487	156,487	100.0	−2.2
2011	158,993	158,726	100.2	0.2

Note: Constant price series is a chain-linked volume measure, with prices referenced to 2010

Source: CSO, National Income and Expenditure Annual Results for 2011 (July 2012), Table A

of goods whose relative prices have risen. In the example in Table 3.1 the price of petrol rose more rapidly than that of books or bananas. Our consumer sensibly reduced her consumption of petrol, but bought more books and bananas. Because it does not take account of these changes in the pattern of spending, the base-weighted price index overstates the impact of the petrol price increase on the cost of living.

An alternative approach, known as the Paasche index after another German economist, uses current year instead of base year weights. That is, we need to calculate the cost of buying the basket of goods bought in year 1 at the prices prevailing in years 0 and 1:

$$\begin{aligned}\Sigma_1^3 Q_{i1}P_{i0} &= \text{the cost of the basket in year 0}\\ &= (Q_{11} \times P_{10}) + (Q_{21} \times P_{20}) + (Q_{31} \times P_{30})\\ &= (8 \times 1.5) + (3 \times 10) + (17 \times 1.10) = 62.4\end{aligned}$$

$$\begin{aligned}\Sigma_1^3 Q_{i1}P_{i1} &= \text{the cost of the basket in year 1.}\\ &= (8 \times 1.75) + (3 \times 12) + (17 \times 1.8) = 80.6\end{aligned}$$

The ratio:

$$\frac{\Sigma_1^3 Q_{i1}P_{i1}}{\Sigma_1^3 Q_{i1}P_{i0}} = \frac{80.6}{62.4} = 1.29$$

When the inflation rate is calculated on this basis it falls from 32.6 per cent to 29.2 per cent.

A second reason why the CPI can overstate inflation is because it fails to take account of the way consumers gain from the introduction of new goods. The list of products that are now within the reach of the ordinary consumer but were unavailable to even the richest person in nineteenth-century Ireland is long: cars, phones, televisions, air travel, exotic food, clothes made from modern fibres and so on. Life-saving antibiotics that sell for as little as €100 a treatment today could not have been bought at any price before World War II. The availability of a wider range of products increases the real value of money. This great boom is not captured in a price index.

Third, the quality of goods and services is continually improving. Recently the most dramatic examples of this have been in computers and electronic gadgets. 'Moore's law' states that the number of transistors on integrated circuits doubles approximately every two years. This has had a huge effect on the storage capacity and processing power of computers, but prices have declined rather than increased as these improvements have been passed on to consumers. For an outlay of €500 today you can buy more computing power than the biggest banks had at their disposal 40 years ago. If you buy a new car today it is loaded with features that a generation ago were 'optional extras', if they were available at all. While some allowance is made for quality improvements in the measurement of the CPI, it is generally felt that not enough is done to reflect the actual pace of improvement.

3.3 The Irish Inflation Record

Irish CPI data are available going back to 1922 on a quarterly basis. Monthly data were introduced in 1997. The GDP deflator is available on a consistent annual basis since 1970.

Figure 3.1 shows how the Irish price level has risen over the period from 1922 to 2011. From a base = 100 in July 1914, the CPI reached a peak of 9,702 in 2008 – that is, in 2008 the price level was 97 times its 1914 level. A basket of goods and services that cost €100 in 2008 would have cost €1.03 in 1914 money. However, as we point out above, care must taken in making this kind of comparison because the basket of goods and services bought in 2007 would have borne little resemblance to that bought in 1914. The graph is on a logarithmic scale so that the slope shows the rate of increase. It may be seen that there was a significant decline in the index in the 1930s and again in 2009 and 2010.

For most purposes, it is more relevant to look at the rate of inflation shown in Figure 3.2 than the price level shown in Figure 3.1. In Ireland, as elsewhere, the rate of inflation has varied greatly over time. We never experienced runaway or hyper-inflation at rates in excess of 100 per cent per annum, as did many European countries after World War I. During the depressed years of the

FIGURE 3.1 Irish consumer price index 1922–2011

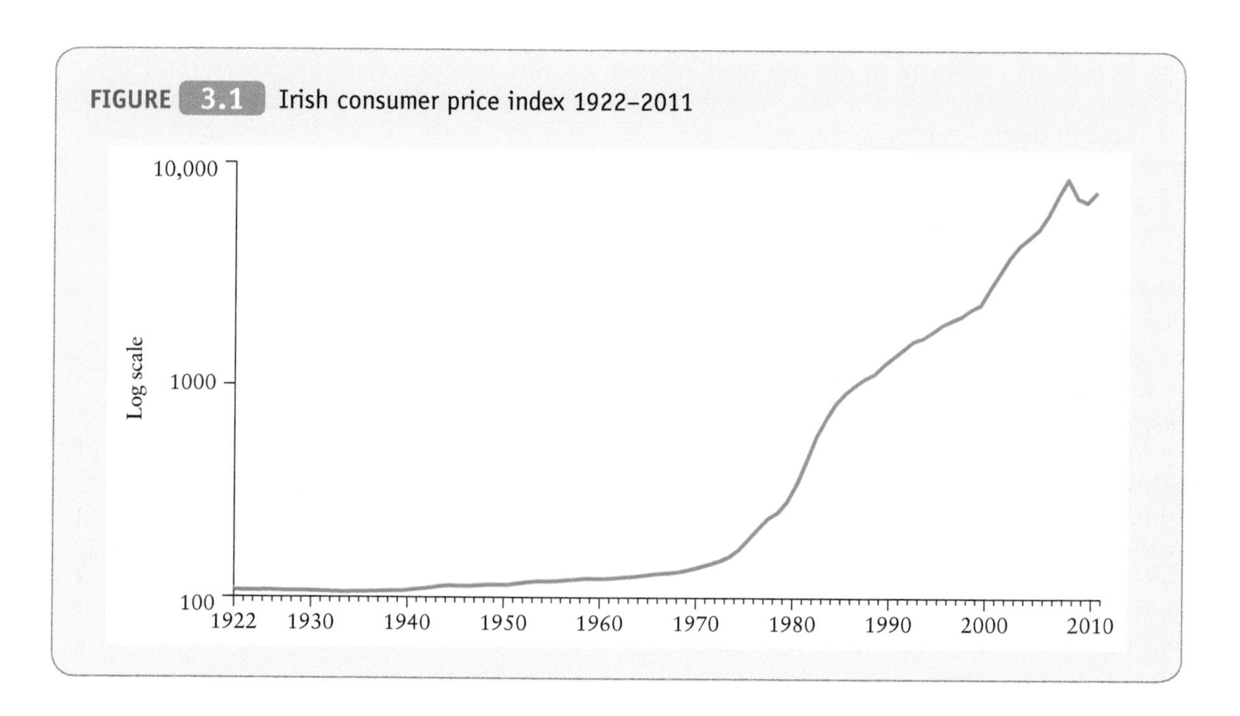

FIGURE 3.2 Two measures of inflation in Ireland, 1970–2011

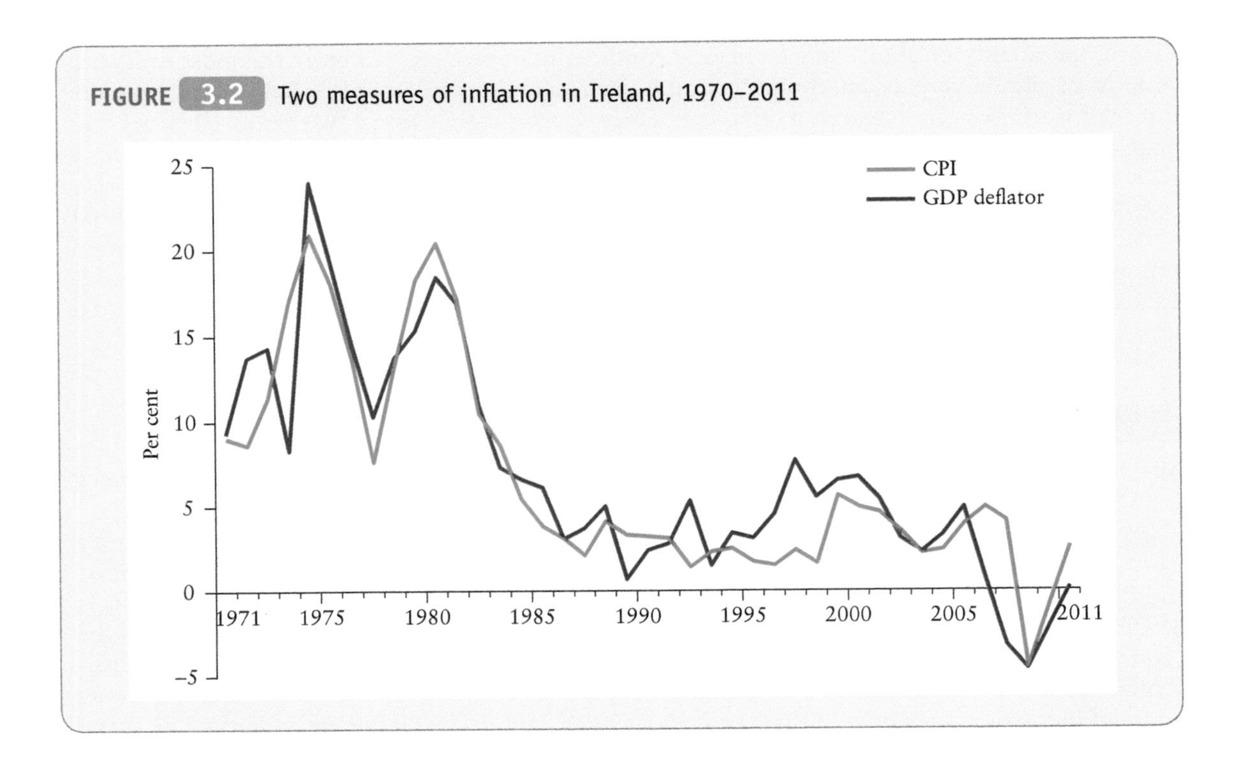

1920s and 1930s the rate of inflation was negative. The CPI in 1933 was 20 per cent below its 1925 level. This was the biggest and most protracted deflation recorded in Ireland since the nineteenth century. After World War II, and following the devaluation of sterling in 1949, the inflation rate was high for a time, but it was subdued during the depressed decade of the 1950s.

In Ireland, as elsewhere in Europe, high inflation became a serious problem during the 1970s. The peak was reached in 1975 when the annual inflation rate was 20 per cent. Our inflation rate was brought under control by the end of the 1980s and was moderate for the next 20 years. In 2009 and 2010 the recession led to the first significant fall in the price level since the 1930s.

Figure 3.2 shows the annual rate of inflation as measured by the CPI and the GDP deflator since 1970. Over the long run the average rates of inflation estimated from the two indices were almost identical – 6.6 from the CPI and 6.8 from the GDP deflator. The general similarity of the two graphs is striking, but in the late 1990s GDP inflation was significantly higher than CPI inflation, while the reverse has been true over the past four years.

As mentioned above, the EU and the ECB favour the use of HICP to measure inflation. The ECB has an inflation rate target of 'close to but less than two per cent'. Figure 3.3 compares Irish HICP inflation with that of the euro area. Only in 2001 and 2008 did inflation move significantly above the ECB target. But the Irish inflation rate was above the Economic and Monetary Union (EMU) rate from 1999 to 2004. During these years the Irish economy was overheating and the rapid rate of increase in prices and wages led to a significant loss of international competitiveness.

The severity of the post-2007 recession in Ireland caused a deeper deflation here than has been experienced in any other EMU country. While this was a reflection of our high unemployment rate, it has helped to restore some of the competitiveness that we lost in the previous decade. However, during 2012 Irish inflation rose back to the euro area average.

FIGURE 3.3 HICP inflation in Ireland and the euro area: monthly data at annual rates, 1999–2012

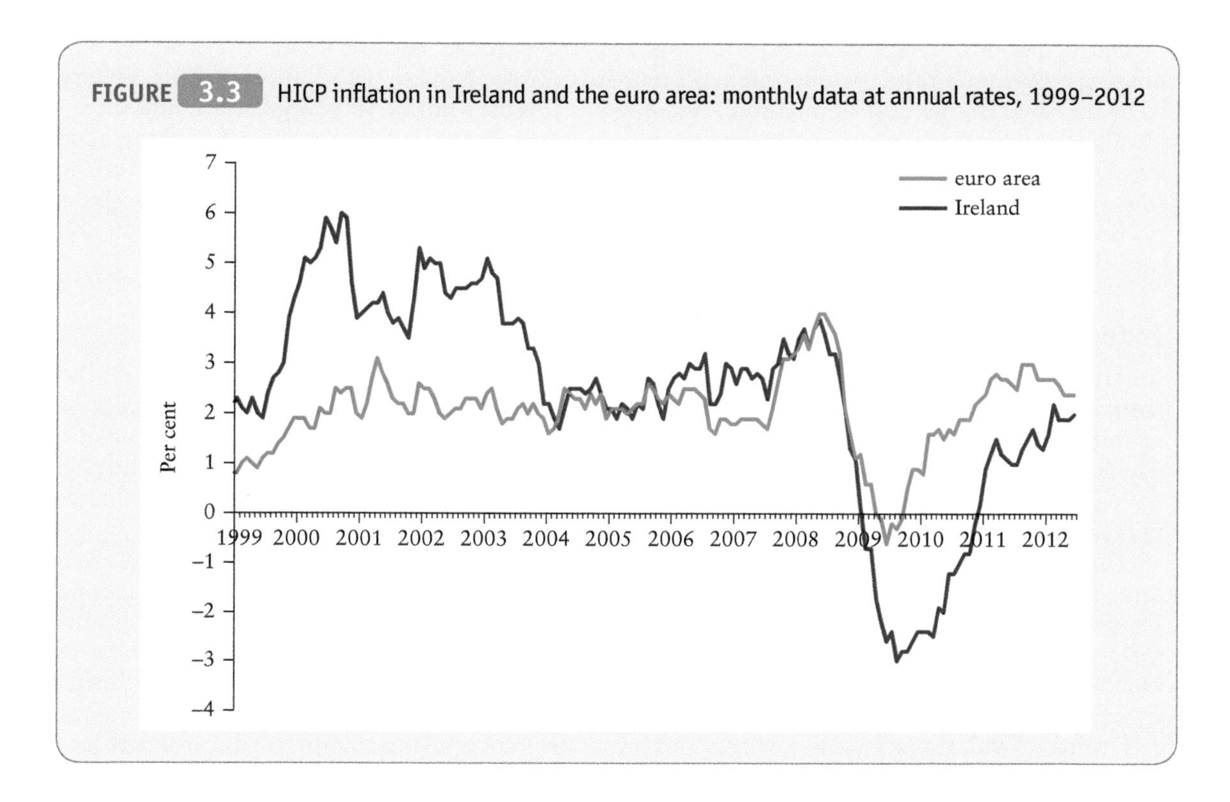

NOTE: In addition to the economy-wide price indices we have discussed here, there are other important price indices relating to particular sectors in the economy. The most commonly cited indices are the manufacturing industry output price index, the wholesale price index, and the agricultural output price index. More recently, great attention has been paid to the index of house prices.

3.4 The Effects of Inflation

Most contemporary Irish students of economics have never experienced high inflation first hand. Since the mid-1980s, inflation in Ireland and most advanced countries has averaged less than five per cent a year. However, in many developing countries very high inflation is still a serious problem; and there is always the danger that inflation could return to haunt us, as it did in the 1970s.

Should we worry about inflation? Should we be willing to squeeze inflation out of the economy if this entails high unemployment and slow growth? To answer these questions we need to consider the costs of inflation.

Transactions costs

There are some obvious, but fairly minor, costs of inflation. When prices are increasing, firms and shops have to print new price lists to inform their customers of the new prices. Customers have to go to some trouble to find out about price changes in order to keep up to date. Economists call these the 'menu costs of inflation'. These costs are not major, but they can cause inconvenience and confusion.

During periods of high inflation people will hold less currency because inflation is eroding its purchasing power. As a result people will make more trips to the bank to withdraw cash. This is referred to as the 'shoe leather cost of inflation'. Again, while this may not be very large, it is a nuisance.

When inflation is high it is also likely to be variable. You can confirm this by looking at Figure 3.2. In the 1970s, inflation was not only high but also very erratic, whereas in the 1990s it was low and stable. Variable inflation can cause confusion and uncertainty. Consumers and businesses do not know what rate of inflation to anticipate from year to year. This introduces a lot of 'noise' into the economy and reduces the efficiency of the price system.

Indexing assets, prices and wages to inflation

Inflation affects the real value of assets. If you had bought shares in a company for €100 and sold them a year later for €110, you would have made a capital gain of €10. However, if inflation was running at 10 per cent the nominal capital gain would have been entirely wiped out by inflation. The Revenue Commissioners no longer allow us to 'index' the price of assets to inflation and nominal capital gains are taxed at 30 per cent. Given the inflation in the economy, the investor incurs a real capital loss.

The failure to index nominal prices and incomes to inflation is a serious issue. If pensions are not linked or indexed to inflation, pensioners suffer a decline in their living standards due to inflation. People who invested in government bonds that paid a fixed dividend (or coupon) have in many instances seen the value of their savings eroded through inflation. In response to this, some governments now issue inflation-linked bonds. The Irish government does not. We discuss this issue in more detail in Chapter 19.

During an inflationary period, wages and prices begin to chase each other in a spiral that leaves no one better off in the long run. Because inflation erodes the value of workers' wages, they claim compensation through large wage increases. This contributes to more inflation and the process can become self-perpetuating.

Table 3.6 shows the percentage change in average hourly earnings and the CPI inflation rate from 1991 to 2012. The percentage change in the real wage is the percentage change in the nominal wage minus the rate of inflation:

$$\%\Delta\text{Real wage} = \%\Delta\text{Nominal wage} - \text{inflation rate}$$

Over the whole period, nominal wages rose at an annual average rate of 3.7 per cent. But inflation averaged 2.5 per cent a year, so real wages rose by only 1.2 per cent a year. There were years when real earnings declined, remained stagnant or increased only marginally (1992 and 2000). Real wages did, however, increase significantly in 1999, 2001 and 2003, and paradoxically the largest increase – over 7 per cent – occurred in 2009. This was when the price level declined and nominal wages did not. However, in this year large income tax increases were imposed, so real after-tax income did not grow.

Over the longer run, real wages are determined by the supply and demand for labour. We develop these concepts in Chapter 4. The relevant point to take away at this point is that inflation introduces confusion into the wage bargaining process. Workers try to compensate for past inflation and anticipate future inflation, and employers try to resist claims for higher nominal wages. Irish policy-makers tried to address this issue over the years by introducing national wage agreements between trade unions, employers and government in an effort to minimise industrial unrest.

Effects on income distribution

Inflation redistributes income between different groups in society. To see this, note that:

$$\text{Real interest rate} = \text{nominal interest rate minus inflation}$$

TABLE 3.6 Real and nominal wage increases

	Increase in industrial earnings (nominal) % (a)	Inflation % (b)	Increase in real wages % (a) – (b)
1991	6.0	3.2	2.8
1992	3.8	3.0	0.8
1993	6.4	1.5	4.9
1994	1.7	2.4	−0.7
1995	2.5	2.5	0.0
1996	4.1	1.6	2.5
1997	3.1	1.5	1.6
1998	5.2	2.4	2.8
1999	5.3	1.6	3.7
2000	6.6	5.6	1.0
2001	8.0	4.9	3.1
2002	6.5	4.6	1.9
2003	6.8	3.5	3.3
2004	4.7	2.3	2.4
2005	3.6	2.4	1.2
2006	3.5	3.9	−0.4
2007	5.8	4.9	0.9
2008	−4.8	4.1	−8.9
2009	2.7	−4.5	7.2
2010	−1.1	−0.9	−0.2
2011	0.0	2.6	−2.6
2012	1.0	2.2	−1.2
Average	3.7	2.5	1.2

Source: CSO database, Earnings and Labour Costs, average hourly earnings

Consider the example of a person who saved and put money in a bank in Ireland in the 1970s. The nominal interest received on the bank deposit was eight per cent (before tax). However, the inflation rate was over 15 per cent. Thrifty people got their savings back in depreciated money. That is, the real interest rate was negative. In effect their savings were being stealthily confiscated by inflation.

Borrowers, on the other hand, paid an interest rate that was lower than the inflation rate. They gained by going into debt and repaying loans in money whose value had declined. In this manner the high inflation of the 1970s transferred substantial amounts of wealth from savers to borrowers. The problem during this period was that high inflation was not anticipated. People who had grown up in the low-inflation environment of the 1950s took a long time to realise that high inflation was here to stay and they passively accepted interest rates that were below the rate of inflation. Even when they woke up to the reality of inflation, they could find no convenient way of investing their savings in inflation-proof assets.

> *By a continuous process of inflation, governments can confiscate, secretly and unobserved, an important part of the wealth of their citizens. By this method, they not only confiscate, but they confiscate arbitrarily; and while the process impoverishes many, it actually enriches some.* (Keynes 1919)

High inflation relative to interest rates was also a key factor underlying the housing boom in Ireland, especially between 2001 and 2007. Interest rates were set by the ECB but, as we saw in Figure 3.3, inflation in Ireland was above that of the euro area and, as a result, real interest rates in Ireland were low or sometimes negative. This encouraged people to borrow and invest far more in the property market than was warranted by the 'fundamentals'.

In general, unanticipated inflation acts like a tax on the weaker groups in society – the elderly living on fixed incomes, people with small savings who receive only fixed-interest payments, and others who are not smart enough or ruthless enough to offset the effects of rising prices on their income and wealth.

Inflation and international competitiveness

Inflation differentials between countries affect an economy's international competitive position and the ability of domestic firms to compete with their international rivals. If, for example, Ireland had an inflation rate of five per cent while inflation in the euro area countries averaged only two per cent, Irish exports would become progressively dearer in the rest of the euro area while imports would become cheaper in Ireland. This would have a negative effect on economic growth and employment in Ireland.

If wage inflation is persistently higher in Ireland than in other countries to which production can be relocated, this too will have a negative impact on the country. In January 2009 the Dell factory in Limerick was scaled down due to its high cost base relative to other locations where the company could manufacture. It is estimated that as many as 10,000 jobs were lost directly and indirectly across the Midwest region as a result. This illustrates the impact of high inflation on a region that has to compete internationally for inward investment.

3.5 Deflation

As we have seen, there were periods of stable or even falling prices in Ireland in the 1920s and 1930s, and during the post-2007 recession.

The effects of deflation are essentially the opposite to those of inflation. Deflation increases the real purchasing power of nominal savings and fixed incomes. Also, as seen in Ireland since 2007, wages in competitive labour markets are more likely than state old age pensions to be cut in response to deflation.

Deflation can help improve a country's international competitiveness. If a country's price level falls faster than that of its competitors, its competitiveness will improve. We can see from Figure 3.3 that since 2007 Ireland has experienced more deflation than other euro area countries. This has helped us to become more competitive.

But deflation poses a problem for monetary policy, which we discuss in detail later in this book. Monetary policy consists, in part, in central banks changing the nominal interest rate to influence real output or inflation. In recessionary times, the central bank may lower nominal interest rates

Box 3.1 Inflation indexation is not always popular

The Minister for Finance in 1924, Ernest Blythe, argued that since the cost of living was falling he was justified in cutting the old age pension for people aged 70 to 80 by 10 per cent, from 10 shillings to nine shillings a week. This led to an outcry, but Blythe remained in the government until the elections of 1932.

It is interesting to note that the reduced pension of nine shillings is equivalent to about €52 in today's money. Today, the actual value of the old age pension is €230 a week and it is paid to people from the age of 66.

to stimulate the economy. However, nominal interest rates cannot fall below zero (although some Swiss banks now charge you for the privilege of having money on deposit with them). Thus if the price level is falling, even if nominal interest rates fall to zero, the real interest rate will increase and this limits the effectiveness of monetary policy.

Just as inflation helps erode the real value of debt incurred in the past, deflation increases the burden of past borrowing. Irish households are now realising the seriousness of deflation for people who borrowed during the boom. Households who borrowed to purchase houses near the price peak are still responsible for the debt they incurred then, even though house prices have plummeted.

Ignoring repayments, the principle of a mortgage remains fixed even if the value of the house falls. House prices fell by at least 50 per cent in Ireland between 2007 and 2012. People who borrowed heavily to purchase at the height of the boom are now in a very unpleasant situation. A person might have borrowed €450,000 to buy a house valued at €500,000 in 2007. The value of the house could have fallen to €250,000 by 2012, but mortgage repayments are not adjusted to take account of this. It is understandable that the borrower will feel aggrieved at having to pay back over the next 20 years perhaps twice as much as the house is worth (as well as the interest on this amount).

The American economist Irving Fisher argued that borrowers cut spending as their debt burden increases and this deepens an economic slump, causing more deflation. He argued that this was a key factor underlying the Great Depression of the 1930s. We now see this effect acting as a significant drag on the recovery of the Irish economy from the post-2007 recession.

Benefits of inflation

Given these adverse effects of deflation it is possible to make an argument that inflation has some benefits to offset the costs we have been discussing.

Inflation erodes the burden of debt, which is fixed in nominal terms. As we shall discuss in a later chapter, most countries emerge from wars heavily indebted, which is like a millstone round the necks of the post-war generation. In fact many countries – such as the United States in the 1950s – inflated their way out of their debt. The rate of inflation was higher than the interest rate on government war bonds and this helped ease the burden on the taxpayer at the expense of those who invested in these bonds.

Another possible benefit of inflation is that it makes it easier to reduce real wages. Recall that the rate of increase in real wages is the difference between the rate of increase in nominal wages and the rate of inflation (see Table 3.6). It is very difficult to get workers and trade unions to agree to a reduction in nominal wages. The argument here is that inflation can make the labour market work more effectively. Suppose that it is necessary for the real wage to fall by two per cent to reduce unemployment. Which of the following two options is best?

$$\text{Nominal wage} = \text{real wage} + \text{inflation}$$

$$\text{Option A: } -2\% = -2\% + 0\%$$

$$\text{Option B: } 3\% = -2\% + 5\%$$

Generally, workers and trade unions will resist any cut in their nominal wages. With the exception of Ireland in the 2007–12 period, it was very rare for nominal wages to decline. Hence option A above may be very difficult to implement.

Option B, on the other hand, lets inflation do the job. If workers suffer from money illusion, they feel better off because their nominal wage has gone up by three per cent. But the inflation rate of five per cent in the background ensures that the real wage declines by two per cent. The main point is that inflation greases the wheels of the labour market and makes the market more flexible.

As the data in Table 3.6 show, in 2009, when the Irish price level fell, nominal wages increased, resulting in a substantial rise in real wages. On the other hand, in 2006 nominal wages rose by 3.5 per cent, but inflation was 3.9 per cent, resulting in a 0.4 per cent fall in real wages. What happened in 2006 was arguably less painful than trying to engineer a reduction in nominal wages.

Finally, it may be the case that businesses are more buoyed up by the prospect of rising prices, even if costs are also rising, than by the prospect of deflation. While very high rates of inflation are disruptive and make it hard to plan the future, the prospect of moderate inflation probably encourages more risk-taking than does the prospect of deflation.

It is for these reasons that central banks target a low but positive rate of inflation. Their task is to avoid higher rates of inflation that could spiral out of control into hyper-inflation and do untold damage to the economy, but they are also aware that a falling price level poses the threat of deflation and the problems associated with it. With this in mind, the ECB has set itself the target of maintaining inflation close to but below two per cent.

In Appendix 3.1 below we provide a brief list of winners of the Nobel Prize in economics. We hope that this appendix will give the reader an insight into how economics, both micro- and macro-, has evolved over the years.

3.6 Key Terms and Concepts

The main topics discussed in this chapter were:

- the measurement of inflation
- Ireland's inflation record
- the effects of inflation.

Appendix 3.1 Winners of the Nobel Prize in economics 1969–2011 and their contributions to economics

1969 Ragnar Frisch and Jan Tinbergen (joint award): for the development and the application of dynamic models for the analysis of economic processes.

1970 Paul Samuelson: for the development of static and dynamic economic theory and his contribution to raising the level of analysis in economic science.

1971 Simon Kuznets: for his empirically founded interpretation of economic growth, which led to a new insight into the economic and social structure and process of development.

1972 John Hicks and Kenneth Arrow (joint award): for their pioneering contributions to general economic equilibrium theory and welfare theory.

1973 Wassily Leontief: for the development of the input-output method and for its application to important economic problems.

1974 Gunnar Myrdal and Friedrich August Von Hayek (divided equally): for their pioneering work in the theory of money and economic fluctuations and for their analysis of the interdependence of economic, social and institutional phenomena.

1975 Leonid Kantorovich and Tjalling Koopmans (joint award): for their contributions to the theory of optimum allocation of resources.

1976 Milton Friedman: for his achievements in the fields of consumption analysis, monetary history and theory and for his demonstration of the complexity of stabilisation policy.

1977 Bertil Ohlin and James Meade (divided equally): for their contribution to the theory of international trade and international capital movements.

1978 Herbert Simon: for his pioneering research into the decision-making process within economic organisations.

1979 Theodore Schultz and Arthur Lewis (divided equally): for their contribution to economic development research with particular consideration of the problems of developing countries.

1980 Lawrence Klein: for the creation of econometric models and the application to the analysis of economic fluctuations and economic policies.

1981 James Tobin: for his analysis of financial markets and their relations to expenditure decisions, employment, production and prices.

1982 George Stigler: for his seminal studies of industrial structures, functioning of markets and cause and effect of public regulation.

1983 Gerard Debreu: for having incorporated new analytical methods into economic theory and for his reformulation of the theory of general equilibrium.

1984 Richard Stone: for his contribution to national income accounting and improving the basis for empirical economic analysis.

1985 Franco Modigliani: for his analysis of saving and financial markets.

1986 James Buchanan: for his development of the contractual and constitutional basis for the theory of economic and political decision-making.

1987 Robert Solow: for his contribution to the theory of economic growth.

1988 Maurice Allais: for his contribution to the theory of markets and efficient utilisation of resources.

1989 Trygve Haavelmo: for his clarification of probability theory foundations of econometrics and his analysis of simultaneous economic structures.

1990 Harry Markowitz, Merton Miller and William Sharpe (one-third each): for their work in the theory of financial economics.

1991 Ronald Coarse: for his discovery and clarification of the significance of transaction costs and property rights for the institutional structure and functioning of the economy.

1992 Gary Becker: for extending the domain of microeconomic analysis to a wide range of human behaviour and interaction, including non-market behaviour.

1993 Robert Fogel and Douglass North (joint award): for having renewed research in economic history by applying economic theory and quantitative methods in order to explain economic and institutional change.

1994 John Harsanyi, John Nash and Reinhard Selten (joint award): for their analysis of equilibria in the theory of non-co-operative games.

1995 Robert Lucas: for the development and application of the hypothesis of rational expectations, and thereby having transformed macroeconomic analysis and deepened the understanding of economic policy.

1996 James Mirrlees and William Vickrey: for their contribution to the economic theory of incentives under asymmetric information.

1997 Robert Merton and Myron Scholes: for a new method to determine the value of derivatives.

1998 Amartya Sen: for his contributions to welfare economics.

1999 Robert A. Mundell: for his analysis of monetary and fiscal policy under different exchange rate regimes and his analysis of optimum currency areas.

2000 The prize was shared between James J. Heckman, for his development of theory and methods for analysing selective samples, and Daniel L. McFadden, for his development of theory and methods for analysing discrete choice.

2001 The prize was awarded jointly to George A. Akerlof, A. Michael Spense and Joseph E. Stiglitz: for their analyses of markets with asymmetric information.

2002 The prize was shared between Daniel Kahneman, for having integrated insights from psychological research into economic science, especially concerning human judgement and decision-making under uncertainty, and Vernon L. Smith, for having established laboratory experiments as a tool in empirical economic analysis, especially in the study of alternative market mechanisms.

2003 The prize was shared between Robert F. Engle, for methods of analysing economic time series with time-varying volatility (ARCH), and Clive W. J. Granger, for methods of analysing economic time series with common trends (cointegration).

2004 The prize was awarded jointly to Finn E. Kydland and Edward C. Prescott for their contributions to dynamic macroeconomics: the time consistency of economic policy and the driving forces behind business cycles.

2005 The prize was awarded jointly to Robert J. Aumann and Thomas C. Schelling for having enhanced our understanding of conflict and co-operation through game-theory analysis.

2006 Edmund S. Phelps: for his analysis of intertemporal trade-offs in macroeconomic policy.

2007 The prize was awarded jointly to Leonid Hurwicz, Eric S. Maskin and Roger B. Myerson for having laid the foundations of mechanism design theory.

2008 Paul Krugman: for his analysis of trade patterns and location of economic activity.

2009 The prize was shared between Elinor Ostrom, for her analysis of economic governance, especially the commons, and Oliver E. Williamson, for his analysis of economic governance, especially the boundaries of the firm.

2010 The prize was awarded jointly to Peter A. Diamond, Dale T. Mortensen and Christopher A. Pissarides for their analysis of markets with search frictions.

2011 The prize was awarded jointly to Thomas J. Sargent and Christopher A. Sims for their empirical research on cause and effect in the macroeconomy.

2012 The prize was awarded jointly to Alvin E. Roth and Lloyd S. Shapley for their work on the theory of stable allocation and market design.

Source: Nobel Prize Internet Archive (http://nobelprizes.com/nobel/).

CHAPTER 4

The Labour Market and Unemployment

4.1 Introduction

We have emphasised that inflation and unemployment are two evils that macroeconomic policy seeks to minimise. In the previous chapter we discussed inflation. In this chapter we turn our attention to unemployment. We discuss the theory of unemployment, review how it is measured and summarise the Irish unemployment record since World War II.

At a theoretical level we can think of unemployment as an imbalance between the supply of and demand for labour. When employers are seeking to employ more people than are available for work, unemployment will fall and wage rates will increase. When more people are seeking work than there are jobs available, unemployment will rise and wages will fall.

To get a deeper understanding of unemployment we look at how the supply of and demand for labour interact in the labour market.

4.2 The Labour Market

The workings of the labour market are best understood by taking a microeconomic approach similar to the one we would take in looking at any 'normal' market. Later on we discuss why the labour market differs in many ways from a normal market.

The demand for labour

We start by describing the demand for labour. To do this we refer back to the concept of the production function that we introduced in Chapter 2.

We assume that markets are competitive and each firm takes the nominal wage (W) and the price level (P) as given. Firms hire more labour if the benefit to them of an extra worker exceeds the cost. The cost to the firm of hiring a worker is the real wage and the benefit is the marginal product of labour (MPL). Recall from Chapter 2 that the production function can be written as:

$$Y = F(K, L)$$

where Y is output, K is capital and L is labour. For simplicity, we ignore technology and natural resources. The MPL is defined as the extra output the firm can produce using an additional unit of labour (holding other inputs fixed):

$$MPL = F(K, L + 1) - F(K, L) \quad (1)$$

The production function for this firm is shown in Figure 4.1. In the upper diagram, increasing employment along the horizontal axis leads to an increase in output (Y) on the vertical axis. The slope of the production function reflects the MPL. It becomes flatter as the level of employment increases. This means that as more labour is hired, output continues to increase but at a diminishing rate. This is the assumption of diminishing returns to labour. The lower diagram shows the MPL at each level

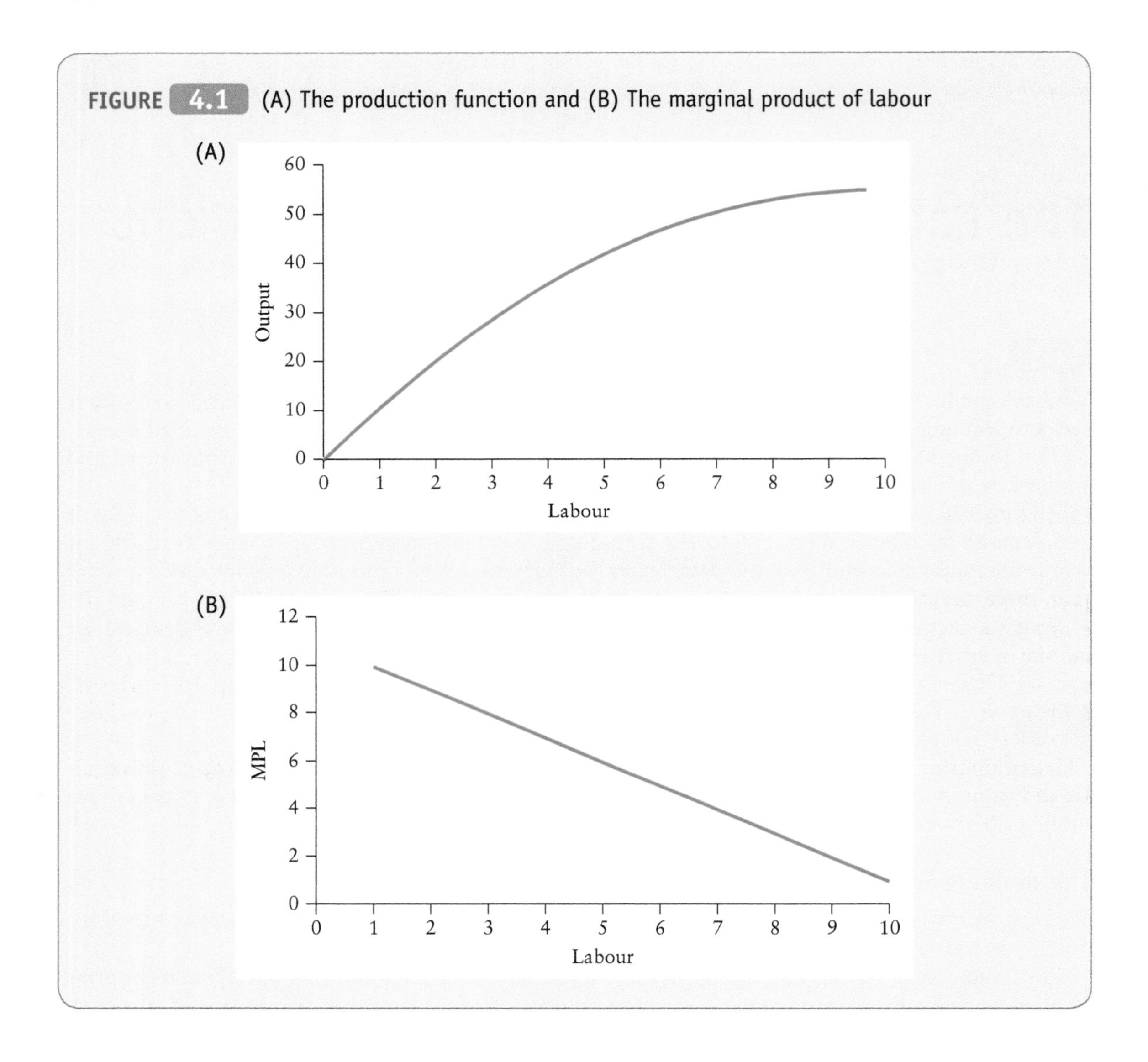

FIGURE 4.1 (A) The production function and (B) The marginal product of labour

of employment. In keeping with the convexity of the production function, this is decreasing along the vertical axis. It may be seen that the extra output produced by worker 6 is 5 units, but the extra output produced by worker 7 is 4 units. This again reflects the assumption of diminishing returns. As more and more labour is applied to a fixed amount of capital, each additional worker becomes less efficient. That is, the MPL declines as the level of employment rises. (Figure 4.1 is based on the data in Table 4.1.)

The basic rule for profit maximisation is that a firm will increase output up to the point where the marginal cost (MC) of producing an extra unit of output is equal to the marginal revenue (MR) from selling it:

$$MC = MR \quad (2)$$

In a competitive market, each firm is so small in relation to the overall market that increases in its output will have no effect on the market price, so the demand curve for the firm's product is horizontal and not downward sloping as in the case of a monopoly. It follows that the firm maximises profit when marginal revenue equals the output price (P). The profit-maximising rule is:

$$MC = P \tag{3}$$

Consider the cost of producing an extra unit of output, MC. We have assumed that the only variable input is labour: the other inputs as given in the production function are fixed in the short run. MC is therefore equal to the cost of hiring one extra worker divided by the number of units of extra output he or she produces. The cost of the worker is the wage rate (W) and the output of the worker is the marginal product of labour (MPL). Hence:

$$MC = W/MPL \tag{4}$$

If, for example, the wage rate is €500 a week and an additional worker produces 20 units of output in a week, the MC of a unit of output is €25. Substituting equation (4) into (3), a firm maximises its profits when:

$$W/MPL = P \tag{5}$$

Rearranging, the profit maximisation rule can be written as:

$$W/P = MPL \tag{6}$$

Equation (6) states that a firm's profits are maximised when the real wage rate (W/P) is equal to the marginal product of labour, MPL. Consider the data in Table 4.1. Suppose the real wage is 5, how many workers should the firm hire? If it hired three workers the MPL would exceed the real wage and profits could be increased by hiring additional labour. Similarly, if it hired 10 workers, the MPL would fall to one, which is less than the real wage. The firm would incur a loss on the last five workers hired. The firm could increase profits by reducing its workforce to six.

We can use this approach to trace out the demand for labour curve, which is labelled $L^d(MPL)$. This indicates that the number of workers demanded is a function of the marginal product of

TABLE 4.1 The marginal product of labour

Labour	Units of output	Marginal product of labour
L	Y	MPL
0	0	NA
1	10	10
2	19	9
3	27	8
4	34	7
5	40	6
6	45	5
7	49	4
8	52	3
9	54	2
10	55	1

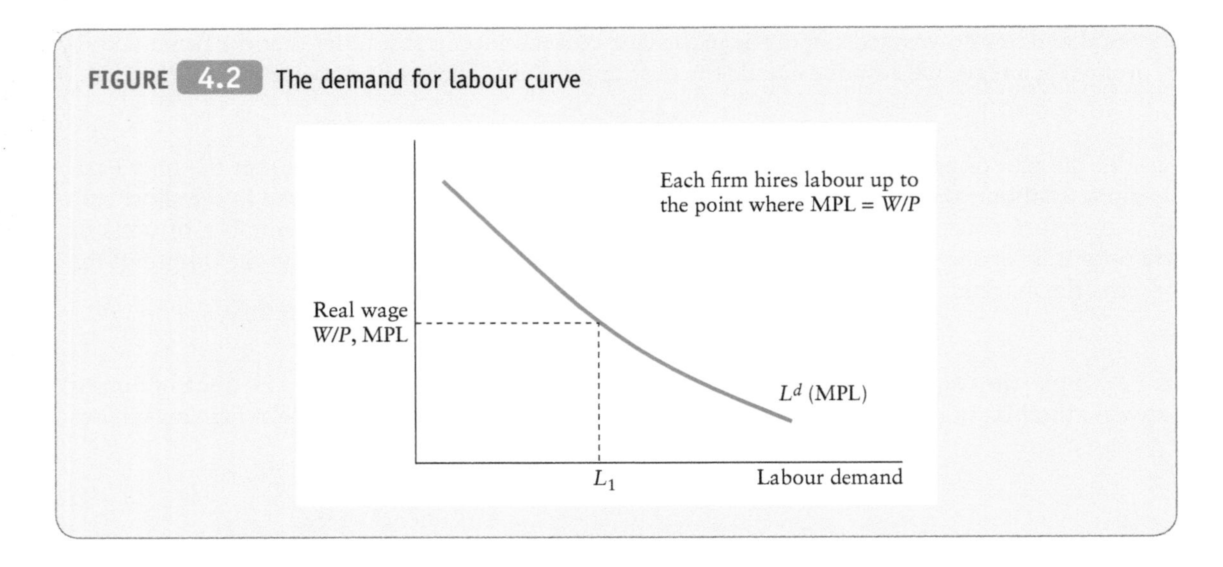

FIGURE 4.2 The demand for labour curve

labour. In Figure 4.2 the real wage is shown along the vertical axis. Picking a particular real wage and reading over to the MPL line we obtain the associated demand for labour along the horizontal axis. For any level of W/P we can read off the profit-maximising level of employment by moving horizontally over to the MPL curve and then vertically down to the X-axis. Because the MPL curve is downward sloping due to diminishing returns, the demand for labour curve is also downward sloping.

The MPL at different levels of employment depends on the level of capital, technology, education and training that are being combined with labour to produce the firm's output. An increase in the capital stock, for example, increases MPL. This shifts the L^d curve outwards and more labour will be demanded at a given wage rate. In Figure 4.3 the demand for labour shifts outward due to an increase in the capital stock and, at the original wage rate, more workers will be employed.

In Appendix 4.1 below, we explain the Cobb–Douglas production function and show how it is related to the distribution of national income and to productivity.

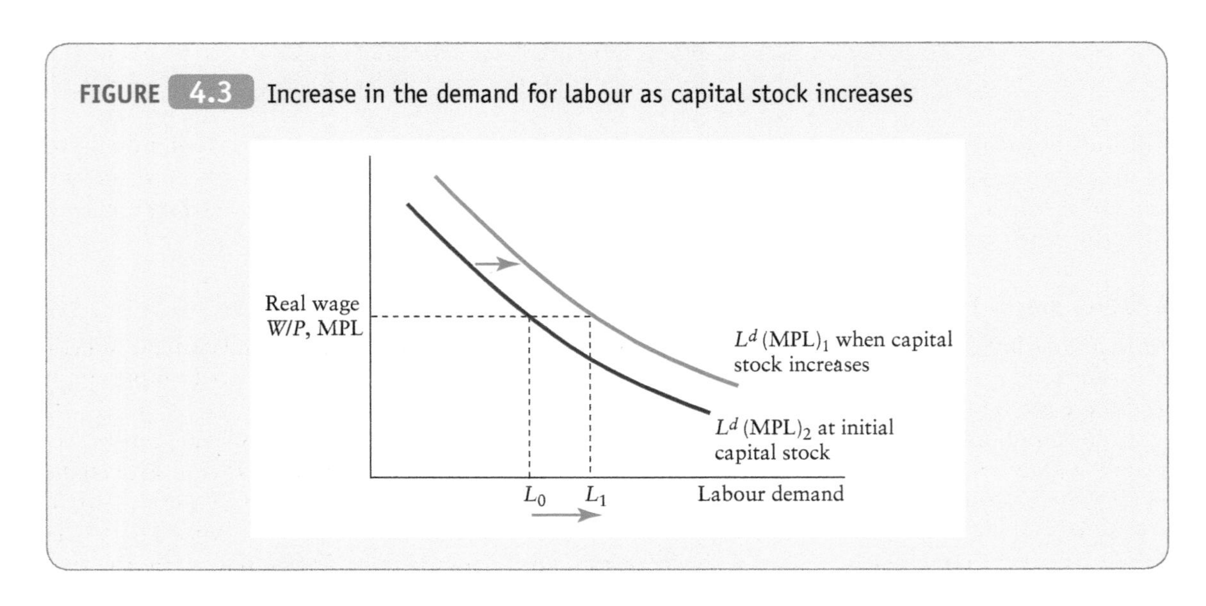

FIGURE 4.3 Increase in the demand for labour as capital stock increases

FIGURE 4.4 The supply of labour

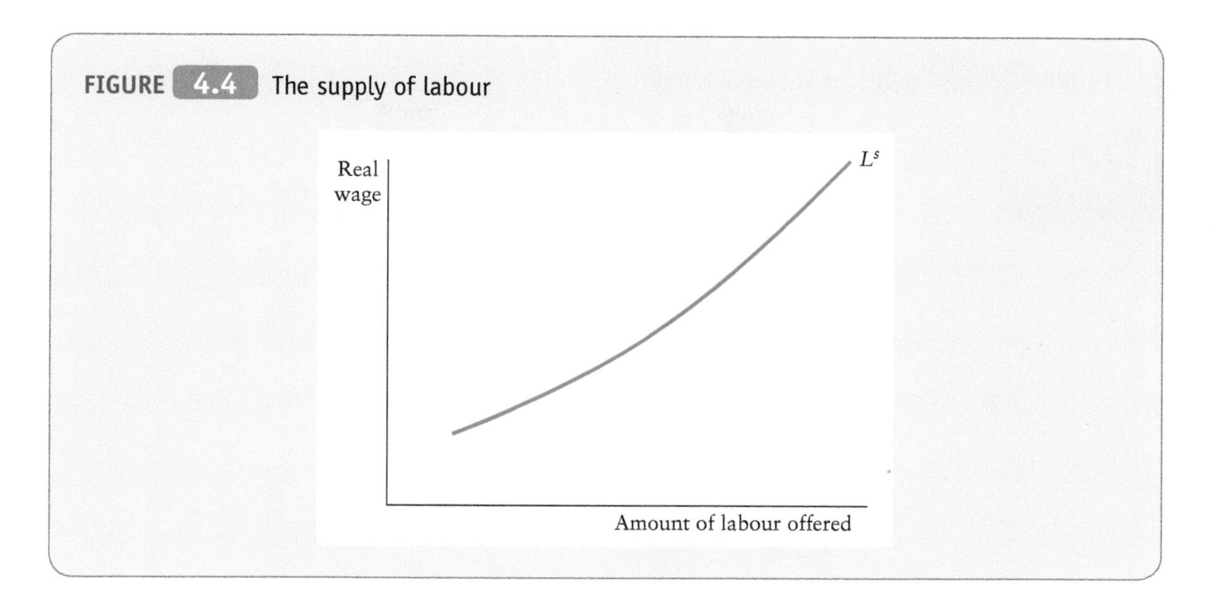

The main point made in Appendix 4.1 is that the MPL is proportional to average labour productivity (Y/L). Therefore W/P should rise when labour productivity is growing. In fact the evidence is consistent with this prediction, as over the long run real wages have risen more or less in line with productivity.

The supply of labour

The other side of the labour market is the supply of labour. In the short run, with a given working-age population, we assume that the supply of labour depends on the real wage, W/P. This reflects the common sense belief that people must be paid more if they are to work longer hours and that it takes a higher real wage rate to induce inactive people into the labour force. The supply of labour function is written:

$$L^s = F(W/P) \tag{7}$$

The labour supply curve, L^s, in Figure 4.4 is upward sloping, reflecting the assumption that as the (real) wage increases workers are willing to work longer hours (overtime) and more people enter the labour force seeking employment.

Over the longer run, factors like the size of the population, its age structure and the participation of different demographic groups in the labour force determine the size of the labour force and the supply of labour. We show how these factors have influenced the size of the Irish labour market over the years in Appendix 4.2 at the end of this chapter.

Labour market equilibrium

As in all markets, the equilibrium in the labour market occurs where the supply and demand schedules intersect. At $(W/P)_0$ in Figure 4.5 firms can hire the number of workers they wish to hire (L_0), and there are no unemployed job seekers.

If the supply of labour exceeds the demand, there is an excess supply of labour. This represents people who would be willing to work at the going wage but cannot find job offers. They are unemployed. On the other hand, if the demand for labour exceeds the supply at the going real wage there will be labour shortages and the real wage will rise. This increase in the real wage will increase the supply and reduce the demand. If there is an excess supply of labour, and unemployment, the real

FIGURE 4.5 Labour market equilibrium

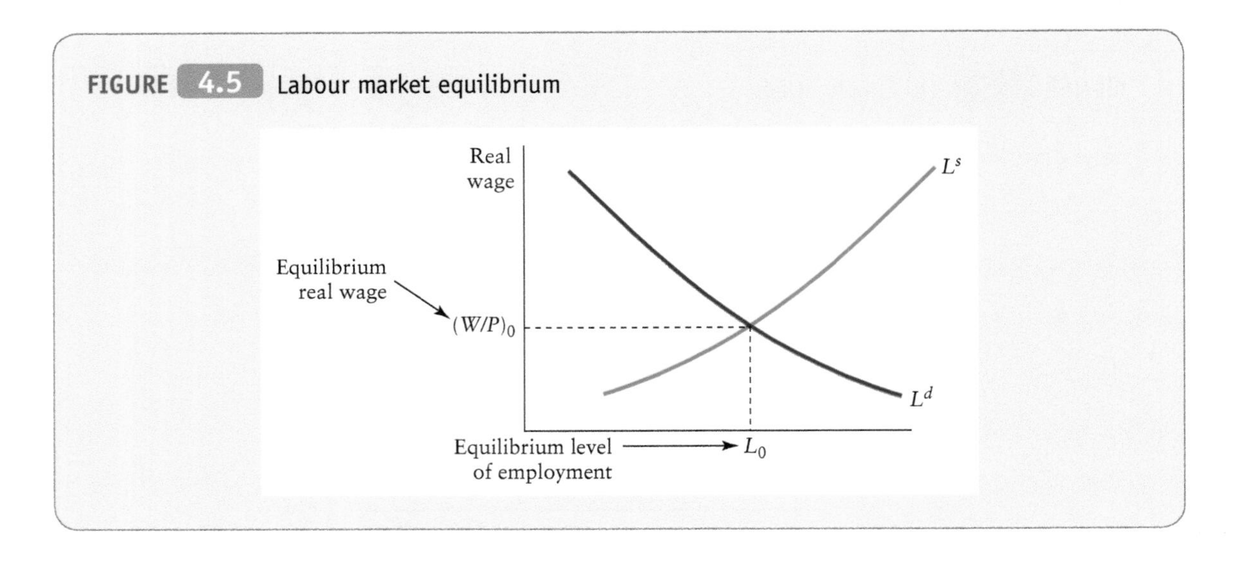

FIGURE 4.6 Unemployment

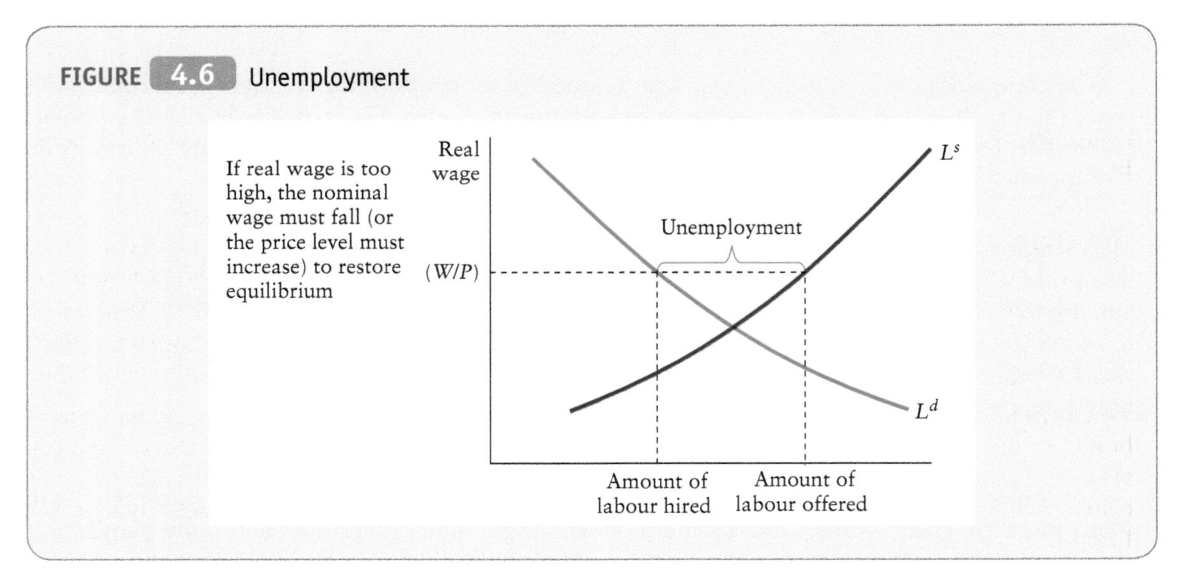

wage should fall, reducing the supply of labour and increasing the demand for labour to restore equilibrium. However, real wages are likely to be sticky or inflexible in a downward direction as workers resist nominal wage cuts. This will lead to persistent unemployment.

Figure 4.6 illustrates the case where the real wage is too high. Either the nominal wage must fall or the price level must rise (or some combination of both) to restore equilibrium. In Figure 4.7, the real wage is too low. Firms would like to hire L_2 labour but only L_1 is supplied, hence there is an excess demand or shortage of labour equal to $L_2 - L_1$. Now the nominal wage must rise or the price level fall to restore equilibrium.

4.3 The Natural Rate of Unemployment

The idea of a 'natural' rate of unemployment was introduced into economics by Milton Friedman and Edmund Phelps in the 1960s. Both were awarded the Nobel Prize in economics. Friedman gave

FIGURE 4.7 Labour shortages

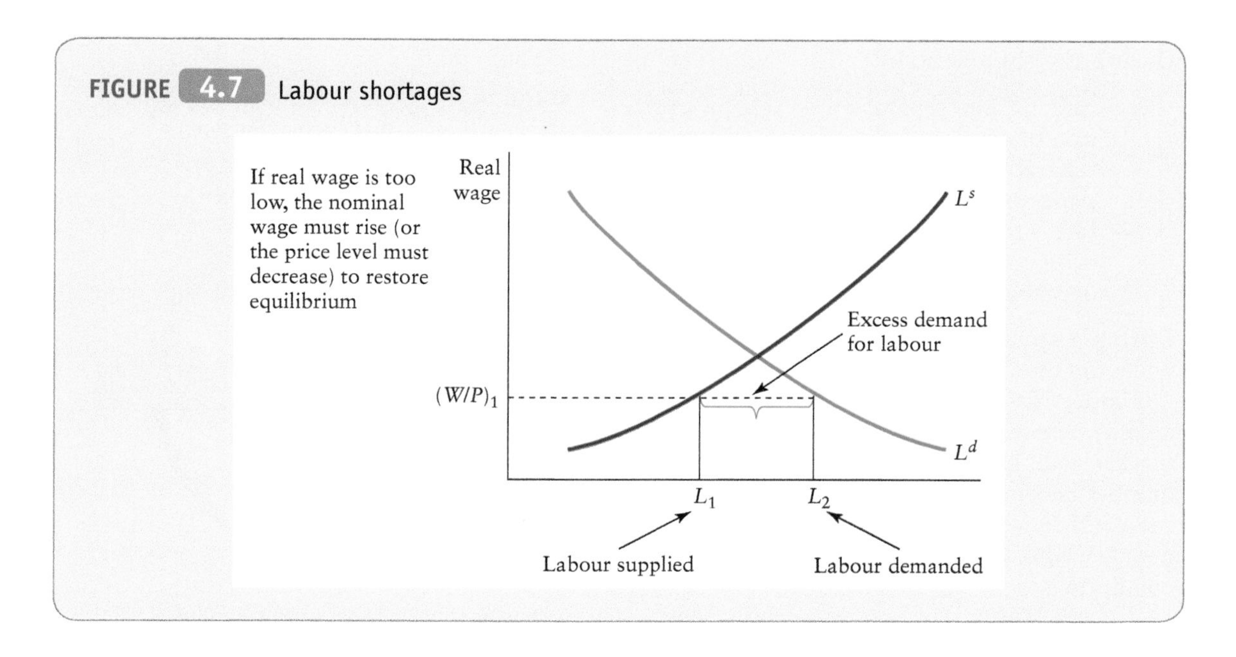

a clear definition of what he meant by this phrase in his 1968 Presidential Address to the American Economic Association:

> *At any moment of time, there is some level of unemployment which has the property that it is consistent with equilibrium in the structure of real wages ... The 'natural rate of unemployment' ... [is] the level that would be ground out by the [economy] ... [given] the actual structural characteristics of the labour and commodity markets, including market imperfections, ... variability in demands and supplies, the costs of gathering information about job vacancies, and labor availabilities, the costs of mobility, and so on.*

This implies that there is unemployment that will persist when the supply and demand for labour on aggregate are balanced and that this unemployment is 'normal' or 'natural' given the structure of the economy. It is the unemployment that arises from the rigidities and imperfections in the way labour markets work. We could call this *natural unemployment.* Unless what Friedman called the 'structural characteristics' of the labour market change, the 'natural' rate is the steady-state rate to which the economy gravitates in the long run. At this unemployment rate no inflationary pressures build up in the labour market, on the one hand, and there is no 'excess' unemployment, on the other. If the economy grows fast enough to stay on its 'natural' growth path, the rate of unemployment will remain stable, fluctuating only marginally round its natural rate.

Unemployment in the steady state

We can develop a simple model that shows how the steady-state unemployment rate depends on two key characteristics of the labour market.

We use the following notation:

E = number of employed workers
U = numbers unemployed
L = the labour force = E + U
U/L = the unemployment rate (per cent)

During any given period:

s = rate of job separation – the proportion of employed workers who become separated from their jobs due to redundancy over the period

f = rate of job finding – the proportion of unemployed workers who find jobs over the period.

During a recession s will rise and f will fall, while the reverse will happen during a boom.

Figure 4.8 shows the flows between employment and unemployment. The labour market will be in a steady state when the number becoming unemployed in each month equals the number of formerly unemployed people who find jobs. The steady-state condition is:

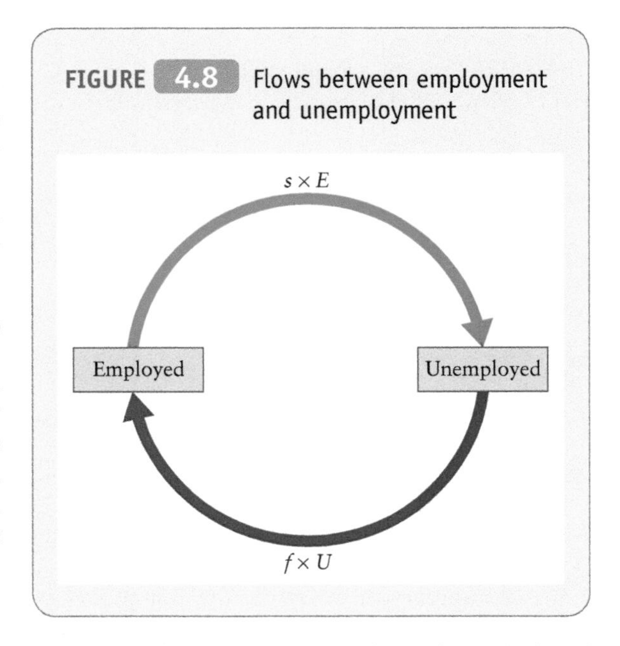

FIGURE 4.8 Flows between employment and unemployment

$$s \times E = f \times U$$

To calculate the unemployment rate corresponding to this, add and subtract U from the right-hand side:

$$f \times U = s \times (E + U - U)$$

or:

$$f \times U = s \times (L - U)$$
$$f \times U = s \times L - s \times U$$

Solve for U/L (unemployment rate):

$$(f + s) \times U = s \times L$$
$$\frac{U}{L} = \frac{s}{(s + f)}$$

To illustrate what this implies, assume that in a stable situation one per cent of employed workers lose their jobs each month ($s = 0.01$) and 19 per cent of unemployed workers find jobs ($f = 0.19$). The steady-state rate of unemployment is:

$$\frac{U}{L} = s/(s + f) = \frac{0.01}{(0.01 + 0.19)} = 0.05 \text{ or 5 per cent.}$$

This model of the steady-state unemployment rate is related to Friedman's concept of a 'natural' rate of unemployment. He believed that the natural rate depends on the structure of the economy and of the characteristics of the labour market. Hence, if s and f are stable, the unemployment rate will settle at $s/(s + f)$. However, if s should rise and/or f fall, the 'natural' rate of unemployment would rise.

What are the factors behind the separation rate and the job finding rate? When the economy falls into a recession, a larger proportion of the employed population lose their jobs (s rises) and it becomes harder for the unemployed to find jobs (f falls). If s were to rise to two per cent and f to fall to ten per cent, the unemployment rate would stabilise at $0.02/(0.02 + 0.1) = 16.7$ per cent. This would be the new 'natural' rate.

This illustrates the concept of *cyclical unemployment*, which accounts for the pronounced variation in the unemployment rate that we have experienced over the business cycle (we give the Irish data below). After a recession, when the economy stabilises, s will fall back, perhaps returning to its pre-recession level. But it is less likely that the rate of job finding among the unemployed, f, will revert back to its previous level. If it does not, the 'natural' rate of unemployment will rise not just in the short run but for a longer period.

We shall see below that during the recession that began in 2008 the rate of job losses soared, but fell back as the economy settled down at a very low growth rate after 2010. The chances of the unemployed finding new jobs remained very low. The steady-state unemployment rate rose from just over four per cent during the boom to close to 15 per cent during and after the recession. Even though the inflow to unemployment slowed down after 2009, many of the recently unemployed became long-term unemployed. The increase in the unemployment rate due to the recession became a more permanent type of unemployment.

Another factor that can contribute to a high steady-state unemployment rate is frequent shifts in the pattern of employment between occupations and sectors. This could be due to changing technology – the introduction of new products and the phasing out of old ones – and the changing pattern of spending over time. More is being spent on health, leisure and education now than 20 years ago, so there is an increased demand for people with skills in these service sectors. A lot of routine manufacturing has been relocated to low-wage developing countries, leading to large-scale job losses in Ireland and other developed countries. This gives rise to a high s and tends to increase the steady-state unemployment rate.

Finally, we should not forget that most young people leaving the education system and entering the labour market experience some initial unemployment. If the rate of inflow to the labour market is high – due for example to a rise in the birth rate 16 to 20 years earlier, the steady-state unemployment rate will rise until the 'baby bulge' has been absorbed into employment.

Seasonal unemployment is a special form of temporary unemployment. Some industries, such as tourism and fishing, are seasonal in nature. During the off-season, people engaged in these industries become temporarily unemployed. One of the puzzles of Irish unemployment is why it does not decline more steeply during the summer months in the tourist areas.

4.4 Frictional and Structural Unemployment

It is customary to talk about different types of unemployment, even though it is never possible to identify who falls into each category. The natural rate of unemployment is made up of frictional and structural unemployment. Cyclical unemployment is due to deviations of actual unemployment from the natural rate.

Natural rate of unemployment

This is the steady-state level of unemployment to which the economy gravitates in the long run. It is the level of unemployment that does not go away even in the long run. As mentioned, it consists of frictional unemployment and structural unemployment and can vary over time. It is also the level of unemployment associated with the potential real growth rate.

Frictional unemployment

This type of unemployment arises because of the time it takes workers to find jobs that suit their skills. In a dynamic economy people's preferences or tastes are ever-changing, new technologies are constantly being introduced and relative prices vary. As a consequence, some firms go out of business, while others open up. There are always people losing their jobs, switching between one job and another, and entering and leaving the labour force. Job vacancies may not match the skills or the occupations of the unemployed.

Unemployment that arises because of changes or friction in particular markets is referred to as frictional unemployment. This type of unemployment arises even when wages are flexible and there is an availability of jobs. It arises because workers have different abilities and preferences, and jobs have different skill requirements. Home ownership, schooling and other factors also limit the geographic mobility of workers. Furthermore, information about job vacancies is imperfect. The social welfare system means that people are not forced to accept the first job offered and instead can spend a long period of time finding suitable employment.

A particular type of frictional unemployment is seasonal unemployment. Some industries, such as tourism and fishing, are seasonal in nature. During the off-season, people engaged in these industries become temporarily unemployed.

Structural unemployment

As explained earlier, there is a particular real wage that ensures that the labour market is in equilibrium. If, for some reason, the real wage is above this equilibrium level, unemployment will result. This type of unemployment is called structural unemployment.

The overall labour market can be thought of as comprising many sub-labour markets. That is, there is a market for construction workers, accountants, engineers and so on. If the wage rate adjusted in all sub-labour markets to ensure that supply equalled demand, structural unemployment would be eliminated.

Let us consider further how these sub-labour markets are expected to adjust to unemployment. If wages rise in the occupations that are in demand and decline in those that are losing out, there will be a flow of workers to the expanding sectors and away from the contracting sectors.

But this process does not happen smoothly or instantaneously. It is limited by the fact that the labour markets for different occupations are quite separate. Dentists do not compete with bricklayers for jobs and unemployed bricklayers cannot easily retrain as qualified dentists!

Structural unemployment is due to the failure of the wage rate to ensure equilibrium in all sub-labour markets. For example, there has been a steady fall in the demand for automobile car workers in Detroit, while the demand for programming engineers in San Francisco has grown by leaps and bounds. However, unemployed automobile workers from Detroit have not thronged to booming Silicon Valley to take up jobs in the IT industry. No matter how far wages fall in Detroit or how high they rise in San Francisco, not many unemployed auto workers are likely to become programmers. It is asking too much to expect flexible wages to overcome all the obstacles to labour market adjustment. For this reason depressed regions continue to record high unemployment for long periods, while booming regions experience labour shortages.

Over the longer run, the biggest structural change in Ireland, as in most countries, has been the decline in the number of people working in agriculture. In 1961 there were 375,000 farmers and farm workers in Ireland. Today there are fewer than 100,000. Farming accounted for more than a third of the labour force then but only five per cent today. However, this change did not cause much structural unemployment because much of it took place through the emigration of farmers' children and the ageing of the farm labour force.

Another reason why structural unemployment can arise is due to forces preventing the wage rate falling to the equilibrium level and clearing the labour market. As explained below, structural unemployment can arise due to minimum wage laws, the power of the labour unions and/or efficiency wages.

4.5 Cyclical Unemployment

This is the deviation of *actual* unemployment from the *natural* rate. It is due to short-run swings in the business cycle. During the contractionary phase of the business cycle, firms lay off workers and unemployment rises. In principle, many of these workers should be hired back during the recovery phase of the business cycle.

A key question is: How long does cyclical unemployment last? The length and depth of the recession is critical in this regard. A protracted recession turns short-term into long-term unemployment and cyclical into structural unemployment. If cyclical unemployment were a short-lived phenomenon it would not be much of a problem. However, the evidence suggests that all too often it turns into structural unemployment and persists for a long time.

This lends great importance to the task of trying to keep the economy growing at a steady pace and avoiding the pronounced business cycles that characterise modern economies. We return to this issue in several later chapters.

Cyclical unemployment in Ireland

The recent upheaval in the Irish economy has seen our unemployment soar and remain high. Table 4.2 shows the changes in employment by sector that occurred between 2006 and 2011. The numbers reflect the impact of the post-2007 recession. Overall the numbers employed fell by 123,000 or six per cent while the numbers unemployed trebled. (The total labour force grew by 129,000.) Two sectors accounted for most of the decline in employment: Construction, where the numbers at work fell by 125,000 due to the collapse of the property market, and Industry, where the numbers at work fell by 48,000. On the other hand, the numbers working in the Educational sector rose 36,000, in Health by 16,000 and in Public Administration by 12,000.

Note that most of those employed in the expanding sectors are on the public payroll. Given the need to cut public spending, the level of employment in these sectors is now likely to decline. To

TABLE 4.2 Numbers at work in Ireland by broad sector of employment (thousands)

	2006	2011	Change 2006–2011
Agriculture and mining	97.0	99.9	2.9
Manufacturing industry and utilities	254.5	206.2	−48.3
Construction	215.2	90.4	−124.8
Wholesale, retail trade, transport, hotels and restaurants	463.7	466.9	3.1
Banking, financial services, real estate	266.4	277.4	11.0
Public administration and defence	101.3	113.5	12.3
Education	127.5	163.7	36.3
Health and social services	271.6	288.0	16.5
Other	132.9	101.3	−31.6
Total at work	1,930.0	1,807.4	−122.7
Unemployed, of which:			
Looking for first regular job	23.4	34.1	10.7
Having lost or given up previous job	150.1	390.7	240.6
Total unemployed	173.5	424.8	251.3
Total labour force, employed + unemployed	2,103.5	2,232.2	128.6

Source: Census of Population 2006 and 2011 (based on principal employment status (PES))

add to the gloomy picture, the banking and finance sector over-expanded during the boom and is now contracting.

The important point is that while overall employment declined, there were some expanding sectors. However, it is unlikely that many of those losing their jobs in construction or manufacturing would find work in the education, health or public administration sectors. Not surprisingly, therefore, the number of people unemployed – especially those who had lost their previous job – trebled.

Many of those who were working in the Irish construction sector before 2008 are unlikely to be able to find employment in Ireland again. They lack the skills needed in any of the growing sectors and occupations and may be too old to retrain. To get any proportion of the 400,000 people classified as unemployed in the 2011 Census back to work would require a resumption of rapid growth, which seems a long way off at present.

This illustrates how cyclical unemployment can turn into structural unemployment. It is simply asking too much of the wage rate to adjust to ensure the elimination of structural unemployment.

Cyclical unemployment and the natural rate of unemployment

Figure 4.9 sheds light on our earlier discussion of the 'steady state' or 'natural' rate of unemployment. Between 1960 and the early 1970s, and again between 2000 and 2007, the unemployment rate fluctuated in a band between four and six per cent. During these years the inflation rate was generally fairly low and stable. It is therefore tempting to identify somewhere in the region of five per cent as the Irish equilibrium rate. However, it is clear that the unemployment rate can remain far above its equilibrium level for long periods. It was above ten per cent for 16 years between 1981 and 1997. In 2012 it is close to 15 per cent. This volatility makes it hard to identify the 'natural' rate of unemployment. It is difficult to say when

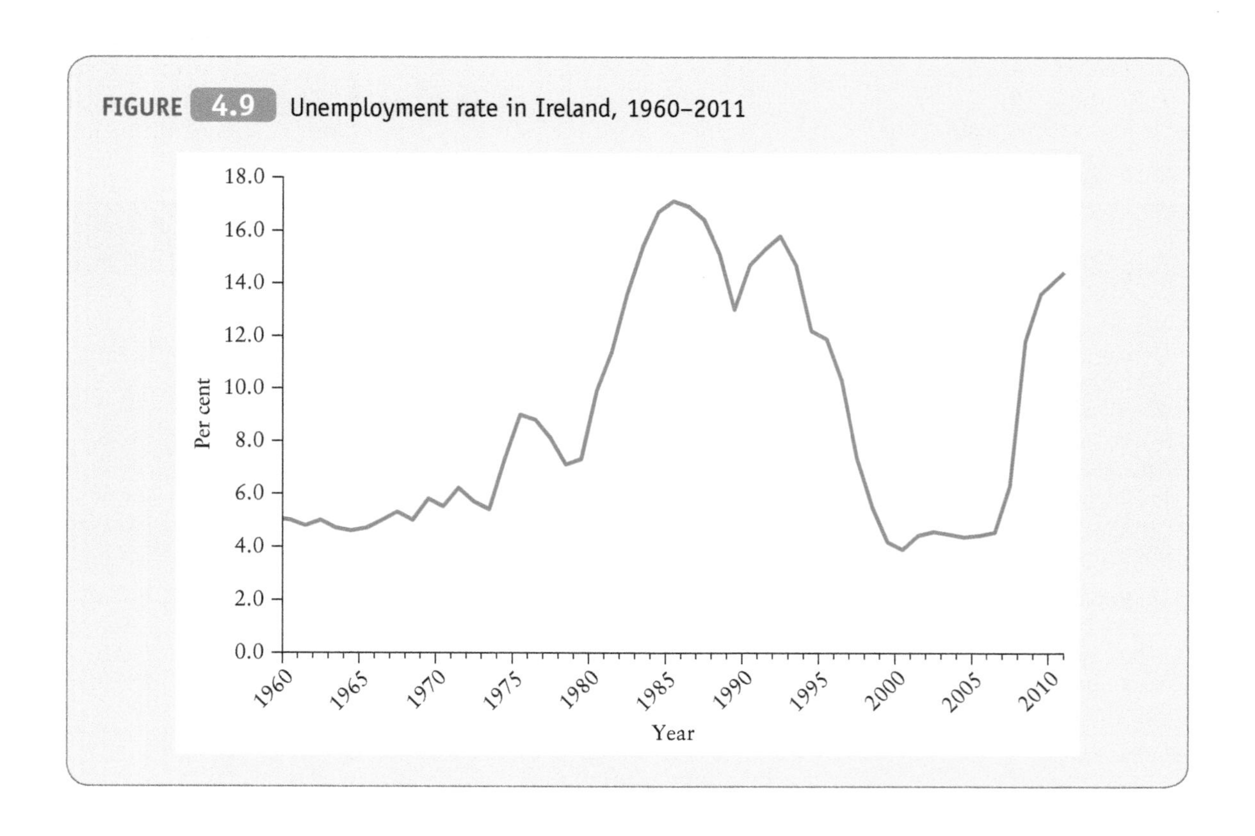

FIGURE 4.9 Unemployment rate in Ireland, 1960–2011

the unemployment rate will fall from its present peak and at what level it will settle when the economy begins to grow again. (Refer to the calculations in Chapter 12.)

For this reason some economists have been critical of the notion of a 'natural' rate to which the unemployment rate tends to revert. The natural rate of unemployment may rise as the actual unemployment rate rises. This has been labelled 'hysteresis'. It is as if your normal body temperature, instead of remaining at 37° Celsius, rose every time you had a fever.

After a decade of high unemployment, in Ireland in the 1990s it was said that our 'natural' rate was in the region of ten per cent, but we enjoyed a much lower rate without excessive inflation some ten years later. The Nobel Prize-winning economist Robert Solow said, 'A natural rate that hops around from one triennium to another under the influences of unspecified forces, including past unemployment rates, is not natural at all' (Layard *et al.* 1991; Solow 1986).

4.6 Why Doesn't the Labour Market Clear?

Most markets generally clear fairly quickly – excess supply and excess demand do not persist for long. So why is the situation different in the labour market? Why should there be any significant unemployment over and above some minimal level of frictional unemployment?

We have already discussed the implausibility of asking wages to adjust in sub-labour markets to eliminate structural unemployment. We now examine some of the reasons why the wage rate is kept above the equilibrium rate, thereby creating further structural unemployment.

The minimum wage

Many governments pass laws stipulating that a minimum wage must be paid to employees. In Ireland the minimum wage for adults is now €8.65 per hour. (It had been cut by €1 an hour at the beginning of 2011 but the new Fine Gael–Labour coalition government restored the former rate after taking office.) When account is taken of employers' Pay-Related Social Insurance (PRSI) of 4.25 per cent the cost of hiring an employee comes to more than €9 an hour. This may exceed what an unskilled and inexperienced worker is worth to an employer. Figure 4.10 shows how a high minimum wage results in unemployment by halting the downward adjustment of the wage rate.

FIGURE 4.10 Minimum wages

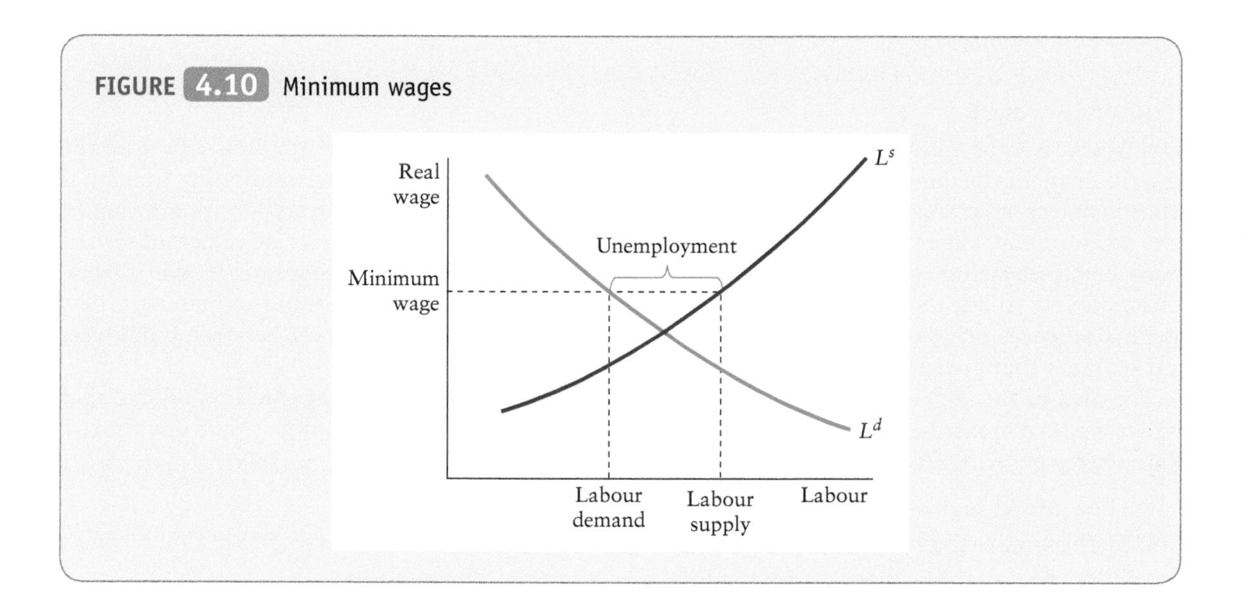

The workers who retain their jobs are, of course, better off, but the workers who lose their jobs or do not get employed are worse off. It is hard to quantify how important the Irish minimum wage is as a cause of unemployment, but it does militate against the provision of entry-level jobs that could provide unemployed young people with valuable work experience.

Trade unions

Trade unions affect how labour markets function. One of their main purposes is to secure higher wages for their members. If they are successful they will push the wage rate above the market clearing rate and increased unemployment will result. In inflationary periods unions seek the indexation of wages: automatic increases in nominal wages to compensate for rises in the cost of living. During the period of high inflation and rising income tax rates in Ireland in the 1970s and 1980s unions targeted real, after-tax pay. They sought to protect their members from the effects not only of inflation but also of higher taxation. This approach stymies the downward adjustment of the cost of employing workers that is needed to help the labour market clear.

It has been argued that there are two ways of organising labour markets that can ensure industrial harmony and low employment. One is the 'corporatist' or 'social partnership' approach that appears to be successful in the Scandinavian countries and Austria and was tried here from the late 1980s onwards. This involves obtaining agreement between trade unions, government and employers about wage increases and other labour market issues. We review Ireland's experience with this approach in Chapter 8. At the other extreme, in the United States union membership is very low and the wage-bargaining process is decentralised. By taking the local balance between supply and demand into account this helps labour markets to adjust.

The worst outcome may be associated with situations where individual trade unions struggle to increase their members' pay but accept no responsibility for the effect of their actions on the national economy. This was the situation in Britain before the Thatcher government broke the power of the unions in the 1980s.

Irish trade union power has declined considerably over the years. It is estimated that almost half of Irish workers were members of a trade union in the early 1990s; by 2006 this proportion had fallen below one-third. None the less, unions remain relatively strong in some public sector areas and are involved in national wage bargaining. By making it harder for employers to cut wages and introduce flexible working practices they may make the adjustment of the labour market to changing economic conditions more difficult.

Efficiency wages

Karl Marx, writing in the mid-nineteenth century, believed that the capitalists of his day used the 'reserve army of the unemployed' to force wages down to the bare subsistence minimum. Industrial relations are not so simple today. The unemployed do not knock at employers' doors offering to take work at any wage they are offered. If they did, employers would probably be reluctant to hire them, being suspicious of a worker who offers to work for less than the going rate. Nor is it usual for employers to ask their employees to accept wage cuts or to threaten to replace them with new recruits at lower wages. In most firms there is an explicit or implicit contract between employers and workers that guarantees a certain stability of wages.

The idea of the 'efficiency wage' has been developed to explain this behaviour. It is argued that higher wages increase worker productivity, which is more valuable to an employer than a wage cut. High wages have the following advantages.

- They attract higher-quality job applicants.
- They increase the motivation and work effort of those who are employed.
- They reduce labour turnover by binding workers to 'good' employers.

By paying above the odds, firms retain a more productive labour force than they would get if they set wages in accordance with fluctuations in the supply and demand for labour. We can think of the reputation of Guinness as employers in the city of Dublin in the last century. A job with the brewery was much more valuable than other available jobs. In return for paying above the odds, the firm got loyal and productive workers. The result, however, could have been more unemployment because fewer workers were hired at the higher wages.

The social welfare system

Modern economies all have highly developed welfare systems that are designed to help the unemployed cope with loss of income while they search for a new job. A relatively generous social welfare system increases search unemployment because it reduces the opportunity cost of being unemployed and the urgency of finding work. This will tend to lower f, the rate at which the unemployed accept job offers, and raise the natural rate of unemployment. A harsh social welfare system deprives the unemployed of the luxury of prolonged job search and encourages or forces them to accept whatever job offers they can get. Perhaps, like Hamlet, the state should be cruel (in the short run) to be kind (in the long run)! But generous Jobseeker's Benefits (JB) allow people more time to search for suitable jobs and this should lead to better matches between jobs and workers. This, in turn, should lead to greater productivity and higher incomes in the longer run.

Replacement ratio

The ratio of what a job seeker can obtain from the welfare system from benefits such as the JB and Jobseeker's Allowance (JA), housing benefits and a medical card, on the one hand, and what he or she would earn by taking a job offer (after taxes, social charges and work-related expenses), is known as the replacement ratio. A high replacement ratio can create a welfare or unemployment 'trap', making it more attractive for people to remain unemployed than to accept a job offer.

$$\text{Replacement ratio} = \frac{\text{net income while unemployed}}{\text{net income while employed}}$$

In 2012 a single person on the adult minimum wage (€8.65 an hour) earned a gross wage of about €330 a week or €17,000 a year. This is just under the PAYE and PRSI thresholds, but it is liable for a Universal Social Charge (USC) of €510, leaving €16,490 a year or €317 a week in take-home pay. When unemployed he or she would be entitled to JB or JA. The rates of payment of JB range from €85 a week, for JB for those previously on low incomes, to €188 (which is the maximum JB and the JA for persons aged 25 and over). The replacement ratio therefore lies in the range €85/€317 to €188/€317 or between 27 and 59 per cent.

This may seem relatively low, and hardly enough to dissuade a person from accepting a job offer, but several other factors need to be taken into account. The individual may be entitled to a range of other benefits such as:

- rent allowance
- medical card
- subsidised local authority housing
- non-cash benefits such as fuel allowances, etc.

Some or all of these would be withdrawn if the unemployed person accepted paid employment.

Moreover, the denominator of the replacement ratio should reflect not just taxes on income but also work-related expenses such as:

- cost of commuting
- childcare costs
- other employment-related expenses, such as having to dress more formally.

Finally, some unemployed people work occasionally in the grey or black economy while still registered as unemployed. In rural Ireland during the summer months there are still lots of opportunities for 'nixers'. The social welfare system finds it hard to crack down on this type of abuse.

The upshot is that the interaction of the tax and social welfare systems can create situations in which an unemployed person does not find it very attractive to 'sign off' the Live Register and accept an offer of employment.

In mid-2012 the ESRI published a working paper entitled *The Cost of Working in Ireland*, which claimed that up to 44 per cent of working parents with children in Ireland would be better off on social welfare. Work-related expenses such as transport, lunches and other outlays were estimated to cost parents up to approximately €10,000 a year. When account is taken of these and PAYE, PRSI, and the USC, it would not be worth many people's while to take up paid employment. This breeds a culture of welfare dependency. However, this paper was later withdrawn by the ESRI amid a storm of controversy. While the calculations have been criticised, there can be little doubt that in certain situations some unemployed people are better off remaining unemployed. (The paper is still available online at http://cdn.thejournal.ie/media/2012/06/ESRI-report.pdf, and a critique of its findings is contained in www.irisheconomy.ie/index.php/2012/06/20/the-costs-of-working-in-ireland-again/.)

There is evidence that countries where the unemployed are entitled to extended benefits have higher levels of long-term unemployment than countries where entitlement is limited. In the USA most unemployment benefits normally run out after six months' unemployment. However, in response to the recession of 2008 President Obama signed a bill that extended the duration of benefits for up to 99 weeks. It has been claimed that this helps account for the slow pace at which the unemployment rate has fallen as the US economy came out of the recession. In Ireland entitlement to JB normally runs out after 15 months, but if a person is still unemployed after this period they may qualify for a move to the means-tested JA. Entitlement to JA, which can last indefinitely, gives a rate of benefit much the same as for JB.

Recently a prominent American economist presented the following estimate of the impact of extending the payment of unemployment benefits in the USA:

> *Suppose that the expansion of unemployment-insurance coverage to 99 weeks had not occurred and I assume the share of long-term unemployment had equalled the peak value of 24.5 per cent observed in July 1983. Then, if the number of unemployed 26 weeks or less in June 2010 had still equalled the observed value of 7.9 million, the total number of unemployed would have been 10.4 million rather than 14.6 million. If the labour force still equalled the observed value (153.7 million), the unemployment rate would have been 6.8 per cent rather than 9.5 per cent.* (Barro 2010)

Tax wedges

Various taxes and levies, such as employer's and employee's PRSI, income tax (PAYE), pay-related social insurance (PRSI) and the universal social charge (USC), drive a wedge between what it costs an employer to hire a worker and the amount that worker actually takes home in his or her pay packet at the end of the week. This has serious implications for the level of employment and unemployment.

The supply of labour depends on the after-tax purchasing power of the worker's income, that is gross income less PAYE, employee's PRSI and the USC. The demand for labour, on the other hand, depends on the total costs of hiring a worker, that is the gross wage plus employer's PRSI.

The average industrial wage is now close to €700 a week. A single person on this income (€36,400 a year) is liable for €4,736 in PAYE, €1,456 in PRSI, and a USC of €1,867. This reduces take-home pay to €28,341, or €545 a week – just 80 per cent of gross pay. But the employer has to pay a further €2,710 in employer's PRSI. So it costs €39,110 to pay an employee enough for him or her to take home €28,341. The tax wedge in this example is almost exactly €10,764 or just over 27.5 per cent of the cost to the employer. Because these taxes and levies are progressive, their burden increases as the level of pay rises.

FIGURE 4.11 The tax wedge

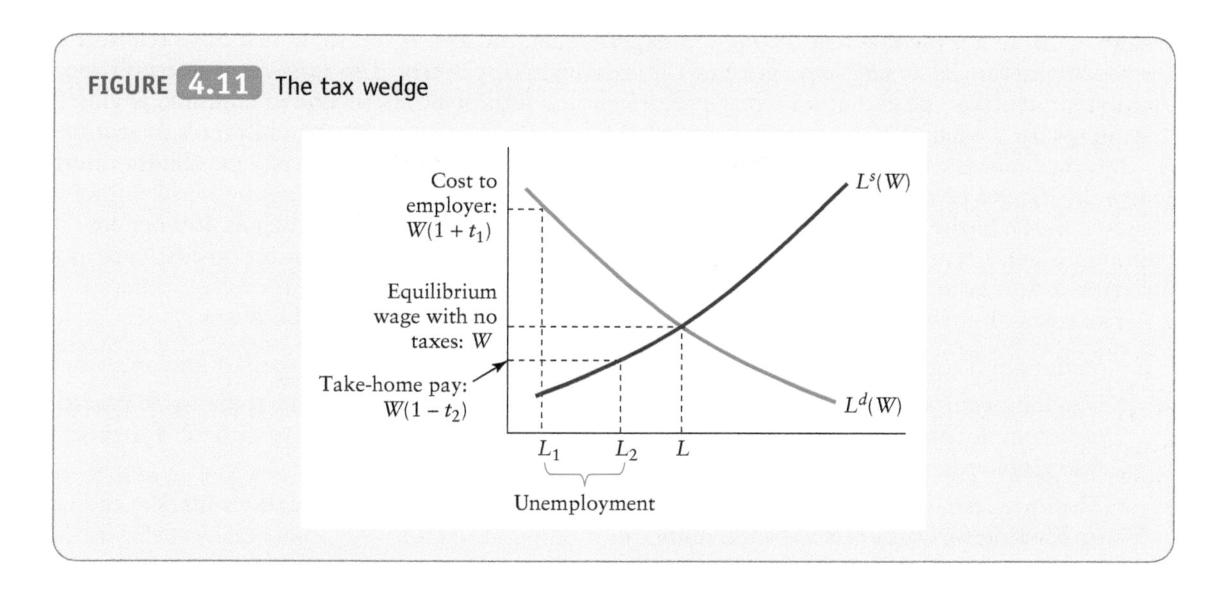

It is also relevant to consider VAT and excise taxes, which reduce the purchasing power of take-home pay when it is spent on goods and services. In Ireland today these would typically amount to another 25 per cent, reducing the purchasing power of take-home pay to €21,800, or about 56 per cent of the employment cost.

The effect of the tax wedge is to move the employer up along the demand for labour schedule leading to a reduction in employment. In Figure 4.11, where we assume the price level is constant, the equilibrium real wage is W and the corresponding level of employment L, where labour supply and demand are equal. If levies on employers are at a rate equal to t_1, the cost of hiring a worker is $W(1 + t_1)$. At this higher cost of hiring, the demand for labour falls to L_1. If taxes and levies on employees equal t_2, take-home pay falls to $W(1 - t_2)$. At this reduced take-home pay the supply of labour falls to L_2. But the demand for labour has fallen more than the supply of labour and a gap opened up between them. We assume that the demand for labour dictates the level of employment (the market is demand-constrained), so employment falls to L_1 and the gap $L_2 - L_1$ represents unemployment.

The size of gap depends on the slope of the supply and demand schedules. The more elastic or flat the schedules, the greater the impact on employment and the higher the level of unemployment that emerges. In Ireland both labour supply and labour demand are likely to be relatively elastic: the supply of labour because of the possibility of emigrating or working in the 'black' economy rather than accepting low after-tax wages; the demand for labour because much of our employment is in internationally traded sectors, where Irish employers are not able to raise their prices in response to higher domestic costs.

Despite this analysis, it should be admitted that social charges like PRSI and USC are relatively low in Ireland by European standards. In Germany, for example, the gap between take-home wages and the total employment cost to an employer is considerably larger than it is in Ireland, yet Germany has reduced its unemployment rate during the current recession.

4.7 The Costs of Unemployment

Unemployment imposes very serious costs on individuals and society. Obviously, becoming unemployed involves a loss of income. In developed countries this loss is shared between the employed and unemployed through the welfare system. This has to be financed by taxes levied on the working population, which act as a drag on the economy. Moreover, these transfer payments do not make up all of the income lost through unemployment and as a result there is a close relationship between the rate of unemployment and the incidence of poverty. The long-term unemployed in particular are likely to end up in a very precarious financial position, unable to continue paying the mortgage on their home, to service existing bank loans and to pay for their children's education.

If forced into the hands of unscrupulous money lenders, they will have to pay exorbitant interest rates. In Ireland interest rates as high as 187 per cent per annum are charged by licensed money-lending firms. In the USA, so-called 'pay-day' loans charge interest rates as high as 400 per cent per annum. Clearly, if an unemployed person is forced to borrow from these institutions they are likely to enter a downward spiral of poverty and hardship.

The costs of unemployment increase the longer a person is out of work because:

- Savings and social welfare payments help tide households over a short spell of unemployment.
- The long-term unemployed tend to lose motivation and self-esteem and come to be regarded as 'unemployable'. Their skills become out of date and it becomes more difficult for them to find employment.
- The long-term unemployed become discouraged, lose contact with the labour market and give up looking for work ('What's the point?').
- The long-term unemployed exercise little influence on the wage-bargaining process. They become 'outsiders'. The 'insiders' who are fortunate enough to still have jobs do not feel any pressure to accept wage cuts that would lead to more employment and help price the long-term unemployed back into employment.
- Unemployed people often have low self-esteem and experience stress and suffering, which increases with the duration of unemployment.

None the less, in our discussion of 'Beyond GDP' in the appendix to Chapter 2 we emphasised that happiness and life satisfaction are not that closely related to the level or growth of GDP. While unemployment does lead to a drop in subjective well-being, the evidence for Ireland shows that self-assessed 'life satisfaction' has not dropped as dramatically as might have been feared since the onset of the recession. This contrasts with the steep fall in this measure in Ireland during the 1980s and in some other countries, notably Greece, during the current recession.

While there has been a tendency for the male suicide rate to rise as the unemployment rate rises, there are countervailing factors. Suicide in Ireland has been correlated with the level of alcohol consumption, and this has fallen since the turn of the century. The net result has been that the suicide rate in 2011 was actually lower than the rates recorded at the peak of the boom in the late 1990s. The level of road accidents and fatalities has also fallen during the recession as the volume of traffic dropped (Walsh and Walsh 2011).

Rising unemployment has a negative impact on the public finances. During the current recession, spending on transfer payments has risen dramatically. The Minister for Finance pointed out in his Budget 2012 speech that 'The financial allocation for jobseekers' payments alone is now over three times the 2006 level.' At the same time, revenue from income taxes, VAT, stamp duties and so on declined and the budget plunged into deficit.

A country with a high rate of unemployment therefore faces the unpalatable prospect of having to impose higher tax rates on the employed population to help support those without work and keep the budget deficit under control. This risks becoming a downward spiral, squeezing household spending and making it harder to get the economy growing again. We discuss these issues in more detail in Chapters 7 and 8.

In addition to the loss of current output and income caused by high unemployed, permanent damage may be inflicted on the economy's productive capacity due to the fall in investment and the loss of skills during a recession. If this is true, the economy's growth trajectory is lowered and the effects of the recession are felt for many years into the future.

4.8 Reducing Unemployment

After the recession of the 1980s, the Irish unemployment rate did not begin to fall appreciably until the economy had been growing rapidly for some years in the 1990s. We are now faced with several more years of fiscal austerity and weak aggregate demand. These facts have increased the urgency of implementing specific labour market policies to reduce the natural rate of unemployment.

The money spent on social welfare could be linked to measures designed to help get the unemployed back to work. These are called 'activation measures' to distinguish them from passively paying income support to the unemployed. Most of them involve encouraging the unemployed to go on training and retraining courses. In some countries the payment of income support to the unemployed is now linked to signing on for such courses. President Clinton pledged to 'end welfare as we know it' when he signed the Personal Responsibility and Work Opportunity Reconciliation Act of 1996. This made it much harder for Americans to remain on welfare without undertaking training or participating in community work programmes. In the UK the Restart Programme introduced in 1997 is believed to have reduced unemployment by inviting the unemployed for an interview after six months and encouraging then to participate in training.

Under its current Agreement with the EU and IMF, Ireland is committed to reforming the way social welfare affects the labour market. The review of this Agreement, published in August 2012, reminded the government of the need to:

> *... ensure that activation services are enhanced to tackle the high and persistent rate of long-term unemployment. In particular, the Department of Social Protection will take steps to improve the ratio of vacancies filled off the live register, focus on re-training the unemployed to reduce the risk of long-term unemployment and ensure appropriate incentives through the implementation of sanctions.*

So far, the reforms that have been implemented have not been radical enough to have a major impact on the level of unemployment. The payment of JB for 15 months and JA for an indefinite period thereafter are features of the Irish social insurance system that contribute to the low rate of job finding. Modernising and streamlining our social welfare system and its interaction with the labour market will be a major test of our management of the economy in the coming years.

4.9 Unemployment in Ireland

We now turn to an account of Ireland's experience in regard to unemployment.

How we measure unemployment

Although unemployment is a topic of grave public concern, its definition and measurement are fraught with difficulties. The labour force statistics published by the EU and the OECD rely heavily on the International Labour Office (ILO) definitions of employment and unemployment. The general principle is that a person is regarded as being unemployed if he or she is actively looking for work, willing to accept a suitable job but cannot obtain one.

A person is employed if he or she is working for pay or profit, or in a family business, for *one* hour or more during the week. (People living on family farms have to be working for 10 hours or more a week to be classified as employed.) People who are neither working nor looking for work are classified as 'not in the labour force' or 'economically inactive'.

There are large grey areas here. What is meant by a 'suitable' job? Should a recent graduate in film studies have to accept a job as a gardener? What are the criteria for 'active' job search? Is it reasonable that working as little as an hour a week is sufficient to qualify a person as 'employed'? (Note also that under this definition a full-time student could be classified as 'employed'.)

Calling unpaid workers in the home, such as housewives and farmers' wives, and diligent full-time students, 'inactive' is clearly a misnomer, but it is consistent with excluding unpaid home production from GDP.

The unemployment rate (UR) is the proportion of the labour force that is unemployed:

$$\text{UR} = \left(\frac{\text{unemployed}}{\text{labour force}}\right) \times 100$$

Since the labour force equals the sum of those who are employed and the unemployed:

$$\text{UR} = \frac{\text{unemployed}}{(\text{employed} + \text{unemployed})} \times 100$$

The unemployment rate can be calculated separately for various population groups (men, women, by age group and educational level).

The labour force participation rate (LFPR) is the fraction of the population aged 15 and over 65 that is in the labour force. It is the economically active population as a percentage of the total:

$$\text{LFPR} = \left(\frac{\text{labour force}}{\text{population}}\right) \times 100.$$

The employment rate (ER) equals the participation rate (LRPR) multiplied by one minus the unemployment rate (UR):

$$\text{ER} = \text{LRPR} \times (1 - \text{UR})$$

NOTE: In most countries the principal source of employment and unemployment data is a household survey, such as the Labour Force Survey (LFS) in Europe or the Current Population Survey in the United States. The first Irish LFS was undertaken by the CSO in 1975. Annual surveys were conducted between 1983 and 1996 and a new quarterly survey, the Quarterly National Household Survey (QNHS), was introduced in 1997. A sample of almost forty thousand households are interviewed. The questionnaire has been refined over the years by the Irish CSO and Eurostat.

Table 4.3 shows the numbers employed and unemployed and the adult population in Ireland in the first quarter of 2012. In the lower half of the table we use these data to derive:

- the unemployment rate (UR)
- the (labour force) participation rate (LFPR)
- the employment rate (ER).

Because of the difficulties of differentiating between those who are 'economically inactive' and the unemployed, it is useful to include the employment rate, which summarises the influence of both the unemployment and participation rates. A high employment rate implies low unemployment and/or high participation in the labour force.

Alternative measures of employment and unemployment are available from the Census of Population, based on what is called a person's 'principal economic status' (PES). This measures how a person classifies him or herself ('employed', 'unemployed' or 'in home duties') rather than applying criteria regarding their work, or lack of it, during a week. On the PES basis a full-time student working a few hours at the weekend would be classified as a student and not as an employed person.

The Irish unemployment record

In Figure 4.9 above we showed the unemployment rate in Ireland from 1960 to 2011. (The data for the earlier years may not be strictly comparable to those for 1975 onwards, when the labour force survey began.) Until the mid-1970s the unemployment rate remained between four and six per cent. Much higher rates were recorded in the 1970s and again in the 1980s. A record

TABLE 4.3 Population aged 15 years and over classified by labour force status, 2012 Q2

		Thousands
Employed	(a)	1,836.2
Unemployed	(b)	323.0
Labour force	(c) = (a) + (b)	2,159.2
Not in labour force	(d)	1,431.9
Total population	(e) = (c) + (d)	3,591.1
		%
Unemployment rate	(b)/(c)	15.0
Participation rate	(c)/(e)	60.1
Employment rate	(a)/(e)	51.1

Source: CSO, Quarterly National Household Survey, Quarter 2 2012 (based on ILO definitions)

unemployment rate of 17.1 per cent was recorded in 1986. However, due to the rapid growth in the 1990s the unemployment rate fell sharply and was stable just above four per cent between 2002 and 2007. The economy enjoyed 'full employment' by any definition over these years. However, when the economy collapsed after 2007, unemployment soared and since mid-2012 it has been stuck close to 15 per cent.

It is clear that there has been a close relationship between the unemployment rate and the rate of growth in real GDP. The level of employment fluctuates with the growth rate, and unemployment falls as employment rises, and vice versa. During periods of recession, such as the 1980s and after 2007, the unemployment rate increased. During the boom period from 1987 to 2007 the unemployment rate fell and remained low. If macroeconomic policy succeeded in stabilising the real growth rate around the potential growth rate, the unemployment rate would be stable at a low level.

The duration of unemployment

A question of great social and economic importance that has a bearing on the definition of the 'natural' rate of unemployment is: How long does the typical entrant to the pool of unemployment remain unemployed?

Figure 4.12 shows unemployment by duration (short- and long-term) since 1998. The long-term unemployed are those who have been out of work continuously for a year or longer. The rate of long-term unemployment proved very responsive to the economic boom, falling from 10.4 per cent in 1988 to an amazingly low 1.3 per cent in 2002. The rising tide of the boom provided employment for many who might have been labelled 'unemployable' during the recession.

During the boom years from 2000 to 2006 the short-term unemployment rate fell to around three per cent and the long-term unemployment rate remained under 1.5 per cent. By any standards these were years of 'full employment'. As the economy went into recession after 2007 the short-term unemployment rate soared, reaching almost 10 per cent in the second half of 2009. It has declined since then as the economy bottomed out and the inflow into unemployment (the separation rate, *s*) dropped. By early 2012 it was below six per cent.

Unfortunately, many of the recently unemployed are not leaving unemployment to take up new jobs or to seek better fortunes abroad. They are instead moving into long-term unemployment in

FIGURE 4.12 Short- and long-term unemployment rates, 1998–2011

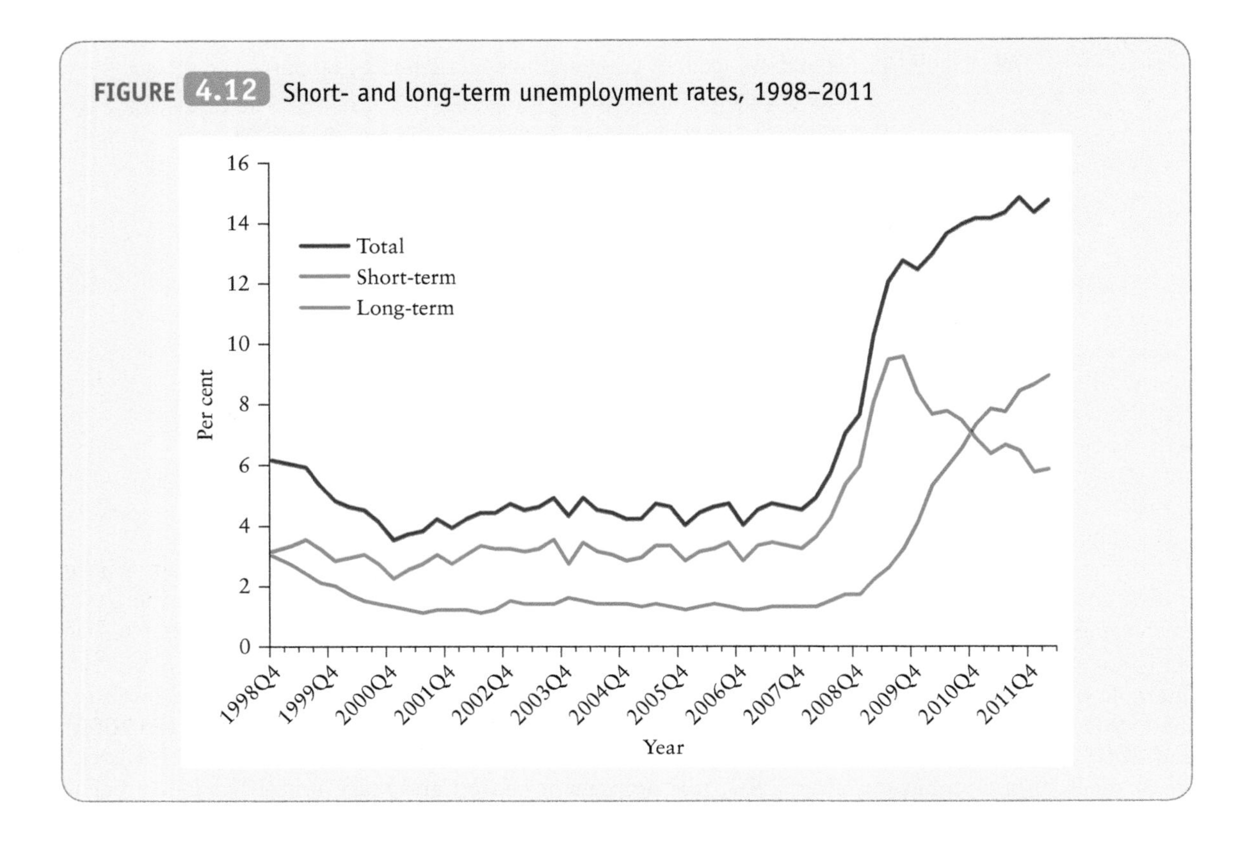

Ireland. Since mid-2009 the long-term unemployment rate has risen steadily and by the first quarter of 2012 had reached 8.9 per cent, accounting for 60 per cent of the total. This is not far off the peak of 10.4 per cent reached at the end of 1988.

The rise in the long-term unemployment rate reflects a fall in f, the rate at which the unemployed find jobs. Thus the 'steady state' or 'natural' rate of unemployment has risen during the recession. Reducing long-term unemployment is the greatest social and economic challenge facing Ireland today.

Who are the unemployed?

The risk of being unemployed differs greatly between population groups. From research in Ireland and other countries (see, for example, Murphy and Walsh 1996), we know that:

- Those with low educational qualifications are much more likely to be unemployed than better-educated individuals; and once they become unemployed, they are more likely to remain unemployed and join the long-term unemployed.
- The youth unemployment rate is much higher than that among people of 'prime working age' – say from age 25 to 44. There is, however, an issue about the measurement of youth unemployment, discussed in Box 4.1.
- Other things being equal, unmarried men are the most likely to be unemployed. This could be because single people are less committed to holding down a job or, alternatively, because those who cannot get a job are less eligible for marriage.
- Men living in large urban areas are more likely to be unemployed than their rural counterparts. Employment opportunities for men appear to be more plentiful in rural areas.

Box 4.1 Measuring Youth Unemployment

The problem of youth unemployment is one of the major issues facing many European countries today. The unemployment rate among Spaniards and Greeks aged 15–24 is about 50 per cent, while the rate for the EU as a whole is about 20 per cent. These are alarming numbers, but they can be somewhat misleading.

As we noted above, the unemployment rate is the numbers 'unemployed' as a proportion of the 'labour force', that is, the sum of the employed and unemployed. The 'unemployed' are those actively seeking work, but not at work.

The problem with using the unemployment rate to measure labour market conditions among young people is that the denominator does not include those who are in the educational system or on full-time training courses. During a recession, more young people stay on in school or college or in training. The unemployment rate may be very high among those who enter the labour market, but it applies to a diminishing proportion of the total. While it is true that half those who are in the labour force are out of work, it is *not* the case that half the Spanish population aged 15–24 is out of work.

As an alternative to the youth unemployment rate some people urge that we should look at the proportion of young people 'not in employment, education or training' (the NEET ratio). We should also consider the employment rate as supplementary information on the state of the youth labour market.

Using data from the Irish Census of Population, between 2006 and 2011 the unemployment rate among people aged 20–24 rose from 13.2 to 34.8 per cent. However, using the NEET ratio, youth unemployment 'only' rose from 13.5 to 25.4 per cent. On the other hand, the employment rate in this age group fell from 60.0 to 39.0 per cent, while the proportion of the group classified as 'students' rose from just over a quarter to over a third.

These figures show that while there is a serious lack of employment opportunities among the young, the problem is perhaps exaggerated by the conventional youth unemployment rate.

TABLE 4.4 Measures of the labour market situation among the Irish population aged 20–24

	2006	2011
Unemployment rate	13.2	34.8
NEET ratio*	13.5	25.4
Employment rate	60.0	39.0
Students as % of total	26.5	35.6

*NEET ratio = not in employment, education or training as % of total

Note: These data are based on the population classified according to 'principal economic status' rather than the ILO conventions used to measure the standard unemployment rate.

Source: Census of Population, 2006 and 2011

- Both men and women are less likely to be employed when there are young children present in the household. Perhaps they choose to devote time to child rearing rather than taking employment at low wages.
- When all other factors are allowed for, those who live in local authority rented accommodation are significantly less likely to be employed than those in other types of housing. This could be due to discrimination or other unknown factors.
- Living in a household with other unemployed and/or inactive adults seems to increase the risk of unemployment. Perhaps like cluster with like, or maybe a culture of not working develops in this situation.

TABLE 4.5 Unemployment rates in Ireland and the main Eurozone countries

	2006	2007	2008	2009	2010	2011
Belgium	8.3	7.5	7.0	7.9	8.3	7.2
Germany	10.3	8.7	7.5	7.8	7.1	5.9
Ireland	4.5	4.6	6.3	11.9	13.7	14.4
Greece	8.9	8.3	7.7	9.5	12.6	17.7
Spain	8.5	8.3	11.3	18	20.1	21.7
France	9.2	8.4	7.8	9.5	9.7	9.6
Italy	6.8	6.1	6.7	7.8	8.4	8.4
Netherlands	4.4	3.6	3.1	3.7	4.5	4.4
Austria	4.8	4.4	3.8	4.8	4.4	4.2
Portugal	8.6	8.9	8.5	10.6	12	12.9
Finland	7.7	6.9	6.4	8.2	8.4	7.8

Source: Eurostat (http://epp.eurostat.ec.europa.eu)

While these findings do not help explain the reasons for fluctuations in the rate of unemployment, they point to policies that might help reduce unemployment, such as training and education and increased geographic mobility.

4.10 Unemployment in the Euro Area

The variation in unemployment rates across the countries of the euro area is of particular interest because, as we discuss in several later chapters, as members of the EMU our monetary policy and to an increasing extent our fiscal policy are determined in Frankfurt and Berlin rather than in Dublin. For a uniform monetary policy to be appropriate to a group of countries they should be at a common point on the business cycle and their unemployment rates not too far apart.

Table 4.5 shows the unemployment rates from 2006 to 2011 in some of the euro area countries. The important point is that, whereas in 2006 unemployment rates in these countries were relatively uniform, they behaved quite differently over the next five years. Unemployment rates soared in Ireland, Spain and Greece, but they remained largely unchanged in Belgium, Austria, Finland, France and the Netherlands, while in Germany the rate fell.

The outcome was that by 2011 the unemployment rates in Spain, Greece and Ireland were multiples of the rates in Germany, Austria, Finland and France. The core of the EU had a very different experience in regard to unemployment during the recession than the peripheral countries. This has very important implications for the viability of the euro area and lies behind some of the tension that has emerged in regard to monetary and fiscal policy during the crisis.

4.11 Key Concepts

The main topics discussed in this chapter were:

- the labour market
- the natural rate of unemployment
- frictional unemployment
- cyclical unemployment

- the costs of unemployment
- why the labour market does not clear
- how to reduce unemployment
- the experience with regard to unemployment
- trends in unemployment in the euro area.

Appendix 4.1 The Cobb–Douglas production function and productivity

The Cobb (Charles)–Douglas (Paul) production function is written as:

$$Y = AK^{\alpha}L^{1-\alpha}$$

where Y is output, A represents the level of technology, K is the capital stock and L is labour. α is a coefficient that tells us how much income goes to capital and how much to labour $(1 - \alpha)$. Note that capital and labour share depends not just on α but also the amounts of K and L and also A. In the USA until recently, $\alpha = 0.3$, hence the ratio of labour income to total income = 0.7. That is, 30 per cent of national income goes to capital and 70 per cent to labour. Despite numerous changes to the US economy over the decades, these coefficients have remained relatively constant.

The coefficient α is also an output elasticity. This states that a one per cent increase in capital would lead to a 0.3 per cent increase in output. Furthermore, as the two coefficients add to 1, the production function exhibits constant returns to scale. The doubling of all inputs will lead to a doubling of output.

MARGINAL AND AVERAGE PRODUCTIVITY

If we now differentiate the production function with respect to both labour and capital we obtain:

$$MPK = \alpha AK^{\alpha-1}L^{1-\alpha} = \alpha Y/K$$
$$MPL = (1 - \alpha)AK^{\alpha}L^{-\alpha} = (1 - \alpha)Y/L$$

These equations state that each factor's *marginal* product is proportional to its *average* product (Y/K) and (Y/L). Rearranging:

$$\text{Capital income} = MPK \times K = \alpha Y$$
$$\text{Labour income} = MPL \times L = (1 - \alpha)Y$$

Because the production function has constant factor shares, the division of national income between L and K is *constant* over time. This conclusion does not, however, appear to be borne out by the Irish data. Wages share of national income fell by 31 per cent between 1981 and 2002, and by 23 per cent over the period 1981–2011.

LABOUR PRODUCTIVITY AND WAGES

The theory of the labour market developed in this chapter states that the marginal product of labour should equal the real wage:

$$MPL = W/P$$

The Cobb–Douglas production function tells us that MPL is proportional to average labour productivity (Y/L). Therefore W/P should rise when average productivity is growing. Is this true or not for the Irish economy? Table 4.6 shows the relationship from 1961 to 2010 using period averages. With the exception of the Celtic Tiger years when productivity rose much faster than real earnings, there is a close link between the two series. This suggests that productivity, as the theory predicts, is the key to higher real wages.

TABLE 4.6 Labour productivity and real wages

Period	Labour productivity (annual % change)	Real wages per head (annual % change)
1961–1973	4.3	4.7
1974–1985	3.7	2.6
1986–1990	3.5	2.3
1991–1995	2.9	1.9
1996–2000	3.7	1.7
2001–2005	2.4	2.4
2006–2010	1.04	0.86

Source: Authors' calculations from CSO data

Appendix 4.2 The supply of labour in the long run

DEMOGRAPHIC FACTORS

The size of the population is the most important determinant of the size of the labour force in the long run. In this appendix we look at the key influences on Ireland's population over past decades.

The basic demographic arithmetic is that the rate of change in the population is the sum of the rate of natural increase (that is, the excess of the birth rate over the death rate) and the net migration rate (immigration minus emigration). That is:

$$\begin{aligned}\text{rate of population change} &= \text{rate of natural increase} + \text{net migration rate}\\ &= (\text{birth rate} - \text{death rate}) + (\text{immigration rate} - \text{emigration rate})\end{aligned}$$

Figure 4.13 shows the birth and death rates from 1871 to 2011. The death rate has fallen steadily and shows no signs of levelling off in recent years. The birth rate, on the other hand, fell steadily from the 1870s to the 1930s but then increased slightly until 1981. It fell quite sharply from 1981 to 1996 but has risen again in the twenty-first century.

Figure 4.14 shows that these changes caused the rate of natural increase to reach a peak of over 11 per 1,000 population in 1981 and then to fall to half that level by 1996. Surprisingly it had risen back almost to its peak level by 2011. The recession has led neither to an increase in the death rate nor to a fall in the birth rate.

While the rising rate of natural increase has been an important component of population change, the net migration rate has been the dominant influence on population change over the decades. The volatility of the migration rate is mirrored in the volatility of the rate of population change.

From the beginning of the nineteenth century, emigration from Ireland was encouraged by easy access to Britain and America. The outflow became a flood after the Great Famine of the 1840s. Over most of the period between 1871 and 1961, and again in the 1980s, the net emigration rate remained high. In the mid-1950s it amounted to 1.5 per cent of the population, a dismal record surpassed at the time only by Communist East Germany. The high rate of net emigration offset the excess of births over deaths and the population fell.

During the 1990s net emigration turned into net immigration, which reached a very high rate during the early years of the twenty-first century. During these years the booming economy and construction sector in particular attracted a large inflow of workers from the EU new accession states, especially Poland. However, following the collapse of 2008, net immigration turned into net emigration. But despite the economic setbacks of recent years the population has continued

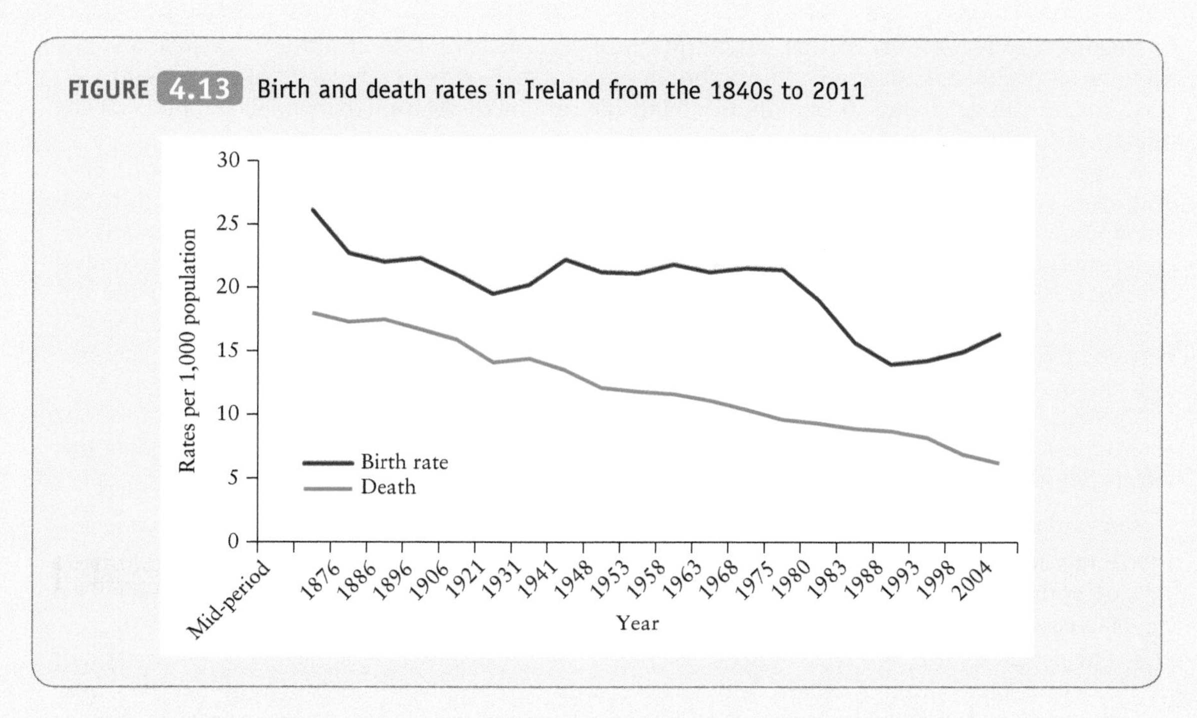

FIGURE 4.13 Birth and death rates in Ireland from the 1840s to 2011

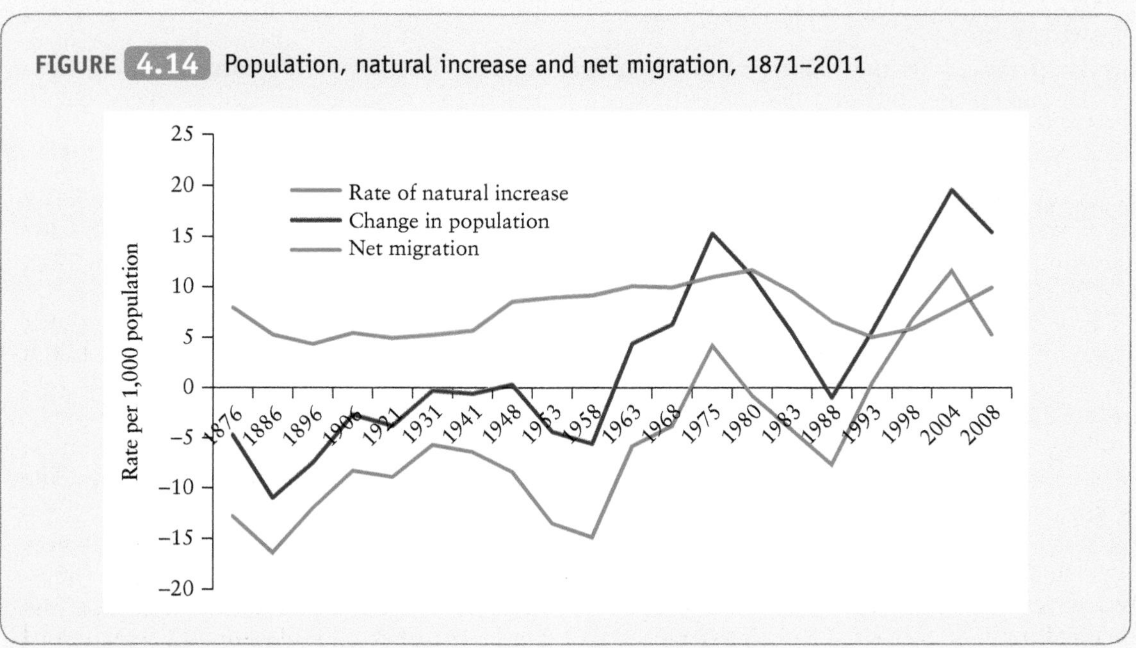

FIGURE 4.14 Population, natural increase and net migration, 1871–2011

to grow due to the high rate of natural increase and because the net emigration rate has not yet reached the levels recorded in the 1980s or 1950s.

Net migration has been strongly influenced by the availability of jobs in Ireland relative to their availability in the countries to which the Irish have traditionally emigrated, which are mainly the richer English-speaking nations. In periods of stagnant or falling employment and living standards in Ireland, like the 1950s, the net emigration rate exceeded the rate of natural increase and the population declined. Conversely, during boom periods such as the early years of the present century, emigration gave way to immigration, and the rate of population growth in Ireland was the highest in Europe.

A consequence of the openness of the Irish labour market and our history of large-scale emigration to Britain since World War II is that there is a close relationship between Irish and British unemployment. When unemployment was high in Ireland in the late 1980s but falling in Britain, emigration resumed and this stabilised the Irish unemployment rate. The behaviour of Irish and British unemployment rates is compared in Figure 4.15. This illustrates the tendency for the UK rate to act as an anchor for the Irish rate. The graph also shows that at present, mid-2012, the gap between Irish and UK unemployment is large and this suggests that Irish emigration may increase as a response.

The heavy emigration of the past, especially during the 1950s, was not only a reflection of our economic stagnation, it may also have contributed to that stagnation due to its adverse economic effects, which including the following:

- A falling population and contracting domestic market act as a deterrent to new investment.
- Emigration distorts the age structure of the population, leading to a relatively high proportion of both young and old dependants, and a relatively small proportion of young adults. This increases the tax burden on the employed population.
- The psychological and social effects of emigration are negative. It is dispiriting if almost half of your school-leaving cohort leaves the country, especially if those who go are the more energetic and enterprising and those who remain behind tend to be conservative and reluctant to take risks.
- Until the 1980s the highest rates of emigration from Ireland were recorded among farm labourers, the sons and daughters of small farmers, and unskilled manual workers, but in

FIGURE 4.15 Unemployment in Ireland and the UK

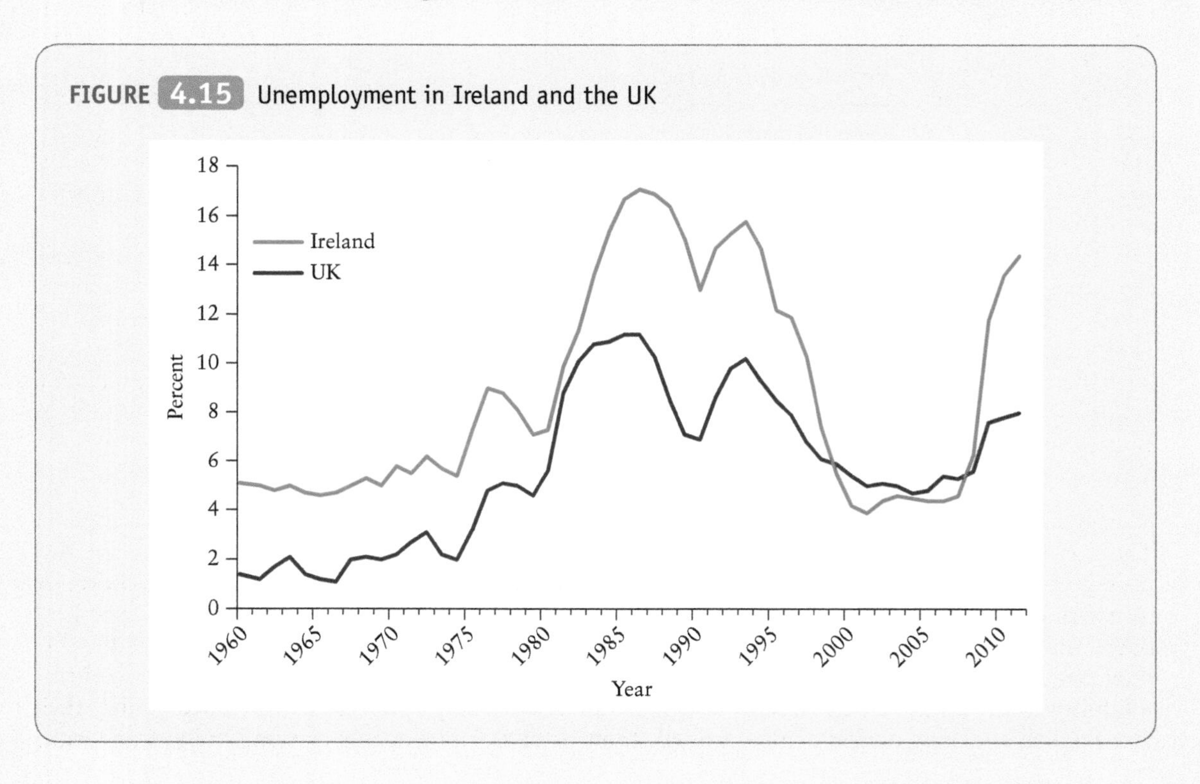

the 1980s and after 2007 the highest rates of emigration were among those with third-level and professional qualifications. This outflow of highly educated young people represents a loss of human capital. The state enjoys no return on public money spent on the education of emigrants.

But while admitting the costs of emigration, we should also take account of some compensating benefits.

- Emigration has afforded many young Irish people the opportunity of raising their living standards.
- Emigration acts as a 'safety valve' and reduces the numbers unemployed in Ireland, relieving pressure on the social welfare system.
- When the performance of the Irish economy picked up in the 1990s, returning emigrants proved to be a valuable source of skilled personnel.

Nevertheless, in light of our exceptional history of mass emigration from the early nineteenth century down to the 1950s, and the recurrence of large-scale emigration again in the 1980s and since 2007, it is reasonable to state that providing young people the opportunity to live and work in their country of birth should be among the goals of Irish macroeconomic policy.

THE LABOUR FORCE PARTICIPATION RATE

Given the size of the population, the supply of labour depends on the labour force participation rate (LFPR). Changes in the LFPR have played an important part in Ireland's recent economic development. Table 4.7 shows the aggregate LFPR for census years since 1961.

In the earlier years of this period the share of the Irish population in the working-age age group (roughly from age 15 to 64) was unusually low in Ireland. This was due to the relatively high birth rate on the one hand, and the high emigration rate on the other. The high birth rate meant that the proportion of children in the population was large, while emigration hollowed out the proportion in the 20–39 age groups. These factors eased as the birth rate declined during the recession of the early 1980s and when emigration turned to immigration in the 1990s.

The most important change in the LFPR among the working age population has been the increase in the rate among women. This has been due to factors such as rising educational attainment among younger women, the decline in family size, and the removal of various legal and institutional barriers to women's employment. (Until the 1970s women had to retire from employment in the civil service and the banks if they got married.)

These forces, as well as the booming economy during the period 1987–2007, combined to raise the overall LFPR. The rate increased significantly after 1980, rising from 40.2 per cent to a peak of 49.8 per cent in 2006. The recession reversed this upward trend and the LFPR dropped back to 48.6 per cent in 2011.

A rising LFPR increases the proportion of the population that is economically active. The *employment dependency ratio* takes into account the proportion of the labour force that is employed. It is the ratio of the non-employed to the employed in the total population:

$$\text{Employment dependency ratio} = \left(\frac{\text{non-employed}}{\text{employed}}\right) \times 100$$

The non-employed population is the total population minus the employed labour force, so this ratio gives an indication of the burden that has to be borne by the employed (through taxation or transfers within households) to support those who are not employed. This is even more significant than the LFPR as an indication of the balance between the 'productive' and 'unproductive' population (using these words in the narrow sense of contributing or not contributing to GDP).

During the 1980s, though the population was increasing, the numbers at work declined. Table 4.7 shows that from the already high level of 168 in 1961, employment dependency ratio

TABLE 4.7 Labour force participation rate and employment dependency ratio

Year		Labour Force		LFPR	Employment dependency ratio
		Total	At work		
Census year	Population	thousands		%	%
1961	2,818.0	1,109.0	1,052.5	39.4	168
1971	2,978.2	1,110.0	1,054.8	37.3	182
1986	3,540.6	1,329.5	1,091.2	37.6	224
1981	3,443.0	1,382.9	1,149.1	40.2	200
1991	3,525.7	1,534.0	1,307.2	43.5	170
2002	3,917.2	1,800.9	1,641.6	46.0	139
2006	4,239.8	2,109.5	1,930.0	49.8	120
2011	4,588.3	2,232.2	1,807.4	48.6	154

Impact of changing employment dependency ratio on living standards
GDP (at constant prices)
Index 1986 = 100

	Total	Per person in employment	Per head of population
1986	100	100	100
2006	315	190	265
Annual average growth rate, 1986–2006			
	5.6	3.1	4.75

Sources: Censuses of Population and NIE

rose to a peak of 224 in 1986. There were more than two people not working to be supported in one way or another by every working person. One of the benefits of the post-1987 boom was that rise in employment combined with the continuing fall in the birth rate and in emigration and led to a steady decline in the ratio, which reached a low of 120 in 2006.

The implications of the fall in this ratio between 1986 and 2006 were very important. Even if labour productivity – output per employed person – had remained unchanged over the period, income per person would have risen significantly due to the rise in the proportion of the population that was employed. This is highlighted in the calculations at the bottom of Table 4.7, which are based on the growth in real GDP, the growth in population and the growth in the employed population between 1986 and 2006. Total GDP grew at an annual average rate of 5.6 per cent over this period, GDP per person at work (or average labour productivity) at 3.1 per cent and GDP per head of population at 4.75 per cent. As we emphasised in earlier chapters, the growth in real income per person is the best guide to the trend in living standards. It could be said that the decline in the employment dependency ratio raised the rate of growth of GDP per head of population from 3.1 to 4.75 per cent or that it accounted for over half the improvement in living standards that took place over these years.

Unfortunately, this source of growth in income per person went into reverse as employment slumped during the post-2007 recession. The costs of paying for the welfare and educational systems are now rising rapidly while the numbers at work are still falling.

Appendix 4.3 The Live Register as a measure of unemployment

An important supplementary source of information on unemployment is the Live Register (LR) monthly returns from social welfare offices, which give the number of people registered for the Jobseeker's Benefit and Allowance. The release contains the warning that 'The Live Register is not designed to measure unemployment. It includes part-time workers (those who work up to three days a week), seasonal and casual workers entitled to Jobseeker's Benefit or Allowance.' Despite this, the figures are widely quoted in the press as a measure of unemployment. Figure 4.16 compares the numbers 'unemployed' as indicated by the LR and the QNHS from 1997 to 2012. The numbers on the LR, as is to be expected, have been consistently higher than the 'unemployed' by the criteria used in the QNHS. However, the two series follow very similar trends. Both were low and stable between 2000 and 2007, both climbed steeply after 2007, and both have levelled off since 2011.

However, the discrepancy between the two totals has varied significantly. In 1999 and 2000 the numbers on the LR were over twice the QNHS unemployed total, but by 2009 the discrepancy had fallen to 50 per cent. With a high unemployment rate it seems that a higher proportion of those on the LR are 'unemployed' in the ILO meaning of the word. It is reassuring to see that the month-to-month variations in the LR can be used as a guide to the trend in unemployment, even if the total tends to overstate the numbers actively seeking work.

FIGURE 4.16 Comparison of Live Register and Quarterly National Household Survey data on 'unemployment'

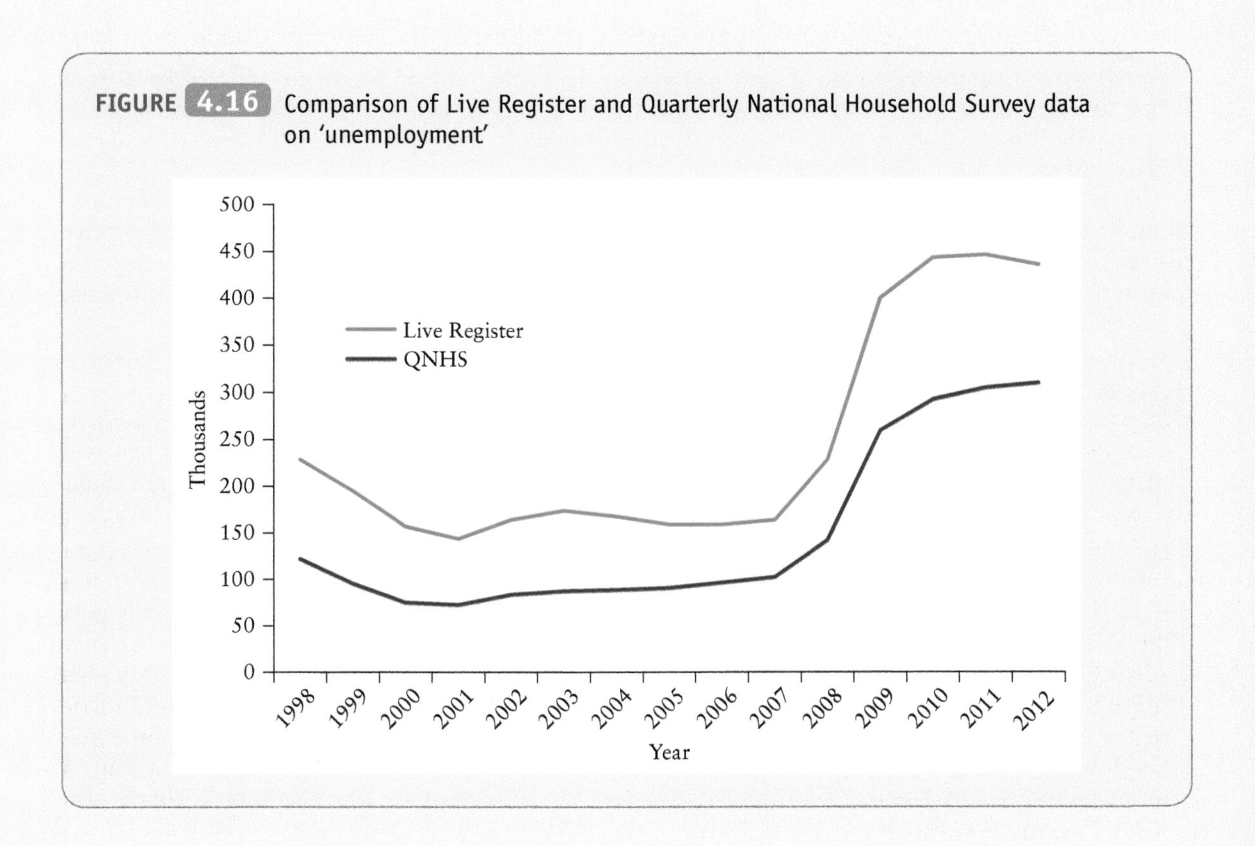

CHAPTER 5

Introduction to the Theory of Income Determination

The ideas of economists and political philosophers, both when they are right and when they are wrong, are more powerful than is commonly understood. Indeed the world is ruled by little else. Practical men, who believe themselves to be quite exempt from any intellectual influences, are usually the slaves of some defunct economist. Madmen in authority, who hear voices in the air, are distilling their frenzy from some academic scribbler of a few years back. (Keynes 1936)

5.1 Introduction

The goals of macroeconomic policy are a high and stable growth rate in real GNP and a low unemployment rate. A low rate of inflation is also desirable, both in its own right and because it helps to achieve the growth and unemployment objectives. As will be explained in later chapters, in pursuing these objectives policy-makers are constrained by the need to avoid excessive fiscal and balance of payments deficits.

In this chapter we outline a macroeconomic model based on the theory of income determination. The aim is to explain the level and changes in national income, unemployment and the price level. The model is used to explain how the economy adjusts to economic shocks – unexpected events that throw it off course. The concluding section discusses the relationship between economic growth and unemployment.

5.2 Macroeconomic Models

Macroeconomic theory uses models to explain how the economy works. Model building involves setting out the way in which variables such as GNP, unemployment and the price level are interrelated. A model can be used to explore how policy variables, such as government expenditure, taxation, interest rates and the exchange rate, affect the economy's performance.

Thus a macroeconomic model should be able to shed light on the Irish boom of the 1990s and the post-2007 recession. It should also be able to suggest policies that will stabilise the economy and keep it closer to its long-run growth path.

It is important to bear in mind that models are based on theories. It is necessary to keep testing economic theories against the facts to make sure that they are consistent with reality. Econometrics is a branch of economics that has developed statistical techniques to estimate the parameters or coefficients of models from the data. Lawrence Klein developed one of the first large-scale macro econometric models of the United States at the University of Pennsylvania in the 1950s. In Ireland, the two most widely used models have been developed by the Central Bank of Ireland and the ESRI.

5.3 Keynes's General Theory

Modern macroeconomics could be said to have commenced with the publication in 1936 of the book *The General Theory of Employment, Interest and Money* by the British economist John Maynard Keynes (1883–1946). He was not entirely modest about what he was attempting to achieve. In a letter to George Bernard Shaw in 1935 he wrote, 'I believe myself to be writing a book on economic theory which will largely revolutionise – not, I suppose, at once but in the course of the next ten years – the way the world thinks about economic problems.'

The inspiration for the book was Keynes's belief that the orthodox or classical model of the day was unable to explain the reality of the Great Depression of the 1930s. At the time he was writing, the industrial countries of the world were in the severest depression in modern history. In the USA, over the period 1929 to 1933, real output fell by 30 per cent, unemployment increased from 3.2 per cent to 25 per cent and the price level fell by 25 per cent. On Tuesday 29 October 1929, stock prices in New York fell by 12 per cent. By June 1932 stock prices had fallen by 85 per cent from their peak. By the time Franklin Delano Roosevelt (FDR) took office in March 1933, the depression was much more severe than anything experienced in the past. Unemployment in Britain increased from 10.4 per cent in 1927 to a peak of 22.1 per cent in 1932. In Ireland, unemployment increased from only 22,858 in 1929 to a peak of 133,319 in 1933.

However, not every European country remained mired in depression throughout the 1930s. In Italy, the Fascist regime had embarked on a public works programme in the 1920s, which averted the worst effects of the Great Depression. After Hitler's accession to power in Germany in 1933, government expenditure was increased and there was a rapid expansion in output and employment. In Sweden a Social Democratic government had maintained a high level of employment by increasing its public works programmes.

Keynes, in a lecture delivered at University College, Dublin in 1933, mentioned that several European countries 'have cast their eyes or are casting them towards new modes of political economy', but he warned that self-sufficiency policies would not be feasible in Ireland without a disastrous reduction in a standard of life which was already none too high. A year after his Dublin visit, Keynes was recommended by the Department of Finance as an outside expert member for the proposed Irish Banking Commission, and de Valera's cabinet rejected his appointment (Keynes 1933; Nolan 2012).

Policy-makers in the English-speaking democracies at this time did not have a macroeconomic model that justified action by governments to move the economy out of the Depression. Keynes's *General Theory* was devoted to developing such a model. At its crudest, what he proposed was relatively simple. If the economy is in a depression, with high unemployment and plenty of unused capacity, government should increase spending or reduce taxation. This would lead to a higher level of economic activity and lower unemployment.

In fact, Keynes's ideas had little immediate impact on policy. The establishment in America, as well as in Britain, remained intellectually committed to the tenets of orthodox or classical economics, which predicted that in due course the economy would right itself. Their main concern was with balancing the budget. In fact, in the early 1930s tax rates were raised and expenditure cut, which had the effect of exacerbating the Depression.

The US government hired photojournalist Dorothea Lange and others to bring the plight of sharecroppers, displaced farm families and migrant workers to public attention. The motive behind this was to persuade Congress to allow the president to increase spending to alleviate the recession, even if this entailed running a budget deficit.

However, only when government spending on armaments soared and vast numbers were mobilised into active military service, as World War II loomed, did unemployment begin to fall rapidly.

The classical model that Keynes was trying to dethrone was based on assumptions that led to the belief that the economy was self-correcting and would quickly return to full employment without active government intervention. Keynes believed that this view was valid only as a 'special case'. (An outline of the classical theory is given in Chapters 19 and 20.)

> *[T]he classical theory ... upon which I was brought up ... dominates the economic thought, both practical and theoretical, of the governing and academic classes of this generation, as it has for a hundred years past. I shall argue that the postulates of the classical theory are applicable to a special case only and not to the general case. ... Moreover, the characteristics of the special case assumed by the classical theory happen not to be those of the economic society in which we actually live, with the result that its teaching is misleading and disastrous if we attempt to apply it to the facts of experience.* (Keynes 1936)

Keynes's difficulty with the classical theory was that it adopted a long-run view of how the economy adjusts. In the long run all prices and wages had sufficient time to adjust to restore equilibrium in the market for goods and services and the labour market. The flexibility of wages and prices helped the economy to automatically revert back to full employment following a disturbance. Given this automatic adjustment, the classical school advocated a non-interventionist policy stance. There was no need for an active fiscal policy.

But for Keynes, macroeconomics had to be about more than just the long run. His famous dismissal of the long-run view of macroeconomic adjustment was written before the Great Depression:

> *The long run is a misleading guide to current affairs. In the long run we are all dead. Economists set themselves too easy, too useless a task if in tempestuous seasons they can only tell us that when the storm is long past the sea is flat again.* (Keynes 1923)

While Keynes was a master of the English language and he wrote to try to influence a wide readership, his books are not easy reading for students today. The sort of macroeconomic models we present in this text were distilled from the work of Keynes's successors. The Oxford economist John Hicks (1904–1989), in particular, formulated a graphical version of the main Keynesian model (the IS-LM model), which we outline in Chapter 11.

We now outline the basic Keynesian theory of income determination. This model will be extended at various stages throughout this book.

5.4 Equilibrium in the Goods and Services Market

At the heart of the macroeconomic model are the concepts of aggregate demand (AD) and aggregate supply (AS). Expenditure on output is demand. AD refers to total spending on the economy's output. Like any demand schedule in microeconomics, the AD schedule relates total spending to the price level. In Section 5.5 we explain why AD is inversely related to the price level.

AS refers to the total amount of goods and services produced in the economy. The AS schedule is a positive function of the price level, as are microeconomic supply schedules. As we shall see, the interaction between AD and AS determines real output, denoted as Y, and the price level, P.

As with any model of supply and demand, there are three possibilities:

$$AS = AD \text{ Equilibrium}$$
$$AS > AD \text{ Excess supply}$$
$$AS < AD \text{ Excess demand}$$

If AS equals AD, the economy is in equilibrium. If AS exceeds AD, there is an excess supply of goods and services. If AS is less than AD, there is an excess demand for goods and services. An excess supply means that firms are producing too much output and this is a signal to cut back on production. Excess demand means that firms are producing too little output and this is a signal to increase production.

As will become apparent, the policy-maker can attempt to influence either the supply or demand side of the economy to move towards the key macroeconomic objective of ensuring that the economy is at the potential level of real output, and the natural rate of unemployment.

NOTE: An important role is played by changes in stocks or inventories in this process. Unplanned changes in stocks arise if the economy is not in equilibrium. Unplanned changes in stocks send signals to firms whether to increase or decrease production. In particular, if AS > AD, stocks build up and this indicates to firms to cut production. Conversely, if AD > AS, stocks will be run down and this indicates to firms to increase production.

We turn now to the derivation of the AD and AS schedules.

5.5 Aggregate Demand (AD)

In Chapter 2 we explained how the national income accountants classify expenditure on national output into the following categories.

	Symbol
Private consumer expenditure	C
Investment	I
Government current expenditure	G
Exports	X
minus Imports	− M

$$\text{Total expenditure} = C + I + G + X - M$$

or

$$\text{Total expenditure} = C + I + G + NX \quad (1)$$

For details of what is included in each category, see Chapter 2.

The aggregate demand schedule

In microeconomics, a demand schedule shows the relationship between the price a firm charges and how much of its product consumers demand. The higher the price, the lower the demand.

There is a similar inverse relationship between the price level (P) and AD in macroeconomics, which we depict in Figure 5.1. The price level is on the vertical axis and the level of real output (Y) on the horizontal axis.

In microeconomics it is easy to understand why a change in price would affect the demand for a firm's output. If a firm lowers its price, consumers will switch their spending from substitute products with a higher price. The demand for the firm's product will increase and the demand for the substitute product will fall. But why should a change in the overall price level affect the aggregate level of output? We give three theoretical explanations for this in Box 5.1.

FIGURE 5.1 The downward-sloping AD curve

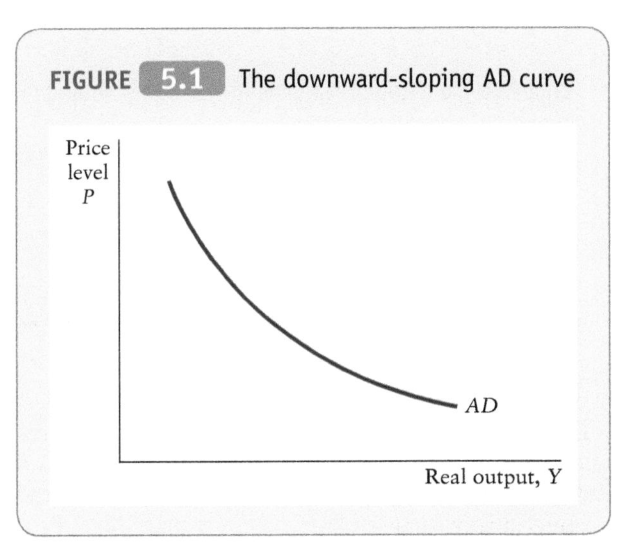

Box 5.1 Why does the aggregate demand curve slope downwards?

Three reasons why the aggregate demand curve slopes downwards:

1. **The competitiveness effect** A fall in the domestic price level relative to the foreign price level will increase price competitiveness of domestic firms (assuming a fixed exchange rate). As a result, domestic firms will capture a greater share of both domestic and foreign markets. In terms of equation (1) above, net exports (NX) rise, and this leads to an increase in AD and subsequently to an increase in real GNP. As explained in a later chapter the effect works through what is known as the real exchange rate. (The real exchange rate is the nominal exchange rate adjusted for domestic and foreign prices.) In short:

$$\downarrow P \rightarrow \downarrow \text{real exchange rate} \rightarrow \uparrow NX \rightarrow \uparrow \text{real output}$$

2. **The real balance effect** This refers to the effect of the price level on the real value of assets and subsequently on the level of consumption. If you hold some of your savings in cash, a fall in the price level will increase the real value (or purchasing power) of your wealth. Because you are now richer, you are likely to feel that you can afford to consume more out of your income. Hence, a decrease in the price level increases households' wealth which, in turn, increases consumption (C) and aggregate demand (AD). In short:

$$\downarrow P \rightarrow \uparrow \text{wealth} \rightarrow \uparrow \text{spending} \rightarrow \uparrow \text{real output}$$

The real balance effect is known as the *Pigou effect* because it was first suggested by Keynes's contemporary at Cambridge University, Arthur C. Pigou (1877–1959).
Realistically, this effect is likely to be small and more than offset by the negative impact of falling asset (house) prices on personal consumption, which we mentioned in the main text.

3. **The liquidity or Keynes effect** Briefly, the argument here is that high interest rates (i) encourage consumers to postpone or abandon expenditure plans because of the high cost of borrowing money. For example, suppose you intend to finance the purchase of a CD player by borrowing from a bank. If interest rates increase, you may decide to make do with your old music system as the cost of finance is too high. On the other hand, low interest rates encourage people to spend because the cost of borrowing is cheap.

As explained in detail in later chapters, there is a relationship between the price level (P) and the interest rate (i). A fall in the price level leads to a fall in the rate of interest. The fall in the interest rate, in turn, leads to increased spending on interest-sensitive components of AD, such as consumer expenditure (C) and investment (I). In short:

$$\downarrow P \rightarrow \downarrow i \rightarrow \uparrow I, C \rightarrow \uparrow AD \rightarrow \uparrow \text{real output}$$

Conversely, a higher price level increases the interest rate. The higher interest rate should lower C and I and, therefore, aggregate demand.

This explanation for the inverse relationship between the price level and real output is called the *Keynes effect*.

A diagram with only the AD curve does not tell us what the level of real output will be. For this we have to include the AS schedule, which we discuss below.

The location of the AD schedule

The location of the AD curve depends on several factors. For a given price level, an increase in any component of AD, such as C, I, G or NX, will shift the AD curve out to the right. A fall in any of the components of AD will shift the curve to the left. To illustrate this, consider point A in Figure 5.2, which corresponds to a price level P_1 and a real output level of Y_1. An increase in, say,

C implies that AD is higher for each level of P, so the AD schedule shifts to the right. B is a point on the new aggregate demand curve, AD_2. Corresponding to this point is a higher level of output Y_2 at the previous price level P_1. Conversely a fall in C will shift the AD back to the left.

FIGURE 5.2 Shifting the AD curve

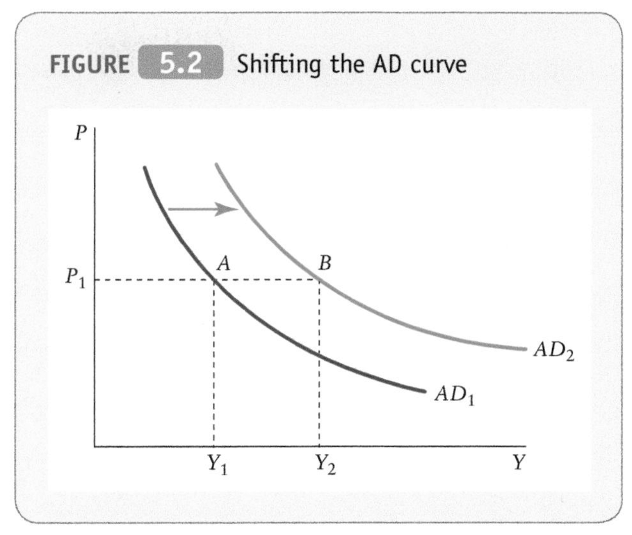

Several major shocks have affected the demand side of the Irish economy in recent times. Because our economy is so open to international trade, any event that triggers a global recession acts like a shock to Irish AD by reducing our exports. The terrorist attack on the World Trade Center in New York City on 11 September 2001 (9/11) led to a sharp decline in air travel and tourism. This reduced our net exports, NX, and shifted the AD curve in to the left. The adverse repercussions on business confidence led to a drop in investment, I, which also shifted the AD schedule inwards.

An example of a change that caused an outward shift in AD is provided by Finance Minister Charlie McCreevy's 2000 Budget, which significantly reduced Irish income tax rates and boosted consumer expenditure, C.

But the most dramatic shock to our economy in the post-war period was due to the world financial crisis of 2007–2008. The sub-prime mortgage crisis in the USA and the collapse of the Wall Street investment bank Bear Stearns in March 2008, followed by Lehman Brothers in September, had a devastating impact on the global economy. There were fears that the world's banking system would implode, with catastrophic consequences for the real economy. Business and consumer confidence collapsed, leading to sharp falls in consumption and investment spending. Falling C and I shifted the AD schedule inwards.

Then the fiscal crisis that emerged in 2008–2009 required large cuts in government spending, G, and increases in taxes, which further reduced C. Finally, the bursting of the bubble in Irish house prices sharply reduced the value of the largest single asset owned by many Irish households – the equity in their house.

During the bubble, soaring house prices had made many households feel wealthy and encouraged them to consume more. In some cases home owners borrowed against the perceived value of their house to finance a new car or a foreign holiday. This process went sharply into reverse after 2007 as house prices plummeted. 'Negative equity' became a problem for some households as the value of their house fell below the mortgage they owed to the bank or building society. People in this situation cut back on their discretionary spending as much as they could and this contributed to the fall in consumption, C.

Figure 5.3 shows how all the domestic components of AD (C, G, and I) fell sharply after 2007 and the economy entered its deepest recession since World War II. From the peak in 2007/8 to end-2011, personal consumption, C, declined by 13 per cent in real terms; public consumption, G, by 15 per cent; and investment spending, I, by 63 per cent. This illustrates the point that investment spending is the most volatile component of AD and the greatest source of instability in the economy.

Consumption spending, public or private, is far less volatile and changes more slowly. Even during a recession, households try to maintain the level of spending they have been accustomed to, and politicians are loath to cut government spending, G. But when business people lose confidence in the future they quickly shelve their investment plans.

FIGURE 5.3 GNP and components of aggregate demand

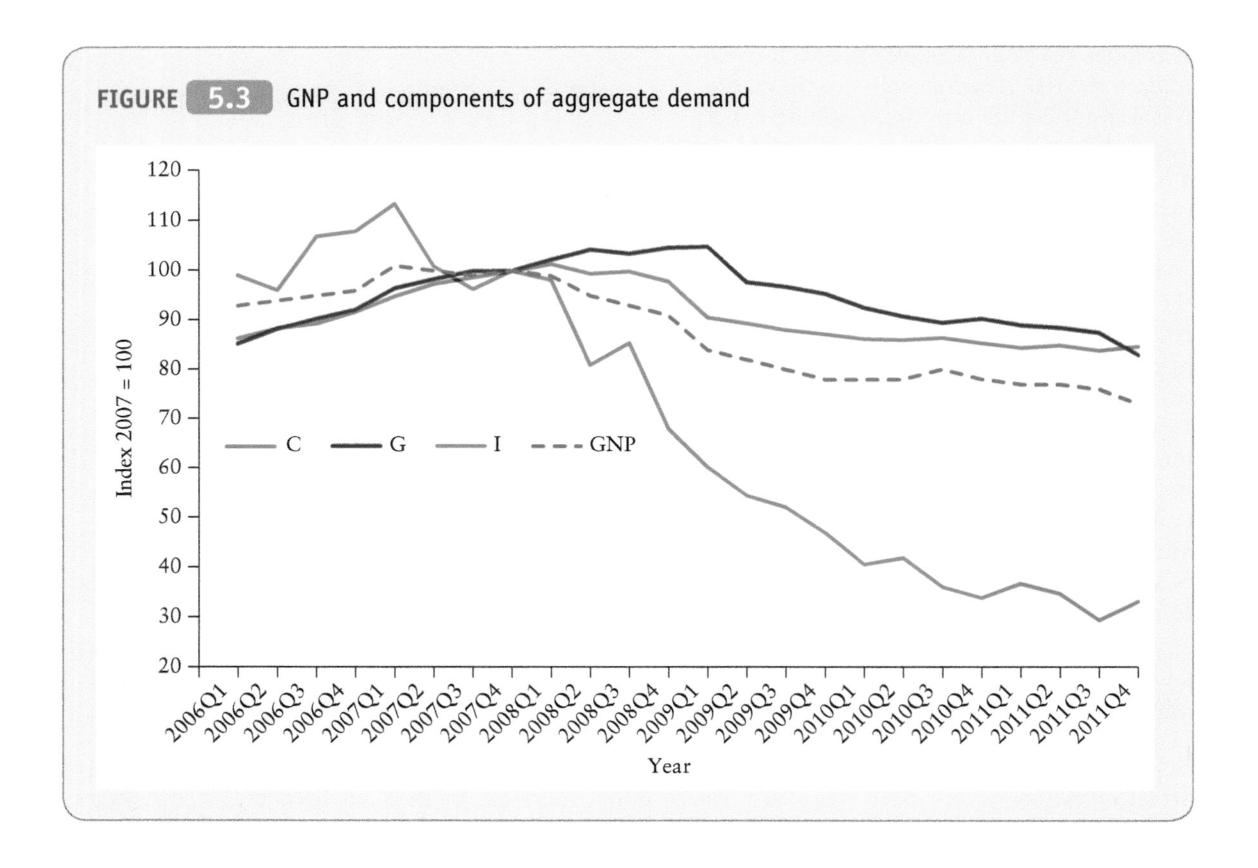

The only component of Irish AD that did not collapse after 2007 was NX. While imports fell sharply (reflecting the fall in imported consumer and investment goods), exports continued to grow.

5.6 Aggregate Supply

Long-run aggregate supply

We explained in Chapters 2 and 4 how output is determined from the production function. Potential output, Y*, corresponds to the level of output that can be produced when all the available factors of production are fully employed. In Figure 5.4 we depict a long-run aggregate supply curve drawn parallel to the vertical axis above the level of potential (or full-employment) output Y*. The schedule is vertical because real output depends on the volume of inputs (land, labour, capital) and not on the price level. This is a key assumption. It is reasonable to believe that in the long run prices do not influence the level of real output. You cannot produce more by simply printing money and raising the price level. If you start

FIGURE 5.4 The long-run aggregate supply curve

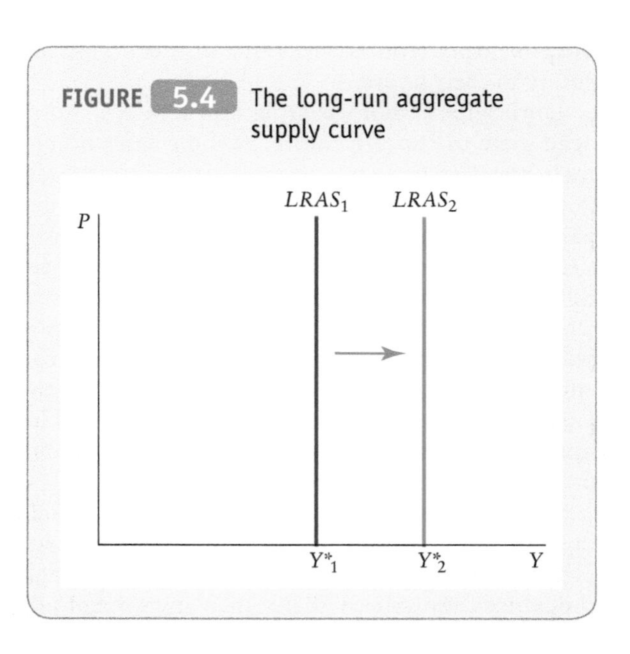

FIGURE 5.5 The long-run effects of an increase in aggregate demand

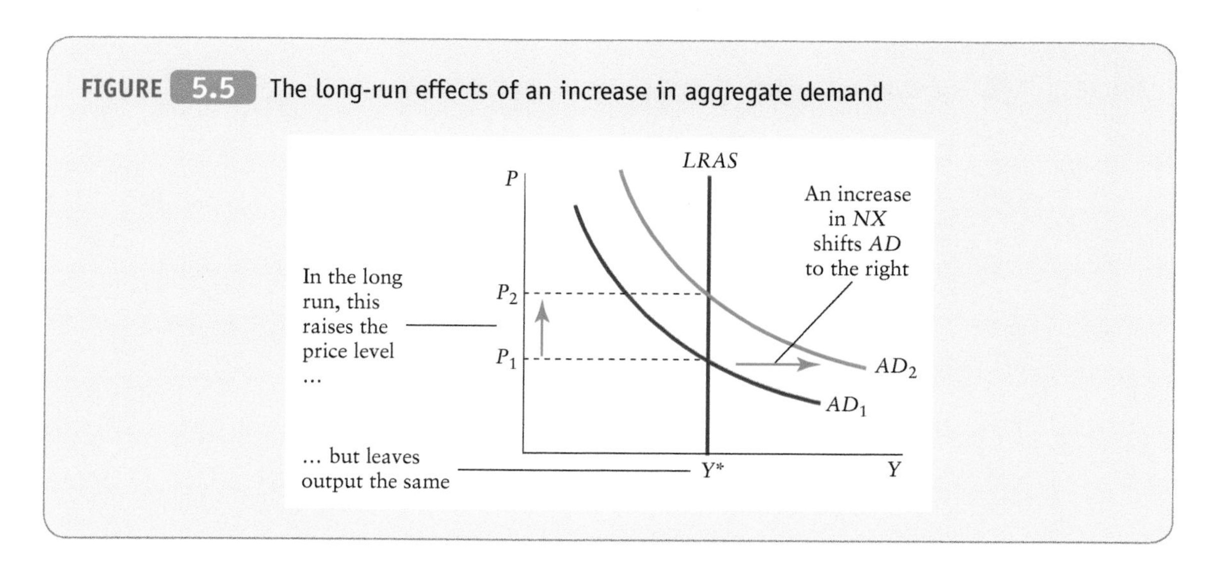

from full employment, more output requires more inputs. In Figure 5.4 the LRAS shifts to the right when the level of inputs increases, due to the growth of the labour force, for example, or an increase in the capital stock. The key point is that to increase Y^*_1 to Y^*_2 the economy requires more inputs (factors of production).

Figure 5.5 shows an AD schedule intersecting the AS schedule. As in any market, the intersection of supply and demand determines the equilibrium. Because the LRAS schedule in Figure 5.4 is vertical, the equilibrium level of output will always be Y*. When AD increases or shifts up, the result is an increase in the price level, P, but the level of output does not increase because the economy's potential output has not increased.

Flexible versus sticky prices

In our diagrams showing the intersection of AD and AS, we have so far assumed that the price level, P, changes in response to changes in AD. This allows the market to clear. Actual output and potential output coincide.

Market clearing requires the assumption that prices are flexible and adjust to equate supply and demand. In the long run there is sufficient time for prices and wages to adjust and it is plausible to assume that prices are flexible. The classical model, developed in Chapters 19 and 20, relies heavily on this assumption.

The Keynesian model, on the other hand, is a short- or medium-run model where at least some prices and costs are 'sticky'. By this we mean that they are slow to adjust in response to changes in supply or demand. As a consequence markets may not always clear and the level of output may not always correspond to the potential level of output, Y*.

Price and wage stickiness or rigidity can be due to a number of factors. Labour contracts may set wage rates for a year or two ahead. As we explain below, the 2010 Croke Park Agreement stipulated that there should be no reduction in Irish public sector wages before 2014. Many Irish commercial leases exclude downward rent reviews. This has been an important rigidity in the property market during the recession. Other rigidities arise because firms enter into agreements to supply raw materials at fixed prices and catalogues specify prices for a season ahead.

The economy's response to shocks depends very much on the flexibility of prices. If prices are not flexible the market will be slow to clear following a shock. This can lead to unemployment or

FIGURE 5.6 The short-run effects of an increase in aggregate demand

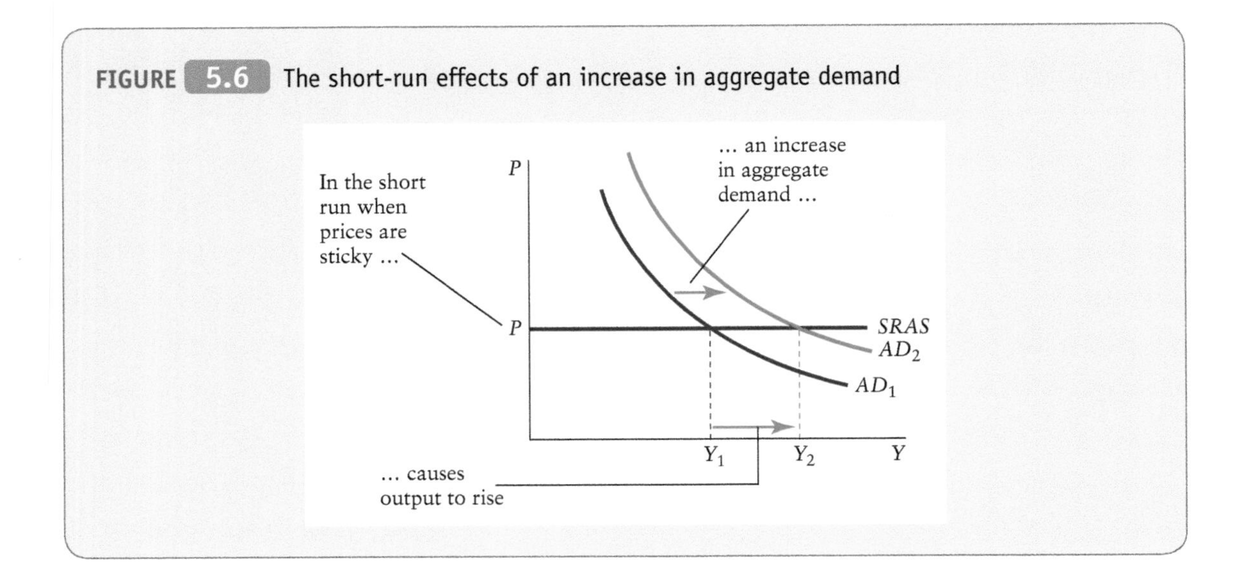

excess demand. The AS schedules in Figures 5.4 and 5.5 depict the long run in which prices are flexible and demand shocks simply change the aggregate price level, P, but do not alter the level of output, which always remains at Y*.

Aggregate supply in the short run

More prices are sticky in the short run than in the long run. As a result the price level affects real output in the short run and actual output can deviate from its potential level. If we take the extreme case where all prices are sticky and firms are willing to sell as much at that price level as their customers are willing to buy, the short-run aggregate supply curve, SRAS, is horizontal. Aggregate supply can expand up to Y*, at which point the economy is fully employed.

Figure 5.6 shows the short-run effects of an increase in aggregate demand. If, for example, an increase in NX moves the AD curve out to the right, with the price level fixed the result is an increase in real output along the horizontal axis.

In the less extreme situation where some prices are sticky and other prices are flexible, the SRAS curve is upward sloping, as in Figure 5.7. As the level of real output rises on the horizontal axis, the overall price level also rises along the vertical axis.

The slope of the aggregate supply curve

Why does the SRAS slope upwards? Why should a firm increase its output when all prices are rising? To answer this question, consider the fact that a firm's profit is equal to total revenue minus total cost:

$$\text{Profit} = \text{total revenue} - \text{total cost} \tag{2}$$

In turn, total revenue equals the price of output (P_q) multiplied by the volume of output (Q). Total cost equals the price of inputs (P_z) multiplied by the volume of inputs (Z), such as raw materials and labour. Substituting into equation (2):

$$\text{Profit} = (P_q \times Q) - (P_z \times Z) \tag{3}$$

We use this equation to offer three reasons why the SRAS curve is upward sloping.

FIGURE 5.7 The short-run aggregate supply curve and sticky prices

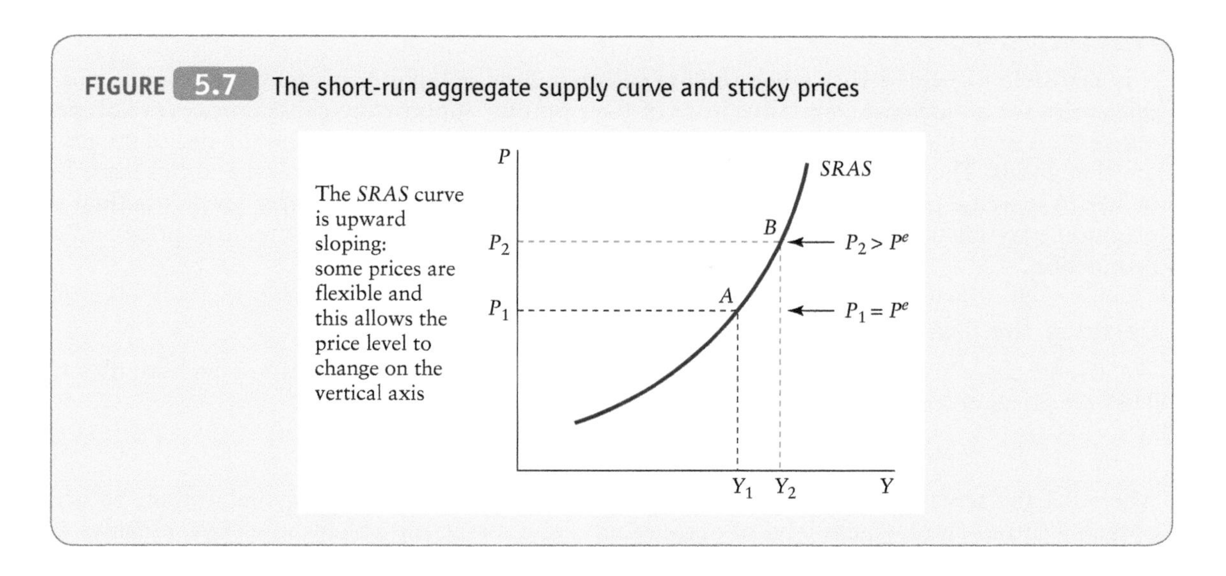
The SRAS curve is upward sloping: some prices are flexible and this allows the price level to change on the vertical axis
P
SRAS
B
P_2
$P_2 > P^e$
A
P_1
$P_1 = P^e$
Y_1 Y_2
Y

Sticky wages

When unions and employers sit down to negotiate wages for, say, the coming year, both sides have in their minds a forecast of the inflation rate for the year. Corresponding to this is an expected price level (P^e). If an agreement is negotiated, workers are locked into a wage deal for a year. If the actual price level, P, turns out to be higher than the expected level, P^e, workers have to wait until the next set of negotiations to try to redress their loss. The implications of this are:

- If $P > P^e$ the firm can make more profits by increasing production

$$\uparrow P \rightarrow \uparrow \text{revenue} \rightarrow \uparrow \text{profit} \rightarrow \uparrow Y$$

- If $P < P^e$ the firm makes less profits and will now cut production

$$\downarrow P \rightarrow \downarrow \text{revenue} \rightarrow \downarrow \text{profit} \rightarrow \downarrow Y$$

In Figure 5.7, the firm is initially at point A and $P = P^e$. If P increases relative to P^e the increase in profit encourages firms to expand output from Y_1 to Y_2. This positive relationship between the price level and the volume of output supplied is reflected in an upward-sloping SRAS curve.

This result depends crucially on the assumption that costs, and wages in particular, do not change as output prices change. If wages remain constant as prices rise, real wages decline and workers will be worse off. The assumption that nominal wages are constant is certainly not valid in the long run.

Sticky prices

Another explanation for the upward-sloping SRAS curve is the belief that prices are sticky. Because of menu costs, some firms do not adjust prices immediately. If there is an unexpected increase in the general price level, but some firms do not raise their prices, their prices will be relatively low. This will lead to an increase in sales and an expansion in production. Conversely, if there is an unexpected decrease in P, some firms now have prices that are too high. Sales will decline and the firm will cut production. This is another explanation for the upward-sloping SRAS curve.

Price misperceptions

It is plausible to believe that when the overall price level is rising firms may mistake the rise in their price for an increase in relative price of their output. Suppose the general price level, P, rises above P^e. A firm is aware of the rise in the price of its output before it notices the rise in the prices of other goods. The producer mistakenly believes that relative prices have risen and this leads him or her to increase production. The same logic applies when the overall price level is falling: the producer may mistake the fall in the firm's output price for a decline in its relative price and cut production.

Deriving the SRAS model

We assume there are two types of firm. The first type is firms whose prices are perfectly flexible. They set prices according to this rule:

$$P^F = P + \alpha(Y - Y^*) \qquad (4)$$

where P is the actual price level, P^F is the price level of 'flexible firms', Y is actual output, Y^* is the potential or full-employment level of output and α is a coefficient which shows how sensitive P is to the output gap.

The second type is sticky-price firms. These firms set prices before they know the outcome for P, Y and Y^*. They therefore base their price decision on expected P, Y and Y^*.

$$P^S = P^e + \beta(EY - EY^*) \qquad (5)$$

The notation is as before, except E denotes expected output, P^e is the expected price and P^s is the price of 'sticky-price firms'. Assume now that sticky-price firms expect actual output to be at its potential level, Y^*, $EY = EY^*$. It follows that $P^S = P^e$.

Assume also that the proportion of sticky-price firms is a fraction, λ. The overall price equation (P) for the economy is:

$$P = \lambda P^e + (1 - \lambda)[P + \alpha(Y - Y^*)] \qquad (6)$$

where λ indicates the proportion of sticky-price firms and $(1 - \lambda)$ the proportion of flexible-price firms.

Subtract $(1 - \lambda)P$ from both sides of equation (6). We obtain:

$$\lambda P = \lambda P^e + (1 - \lambda)[\alpha(Y - Y^*)] \qquad (7)$$

Divide both sides of equation (7) by λ:

$$P = P^e + [(1 - \lambda)\alpha/\lambda](Y - Y^*) \qquad (8)$$

Let $\phi = (1 - \lambda)\alpha/\lambda$, we can write:

$$P = P^e + \phi(Y - Y^*) \qquad (9)$$

This aggregate price equation states that the two main factors determining the overall price level are the expected price level, P^e, and actual output (Y) relative to the potential level of output (Y^*). If firms expect higher prices, they will set actual prices higher in advance. This pushes up the actual price level.

If the economy is over-heating, and $Y > Y^*$, firms with flexible prices will increase prices. The more flexible firms there are in the economy (the smaller λ), the more responsive is P to the output gap $Y - Y^*$.

We can now derive the SRAS curve by solving equation (9) for Y.

$$P - P^e = \phi Y - \phi Y^* \qquad (10)$$

Or

$$\phi Y = \phi Y^* + P - P^e \tag{11}$$

Divide both sides by ϕ.

$$Y = Y^* + 1/\phi(P - P^e) \tag{12}$$

Or setting δ equal to $1/\phi$:

$$Y = Y^* + \delta(P - P^e) \tag{13}$$

This is the equation underlying the SRAS curve. As Y and P are positively related, the SRAS curve is upward sloping.

The location of the SRAS curve

The same factors that shift the LRAS curve also affect the SRAS curve. For example, an increase in labour, capital, natural resources and technology all move the LRAS and SRAS curves to the right. However, the SRAS curve is also affected by the expected price level (P^e). We now explain why this is the case.

The determinants of the expected price level, P^e, will be discussed in more detail later in this book. We summarise this discussion here by noting that *adaptive expectations* refers to the situation where people and firms tend to extrapolate recent rates of inflation into the future. High current inflation gives rise to high expected inflation. The simplest rule of thumb would be that next year's rate of inflation will be much the same as this year's. This approach will lead to mistakes when there are shocks that change the rate of inflation.

Rational expectations, on the other hand, refers to the situation where people and firms make use of all available information, including the implications of changes in policy, in formulating expectations. It plausibly assumes that people look forwards, not backwards, when forecasting the future price level. They take all relevant information into account, including expected changes in input prices, exchange rates, interest rates, political developments and so on.

We emphasise that firms are concerned about their cost base and profit level. Referring back to the profit function (equation (3)), an expected increase in the price of inputs such as wages or raw materials will motivate firms to raise output prices to maintain profits.

$$(\uparrow P_z \times Z) \rightarrow \uparrow P^e \rightarrow (\uparrow P_q \times Q) \rightarrow \text{Constant profit}$$

In Figure 5.8, the anticipated increase in the cost base leads to an increase in P^e and the SRAS curve shifts upwards from A to B. At B, real output is unchanged, but the price level has increased from P_1 to P_2. By moving the SRAS curve upwards in this way, we can examine the relationship between the new, higher price level and the original level of real output. Conversely, an expectation of lower input prices is reflected in a decrease in P^e and the SRAS curve shifts downwards.

FIGURE 5.8 An increase in price expectations

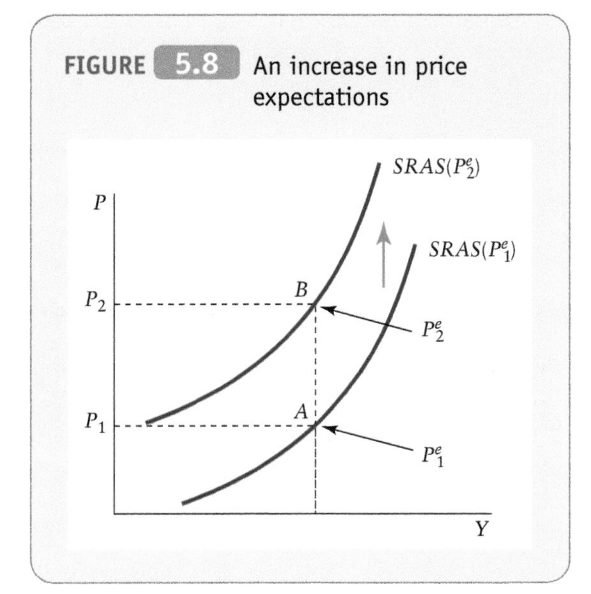

In terms of equation (13):

$$Y_1 = Y^* + \delta(P_1 - P^e)$$

If P^e increases, firms will pass this on in higher P. For a given Y, if we shift the SRAS curve upwards, we can examine the relationship between the initial Y and the new higher level of P. Conversely, a fall in P^e will be reflected in a lower level of P. We now shift the SRAS curve downwards to examine the relationship between the original level of Y and the new lower level of P.

Productivity is an important influence on the location of the SRAS curve. If more output is obtained from the same, or fewer, inputs, productivity has increased. This occurs when technology improves or there is an improvement in working practices. An increase in productivity reduces costs. The expected price level and the SRAS curve shifts down to the right. In contrast, a decrease in productivity raises the expected price level and the SRAS curve shifts upwards to the left.

The Irish economy has been buffeted by many supply-side shocks over the years. By far the most important of these have come from changes in oil and energy prices. Fuel and energy are major components of production costs throughout the economy. When energy prices rise it is to be expected that the price level will rise and this shifts the SRAS curve up and to the left. Adverse shocks like this were the cause of the global recession in the 1970s. More local shocks can also have serious repercussions. The prolonged drought in the US Midwest during the summer of 2012 sent food prices soaring, with the result that inflation expectations were revised upwards. New environmental protection laws designed to reduce carbon emissions impose higher costs on energy-intensive sectors, and this too shifts the SRAS curve upwards.

The key point is that any event or new policy that causes the actual price level, P, to deviate from the expected price level, P^e, will lead to a shift of the SRAS curve. Price expectations determine the position or location of the SRAS curve.

5.7 Equilibrium

In Figure 5.9, the long-run aggregate supply (LRAS), SRAS and AD curves are brought together. The LRAS curve is vertical above the horizontal axis at Y* and the equilibrium price, P_1, and output level, Y_1, are at A.

Recall that changes in stocks act as a signal to firms as to whether production should be increased, reduced or left unchanged. At A there are no unplanned (unanticipated) changes in stocks. This is the key to the concept of equilibrium in the market for goods and services.

If the price level is lower than P_1, as at P_2, SRAS is less than AD. The excess demand will lead to an unplanned reduction in stocks. In order to ration the available supply among those trying to buy it, firms will raise prices. As the price level rises, this encourages firms to increase production (along

FIGURE 5.9 Equilibrium in the goods and services market

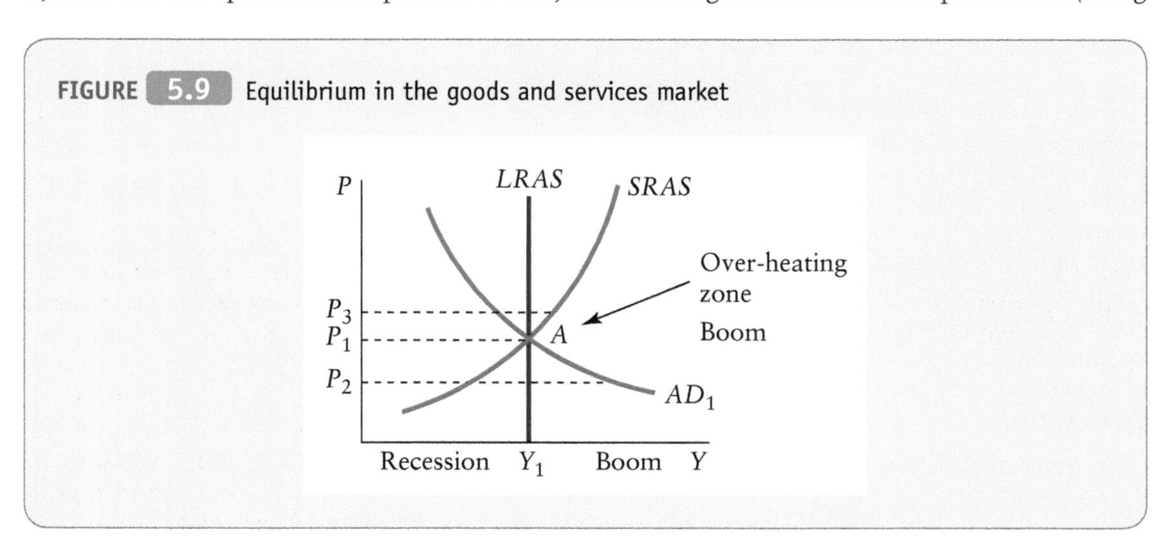

the SRAS curve) and reduces the demand for goods (along the AD curve). Eventually equilibrium will be restored at A.

Similarly, if the price level is higher than P_1, at P_3, SRAS exceeds AD and there is an excess supply of goods and services. There will be an unplanned increase in stocks. Firms will lower prices in order to clear unwanted stocks. As the price level falls, firms will cut production (along the SRAS curve) and the demand for goods and services will increase (along the AD curve). Again, equilibrium will be reached at A.

In our discussion of shifts in the AD and AS schedules, we assume that equilibrium is quickly re-established following a disturbance. In reality, of course, it takes time for markets to adjust and there will be an interim while the economy moves to a new equilibrium.

Output gaps

Both aggregate demand and aggregate supply are constantly buffeted by shocks that cause the economy to move away from full employment. When the economy is not at full employment, an output gap emerges, defined as:

$$\text{Output gap} = \text{actual real GNP (Y)} - \text{potential real GNP } (Y^*) \quad (14)$$

It is usually expressed as a percentage of potential output, $(Y - Y^*)/Y^*$.

When actual real GNP is below potential real GNP, the output gap is negative and unemployment is above the natural rate. The economy is operating below capacity and the economy is in recession or over-cooling. When actual real output is above potential output, the output gap is positive and the economy is said to be over-heating. Labour shortages will become widespread as the unemployment rate falls below its natural rate, causing upward pressure on wages. Firms will pass on their rising costs by increasing output prices.

A key question is: How does the economy revert back to the LRAS line following a shock?

5.8 Adjusting to Demand-side Shocks

Starting from A in Figure 5.10, if the economy is hit with an adverse demand-side shock that reduces consumption, investment or net exports, the AD curve shifts from AD_1 to AD_2. At price level P_1 there is excess supply measured by the distance AB. The price level will fall and this increases demand from B to C along the AD curve and reduces supply from A to C along the SRAS curve. A new equilibrium is established at C where AD equals SRAS and both the price level and real output have fallen. The new short-run equilibrium is to the left of the LRAS line and actual output is now less than potential real output and unemployment is above the natural unemployment level. How does the economy adjust out of this recession?

The key variable in the adjustment process is the real wage (W/P). Corresponding to point A in Figure 5.10 is a unique real wage which is related to prevailing price expectations. When the economy moved to C, the actual price level fell unexpectedly and because the nominal wage remained unchanged, the real wage increased.

If workers reduce their price expectations in line with the new lower actual price level they accept a cut in nominal wages and the SRAS curve will shift down to the right This moves the economy from C to D and the economy returns to Y^*. (Recall that price expectations determines the location of the SRAS curve.) At D the original real wage is restored because the fall in nominal wages is exactly equal to the fall in the price level.

This analysis illustrates the difference between the economy in the long and short runs. Along the LRAS schedule the real wage is constant. As the economy moves from A to D the change in nominal wages offsets the change in the price level, and real wages remain constant. But as the economy moves along the SRAS schedule, sticky nominal wages imply that real wages change as the price level changes. Wage flexibility plays a key role in the adjustment mechanism.

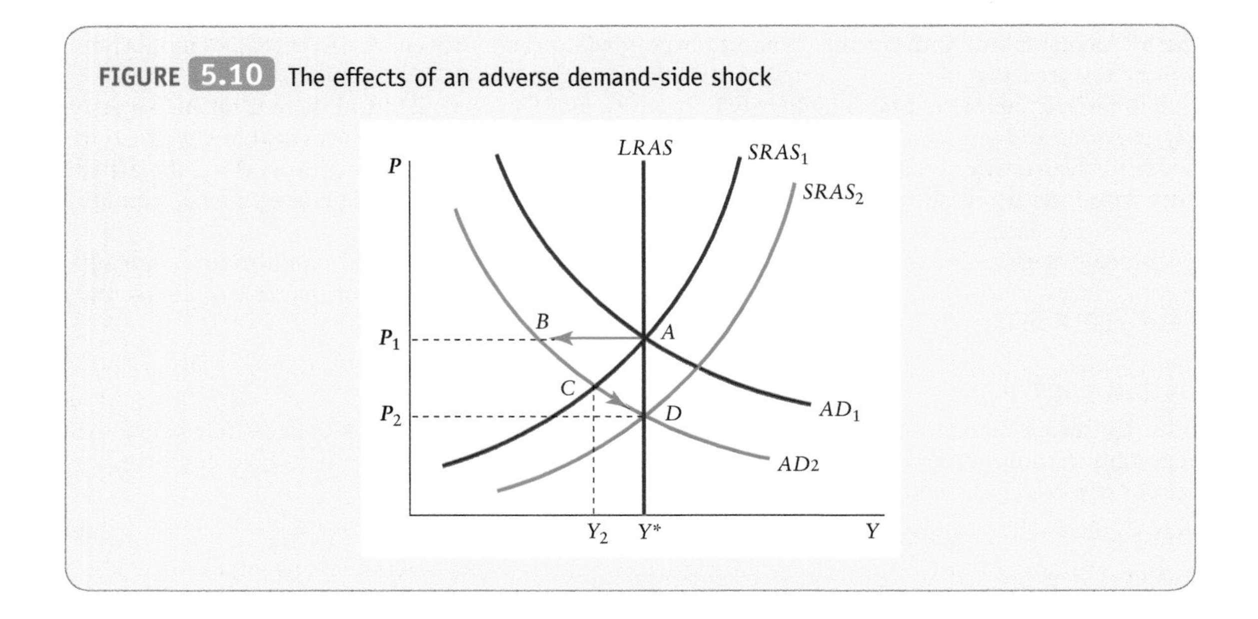

FIGURE 5.10 The effects of an adverse demand-side shock

The Keynesian perspective

As mentioned earlier, the classical school of economics takes a long-run perspective on the adjustment process. As all prices and wages adjust in the long run, the economy will eventually revert to the full-employment equilibrium following a disturbance. The classical school believes that adjustment will occur without active intervention by policy-makers. It therefore favours a non-interventionist policy philosophy.

Keynesian economists argue that point C in Figure 5.10 represents equilibrium because aggregate supply equals aggregate demand and there is no unintended accumulation of stocks. Most important, Keynes argued that nominal wages are inflexible in a downward direction and the economy could remain at C for quite a long time. The SRAS curve will not move down to the right and the economy will remain to the left of potential output for as long as nominal wages remain stuck at their pre-recession level.

If the adjustment takes a long time to work through the economy it will be very costly in terms of lost output and excess unemployment. This was the case during the Great Depression of 1929–1939 and in Ireland in the mid-1980s. During the current recession we are facing the prospect that the unemployment rate will remain considerably above any reasonable definition of the natural rate for many years.

Keynes believed that active policy measures are needed to resort full employment more quickly. If the economy is at C in Figure 5.10, an increase in government expenditure and/or a cut in tax rates would shift the AD curve back to its original position at A. The economy would revert to Y* and unemployment would fall back to its natural rate.

Government could attempt to increase aggregate demand indirectly by influencing the levels of consumption (C), investment (I) or net exports (NX). Cuts in VAT rates, car scrappage schemes, and incentives for investment are examples of measures that have been taken in Ireland to boost the non-government components of aggregate demand. But governments may prefer to rely on direct measures and raise their own contribution to aggregate demand.

A recent example of this is the 2009 'stimulus package' introduced by the Obama administration to shorten the current recession in the USA. This involved spending about $800 billion on infrastructure, education, health, and energy, providing federal tax incentives for investment, and expanding unemployment benefits and other social welfare provisions. This is an important example of implementing the Keynesian recommendation to stimulate aggregate demand to shorten recessions.

Policies designed to stabilise the economy and reduce the severity of short-run fluctuations are not confined to fiscal policy. The authorities may also use monetary, exchange rate and incomes policies to combat the effects of adverse demand and supply side shocks. These are discussed in later chapters.

Trade-offs between policy goals

A demand stimulus may create a policy dilemma. An expansionary fiscal policy increases AD and should reduce unemployment, which is desirable, but if this comes at the expense of higher inflation, there is a cost. There may be a trade-off between the policy goals of price stability and low unemployment. Fiscal stimulus also involves running budget deficits, which have to be financed through borrowing. This adds to the national debt. Rising debt levels place a limit on the use of active fiscal policy as a counter-cyclical policy.

Wage flexibility

In view of the key role of wage–price flexibility in the adjustment process, it is natural to ask: How flexible are prices and wages in Ireland? We presented data on real and nominal wage changes in Ireland in Table 3.6. Referring back to that table it may be seen that over the entire period from 1991 to 2011 there were only two years – 2008 and 2010 – when nominal wages fell. However, there were additional years – 1994, 2006 and 2010–12 – when real wages fell because the rise in nominal wages did not fully compensate for the rise in the price level.

In Table 5.1 we take a more detailed look at how nominal wage rates behaved since the onset of the current recession in 2008. (We show hourly wage rates rather than weekly earnings because the latter are affected by the number of hours worked.) In the second column we show the percentage change in nominal hourly earnings between the first half of 2008 and the first half of 2012. This summarises what happened to wages over four years of recession.

The hourly wage rate for all employees averaged across all economic sectors rose by 2.4 per cent. Over the same period the price level, as measured by the CPI, *fell* by one per cent, so real wages rose by 3.4 per cent. Over this four-year period, when the unemployment rate trebled, there was no downward adjustment of real or nominal wages across the Irish economy.

However, the pattern varies across sectors. Nominal hourly wage rates fell in seven sectors and rose in eight. Perhaps not surprisingly, the biggest reductions were recorded among employees in the financial, insurance and real estate, public administration and defence, and construction sectors. On the other hand, earnings rose by 8 per cent in the education sector and by 7.5 per cent in manufacturing industry.

The government implemented special measures that affected the pay and taxation of public service employees in the Budgets of 2009 and 2010. Employment in the public sector was also reduced. These measures were designed to contain the fiscal deficit. The new levies on pay in the public service reduced after-tax income but did not affect gross pay. However, in January 2010 a cut in public sector employees' gross pay was imposed on a sliding scale from five per cent for the lowest paid to 15 per cent for the highest paid. This is reflected in the data for the public administration (although not for the education sector) in Table 5.1. This does not, however, reduce labour costs as the additional taxation is used to finance the government budget deficit.

However, in June 2010, shortly after the cut in nominal wages was implemented, the government and the public sector unions signed the Croke Park Agreement. This stipulated that there would be no further cuts in public sector rates of pay over the period 2010–2014. Despite the crisis in the public finances and the high level of unemployment, nominal wage rigidity was built into the public service wage bill for a three-year period.

TABLE 5.1 Average hourly earnings by sector

NACE economic sector	2012 as % of 2008*
Mining and quarrying	112.1
Manufacturing	107.2
Construction	95.0
Wholesale and retail trade, etc.	103.7
Transportation and storage	98.3
Accommodation and food service activities	98.4
Information and communication	105.2
Professional, scientific and technical activities	102.9
Administrative and support service activities	100.2
Public administration and defence, etc.	92.9
Education	108.5
Human health and social work activities	99.0
Electricity, utilities	95.4
Financial, insurance and real estate	91.0
Arts, entertainment, recreation, etc.	103.2
All sectors	102.4

***Average** of Q1 and Q2 of both years

Source: CSO, Quarterly Survey of Earnings and Labour Costs

It should also be noted that, in the public sector, there have been significant cuts in the wage and salary rates being offered to new entrants. For example, newly recruited teachers are now earning up to one-third less than their counterparts did a few years ago and similar cuts to starting salaries have been implemented in the health services. Obviously in a period of falling public service employment it will take some time before these cuts are reflected in average wage rates.

Overall, it is hard not to draw the conclusion that, harsh though the fall in real after-tax earnings has been in both the private and public sectors, and despite an enormous number of job losses and the crisis level of unemployment, real wages have proved very inflexible. In terms of the AD–AS analysis in Figure 5.10, there is little evidence of the fall in nominal wages that would be required to shift the SRAS downwards by the amount needed to restore the economy to its potential real output at Y*.

Expansionary demand-side shocks

In Figure 5.11 the economy is initially at A and output is at its potential level, Y*. The government – facing an election – might pursue an expansionary fiscal policy (increasing expenditure or cutting tax rates) in the belief that real output could be increased and unemployment reduced. This would shift the AD out to the right. Initially there would be excess demand measured by the distance A–B. Unless output expands, the price level will rise and this will reduce demand (from B to C) and increase supply (from A to C) and a new equilibrium will be established at C. The economy is now operating above its potential Y* and the expected price level will rise. How does the economy adjust to this over-heating (inflationary) situation?

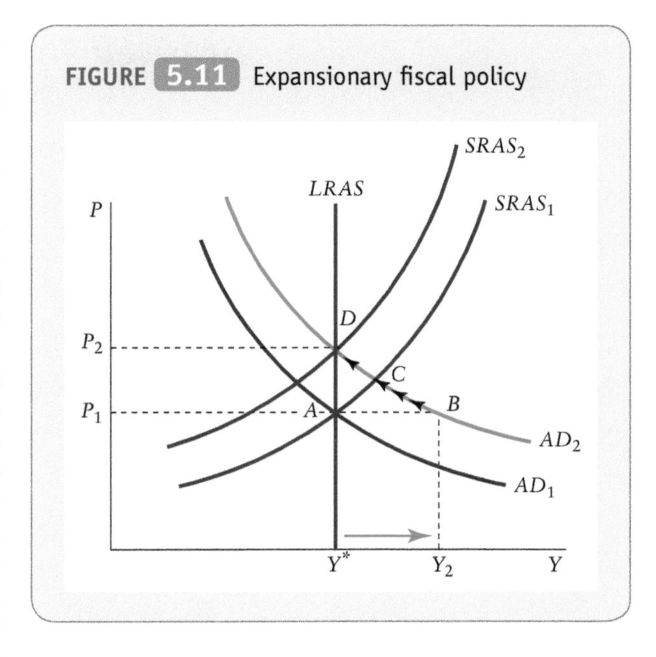

FIGURE 5.11 Expansionary fiscal policy

The $SRAS_1$ curve is drawn for given price expectations (P^e). The increase in the price level from P_1 to P_2 is unexpected and workers have bargained for too low a nominal wage. The unanticipated increase in the price level has reduced the real wage workers actually receive. At the first opportunity, workers will try to redress the situation and demand higher wages in line with the new level of prices. This causes the SRAS curve to shift up and to the left. The economy moves to D and back to its potential level of output, Y*. At D, the original real wage is restored because the percentage change in the price level from P_1 to P_2 equals the change in nominal wages. The effect of the expansionary fiscal policy has been a temporary increase in real output (which may get the government re-elected), but the price level is now at a higher level.

The key question is: How long does it take to get from A to D? The answer once again is that it depends on the flexibility of prices and wages. In the previous section we gave the evidence concerning wage flexibility in Ireland during the current recession. We saw that nominal wages have been sticky despite the size of the output gap.

But note that there is a lack of symmetry with the adverse-shock case. Nominal wages fall slowly (if at all) to reduce real wages and shorten the recession, but nominal wages are likely to rise quickly when the economy is operating above Y* and the labour market is overheating. At the height of the boom in 2001, Irish nominal wages increased by eight per cent and real wages by over three per cent.

5.9 Adjusting to a Supply-side Shock

Consider now the effect of an adverse supply-side shock such as an increase in the price of oil. Suppose the economy is initially at A in Figure 5.12. Output is at its level Y* and the price level is P_1. How do increases in oil prices impact on the economy?

Higher oil prices affect a whole range of raw materials and increase firms' costs. Petrol prices, electricity charges, heating bills and so on all increase. This raises price expectations and the SRAS curve shifts in to the left. The

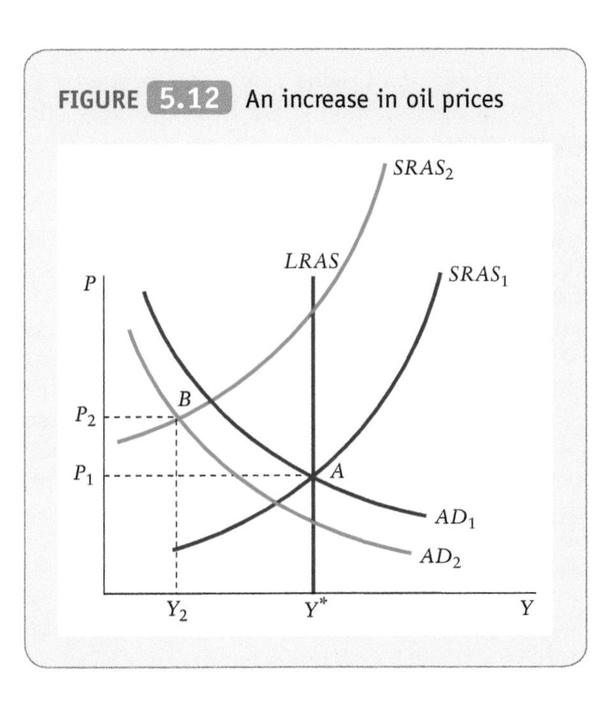

FIGURE 5.12 An increase in oil prices

FIGURE 5.13 Wholesale price of fuel oil: Ireland, 2000–2012

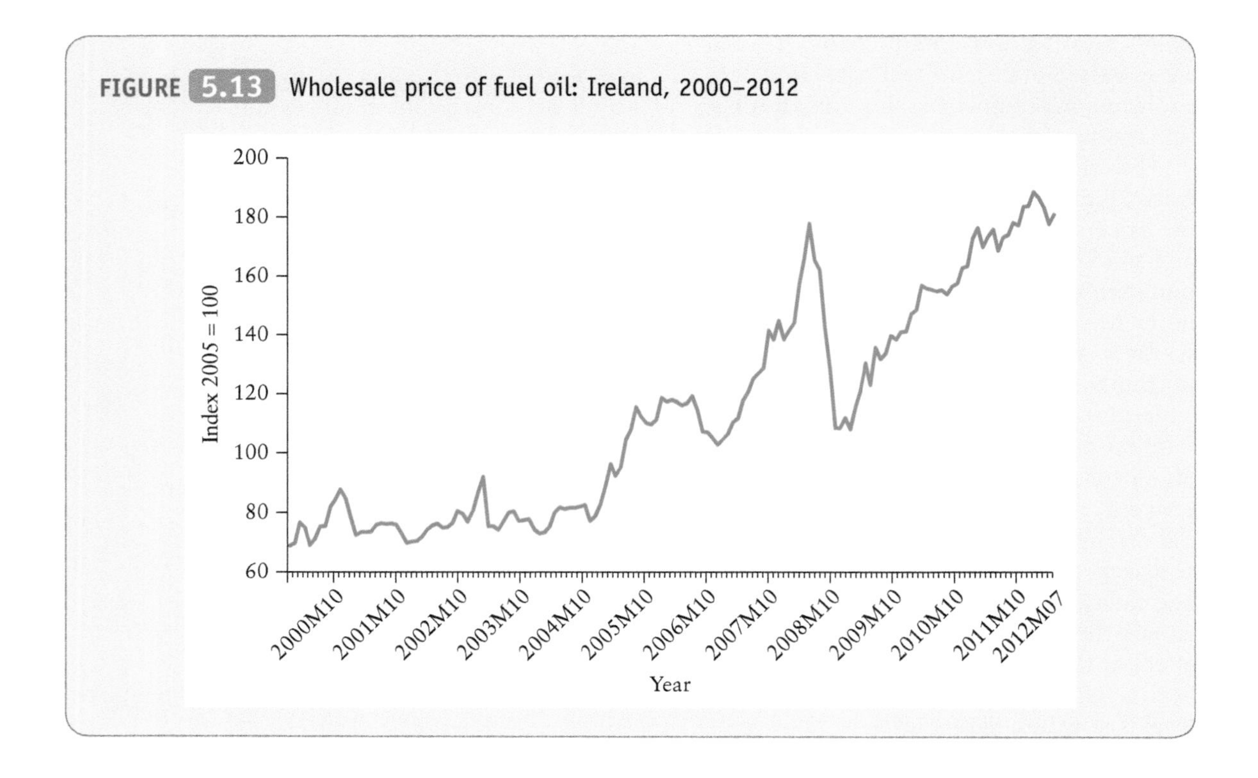

increase in oil prices also shifts the AD curve down by lowering investment, I, as firms cut back on their investment plans and raises imports, M, because the cost of imported fuel has risen. As drawn in Figure 5.12, the movement of the SRAS curve is greater than the movement of the AD curve. Equilibrium is re-established at B, where the price level has increased and real output has fallen. Unemployment will also have increased. All of the key macroeconomic variables have deteriorated. The combination of rising prices and falling output has been labelled *stagflation*.

A small open economy like Ireland is very vulnerable to external shocks. Figure 5.13 shows the wholesale price of fuel oil in Ireland between 2000 and 2012. Between 2005 and 2007 oil prices increased by 125 per cent and then fell by 35 per cent in 2008, but have risen by almost 70 per cent between 2009 and mid-2012. This volatility buffets the economy and moves it away from its LRAS curve.

A shock to either AD or AS may not only move the economy away from Y* in the short run, it could permanently lower the economy's growth potential. We have stressed that there is no easy way to move an economy back to its LRAS curve after it has been hit by an adverse shock. The degree of real wage flexibility is limited. The government's budget deficit will increase as the economy goes into recession, which makes a fiscal stimulus problematic from the public finance point of view.

Thus the economy can get stuck at a point to the left of potential real output. A prolonged recession may lead to the virtual cessation of investment in new capital. This would lower the future productive capacity of the economy as the current stock of capital depreciates. High unemployment and falling real wages could cause some people to drop out of the labour force, while long-term unemployment leads to loss of skills and motivation. These effects of a recession would cause the potential output schedule to shift to the left and intersect the SRAS and AD curves to the left of the original LRAS curve.

Figure 5.14 shows the actual level of real GNP from 2003 to 2011. It also shows a line that extrapolates the trend in GNP over the pre-recession years (2003–2007) forward to 2011. This is a

FIGURE 5.14 Real GNP relative to its trend, 2003–2011 (log scale)

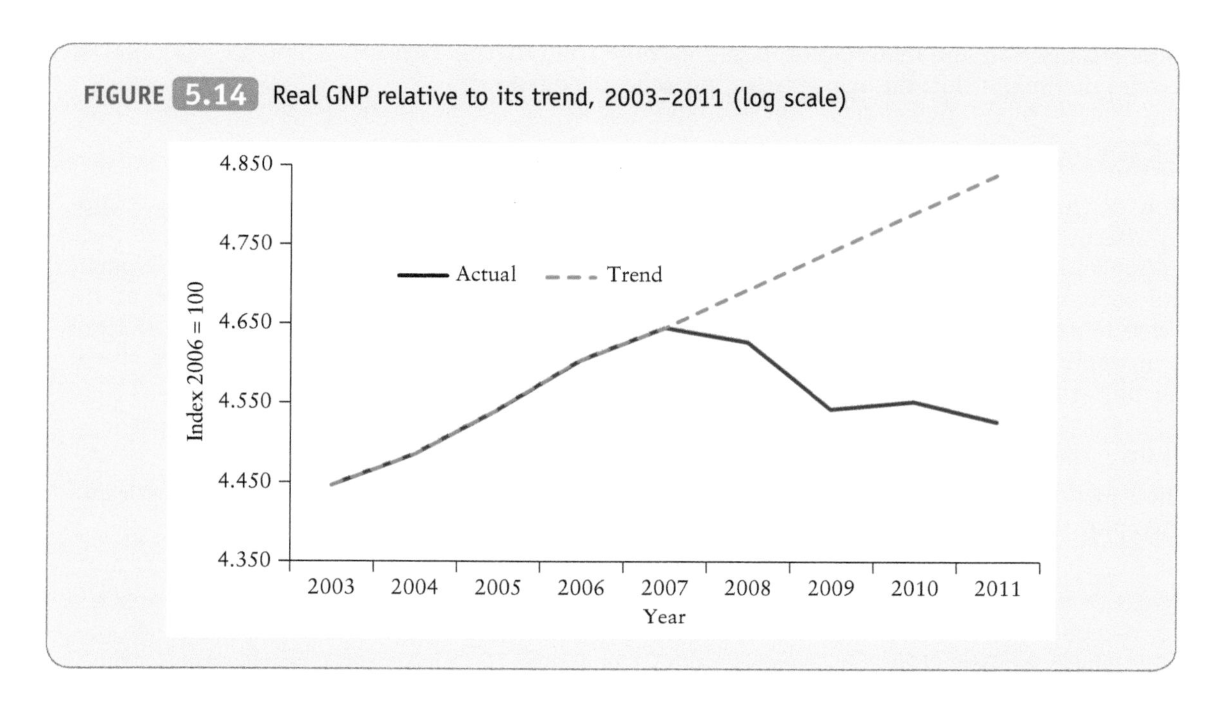

rough estimate of where the economy might have been in 2011 had the pre-recession growth rate been maintained. On the basis of this calculation, the economy would have been one-third larger in 2011 than it actually was. While the assumption that growth could have continued at the rate recorded between 2003 and 2007 is unrealistic in view of the bubble-like nature of the boom, the calculation nonetheless highlights how much has been lost due to the recession. The likelihood is that we may never recover much of the output lost during the recession.

Supply-side economics

A favourable supply-side shock or a policy initiative that moves the SRAS curve outwards raises output and lowers unemployment and inflation. Policies that produce these results are called 'supply-side economics'. Versions of supply-side economics became popular in the 1980s during the Reagan administration in the USA and the Thatcher era in Britain. They were vigorously endorsed by the Republican Party in the 2012 US Presidential campaign. Paul Ryan, the Republican vice-presidential candidate, is an economist who ardently believes that the key to greater prosperity lies in lower taxes, especially income and capital gains taxes, reduced regulation on business and cuts in welfare benefits. In the terminology of this chapter, he believes that these policies would shift the aggregate supply curve to the right, leading to higher output, lower unemployment and lower inflation. If Ryan's economic philosophy were implemented, the US economy would serve as a laboratory for the effectiveness of supply-side economics.

In Ireland there is a constant search for policies that would enhance productivity and shift the SRAS schedule outwards. An example is contained in the report called *Building Ireland's Smart Economy: A Framework for Sustainable Economic Renewal*, published in 2008 (Department of the Taoiseach 2008). This report contained a long list of proposals designed to increase the productivity of the Irish economy. For example, it was proposed to 'invest heavily in research and development, incentivise multinational companies to locate more R&D capacity in Ireland, and ensure the commercialisation and retaining of ideas that flow from that investment'. These are examples of policies that might shift the aggregate supply schedule outwards.

5.10 Real GNP and Unemployment

How do the fluctuations in output associated with shifting aggregate demand and aggregate supply affect the unemployment rate? Firms hire additional workers when they wish to expand their output and shed workers when output is falling. The labour force is the sum of employment and unemployment, and the labour force does not change much in the short run. Hence, an increase in real output will lead to an increase in employment and this, in turn, will lead to a fall in unemployment. Conversely, a fall in real output will lead to a fall in employment and a rise in unemployment.

Okun's law

The American economist Arthur Okun noticed the close relationship between GDP growth and unemployment in the 1960s and formulated what became known as Okun's law.

NOTE: Arthur Okun (1928–1980) became Professor of Economics at Yale in 1963. He was made a member of John F. Kennedy's Council of Economic Advisers in 1964 and became chairman of this council in 1968. Using 1950s data for the US economy, he found that a one percentage point increase in the unemployment rate was associated with a three percentage points fall in real GDP. He later commented: 'This "rule of thumb" held up so well over the next decade that some of my professional colleagues called it Okun's Law.'

In Figure 5.15 we show the rate of change in real GNP on the horizontal axis and the change in the unemployment rate on the vertical axis for the period 1970–2011. It can be seen that the unemployment rate fell during periods of rapid growth. For example, from 1987 to 2007 the economy grew very rapidly, employment expanded at an unprecedented rate and the unemployment rate fell to a historic low. The most dramatic year was 1998 when real GNP grew by 7.8 per cent and the unemployment rate fell by three percentage points (from 10.3 to 7.4 per cent). Conversely, during periods of falling output, such as the mid-1980s and after 2007, employment fell and unemployment rose. The worst year was 2009, when real GNP fell by eight per cent and the unemployment rate rose from 6.3 to 11.8 per cent.

Okun's aim was to convince President Kennedy to implement expansionary fiscal policies by showing him how much output was lost by tolerating a high rate of unemployment. We turn this around and ask: How fast must GNP grow to prevent the unemployment rate from rising? The regression line fitted to the points in Figure 5.15 is highly significant statistically and shows that changes in real GNP have been closely linked to changes in unemployment over the years. The line slopes downwards, indicating that as the growth rate increases along the horizontal axis, the unemployment rate falls on the vertical axis. We estimated the equation

$$\Delta U = \alpha - \beta(\%\Delta \text{real GNP}) \tag{15}$$

where ΔU is the change in the unemployment rate, $\%\Delta GNP$ is the percentage change in real GNP, α is an intercept and β is the slope of the line relating the two variables. Using data over the period 1970–2011, we obtained the following result:

$$\Delta U = 1.43 - 0.34[\%\Delta \text{real GNP}] \; R^2 = 0.67$$

This suggests that for every one per cent increase in real GNP, unemployment falls by 0.34 percentage points (one-third of a percentage point).

FIGURE 5.15 Okun's law, Ireland, 1970–2011

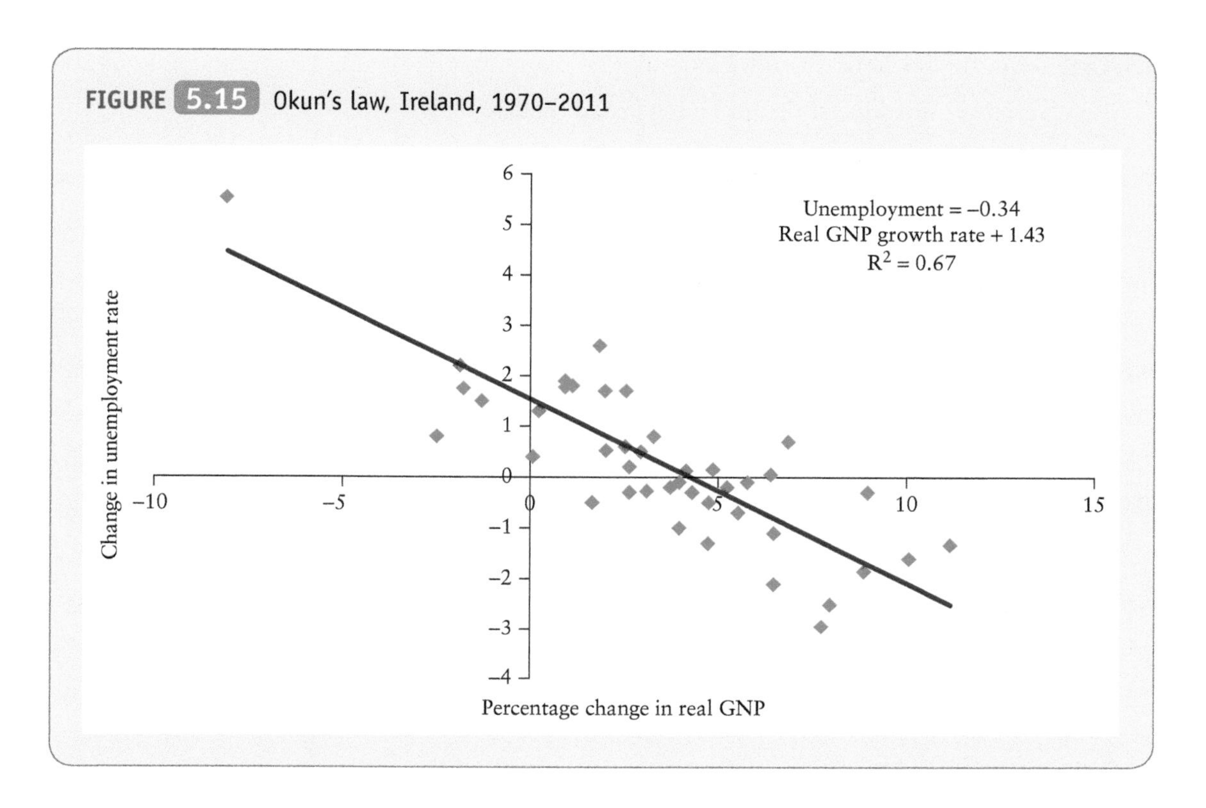

We can use our estimated Okun's law equation to estimate how fast the Irish economy must grow just to prevent the unemployment rate from rising. Setting $\Delta U = 0$, we have:

$$0.34(\%\Delta\text{real GNP}) = 1.43$$

which yields the following estimate of the rate of GNP growth required to stabilise the unemployment rate:

$$\%\Delta\text{real GNP} = \frac{1.43}{0.34} = 4.2$$

Given that none of the forecasts for the Irish economy over the next few years suggests that we shall return to four per cent growth in GNP, the prospects are for the unemployment rate to remain high or even to continue to increase.

One limitation of the simple Okun's law in the Irish context is that it does not allow for net migration, which has been such an important influence on our economy over the decades. In Chapter 4 we discussed the manner in which Irish migration responds to the differential between Irish and British unemployment rates. One of the reasons our unemloyment rate was so high in the 1980s was that the UK economy was also in recession and the USA tightened its immigration laws, leaving young Irish people more or less trapped in our recession-ridden economy.

This is not the case today, when people are freer to move to the USA, Britain, Canada, Australia and New Zealand. (It is noticeable that all of these favoured destinations of Irish emigrants are outside the euro area!) Our unemployment rate would undoubtedly be higher were it not for this safety valve.

The other side of the coin is that in the absence of significant immigration the credit-fuelled boom of the early years of the present century would have been choked off by labour shortages and led to soaring wage inflation.

5.11 Key Terms and Concepts

In this chapter we introduced the following broad themes:

- the idea of a macroeconomic model
- the Keynesian theory of income determination
- the concepts of aggregate supply and aggregate demand
- the concept of potential real GNP and the natural unemployment rate
- output gaps and how these relate to changes in unemployment and inflation
- equilibrium in the goods and services market
- demand-side and supply-side policies
- how economies adjust to demand-side and supply-side shocks
- Okun's law – the relationship between changes in real GNP and the unemployment rate.

CHAPTER 6

The Consumption Function and Income Determination

6.1 Introduction

In Chapter 5 we discussed the role of aggregate demand in determining output and employment. In this chapter we focus on the largest component of aggregate demand: personal consumer expenditure, C. The first part of the chapter explains the consumption function, which plays a key role in macroeconomic theory and policy. This is followed by a discussion of the multiplier, which is an integral part of Keynesian theory and has an important bearing on the effectiveness of fiscal policy in regulating the business cycle. The concluding sections of the chapter examine two important extensions of the Keynesian consumption function: the life cycle hypothesis; and the permanent income hypothesis.

6.2 Income, Consumption and Saving

In Chapter 2 we saw that personal consumption expenditure, C, accounts for just over 50 per cent of GDP or aggregate demand, AD, in Ireland. The study of consumption is therefore important not just in its own right but for our understanding of the determination of output, income and employment.

Although we are primarily concerned with consumption expenditure aggregated over all types of consumer goods and services, it is of interest to look at the composition of this expenditure. Table 6.1 shows the breakdown of personal consumption into its main components, such as housing, food, transport and communications, recreation and entertainment, and alcoholic beverages. The housing component includes the rent imputed to living in owner-occupied homes. The proportion spent in Ireland on alcoholic beverages (7.7 per cent) is high by international standards. Note that expenditure outside the country is subtracted from the total (it is not part of Irish aggregate demand) but spending by visitors to Ireland is included.

The data in Table 6.1 are totals for all the households in the country. When households are classified by income group, important differences in consumption patterns are apparent. In particular, people on low incomes spend a higher proportion of their income on necessities such as food and housing. As income increases, the proportion of income spent on clothing, transport and leisure activities rises. High-income households buy better-quality food, but they spend a smaller proportion of their income on it.

The consumption function

Given the importance of consumer expenditure in total expenditure, it is important to identify the factors that influence it.

Disposable income (Y^d) is equal to gross income (Y) minus taxation plus transfers – that is, the difference between what households receive from the state in various benefits (pensions, welfare

TABLE 6.1 Irish personal consumption by category, 2011

	€ billion	%
Food and non-alcoholic beverages	7.9	9.6
Alcoholic beverages (total, including pubs)	6.4	7.7
Tobacco	2.2	2.7
Clothing and footwear	3.2	3.8
Housing (rent, local government charges, repairs and decorations)	13.3	16.1
Fuel and power (excluding motor fuels)	3.0	3.7
Household equipment and operation	3.9	4.8
Transport and communication	12.6	15.3
Recreation, entertainment and education	8.7	10.5
Professional services (medical, etc.)	8.6	10.4
Miscellaneous goods and services	11.4	13.8
Expenditure outside the state	4.5	5.5
Expenditure by non-residents	−3.2	−3.9
Total personal consumption of goods and services at current market prices	82.5	100.0

Source: CSO, National Income and Expenditure 2011, Table 13

entitlements, etc.) and what they pay in taxes on income. We shall call this difference 'net taxes' and denote it by the label NT.

$$Y^d = Y - NT \tag{1}$$

Disposable income is used for consumer expenditure (C) or is saved (S). What is left over out of disposable income after consumption is defined as personal saving. (This is a flow, as distinct from *savings*, which is the stock of accumulated saving.)

$$Y^d = C + S \tag{2}$$

In 2011 (for which data were published in mid-2012) personal consumption expenditure accounted for 75 per cent of personal income, taxes on personal income and wealth for 21 per cent, and personal saving for four per cent. If we concentrate on personal *disposable* income, Y^d – personal income *minus* taxes on personal income – we find that five per cent was saved and 95 per cent consumed.

Keynes argued that the main determinant of consumer expenditure is current disposable income, Y^d. He labelled the relationship between income and consumption the *consumption function*, which can be written:

$$C = \alpha + mpc \times Y^d \tag{3}$$

where α is the intercept term and mpc is the marginal propensity to consume. Equation (3) makes consumption expenditure a function of disposable income. The direction of causation runs from Y^d to C. Because Y^d causes changes in C, Y^d is referred to as the explanatory (or independent) variable, and C as the dependent variable.

In order to illustrate how the consumption function is derived, consider the data on Y^d, C and S given in Table 6.2 for a hypothetical cross-section of households at a point in time. Household A has an income of €10,000 and consumption of €9,000 per annum. Household B

TABLE 6.2 Household disposable income, consumption and saving

	Disposable income	Consumption	Saving	APC	APS
A	10,000	9,000	1,000	0.90	0.10
B	15,000	12,000	3,000	0.80	0.20
C	20,000	15,000	5,000	0.75	0.25
D	25,000	18,000	7,000	0.72	0.28
E	30,000	21,000	9,000	0.70	0.30
F	35,000	24,000	11,000	0.68	0.32
G	40,000	27,000	13,000	0.67	0.33

has an income of €15,000 and spends €12,000, and so on for the richer households, C to G. Table 6.2 shows that as disposable income increases, households spend less and save more as a proportion of income.

Figure 6.1 plots the relationship between disposable income and consumption given in Table 6.2. Consumption expenditure is shown on the vertical axis and disposable income on the horizontal axis. Point B in Figure 6.1 corresponds to consumption expenditure of €12,000 and income of €15,000. The remaining points in Figure 6.1 correspond to the other households in Table 6.2.

The line joining A, B, C and so on is the consumption function for this cross-section of households. The intercept is the point where the consumption function cuts the vertical axis. It corresponds to the α term in equation (3) above. The intercept can be thought of as the level of consumption spending that is independent of the level of Y^d and is referred to as *autonomous consumption*.

The slope of the consumption function summarises how consumer expenditure reacts to changes in disposable income. It is called the marginal propensity to consume (mpc) because it tells us consumers' *propensity* to consume out of *marginal* or additional income.

FIGURE 6.1 Illustration of a consumption function

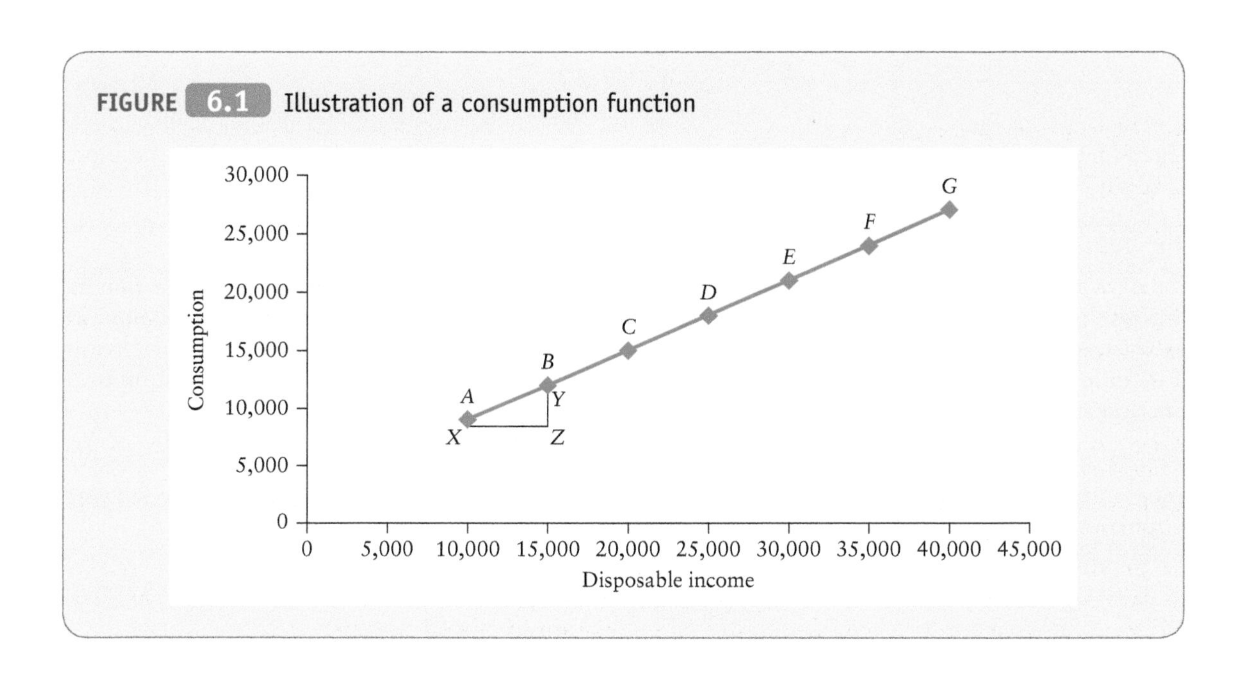

If we take the first difference of equation (3) we can write:

$$\frac{\Delta C}{\Delta Y^d} = \text{mpc} \qquad (4)$$

where Δ denotes the change in a variable. The mpc is a positive number which is generally greater than zero but less than or equal to 1: $0 > \text{mpc} \leq 1$. An mpc of 0.9 means that for every €1 increase in income, spending increases by €0.90.

The hypothetical data on income and consumption in Table 6.2 can be used to calculate the mpc. In the triangle labelled XYZ, the distance XZ represents the change in disposable income, and the distance ZY represents the change in consumption expenditure. The slope of the consumption function XY is the ratio ZY/XZ and equals $\Delta C/\Delta Y^d$, the mpc. As household income increases from €10,000 to €15,000, consumption expenditure increases from €9,000 to €12,000. The mpc is therefore 0.6.

$$\text{mpc} = \frac{\Delta C}{\Delta Y^d} = \frac{(€12{,}000 - €9{,}000)}{(€15{,}000 - €10{,}000)} = 0.6 \qquad (5)$$

NOTE: Because the consumption function in Figure 6.1 is linear, the mpc is the same at all points on the line. (The reader can confirm this by calculating the mpc for the range of income and expenditure given in the table.) We have presented a linear consumption function for illustrative purposes. In reality, it is possible that the mpc would decrease at higher levels of income because the richer a household becomes, the larger the proportion of any further increase in income that is likely to be saved. If a line is non-linear, each point on the line has a different slope. The slope at a particular point on the curve can be calculated by drawing a line tangent to the curve at that point. The slope of the tangent line gives the slope of the curve at that point.

The saving function

As we have noted, by definition consumer expenditure and saving must sum to disposable income. Because C depends on Y^d, it follows that S also depends on Y^d. The relationship between S and Y^d is referred to as the saving function.

$$\text{Since } Y^d = C + S$$
$$S = Y^d - C$$
$$S = Y^d - \alpha + \text{mpc} \times Y^d$$
$$S = -\alpha + (1 - \text{mpc}) \times Y^d$$

where (1 − mpc) is the marginal propensity to save, mps. The mps is equal to one *minus* the mpc. That part of an increase in disposable income that is not consumed is saved.

The average propensities to consume and save

The data on a cross-section of households presented in Table 6.2 were constructed to show that as disposable income increases, households spend less and save more as a proportion of income. In contrast, with a linear consumption function the *average* propensity to consume (or the proportion of income consumed) always falls as income rises. This may be seen by dividing the consumption function by Y:

$$\text{Average propensity to consume (apc)} = \frac{C}{Y^d} = \frac{\alpha}{Y^d} + \text{mpc}$$

Since α and mpc are constants, the apc falls as Y^d rises. This implies that people consume smaller proportions of their disposable income at higher income levels.

Similarly, the average propensity to save, aps, may be written:

$$\frac{S}{Y^d} = -\frac{\alpha}{Y^d} + \text{mps}$$

And since $-\alpha/Y^d$ falls as Y^d increases, the aps rises as Y^d rises. Keynes argued, on the basis of his own intuition rather than a detailed study of the data, that consumption would decline (and savings would rise) as income rose. Keynes put it as follows in the *General Theory*:

> *The fundamental psychological law, upon which we are entitled to depend with great confidence both a priori from our knowledge of human nature and from the detailed facts of experience, is that men are disposed to increase their consumption as their income increases, but not by as much as the increase in income.* (Keynes 1936)

This led him to worry about the problem of the economy coping with an increasing stream of saving as income increased. As explained in Chapter 9, personal saving in banks and other financial institutions is used to finance investment, I, by firms. Keynes worried that it would be difficult to find new profitable investment outlets in line with the rise in saving and that, in certain circumstances, this could push the economy into recession.

Keynes praised the ancient Egyptians for building pyramids and the people in the Middle Ages for building cathedrals, because these activities used up their saving and provided employment. Furthermore, because there was no tendency for the rate of return from building pyramids or saying masses to fall: 'Two pyramids, two masses for the dead, are twice as good as one; but not so two railways from London to York.'

The Japanese economy has been in the doldrums since the 1980s and has a high propensity to save. The lack of profitable outlets for saving have contributed to this stagnation. Other examples of the problem of finding profitable outlets for saving are the over-investment in electronics/telecommunications technology in the late 1990s and, of course, the building boom in Ireland between 2000 and 2007. Many blame the bubble in the housing market in the USA and some European countries over this period on the availability of cheap credit chasing a limited number of profitable outlets.

The evidence for a declining apc was, however, shaky. In the mid-1940s Nobel Prize-winner Simon Kuznets (1901–1985) presented evidence that the apc was equal to 0.87 throughout the periods 1869–1898, 1884–1913 and 1904–1933. This meant that the ratio of consumption to income was relatively stable and that the apc did *not* decline as disposable income increased. (Note here that Kuznets's evidence is 'over time', whereas the data in Table 6.1 is cross-section data at a 'point in time'.) Later in this chapter we explain how theories of consumer behaviour have been developed to reconcile this apparent conflict between Keynes and Kuznets.

The consumption and saving functions are very important building blocks in macroeconomic theory. As we shall see later in this chapter, the consumption function partly determines the effectiveness of fiscal policy. It is therefore appropriate to look now at the Irish data on the behaviour of personal income, consumption and saving over decades.

6.3 Personal Income, Consumption and Saving in Ireland

Figure 6.2 shows the percentage change in personal dispoable income and in personal consumption expenditure over the period 1971–2011. Note that the data are in current prices, so both series reflect the rate of inflation. Nonetheless, it is clear that there has been a very strong relationship between the two variables.

We can use the same data to get a rough estimate of the mpc for the Irish economy. Figure 6.3 displays the same two series as Figure 6.2, but now they are shown on an X–Y scatter diagram. The slope of the best-fit or regression line drawn through this scatter plot is an estimate of the marginal propensity to consume (mpc). The estimate we obtain is 0.86. This suggests that 86 per cent of any change in disposable income is consumed. The implied marginal propensity to save (mps) is 0.14.

FIGURE 6.2 Changes in personal disposable income and personal consumption expenditure, Ireland 1971–2011

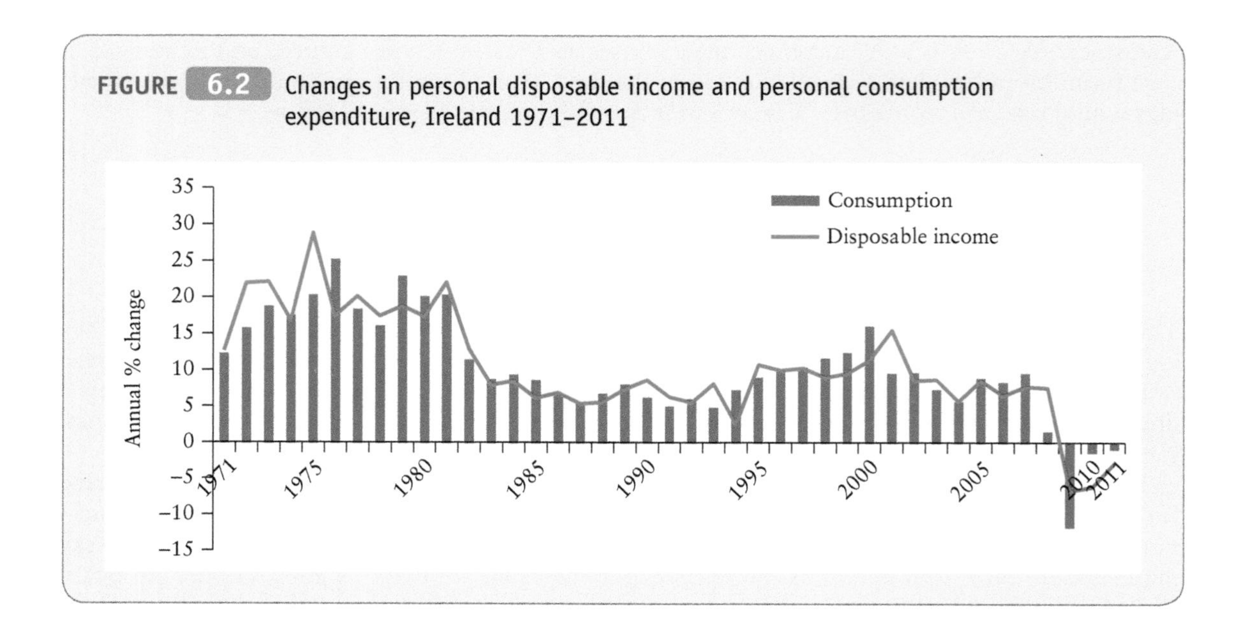

FIGURE 6.3 The Irish consumption function, 1970–2011

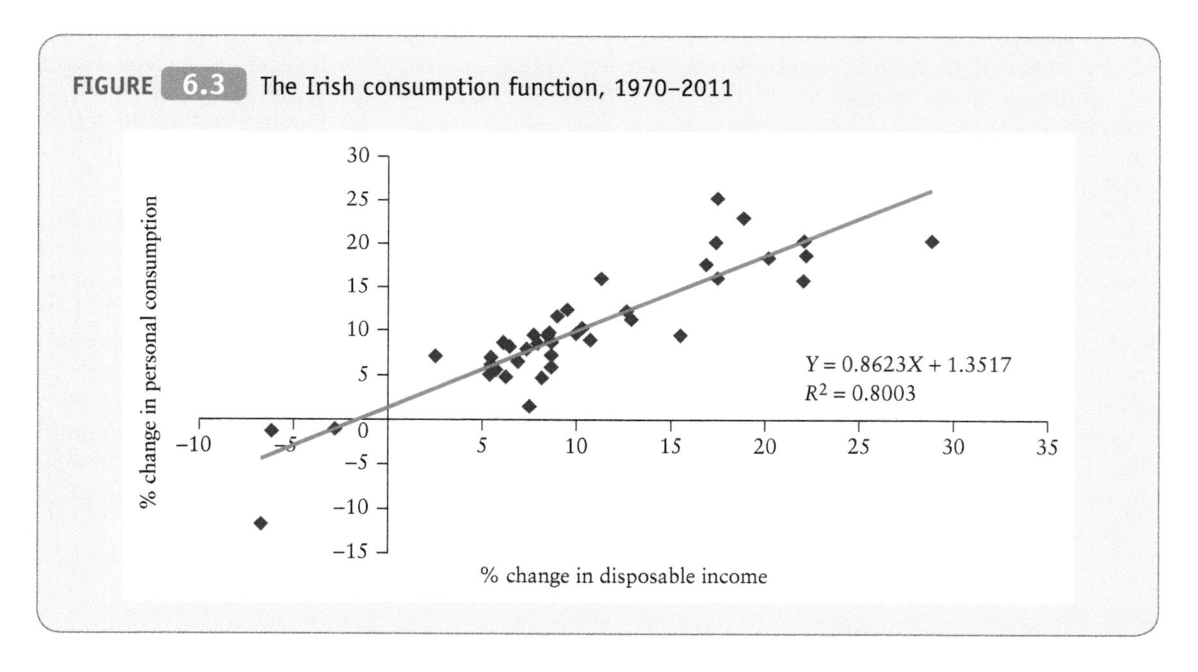

This consumption function is a simple one. It does not take into account any of the influences on consumption other than current year's income. Yet it gives a reasonably good account of the year-to-year variations in consumption.

Figure 6.4 shows the ratio of personal consumer expenditure to personal disposable income for the Irish economy over the period 1970–2011. The average apc over the whole period is 0.93, which is somewhat above the Kuznets figure of 0.87 discussed above. For most of the 41 years covered in the series, the apc lay between 0.90 and 0.95. However, it is notable that it fell sharply in two recession years – 1975 and 2009. A rise in the saving ratio is a natural reaction to the

FIGURE 6.4 Personal consumption/personal disposable income ratio, Ireland 1970–2011

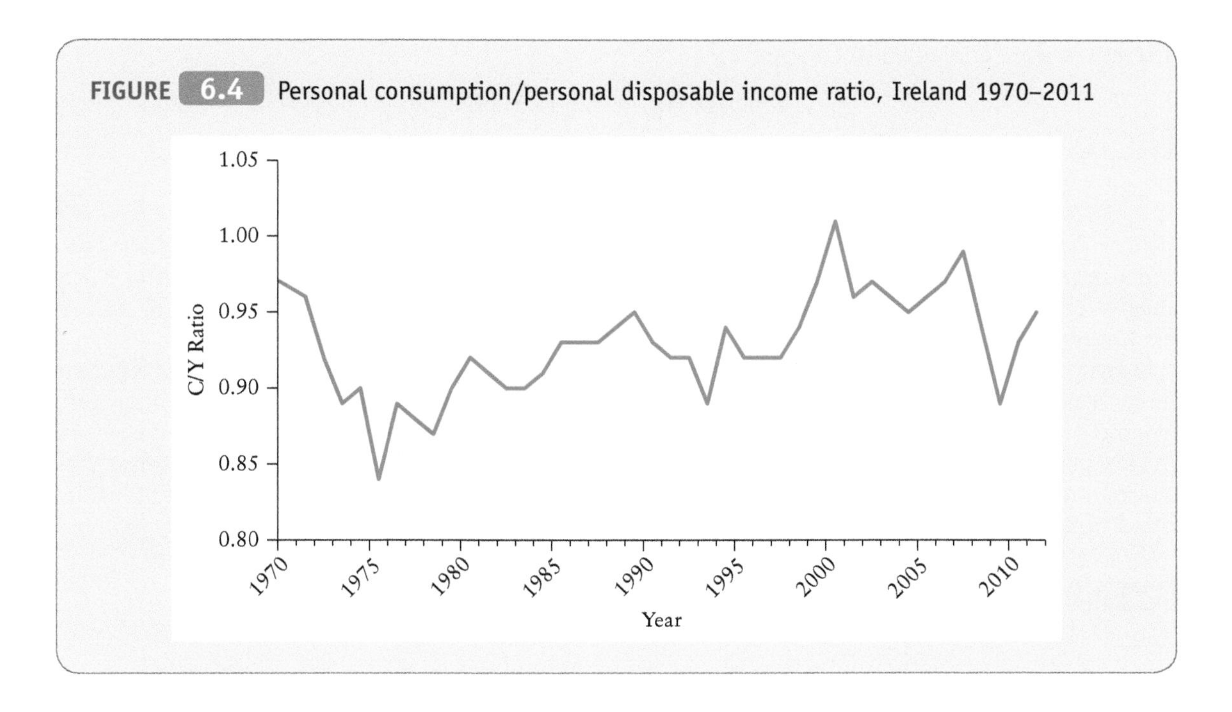

uncertainty created by rising unemployment and falling income. The saving ratio fell from 1992 through to the turn of the century, reflecting the expansion in credit that fuelled the boom. In fact in 2001 consumption exceeded disposable income, the gap being made up by borrowing.

6.4 The Keynesian Multiplier

In Chapters 2 and 5 we defined aggregate demand, AD, for an open economy as being equal to personal consumption expenditure (C), investment (I), government consumption expenditure (G) and net exports (NX). When the economy is in equilibrium, real output (Y) equals AD. Hence:

$$Y = AD = C + I + G + NX \tag{6}$$

An important issue in macroeconomic analysis is assessing by how much an increase in total expenditure raises Y. As a first approximation it might be expected that Y rises by the same amount. However, according to Keynesian multiplier theory, equilibrium Y will actually increase by a multiple of the initial increase in spending. This concept of the multiplier is a central idea in Keynesian economics. The multiplier is defined as:

$$\text{Multiplier} = \frac{\text{Change in equilibrium Y}}{\text{Initial change in AD}}$$

The idea of the multiplier increased the appeal of Keynesian theory in the 1950s and 1960s. After all, if every additional €1 billion spent by the government boosts Y by some multiple of €1 billion, additional spending would appear to be justified as long as there are unemployed resources in the economy. Conservatives, however, are wary of the way this theory seems to promise 'something for nothing'.

An intuitive explanation

To simplify matters, we use the label Y throughout this section to signify national income, national output and disposable income, without going into the distinctions between these magnitudes. (The differences were explained in Chapter 2.)

$$Y = AD \equiv C + I + G + NX \tag{7}$$

We can write the consumption function as:

$$C = \alpha + mpc \times Y \tag{8}$$

If there is an increase in government consumption expenditure, G, aggregate demand increases. Firms respond to the higher level of demand by producing more goods and services, and Y increases. This, in turn, will cause employment to increase and unemployment to fall. At the end of this first round, Y has increased by exactly the amount of the initial increase in G.

However, that is not the end of the process. In the second round we take account of the fact that the increase in Y raises C via the consumption function. This leads to another increase in aggregate demand and Y. The consumption function has a feedback effect that leads to further increases in Y. This process will continue into third, fourth and successive rounds because the economy has entered into a rising income-consumption spiral. The process and the feedback from Y to C is depicted in Box 6.1.

Box 6.1 The multiplier process

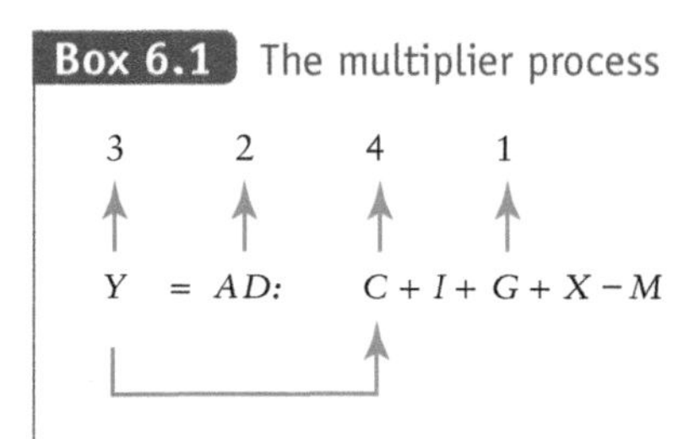

Two important points need to be made relating to the multiplier process. First, the process eventually comes to an end because the mpc is less than 1. In each successive round the increase in consumption is the mpc times the increase in Y. If the mpc is equal to 0.8, an increase of €1 billion in Y will lead to a €0.8 billion increase in consumption. In the next round, Y rises by €0.8 billion and C rises by a further €0.64 billion (that is, the €0.8 billion increase in Y times the mpc). Thus the increases in consumption taper off in successive rounds. The smaller the mpc, the sooner the expansion comes to a halt. Conversely, the higher the mpc, the longer it lasts.

The second point is that the multiplier assumes that the short-run aggregate supply (SRAS) curve is horizontal, so that additional output is forthcoming in response to increased demand, without any rise in the aggregate price level. For this to be true, there must be significant unutilised resources (especially labour) in the economy.

Keynes argued that the slope of the SRAS curve is not uniform at all levels of real Y but is actually kinked. That is, it takes on different slopes depending how close the economy is to potential output, Y^*. When there is a great deal of excess capacity in the economy and the unemployment rate is high, the SRAS curve is likely to be horizontal. A shift to the right in the AD curve leads to an increase in real Y without having a marked increase in the price level. Note that a horizontal SRAS curve also corresponds to the case where prices are fixed. As explained in Chapter 5, this relates to the very short run.

As Y^* is approached, the SRAS curve begins to slope upwards. Any further shift of the AD curve to the right will lead to some mixture of increases in the price level and real output. As the economy moves to the right of Y^*, the SRAS curve becomes vertical. A shift of the AD curve to the right will now result only in higher prices and have no impact on real Y.

FIGURE 6.5 The multiplier process (assuming a horizontal short-run aggregate supply curve)

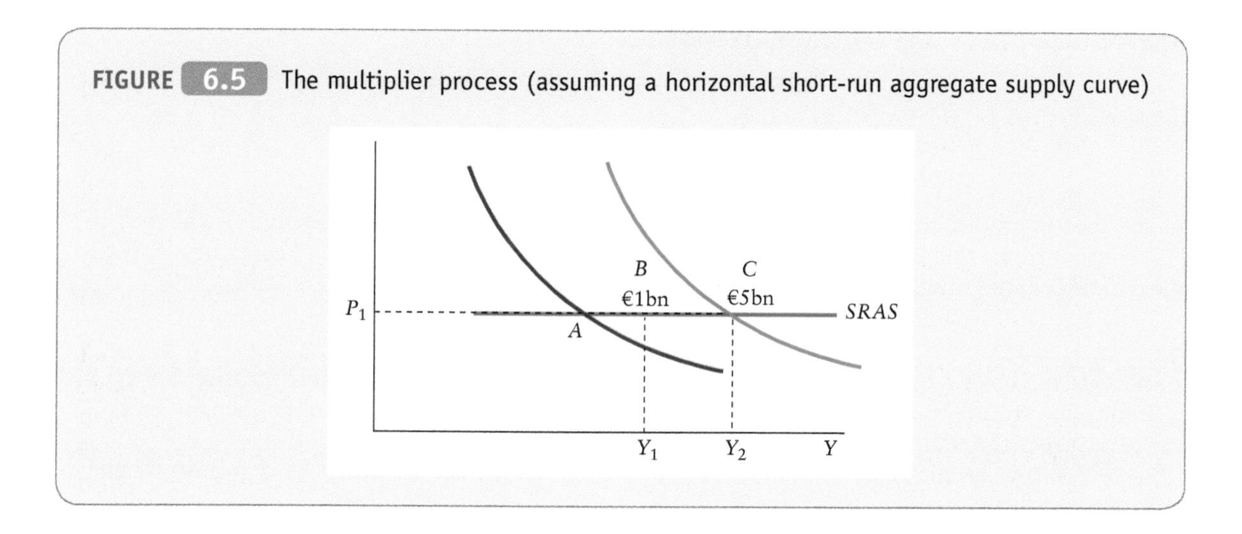

Figure 6.5 shows the multiplier process based on a horizontal SRAS curve. If the economy is initially at A, an increase in government expenditure will shift the AD curve to the right and the economy moves to B and real output increases by €1 billion. In the final equilibrium real output has risen to €5 billion (this assumes the multiplier is 5) and the price level remains unchanged.

Hence, the multiplier really relates to a situation where the aggregate price level (P) is fixed due to the overhang of spare capacity in the economy. This may be realistic in a situation where there are considerable unemployed resources in the economy, and rising prices is not a factor to be reckoned with, which of course was the case when Keynes was writing in the 1930s.

The multiplier process relates to a change in any of the components of aggregate demand. It can also be applied to local or regional situations. A pertinent example of the multiplier effect relates to the loss of 1,900 jobs at the Dell facility in Limerick in January 2009. To lower its production costs, Dell decided to move part of its production facility to the Polish city of Lodz. A report by Forfás predicted that 2,510 workers would be made redundant by Dell with the consequent loss of almost 7,000 other jobs in related companies. One supplier, RR Donnelley, which was entirely dependent on Dell, closed, making 477 workers redundant. It was estimated that the payroll loss for Dell workers would take as much as €117 million of disposable income out of the local economy, resulting in the loss of around 350 jobs in local shops. The redundancies would also result in a €173 million loss to the exchequer through a reduction in PAYE and PRSI contributions as well as corporation tax.

The multiplier formula

In order to derive the multiplier formula, consider the following equations:

$$Y = AD \qquad \text{Equilibrium condition} \tag{9}$$

$$AD \equiv C + I + G + NX \qquad \text{Aggregate demand} \tag{10}$$

$$C = \alpha + (mpc \times Y) \qquad \text{Consumption function} \tag{11}$$

To derive the multiplier formula, substitute (10) into (9) to obtain:

$$Y = C + I + G + NX \tag{12}$$

Now substitute (11) into (12):

$$Y = \alpha + (mpc \times Y) + I + G + NX \tag{13}$$

Bring the (mpc × Y) term over to the left-hand side:

$$Y(1 - \text{mpc}) = \alpha + I + G + NX \quad (14)$$

Divide both sides by (1 − mpc) to obtain:

$$Y = \left[\frac{1}{(1 - \text{mpc})}\right](\alpha + I + G + NX) \quad (15)$$

We see that if any of the terms (α, I, G or NX) change, the level of equilibrium Y changes by 1/(1 − mpc) times this change. The multiplier therefore equals 1/(1 − mpc). For example, if the mpc equals 0.8, the multiplier is:

$$\text{Multiplier} = \frac{1}{(1 - 0.8)} = 5$$

An increase in G of €1 billion would raise Y or national income by €5 billion. If the mpc were 0.9, the multiplier would be 10. We see immediately that the higher the marginal propensity to consume, the larger the multiplier.

Box 6.2 shows an alternative method of deriving the multiplier formula. We demonstrate that if a process such as:

$$\text{multiplier} = 1 + MPC + MPC^2 + MPC^3 + \ldots,$$

then it is a mathematical fact that the process is equal to:

$$\frac{1}{(1 - MPC)}$$

Box 6.2 Deriving the multiplier formula

An increase in government spending sets off the multiplier process:

1 Increase in G = €1 billion.
2 + Second round = mpc × €1 billion.
3 + Third round = mpc(mpc × €1 billion).
4 + Fourth round = mpc3 × €1 billion.
• •
• •

Total increase in Y = $(1 + \text{mpc} + \text{mpc}^2 + \text{mpc}^3 + \ldots) \times$ €1 billion

As shown below, a multiplier process equal to $1 + \text{mpc} + \text{mpc}^2 + \text{mpc}^3 + \ldots$ is equal to 1/(1 − mpc), as long as mpc is between 0 and 1.

Proof:

For mpc < 1

$$z = 1 + \text{mpc} + \text{mpc}^2 + \text{mpc}^3 + \ldots, \quad (1)$$

Multiply both sides by mpc.

$$\text{mpcz} = \text{mpc} + \text{mpc}^2 + \text{mpc}^3 + \text{mpc}^4 + \ldots, \quad (2)$$

Subtract 2 from 1:

$$z - \text{mpcz} = (1 + \text{mpc} + \text{mpc}^2 + \text{mpc}^3 + \ldots) - (\text{mpc} + \text{mpc}^2 + \text{mpc}^3 + \text{mpc}^4 + \ldots)$$

$$z - \text{mpcz} = 1$$

$$z(1 - \text{mpc}) = 1$$

$$z = \frac{1}{(1 - \text{mpc})}$$

We know from our earlier discussion that the mpc and the mps must sum to 1. It follows that (1 – mpc) is equal to mps and the multiplier formula can be rewritten as:

$$\text{Multiplier} = \frac{1}{\text{mps}}$$

An mpc of 0.8 implies an mps of 0.2. Inserting this value for the mps into the above formula, the multiplier again equals 5. The higher the mps, the lower the multiplier; the lower the mps, the higher the multiplier.

Generalising the multiplier

Saving is only one possible leakage from the flow of aggregate demand that reduces the multiplier. In this section we consider two other leakages, namely taxes and imports. All of these leakages reduce the multiplier.

The size of the multiplier depends on how much of an initial increase in Y is passed on through an increase in C. In an open economy, much of any increase in expenditure will leak abroad in the form of additional imports, M, which is spent on the output of some other economy. Clearly, this does nothing to stimulate the level of output in the domestic economy. Similarly, we have to take account of the fact that taxes on income and expenditure divert a sizeable proportion of additional consumer income to the government. This is another leakage from the multiplier process.

These additional leakages tend to bring the multiplier process to a halt sooner than would be the case where the only leakage was saving. We now consider how these leakages affect the value of the multiplier. The algebra is set out in Appendix 6.1.

Taxes

If there is a single flat rate of tax on income, the relationship between tax revenue (T) and Y is given by the following equation:

$$T = \text{mpt} \times Y \tag{16}$$

where mpt is the marginal tax rate or marginal propensity to tax, and $0 < \text{mpt} < 1$. If the flat rate of tax was 30 per cent, the mpt would equal 0.3. Allowing for a tax of this type, the multiplier formula becomes:

$$\text{Multiplier} = \frac{1}{(\text{mps} + \text{mpt})} \tag{17}$$

The formula contains the sum of the 'marginal propensities to leak' (that is, to tax and save) in the denominator. Hence, the larger these leakages from extra income, the smaller the multiplier. This general principle holds true even for the most complicated models.

Imports

The third possible leakage is due to the relationship between Y and imports. The relationship may be expressed as:

$$M = \delta + (\text{mpm} \times Y) \tag{18}$$

where δ is an intercept term, and mpm is the marginal propensity to import, and $0 < \text{mpm} < 1$. If, for example, mpm equals 0.4, then equation (18) states that 40 per cent of any increase in Y is spent on imports. As shown in Appendix 6.1, the multiplier with saving, taxation and import leakages is:

$$\text{Multiplier} = \frac{1}{(\text{mps} + \text{mpt} + \text{mpm})} \tag{19}$$

Once again, the denominator is the sum of all the leakages from the multiplier process. We apply this to the Irish economy below.

Tax multiplier

Suppose instead of changing government expenditure, taxes on income are lowered or increased. How does this affect output?

If taxes *fall* by ΔT (disposable) income rises by this amount and consumption and aggregate demand *increase* by the mpc $\times$ ΔT. So initially $\Delta AD = \Delta C = \text{mpc} \times \Delta T$.

To find the effects of this initial change in AD on the final equilibrium level of Y, we need to apply the multiplier to it. Using our simplest multiplier $(1/(1 - \text{mpc}))$, we derive the tax multiplier:

$$\text{Tax multiplier} = \frac{-(\text{mpc} \times \Delta T)}{(1 - \text{mpc})}$$

(The negative sign reflects the fact that tax cuts increase AD and vice versa.) If, for example, the mpc were 0.8, the tax multiplier would be 4. The comparable government expenditure multiplier would be $\Delta G \times (1/(1 - \text{mpc}))$ which is 5. The tax multiplier is lower because some of the tax cut is saved in the first round and leaks away from AD.

Another relevant formula is the 'balanced budget multiplier'. This shows that an equal decrease (or increase) in tax revenue and government expenditure has a multiplier of 1, and not zero as might be expected. If the government raises tax receipts by €1 billion, AD will fall by mpc × €1 billion. If it raises government consumption, G, also by €1 billion, AD rises by €1. The combined effect of these two changes in AD on the final equilibrium level of Y is the sum of the two changes (increase in tax and the increase in spending) each multiplied $1/(1 - \text{mpc})$, that is:

$$-(\text{mpc} \times €1 \text{ billion}) \times \left[\frac{1}{(1 - \text{mpc})}\right] + €1 \text{ billion} \times \left[\frac{1}{(1 - \text{mpc})}\right]$$

Assume that mpc equals 0.8:

$$(-0.8 \times €1 \text{ billion}) \times \left[\frac{1}{(1 - 0.8)}\right] + €1 \text{ billion} \times \left[\frac{1}{(1 - 0.8)}\right]$$

$$= (-€4 \text{ billion}) + (€5 \text{ billion}) = 1$$

The balanced budget multiplier is therefore 1, not zero.

Summary

Any change in the level of a component of aggregate demand, such as investment (I), government consumption expenditure (G), net exports (NX) or the autonomous component of personal consumption (C) or imports (M), affects the equilibrium level of Y. The final change in equilibrium Y is greater than the initial change in aggregate demand. The ratio between the two is defined as the multiplier. Leakages take the form of saving, taxes and imports. The larger the leakages from the multiplier process, the smaller the multiplier and, conversely, the smaller the leakages, the larger the multiplier.

Many more complex multiplier formulae can be derived. The models outlined here do not include a financial or money market, which we have not yet discussed. When the model is expanded to include a money market, the multiplier formula becomes even more complex. As a consequence, in recent years simple multiplier analysis of the type presented here has lost much of its prominence in economics.

Some textbooks elaborate multiplier formulas, presumably in the belief that a bit of algebra is good for the student's soul! However, it is far more important that the student understands the basic concepts, and the issues at stake, in the application of the Keynesian model, than that he or she spends a lot of time deriving complicated multiplier formulas.

The multiplier in the Irish economy

Ireland is a small economy that is extremely open to international trade. Furthermore, the marginal rate of income tax and the indirect tax rates applied to discretionary spending are high. These considerations would lead us to expect that the multiplier would be low. A survey of the available research confirms this. There is widespread agreement that mps = 0.26, mpt = 0.24 and mpm = 0.4 are realistic values for the parameters that enter into the calculation of the multiplier. Inserting these values into the formula given above yields the following result:

$$\text{Multiplier} = \frac{1}{(0.26 + 0.24 + 0.4)} = 1.11 \quad (20)$$

This implies that an increase in G, C, I or X, or a reduction in M of €1 billion would raise Y by €1.11 billion. Under these conditions 'multiplier' is somewhat of a misnomer. The leakages are so large that Y only increases by marginally more than the initial increase in AD itself. In addition to small multipliers, there are other considerations that suggest that fiscal policy will not have any long-lasting effect on Y (see Chapter 7). Thus one of the alluring features of the simple Keynesian model, the idea that an increase in government spending results in an increase in the equilibrium level of Y equal to a multiple of the original stimulus, has to be modified to take account of Irish conditions. Nonetheless, increased total expenditure does tend to increase the equilibrium level of Y.

6.5 Alternative Theories of Consumer Behaviour

In the 1950s the apparent conflict between Keynes's intuition that the average propensity to save would rise over time and Kuznets's evidence to the contrary led to the refinement of theories of consumer behaviour. Two of the most influential contributions have been the life cycle hypothesis and the permanent income hypothesis.

Keynes's theory states that current consumption depends only on current income. However, the American economist Irving Fisher suggested that current consumption is instead a function of the present value of lifetime income. The timing of income is irrelevant because the consumer can borrow or lend between or across periods. If, for example, a consumer learns that her future income will increase, she can spread the extra consumption over both periods by borrowing in the current period. A student investing in third-level education could expect her income to rise when she obtains her degree, so she will borrow while she is in college and repay when she graduates.

The basic assumption is that a consumer is forward-looking and chooses consumption for the present and future to maximise lifetime satisfaction. Consumers' choices are subject to an intertemporal budget constraint, a measure of the total lifetime income available for present and future consumption. Fisher's theory of consumption provides the basis for much subsequent work on consumption. We now turn to a discussion of two of the most influential long-run theories of consumer behaviour.

The life cycle theory of consumption

The life cycle theory of consumption was developed by Franco Modigliani, who was awarded the 1985 Nobel Prize for economics. He argued that a household's consumption does not depend only on its current disposable income, as in the Keynesian consumption function, but rather on its lifetime income.

NOTE: The life cycle hypothesis was developed by Modigliani in conjunction with Richard Brumberg. See Modigliani and Brumberg (1954).

Disposable income changes over the life cycle. Typically, an individual has no income in the first 18 years of life, while at school. Once he or she starts work, income rises rapidly, reaching a peak in mid-life. On retirement at, say, 65 there is a sharp decline in income and the individual has to live on a pension, typically half pre-retirement income. The life cycle hypothesis assumes that people prefer to maintain a constant or slightly increasing flow of consumption over their lifetime to a situation where consumption depends completely on current income. They can achieve this if they are willing to save at those periods in their lives when their earnings are high and to dis-save when their income falls. This would involve dis-saving early and late in life, and saving during the peak earning years. This is referred to as consumption smoothing.

This pattern of consumption is depicted in Figure 6.6. The horizontal consumption line shows a constant level of consumption over the person's working life. It is assumed that the person saves during his or her working years and this increases wealth. Following retirement, the person has a reduced income from a pension and dis-saves by running down wealth. The saving over the working years is used to finance consumption in retirement so that over the life cycle consumption equals income.

FIGURE 6.6 The life cycle hypothesis

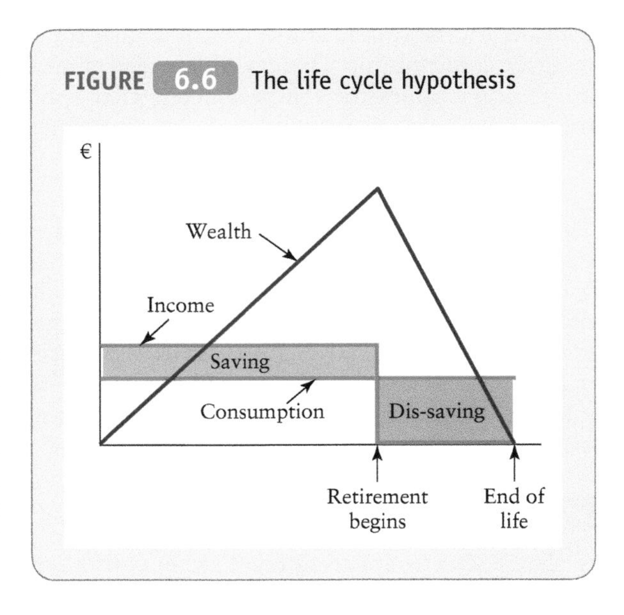

This theory predicts that changes in current disposable income (Y^d) have much less influence on consumption expenditure (C) than would be expected from the Keynesian consumption function we introduced above. Individuals are supposed to take the long view and set their consumption targets in line with their expected lifetime income, rather than simply adjusting consumption to day-to-day fluctuations in income.

Extensions to the life cycle hypothesis

The life cycle hypothesis can be extended in a number of ways. Consumption can be expressed as a function of disposable income and wealth. The greater a person's wealth the higher will be consumption, and vice versa. This means that changes in wealth brought about by a stock market crash can lead to a fall in consumption and thereby help push the economy into recession. This seems to be what has happened following the stock market crash in 2007. Studies have found that house prices have a far bigger wealth effect than stock prices – more people own their house than own stocks and shares. Hence, the fall in house prices after 2007 reinforced the fall in the stock market and helps explain the seven per cent fall in consumer spending in 2009.

NOTE: Income, consumption, saving, and investment are *flow* variables. They measure how much is earned, consumed, saved and invested over a period of time. Savings, wealth and the capital stock are, on the other hand, stock variables. They measure the value of assets at a point in time.

The introduction of wealth also reconciles the apparent disagreement between Keynes and Kuznets. In Figure 6.7 wealth determines the intercept (or location) of the short-run consumption function. Over the long run, wealth increases significantly and this shifts the short-run consumption function upwards. As the short-run consumption functions shift up, the points A, B and C in the diagram map out the long-run consumption function. Thus, even if each short-run consumption function displays a declining APC (as advanced by Keynes), the long-run consumption function cuts through a series of upward-shifting short-run consumption functions. Hence, the long-run consumption function is much steeper than the short-run consumption functions. The long-run APC can be constant (as Kuznets's data suggested), even though the short-run APC is declining.

FIGURE 6.7 The long- and short-run consumption function

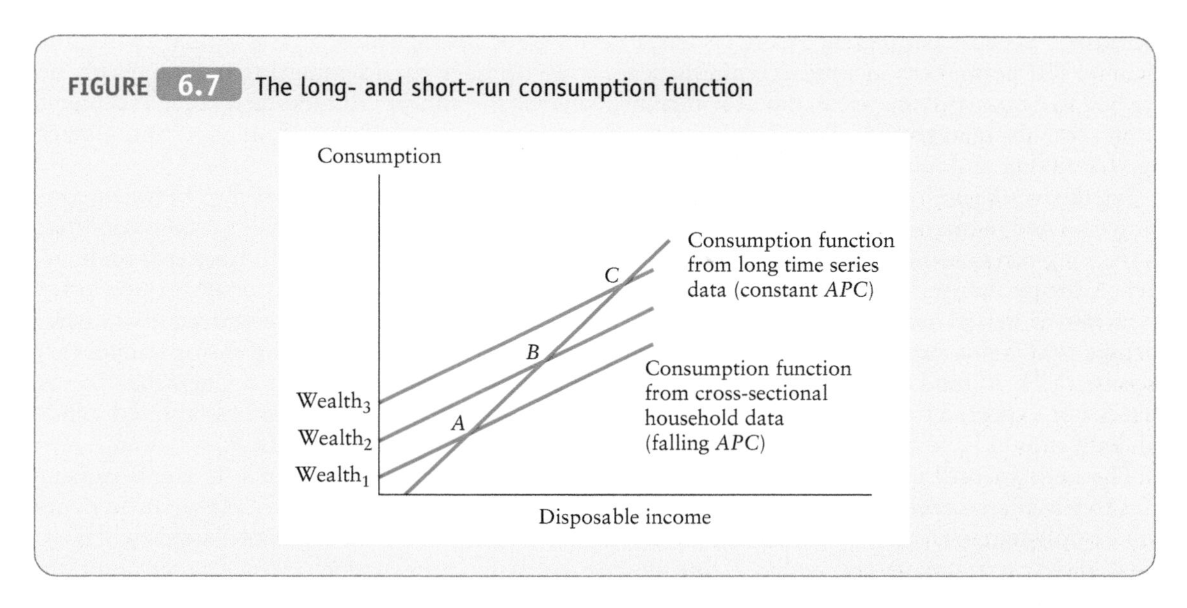

From the life cycle hypothesis it also follows that changes in the retirement age and the presence of social welfare or a state pension have an impact on saving and therefore consumption. A lower retirement age suggests that people will save more during their working years and lifetime consumption will, as a result, be lower. In contrast, the existence of social welfare or a state pension means that people do not need much saving to maintain consumption in their retirement period. Hence, the saving rate will be lower.

Finally, the age distribution of the population can have an important bearing on aggregate saving and consumption. A stationary or declining population, such as that of many European countries today, implies a high proportion of elderly people. This, in turn, implies that many people are living off past saving, which will depress the aggregate saving ratio.

The permanent income hypothesis

The permanent income hypothesis was developed by Milton Friedman, 1976 Nobel Prize-winner in economics (Freidman 1957). The permanent income hypothesis is similar in many respects to the life cycle hypothesis. The permanent income hypothesis argues that current consumption depends on permanent income (YP):

$$C = f(YP) \tag{21}$$

The equation reads: consumer expenditure is a function of permanent income. In Friedman's original exposition of the theory, no precise definition of permanent income was given. However, we can think of permanent income as being equal to a weighted average of current and past incomes. An example is:

$$YP_t = 0.6Y^d_t + 0.3Y^d_{t-1} + 0.1Y^d_{t-2} \tag{22}$$

where Y^d_t is disposable income in time t, Y^d_{t-1} is disposable income in time $t - 1$ and Y^d_{t-2} is disposable income in time $t - 2$. Equation (22) says that today's permanent income is equal to 60 per cent of this year's disposable income plus 30 per cent of last year's income plus 10 per cent of income two years ago. Note that the weights used in the calculation tend to get smaller the further we go back in time.

The basic idea underlying equation (22) is that people base their consumption patterns on income averaged over good and bad times. Irish farmers, for example, do not splurge the proceeds of an exceptionally good harvest because they know from experience that there will be bad harvests in the future! Because permanent income is based on long-run average income, it is similar to lifetime income. The permanent income hypothesis does, however, have the advantage that it can easily be applied to aggregate time series data for income, whereas the concept of lifetime income is difficult to measure using aggregate data. The life cycle hypothesis, on the other hand, allows for a greater role for saving and initial wealth.

Friedman's basic hypothesis is that there is a constant proportional relationship between consumption and permanent income. This means that the apc out of permanent income is constant (that is, the long-run consumption to income ratio is constant). This squares well with Kuznets's findings. Hence, the permanent income hypothesis can explain why the apc is supposedly constant over time.

However, actual income is highly variable and the proportion of it that is consumed also varies. Income that is not expected to be repeated in the future is referred to as transitory (or temporary) income (YT). A good example of such income would be a once-off legacy or a Christmas bonus that is not expected to be repeated. According to Friedman's theory this type of unexpected windfall gain should have a weak effect on consumption – most of it will be saved.

The permanent/transitory distinction is important in the context of tax cuts. If a government tries to stimulate spending by cutting taxes, consumers may not respond if they believe the tax cuts will be only temporary. If eventually the government has to revise its tax cuts, households will have enjoyed only a transitory rise in disposable income that will not have much effect on consumption.

In 1978 Robert Hall extended Friedman's analysis by incorporating the assumption of rational expectations into the permanent income hypothesis: people use all available information to forecast future variables like income. These forward-looking consumers would then base consumption on expected future income.

Some recent research has moved away from the assumption, inherent in the above theories, that consumers are rational and act to maximise lifetime utility. These studies consider the psychology of consumers and ask, for example, why people in some countries are not saving enough for retirement. If consumers are imperfect decision-makers and respond to the 'pull of instant gratification', saving will be much lower relative to the saving level of a perfectly rational lifetime utility maximiser.

6.6 Key Terms and Concepts

The main points discussed in this chapter were:

- the consumption and saving functions
- the relationship between personal disposable income, consumption and saving in Ireland
- the multiplier effect and how its size depends on the saving, tax and import leakages
- the multiplier under Irish conditions
- life cycle and permanent income theories of consumption.

Appendix 6.1 Deriving the multiplier formula with saving, taxation and import leakages

The notation c, s, t and m is used to denote the marginal propensity to consume (mpc), the marginal propensity to save (mps), the marginal propensity to tax (mpt) and the marginal propensity to import (mpm), respectively. The equilibrium condition is:

$$Y = C + I + G + X - M \qquad (1)$$

The behavioural relationships underlying the equilibrium condition are:

$$C = \alpha + (c\,Y) - T \qquad \text{Consumption function} \qquad (2)$$

Note that the consumption function here is slightly different from the Keynesian consumption function. Here consumption is a fraction of income (cY) and taxation (T) is then deducted. This is not the same as saying consumption is a function of disposable income. The amendment is, however, necessary to arrive at the simple multiplier formula.

$$T = tY \qquad \text{Tax function} \qquad (3)$$

$$M = \beta + mY \qquad \text{Import function} \qquad (4)$$

The letters α and β denote the intercept terms in the consumption and import equations respectively. The coefficients c, t and m show how C, T and M react to changes in Y. The consumption function here differs from the over-simplified multiplier formula given in the main text in that consumer expenditure is determined by gross income and by taxation. Previously, consumer expenditure depended only on gross income. Here the consumption function states that a change in gross income affects consumer expenditure via c, whereas a change in taxation has a direct effect on consumer expenditure.

Substitute equation (3) into equation (2).

$$C = (\alpha + cY) - (tY) \qquad (5)$$

or

$$C = \alpha + (c - t)Y \qquad (6)$$

Substitute equations (6) and (4) into the equilibrium condition (1).

$$Y = \alpha + (c - t)Y + I + G + X - \beta - (mY) \qquad (7)$$

$$Y - (c - t - m)Y = \alpha - \beta + I + G + X \qquad (8)$$

or

$$Y(1 - c + t + m) = \alpha - \beta + I + G + X \qquad (9)$$

Recall that $s = 1 - c$.

$$Y(s + t + m) = \alpha - \beta + I + G + X \qquad (10)$$

Divide both sides by the term in brackets:

$$Y = [1/(s + t + m)] \times (\alpha - \beta + I + G + X) \qquad (11)$$

The term $[1/(s + t + m)]$ is the multiplier formula when saving, taxation and import leakages are allowed for. Note that the minus sign on the import intercept term, β, indicates that an increase in imports, not brought about by a change in national output or income, will decrease Y via the multiplier formula. As before, an increase in α, I, G or X will increase Y via the multiplier formula, and vice versa.

It is clear that taking taxation and imports into account lowers the value of the multiplier. For example, if s, t and c equalled 0.26, 0.24 and 0.4 respectively, the crude multiplier that ignored taxes and imports would be equal to 3.84. However, the more realistic multipliers that include taxes and imports would be equal to only 1.11. The latter value is more relevant in Ireland's very open and taxed economy.

CHAPTER 7

Introduction to the Theory of Fiscal Policy

7.1 Introduction

The Keynesian theory of income determination discussed in Chapter 5 suggests that governments can use fiscal policy to dampen the fluctuations in economic activity that would otherwise occur over the business cycle. We saw in Chapter 2 that the growth rate of Irish real GNP has been very erratic over the years. For example, the recession of the 1980s was followed by the boom of the 1990s and this was followed by the deep recession that began in 2008. The evidence is that Irish economic policy has not been very successful in regard to maintaining a high and stable growth rate.

In this chapter we outline the theory of fiscal policy. We discuss how to assess the stance of fiscal policy, distinguishing between 'automatic' and 'discretionary' changes in government expenditure and tax receipts. We discuss the problems encountered in implementing a successful fiscal policy, how changes in tax rates affect the supply side of the economy, and the implications of fiscal deficits for the debt/GNP ratio. In Chapter 8 we look in detail at the Irish record on implementing fiscal policy.

7.2 Fiscal Policy

According to Keynesian economic theory, fiscal policy can be used to keep the actual real growth rate close to the potential real growth rate over time.

> **NOTE:** We use the symbol Y* to refer to the level of output the economy can produce with a fully employed labour force, and the available physical (machinery and plants) and human (education and experience) capital stock and technology. This is the potential or full-employment level of real output.

In Figure 7.1, the rate of growth in Y* is indicated by a horizontal line. It is assumed that the economy is capable of averaging a steady three per cent annual real growth rate over the long run. Once an economy is mature and using the latest available technology the rate of growth of potential output depends on the rate of growth of the labour force, the capital stock and advances in technology. There is no agreed figure for the long-term potential growth rate of the Irish economy, but a figure of three per cent seems realistic now that the 'catch-up' phase of the boom years is over. Bear in mind that this is the growth in total Y, not per capita Y, so some of it is due to the growth of the population and labour force. We discuss the determinants of growth in the long term in Chapter 22.

The actual growth rate is shown crossing and re-crossing the potential real growth rate line. The 'output gap' is the gap between actual and potential output as a percentage of potential output, that is $(Y - Y^*)/Y^*$. When this is negative, firms find they have excess capacity and workers will be laid off. Employment decreases and unemployment increases. The economy is in recession. When it is negative, the distance from the actual and potential growth rates may be called the unemployment gap.

FIGURE 7.1 Stabilisation policy

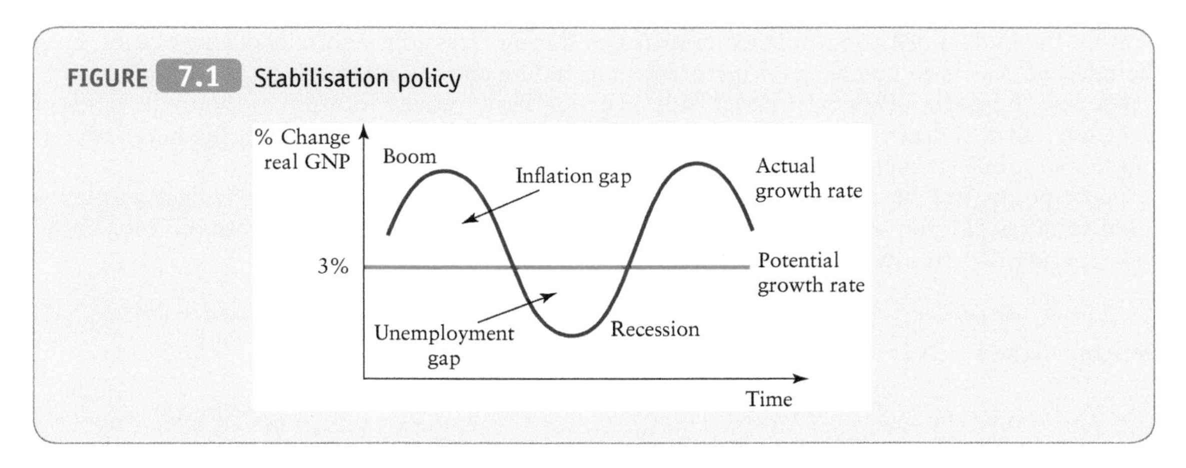

When the output gap is positive the economy is running above its long-run potential, firms are operating above full capacity, labour shortages emerge and there is upward pressure on wages. The economy is over-heating. These wage increases tend to be passed on by firms in higher output prices. The result is inflation. For this reason, the positive distance between the actual and potential growth rates may be referred to as an inflation gap.

The objective of stabilisation policy is to keep the actual level of Y as close as possible to the potential level Y* and avoid inflation and unemployment gaps.

As explained in Chapter 5, the location of the aggregate demand (AD) curve is determined by consumption expenditure (C), investment (I), government expenditure (G), exports (X) and imports (M). An increase in C, I, G, X or a fall in M will shift the AD curve out to the right and vice versa. Stabilisation policy is an attempt by government to offset the instability caused by fluctuations in the private sector components of aggregate demand. For example, if the economy begins to move into a recession because of, say, a fall in X, the government could counter this by increasing G. Alternatively, it could stimulate C by reducing tax rates and/or increasing transfer payments or providing incentives to stimulate I.

Similarly, if prices are rising because of an excess demand for goods and services, the Keynesian prescription is for government to cut expenditure and/or raise tax rates, thereby dampening the inflationary pressure. These discretionary fiscal measures would be counter-cyclical – injecting additional spending when the economy goes into recession, and withdrawing it when the economy is booming. If properly implemented, an active fiscal policy would keep the actual level of Y, and its growth rate, close to Y* and its growth rate. This would tend to dampen the business cycle.

7.3 Assessing the Stance of Fiscal Policy

In the previous section we dealt with government spending and taxation as if they were completely exogenous, that is, as if they could be set precisely at a level decided by the government. In reality, the levels of government spending and taxation are strongly influenced by the business cycle.

Automatic stabilisers

During a recession government tax receipts fall and government expenditure automatically increases. For example, as unemployment rises, households and companies are making less money and income tax and VAT receipts decline. As unemployment rises, the government must pay out more money in social welfare and other transfer payments. The process goes into reverse during an expansion. In this case, tax revenue rises and government expenditure on social welfare falls. As a result, the budget deficit automatically increases during recessions and falls during booms, even though there has been no change in government spending and tax rates.

Because the government is automatically injecting more money into the economy in times of recession and withdrawing more in boom periods, cyclically induced changes in the budget act as automatic stabilisers on the economy.

These points can be illustrated graphically (Figure 7.2). The government's budget surplus is equal to taxes (T) minus government expenditure on current goods and services (G) plus social welfare and other transfer payments (SW).

$$\text{Budget surplus} = T - [G + SW] \quad (1)$$

Defining net taxes (NT) as being equal to T minus SW:

$$NT = T - SW \quad (2)$$

NT is that portion of government tax revenue and spending that varies with fluctuations in nominal output or GNP. Current expenditure (G), on the other hand, is assumed to be constant and does not vary with changes in GNP. In Figure 7.2, NT and G are shown along the vertical axis. Nominal GNP is shown on the horizontal axis. As government expenditure, G, is assumed to be constant at all levels of GNP it is represented as a horizontal line. The net taxes (NT) line, on the other hand, is positively sloped. This is because more tax revenue is collected and less is paid out in social welfare as GNP increases. Conversely, as GNP falls, less is collected in taxes and more paid out in social welfare and NT decreases.

In Figure 7.2, a vertical line has also been included to indicate potential nominal GNP (Y^*). (Note that in this section we use Y^* to denote nominal and not real potential output.) This reference line will become useful in assessing the stance of fiscal policy. Consider the point A in the diagram, corresponding to Y^*. Government expenditure equals net taxes and the budget is balanced. To the left of Y^* there is a budget deficit (expenditure exceeds revenue), and to the right a budget surplus (expenditure is less than revenue).

It is clear from the diagram that the budget balance automatically changes as Y changes along the horizontal axis. If, for example, we start from Y_1 and move to Y_2, net taxes move up along the NT line and the government's budget swings automatically from deficit to surplus. This means that as the economy moves out of a recession, the government's budget surplus will automatically increase. Conversely, as the economy contracts, the budget surplus automatically falls.

FIGURE 7.2 Automatic stabilisers

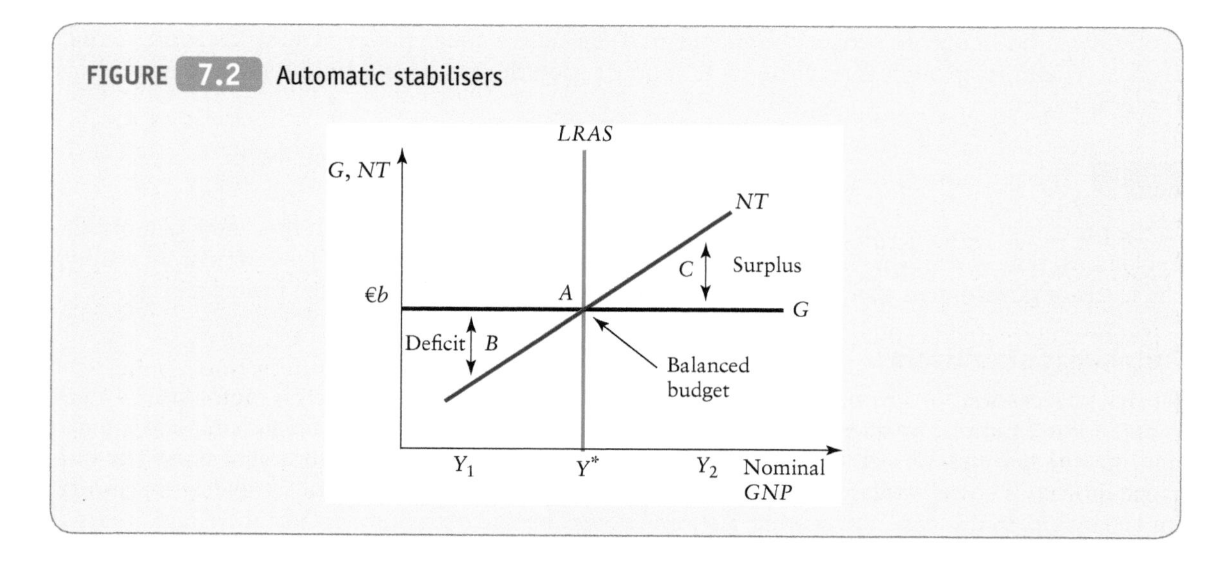

FIGURE 7.3 Discretionary changes in the budget balance

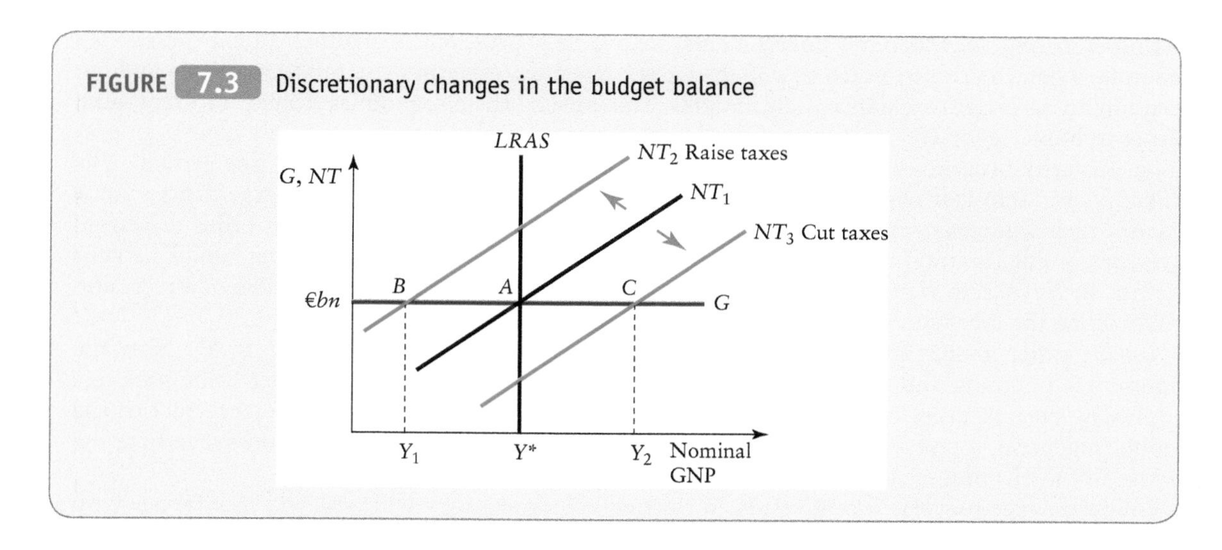

Discretionary fiscal policy

Figure 7.2 can be modified to clarify the distinction between automatic and discretionary changes in the budget balance. Discretionary budget changes arise when the government deliberately changes the stance of fiscal policy by changing tax rates, the level of social welfare benefits, or the level of its expenditure on goods and services.

Figure 7.3 shows an increase in taxes or/and a cut in SW shifting the NT line upwards to the left. This initially gives rise to a budget surplus. GNP would now have to fall to Y_1 for the budget to be balanced (point B in the diagram). Conversely a cut in taxes or/and an increase in SW shifts the NT line downwards to the right. GNP would now have to rise to Y_2 for the budget to balance (point C in the diagram). Similarly, a cut in government consumption shifts the government expenditure (G) line downwards and vice versa.

Each of these changes represents a policy decision by the government. They are discretionary policy changes that result in the budget being balanced at different levels of GNP. At what level of GNP should the government attempt to balance the budget?

The full-employment budget

The relevant budget balance from a policy perspective is the budget balance corresponding to the potential, or full-employment, level of output, Y^*. The government should choose a combination of tax rates and levels of expenditure that would result in a balanced budget if the economy were at Y^*.

In Figures 7.2 and 7.3 the vertical line represents potential GNP, Y^*. At this point, $NT = G$ and the budget is balanced. To the left of potential GNP, the economy is in recession and the government should tolerate the resultant budget deficit. In contrast, to the right of potential GNP the economy is over-heating (running above capacity) and the government should run a surplus.

Discretionary fiscal policy should be counter-cyclical. It should be expansionary in times of recession and contractionary in boom times. Only if this is the case will policy succeed in dampening the business cycle and keeping the economy close to full-employment output, Y^*.

The problem is that in some cases, governments behave like households and pursue a policy of always trying to balance the budget. To illustrate this, suppose in Figure 7.3 GNP falls from Y^* to Y_1. The economy goes into recession and a budget deficit emerges. If the government, in an effort to balance the books, responds by cutting expenditure or raising taxes, this would push the economy further into recession. This policy would be pro-cyclical, making the business cycle more rather than less pronounced.

Unfortunately, all too often governments behave in a pro-cyclical manner. In the 1930s, for example, when the recession led to collapsing tax revenues, governments raised tax rates and cut spending in an effort to balance their budgets. This pushed their economies deeper into recession. Closer to home, since 2007 countries like Greece, Portugal, Ireland, Spain and Italy have been pursuing 'austerity programmes' under pressure from the IMF, the EU and the ECB (the Troika). The official view, identified with the German establishment, is that countries with large deficits must balance their budgets even when unemployment is far above its natural level in order to restore investor confidence and lay the foundations for recovery and growth in the long run. This runs against the Keynesian view that embarking on an austerity programme in the middle of a recession will prolong the recession and make it harder to balance the budget.

On the other hand, suppose that in Figure 7.3 the economy moves from Y* to Y_2. Now the economy is booming and a budget surplus emerges. If the government attempts to eliminate this surplus by cutting taxes or increasing expenditure, the result will be to add further fuel to the boom. In general, a policy of always balancing the budget can be pro-cyclical and exacerbate the swings in the business cycle.

Politicians face perverse incentives. If an election is looming they will wish to curry favour with voters by cutting taxes and raising expenditure regardless of the possibility that the economy is already at Y* or even over-heating. On the other hand, if the economy is plunged into a recession, they will find it hard to borrow the money needed to stimulate aggregate demand. They will be forced by the ever-vigilant bond market to try to balance the books, even if this intensifies the recession.

In evaluating the conduct of fiscal policy, economists need to gauge whether government policy is expansionary, neutral or deflationary and whether policy is appropriate to the needs of the economy. In attempting to assess the stance of fiscal policy, the budget balance at potential GNP, Y*, is more relevant than the actual budget balance. An examination of the actual budget balance without adjustment for built-in stabilisers can give a misleading picture of the direction of fiscal policy.

Structural budget balance

A key concept is the structural budget balance. This refers to what the underlying budgetary outcome is when temporary shocks are stripped out of the picture. To calculate the structural deficit, we need to see what the deficit would be if the economy were at or close to potential output. In Figure 7.3 at Y* the budget is balanced as expenditure equals revenue. There is no structural deficit. At Y_1, however, because the economy is no longer at full employment a budget deficit has emerged. Deficits that arise from once-off falls in revenue or increases in expenditure are deemed not to be structural. A structural deficit is a deficit that would persist even if these temporary shocks were absent and the economy back at full employment.

It is theoretically important to separate the elements of an actual deficit that are due to temporary factors, such as a once-off transfer payment to a less developed country following an earthquake, and structural factors, such as a fundamental fall in property taxes following the collapse of the housing market. This is no easy task. In practice it is not easy to distinguish between once-off and structural changes in tax or spending. Moreover, it is also necessary to measure potential or full-employment output, Y*, and this is not a simple matter. It requires an estimate of the rate of unemployment corresponding to 'full employment' and over time it calls for an estimate of the economy's underlying potential growth rate. There is no agreed methodology for preparing these estimates. It is a lot easier to illustrate it in a diagram, as we have done in this chapter, than to operationalise it for national budgetary practice.

For example, in Ireland in 2012 the unemployment rate is close to 15 per cent. This has led to massive spending on Jobseeker's Allowances and other welfare payments and a huge loss of income tax receipts. When calculating the structural deficit, how much of an adjustment should be made for these 'exceptional' factors? This depends on the view you take about how long it will be before the economy returns to a 'normal' or 'full-employment' level of activity.

As recently as 2008 the unemployment rate was below five per cent, but it is likely to be a long time before it approaches this level again. Meanwhile, how much of the excess unemployment should be treated as 'temporary' and how much as 'structural'? One of the depressing features of a recession is that the longer it lasts the more actual unemployment becomes structural because the proportion of the unemployed who have been out of work for a long time rises. The so-called 'natural' rate of unemployment tends to rise in line with the actual rate. (This process is called 'hysteresis' and was discussed in Chapter 4.)

Yet, although it is a highly technical concept, the idea of the 'structural budget balance' was built into the wording of the Fiscal Compact on which Irish voters had their say in a referendum in 2012.

7.4 Problems in Implementing Fiscal Policy

The Keynesian idea of using fiscal policy to stabilise the economy is appealing, but experience has shown that it is in practice very difficult, if not impossible, successfully to fine-tune the economy in this manner. In fact, we shall see in the next chapter that the Irish record on this front has been poor. Let us consider some of the factors that make it difficult to implement a successful counter-cyclical fiscal policy.

Lags

If the economy experiences an adverse shock and is going into recession, the government should adopt an expansionary fiscal stance. But the response is likely to be delayed. It takes time to recognise what is happening to the economy (the recognition lag). Only a limited amount of timely economic data is available. Information on key variables becomes available gradually and in Ireland, as in other countries, the first estimates of GNP in particular may be revised significantly in subsequent quarters. While numerous unofficial estimates are prepared, economists often fall back on extrapolating recent trends and fail to anticipate turning points. The magnitude of the downturn of 2007/8 took everyone by surprise.

Second, policy-makers have to decide which mix of tax and expenditure changes are appropriate to deal with a downturn. This is an extremely political matter in all countries, with some people strongly opposed to increased expenditure and others strongly opposed to tax cuts. If more money is to be spent, should it go on roads or education? How many projects are 'shovel ready' – that is, even if there were no budget constraint, how many worthwhile projects could get under way in the morning? If extra money is made available, what is the most effective way to spend it? If taxes are to be cut, what is the fairest and most effective way of doing this?

These lags are referred to as inside lags. There is also the outside lag between implementing a policy and when it actually affects aggregate demand. Allowing for the multiplier (which we discussed in Chapter 6), the effects of fiscal policy will tend to be spread out, at a diminishing rate, over two or three years.

The problem with these lags is that by the time the fiscal policy takes effect economic conditions in the country may have altered. The implication is that the policy could be inappropriate by the time it becomes effective and end up destabilising instead of stabilising the economy.

Figure 7.4 shows the economy adjusting back towards the long-term growth rate of potential real output, Y*, after having been hit by an adverse shock. Initially, the economy falls below its potential growth rate and into recession. After a time the government recognises the downturn and sets about implementing an expansionary fiscal policy. Because of the recognition, decision, implementation and outside lags, this policy will take some time to impact on the economy. Suppose that nine months later the economy had already begun to right itself due, for example, to an upturn in export markets. The growth rate starts to move back towards the potential rate. Six months later,

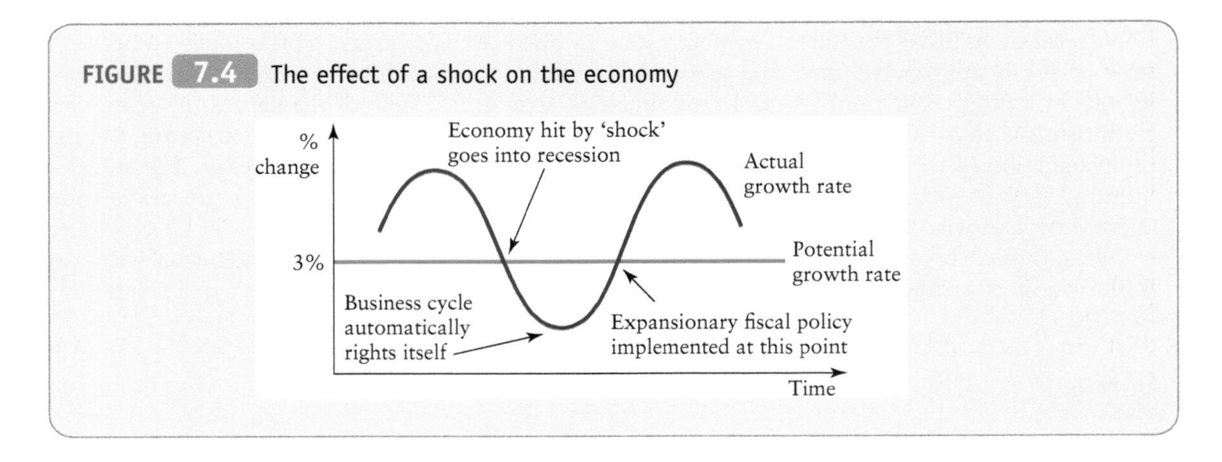

FIGURE 7.4 The effect of a shock on the economy

the expansionary fiscal policy kicks in and causes the economy to over-heat. Because of its timing, the fiscal stimulus destabilises rather than stabilises the economy.

How big a response?

Another difficulty arises from the problem of deciding how much additional demand the government should inject into or withdraw from the economy. The appropriate amount to spend to counter a fall in aggregate demand can only be calculated on the basis of an exact knowledge of how the shock hits the economy and the relevant multipliers. Clearly, assessing correctly the extent of the shock is very problematic. In Appendix 6.1 at the end of Chapter 6 we illustrated how the multiplier is calculated for a small, open economy like Ireland. It was clear that such a calculation requires estimates of a large number of parameters that summarise how the economy behaves. This, in turn, requires estimating a model of the economy and experience shows that such models have to be constantly updated and revised if they are to provide useful guides for economic policy.

The political economy of fiscal policy

Policy-makers are not disembodied technicians, unaware of political realities. In democracies economic policy is influenced by the desire of politicians to get re-elected, which depends on delivering results such as low inflation and unemployment. Political parties tend to attach different relative weights to these objectives. Since World War II, German politicians have placed great emphasis on maintaining a low inflation rate, believing that this is crucial to the long-run stability of the economy. On the other hand, until recently at least, Italian politicians were willing to condone high inflation, believing that lower unemployment could be bought by tolerating higher inflation. There were also differences between left-wing and right-wing parties within these countries, with the right-of-centre parties stressing the importance of low inflation, and left-of-centre parties attaching greater importance to maintaining low unemployment.

The electoral cycle also has an important influence on policy. During the 1978 general election, for example, Irish political parties vied with one another in extravagant promises to the electorate, including the abolition of rates (property taxes on domestic property). After the election, increases in expenditure and cuts in taxation were implemented when the economy had already started to grow rapidly. Furthermore, politicians find it much easier to implement expansionary than deflationary policies. Hence there is an asymmetry, with politicians keen to 'do something' when a recession strikes, but reluctant to introduce measures to curb an over-heating economy.

One way around the problem created by the political cycle is to create independent economic policy-making institutions. Following the example of the American Federal Reserve System and the German Bundesbank, many European governments, including the British government, have given their central banks increased autonomy and the independence to withstand demands for inflationary financing of government deficits. One of the key features of the EMU is that the ECB should be 'above politics' and certainly above national politics. The participating countries relinquished control over their monetary policy to the ECB and in this they hope to gain the anti-inflation credibility that a strong and independent central bank enjoys.

However, during the current crisis there is considerable controversy over whether the ECB is still as independent as it should be. During 2012 the Bundesbank became increasingly critical of what it saw as the willingness of the ECB to take decisions that would please politicians in Paris, Rome, Madrid and Dublin rather than adhering rigidly to its original anti-inflation mandate. The introduction of the Fiscal Compact during 2012 was designed to assuage these concerns and narrow the range of fiscal options open to politicians in the EMU countries.

Crowding out

Another issue that may reduce the effectiveness of fiscal policy is referred to as 'crowding-out'. The aggregate demand (AD) identity:

$$Y = AD \equiv C + I + G + NX \tag{3}$$

states that the total output of goods and services (Y) equals aggregate demand (or total expenditure). This, in turn, can be broken down into consumer expenditure, investment, government expenditure and net exports. Suppose the government increases G in order to boost total expenditure and raise Y. Assuming the government incurs a budget deficit, the extra spending will have to be borrowed in financial markets. This increase in the demand for funds on the money markets can cause interest rates to rise (this effect will be elaborated upon in Chapter 10). The higher interest rates, in turn, can reduce consumer expenditure (C) and private sector investment (I). As C and I fall, the level of aggregate demand decreases. In terms of equation (3) above, the initial increase in G is completely offset by the fall in C and I and Y is unchanged. Government expenditure has crowded out consumption and investment. In this case, there is 100 per cent crowding out and fiscal policy has no impact on aggregate demand.

In practice, the degree of crowding out is likely to be considerably less than 100 per cent, but so long as it is not zero it diminishes the effectiveness of fiscal policy. With crowding out, the net effect of fiscal policy on aggregate demand is less than the increase in G. The important point is that the ultimate effect on Y is smaller than that suggested by the multipliers we derived in Chapter 6, which took no account of crowding out.

The Barro–Ricardo equivalence theorem

Another consideration that may reduce the effectiveness of fiscal policy arises from the effect of government deficits on the behaviour of households. In an influential article published in 1974, the Harvard economist Robert Barro proposed the idea that increases in government debt could result in a fall in private sector consumption. In terms of equation (3) above, the increase in G is offset by a fall in C. The classical economist David Ricardo (1772–1823) appeared to have entertained the same idea, hence the theorem is now known as the Barro–Ricardo equivalence theorem.

The bones of the proposition are as follows. Suppose the government lowers taxes without cutting its spending and finances the ensuing deficit by selling bonds to the public. These bonds must be redeemed (with interest) at some time in the future. Households' current disposable income rises due to the tax cut, but future disposable income will fall by an equivalent amount because of the necessity of repaying the debt. Thus, households' long-run or permanent income (see Chapter 6) does not change. If households are rational (far-seeing individuals who care about future generations), their consumption should be unaffected by the tax cut. However, if the present generation is willing to pass the increased debt on to future generations they feel better off as a result of the tax cut and consumption will increase.

The Irish experience offers some support for the Barro–Ricardo equivalence theorem. When the fiscal deficit was very large in the first half of the 1980s, the private sector saving ratio was very high; when the public sector deficit was brought under control in the later 1980s, the private sector saving ratio fell. Since the start of the current crisis, the private sector's saving ratio has risen rapidly.

Supply-side shocks

Fiscal policy is not an effective policy response to dealing with an adverse supply-side shock.

In Figure 7.5 the economy is initially at point A, where the price level is P_1 and real output is Y_1. Suppose now the economy is hit by a supply-side shock which shifts the SRAS curve up to the left. As the economy moves to point B, real output falls and the price level increases to P_2. If the government now introduces an expansionary fiscal policy to increase real output, the AD curve moves up to the right and a new equilibrium is achieved at the point C. The difficulty, however, is that there is a further increase in the price level. So while the fiscal policy can (in certain circumstances) deal with the fall in real output it cannot simultaneously counteract the increase in prices. Other measures are required to deal with supply-side shocks, such as increased investment in new technologies, greater labour force flexibility and so on.

FIGURE 7.5 An adverse supply-side shock

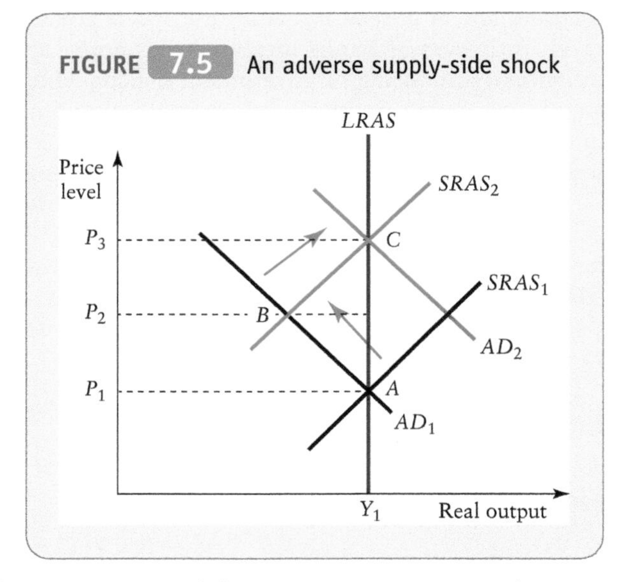

Summary

From the above discussion it should be clear that in practice the use of fiscal policy to stabilise the economy is not an easy task. While the basic idea seems simple, its implementation is fraught with difficulties. Moreover, economists have become increasingly sceptical of some of the assumptions underlying the Keynesian model. Nonetheless, policy-makers continue to try to use budgets to reduce the fluctuations in economic output. And there are examples of some successes. Most economists would reckon that the 'stimulus packages' introduced by the Obama administration in the USA in 2010 mitigated the effects of the Great Recession on the US economy.

7.5 Taxation and the Supply Side of the Economy

Up to this point, our emphasis has been on how taxation affects the demand side of the economy. But ever since Adam Smith, economists have recognised that taxation also affects the supply side of the economy by affecting the incentives to work and save. This affects the level and composition of output and income. If these effects are large they can have surprising results. Under certain conditions, it could be that tax cuts increase, rather than decrease, tax revenue. This argument has been put forward by the University of Southern California economist Arthur Laffer, who reputedly first drew the *Laffer curve* on a napkin in a Washington restaurant to explain the point to a reporter.

The Laffer curve depicts the relationship between the average tax rate (vertical axis) and the tax revenue to the government (horizontal axis). This is illustrated in Figure 7.6, which shows how much revenue is obtained from different average rates of income tax. There are two rates where no tax revenue is collected – zero and 100 per cent. In the first case, there is no tax and therefore no revenue. In the second case, all income would be taken in tax and there would be no incentive to work. If no one works there is no income to tax and revenue is zero. Between these two extremes, it is argued, revenue first increases and then decreases as the tax rate rises.

FIGURE 7.6 The Laffer curve

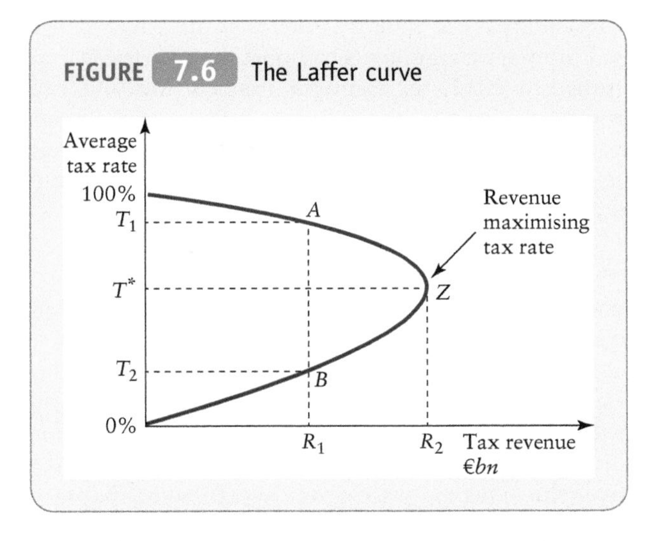

In Figure 7.6 the revenue-maximising tax rate is T*. Moreover, the same amount of tax revenue can be obtained at high or low tax rates: T_1 and T_2 generate the same revenue, R_1. It follows, therefore, that government could cut the tax rate from T_1 to T_2 without suffering any loss of revenue.

More generally, if the tax rate is below T* an increase in the tax rate leads to an increase in revenue. This is what is normally expected. However, if the tax rate is above T*, we have the surprising result that an increase in the tax rate leads to a reduction in revenue. In this situation, the government raises the tax rate in order to generate extra revenue and finds that its tax receipts fall. If it lowered the tax rate it would generate extra revenue.

Part of the explanation for this paradoxical result is that above T* an increase in the tax rate reduces revenue related to work incentives. High tax rates discourage people from working. If people work less, their taxable income falls and so do tax receipts. In the past, marginal income tax rates have been very high in Ireland. Rates were reduced in the early years of this century, but after recent increases they are quite high in certain circumstances. In 2012, for example, an unmarried employee earning above €32,800 a year would have to pay 41 per cent income tax on additional income, a USC of seven per cent and PRSI at four per cent.

Thus it could happen that if he or she were to do a few hours' overtime, out of every €100 additional income earned, 52 per cent would be taxed away in one form or another. A university lecturer, for example, might be offered €3,000 to teach an evening course. The take-home pay corresponding to this would be only €1,440. If the lecturer decided that the after-tax purchasing power of the lecture fee was not worth the time and effort involved, he or she would stay at home in the evenings instead of going out to teach an extra course. If enough people reacted in this way, the course would not go ahead and the economy would shrink (although admittedly by the smallest amount!). On the other hand, a reduction in the marginal tax rate would make it worthwhile to teach the course, output would rise and tax receipts would be more buoyant.

In addition to discouraging work effort, high tax rates create many other undesirable incentives. People are encouraged to switch from the formal economy into the informal or 'black' economy, to take money out of the country and place it in foreign tax havens ('capital flight'), and even to emigrate. High tax rates also encourage people to shop in countries where indirect taxes are low. Tax rates in Ireland, for example, cannot move too far out of line from the tax rates that obtain in the UK. High tax rates on spirits, petrol and electrical goods led shoppers from the Republic to purchase these items in Northern Ireland in the mid-1980s. When the tax rates were cut towards the end of the decade, more was spent in the Republic and revenue rose. These effects of high tax rates are consistent with the existence of a Laffer curve.

NOTE: There are a number of reasons, however, why tax cuts may not have the dramatic effects predicted by this theory. It is possible, for example, that lower taxes might encourage people to work less because after the tax cut they can obtain the same level of take-home pay with less effort; they may decide to enjoy more leisure at the same income, which they can now earn by working less. This would offset the effects predicted by Laffer. Moreover, for the Laffer curve to be bell-shaped, the reduction in taxes has to boost real output by an amount sufficient to more than compensate for the initial loss of tax revenue.

It is not easy to identify where on the Laffer curve the economy is. Special interest groups often use Laffer-type arguments to boost the case for tax cuts on their products. The Irish tourist industry claimed in 2012, for example, that cutting VAT rates on 'hospitality-related' expenditure would provide a boost to the industry and be 'self-financing'. Subsequent evaluations of these claims showed that this does not seem to have been the case. In the 2012 American presidential debates the Republicans argued that cutting income taxes would prove self-financing, but most economists remain sceptical of this view.

Tax rates and the AD, AS diagram

Economists are generally agreed that changes in taxation impacts on the supply side of the economy. Disagreement, however, arises on the extent of this impact. In the left-hand diagram in Figure 7.7, we assume the economy is initially in recession and output is below its full-employment level. Keynesian economists agree that a tax cut will shift both the aggregate demand (AD) and SRAS curves to the right. The AD curve moves because the tax cut leads to an increase in consumer expenditure (C) and therefore AD. On the supply side, for the SRAS curve to move to the right, the tax cut must lower the expected price level. Recall from Chapter 5 that the expected price level determines the location of the SRAS curve.

The Keynesian view is that the shift in the AD curve will be greater than the movement of the SRAS curve. As shown in the left-hand diagram, the economy moves from the point A to B and both the price level and real output increase. (Note that the greater the movement of the SRAS curve, the lower the change in the price level and the greater the increase in real output.) Hence, we obtain the standard Keynesian result, that an expansionary fiscal policy generates more real output but also increases the price level.

Supply-side economists such as Arthur Laffer, on the other hand, assert that the shift of the SRAS curve to the right will be approximately equal to the movement of the AD curve. As can be seen in the right-hand diagram in Figure 7.7, the result is a much bigger increase in real output (less stimulus is required) and little or no effect on the price level. Some supply-side economists go further and argue that the movement of the SRAS curve will be greater than the movement of the AD curve. In this case, the increase in real output will be accompanied by a fall in the price level.

FIGURE 7.7 Taxation and the AS curve

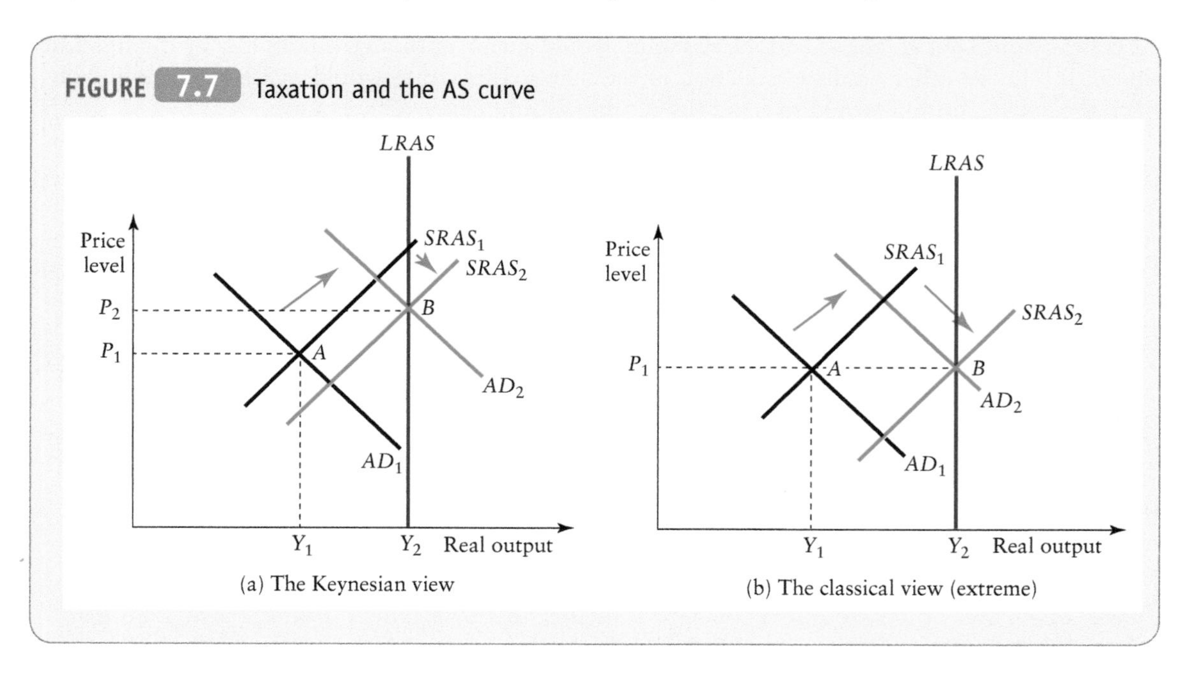

The dispute between the Keynesians and the supply-siders is, therefore, one of quantifying the effect of the tax change on the SRAS curve. In the context of stabilisation policy, it is clear that the Laffer curve and the effect of tax changes on the SRAS curve create more uncertainty about the effects of fiscal policy on the economy.

7.6 The Dynamics of Debt Stabilisation

A key question facing nations over the longer term is: What will happen to the economy if we continue to run budget deficits and borrow as we have in the past? Specifically, what will happen to the national debt to GDP (or national income) ratio if we persist in running budget deficits? No country can contemplate the prospect of a steadily rising debt/GDP ratio for the simple reason that this would result in an ever-increasing burden of interest payments relative to income. Taxpayers would have to pay more and more of their income in taxes to pay for past borrowing.

Furthermore, if the debt/GDP ratio 'gets too high', investors worry that the government will default on the debt and demand higher interest rates to compensate them for the increase in the perceived risk associated with lending to the government. Whereas in good times buying government bonds (sovereign debt) was regarded as being as close as possible to a risk-free investment, we see in recent years that there is now believed to be a very real risk that some governments may default on their debt and hence higher interest rates are being demanded to compensate for the risk associated with holding Greek, Portuguese, Spanish and Irish government bonds.

As the debt/GDP ratio rises, the economy suffers in many ways. Taxpayers see no current benefits from the money they have to pay in taxes for this purpose. Taxes paid to service past debt are perceived as being diverted from financing current spending on health and education, for example. It has been suggested that as the debt/GDP ratio rises above 90 per cent the economy enters a danger zone, with investors becoming increasingly reluctant to finance further borrowing and the burden of the debt tending to impede future growth. Sooner, rather than later, the process of a rising debt/GDP has to be reversed (Reinhart and Rogoff 2009).

This is now an important issue for Ireland, whose debt/GDP ratio has ballooned in recent years, reflecting the collapse of tax revenues in Ireland in 2008 and the cost of recapitalising the banks. The Irish budget deficit reached a record 40 per cent of GNP in 2010. While we were fortunate in that the level of debt/GDP ratio was reasonably low (23 per cent of GNP) in 2007, borrowing at the rate that occurred since 2008 inevitably led to a ballooning of the debt and with a declining GDP the debt/GNP ratio soared. It reached 117.7 per cent in 2012 and is still rising.

A major factor contributing to the rise in the debt/GNP ratio was the need to recapitalise the Irish banks. A capital injection by the government of €64 billion into the main banks was necessary to save the banking system from collapse. This injection of funds was treated by the European Statistical Office (Eurostat) as sovereign debt and included in the definition of debt used to assess the debt/GDP ratio. This increased the debt/GDP ratio by about 40 percentage points.

To answer the question of how the debt/GDP ratio can be stabilised, let us set out a simple model. Government expenditure may be divided into two components: its normal current (including transfer payments) spending and capital spending, G; and interest paid on past borrowing. If we denote the stock of national debt as D and the interest rate payable on this debt as i, debt service equals iD and total government spending equals $G + iD$.

If we concentrate on tax revenue, T, as the government's main source of funds, the general government deficit (GGD) or fiscal deficit is the shortfall of government spending over tax revenue:

$$GGD = G + iD - T \tag{4}$$

If debt service is excluded from the deficit, and attention is confined to government's spending on goods and services, G, we obtain what is called the primary deficit, PD:

$$PD = G - T \tag{5}$$

If we denote borrowing as ΔD (that is, the change in national debt) the government's budget is:

$$\Delta D = G + iD - T \tag{6}$$

The absolute level of the national debt would be stabilised if the budget was balanced. The budget constraint now becomes:

$$\Delta D = G + iD - T = 0 \tag{7}$$

This implies that to stabilise the level of the national debt the government must run a primary budget surplus equal to the interest on the national debt:

$$T - G = iD \tag{8}$$

The government must pay the interest on past debt out of current tax receipts. We can express these magnitudes as percentages of GDP by dividing equation (7) through by GDP. This gives us:

$$\frac{\Delta D}{GDP} = \frac{G}{GDP} + \frac{iD}{GDP} - \frac{T}{GDP} \tag{9}$$

Writing ratios to GDP in lower case letters (D/GDP = d, etc.) this becomes:

$$\frac{\Delta D}{GDP} = (g + id) - t \tag{10}$$

(Note that ΔD/GDP is not the same as Δd because it is ΔD in the numerator.) Stabilising the debt/GDP ratio implies ΔD/GDP = 0

$$\frac{\Delta D}{GDP} = (g + id) - t = 0$$

or

$$t - g = id$$

This implies that the debt will stabilise if the primary budget surplus equals the interest rate times the debt/GDP ratio. In a growing economy the question of interest is: What are the conditions under which the debt/GDP ratio, d, will be stabilised or reduced? To obtain the necessary condition, we need to introduce the nominal (not the real) growth rate into the analysis. (The nominal growth rate includes changes in the price level.) This can be done as follows. By definition,

$$d = \frac{D}{GDP}$$

Rearranging:

$$D = d \times GDP$$

Total differentiation gives:

$$\Delta D = d \times \Delta GDP + GDP \times \Delta d$$

Dividing both sides by GDP yields:

$$\frac{\Delta D}{GDP} = d \times \frac{\Delta GDP}{GDP} + \Delta d$$

Letting y equal the rate of growth of nominal GDP (that is, ΔGDP/GDP):

$$\frac{\Delta D}{GDP} = d \times y + \Delta d$$

Setting this equation equal to equation (10) above, we obtain:

$$g + id - t = d \times y + \Delta d \tag{11}$$

Rearranging:

$$\Delta d = g + id - t - d \times y \tag{12}$$

or

$$\Delta d = g - t + (i - y)d$$

The goal of stabilising the debt/GDP ratio implies setting d = 0, which implies:

$$g - t + (i - y)d = 0$$

or

$$t - g = (i - y)d \tag{13}$$

This crucial equation states that to stabilise the debt/GDP ratio the primary budget balance as a percentage of GDP (t – g) must be equal to or greater than the difference between the rate of interest and the rate of growth of nominal GDP times the initial ratio of debt to GDP, $(i - y)$d.

The crucial term in this equation is $(i - y)$: that is, the gap between the nominal rate of interest and the rate of growth of nominal GDP. At the time of writing (mid-2012) countries like Spain and Italy are facing interest rates close to seven per cent on their medium-term debt, while their economies are recording negative real growth rates and inflation is very low, under two per cent. The gap between i and y is therefore four or five per cent, implying that if the debt/GDP ratio is not to continue to grow, and become unsustainable, very large primary surpluses will have to be achieved.

The algebra can be applied to show that the condition in the Fiscal Compact that governments may not run (structural) deficits in excess of 0.5 per cent of GDP implies that they will have to run large primary budget surpluses until such time as the debt/GDP ratio falls.

Forecasting the Irish debt/GDP ratio

We can apply the model to the present Irish situation by using a set of projections published by the ESRI (FitzGerald and Kearney 2011). In Table 7.1 forecast nominal GDP is given in line E and the projected debt/GDP ratio in line G. It can be seen that gross debt as a percentage of GDP is forecast to peak in 2012 at 112.5 per cent and fall back to 103.2 per cent by end 2015. Clearly the return to the low debt/GDP level of the early 2000s is going to be a slow and arduous process.

The implications of these calculations are enormous. Taxpayers today and tomorrow will have to pay higher taxes, not to finance better public services such as health and education, but to pay for past borrowing. Not all of this past debt was incurred for worthwhile uses and, even when it was, taxpayers soon forget that better roads and schools have to be paid for into the future.

The public may accept high levels of taxation to sustain good schools and hospitals, to build better roads and water treatment plants, and to support the elderly and the young. However, they are unlikely to accept an increasing tax burden in the face of declining levels of spending on schools, roads, hospitals and support for pensioners and children. 'Honouring the obligation to service past debts' is not a very catchy election slogan.

This is the dilemma being faced today by democratic governments across Europe. In 2012, Greece resorted to the alternative of defaulting on the national debt, but not on the scale that is required to alleviate the problem. Nonetheless it remains shut out of the normal bond markets.

Portugal and Ireland have so far succeeded in avoiding default by obtaining 'bailouts' from the Troika. This gave them access to loans at approximately three per cent, compared with the much higher rates that would have to be paid on the bond market (if any money could be raised there).

TABLE 7.1 Forecasting the debt/GDP ratio

	Borrowing flows		2010	2011	2012	2013	2014	2015
A	General government deficit	€ bn	49.9	15.1	12.6	10.5	6.3	3.2
	Primary deficit	€ bn	44.9	9.7	6.3	1.9	−2.9	−6.3
	Debt interest	€ bn	5	5.4	6.2	8.5	9.1	9.5
B	Bank capitalisation	€ bn		17	0	0	−3	0
C	Change in liquid assets	€ bn		−8.8	−2.3	−4.3	0	0
D	Total new borrowing	€ bn (A + B + C)		23.3	10.3	6.2	3.3	3.2
E	Forecast nominal GDP	€ bn	155.9	157.3	161.5	169.4	175.0	188.2
F	Total gross government debt	€ bn	148.1	171.4	181.7	187.8	191.1	194.3
G	% of GDP	%	95	109	112.5	110.9	109.2	103.2

Source: FitzGerald and Kearney 2011

But in return for this, they have agreed to a very rigorous schedule of expenditure cuts and tax increases that will, it is hoped, bring the fiscal deficit to a sustainable level (three per cent of GDP) by 2015.

At the time of writing, in mid-2012, it is still far from clear whether the austerity package we have agreed with the Troika can be successfully implemented and whether it will succeed in stabilising the Irish public finances. We review in more detail the way fiscal policy has been pursued in the past and the current Irish fiscal situation in the next chapter.

7.7 Key Terms and Concepts

The main points discussed in this chapter were:

- the government's budget and the characteristics of government expenditure and taxation
- fiscal policy
- automatic fiscal stabilisers
- defining and measuring the structural budget balance
- the difficulties of implementing an appropriate fiscal policy
- taxation and the supply side of the economy
- the dynamics of stabilising the debt/GDP ratio.

CHAPTER 8

Fiscal Policy and Economic Planning in Practice: The Irish Record

8.1 Introduction

In this chapter we use the ideas we developed in Chapter 7 to look at how fiscal policy has been conducted in Ireland. We start with a picture at the budgetary situation in Ireland in 2012. This includes an account of how the post-2007 recession has devastated the Irish public finances.

We then present an overview of the longer-term trends in Irish public revenue, expenditure and the deficit. This is followed by an examination of the broad framework within which fiscal policy has taken place, summarising the various approaches to 'economic planning' that have been adopted in Ireland since the 1950s.

Finally, we evaluate the conduct of Irish fiscal policy, paying particular attention to the key issue of whether it has helped stabilise the economy and dampen swings in the business cycle.

8.2 The Budget Framework

The government budget is divided into a current and a capital account. Current expenditure is of a day-to-day nature. It does not result in the creation of fixed assets. Current revenue is income from taxes, levies and charges. The balance between current receipts and expenditure is the current budget balance.

Capital expenditure involves the creation of assets such as schools, hospitals and roads. Capital revenue consists of interest on stocks owned by the government, loan repayments and capital grants received from the EU. The excess of the central government's capital expenditure over capital revenue is called the capital budget deficit.

The sum of these two deficits constitutes the total Exchequer balance.

Table 8.1 presents a summary of the 2013 Budget. The second last line is the gap between total receipts and total (current plus capital) spending, the total Exchequer balance. It is the amount of money the government must borrow to cover the excess of spending over revenue. In 2013 this came to €15.4 billion or 9.2 per cent of GDP. (We relate the fiscal magnitudes in this chapter to GDP, rather than GNP, because that is the international practice.)

NOTE: The word 'exchequer' comes from the Norman French word for the Treasury, the government department responsible for collecting and managing the state's revenue.

Table 8.1 also shows a different measure of the deficit, the general government balance (GGB). This is used by the EU in assessing the state of the public finances. Until recently the differences between

TABLE 8.1 Irish Exchequer receipts and expenditure 2012

		€ billions	% GDP
	Current expenditure	49.9	29.8
	Current revenue	40.3	24.0
A1	Current budget surplus (+)/deficit (−)	−9.6	−5.7
	Capital expenditure	7.8	4.7
	Capital revenue	2.0	1.2
A2	Capital budget surplus(+)/deficit (−)	−5.8	−3.5
A3 = A1 + A2	Exchequer balance	−15.4	−9.2
	General government balance (GGB)	−12.6	−7.5

Notes: The difference between the exchequer balance and the GGB is discussed in the text. Spending and revenue are shown relative to GDP, rather than GNP: this is international practice when comparing countries' fiscal situations.
Source: Department of Finance, Budget 2013, Economic and Fiscal Outlook, Table 9

the two measures were technical and small, but since 2009 they have been very significant, because of two factors:

1. The money used by the government to acquire equity in the banks is included in the Exchequer balance but not in the GGB.
2. The issue of the promissory notes to the Irish Bank Resolution Corporation (the remains of Anglo Irish Bank), which we discuss in Chapter 10. In 2010 €31.4 billion was added to GGB in respect of these notes but was not included in the Exchequer balance. In January 2013, the promissory notes were replaced by long-term bonds.

In 2013 the GGB was projected at −7.5 per cent of GDP, significantly lower than the Exchequer balance. The Exchequer deficit can be financed from four sources. The government can:

1. sell bonds to the general (or non-bank) public;
2. borrow from the central bank;
3. borrow from commercial banks;
4. borrow from abroad.

As we shall discuss in more detail in Chapter 9, the Maastricht Treaty that governs the EMU prevents the ECB from lending to finance government deficits. However, one way of circumnavigating this rule is for the commercial banks to borrow from the ECB and then use this money to buy government bonds (lend to the government). Since the crisis of 2008, national governments have been borrowing from the ECB. This has led to the ECB launching a major programme of bond purchases for some of the euro area countries.

Borrowing from abroad involves selling bonds to non-residents or borrowing directly from foreign banks. Borrowing increases indebtedness, within the country and/or to external creditors. As we saw in the previous chapter, there is great concern when the level of indebtedness rises relative to GDP. An increasing level of debt implies that a heavier tax burden must be borne by today's and tomorrow's taxpayers just to pay for past borrowing. This highlights the importance of using borrowed money for productive purposes that yield a return to the economy and not to finance wasteful spending. The yield on the uses to which borrowed money is put should be high enough to justify the burden that servicing the debt will impose on future taxpayers.

8.3 The Impact of the Recession on the Irish Public Finances

The recession that developed in Ireland in 2008 had devastating effects on the Irish public finances. Here we give a broad outline of these effects. Figure 8.1 shows current, capital and total Exchequer spending as a percentage of GDP from 2000 to 2012. Current spending dominates the total and also accounts for most of its variability. Between 2000 and 2007 spending relative to GDP was very stable at around 25 per cent. However, the graph brings out clearly the way the recession led to a ballooning of public spending relative to GDP. Unfortunately, this had nothing to do with increasing the provision of better public services, such as health and education, but simply reflected the impact of the decline in the economy on the demands on the Exchequer.

Between 2006 and 2012 current spending surged from 21 to almost 40 per cent of GDP. Even if the level had remained unchanged, it would have risen as a proportion of GDP because GDP was 25 per cent lower (in current prices) in 2012 than in 2006. But to make matters worse the recession led automatically to large spending increases under two headings:

1. National debt interest payments rose from €1.8 billion to €7.8 billion. This was due to the impact of the huge Exchequer deficits on the national debt.
2. Transfer payments to households rose from €20.4 billion to €28.3 billion. This was mainly due to an increase in welfare payments to the unemployed and others affected by the recession.

FIGURE 8.1 Exchequer spending as a percentage of GDP, 2000–2012

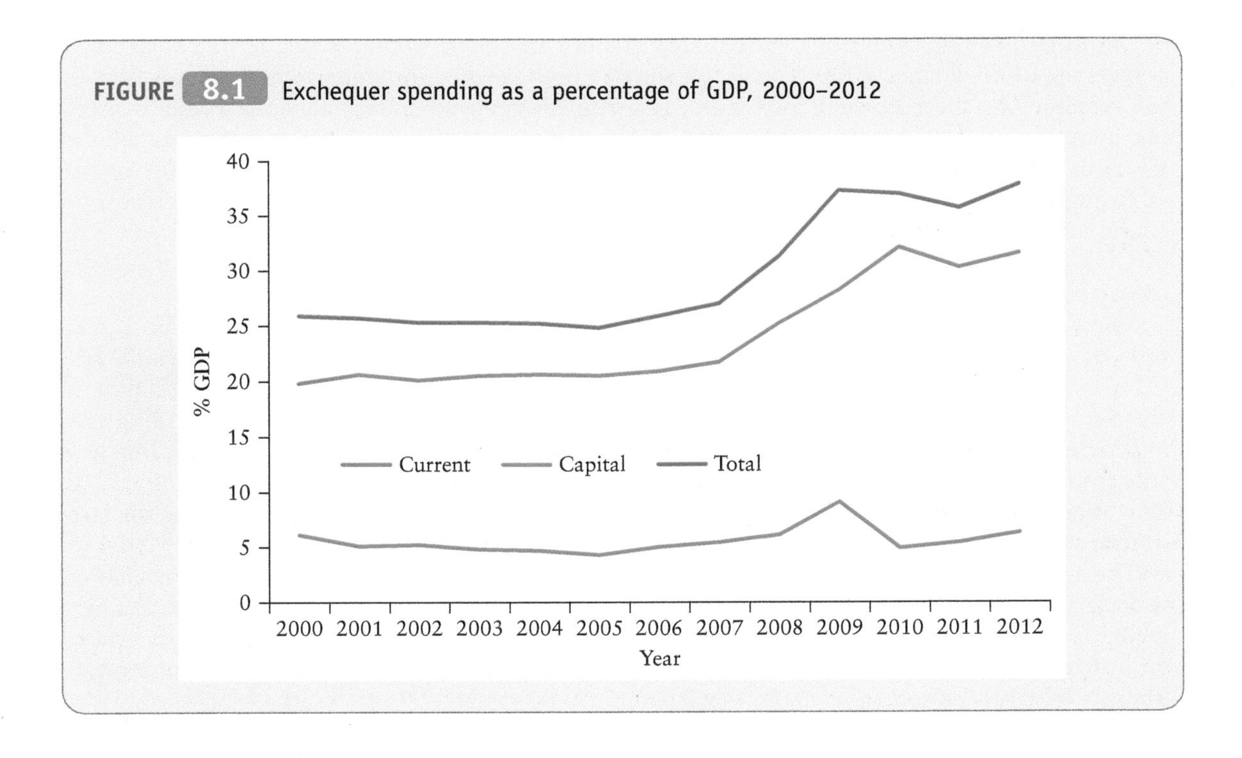

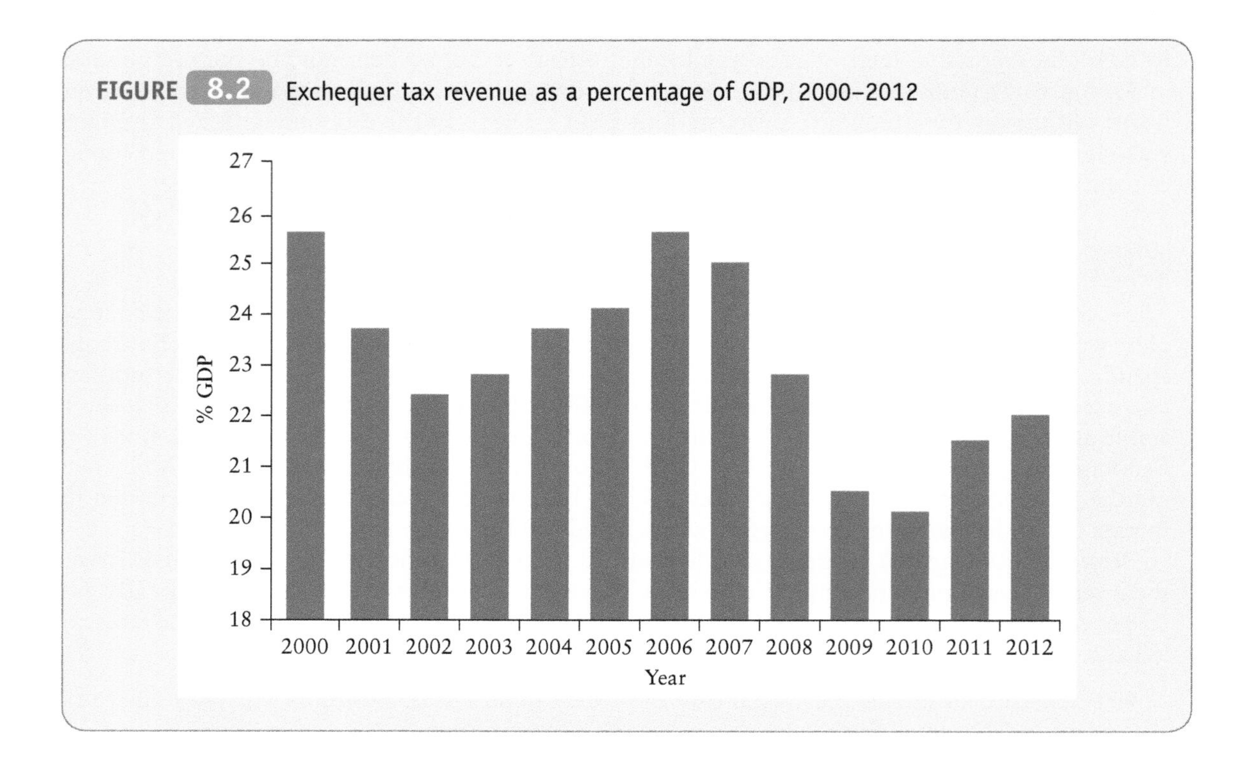

Despite recent cutbacks in the public capital programme, capital spending is still over six per cent of GDP, higher than it was on average between 2000 and 2007 and higher than in many other European countries.

Turning to the revenue side of the budget, Figure 8.2 shows total Exchequer tax receipts as a percentage of GDP since 2000. The graph shows how the recession undermined the government's tax revenue. As the recession took hold, government revenue collapsed, despite major income tax increases in the Budgets of 2009 and 2010. Between 2007 and 2010, tax receipts fell from €47.2 billion to €31.5 billion. As a percentage of GDP they fell from 25.0 in 2006 to 20.1 in 2010.

Falling revenue and rising expenditure led inevitably to a large increase in the public sector deficit, however we measure it. Figure 8.3 shows the Exchequer balance and the GGB as a percentage of GDP from 2000 to 2015. The figures for 2012 and later are projections based on the government's agreement with the Troika, as reviewed in spring 2012.

The remarkable transformation in the public finances is clear from this graph. Both measures of the public balance were in surplus if we take the totals for the period 2000–2007. Over this period we were actually paying down our national debt and relative to GDP it was shrinking rapidly. However, following the economic collapse after 2007, with spending rising and revenue falling, the deficit soared. It had reached 15 per cent of GDP by 2009, but worse was to come. The GGB measure of the deficit rose to an amazing 32 per cent of GDP in 2010. This includes about €32 billion (or 20 per cent of GDP) that was used to recapitalise the banks in that year.

The Exchequer balance, on the other hand, stabilised in the region of 11 per cent of GDP and is projected to decline sharply between 2012 and 2015 according to the terms of the Troika agreement. The realisation of this plan for restoring balance to the public finances depends crucially on how rapidly the economy grows and how successful the government is in implementing tough budgets over this period.

FIGURE 8.3 Government budget balances, 2000–2015

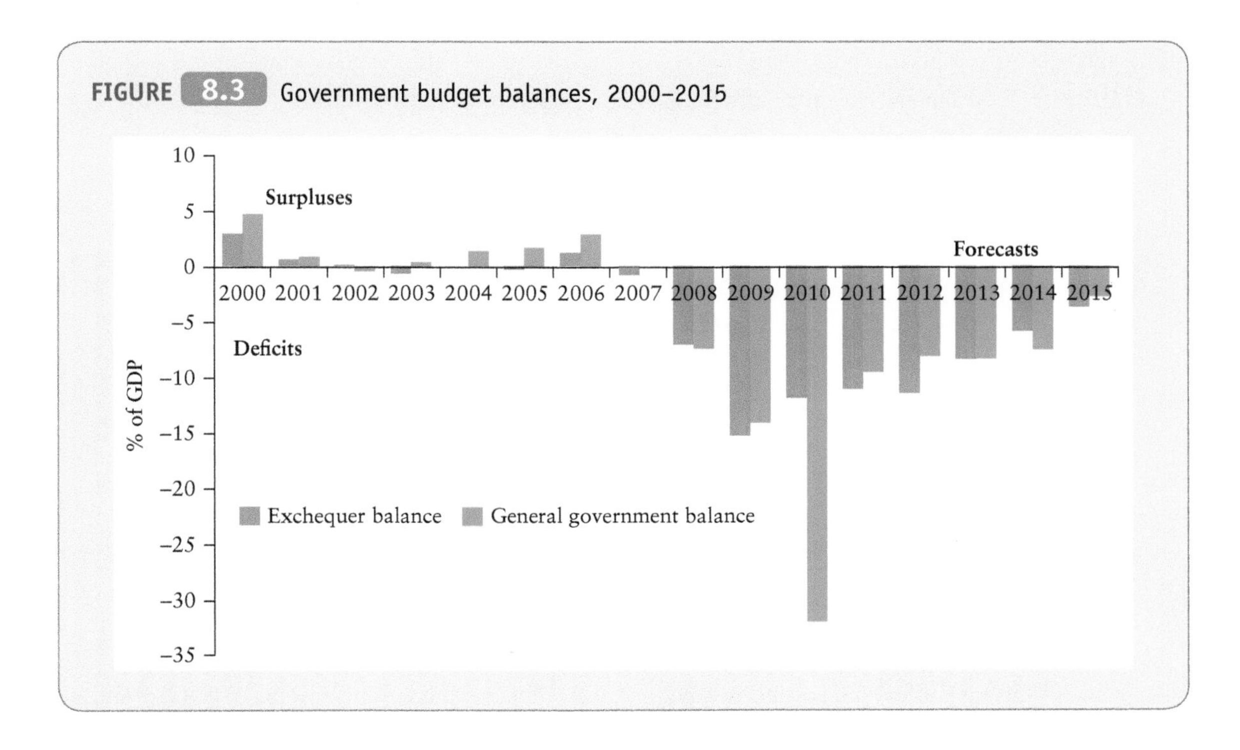

The restrained fiscal policies pursued prior to 2007, combined with rapid economic growth and low interest rates, shrank our national debt relative to GNP. From a peak of over 100 per cent at the end of the 1980s, the debt/GNP ratio fell to a low of 25 per cent in 2006 (Figure 8.4). This undoubtedly generated some complacency in Irish political circles; it seemed as if the country was very securely placed to weather any temporary setbacks that might come our way.

However, our fortunes were reversed with frightening speed due to the scale of borrowing required to finance the massive deficits incurred after 2007. By 2012 the debt/GDP ratio was back over 117 per cent and still rising. Stabilising this ratio is now the crucial challenge facing the country.

The tax take

The broad categories of tax revenue are:

- customs duties (a small category because our trade with the rest of the EU is not subject to these duties)
- income tax (now the largest source of revenue)
- excise taxes (on alcohol, tobacco, petrol, etc.)
- capital acquisitions tax (CAT), capital gains tax (CGT) and stamp duties (taxes incurred when buying, selling or transferring assets)
- corporation tax and VAT (second to income tax as a source of revenue).

Table 8.2 shows how much was raised under these headings in 2007 and 2011. It is striking that despite the significant increases in the tax rates in the 2009 and 2010 Budgets the yield from income tax was much the same in 2011 as it had been in 2007.

FIGURE 8.4 General government debt as a percentage of GNP, 1970–2015

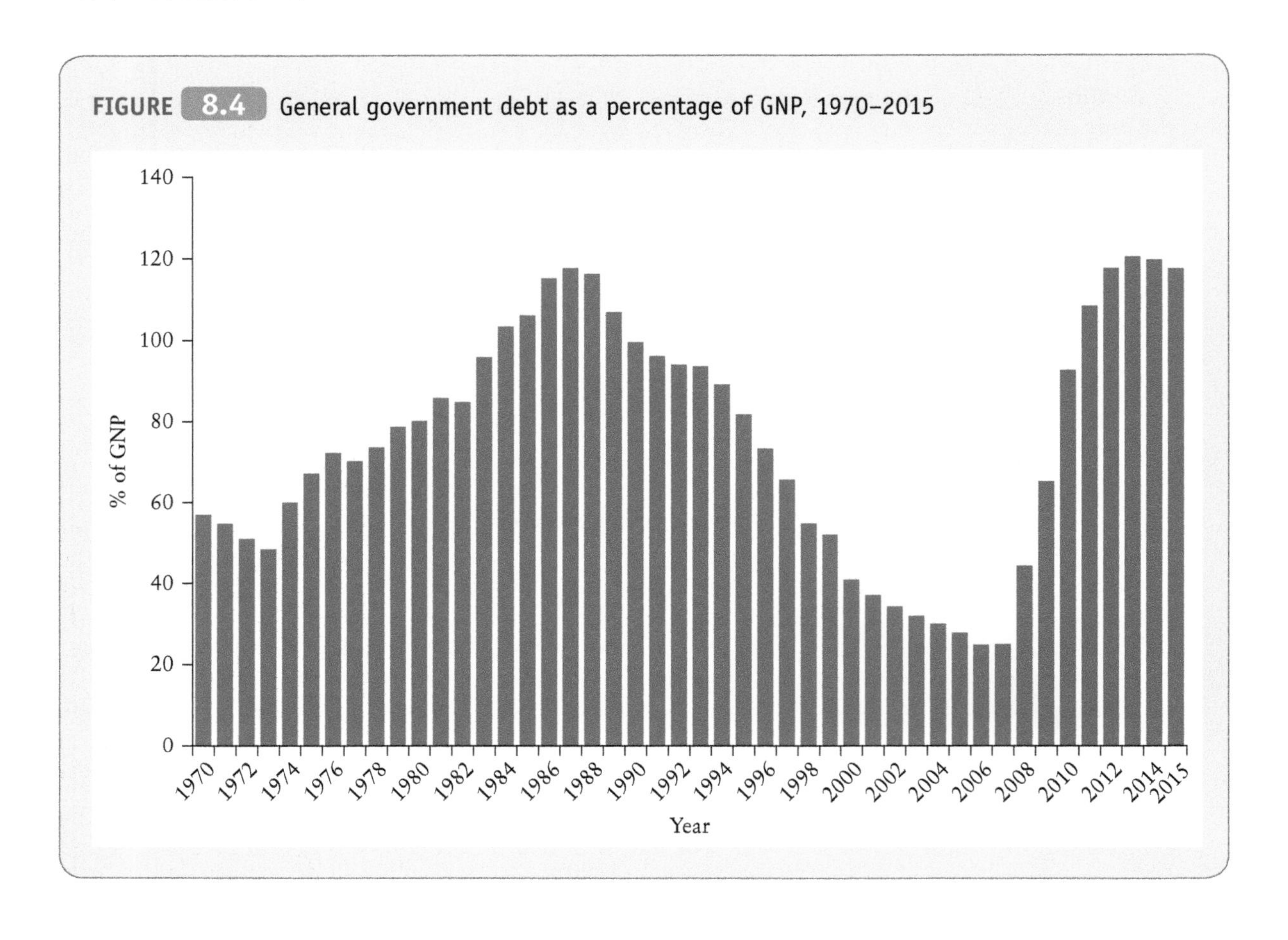

TABLE 8.2 Changes in tax receipts by category

	Year				
	2007		2011		
Tax	€ billion	% of total	€ billion	% of total	Percentage change 2007–11
Customs	0.3	0.6	0.2	0.7	−9.6
Excise duty	5.8	12.4	4.7	13.7	−19.9
CGT, CAT, stamp duty	6.7	14.1	2.1	6.0	−69.3
Income tax	13.6	28.7	13.8	40.5	1.7
Corporation tax	6.4	13.5	3.5	10.3	−44.9
VAT	14.5	30.7	9.7	28.6	−32.8
Total	47.2	100.0	34.0	100.0	−28.0

Note: CGT = capital gains tax; CAT = capital acquisitons tax

Source: Department of Finance Database

The collapse of receipts from CAT, CGT and stamp duties following the property market crash is striking. In 2011 they brought in less than one-third of their 2007 yield. One of the criticisms of the way the public finances were managed during the boom was that too much reliance was placed on the continuation of the bonanza yield of these taxes.

Excise revenue also fell after 2007, reflecting among other factors the fall in consumption of petrol due to declining traffic volumes.

NOTE: In Budget 2008, released in December 2007, the projected yield from CAT, CGT and stamp duties in 2008 was €6.5 billion – roughly its level in 2007. The actual yield of these taxes in 2008 was only €3.8 billion.

VAT is an *ad valorem* tax, levied as a percentage of the pre-tax price of goods and services. Its yield rises automatically with inflation and falls with deflation. Thus both the falling volume of sales and the low inflation rate contributed to the fall in VAT revenue between 2007 and 2011.

Excise duties, on the other hand, are specific taxes, levied in terms of so much per unit. They have to be raised to prevent inflation eroding their real value. The rates of excise on the 'old reliables' (tobacco and drink) are relatively high in Ireland compared with most other EU countries, while petrol is taxed more heavily in the UK, France and some other continental countries. Ireland is particularly vulnerable to avoidance (through cross-border imports) and evasion (through smuggling of untaxed drink and, especially, tobacco) on items on which our excise rates are higher than those in the UK.

Many commentators have drawn attention to Ireland's narrow tax base and the absence of taxes on wealth, especially land and property. The programme that Ireland agreed with the Troika in 2010 includes a commitment to re-introduce taxes on domestic property. However, the Household Charge introduced in 2012 has proved very unpopular and steps have yet to be taken to collect it from a large minority of those who are liable. It remains to be seen how successful the new and comprehensive system of domestic property taxation introduced in Budget 2013 will be.

Having presented this overview of the recent developments in the Irish public finances, we turn to a historical review of the evolution of the fiscal policy over the years.

8.4 Economic Planning

Our account of Ireland's current budgetary problems leads to the basic question: How have successive governments approached the planning of spending and taxation? Behind this lies another question: How have successive governments viewed the role of the state in the economy? We shall try to shed light on these issues by reviewing the history of 'economic planning' in Ireland. We look briefly at the evolution of policy from the 1950s to the current decade, and in more detail at the framework that dictates our approach to these issues now that we are adhering to an agreement with the Troika that is designed to bring our fiscal situation back into a sustainable situation over the coming three years.

The origins of economic planning in the 1940s and 1950s

The budgetary concept of a public capital programme was introduced after World War II in an attempt to systematise the public sector's annual spending on capital and development projects. This was linked to our participation in the post-war Marshall Plan because, as a condition of receiving aid, the US authorities wanted to see integrated proposals for spending it. The Department of Finance was opposed to borrowing, even on very favourable terms, for ambitious new projects, but the Department of Foreign Affairs, where Seán MacBride was minister, prepared a long-term development plan.

These tentative steps towards planning were overtaken by the stagnation of the early 1950s and the crisis of 1955–1956, when living standards and employment fell and emigration soared. The crisis was triggered by a number of factors. One of them was an abortive attempt to decouple Irish from British interest rates in 1955. The London discount rate was raised by 1.5 per cent, but the Irish banks were persuaded by the minister for finance not to follow suit, as they normally would. With Irish interest rates below British rates, there was a substantial outflow of reserves form the Irish banking system. The fiscal authorities responded to the crisis in early 1956 by imposing heavy import duties. This induced a domestic recession and led to a surge in emigration, which reached the post-war record level of 1.8 per cent of population in 1957 (Honohan 1994).

The crisis of the 1950s was severe and very disappointing to those who had hoped that an independent Ireland would be able to offer decent economic prospects to its young people. T. K. Whitaker, who was secretary of the Department of Finance at the time, commented, 'The mood of despondency was palpable. Something had to be done or the achievement of national independence would prove to have been a futility. Various attempts were made to shine a beam forward in this dark night of the soul.'

In early 1958, a survey of the economy was prepared in the Department of Finance and was published in November under the title *Economic Development*. This survey provided the basis for the First Programme for Economic Expansion, which was published soon after. The First Programme proposed three main policies to escape from the recession.

1. Public expenditure should be switched from non-productive to productive projects. In particular, capital spending on local authority housing and hospitals was to be reduced and spending on agriculture and industry increased.
2. Priority was to be given to a significant reduction in taxation, particularly income taxation, because 'high taxation is one of the greatest impediments to economic progress because of its adverse effects on saving and on enterprise'.
3. It was also suggested that the increase in wages and salaries in Ireland should lag behind that in Britain.

The hope was that agriculture would still serve as the engine of growth for the economy.

> **NOTE:** Out of a total of 212 pages of text in the First Programme, 100 were devoted to a detailed discussion of agriculture, forestry and fisheries. (The headline in the *Irish Independent* proclaimed, 'Easier credit schemes for farmers proposed'!) The same emphasis on rural development was apparent in the report of the Commission on Emigration published in 1954. That report looked mainly to agriculture to halt the outflow of population.

The conflict between trying to increase agricultural output while at the same time maintaining exceptionally high protective tariffs on industrial products was not discussed. In fact, the failure of protectionism and the need to move to an export-oriented strategy were not explicitly addressed. Although it was acknowledged that tariffs 'might impair the incentive to reduce costs and increase efficiency', the enthusiasm for free trade was muted.

The Programme set a target of achieving 11 per cent growth in the volume of GNP over the period 1959–63, but growth of 23 per cent was actually achieved (Figure 8.5). However, the improved performance was not attributable to any of the policies introduced in the Programme for the reason that few of its recommendations were implemented.

- The burden of taxation was not eased. Instead, income tax, in particular, rose inexorably.
- There was no rise in the level of manufacturing investment.
- Agriculture did not prove to be an engine of growth. Even after entry into the European Economic Community (EEC) and a massive injection of subsidies from the Community,

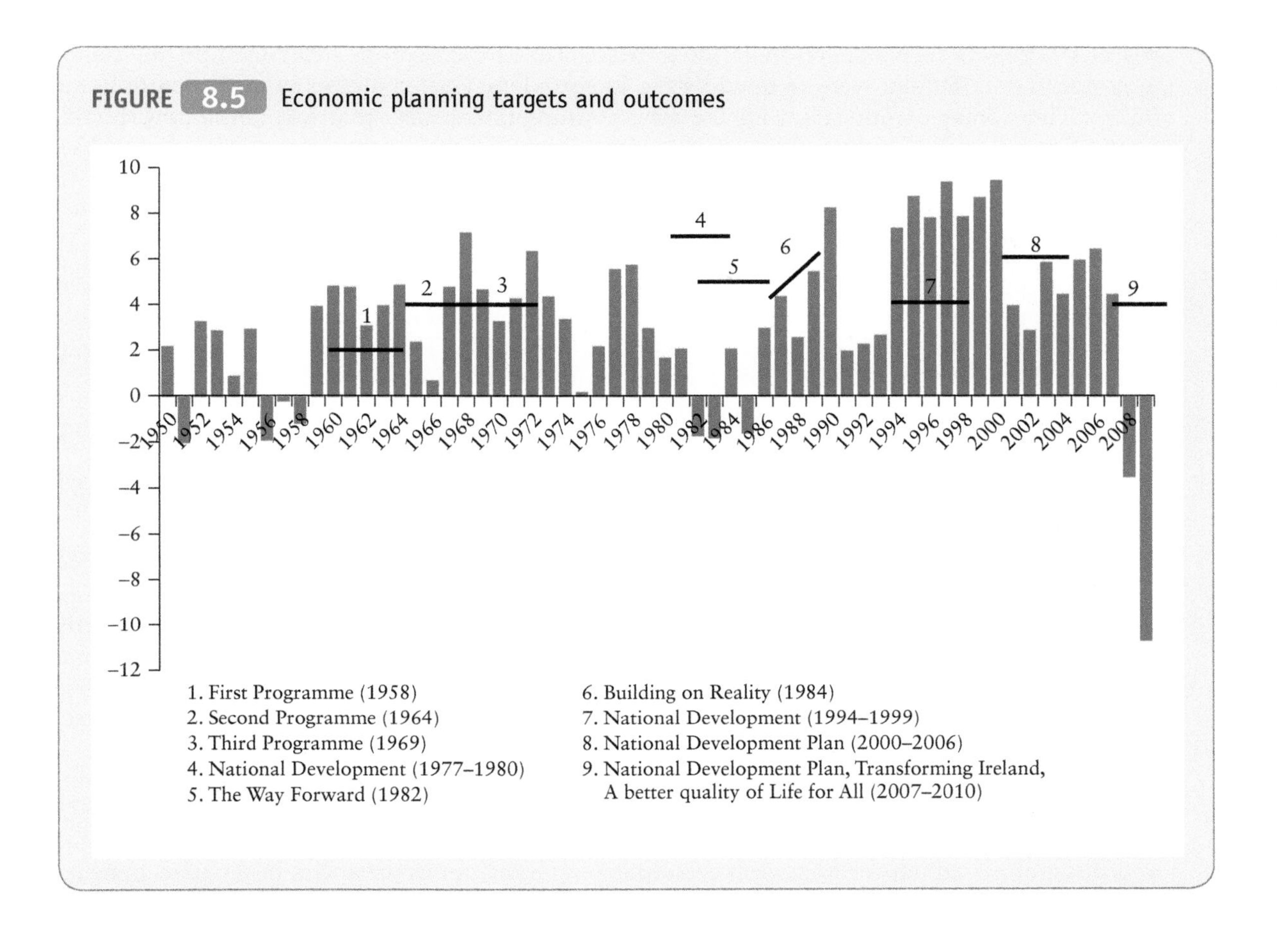

FIGURE 8.5 Economic planning targets and outcomes

the agriculture share of GNP declined steadily and the number employed on family farms continued to fall.

- The role of economic locomotive was assumed by industry, as the scale of the inflow of foreign capital far exceeded that in the First Programme's projections.
- Growth resumed in 1958/59, before any of the new policies could have taken effect.

The First Programme was not the last to contain targets and projections that proved very wide of the mark. Figure 8.5 shows the projected or target growth rates in real GNP cited in each of the economic programmes since the 1950s with the actual growth rate recorded in the relevant period. It can be seen that the projections bear little resemblance to the actual outcome. This highlights the point that large-scale planning of the sort attempted in Ireland in the past has such a poor track record that its value is called into question.

Due to the rapid expansion of the world economy during the 1960s the Irish economy recovered more or less spontaneously from the protracted recession of 1954–58. This was helped by the opening up of the economy, the dismantling of protectionism, which was only reluctantly envisaged in the Programme.

There is, however, no doubt that the First Programme captured the imagination of a much wider population than would normally be aware of a detailed discussion of economic policy. It served to gain acceptance of the importance of economic development as a policy objective. Up to this point, the weight of religious, nationalistic and left-wing opinion in Ireland was suspicious of material prosperity. Projects such as developing the transatlantic air connections with Shannon and building motorways in Dublin were rejected by the Labour–Fine Gael coalition as favouring only the wealthy. There was no enthusiasm for the mass consumption society that was developing in continental Europe and belatedly in Britain. Hostility to 'materialism' was widespread (Garvin 2004).

Economic planning in the 1960s and 1970s

It was inevitable that the dramatic improvement in the performance of the Irish economy in the years following the publication of the First Programme would be attributed to the Programme itself and that the planning exercise was repeated in a much more ambitious form in subsequent years. A Second Programme (1964–70) was published in 1964 and a Third Programme, Economic and Social Development, 1969–72 in 1969. These contained much more detailed statistical analyses of the Irish economy than had been attempted in 1958.

Both of these programmes projected a growth rate of four per cent a year in real GNP, which was the actual growth rate during the recovery from the deep recession of the 1950s. However, as may be seen from Figure 8.5, the projections of the growth of the economy proved as wide of the mark during the Second and Third Programmes as they had been in the First.

The greater detail contained in the later documents drew attention to their increasing lack of relevance as the planning periods progressed. The Second Programme was based on the assumption that Ireland would be a member of the EEC by 1970. France's veto of British entry shortly after its publication provided a rationale for abandoning the Programme. It also became clear after the publication of the Third Programme in 1969 that the targets contained in this, especially those relating to employment, would not be achieved. Thus the exercise in planning that was a central feature of Irish economic policy in the 1960s seemed to end in failure.

The degree of disillusionment with the process of planning in the turbulent economic circumstances of the 1970s is reflected in the words of the Minister for Finance, Richie Ryan, in his 1975 budget speech: '. . . of all the tasks that could engage my attention, the least realistic would be the publication of a medium- or long-term economic plan based on irrelevancies in the past, hunches as to the present and clairvoyance as to the future . . .'

Economic planning in the 1980s

Irish economic planning enjoyed renewed popularity after the formation of a new government in 1977. A Department of Economic Planning and Development was created. A plan called National Development 1977–1980 was published, containing specific targets for the growth of output and employment and the reduction in unemployment. It was envisaged that the public sector would provide an initial boost to the economy, after which the private sector would take up the running ('pump priming'). This required increased government spending and recruitment in the public sector. The optimistic projections on which the plan was based were rendered irrelevant by the second oil price crisis in 1979. With hindsight it is evident that the plan hindered, rather than helped, the adjustment of the economy to this shock.

Subsequent government statements on national development focused on the constraints facing the economy, rather than on specific targets for sectoral output. Following entry into the European Monetary System (EMS) in 1979, it was recognised that pay moderation was essential if competitiveness was to be improved. In 1981 the coalition government established a Committee on Costs and Competitiveness. Its report set out calculations of a wage norm based on forecast increases in our competitors' wage costs and likely changes in exchange rates. The idea was that if this norm were adhered to, there would be no deterioration in the country's competitiveness. Unfortunately, the norm proposed in October 1981 was rendered inappropriate almost as soon as it was published by a weakening of sterling. (The fall in sterling meant that greater wage moderation was required if Ireland was to maintain its competitiveness with the UK.)

A planning document, *The Way Forward*, prepared by the Fianna Fáil government during 1982 became the manifesto on which the party fought (and lost) the second general election of 1982. This document contained optimistic forecasts of economic growth based on a dramatic improvement in our international competitiveness, to be achieved by 'moderate pay increases combined with increases in productivity'.

In March 1983 the new coalition government established an independent National Planning Board to prepare a study that would form the basis for a new plan. (One of the authors of the present book, Brendan Walsh, was a member of the Committee on Costs and Competitiveness and of the National Planning Board.)

Proposals for Plan 1984–87 was published in April 1984. This document differed fundamentally from its immediate predecessors, and in some ways returned to the spirit of the First Programme, by presenting very detailed sectoral policy recommendations. It contained no fewer than 241 recommendations, ranging over many aspects of economic and social policy. The recommendations included:

- reducing the level of public sector borrowing by expenditure cuts rather than increased taxation
- increasing the efficiency of the public sector through privatisation and deregulation: the high costs of monopolistic state companies were acting as a drag on the ability of the private sector to compete internationally
- special targeted measures to alleviate the problem of long-term unemployment
- an emphasis on the goal of stabilising the debt/GNP ratio and reducing the level of taxation.

In many respects the package proposed resembled a structural adjustment programme of the type agreed between Ireland and the EU–ECB–IMF Troika in 2010.

The coalition government's plan, *Building on Reality*, was published in autumn 1984. This generally endorsed the policy recommendations contained in *Proposals for Plan*. It forecast that total employment would increase over the next three years as employment in private sector services grew rapidly and industrial employment began to recover from the recession. These projections proved too optimistic. The public finances continued to deteriorate until 1987 and employment did not begin to recover until 1988.

National wage agreements

Ambitious, large-scale economic plans of the type described in the previous section faded away in the mid-1980s. Economists were increasingly sceptical of the relevance of such exercises in a small, open economy like Ireland. This was, in turn, partly influenced by a renewed belief in the UK and the USA in market forces and the harmfulness of government interference in the productive areas of the economy. One issue that remained on the government's agenda, however, was how to deal with pay.

In Britain in the 1980s the power of the unions was undermined by confrontations, such as the one that crushed the miners' strike in 1984, and subsequent legislative changes. However, in Ireland there was no political agenda to curb union power. Instead the centralised approach to wage bargaining adopted in the 1970s returned to fashion.

The minority Fianna Fáil government that was formed in 1987 published a *Programme for National Recovery 1987–90* in October 1987. This programme was influenced by the successful experience of countries, such as the Netherlands, Austria, Norway and Sweden, that placed great emphasis on agreements between employers, trade unions and the government to adhere to specific increases in wages and salaries over a three-year period. A reduction in the rate of income tax was promised, and the prospect of increases in employment in selected state-sponsored enterprises was held out.

This approach was embodied in a series of successive programmes, such as:

- Programme for National Recovery (1988–90)
- Programme for Economic and Social Progress (PESP) (1991–94)
- Programme for Competitiveness and Work (1994–96)
- Partnership 2000 (1997–99)
- Programme for Prosperity and Fairness (2000–2003)
- Sustaining Progress (2003–2006)
- Towards 2016 (2006–2008).

These national agreements were hailed as examples of 'social partnership', that is co-operation between trade unions, employers, farmers and government on a broad economic agenda. The approach is also referred to as 'corporatism' because it gives a role to some but not all citizens as members of organisations rather than just as individuals. Supporters of this approach give it credit for maintaining industrial peace after the 1980s and providing a stable framework for business and moderating wage costs. Some have viewed the agreement as one of the reasons underlying Ireland's economic success after 1990.

However, national wage agreements can also be criticised for imposing a uniform wage increase on all sectors of the economy and being tailored to the needs of stronger unionised sectors (including the public sector), rather than those of small and medium-sized firms facing severe international competition. They also favoured trade union members over non-members and the self-employed.

A weakness of the partnership process became clear under the Programme for Prosperity and Fairness. This provided for a 15.75 per cent increase in wages over the period 2001–2004, but supplementary pay increases were provided in Budget 2001 to compensate for higher than expected inflation. Renegotiating national wage agreements in the light of unanticipated increases in inflation violated the idea that these agreements provided a stable and predictable framework for wage increases over the medium term.

A wider issue that emerged in the new century was the level of pay in the public sector relative to that in the private sector. Towards the end of the 1990s, the public sector unions argued that their members had not participated sufficiently in the prosperity of the 'Celtic Tiger' boom. Responding to the trade union argument that it was 'pay-back time' for the moderation they had exercised and the contribution they had made to the boom, it was agreed to undertake an exercise in 'public service benchmarking'.

The idea was to evaluate the job content of a wide range of public sector jobs and compare their rates of pay with comparable jobs (or jobs of equal value) in the private sector. This raised a host of issues about, for example, the value of the exceptionally generous pension provision in the public sector, the generally more secure and less stressful working environment, and so on. Also it was not always possible to find comparable jobs in the private sector. Is a private security job comparable to that of a member of the Garda Síochána? Standard human resource management metrics were applied to tackle these issues.

The Public Sector Benchmarking Body met for the first time in November 2000 and published its first report in June 2002. A range of pay increases was recommended, giving rise to an overall increase of 8.9 per cent in public sector pay. This was over and above any entitlements to pay increases under the Programme for Prosperity and Fairness, which were also awarded to public sector workers. Senator Joe O'Toole commented at the time that the benchmarking process was 'like an ATM for public service workers'.

Moreover, the highest level of public service pay was not included in the benchmarking exercise, but separate pay awards were also made by the Review Body on Higher Remuneration in the Public Sector. A pay increase of 7.5 per cent was recommended for higher civil servants in 2005–2006, and a variety of other substantial increases were awarded at later dates (Kelly *et al.* 2008).

A second benchmarking exercise was undertaken in 2006 and the report published in December 2007. (One of the authors of this book, Brendan Walsh, served on the second benchmarking body.) This time the evidence presented to the body warranted pay increases only in a very limited number of public sector jobs and virtually no special public sector pay awards were made. With hindsight we can say that this was a fortunate outcome because a second wave of across-the-board pay increases in the public sector would have made the budgetary crisis of 2008 even more disastrous than it was.

Meanwhile, the main partnership process trundled on. The seventh social partnership agreement, called Towards 2016, which was concluded in June 2006, provided for cumulative wage increases of 10.4 per cent over the period to early 2008. This agreement contained many aspirations for continuing improvements in the social welfare system.

The partnership process was greatly weakened by developments in 2008. For one, the Irish trade union movement had become progressively weaker over the years, and the post-2007 recession accelerated this process. Trade union density (membership as a proportion of the labour force) had declined from roughly 60 per cent in the 1980s to 30 per cent in recent years, and membership had become increasingly concentrated in the public services.

The scale of the economic crisis that hit the country after 2007 made many of the aspirations of Towards 2016 unrealistic. In September 2008 a new 21-month pay award was agreed but, following an 11-month pay freeze, the government rescinded on paying the first 3.5 per cent pay instalment in light of the fiscal deficit that had emerged. It could be said that this ended the partnership process.

Budget 2009 acknowledged the vastly changed economic landscape and the need to introduce special measures to deal with the new realities. An income levy of one per cent on incomes up to €100,000 and two per cent above that level was introduced. In February 2009 a pension levy was imposed on public sector workers, rising from five per cent to 9.6 per cent depending on salary. A supplementary budget was introduced in April 2009 that raised the income levy to two, four and six per cent, depending on income, and doubled the health levy. In 2011 the old system of levies was replaced by a Universal Social Charge (USC). If liable to the higher marginal rate of income tax, workers in the private sector, paying full rates of PRSI, now face a combined income tax plus USC plus PRSI of 52 per cent on marginal income.

In Budget 2010 public sector pay was cut by between five and 15 per cent. In Budget 2011 public sector pensions were cut on a sliding scale of up to eight per cent. The cumulative effect of these measures has been a very significant reduction in public service take-home pay and pensions completely outside the terms of national wage agreements.

Short-run, emergency fiscal measures swamped the medium-term vision that had been the core of the partnership approach. The process gradually tapered off into a series of agreements dealing mainly with workers in the public service, notably the Croke Park Agreement signed in 2010. While providing for increased flexibility in public sector work practices, it was also agreed that there would be no further reductions in rates and no compulsory redundancies until 2014.

National development plans

Even when ambitious but largely futile national planning exercises were abandoned after 2000, the need to take an orderly approach to the government's capital spending was still recognised. Increased funding for infrastructure projects became available from the EU in the 1990s and this required a more systematic approach to project evaluation. The EU was not prepared to give the Irish government money to spend on projects unless it could be shown that these had a sound economic and social justification. The response was to prepare more detailed public capital programmes, based on cost-benefit appraisals. Although called 'plans', these capital programmes differed fundamentally from the discredited attempts at macroeconomic planning of the 1960s and 1970s.

In October 1993 the coalition government published the *National Development Plan: 1994–1999*. This plan envisaged spending €28 billion between 1993 and 1999 on a whole range of areas including industry, natural resources, tourism and transport. Expenditure was funded by the EU (39.4 per cent), the Irish public sector (42.2 per cent) and the private sector (18.4 per cent). The basic objective was to create jobs by developing the agricultural, industrial and services sectors, by improving infrastructure and by developing the skills of the workforce through education and training. The plan anticipated an annual real growth rate of 3.5 per cent from 1994 to 1999. This target proved too pessimistic. The period from 1994 to 2000 was characterised by an unprecedented growth of output and employment that was not anticipated at the time this Plan was drafted. This provides yet another illustration of the inability of policy makers to foresee the behaviour of a small open economy.

The National Development Plan 2000–2006 proposed spending €51.5 billion over the seven years of the plan. Most of the money was to be put into upgrading the national road network, improving public transportation, reducing environmental pollution and addressing housing shortages. Money was also earmarked for developing human resource skills and tackling deprivation and poverty.

The last of these plans, the National Development Plan 2007–2013 was launched in January 2007. Subtitled 'Transforming Ireland: A Better Quality of Life for All', it proposed a €184 billion capital spending programme over seven years, with 'economic infrastructure' and 'social inclusion' the two largest components, amounting together to 57 per cent of the total.

These plans have been repeatedly criticised by economists for including large projects for which no adequate cost-benefit studies were published. Examples include the Dublin Port Tunnel and Dublin Airport Terminal 2. In addition, the extraordinary cost over-runs associated with many of the projects have not been properly investigated. A spectacular example was the Green and Red Dublin Luas network, which was costed at €254 billion but eventually cost €770 billion to build.

This problem with the planning of Irish capital spending continues. Despite the lack of evaluation of previous large-scale projects, the most recent National Development Plan contained commitments to:

- reopen the Western Rail Corridor between Ennis and Claremorris
- complete the Metro North line from Dublin city centre to Swords via Dublin Airport
- a phased development of the (Dublin) Metro West line.

Critics point out that the 2007 Plan showed how little had been learned from the experience of capital budgeting during the boom period. It was inevitable that the economic crash and the harsher fiscal realities would lead to a sharp reduction in capital spending, but even in 2012 it is still running at a high level relative to GDP by European standards and too much of it is based on political rather than economic rationales.

NOTE: Perhaps the most notorious example of grandiose spending proposals that were not supported by cost-benefit appraisal were the plans for a National Sports Campus with a capacity of 75,000 in Abbotstown, north Dublin – labelled the 'Bertie Bowl' because it was favoured by former Taoiseach Bertie Ahern. This was not included in the National Development Plan and controversy raged over its likely cost as well as over its potential benefits. No systematic cost-benefit appraisal of the project was ever published. After much disagreement it was finally shelved in September 2002, but it had already cost the taxpayer about €500 million. In recent years the capital city has handled all its major sporting commitments as well as many large concerts in Croke Park and the new Aviva Stadium.

The new era of economic austerity led to a major reduction in the scale of capital spending and many projects that had been dreamed of before the crisis have been postponed. Nonetheless, the culture of bringing forward capital spending without transparent evaluation procedures persists.

In 2012 the government released details of a 'stimulus package' for capital projects which will see funding provided through the National Pension Reserve Fund (NPRF), future sales of state assets, and public–private partnerships funded by the European Investment Bank (EIB). Two additional road projects are included in the package – the N17/N18 Gort to Tuam motorway and motorways and bypasses round New Ross and Enniscorthy in Wexford. Despite the expensive planning mistakes of the recent past, these projects have been justified on vague criteria such as completing regional road networks and job creation. (Highway construction is not labour-intensive!) It is not clear that either of them would pass the test of careful analytical scrutiny in these austere times.

Summary

Economic planning of the type undertaken by successive Irish governments in the 1960s is now unfashionable. The Irish government has moved from ambitious macroeconomic plans that were inherently incapable of being successfully implemented to looser 'indicative plans' or 'programmes'. Centralised wage deals were a key feature of these. They were credited with restoring industrial peace and facilitating the non-inflationary economic growth recorded down to 2007. However, this process was already unravelling due to large-scale public service pay awards that were made outside the central agreements and the renegotiation of agreements to take account of unanticipated inflation after 2001. The post-2007 crisis dramatically reduced the scope for national wage agreements and, as of 2012, all that remains is an agreement covering pay and terms of employment in the public service until 2014.

Parallel with the large-picture 'Programmes', the government introduced a series of capital spending programmes, or National Development Plans, that ran from 1994 to 2013. These set out priorities for spending on economic and environmental infrastructure, social housing, education and training. Much was achieved under these Plans, although not in the most cost-effective manner. Many grandiose projects were included for reasons of local political advantage or simply as flagship projects that lacked real economic justification. The crisis in the public finances since 2008 has forced a reduction in the scale of capital spending, although it remains high relative to GDP by European standards and the 'stimulus package' launched in 2012 included projects for which cost-benefit appraisals have not been published.

8.5 Irish Fiscal Policy in Historical Perspective

Even if we accept the negative view of economic planning and programming taken in the foregoing review, it is still possible to believe that government fiscal policy has a role to play in smoothing the economy's growth path by adjusting its contribution to aggregate demand along the lines described in Chapter 7.

In section 8.3 above we discussed the impact of the post-2007 recession on the public finances and outlined the crisis we face on this front and how it constrains our freedom of action in regard to fiscal policy.

In this section we look back and provide a historical perspective on Irish fiscal policy from the 1970s to the outbreak of the current crisis.

Figure 8.6 shows the total Exchequer balance and the current budget balance (which is part of the total) as a percentage of GNP from 1973 to 2007. (We noted earlier that until 2008 the Exchequer balance was very similar to the GGB.) There were three distinct sub-periods. From the early 1970s until the late 1980s the country incurred very large Exchequer deficits. The Exchequer borrowing requirement (EBR) was over 10 per cent of GNP in eight of these years. Over half the total Exchequer deficit was accounted for by the current budget deficit, which reached almost eight per cent of GNP in some years.

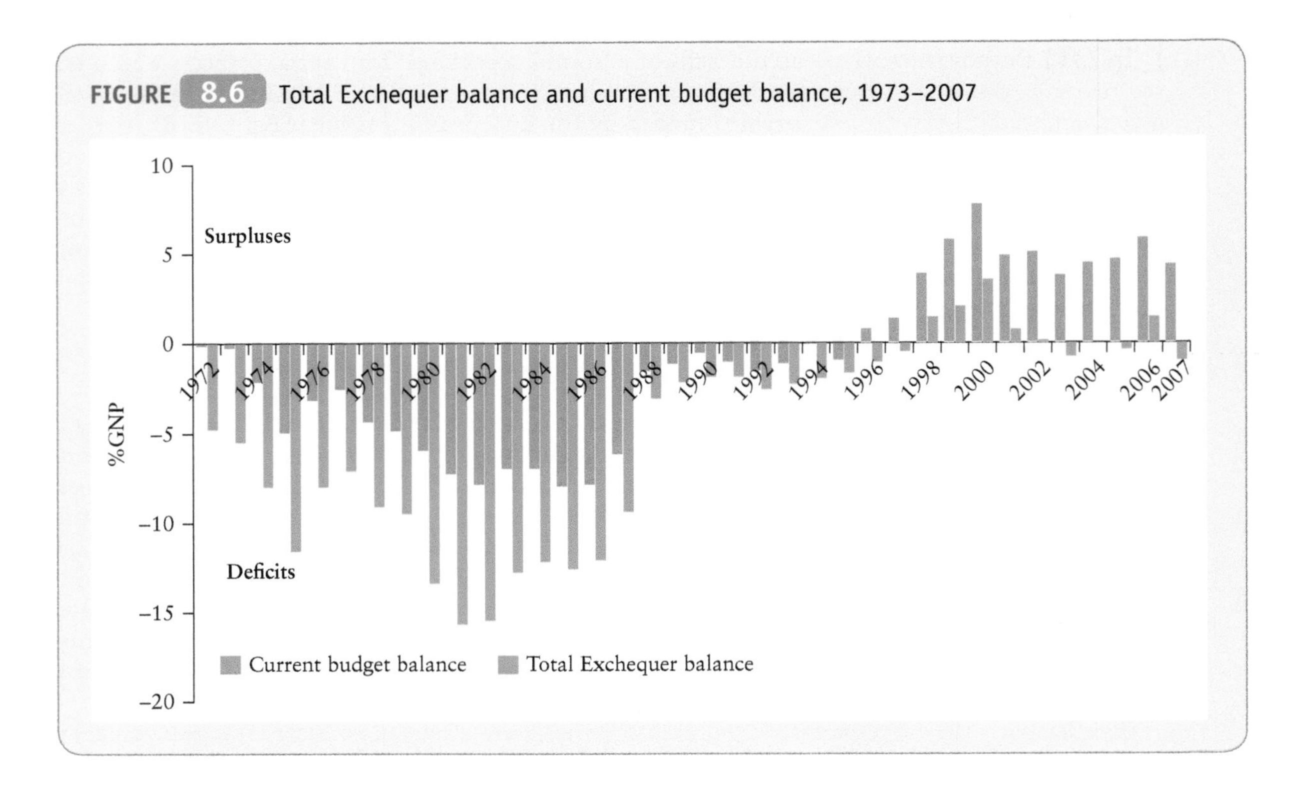

FIGURE 8.6 Total Exchequer balance and current budget balance, 1973–2007

A high level of borrowing for 'capital' purposes contributed to the large Exchequer deficits in the 1980s. Unfortunately, much of this borrowing was not used for worthwhile investment in roads, schools and hospitals, but was pumped into loss-making state enterprises such as Nitrogen Éireann Teo, Aer Lingus, Córas Iompair Éireann, Bord na Móna and many others. In later years the gap between the two was smaller and reflected mainly the state's investment in capital formation.

A dramatic improvement occurred after 1988. The Exchequer deficit fell to a sustainable two per cent of GNP and the current budget was balanced. By the middle of the 1990s surpluses began to emerge on the current budget and the overall balance fell close to zero. Some exceptionally large current budget surpluses were recorded during the boom years of the early twenty-first century, which helped finance a higher level of capital spending.

These large swings in the public finances were mainly driven by swings in the performance of the economy. The deficits of the 1980s could be blamed on a static economy that was choked by steadily rising tax rates. High unemployment led to higher social welfare spending and slow growth caused tax receipts to slump. The current budget deficit reached an unsustainable level of eight per cent of GNP despite several austerity budgets. The 'automatic stabilisers' were in operation but they did not stabilise the economy.

The improvement in the late 1980s owed something to the switch of emphasis from tax increases to spending cuts, but it was mainly due to a resumption of growth. That, in turn, owed much to external factors. Once again, the further improvement in the public finances towards the end of the 1990s reflected the accelerated growth of that period rather than discretionary changes in fiscal policy.

We turn now to different phases of the period between 1973 and 2007 and the economic philosophy of the ministers who were responsible for fiscal policy over these years (see Box 8.1).

Box 8.1 Finance ministers from the foundation of the state to 2012

1	Eoin MacNeill	22/01/1919
2	Michael Collins	02/04/1919
3	William T. Cosgrave	26/08/1922
4	Ernest Blythe	06/12/1922
5	Seán MacEntee	09/03/1932
6	Seán T. Ó Ceallaigh	16/09/1939
7	Frank Aiken	19/06/1945
8	Patrick McGilligan	18/02/1948
9	Seán MacEntee	14/06/1951
10	Gerard Sweetman	02/06/1954
11	James Ryan	20/03/1957
12	Jack Lynch	21/04/1965
13	Charles J. Haughey	16/11/1966
14	George Colley	09/05/1970
15	Richie Ryan	14/03/1973
16	George Colley	05/07/1977
17	Michael O'Kennedy	12/12/1979
18	Gene Fitzgerald	16/12/1980
19	John Bruton	30/06/1981
20	Ray MacSharry	09/03/1982
21	Alan Dukes	14/12/1982
22	John Bruton	14/02/1986
23	Ray MacSharry	10/03/1987
24	Albert Reynolds	25/11/1988
25	Bertie Ahern	14/11/1991
26	Ruairi Quinn	15/12/1994
27	Charlie McCreevy	26/06/1997
28	Brian Cowen	29/09/2004
29	Brian Lenihan	07/05/2008
30	Michael Noonan	09/03/2011

1972–77: Departure from fiscal rectitude

Before the 1970s, Irish ministers for finance did not consciously attempt to implement an active fiscal policy. Annual budgets were framed primarily to raise the money needed to finance the government's day-to-day spending. Although borrowing was incurred to finance the Public Capital Programme, fiscal policy was not consciously used as an instrument of demand management or to try to reduce the level of unemployment. This situation changed radically after the first oil shock in 1973.

The year 1973 was a watershed in Western economic history. The Organisation of Petroleum Exporting Countries (OPEC) raised crude oil prices from $3 to $12 a barrel. This was a severe shock to both the demand and the supply sides of economies dependent on imported energy. On the demand side, the enormous price rise greatly increased expenditure on imports because there was little scope in the short run for reducing dependence on imported energy.

An increase in the price of imports shifts the aggregate demand (AD) schedule down to the left. On the supply side, the increase in the cost of a basic input has the effect of shifting the short-run aggregate supply (SRAS) schedule up to the left. Putting the two effects together, real output falls and the price level increases. This combination of falling output and rising prices is known as stagflation. This is what happened throughout the developed economies in 1973/4 and again in 1979.

The immediate policy response to the oil crisis was to try to maintain the level of aggregate demand by increasing government spending without any corresponding increase in the level of taxation. However, an expansionary fiscal policy was not an adequate response to the oil price shock. An expansionary fiscal policy will shift the AD curve upwards to the right. The result will be an increase in real output but also a further increase in the price level. Hence the fiscal policy exacerbates the inflation problem.

In 1975 the government recognised the need to dampen the inflationary pressures that were building up. Food subsidies and tax cuts were introduced in a mini-budget in mid-1975 in the hope that this would moderate wage inflation. In fact it increased the current budget deficit and added to inflationary pressures. By 1975, the current budget deficit and the GGD increased to 5 per cent and 11.6 per cent of GNP respectively. The national debt/GNP ratio climbed steadily (see Figure 8.4).

In a reversal of policy, in 1976 Minister for Finance Richie Ryan raised taxes and curbed expenditure as the economy began to recover. A wealth tax was introduced, and VAT on wine, spirits and petrol was introduced. (This earned him the title 'Minister for Hardship' and 'Red Richie' in the media.) As a result of these corrective measures, combined with a recovery in economic growth, the current budget deficit fell to 2.6 per cent of GNP, and the GGD to 7.1 per cent, in 1977. It appeared that the economy had weathered the oil crisis and the public finances were moving in the right direction.

In fact the structural problems created by the oil price shock remained unresolved and Ireland, like most other OECD countries, was still vulnerable to further increases in the price of oil. It was not until after the second oil price shock, at the end of the 1970s, that investment in energy conservation began in earnest.

1977–81: Going for broke

The general election of 1977 destroyed the chances of maintaining progress towards restoring order in the public finances. The political parties vied with one another in promising to cut taxes and raise expenditure. (Both major parties claimed credit for proposing the idea of abolishing rates on private houses.) The incoming Fianna Fáil government exceeded their manifesto commitments to tax cuts and increased expenditure.

Minister for Finance George Colley in his 1978 budget increased income tax allowances and public sector pay and abolished rates and the wealth tax. A total of 11,250 new posts were authorised in the public sector between mid-1977 and the end of 1978. As a result of these measures, in 1979 the current budget deficit increased to 4.9 per cent and the GGD to 9.5 per cent of GNP. This occurred at a time when the economy was already growing at an unsustainable rate: real GNP expanded by 5.6 per cent in 1977 and was forecast to continue to grow rapidly in 1978 even if there had been no fiscal stimulus. Employment and real earnings were increasing rapidly and for the first time ever there was substantial net immigration to Ireland.

The rationale for the 1978 budget was, first, the need to reduce unemployment which, although falling, was still above its 1973 level. Second, borrowing from the ideas of Arthur Laffer that we discussed in Chapter 7, the policy was described as a 'self-financing fiscal boost'. It was believed that the increase in the real growth rate would generate extra taxes, which would quickly eliminate the budget deficit. The tax cuts would be self-financing.

Events between 1978 and 1980 confounded the hope that the budget deficit would be quickly eliminated. A second oil price shock occurred in 1979 and the price of crude oil rose to over $40 a barrel. The rate of growth of real GNP fell to 1.7 per cent in 1980 and to −1.7 per cent in 1982. By 1982, the current budget deficit rose to 7.2 per cent and the GGD to 11.1 per cent of GNP. The national debt/GNP ratio had increased to 85 per cent and was still rising rapidly (see Figure 8.4).

Of even greater significance was the fact that the real growth rate had fallen to −1.7 per cent, unemployment was up to 10 per cent, inflation rose to 20 per cent and the current account balance of payments deficit rose to 11 per cent of GNP. The Irish economy was clearly in a deep crisis.

The fiscal deficit was already so large and the level of the national debt was growing so rapidly that no scope remained for trying to offset the deflationary impact of the oil price increase through an expansionary fiscal policy.

NOTE: The budget deficits incurred after 1973 and our resort to external borrowing to finance them had turned us into a net debtor country by 1980: the level of our external public debt had reached £2,207 million, whereas our official external reserves were only £1,346 million.

There was little general awareness of the speed with which the country was being plunged into debt and the implications for the future tax burden. Some economists argued that there was no need to worry about further external borrowing because our international credit rating was still sound and additional borrowed money could be used to generate employment and create valuable assets. But in reality much of the borrowed money was wasted – it went to finance day-to-day expenditure or projects with a rate of return that was much lower than the rate of interest. Further borrowing for such purposes was not warranted, regardless of the willingness of international bankers to lend to the country. Moreover, the growth of public sector debt throughout Eastern Europe, Africa and Latin America was to trigger off an international crisis in 1982 that completely changed the attitude of international creditors to countries in Ireland's situation.

This phase of Ireland's economic history illustrates many of the points made in Chapter 7 concerning the problems of successfully implementing a stabilisation policy:

- There was confusion about how rapidly the economy was growing.
- The policies that were implemented began to take effect long after the conditions they were designed to address had changed.
- The desire of politicians to be elected prevailed over economic analysis.

1981–86: Picking up the pieces

In mid-1981 a new coalition government consisting of Fine Gael and the Labour Party was elected and in early 1982 a deflationary budget was introduced to try to correct the deteriorating fiscal situation. The Minister for Finance, John Bruton, promised to phase out the budget deficit over four years. A VAT rate of 18 per cent was imposed on children's clothing and footwear. (There had been zero VAT on children's footwear and one minister expressed concern that women with small feet were availing of this!) Excise duties, income tax, postal and phone charges were all increased and income tax allowances were reduced. The independent socialist TD for Limerick East, Jim Kemmy, could not support the tax on children's footwear and defected to the Opposition benches. The budget was defeated by 82 votes to 81 votes. John Bruton remains the only minister for finance not to have his budget ratified by the Dáil.

This led to another general election and a minority Fianna Fáil government supported by the Workers' Party was returned to office. In November 1982, the Workers' Party withdrew their support and another general election saw the return of a Fine Gael–Labour Party coalition.

The financial and economic crisis continued to intensify. By 1984, the national debt/GNP ratio was over 100 per cent and was still rising. This was clearly an unsustainable trajectory. The gravity of the economic crisis facing the country was now widely appreciated. The main political parties agreed that restoring order to the public finances had to take precedence over trying to reduce the level of unemployment.

The approach taken by the coalition government over the period 1982–86 of raising the level of taxation and reducing current expenditure was not successful. The following reasons can be advanced for the failure.

- A ban on public sector recruitment did not bring the wage bill under control.
- Rising unemployment caused social welfare (transfer payments) to increase.
- The accumulating national debt and rising interest rates caused debt interest payments to increase.
- Higher tax rates did not yield more revenue, due to the stagnation of the economy. Minister for Finance Alan Dukes's 1983 budget set a record for tax increases but produced hardly any reduction in the current budget deficit. This lent some support to the Laffer hypothesis and led to a belief that tax cuts would be more appropriate in Ireland's circumstances, even if they led to still larger deficits in the short run.

The result was that by 1986 the current budget deficit had reached 7.3 per cent and the general government deficit GGD nine per cent and the debt/GNP ratio continued to rise. The narrowing gap between the total and current deficits showed that the coalition government found it easier to reduce capital than current spending.

In the autumn of 1986 disappointing Exchequer returns led to further loss of confidence in the economy, which was manifested in nervousness on the foreign exchange markets and a three percentage-point increase in Irish relative to UK interest rates. It had become clear that the strategy of raising taxes was self-defeating. The economy was shrinking under the increasing burden of taxation and capital was fleeing the country for more benign environments. (It is estimated that in 1986 the private capital outflow reached over £1 billion, despite exchange controls.)

The public finances were on a downward spiral due to the operation of the 'automatic stabilisers' – falling revenue and rising transfer payments. It was generally accepted that the problem had to be tackled through drastic cuts in expenditure rather than further tax increases, but the coalition government split and fell on this issue. The cuts in current expenditure proposed by the Minister for Finance, John Bruton, in the draft *Book of Estimates* in October 1986 were not acceptable to his Labour Party partners in government, who still favoured maintaining a high level of expenditure and trying to reduce the deficit by increasing taxation.

1987–91: Order restored

The formation of a minority Fianna Fáil government in January 1987 initially increased the economic uncertainty. While in opposition the party had vehemently attacked what they had labelled the 'monetarist' or 'Thatcherite' policies of the coalition government. They fought and won the election with promises of higher government spending. However, once in office the new government, with the support of the main opposition parties, tackled head-on the problem of curbing government expenditure. In the 1987 budget, the Minister for Finance, Ray MacSharry, reduced current government spending by more than had been proposed by Fine Gael in the draft *Book of Estimates* that had led to the downfall of the coalition government (earning him the nickname Mac the Knife). There were some cuts in public spending, a public sector pay freeze, and an embargo on public sector recruitment.

The restoration of order in the public finances gained momentum in the January 1988 Budget when an unprecedented three per cent reduction in government spending was passed. This cut in expenditure was with the support or abstention of the main opposition parties and came to be known as the Tallaght Strategy – so-called after a speech supporting the government in its economic and Northern Ireland policies was made by the Opposition leader Alan Dukes in Tallaght, County Dublin. By the end of 1988, the current budget deficit fell to 1.5 per cent and the Exchequer deficit to 2.3 per cent of GNP (Figure 8.6).

The 1988 Budget also proposed a tax amnesty (known as the Tax Incentive Scheme), with the objective of collecting £30 million in unpaid taxes. This was a recognition of the significant scale of tax evasion that had grown up as tax rates rose to penal levels. During 1988 over £500 million was raised from this source and from the application of a new system of self-assessment of income tax to the self-employed. These amounts far exceeded the most optimistic forecasts. It is believed that a significant amount of money had been hoarded outside the financial system and, once the tax was paid on this money, the funds came back into the economy and boosted expenditure on goods and services. In addition, as growth resumed, other sources of revenue (VAT and excises) were buoyant and expenditure was held below the level projected in the budget.

The 1990s

During the 1990s, especially after 1993, the Irish economy experienced an unprecedented combination of rapid growth and low inflation. Indeed, as we have noted, its performance over these years was remarkable by any standards. The stance of fiscal policy moved away from the failed stabilisation policies of earlier years. Policy became dominated by the objective of qualifying for membership of the EMU in 1999. This entailed achieving a government deficit of less than three per cent of GDP and a debt/GDP ratio of 60 per cent. In May 1998, Ireland was deemed to have met the entry criteria and was invited to join the new common currency club, the EMU.

Exceptionally high growth rates continued into the new century, unemployment dropped to historically low levels, inflation remained relatively subdued, and the public finances remained within the restrictions placed on members of the EMU under the 'excessive deficits procedure'. This was more than could be said for countries like Germany, whose public finances were in disarray following the reunification of West and East Germany.

Yet it can be argued that the stance of Irish fiscal policy was relatively expansionary during the boom years, tending to fuel the flames of the strong expansion that was already under way. Particularly during the period from 2003 to 2007 larger budget surpluses should have been run, but this was contrary to the stated philosophy of the Minister for Finance Charlie McCreevey, who famously stated: 'when I have it I spend it, and when I don't, I don't'. He seemed to believe that the tax-cutting measures in his five budgets would increase the supply side of the economy and facilitate a higher sustainable growth rate in the long run. Although a National Pension Reserve Fund was launched in 2001, with hindsight it is now clear that it would have been prudent to have kept a tighter rein on current spending and to have proceeded more slowly with tax reductions during the boom.

The crisis of 2008

We have already discussed in some detail the impact of the post-2007 recession on the Irish economy. We saw that it had a devastating effect on the public finances. Ministers of finance had become excessively dependent on cyclically sensitive tax receipts, especially stamp duties on property transactions, capital gains taxes and capital acquisitions taxes. As we showed in Table 8.2, these sources of revenue dried up suddenly as the housing and stock markets collapsed. At the same time rising unemployment and a fall in consumer spending led to significant falls in income tax, VAT and excise tax receipts, while social welfare payments ballooned. As a result, the budget deficit soared.

In addition, the government was forced to inject funds into the banking system. Overall debt and borrowing was becoming unsustainable and the interest rate facing our National Treasury Management Agency (NTMA) when borrowing on international money markets began to rise.

In order to reduce the budget deficit, the Minister for Finance, Brian Lenihan, in Budget 2009, invoked a 'call to patriotic action'. He introduced a series of budgets designed to cut the current budget deficit to 6.5 per cent. While it was clearly pro-cyclical to raise taxes and cut expenditure as the economy plunged into recession, the minister had no choice. The hard realities of having to borrow on the scale now facing the Irish Exchequer demanded immediate corrective action. As we noted above, the austerity package targeted public sector pay with several levies and pay cuts. It is estimated that public sector net salaries are down between 13 and 21 per cent as a result of these measures. At the same time, of course, unemployment has reduced a lot of private sector incomes to the level of the Jobseeker's Allowance.

So far the burden of adjustment has relied more heavily on increasing taxation rather than cutting public expenditure. The Special Group on Public Service Numbers and Expenditure Programme, widely referred to as An Bórd Snip Nua, chaired by economist Colm McCarthy, reported in June 2009 and identified the possibility of €5.3bn of savings in public spending including 17,300 public service job cuts and a five per cent cut in social welfare. In the following three years little action was taken to implement these recommendations.

Despite the progress made by the Irish government in tackling its fiscal imbalances during 2010, external events blew the economy off course. In the course of the year the Greek economic crisis became unmanageable and the government could no longer access sufficient funds on the bond markets to fund its day-to-day spending.

In May 2010 the Greek government finally applied to the Troika for an agreement to borrow €120 billion. This tended to focus the attention of the bond markets on the situation in Ireland and Portugal. The sudden deterioration in the fiscal balances in the weaker (peripheral) countries of the EU re-awakened markets to sovereign risk and the possibility that governments might default on their borrowings. The spill-over impact of the deterioration of one country's public finances on the ability of other comparable countries to borrow is known as 'financial contagion'.

The increased reluctance of bond purchasers (such as banks, insurance companies and pension funds) to accept the risk of holding the debts issued by countries in fiscal difficulties compounded the problems facing Ireland in 2010. Initially, the fear of default seemed to be confined to the peripheral countries of Europe, but by 2012 these fears had begun to spread even to countries like France and Belgium.

The fiscal correction of 2008–2010, which amounted to taking €14.6 billion out of the economy, failed to convince the international bond markets that Ireland's creditworthiness was improving. The spread between Irish and German bond yields widened significantly. On 18 July 2011, the yield on a 10-year Irish government bond was 14.08 per cent compared to 2.25 per cent on a similar German bond.

The Irish banks experienced massive deposit flight and were kept solvent only through overdrafts from the Irish and European Central Banks. This overdraft totalled €120 billion in September 2011. However, more money was now needed to recapitalise the government-guaranteed banks at a time when the government was effectively shut out of international credit markets. In November 2010, after protracted denial that it needed help, the government was forced to negotiate an agreement from the Troika. A combined rescue package of up to €85 billion was agreed.

Table 8.3 shows how the Troika agreement is funded. Of the €85 billion, the Irish government is contributing €17.5 billion from the National Pension Reserve Fund and cash balances. The IMF is contributing €22.5 billion and Sweden, UK and Denmark are also making a contribution. In return

TABLE 8.3 How the Troika agreement is to be funded

	€ billion
National Pension Reserve Fund	12.5
Cash reserves	5.0
Ireland	17.5
IMF	22.5
European Commission	22.5
European Financial Stability Fund	17.7
UK bilateral loan	3.8
Sweden bilateral loan	0.6
Denmark bilateral loan	0.4
Total package	85.0
Package net of own resources	67.5

Source: Department of Finance, *Stability Programme Update 2011*

for credit up to the €85 billion over three years, the Irish government is committed to bringing the budget deficit below three per cent of GDP by 2015.

Note that the bailout is not a 'handout'. It is a set of loans with relatively high interest rates. Initially a rate of 5.8 per cent was charged on the IMF loan and four per cent to the EU funds, but this was later renegotiated down. These interest rates are, of course, much lower than those at which Ireland would have been able to borrow on the world's bond markets, if we could have borrowed on any terms.

Of the adjustment envisaged in the Troika agreement, approximately two-thirds is to be expenditure reductions and one-third tax increases. Taking into account the €14.08 billion in expenditure cuts introduced by Minister Brian Lenihan in 2010, the total austerity measure over the period 2008–2014 will amount to €30.4 billion. This amounts to austerity measures equivalent to 20 per cent of GDP over the adjustment period.

8.6 Is There Such a Thing as an Expansionary Fiscal Contraction?

One of the justifications made for the imposition of austerity on countries, like Ireland, that are in deep recession is that, contrary to the traditional Keynesian view of fiscal policy, a fiscal correction or contraction can actually lead to rapid economic recovery. This has been labelled the 'expansionary fiscal contraction' (EFC) hypothesis. The economists who coined the label EFC in 1990 used the examples of Denmark and Ireland as case studies to support their case (Giavazzi and Pagano 1990).

Recall that the performance of the Irish economy during the period 1987 to 1990 was extraordinary. Despite the deflationary fiscal policy, the GNP real growth rate rose markedly. The fact that a reduction in the fiscal deficit was followed by an increase in economic growth seemed to refute the conventional Keynesian view of fiscal policy.

This view relies on the following application of our AD-AS model from Chapter 5. The equilibrium condition in the goods and services market is:

$$AD \equiv C + I + G + NX \quad (1)$$

(As before, aggregate demand (AD) or total expenditure on GDP is broken down into consumer expenditure (C), investment (I), government expenditure (G) and net exports (NX).)

According to EFC, the contraction in G could be more than offset by increases in C and I, with the result that there would be a net increase in AD. A crisis of confidence arising from the lack of credibility of the government's commitment to restoring order to the public finances and an ever-increasing tax burden had led to capital flight and a widening interest rate differential between Ireland and Britain. Once the financial markets became convinced that the government was intent on reducing the borrowing requirement, the capital outflow subsided, and this facilitated a reduction in domestic interest rates. Increased confidence and lower interest rates led to a recovery in C and I, which helped offset the contractionary effects of the fiscal retrenchment.

NOTE: The Mundell–Fleming model outlined in Chapter 16 predicts that a deflationary fiscal policy will lead to a fall in the price level and an improvement in price competitiveness. This, in turn, should increase exports and decrease imports and thereby facilitate economic recovery. Other adjustment mechanisms are explained in different chapters of this book.

However, subsequent research on the Irish experience in the late 1980s focused on the importance of external factors in the recovery. These included the collapse of world oil prices, higher farm prices, and accelerating growth in the UK economy. They were reinforced by an improvement in our international competitiveness following the successful eight per cent devaluation of the Irish pound in August 1986. This devaluation contributed to an upsurge in net exports in 1987. Interest rates began to fall in the wake of the devaluation, before the 1987 Budget. Thus, an alternative, more conventionally Keynesian explanation for Ireland's recovery is available, and the value of the EFC hypothesis is in doubt (Bradley and Whelan 1997).

This controversy is of far more than local interest. A version of the EFC hypothesis is very influential today. The argument is that the way for the distressed peripheral economies of Europe to escape from the current recession is to restore confidence by implementing fiscal austerity programmes. The Nobel Prize-winning economist Paul Krugman has dismissed this hope as the 'confidence tooth fairy' approach to the problem. The evidence from Ireland in the late 1980s certainly suggests that unless the economy receives a strong boost from the net export sector, fiscal austerity alone will not bring about recovery.

The measures we have agreed with the Troika would seem to run counter to what would be appropriate to help the Irish economy recover quickly from the recession. However, the constraints we face make it impossible for us to reject austerity and introduce a stimulus package of our own. The orthodox – German – view is that countries in such a fiscal plight must restore the confidence of world bond markets and private sector investors by implementing rapid and even drastic expenditure cuts and tax increases.

A majority of academic economists would probably side with Paul Krugman's critical view of this orthodoxy and scepticism as to whether austerity can restore investors' and consumers' confidence by deflating the economy during a recession.

The European view of the appropriateness of austerity shifted somewhat against the German view during 2012 with the election of a socialist government headed by François Hollande in France, the collapse of the Spanish banking system and that country's recourse to the EU for a bail-out, and the increasing pressure on Mario Monti's 'technocratic' (i.e. non-elected) government in Italy. At least the idea of a 'growth compact' as a complement to the Fiscal Compact has gained ground and governments have agreed to a modest stimulus package for Europe.

In this situation, all Ireland can do is to hope that a more Keynesian view will prevail in Europe, that the debt burden on the country will be alleviated and that growth will resume in the world economy.

8.7 Evaluating Irish Fiscal Policy

This narrative of the measures introduced by successive ministers for finance in their budgets against the backdrop of the rate of growth of the economy needs to be supplemented by a more technical analysis of the conduct of fiscal policy. This analysis would identify the 'discretionary' and 'automatic' components of changes in budget revenue and spending.

A recent analysis along these lines (Bénétrix and Lane 2011) reaches conclusions that are broadly similar to those we drew from the narrative above. The authors show that Irish fiscal policy was pro-cyclical during the boom period 1999–2007, in the sense that discretionary fiscal measures tended to fuel rather than dampen the boom. Moreover, the response to the crisis after 2007 was dictated by the scale of the collapse in tax revenues and an appropriate fiscal stimulus could not be supplied. As a result, the fiscal contraction was once again pro-cyclical and contributed to the scale of the recession in Ireland. They conclude:

> *With hindsight we can see it would have been better to have run larger surpluses during the good years and even accumulated a liquid rainy-day fund that might have been deployed as a buffer against the impact of the severe negative economic shock that came.*

Similarly, an analysis of recent fiscal policy found it to be 'deeply pro-cyclical' (Kearney 2012).

One mitigating factor is that, for reasons we discussed in Chapter 7, the fiscal multipliers in Ireland are probably very low due to the high marginal propensity to import and tax. This implies that even if fiscal policy had been less pro-cyclical, this might not have led to a very marked improvement in the performance of the economy.

8.8 The End of History?

In 2012 Ireland entered a new era in regard to how economic policy will be conducted. In a referendum held on 31 May the country approved by 60 per cent to 40 per cent, on a turnout of 50 per cent, the Thirtieth Amendment of the Constitution. This commits the country to ratify the Treaty on Stability, Coordination and Governance in the Economic and Monetary Union, better known as the Fiscal Compact.

While the Compact is complicated by a lot of legal jargon, the key provision is Article 3, according to which we have to limit the country's 'structural deficit' to 0.5 per cent of GDP. A time frame and a road map of how we have to reach and adhere to this target is laid out.

Although our membership of the EMU had already placed many restrictions on the scope for an independent fiscal policy, the new Compact makes these stricter and more binding legally.

The chequered era of an independent Irish fiscal policy, as we have recounted in this chapter, is now over. How successful the new regime will be remains to be seen.

8.9 Key Terms and Concepts

In this chapter, we have reviewed the stance of fiscal policy since the 1970s. We showed that:

- The timing of fiscal policy has been pro-cyclical; that is, it has tended to amplify rather than dampen the business cycle.
- The most conspicuous effect of deficit spending was to increase the burden of the national debt.
- Between the late 1980s and the economic crash of 2008, we succeeded in reducing the debt/GDP ratio and meeting the fiscal criteria required to gain admission to the euro area.
- We also reviewed the economic downturn and the austerity programme introduced by the Troika.

CHAPTER 9

Money and Banking

9.1 Introduction

The initial sections in this chapter discuss what money is and the types of money used in modern economies. This involves an account of the modern banking system and of the functions of a central bank. We pay particular attention to the evolving role of the ECB in the euro area. We conclude with a brief discusison of the role of the inter-bank market and credit in the recent financial crisis.

9.2 What is Money?

Money performs four basic functions. The most important of these is its role as a medium of exchange. It also serves as a unit of account, a standard of deferred payment, and a store of value. We discuss each of these functions in turn.

Medium of exchange

Without money an economy would have to operate on a barter system: all transactions would involve the exchange of goods and services directly for other goods and services. A farmer, for example, would have to exchange the output of his farm for clothes and other necessities. A doctor, in return for medical services, would receive goods or services from her patients. Such a system would involve enormous transaction costs. To complete a transaction there would have to be a double coincidence of wants – each party to a deal would have to want what the other was offering. A hungry doctor and a sick farmer, for example, would be able to do business, but if an economics lecturer wanted a haircut he would have to find a hairdresser interested in an economics lecture. Most people would find it difficult to complete the range of transactions involved in daily life. As a result, people would be pushed towards self-sufficiency, which is very inefficient.

Adam Smith, in *The Wealth of Nations* (1776), gave a famous illustration of the benefits of the division of labour based on the working of a factory that made nails. By specialising in a single type of product, the workforce becomes very efficient and the scale of production expands beyond what would be possible under a barter system. Under barter, people are forced to be more or less self-sufficient and cannot devote themselves to a particular skill or trade. Occupations requiring a high degree of specialisation, such as engineering, accountancy and teaching, would not come into existence. As a consequence, productivity would remain low. Barter is costly and inefficient and almost all societies have abandoned it in favour of money.

In a money economy, goods and services can be sold for money that can be used to purchase other goods and services. The use of money as a medium of exchange is a very significant social development. It greatly reduces the cost of doing business and encourages people to specialise and trade. People can concentrate on what they are best at and become more efficient at it. They can sell the output that is surplus to their needs and buy what they want with the proceeds. This is a much more efficient arrangement than a barter system. While the desire to accumulate too much money may be 'the root of all evil', the use of money is a major benefit to all societies!

Unit of account

Once people become involved in trading, they need a unit of account in which to quote prices and compare whether something is dear or cheap relative to other items. Money serves this important function. Usually the same currency unit is used as a medium of exchange and a unit of account. It is possible, however, to use a unit of account that is not actually in circulation as money. The IMF, for example, uses special drawing rights (SDRs) in its dealings with member states. A number of multinational firms operating in Ireland use dollars as their unit of account but make payments in euro. In horse racing, the Thousand Guineas is a classic race, but bets are no longer accepted or paid out in guineas.

Standard of deferred payment and store of value

These functions allow us to link the present with the future when doing business. Loans, leases and other contracts have to specify amounts to be paid in the future – that is, they need a standard of deferred payment. Money serves this purpose. Money allows people to save some of their income and use it to purchase things in the future. It acts as a store of value. However, there are risks involved in using money in this way. In inflationary periods money loses value over time. Inflation is a threat to the efficiency of a modern economy, but people can specify contracts that take inflation into account (this is called *inflation indexation*). Very high rates of inflation will prompt people to look to other assets, such as foreign currencies, land, works of art and other 'collectibles' to use as a store of value. All these ways of coping with inflation involve costs.

9.3 Types of Money

Over the centuries, money has taken a rich variety of forms. Whales' teeth in Fiji, feather money in Santa Cruz, dogs' teeth in the Admiralty Islands, boar tusk in New Guinea, beeswax in Borneo, tea brick currency in Mongolia, reindeer in Asiatic Russia, salt in Ethiopia, silk and salt in China, and cocoa beans in Mexico are some examples of what has served as money in different societies. The names applied to money have also varied.

NOTE: Some years ago, in a letter to the *Irish Times*, the current governor of the Central Bank of Ireland, Patrick Honohan, wrote:

> *Sir, I am afraid your correspondent [name withheld] has got the wrong end of the stick. He disdains the use of the term 'sterling' to mean the British pound on the grounds that this is just a propaganda term meaning 'the real thing'. On the contrary, English silver penny coins were called 'sterlings' as much as 900 years ago. Thus the pound sterling was, originally, a pound weight of sterlings. It was because of the high quality of these sterlings that – from the late 17th century on – the term came to mean something like 'the real thing'. Soon thereafter the gold guinea, and then the sovereign, wholly replaced silver coins in England, but the term 'sterling' survived. The connotation of excellence has, of course, been rather tarnished in more recent times. What's in a name? Mention of the guinea brings to mind the currency of Guinea, called the Syli, and which had the misfortune to live up to its name, before it was eventually replaced. When it comes to our own currency, I confess to a preference (unless as Gaeilge) for 'pound' rather than 'punt', if only to avoid the connotation of something small and flat-bottomed, prone to sinking if not looked after properly.*

There are two basic types of money: commodity money and fiat money.

Commodity money

It was natural that intrinsically valuable commodities would be the first money. Over the centuries silver and gold emerged as the preferred form of commodity money. The Irish word for money, *airgead*, derives from the Latin for silver. The scarcity, durability and divisibility of these precious metals made them very suitable for use as money. However, all commodity money suffers from the disadvantage that it ties up a valuable commodity and diverts it from other uses. When silver is used to make coins, the supply of silver to jewellers is reduced.

Cattle have been very widely used to store wealth. (The Latin words for cattle and money are, respectively, *pecus* and *pecunia*, whence the English word 'pecuniary'.) In ancient Ireland the ownership of cattle was a mark of social rank, as it still is today among the Maasai and other communities in Africa.

Fiat money

Fiat money is money that does not have any intrinsic value. Virtually all the notes and coins in circulation throughout the world today fall into this category. Their intrinsic value is very small compared to their value in exchange. For example, the paper and cloth used to make a €50 note are worth almost nothing. The note is only valuable because of the elaborate measures taken to prevent counterfeit notes from circulating. The so-called silver coins used in Ireland until 2002 were in fact made from a cheap cupro-nickel alloy. But even though the coins we use today are made of very cheap metal, the process of minting them is quite expensive.

The move from commodity money to fiat money happened in stages. Initially, bank notes were convertible into something of intrinsic value, usually gold or silver. Most paper notes had been convertible into gold until World War I. The US dollar maintained limited convertibility into gold until President Nixon finally broke the link in 1971. There is no longer a 'promise to pay the bearer' in gold on any of the notes in circulation today. They are 'inconvertible'. Their value derives from the fact that a central bank has a monopoly on issuing them and they are legal tender in a country. (Legal tender is the currency that must be accepted in payment of debts and taxes.) Because it derives its value ultimately from a government decree, it is known as fiat money, from the Latin meaning 'let there be money'.

Circularity in its acceptance

Whatever is used as money, it must achieve circularity in its acceptance. The only reason people accept paper money in payment is because they are certain that other people will also accept it when they want to purchase goods and services at a later stage. If people had the slightest suspicion that a particular type of money could not be spent, they would not accept it as payment. In recent years doubts about the future of the euro have given rise to the purchase of sterling or US dollars just in case the European currency should suddenly lose its value.

If fiat money is to be accepted it must not be easy to reproduce or counterfeit. Counterfeiting can be a serious problem for a government because if it were practised on a large scale it would undermine the economy. A great deal of effort went into the design of the euro notes and coins in order to ensure that they could not be easily forged. They have elaborate serial numbers, embedded holograms, and inks that change colour under ultraviolet light, and there is a special scratch card to identify fakes. A special intaglio (carving) press is used to print the notes. Special ink is put into the recesses of the engraving. Pressure is then applied, which forces the ink out of the recesses, creating an embossed effect on the front of the paper with an indent effect on the back. The 'paper' used to make the notes is 75 per cent cotton and 25 per cent linen.

According to Keynes, the Communist leader Vladimir Lenin claimed that the best way to undermine an advanced economy is to undermine its currency.

> *Lenin is said to have declared that the best way to destroy the Capitalist System is to debauch the currency. Lenin was certainly right. There is no subtler, no surer means of overturning the existing basis of society than to debauch the currency. The process engages all the hidden forces of economic law on the side of destruction, and does it in a manner that not one man in a million is able to diagnose.* (Keynes 1919)

Box 9.1 Euro coins and notes

The euro area money supply is controlled by the ECB, but the task of minting the coins and printing the notes is decentralised to the national central banks. The coins carry national symbols on one side, for example the Irish harp and the German eagle.

The notes carry a serial number that allows you to identify the country that issued them. The first letter is specific to a country. T is for Ireland, X for Germany. If you sum the 11 digits in the serial number, and sum again until you get a single digit, that 'check sum' is unique to a country or two countries. Ireland's check sum is 6, Germany shares 2 with Malta.

If you keep track of the notes in your wallet you will notice that serial numbers beginning with T form a much higher proportion of the total that is warranted by Ireland's share of the euro area M1, which is less than two per cent. This is because the notes printed in Ireland are put into circulation in the first instance through Irish banks.

During World War II, the Germans attempted to flood Britain with forged sterling notes in order to disrupt the war economy. When gold and silver coins were in circulation, debasing them in one way or another was brought to a fine art. 'Clipping' referred to clipping small pieces off the edges of coins that could be collected and reused as silver or gold. The authorities responded by milling the circumference of coins. A second practice was sweating: gold coins were put in a bag, which was shaken vigorously. The dust at the bottom of the bag that flaked off the coins was the profit. Governments and monarchs were not above cheating by adding a cheap metal alloy to the precious metals in the manufacture of legal tender.

Gresham's law

Sir Thomas Gresham (1519–1579), Queen Elizabeth I's currency dealer in Antwerp, noticed that bad money tended to drive out good. This is known as Gresham's law. We can illustrate this by considering what would happen if a country had coins minted with a high silver content (as was the case with the Irish florins and half-crowns until the 1940s). If the government subsequently puts into circulation coins of substantially lower silver content but with the same face value (as happened in Ireland after 1942) the latter will quickly replace the former. Anyone coming across an older coin, with a high silver content, would hoard it. Florins and half-crowns from the early 1940s quickly disappeared from circulation and are now very valuable. The only way to get the 'good' money back into circulation would be to change the rate of exchange between the two types of money, so that a good coin would be worth more a bad coin.

In the USA in the nineteenth century both gold and silver coins circulated as legal tender (this system is known as bimetallism). The ratio of the value of gold to silver was set at various ratios to try to ensure that both types of coins remained in circulation, but in 1873 silver was demonetised, putting America on a gold standard. However, a shortage of gold restricted the money supply and led to falling prices (deflation) and recession. William Jennings Bryan was the Democratic congressman for the silver-producing state of Nebraska. In 1896 he gave a speech in favour of bimetallism that included the famous slogan 'We shall not crucify mankind on a cross of gold.' Eventually the crisis was eased when new goldmines in the Klondike and South Africa provided enough gold to meet the demand for monetary purposes by the end of the nineteenth century.

9.4 The Banking System in a Modern Economy

The financial system is the group of institutions in a modern economy that channels savings to investors. It brings together people with excess funds (savers) and people who want to invest but need funds (borrowers).

NOTE: Saving holds back resources from consumption, while investing uses those resources to create capital. 'Savings' refers to accumulated wealth.

The principal motive for saving is to smooth consumption over one's lifetime. The clearest example of this is the way people set aside money when they are employed in order to build up a pension to allow them to maintain their lifestyle in retirement. People also save in order to accumulate money for special purchases, such as providing for their children's education and dealing with possible future illnesses. Buying insurance policies is an efficient way of saving for many purposes. People take out mortgages to buy houses and make period repayments until the mortgage is paid off. These payments are a form of saving.

Borrowers, on the other hand, borrow to fund businesses and to invest in new ideas and innovations that they hope will generate future wealth. Borrowers obtain money from the financial system knowing that they will have to pay it back with interest in the future. Lenders place money with financial institutions to earn interest while keeping their capital intact. This allows them to share in the wealth generated by businesses without having to get directly involved in running them.

There are many ways in which savers provide funds to borrowers. They can do so directly through the bond market or the stock exchange, or they can use financial intermediaries, such as high street banks, investment banks and various types of investment funds. In this chapter we focus on the core banking system.

The familiar 'high street' banks are deposit-taking institutions. They accept funds from the public and place them on account. Accounts differ depending on how easily and quickly money can be withdrawn from them. (Formerly an important distinction was whether or not cheques could be written on an account, but in the days of internet banking, electronic money transfers and credit cards this is less relevant.)

The definition of the 'money supply' is very important but it is not straightforward. Obviously, the notes and coins in circulation should form part of the money supply, but in a modern economy they are only the small change needed to lubricate the system. Various types of bank deposits and other financial products now dominate the payments system and form part of the money supply.

In Ireland, before we joined the EMU, there were two definitions of the money supply. The narrow definition was M1, which included currency in circulation plus current accounts with banks. Current accounts could be accessed immediately and cheques written against them. A broader definition was called M3, which equalled M1 plus deposit accounts, which were less liquid than current accounts.

When the EMU was launched in 1999 the new currency area was switched to 'the euro area's money supply' and the former Irish money supply was replaced by 'Ireland's contribution to the euro area's money supply'.

In mid-2012 euro area M3 equalled almost exactly €10,000 billion (ten trillion euro). Table 9.1 gives the breakdown of this total between the three measures of the money supply used by the ECB: M1, M2 and M3. Moving from M1 to M3 involves going from the narrowest definition of the money supply (currency in circulation plus overnight deposits) to broader definitions of money that include short-term deposits and other liquid bank liabilities. Note that currency in circulation constitutes less than nine per cent of the broad money. Table 9.1 also shows that Ireland's contribution to the euro area money supply amounts to about two per cent under all headings. This is quite similar to the share of the euro area's GDP that is produced in Ireland (1.7 per cent).

The characteristic that determines whether a deposit with a bank is included in the money supply is its liquidity; that is, how quickly and easily it can be accessed and spent. M1 is equal to currency in circulation plus overnight deposits, which can be withdrawn the day after they are lodged. M2 includes M1 plus deposits and loans with maturity of up to three months, while M3 includes M2 plus a small amount of less liquid liabilities.

TABLE 9.1 The euro area money supply and Ireland's contribution to it, July 2012

	Column	Euro area € bn	Ireland's contribution € bn	Ireland's share of euro area
Currency in circulation	(1)	861	13	1.5%
Overnight deposits	(2)	4,032	81	2.0%
M1	(3) = (1) + (2)	4,893	94	1.9%
Deposits of maturity up to 2 years	(4)	1,877	69	3.7%
Deposits redeemable at notice of up to 3 months	(5)	2,007	12	0.6%
M2	(6) = (3) + (4) + (5)	8,777	177	2.0%
Repos, money market fund shares and debt with maturity of under 2 years	(7)	1,150	8	0.7%
M3	(8) = (6) + (7)	9,927	185	1.9%

Note: Repos are loans against which securities have been used as collateral.

Sources: ECB Monthly Bulletin, July 2012, Table 2.3; and Central Bank of Ireland Money and Banking Statistics, July 2012, Table A.3

NOTE: The old Irish money supply related to Irish residents only. The euro area definitions of a country's contribution to money supply include deposits by all euro area residents. If a German firm or a Spanish bank or a French person has an account in Ireland, that is part of Ireland's contribution to the euro area money supply.

The control of the money supply is a key instrument of monetary policy because of the link between the amount of money in circulation and the rate of inflation. This raises the question: Which measure of the money supply should the ECB try to control? The M1 series is more volatile than the other two as people substitute between short-term deposits and cash, so the ECB has decided that the M3 should be used for policy purposes.

A commercial bank's balance sheet

To understand the role of the banks in a modern society we need to outline the principal features of a commercial or 'high street' bank's balance sheet. Table 9.2 presents a simplified balance sheet for a commercial or high street bank that is in the euro area. The bank's liabilities consist of the money they have taken in from depositors, money they have borrowed on the inter-bank market, and money they have raised by issuing bonds. All of this money is owed to others and the bank has to be prepared to repay it. Some short-term deposits have to be paid on demand and bonds have various maturity dates.

The bank's assets consist of cash and deposits with the ECB; government and corporate bonds it owns; money it has loaned to other banks on the inter-bank market; loans and advances to households (including mortgages) and businesses. The problem is, of course, that the assets are less liquid than the liabilities. While cash in the till and deposits with the ECB are 'real money', loans and advances to households, businesses and other banks are far less liquid.

TABLE 9.2 A simplified commercial bank balance sheet

Assets	Liabilities
Reserves (cash and deposits with ECB)	Deposits
Government and corporate bonds	Inter-bank borrowing
Inter-bank loans	Bonds outstanding
Loans and advances to business	Shareholders' equity
Loans and advances to households (including mortgages)	
Total	Total

As we learned in Ireland after 2007, an extraordinary proportion of Irish banks' assets were property-related – mortgages, loans to developers, loans to other banks that also invested in property. When the property market crashed the value of the assets plummeted, leaving a big hole in the banks' balance sheets. Cash reserves and shareholders' capital were totally inadequate relative to the losses suffered and the banks were soon seen to be insolvent. Without the government's guarantee of deposits and its eventual 'recapitalisation' of the banks the whole system would have imploded, with disastrous consequences for the country.

The equity capital that is shown on the right-hand side of the balance sheet is extremely important. It comes from money put up by investors by buying equity (shares) in the bank and from retained earnings. When some of the bank's assets become 'non-performing' (that is, tank), like much of the real estate for which so many millions were advanced during the recent Irish property bubble, this capital acts as a buffer to cover the bank's liabilities.

It seems reasonable that the first thing to suffer as a result of imprudent lending should be the owners' stake in the bank. The question of whether investors who bought bank bonds, in some cases enjoying high interest returns on them, should also be 'burned' when the bank gets into difficulty is contentious (see Box 9.2).

Box 9.2 Types of bank debt

We explained in the text that if a bank suffers losses on its loans the owners' equity in the bank is the first line of defence. This can be reduced or wiped out in order to keep the bank solvent and allow it to continue trading. But losses on the scale incurred by Irish banks during the property crash were far greater than the banks' core capital. The Irish government stepped in and guaranteed that depositors with the banks would not suffer losses, but the status of other creditors and bondholders was not clear-cut.

There is a pecking order among the different type of bonds the banks issue. As the names imply, 'senior debt' or 'senior loans' take priority over 'junior debt' or 'subordinated debt'. A higher interest rate is paid on the junior debt in return for the greater risk attached to it.

When banks like Anglo Irish Bank went bankrupt, the government decided that senior bondholders were fully covered by the bank guarantee. The ECB took a strong line on this, arguing that senior bondholders should enjoy the same protection as depositors, although they had been attracted by higher interest rates that were a reward for taking on more risk.

Junior bondholders have, however, suffered losses (or 'haircuts') on their investment, reaching as high as 90 per cent in the case of Anglo Irish Bank. The legal rights of those who held bank bonds are now being argued in various European courts.

Bank profits

The rate of interest paid by banks on deposits is lower than the rate they charge on loans. For example, in 2012 the commercial banks in Ireland paid 0.1 to 1.0 per cent on deposits less than €5,000 and charged 11.5–12.75 per cent to category A borrowers (i.e. personal and retail borrowings) on term loans. Of course, they pay higher rates of return on larger and longer-term deposits and to their bond holders. The differential between the interest they pay on their liabilities and what they earn on their assets is the main source of bank profits. (Banks also charge their customers a host of different fees for various transactions, but they do provide 'free' banking to people aged over 60.)

NOTE: Bank profits have always been the subject of much criticism by the public. The Irish Banks' Standing Committee (IBSC), set up in 1920, comprised representatives of both southern and northern banks, to agree common interest rates and bank charges. This suggested that a cartel had been formed with the objective of making supra-normal profits from bank customers. Criticism focused, in particular, on the spread between deposit and lending rates. It was pointed out that deposit rates were lower and lending rates higher than similar rates in the UK. The concern at the outflow of large deposits from Ireland to the UK added weight to this argument. The IBSC is still in existence, but it no longer sets interest rates for the banks, and its influence has been eroded by the entry of new financial institutions into the banking market.

Fractional reserve banking

It is clear from the banks' balance sheets that modern banking is based on a system of fractional reserves. The banks rely on the belief that the public is not going to withdraw all the money they have deposited at once. Over time, new deposits are likely to match withdrawals. If this is the case it is not necessary to back all these deposits with cash in the till. Only a fraction of the value of deposits needs to be covered by ready cash. The rest can be either loaned out or used to purchase interest-bearing securities such as government stock or corporate bonds. If a bank has sufficient reserves to meet normal outflows, the public's confidence will remain high and the fractional reserve system will work well. The bank will earn interest from its loans and advances and the public will enjoy the convenience of having money on deposit. But a loss of confidence in the banking system can spread like wildfire, leading to a run on the banks as everyone scrambles to withdraw money ahead of everyone else.

NOTE: The fractional reserve system was developed by goldsmiths in the Middle Ages. People used to place gold and other valuables with them for safe keeping. At first they simply stored the gold in a vault for a small fee and issued receipts that could be used at a later stage to reclaim the gold. However, it soon became apparent that it was most unlikely that all of the depositors would withdraw all their gold at the same time. They realised it was possible to make profits by lending out most of the gold and charging interest on the loans. Of course, a certain proportion of the gold had to be kept on hand to meet any withdrawals that would arise. This would reassure depositors, and as long as they had confidence in the system, only a small proportion of the gold would actually be withdrawn. The rest could be put to work to earn interest for the goldsmiths turned bankers.

In Europe, the ECB sets a required liquidity ratio known as the minimum reserve. This ratio applies to all banks and financial institutions. In 2012 the minimum reserve stipulates that one per cent of 'relevant liabilities' must be kept in reserves. (See, for example, www.ecb.int/mopo/implement/mr/html/calc.en.html.)

Minimum reserve ratio = 1 per cent of relevant liabilities

'Relevant liabilities' comprise mainly short-term deposits (overnight and up to two years' agreed maturity). The reserve requirement does not apply to deposits with over two years' maturity. Thus, for every €100 the banks have in current and deposit accounts, a minimum of €1 must be kept in notes and coins plus deposits at the ECB. The purpose of the minimum reserve ratio is to ensure that the banks have adequate liquid assets to meet demands for cash by their depositors.

In addition to maintaining specified amounts of liquid assets as reseves, banks in most countries also pay for insurance that covers depositors up to a specified amount. These insurance schemes are usually run by the central bank. In the USA the Federal Deposit Insurance Corporation (FDIC) was established in 1933 to put a halt to runs on the banks. It now guaratees up to $250,000 per depositor (100 times the limit set in 1933). The scope and involvement of the FDIC in the American banking system was expanded in the wake of the collapse of Lehman Brothers in 2008 and it has played a major role in taking over insolvent banks and resolving the bank debt crisis in the USA.

The Central Bank of Ireland requires licensed banks to participate in its Deposit Guarantee Scheme. Up to 2008 the first €20,000 of deposits were guaranteed. However, following the collapse of Northern Rock in 2007, the ceiling was lifted to €100,000. In September 2008 a much wider series of measures was introduced 'to maintain the stability of the financial system of the state', widely known as the Bank Guarantee. We discus this in more detail later.

Bank crises

As long as the public believes the bank is 'sound' it need not keep very much aside as a buffer against losses. The incentive is for the banker to minimise the money that is held in its vault and put as much as possible out as loans and advances to earn money for the bank's owners. If depositors become nervous about the bank's lending practices they will begin to withdraw money in larger than normal amounts and could eventually start a 'run' on the bank. In this manner, loss of confidence in the bank can lead to panic and eventually the collapse of individual banks that do not have enough liquid assets to cover the demands of nervous depositors for cash.

By 2006, a leading international economics textbook was able to claim that major banking crises belonged in the history books: 'Today, bank runs are not a major problem for the banking systems of advanced economies.' Students were told that they would only see bank runs depicted in films like *Mary Poppins* and *It's a Wonderful Life*. But on 14 September 2007, Northern Rock, which used to be a small building society based in Newcastle upon Tyne, had to seek liquidity support from the Bank of England as fears about its solvency spread. Northern Rock had grown very rapidly by borrowing on the world inter-bank market, using the money to finance mortgages. As the 'subprime' (i.e. dodgy or high-risk) mortgage crisis spread across America, people began to look more critically at the type of loans Northern Rock had been making. This was an example of 'contagion', the process whereby trouble in one banking system spreads internationally. Queues formed outside its Dublin branch as anxious depositors withdrew their money. The bank was nationalised on 22 February 2008.

The collapse of the US bank Bear Stearns in March 2008 and of Lehman Brothers in September of that year caused a global financial panic. The banks stopped lending to each other as the banks were not sure of the extent of bad debts on balance sheets. Inter-bank lending dried up and fear of a run on the banks led to deposit flight. The banking crisis quickly found its way to Ireland.

These panics represented a failure of the banking regulatory system in Europe and America. Banks are regulated by national banking authorities – usually the national central bank – in line with rules laid down under what are known as the 'Basel Accords'. The first of these dates from 1988, but we are now on Basel III (2010–11), which addressed some of the weaknesses in the regulatory system revealed by the crisis of 2007–8.

Bank regulation should maintain confidence in the banking system and minimise the risk of a run on the banks. Banks are required by law to keep minimum reserves in relation to their deposits. The assets that banks acquire with their depositors' money are classified according to their riskiness. Banks must hold six per cent of their risk-weighted assets as Tier I capital (equity and cash). This capital is there to absorb losses on the bank's lending.

> **NOTE:** Risk-weighted assets are the total of all assets held by the bank weighted by credit risk. The credit risk is normally determined by the country's central bank. Assets like cash and coins have zero risk weight, while some high-risk loans have a risk weight up to 100 per cent of their face value.

One of the problems facing European banks today is that they hold substantial amounts of sovereign debt (bonds issued by national governments). In the past it was believed that such debt was almost riskless and it was given AAA ratings by the credit rating agencies. It was believed that European governments would not default. But the fiscal crisis led the Greek government to a partial default on its debt in 2012, and the bonds issued by Portugal, Ireland, Spain, Italy and some other EMU countries have been downgraded by the rating agencies.

The lesson of the past five years is that modern banking, which in good times rewards risk-taking by the bonuses paid to its senior executives and soaring share prices and dividends for its shareholders, is extremely unstable. Without massive state intervention, including large-scale nationalisations, whole banking systems would have collapsed in 2008. The consequences for the well-being of ordinary citizens are literally unimaginable.

9.5 Money Creation in a Modern Economy

In a modern economy, where bank money is the most important type of money and the banks operate on fractional reserves, an inflow of cash will cause a multiple expansion of the money supply. This process is illustrated by reference back to Table 9.2. It is assumed that (a) there is only one bank in the country, (b) the minimum reserve requirement is 10 per cent, and (c) the bank does not keep any excess reserves. On the liability side of the balance sheet are deposits and inter-bank borrowing. On the asset side, there are entries for bank reserves and bank lending.

Let us explore what happens when there is a net inflow of reserves (cash) to the bank. Suppose someone receives €1,000 from abroad in return for some service and deposits it in the bank. Given the 10 per cent reserve requirement, the bank will keep €100 in reserve and can make a loan of €900. Suppose the loan of €900 is used to purchase a computer. A local shop receives €900 in exchange for the computer and lodges it with its bank. Hence the computer loan has, in the second round, resulted in the creation of a deposit of €900. The bank again keeps 10 per cent (€90) of the new deposit in reserve and loans out the remainder (€810).

The process need not end there. The borrower of €810 from the bank purchases a CD player from another local store. The store, in turn, deposits the €810 with its bank. Once again the bank will keep 10 per cent in reserves and lend out the rest. This process will go on, but the amount loaned out at each successive stage dwindles because a fraction has to be held as reserves.

Table 9.3 shows what happens to M3 as this process unfolds. As bank deposits increase in each round, so too does the money supply. Given a minimum reserve ratio of 10 per cent, the initial €1,000 deposit will eventually lead to a €10,000 increase in the money supply. However, if somewhere along the line someone hoards the money and keeps it out of the banking system, the expansion of the money supply would halt. The money-creation process only works when the money lent out finds its way back into a bank as a deposit. The process also works in reverse. If a bank loses reserves, there will be a multiple contraction of credit.

TABLE 9.3 The money creation process

Round	ΔM3	Δ Currency + Deposit Accounts
1	1,000	1,000
2	900	900
3	810	810
...	...	...
...	...	...
...	...	...
	10,000	10,000

The money multiplier

The final increase in the money supply can be calculated using a formula for the money multiplier.

$$\text{Money multiplier } (m) = \frac{1}{\text{minimum reserve requirement}}$$

In the above example, $m = 1/0.1 = 10$, so that:

$$\text{Change in M3} = (\text{m}) \times (\text{initial increase in reserves})$$
$$€10{,}000 = 10 \times €1{,}000$$

Note that the higher the minimum reserve requirement, the lower the money multiplier. A reserve requirement of 20 per cent (0.2), for example, gives a money multiplier of 5, but a reserve requirement of 3 per cent (0.03) gives a money multiplier of 33.3. The less money that has to be held in the form of reserves, the greater the final increase in the money supply following an initial increase in reserves. However, we must bear in mind that this example is based on a very unrealistic example in which people do not increase their holdings of currency. Later in this chapter, a more realistic example, which allows for currency leakage, is worked out.

NOTE: The money multiplier should not be confused with the aggregate demand multiplier discussed in Chapter 6. That multiplier relates increases in aggregate demand to increases in real output or GNP, whereas the money multiplier relates a change in a bank's reserves to the final change in the money supply.

9.6 The Role of a Central Bank

The main functions of a central bank are:

- to issue the national currency
- to act as banker to both the commercial banks and the government
- to supervise the orderly operation of the financial system
- to conduct monetary and exchange rate policies so as to safeguard the integrity of the country's money.

Central banks are normally national institutions, like the Bank of England (UK), the Federal Reserve Bank (USA) and, for example, Norges Bank (Norway). However, with the launch of the EMU in

June 1998 a new supra-national central bank was created, called the European Central Bank (ECB) and located in Frankfurt. This performs many (but not all) of the functions of a national central bank for the 17 member states of EMU, including Ireland. The national central banks are still in existence, of course, and act as the ECB's agents in member states.

NOTE: Since 2011 the President of the ECB has been Mario Draghi, who earned a PhD in economics at Massachusetts Institute of Technology and was a professor of economics at the University of Florence before becoming President of the Bank of Italy in 2006.

The ECB is responsible for issuing the notes and coins that circulate in the euro area. (Some of the mechanics of this are discussed in Box 9.1.) Crucially, it is also responsible for setting monetary policy in the euro area. This 'one size fits all approach' is a key feature of the currency union.

The body responsible for deciding monetary policy is the ECB executive board, which has six members: the president and vice-president of the bank and governors of four of the 17 national central banks of the euro area. Thus the national central banks continue to have a say – although only indirectly – in the formulation of monetary policy. In practice the bigger countries of the euro area tend to exert the greatest influence on policy.

Table 9.4 shows a simplified version of the structure of the ECB's balance sheet as of 31 August 2012. The amount of euro currency in circulation is shown on the liabilities side of the balance sheet. Deposits from both commercial banks and governments lodged at the ECB are part of its liabilities. The ECB serves as banker to the banks and to governments.

Gold constitutes just 14 per cent of the ECB's assets. Foreign currency claims or external reserves amount to another 10 per cent. Thus just 24 per cent of the backing for the euro consists of external assets. By far the biggest component (46 per cent) of the bank's assets is 'lending to euro area banks'. Thus the euro is being backed by loans to commercial banks in the member states of the EMU. We might take comfort from the idea that these banks, in turn, are backed by their governments. But there are clear grounds for concern at the extent to which the system has become a method of supplying liquidity to euro area banks.

This is also clear from the structure of the ECB's liabilities, over one-third of which consist of deposits due to euro area banks. Over the last two years the ECB has loaned enormous sums of money to the euro area banks against the collateral of their governments' securities. This side-stepped the

TABLE 9.4 Simplified ECB balance sheet, August 2012

Assets	€ billion	Liabilities	€ billion
Gold	434	Banknotes in circulation	896
Foreign currency claims	312	Euro area banks' deposits	1,103
Lending to euro area banks	1,430	Other liabilities	594
Euro area securities	629	Revaluation accounts	410
Other assets	281	Capital and reserves	86
	–		–
Total	3,086		3,089

Note: Totals do not add up due to rounding.

Source: ECB Consolidated Financial Statement of the Eurosystem as at 31 August 2012

prohibition on lending directly to governments and provided the banks with deposits with the ECB that ensure their day-to-day liquidity.

As both its assets and liabilities have been growing, the ECB's balance sheet has more than doubled since mid-2007. Since most of the liabilities of a central bank form part of the money supply, such a rapid expansion of its balance sheet could lead to inflation in the future. Furthermore, in September 2012, as part of the commitment to preventing the euro area from disintegrating, Mario Draghi announced that he would commit unlimited funds to purchasing government bonds for countries – such as Spain and Italy, but perhaps also Ireland – where bond yields were unsustainably high.

While this commitment is subject to the countries adhering to strict fiscal discipline, along the lines of Ireland's Agreement with the Troika, it raises the prospect of a further massive expansion of the ECB balance sheet.

Seigniorage

Seigniorage refers to the return to a government or central bank from issuing money. In the Middle Ages, feudal lords (seigneurs) had the right to mint coins on their estates. Today, central banks have a monopoly on this right. The profit that accrues to central banks from the currency outstanding is called seigniorage. It arises, for example, because a central bank can use notes that pay no interest to purchase interest-bearing assets like bonds.

> **NOTE**: Suppose you had a machine at home that produced bank notes and that these bank notes were generally accepted by everyone. How nice it would be! You could print off some notes (raise 'revenue') and go and buy goods and services. That is, in effect, what the government can do. They are creating 'revenue for the government' without raising taxes or selling bonds. This 'revenue' is call seigniorage.

In the USA seigniorage is estimated to account for about three per cent of total government revenue. This is an exceptionally large figure due to the willingness of foreign central banks, companies and individuals to use the US dollar as a store of value and a medium of exchange. However, when inflation was running at a very high rate in Italy and Greece in the 1970s, seigniorage accounted for more than 10 per cent of total government revenue.

In countries experiencing hyperinflation, seigniorage is often the government's main source of revenue. Indeed, when printing money is viewed as an easy source of revenue for the government it can become the cause of hyperinflation.

The concept of an *inflation tax* is closely related to seigniorage. Inflation reduces the real value or the purchasing power of money. Hence, inflation acts as a form of tax on holders of money. The fall in the real value or purchasing power of the money supply benefits the central bank and government by reducing the real value of their liabilities. The losers are, of course, the public who hold money and see its purchasing power decline.

A central bank is a profitable institution. The surplus or profit of the income earned on Europe's official external reserves plus net lending minus the ECB's operating expenses is turned over to the national governments.

Lender of last resort

Traditionally an important function of a national central bank is to serve as a *lender of last resort (LOLR)*. This role is related to issues that have arisen about the behaviour of the ECB during the post-2007 crisis.

To understand what the LOLR function entails, recall that commercial banks do not have all of their depositors' money available to pay out over the counter on demand. Most of it has been used for short- and medium-term loans that cannot be called in immediately. The idea of LOLR originated in England at the beginning of the nineteenth century. The reformer and banker Henry Thornton wrote an influential book on credit and banking in 1802. In it he spelled out the basic elements of sound central bank practice regarding lending to 'distressed' banks.

However, the founder of *The Economist*, Walter Bagehot (1826–1877) is most often credited with establishing modern LOLR theory. He expanded on Thornton's work, without referring to him by name. Both authors justified the need for an LOLR, whose role, they argued, was:

> *(1) to protect the money stock, (2) to support the whole financial system rather than individual financial institutions, (3) to behave consistently with the longer-run objective of stable money growth, and (4) to preannounce its policy in advance of crises so as to remove uncertainty.* (Humphrey 1989)

Bagehot suggested that, in a liquidity crisis, a central bank should lend freely, at a high rate of interest relative to the pre-crisis period, to any borrower with good collateral. This could be bonds that would normally be accepted by the central bank valued somewhere between panic and pre-panic prices. He also recommended that the quality standards on collateral taken by the Bank of England during a crisis should be relaxed. However, institutions without good collateral were assumed to be insolvent and should be allowed to fail and wound up.

Thus the LOLR approach implies that a central bank should be ready to lend to *solvent* banks that are encountering *liquidity* problems due to their inability to raise cash in the short run to redeem their obligations to depositors. The two italicised words are crucial, but they have no easy definition. It is never easy to distinguish between banks that are fundamentally insolvent and those that are only facing short-term liquidity problems.

Perhaps an analogy with a rich individual may help. If he has borrowed heavily but invested shrewdly in paintings and objets d'art that have greatly appreciated in value, he is surely solvent. But if his creditors come knocking at his door seeking immediate repayments of their loans (due to their need to repay their creditors) our collector friend may find it hard to come up with the money in the short term. Selling valuable paintings is not something to rush into. Catalogues have to be prepared, rich clients lined up and the scene set. But meanwhile the creditors are knocking at the door. In this situation a shrewd financier should be prepared to lend (against the collateral of some of the best paintings) to tide the collector over the period before he can sell enough of his assets to bring in the cash to satisfy his creditors. This is the role of an LOLR.

But suppose our friend had borrowed money to invest in the latest 'modern art' fad and the bottom had fallen out of the market for the artists he thought would be the Picassos of their generation. In this case, a shrewd banker would not be willing to lend money to help him repay his debts against the collateral of these paintings. The collector would be rightly regarded as insolvent and his creditors would have to resort to the commercial courts to try to claw back some of the money they had foolishly loaned to him.

The Bagehot doctrine recommends that central banks should provide massive support for solvent banks that experience temporary liquidity difficulties in order to fend off a widespread loss of confidence in the banking system. On the other hand they should set up mechanisms to dissolve banks that are clearly insolvent so that they can resolve their liabilities to depositors.

The problem with the ECB as the crisis broke in 2007 was that it had no clear mandate as an LOLR and tended to mistake insolvency for illiquidity. For far too long it refused to recognise that institutions like Anglo Irish Bank were not just in need of short-term loans to tide them over a bad patch, but that they were fundamentally insolvent. The real estate for which billions had been borrowed in the years before the crash was now virtually worthless and could not be accepted as collateral for bail-outs.

The ECB stood back during the early stages of the crisis. It insisted that it carried no blame for not having averted the crash by tighter regulation before 2007: that, apparently, was a function that still resided with the national central banks. Ultimately the Irish government and taxpayer had to bear the cost of bailing out the insolvent Irish banks.

Major flaws in the design of EMU became apparent during the crisis. There was no uniform, euro-wide system of bank regulation. The ECB was not responsible for bailing out troubled banks. It had no mandate for resolving the liabilities of insolvent banks. There was no EMU-wide bank deposit insurance system. This was in stark contrast to the Federal Reserve Bank and the Federal Deposit Insurance Corporation in the USA, where the banking crisis was resolved much faster than has been the case in Europe.

However, between December 2011 and February 2012, the ECB lent €1 trillion to euro area banks to help stem the financial crisis, but all of this had to be guaranteed by the sovereign states (including Ireland) and treated as part of their general government debts. As a result of the banking crisis, countries like Ireland, and subsequently Spain, became unable to borrow on the world bond markets because of the overhang of debt arising from trying to rescue their banking systems.

We mentioned the impression conveyed in many textbooks written prior to the crisis that bank failures were a thing of the past and that modern bankers need not be unduly concerned. This was, of course, incorrect. There had been many large bank failures in advanced countries since the World War II. Here are some important examples:

- Continental Illinois Bank of Chicago, one of America's largest banks, collapsed in 1984 as a result of losses on its loans.
- Bank of Credit and Commerce International (BCCI) in 1991 had its banking licence revoked, first in the USA and then in Britain. Depositors worldwide lost billions of pounds in the largest bank collapse in history.
- Savings and loans associations in the USA collapsed in the 1990s. (These are known as 'building societies' in Britain and Ireland.) In 1995 it was estimated that the total cost of resolving the 747 failed institutions was $87.9 billion.

Before the recent crisis there had been several examples of failed banks and financial institutions in modern Ireland:

- Irish Trust Bank and Merchant Banking closed in 1976 and 1982 respectively. Depositors with these banks lost a significant proportion of their money.
- The Private Motorists Protection Association and the Insurance Corporation of Ireland (ICI), a wholly owned subsidiary of Allied Irish Banks (AIB), were placed under administration in 1983 and 1985 respectively. It is believed that the ICI collapse cost AIB losses of around €127 million. These losses were paid for by a levy on other insurance companies and by subventions from the Irish taxpayer.

The list is long and it makes one wonder why we were so unprepared for the crash that shook our banking system to its core in 2008.

9.7 High-powered Money and the Money Multiplier

The main liabilities of a central bank – currency in circulation and commercial banks' deposits – are referred to as 'high-powered money' or the 'monetary base'; 'high-powered' because changes in commercial banks' reserves have a multiple impact on the money supply. Simplifying greatly, we can write that high-powered money (H) is equal to currency (CU) plus commercial bank reserves at the Central Bank (RE).

$$H = CU + RE \qquad (1)$$

Using this definition we can present a more complete version of the money multiplier than the simple one introduced earlier. We assume that people hold currency in proportion to their current and deposit accounts (D):

$$CU = c_p D \tag{2}$$

where $0 < c_p < 1$. If c_p was equal to, say, 0.1, this means that for every €1 held in current and deposit accounts, the public holds 10 cents in currency. Because of the minimum reserve, licensed bank reserves at the central bank are also related to current and deposit accounts.

$$RE = r_b D \tag{3}$$

Again, $0 < r_b < 1$. If the minimum reserve ratio were 10 per cent, r_b would be at least 0.1. The banks can, however, keep excess reserves if they wish. If equations (2) and (3) are inserted into equation (1), we obtain:

$$H = (c_p + r_b)D \tag{4}$$

Recall that M3 is equal to currency plus current and deposit accounts.

$$M3 = CU + D \tag{5}$$

Substitute equation (2) into equation (5):

$$M3 = (c_p + 1)D \tag{6}$$

The final step in deriving the relationship between M3 and H is to take the ratio of equation (6) to equation (4):

$$\frac{M3}{H} = \frac{(c_p + 1)}{(c_p + r_b)} \tag{7}$$

or

$$M3 = \frac{(c_p + 1)}{(c_p + r_b)} \times H \tag{8}$$

This version of the money multiplier relates high-powered money to the overall money supply and allows for currency leakages. If $c_p = 0$ (the public does not increase currency holdings as deposits increase) we obtain the earlier version of the multiplier.

We can calculate the money multiplier in the euro area in May 2012. At that time, currency = €861 billion, bank reserves = €107 billion and deposits €19,253 billion (part of this reserve base is subject to a 0 per cent reserve coefficient).

$$c_p = \frac{CU}{D} = \frac{861}{9{,}927} = 0.086$$

$$r_b = \frac{RE}{D} = \frac{107}{9{,}927} = 0.01$$

The money multiplier is equal to

$$\frac{(c_p + 1)}{(c_p + r_b)} = \frac{(0.086 + 1)}{(0.086 + 0.01)} = 11.3$$

This means that an increase of €1 in high-powered money would lead to an increase of €11.3 in the money supply. An increase in currency holdings in relation to deposits (c_p) will reduce the money multiplier. Similarly, as we noted earlier, an increase in r_b will decrease the money multiplier.

High-powered money is increased whenever the ECB increases its assets or its liabilities. As discussed in Chapter 19, the quantity theory of money predicts a long-run relationship between the growth rate of the money supply and inflation. To keep inflation relatively low, it is necessary to constrain the growth in high-powered money and the money supply.

However, as mentioned above, the ECB balance sheet doubled since 2007. This may have significant long-term implications for the euro area inflation rate. But these are not normal times. Clearly, the ECB is not attempting to constrain high-powered money or the money supply and is instead injecting liquidity into the financial system in order to keep the euro area banking system and sovereign bond market afloat.

There is also the possibility that if the ECB tries to control one definition of the money supply, the public will switch into near substitutes outside this definition to side-step the control. This tendency has been called 'Goodhart's law', after Professor Charles Goodhart, formerly of the London School of Economics, who drew attention to this problem.

Despite the problems of fine-tuning the money supply, international experience shows that it is not possible to have a sustained expansion of the money supply without an increase in the monetary base. Hence the ECB's balance sheet is at centre stage of monetary policy in the euro area.

9.8 Monetary Policy

The key role of a central bank is to 'protect the integrity of the nation's currency'. This implies maintaining price stability – that is, keeping inflation low. The ECB interprets this to mean an inflation rate 'close to but below 2 per cent'. Central banks are judged successful if they achieve a low rate of inflation and, linked to this, prevent the currency from falling in value (depreciating) relative to other currencies.

The prerequisite for success in this area is generally seen as independence from political interference. Central bankers have to be free to take unpopular decisions – such as raising interest rates – even if this is awkward for politicians facing elections. For that reason, the governors of central banks in Europe and the USA are appointed for long terms and cannot be removed by politicians.

The independence of the ECB is absolute. It is laid down in Article 130 of the Treaty on European Union:

> *[T]he ECB's independence is laid down in the institutional framework for the single monetary policy (in the Treaty and in the Statute). Neither the ECB nor the national central banks (NCBs), nor any member of their decision-making bodies, are allowed to seek or take instructions from EU institutions or bodies, from any government of an EU Member State or from any other body. EU institutions and bodies and the governments of the Member States must respect this principle and not seek to influence the members of the decision-making bodies of the ECB.* (www.ecb.int/ecb/orga/independence/html/index.en.html)

During the current EMU crisis these provisions have caused tension between politicians who believe the ECB is not doing enough, or is doing too much, to help resolve the crisis. Moreover, Article 123 of the Treaty prohibits the Bank from indulging in the 'monetary financing of governments'. This has been interpreted as ruling out purchasing bonds issued by the governments of the member states. This would restrict the instruments of monetary policy available to the ECB compared with, for example, those available to the Bank of England and the Federal Reserve Bank.

However, in September 2012 ECB President Mario Draghi announced that the bank was now prepared to commit unlimited resources to buy short-term government bonds, provided strict conditions were met.

As mentioned, most central banks are of the opinion that there is a close link between changes in the money supply and inflation (the quantity theory of money). If central banks can control high-powered money (or the money supply), theoretically they can control the inflation rate. Central banks can use a range of instruments to control the money supply or, more broadly, liquidity in the economy.

Open market operations

Open market operations (OMOs) consist of buying and selling government stock (bonds) on the 'open market' in order to influence the money supply. If the central bank buys government stock, it writes a cheque on itself that it gives to the seller of the bond. The bond seller then lodges this cheque in a bank deposit and the money creation process starts to unfold. This was traditionally the most important and frequently used instrument of monetary policy.

In terms of the ECB's balance sheet (Table 9.4) the entry for government securities increases on the asset side and bank reserves increase on the liability side. The monetary base or high-powered money increases and sets off a multiple expansion in the money supply. Until recently the ECB did not directly purchase government bonds. It purchased them from euro area member banks. By exchanging deposits with the ECB for these bonds, the banks gained increased reserves and the money supply increased.

Conversely, if the ECB wishes to reduce high-powered money it sells bonds to the commercial banks. The banks pay for the bonds by reducing their deposits and this sets the money creation process into reverse. In terms of the ECB balance sheet, government bonds are reduced on the asset side and commercial bank reserves on the liability side. High-powered money and, via the money multiplier, the rate of growth in the money supply decrease.

As a response to the euro crisis, the ECB has purchased government bonds on a large scale, especially from countries where yields had risen far above the low yields prevailing in Germany. This programme of monetising the debt of government is controversial. Orthodox thinking in German economic circles has opposed this strategy and fears that it will prove inflationary.

Quantitative easing

The yield on bonds of different maturities varies. Short-dated bonds, such as exchequer bills that are redeemable within three months, usually have lower yields than medium- and long-dated securities that do not mature for five or ten years. If investors expect interest rates to rise over time, this will push long bond yields higher. A graph showing yields on the vertical axis and maturities (from short to long) on the horizontal axis is called the *yield curve*. The yield curve reflects the term structure of interest rates. If longer-dated securities have higher yields than short-dated ones, the yield curve will be positively sloped. This is the normal situation, because there is always some risk that the rate of inflation will rise over the longer run. The slope of the yield curve provides information on the public's expectations about interest rates in the future.

Quantitative easing (QE) is similar to OMOs but involves central banks purchasing bonds of longer maturity than the short-term bills typically involved in OMOs. Through QE the central bank hopes to push interest rates down at the longer end of the yield curve. As mentioned, the yield curve typically shows higher interest rates on longer term than on shorter-term securities. QE is a relatively new and controversial instrument of monetary policy. It is implemented in the USA by the Federal Reserve and in the UK by the Bank of England. It was introduced in the euro area by the ECB when the yields on the short-term bonds (typically traded in OMOs) had fallen close to zero but there was still a lack of liquidity in the banking system and the fear of deflation was growing. The second wave of quantitative easing in the USA was known as QE2, which invited comparisons with the decommissioned luxury ocean liner.

The central bank's interest rate

The interest rate a central bank charges on its lending to the commercial banks and the government has different names in different countries. In Britain it used to be known as the Bank Rate, then the Minimum Lending Rate, but now the only rate set by the Bank of England is the Bill Discounting

Rate. In Germany the rate set by the Bundesbank was called the Lombard Rate. In Ireland the rate set by the Central Bank of Ireland was called the short-term credit facility (STCF).

In the USA the rate charged by the Federal Open Market Committee (FOMC) to the commercial banks is known as the Discount Rate. However, the commercial banks also borrow and lend to each other and the interest rate they charge each other is known as the Federal Funds Effective rate. The FOMC meets every seven weeks or so and sets a Federal Funds Target rate. The FOMC then engages in open market operations to ensure the effective rate and the target rate are very similar. For example, if the effective rate is greater than the target rate, FOMC will inject money (or liquidity) into the market. This additional supply of money drives down the effective rate towards the target rate. Conversely, if the effective rate is below the target rate, FOMC will withdraw money or liquidity from the market, thereby driving up the effective rate.

The American banking system provides a good example of how a central bank conducts OMOs and interest rate policy. The FOMC is probably the most important monetary policy-making institution in the world. American interest rates have a major influence on interest rates all over the world, but foreign interest rates do not have much effect on them, so the FOMC is relatively free to conduct an independent policy in this area.

The main ECB rate is known as the main refinancing interest rate (MRIR). The MRIR rate has a very important effect on all the interest rates (deposit and lending) set by the commercial banks in Europe. The commercial banks in Europe will pass on changes in the MRIR rate to their customers (see Chapter 17). This allows the central bank to influence the whole structure of interest rates in the economy. This makes the central bank a very powerful institution. More often than not, a central bank uses its interest rate to indicate its intentions or 'send a signal' to the commercial banks. When it raises its interest rate, this is taken as a signal to the commercial banks to curtail credit.

Reserve requirements

Earlier in this chapter we discussed how central banks set reserve requirements to ensure that banks have sufficient liquid assets to meet day-to-day withdrawals by depositors. If the central bank increases the reserve ratio the banks have to contract their lending in order to meet the new requirement. In fact, because it is a relatively blunt instrument that could lead to severe changes in liquidity, the reserve ratio is changed only infrequently.

Credit guidelines

A central bank can try to dictate to the banks by how much they can increase their lending over a specified period of time. If the banks exceed the guideline, they can be subject to penalties. Credit guidelines are asymmetrical in the sense that banks can be restrained from exceeding the ceiling but cannot be forced to go up to it. If the demand for credit is weak, banks will not be able to reach the ceiling. Credit guidelines were first used in Ireland in the mid-1960s and were abandoned in the 1980s. There are not used by the ECB.

9.9 The Credit-fuelled Property Bubble and the Crash

Before Ireland joined the euro area in 1999, the ability of banks to make loans depended on their success in attracting deposits. To attract deposits from the Irish public the main banks had branches in every city and in the bigger towns all over Ireland. However, after Ireland joined EMU in 1999, Irish banks found it easier to access funds from other European banks on the inter-bank market. This was part of a global trend towards greater international capital mobility but it was facilitated by the removal of the exchange rate risk through the use of a common currency in the euro area. Before the introduction of the euro, if a bank borrowed German marks and made a loan in Irish pounds, it was exposed to an exchange rate risk. If the Irish pound depreciated relative to the

German mark the bank would incur a loss as the borrowings had to be repaid in German marks. There were ways of insuring against this risk in the foreign exchange markets, but these involved costs.

With the liberalisation of capital flows and the removal of exchange rate risk, small banks, like Anglo Irish Bank, which had only six branches in Ireland and a very narrow deposit base here, were able to access inter-bank funds round the world and expand loans at an astonishing rate. The borrowed money was often quite short-term and had to be rolled over from week to week or month to month. The crisis that erupted in September 2008 led to a sudden drying up of inter-bank lending, which threatened the stability of the banking system that had become dependent on it. Only the large-scale provision of liquidity (in the form of loans) by the central banks like the Federal Reserve and the Bank of England averted widespread bank closures.

Box 9.3 LIBOR

The London Interbank Offered Rate (LIBOR) is the average interest rate that leading banks in London estimate they would be charged when borrowing from other banks. It is the primary benchmark, along with the *Euribor*, its European counterpart, for short-term interest rates around the world. It is therefore one of the most important prices in the financial universe.

Early in 2012 a major scandal erupted when it was learned that the US Department of Justice was conducting an investigation into misreporting of the data used to compile LIBOR. Barclays Bank was fined $200 million for its part in the fraud. By the middle of the year the chairman and the most senior officers of Barclays had resigned. In June it was announced that the UK Serious Fraud Office had initiated another investigation into the manipulation of interest rates. In December 2012 Union Bank Suisse was fined a record $1.5 billion for misreporting interest rates.

The reason why banks provided false information for the compilation of LIBOR is that they did not want it to be known that they were being charged high interest rates when they borrowed on the inter-bank market. High interest rates act as a signal that lenders are concerned about the borrower's creditworthiness.

From 1999 onwards Irish bankers were influenced by the psychology of the moment. When the boom in property and land started, banks provided loans to developers to buy land at inflated prices in the hope of quick construction of houses, apartments and offices that could be sold off at even more inflated prices. Rather than relying on their traditional deposit base for funds to make loans, they increasingly had recourse to the international inter-bank market. It should be noted that this enthusiasm for cross-border lending was not confined to members of the euro area. British and Icelandic banks also participated in this market and some of the biggest banks lending to Irish banks were based in the UK.

As the Irish property boom turned into one of the biggest property busts in history, the recklessness of the Irish banks' lending was exposed. They realised that they had loaned out depositors' money, as well as money borrowed from foreign banks, for projects that had no hope of success.

In theory, the banks had the property against which they had loaned as collateral, but when the boom turned to bust after mid-2007, the value of the assets used as collateral by the developers and banks collapsed. Moreover, foreclosing on this collateral was much more complicated than it seemed. First, the value of the collateral had shrunk dramatically, in some cases to less than 10 per cent of the amounts the banks had advanced, so it was of little value to the lender, who did not want to get into the business of managing empty housing estates and vacant shopping centres. Second, Irish property developers were quick to hire lawyers and accountants to shield their personal assets – often in exotic tax havens – from seizure by the banks. Assets were transferred to the spouses of developers beyond the reach of the banks. We return to the aftermath of the housing crash in Chapter 21.

On 28 September 2008, it was feared that the Irish banking system was collapsing and the government put in place a guarantee arrangement to safeguard all deposits (retail, commercial, institutional and inter-bank) as well as bonds, senior debt and dated subordinated debt in Bank of Ireland, Allied Irish Banks, Anglo Irish Bank, Irish Life and Permanent, and the Irish Nationwide Building Society. Total liabilities covered under the scheme amount to approximately €485 billion. Relative to GDP, the scale of this bank guarantee was unprecedented anywhere in the world.

The government's view was that the banks had to be rescued because otherwise they might bring the whole financial system crashing down. They were regarded as 'too big to fail', even if this was clearly implausible in the case of Anglo Irish Bank and Irish Nationwide.

Anglo Irish Bank losses for 2009 and 2010 came to approximately €30 billion (see Chapter 21). This bank was never of 'systemic' importance to the Irish economy. It operated essentially as a gambling casino on the fringes of the Irish financial system (but it was regulated by and had a banking licence from the Central Bank of Ireland). Yet it was covered by the extended liability guarantees offered in 2008 and has cost the Irish taxpayer in excess of €25 billion.

The whole episode raises several thorny issues. First, four years later, there is continuing uncertainty and even mystery as to why the Fianna Fáil government of the day acted as it did. Was it fright at the prospect of the collapse of the whole Irish banking system? Was it favouritism towards well-connected bankers with political links? Was it just ignorance and lack of experience of anything on the scale of the crisis that broke in September 2008? Until there is a full and open hearing into the event of that fateful month these questions cannot be answered.

In a crisis of the type that exploded in 2008, governments are faced with difficult choices. They can stand back and let the weaker banks go to the wall. This would be in accordance with the free enterprise, laissez faire philosophy preached by many who advocated light regulation of the banking system in the years before the crisis. But the implications of the collapse of major banks terrify governments. Powerful groups in all countries argue that intervention to bail out the banks is absolutely necessary. However, when governments bail out banks that have lent money recklessly they create *moral hazard* and set up perverse incentives for future bank executives.

In this context moral hazard means encouraging a reckless attitude towards risk among bankers. Why should they worry about taking risks in the hope of gaining large profits? If things go right they will be enriched; if things go wrong someone else will pick up the cost. The Irish bankers who landed the Irish economy in an unprecedented mess have not been punished in any significant manner. They were removed from their executive posts but were amply compensated with golden handshakes and generous pensions. Their successors will no doubt some day dream of earning excess profits by taking a little more risk than their competitors and the whole bubble of reckless lending will begin to inflate again. 'This time it's different', we will be told.

9.10 Key Terms and Concepts

In this chapter we introduced the subject of money and banking and reviewed their history in Ireland from the earliest times to the present. The main points discussed included:

- the functions of money, the most important being its role as a medium of exchange
- fractional reserve banking
- the role of a central bank
- how money is created
- high-powered money and the money multiplier
- banking crises
- inter-bank lending and the property bubble.

CHAPTER 10

Money and Interest Rates in a Closed Economy

10.1 Introduction

In this chapter we discuss the theory of the demand for money. We start with an overview of the topic, then show how the supply and demand for money determines the rate of interest. The money market is then combined with the goods and services market to create a more realistic model of the macroeconomy. The link between the money market and the goods and services market is the relationship between the rate of interest and interest-sensitive expenditure. Using the expanded model, issues such as the relative effectiveness of fiscal and monetary policy are discussed, as well as the concept of 'crowding-out'.

10.2 Overview of Monetary Policy

We begin this chapter with a brief overview of how the money supply affects aggregate demand, output and employment. Figure 10.1 presents an overview of the key diagrams underlying the analysis. The lower diagram left-hand side shows equilibrium in the money market. In this market, the supply (M^s) and demand (M^d) for money determines the nominal interest rate (i). An increase in the money supply, for example, will shift the M^s line out to the right and this reduces the nominal interest rate along the vertical axis (diagram lower left).

The diagram on the lower right-hand side shows the interest-sensitive expenditure (IE) line. This line illustrates an inverse relationship between the real interest rate (r) and interest-sensitive expenditure such as personal consumption expenditure, investment and net exports (exports minus imports). Assuming the price level is initially constant, the previous reduction in the nominal interest rate leads to an equal fall in the real interest rate (via the Fisher equation – see section 10.5 below) and this leads to an increase in expenditure. The IE line acts as the link or bridge between the money market and the goods and services market.

The upper diagram represents equilibrium in the goods and services market. This is the familiar short-run aggregate supply (SRAS) and aggregate demand (AD) model developed in Chapter 5. The vertical line represents the long-run AS curve (LRAS) or the potential real output line. The main point is that changes in interest-sensitive expenditure (brought about by changes in the real interest rate) shift the AD line up to the right.

Taking the three diagrams together, the central bank can influence real output and the price level as follows.

- An increase in the money supply leads to a fall in the nominal interest rate.
- Via the Fisher equation, the nominal interest rate leads to an equal fall in the real interest rate.
- Via the IE line, this leads to an increase in expenditure.

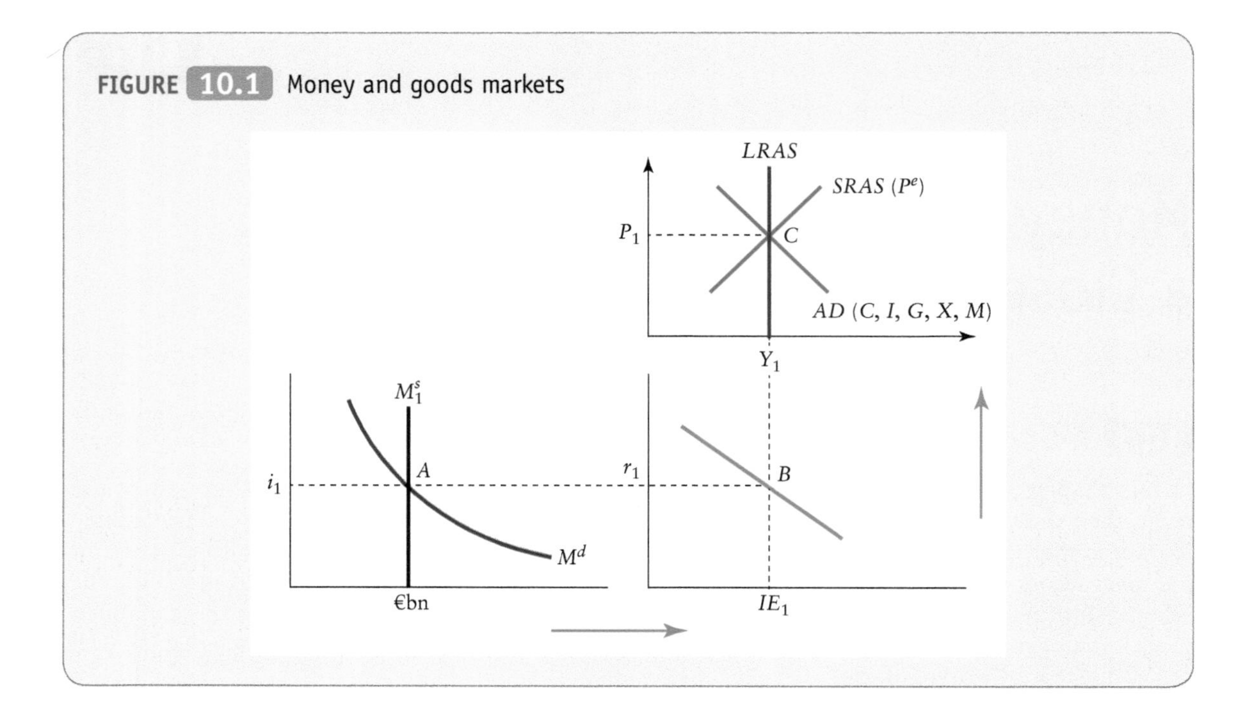

- The rise in expenditure shifts the AD curve out to the right and in the short run both real output (Y) and the price level increase. However, in the longer term, the economy will revert back to potential real output. The overall effect of the increase in the money supply is to increase the price level.

In short:

$$\uparrow M^s \rightarrow \downarrow i \rightarrow \downarrow r \rightarrow \uparrow IE \rightarrow \uparrow AD \rightarrow \uparrow Y \rightarrow \downarrow U \text{ and } \uparrow P$$

Conversely, a reduction in the money supply will, in the long run, lead to proportionate decrease in the price level. We now examine the various strands of this analysis in more detail.

10.3 The Demand for Money

At first sight, the concept of the demand for money (M^d) may appear rather odd. If you ask someone what is his or her 'demand for money', the answer is likely to be 'infinite' or something to that effect. However, the term 'demand for money' is used by economists in a rather special way and does not refer simply to the desire to be rich.

To understand what economists mean by the demand for money, we start from the consideration that wealth can be stored in many forms: money, government stocks, company shares, works of art, houses and so on. Why do people keep some of their wealth in money as opposed to the alternatives? Keynes's theory of *liquidity preference* provides answers to this question.

There are two important differences between money and the alternatives.

- Money is liquid: that is, its value is known and it can be easily and quickly converted into purchasing power. On the other hand, government stocks, company shares and other stores of value give a return, but they are in varying degrees illiquid. That is, they cannot be used as a medium of exchange and it can take time to convert them into cash. Moreover, the value of these assets can change, giving rise to some uncertainty as to how much they are really worth.

- Money does not give a return over time, whereas other assets do. However, the borderlines between the different categories of asset are not rigid. Some liquid assets such as deposit accounts and some current accounts earn interest.

These considerations shed light on the reasons why people forgo the return available on interest-bearing assets and keep some of their wealth in money or cash.

Keynes analysed the reasons for holding money under the headings of the transaction, precautionary and speculative motives. Let us examine each of these in turn.

Transaction and precautionary motives

People need money for transaction purposes – to do their shopping, buy lunch, pay bus fares, etc. No matter how rich one is, it is hard to purchase a meal or groceries without paying with money or some form of credit card. A credit card acts as money because the banks pays on your behalf and you repay the bank by a specified date. Keynes described the transaction motive for holding money as the need 'to bridge the interval between the receipt of income and its disbursement'.

The precautionary motive is the desire to hold money to cater for unexpected contingencies (accidents, illness, etc.) or opportunities that may arise. According to Keynes, people hold money to 'provide for contingencies requiring sudden expenditure and for unforeseen opportunities of advantageous purchases'.

It is reasonable to assume that the amount of money demanded for transactions and precautionary reasons depends on the level of income. The richer a person is, the more expensive her lifestyle and the more money she needs for transaction and precautionary reasons. The same is true at the macro level. As national income or nominal output increases, there is an increase in the demand for money for transaction and precautionary purposes. An increase in nominal output leads to an increase in the demand for money and a fall in nominal output reduces the demand for money. The transaction and precautionary motives for holding money may therefore be written as:

$$M^d = L(\text{nominal output}) \qquad L_1 > 0 \tag{1}$$

Equation (1) states that the demand for money is a function of nominal output. The $L_1 > 0$ indicates that an increase in output increases the demand for money and vice versa. $L(\ )$ denotes function of.

The speculative demand for money

In addition to the desire to hold money to finance day-to-day transactions and eventualities, Keynes believed that people hold money with the 'object of securing profit from knowing better than the market what the future will bring forth'. He called this the speculative motive. To understand the speculative motive we need to look at the workings of the bond market.

The bond market

Bonds are issued by countries and companies as a way of obtaining money from investors. The bonds issued by a company differ from shares in the company in an important way.

Shareholders own a proportion of the company and have voting rights that give them some control over the operations of the company. This ownership entitles them to an uncertain dividend that depends on the profits of the company. On the other hand, bondholders lend money to a company for a specific period of time and do not have any control over the company's affairs. Bonds pay a fixed monetary return (*coupon*) until the maturity date, so the bondholder knows with certainty how much income she will receive from the bond. For example, a bond with a face value of €2,000 and a coupon of €100 that matures in the year 2020 entitles the bondholder to a sum of €100 every year until 2020 and repayment of the €2,000 principal in 2020.

TABLE 10.1 The relationship between interest rates and bond prices

1. Interest rate on bank deposit	20%	10%	5%
2. Fixed bond coupon	€10	€10	€10
3. Price of bonds	€50	€100	€200
4. Yield on bonds (= coupon/price)	20%	10%	5%

Governments as well as companies issue bonds. Bonds issued by governments are known as 'sovereign debt'. Traditionally the bonds issued by governments of the main industrialised countries were regarded as the safest place for investors to place their money. While the return might be low, the capital would be secure. There was no fear that the country would default, i.e. renege on paying interest on the debt and eventually redeeming the principal.

A bond that is never redeemed but that pays an income indefinitely is known as a *perpetuity*. Historically the British government used to issue this type of bond, whose main attraction to the investor was the steady flow of income it provided and the security of being able to sell it on the open market at any time with little risk of losing any of the original investment. Bonds issued by certain national governments are known as 'gilts'. The term originally referred to the debt securities issued by the Bank of England, which had a gilt (or gilded) edge. The term is still used in the UK and Ireland.

Bonds also provide investors a convenient medium for trying to make capital gains. To see how this may be done, we need to consider what determines bond prices and bond yields. Consider the data in Table 10.1.

- Line 1 displays three rates of interest on bank deposits.
- Line 2 shows the fixed coupon payable on a government bond. This is assumed to be €10.
- Arbitrage should now ensure that the yield (per cent) on the bond is equal to that on bank deposits. The yield on a bond is defined as the coupon divided by the price of the bond. If the coupon is €10 and the price of the bond is €100, the yield is 10 per cent. (See Box 10.1 for a discussion of the concept of arbitrage.) The price of the bond required to ensure that the bond yield is the same as the interest rate is given in line 3.
- The only way for the yield on bonds to change, given that the coupon is fixed, is for the price of the bond to vary. (We assume that it is a perpetuity, so that what matters to an investor is its current and future yields, rather than its value at maturity.) Line 4 shows the bond prices that equalise the yield on bonds with that on the bank account.
- Notice what happens when the interest rate falls from 20 to 10 to five per cent. Arbitrage will ensure that the yield on government bonds also falls from 20 to 10 to five per cent. For this to happen, the price of the bond must rise from €50 to €100 to €200. Therefore, as interest rates fall, bond prices rise and, conversely, as interest rates increase, bond prices fall.
- The inverse relationship between interest rates and bond prices means that bondholders stand to make a capital gain when interest rates fall. Conversely, bondholders incur a capital loss when interest rates rise. Investors should therefore buy bonds if they expect interest rates to fall and sell them if they expect interest rates to rise. This strategy provides the basis of the Keynesian speculative motive for holding cash.

Since the early 1980s nominal interest rates have been falling in the main industrial countries. As the rate of inflation declined throughout, nominal interest rates fell from the peaks recorded in the early 1980s to the very low levels now recorded in the largest industrialised countries like the USA, Britain and Germany. This has given rise to a long bull market in bonds. (A bull market is one in

Box 10.1 Arbitrage

Arbitrage is defined as buying a commodity or a currency in one market and selling it in another with a view to making a profit. The effect of arbitrage is to equalise returns across markets. For example, if the price of gold was lower in London than in New York, speculators could make a profit by buying in London and selling in New York. But the increased demand for gold in London would drive up the London price, while simultaneously the increased supply in New York would drive down the New York price. In a short space of time the two prices would converge. Arbitrage is particularly effective in financial markets because information on prices and yields all over the world can be readily obtained. As a result, investors will buy and sell comparable assets until their yields are equal. We are assuming that arbitrage ensures that the yield on the bond is equal to the interest rate obtainable from a bank deposit. In reality, risk, transaction costs and other factors have to be taken into account, and strict equality between the yields on different types of assets will not exist.

which asset prices are rising.) Investors in bonds enjoyed not only the annual coupon or income but also a consistent capital gain. A basket of stocks returned a mere 19 per cent from the start of 2000 through 2011, while a basket of bonds returned about 113 per cent through a combination of rising prices and interest earnings.

The fact that interest rates on 10-year US bonds are now below two per cent has led many to believe that they have nowhere to go but up. If economic recovery gets under way again it could drive interest rates higher, causing bond prices to fall.

NOTE: There are many different interest rates, for example the rates on short- and long-term government stocks, on low- and high-risk company bonds (the latter became known as 'junk bonds' during the 1980s), as well as the rates charged by the banks on loans and paid on deposits. The bonds issued by the 'peripheral' countries of the euro area – including Ireland – have been treated as junk bonds by investors in recent years due to the perceived risk of default. Yields on these bonds soared while yields on bonds issued in the 'core' countries (such as Germany, the Netherlands and Austria) have fallen. Nonetheless, as market conditions for the 'peripheral' countries improved somewhat after 2011, their yields have fallen and the bond prices have risen. Investors who 'took a punt' on Irish bonds in 2010 enjoyed high yields and capital gains over the following two years.

Keynes's 'natural rate of interest'

Keynes believed in the existence of a 'natural' rate of interest. He argued that departures from this rate are viewed as temporary. If interest rates rise above the natural rate, the expectation will be that they will eventually fall. Similarly, if interest rates fall below the natural rate, the expectation will be that they will rise.

Suppose, for example, that the natural rate of interest is considered to be five per cent and interest rates increase from five per cent to eight per cent. Investors holding bonds suffer a capital loss. However, the expectation now is that interest rates will fall back to the natural level of five per cent at some time in the future. Investors should therefore reduce their money holdings and purchase bonds in anticipation of making a capital gain. Hence the rise in the interest rate from five to eight per cent is associated with a fall in the demand for cash balances.

Conversely, a fall in the interest rate from five to three per cent gives rise to the expectation that interest rates will rise in the future. Investors should get out of bonds and into money to avoid making a capital loss. The fall in the interest rate is, therefore, associated with an increase in the demand for money.

This relationship between the interest rate (i) and the demand for money can be written:

$$M^d = L(i) \qquad L_1 < 0 \tag{2}$$

where $L_1 < 0$ indicates that an increase in the interest rate causes a fall in M^d, and vice versa.

NOTE: The inverse relationship between the interest rate and the demand for money could also be explained in terms of the opportunity cost of holding cash. As we saw above, wealth held as cash does not earn a return, whereas wealth held as bonds or in other assets does. By holding cash, a person is therefore forgoing the interest that could have been earned on bonds, for example. Thus, when the interest rate is high, the opportunity cost of holding cash balances is also high, and it is to be expected that the public will economise on their holdings of cash. It is therefore only realistic to include the rate of interest among the determinants of the demand for money.

The total demand for money

Combining equations (1) and (2) we can account for all the motives for holding money and write the demand for money function as:

$$M^d = L(\text{nominal output}, i) \qquad L_1 > 0, L_2 < 0 \tag{3}$$

Equation (3) states that the demand for money is a function of nominal output and the interest rate. The terms L_1 and L_2 indicate how the explanatory variables (nominal output and i) influence the dependent variable (M^d). Separating nominal output into its real (Y) and price components, equation (3) can also be rewritten as:

$$M^d = L(Y, P, i) \qquad L_1 > 0, L_2 > 0, L_3 < 0 \tag{4}$$

Equation (4) states that the demand for money is positively related to both real output (Y) and the price level (P), but negatively to the rate of interest.

A demand for money schedule is drawn in Figure 10.2. The nominal rate of interest is on the vertical axis and the demand for money on the horizontal axis. The relationship between the interest rate and the demand for money is shown by movements along the line. An increase in interest rate from i_1 to i_2 leads to a decrease in the demand for money. Conversely, a decrease in the interest rate increases the demand for money.

Nominal output determines the position (or location) of the demand for money curve. An increase in nominal output (Y × P) shifts the M^d schedule to the right; a fall in nominal output shifts it to the left.

FIGURE 10.2 The demand for money curve

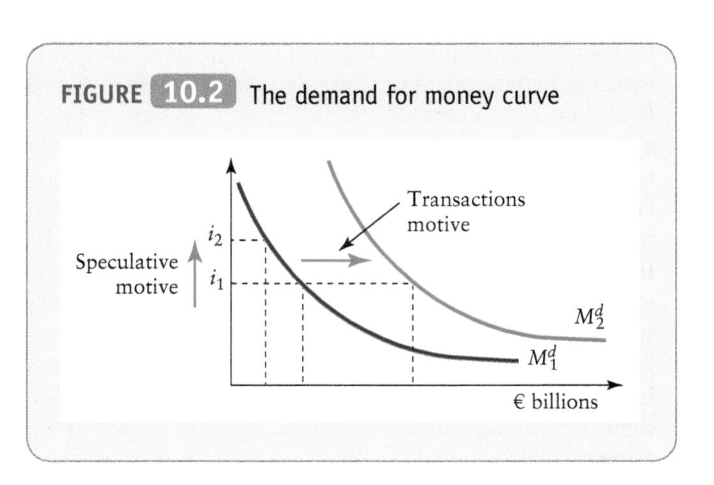

Note that the slope of the demand for money curve is not linear. At low interest rates the curve becomes flat or horizontal. The reason for this is that at low interest rates there may be unanimity among investors that interest rates will rise in the future. That is, investors expect bond prices to fall. In order to avoid speculative losses in the bond market, investors therefore keep their wealth in money. At low rates of interest, the demand for money is virtually infinite as no one wants to hold bonds. This is reflected in the diagram in the flat portion of the demand for money curve.

FIGURE 10.3 Money market equilibrium

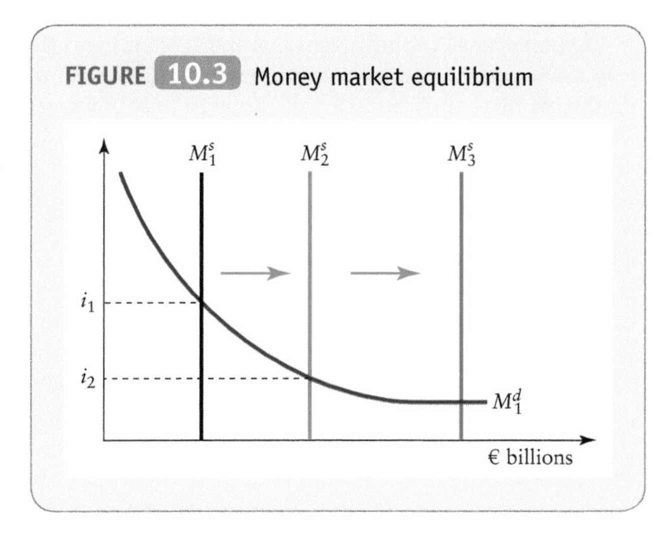

10.4 Money Market Equilibrium

In Figure 10.3 the money supply (M^s) schedule is combined with a demand for money (M^d) schedule. The money supply is shown as a vertical line, which indicates that changes in the interest rate do not affect the supply of money. This assumes that the money supply is completely controlled by the monetary authorities or central bank. Put another way, we are assuming that the money supply is exogenous. (If changes in interest rates had a positive effect on the money supply, the M^s curve would slope upwards to the right.)

The rate of interest is the price of money and, like other prices, it is determined by the forces of supply and demand. At an interest rate of i_1, the supply and demand for money are equal. The money market is in equilibrium.

NOTE: If the interest rate is above i_1, there is an excess supply of money and the interest rate will fall towards the equilibrium rate. If the interest rate is below i_1, there is an excess demand for money and the interest rate will rise to the equilibrium rate.

Figure 10.3 also illustrates what happens to the interest rate when the central bank increases the money supply through open market operations (OMOs). The money supply (M^s) line moves out to the right and the interest rate falls from i_1 to the new equilibrium level, i_2. An increase in the money supply therefore reduces the nominal interest rate. Conversely, a reduction in the money supply leads to an increase in the interest rate.

As mentioned, the demand for money schedule is horizontal at low interest rates. An increase in the money supply along the flat portion of the demand for money curve would not lower interest rates and monetary policy is in this case ineffective. This situation is known as the *liquidity trap*. Examples of a liquidity trap are Japan in the 1990s and the USA and the euro area after 2010. In 2012, the main policy interest rate was one per cent in the USA and 0.75 per cent in the euro area. Since nominal interest rates cannot fall below zero (unless investors are to be charged for putting money on deposit, as has happened recently in Swiss banks), there is little or no scope for the monetary authorities to further stimulate the economy through reductions in the nominal interest rate.

This situation implies that there is a 'zero lower bound' to policy interest rates, which limits the effectiveness of monetary policy. The manner in which the Fed in the USA and, to a lesser extent, the ECB have pushed their policy interest rates down in reaction to the current recession has highlighted this issue. With interest rates close to zero but unemployment still high (and in some countries rising), what instruments of monetary policy are left to central banks to stimulate the economy?

One answer is to indulge in quantitative easing, QE. As mentioned in Chapter 9, QE involves central banks purchasing bonds of longer maturity than the short-term bills typically involved in OMOs. By this strategy the central banks hope to push interest rates down at the longer end of the yield curve. The yield curve is normally upward sloping, indicating higher interest rates in the longer term. QE is an attempt to bring down long-term interest rates.

Between November 2008 and September 2012 the US Federal Reserve Bank conducted three rounds of QE, purchasing a total of $2 trillion of securities. The Bank of England started QE in 2009 and by mid-2012 had purchased about £375 billion of assets.

The ECB, on the other hand, has been more cautious in its approach to QE, which it calls an 'unconventional' policy instrument. However, at the end of 2011 it loaned about €500 billion of three-year loans to the banks and in March 2012 it announced a second wave that could reach €1 trillion. As we explained in Chapter 9, in September 2012 the ECB launched a major bond-purchasing programme to stabilise the euro area bond market. It is being called 'outright monetary transactions' (OMT) rather than QE because it is planned to offset ('sterilise') the bond purchases with sales of other assets. This is intended to stabilise the high-powered money supply.

These initiatives are very different from the restrictive monetary policy pursued by the major countries during the Great Depression. It is to be hoped that they will avert a recurrence of the persistent deflation and high unemployment that characterised the 1930s.

Shifts in the demand for money curve

As mentioned above, an increase in nominal output will shift the demand for money (M^d) curve upwards to the right. As shown in Figure 10.4, if the money supply is held constant, the result will be an increase in the interest rate from i_1 to i_2. Similarly, a fall in nominal output will shift the M^d curve downwards and, assuming the money supply is constant, interest rates will fall. This effect is important when we come to discuss the 'crowding-out' effect later in this chapter.

Note that if the demand for money curve is very volatile and the central bank wants to keep the interest rate constant it will have to vary the money supply. For example, an increase in the demand for money can be offset by an increase in the money supply and the interest will remain constant (not shown, but the reader should redraw Figure 10.4 to illustrate this point). There is an important implication: if the demand for money is volatile, the central bank can control either the money supply or the interest rate, but not both simultaneously. If the interest rate is to remain constant, the central bank loses control of the money supply. Alternatively, if the money supply remains constant the interest rate will vary in line with the demand for money.

In the case of the euro area, the ECB decides on its main refinancing interest rate (MRIR), the rate it charges on loans to commercial banks, and then uses OMOs to change the money supply. Hence, the ECB is targeting the interest rate and therefore loses control over the euro area's money supply. In the USA, the Fed follows a similar policy as it targets the federal funds' effective rate. Both of these central banks favour an interest rate target over a money supply target.

FIGURE 10.4 Increase in the demand for money

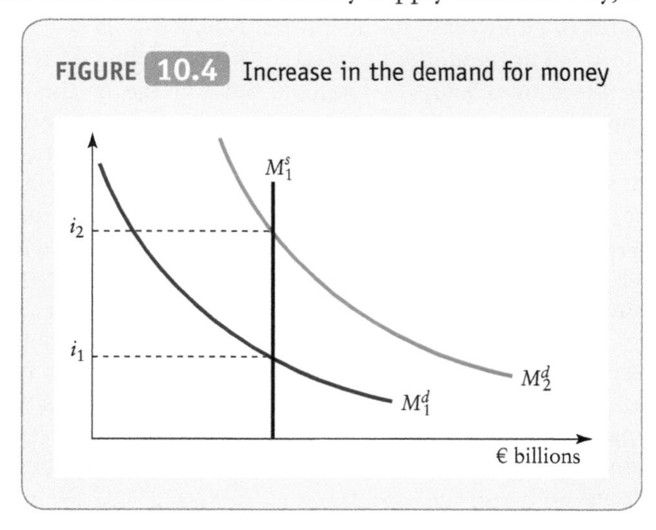

10.5 Nominal and Real Interest Rates

At this point it is important to make a distinction between real and nominal interest rates. The nominal interest rate, i, is the rate quoted in the newspapers or by banks and issuers of bonds. The real rate, r, is defined as the nominal interest rate minus the inflation rate, π.

Real interest rate = nominal interest rate − inflation rate

or

$$r = i - \pi \tag{5}$$

Equation (5) is referred to as the *Fisher equation* after one of America's greatest economists, Irving Fisher (1867–1947), who taught at Yale University. Since interest rates are forward-looking (interest is paid or charged over the next six months or a year), and as we do not know what the rate of inflation will be in the future, the Fisher equation should be stated in terms of *expected* inflation (π^e).

$$r = i - \pi^e \tag{6}$$

Rearranging equation (6), we can also state that the nominal interest rate is equal to the real interest rate plus the expected inflation rate.

$$i = r + \pi^e \tag{7}$$

According to this equation, if the real interest rate is stable, a rise in the expected rate of inflation will lead to a one-to-one increase in the nominal interest rate. This is known as the *Fisher effect.*

We have talked about 'the' interest rate, but, as we pointed out earlier, there is a whole array of interest rates. As we saw in Chapter 9, lower rates are received by depositors than are paid by borrowers – this is how banks make their profits. Furthermore, liquid deposits attract lower interest than long-term deposits and risky borrowers pay higher interest rates than more secure borrowers. The interest rate payable on different types of mortgage also varies. Interest on 'tracker' mortgages is set at the ECB's main refinancing rate plus one per cent, which came to 1.5 per cent in mid-2012, whereas the interest rate on standard 'variable rate' mortgages is over four per cent. (The banks are now losing money on tracker mortgages because they have to pay a higher rate to attract depositors.)

Figure 10.5 shows the nominal interest rate and the inflation rate in Ireland between 1975 and 2012. The interest rate we have used is an average of the interest rates charged on mortgages. The difference between the two series is the real interest rate and is shown in Figure 10.6.

It can be seen that the nominal interest rate was well above the inflation rate from 1985 to 1997. During these years the high real interest rate acted as a drag on the economy and kept the lid on house prices. There was a dramatic fall in the real interest rate following our entry into EMU. From 2000 to 2008 the real interest rate was close to zero. The fall in the real interest rate in 1999 and the negative rate up to 2007 were due to the convergence of Irish nominal interest rates to the euro area level, which in turn reflected the low rates prevailing in Germany. Low real interest in Ireland early in the century coinicided with a period of very rapid real growth and an explosion in house prices. Following the collapse of the housing market and the wider economy in 2007, falling prices or deflation resulted in a rise in the real interest rate.

Thus over the past 15 years the real interest rate has moved counter-cyclically, tending to amplify the fluctuations in the economy. This was a consequence of the transfer of monetary policy to the ECB after entry into the euro area. An independent Irish central bank could have raised interest rates as the asset price boom got under way and unemployment plummeted in the early years of the twenty-first century and lowered them to offset the recession after 2007.

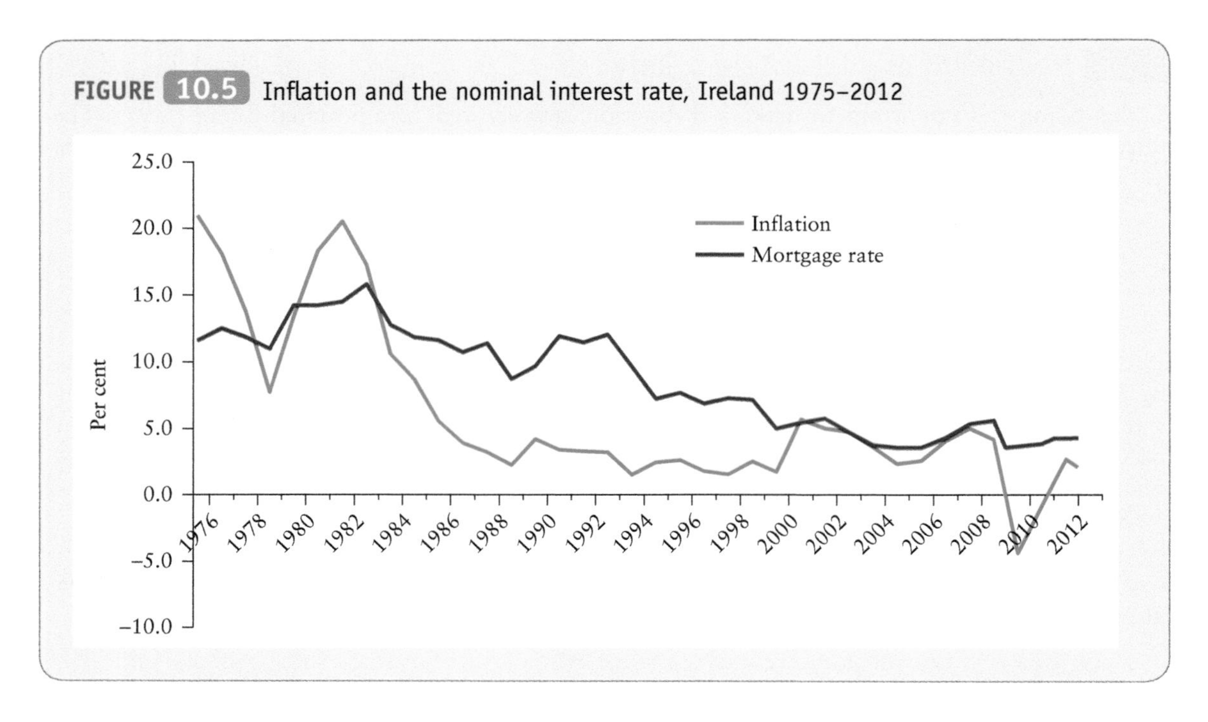

FIGURE 10.5 Inflation and the nominal interest rate, Ireland 1975–2012

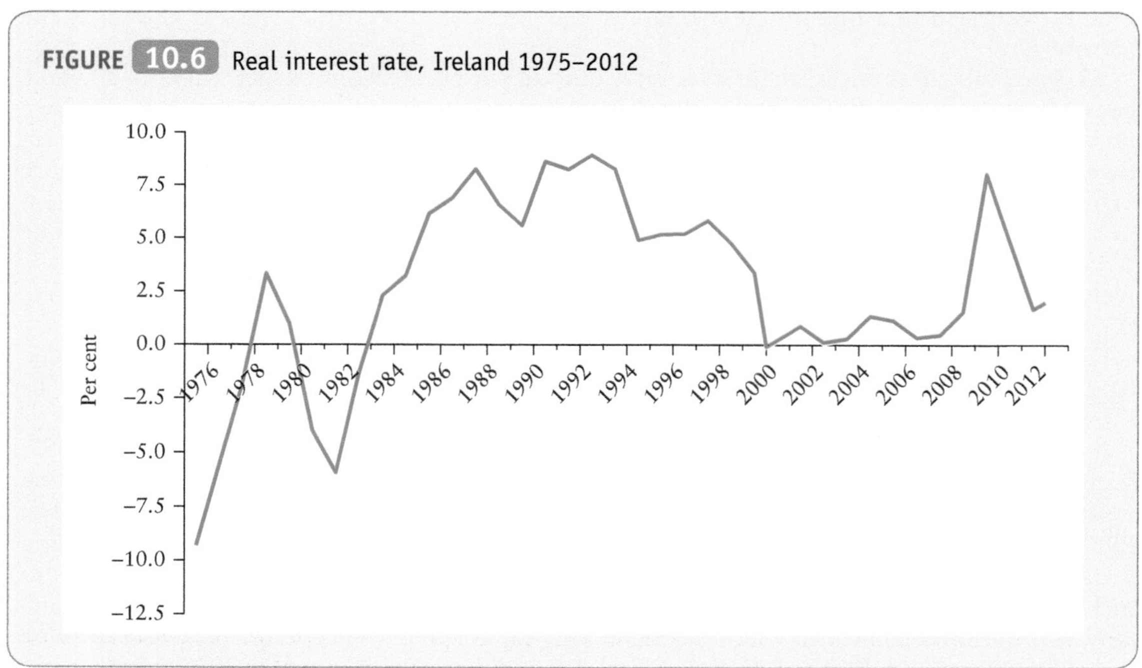

FIGURE 10.6 Real interest rate, Ireland 1975–2012

10.6 Aggregate Demand and Interest Rates

In this section we explain how changes in the interest rate impact on interest-sensitive expenditure (IE), which in turn affects the AD curve. Changes in the AD curve will affect real output (Y), the price level and unemployment. We are assuming here that there is a one-for-one relationship between the nominal and real interest rates. Referring back to the Fisher equation, a decrease in the nominal rate is reflected in a fall in the real interest rate. This will be the case in the short run when the price level is constant.

Consumer expenditure

Changes in the real interest rate (r) can be expected to influence personal consumption expenditure (C), which is a key component of aggregate demand. A decrease in the real interest rate could be expected to increase C and vice versa. The fall in real interest rates in the late 1990s and early 2000s, for example, encouraged more people to take out loans and to increase expenditure. Conversely, if real interest rates were to rise to a high level this would encourage people to cut expenditure and pay off expensive loans.

The consumption function outlined in Chapter 6 can be expanded to include the real interest rate. In this case, C becomes a function of real disposable income and the real interest rate. A change in the real interest rate can be expected to affect autonomous personal consumption expenditure.

Investment

Investment (I) consists of creating assets such as building roads, factories, houses and equipment. Consider a firm that is contemplating investing in, say, new plant or machinery. It has three possible ways of financing this:

1. using retained earnings or profits
2. borrowing from a bank
3. selling new shares in the company on the stock exchange.

The main sources of finance for private sector investment are retained earnings and bank borrowing. Because banks charge interest on their loans, it is easy to see why there is an inverse relationship between investment and the interest rate. A higher rate of interest will tend to discourage borrowing for investment. Conversely, a lower interest rate will tend to encourage borrowing for investment.

But the rate of interest should also be taken into account when retained earnings are being considered to finance an investment project. Firms should take account of the opportunity cost of using retained profits. Retained earnings could be used to purchase government bonds and thereby earn a rate of return. The investment project should offer a rate of return that at least matches the return from bonds.

Similarly, a firm's ability to raise money through the stock market depends on whether it can convince investors that the investment project will generate a return that is comparable to what they could earn from investing in bonds. Thus, the rate of interest will affect a firm's investment plans, regardless of which of the three sources of funds it uses.

In Appendix 10.1 at the end of this chapter we explain the concept of net present value and show how it is used to evaluate the profitability of an investment project.

Net exports

Although we are dealing with a closed economy in this chapter, it is appropriate to introduce one departure. Changes in the interest rate also affect net exports (NX). As explained later in the book, changes in the interest rate will affect the exchange rate and this, in turn, will impact on NX. In particular, a rise in euro area interest rates, *ceteris paribus*, will lead to an appreciation of the euro exchange rate. This in turn will make euro area exports more expensive and imports cheaper. The result will be a fall in NX.

Conversely, a fall in euro area interest rates, other things being equal, will lead to a depreciation of the euro exchange rate. This will make euro area exports cheaper or more competitive and imports dearer. The result is a rise in NX.

Summary

This inverse relationship between the real interest rate, on the one hand, and C, I and NX is known as the interest-sensitive expenditure (IE) schedule and it is illustrated in Figure 10.7. The interest rate is measured along the vertical axis and expenditure (C, I and NX) along the horizontal axis. This curve is particularly important as it acts as the bridge between the money market and the goods and services market.

If changes in the rate of interest have a weak effect on expenditure, then the IE curve will be steep (inelastic). If, on the other hand, changes in the rate of interest have a strong effect on expenditure, the IE curve will be flat (elastic). As we shall see, the slope of this IE schedule has an important bearing on the relative efficiency of fiscal and monetary policy.

FIGURE 10.7 The interest-sensitive expenditure curve

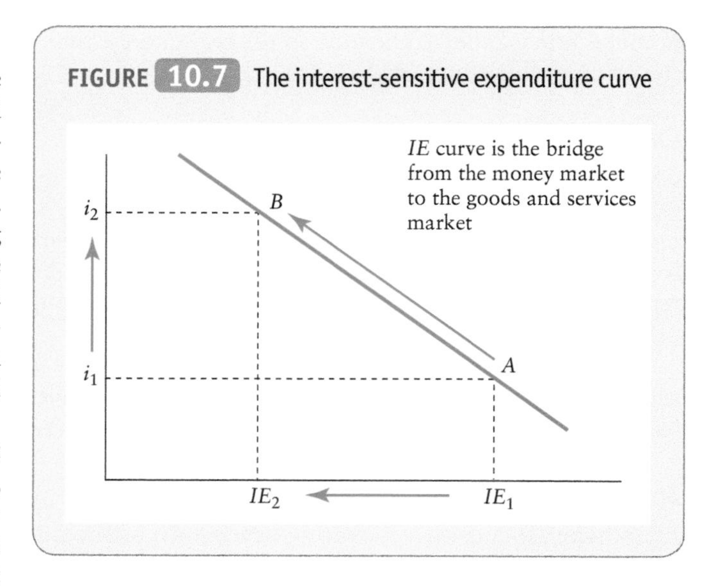
IE curve is the bridge from the money market to the goods and services market
i_2
i_1
B
A
IE_2
IE_1

10.7 Monetary Policy in a Closed Economy

We now incorporate our model of the money market and the IE curve into the AS/AD model developed in Chapter 5. The expanded model of the economy contains two markets: the goods or product market; and the money market. In the goods market, the interaction of the short-run aggregate supply (SRAS) and the aggregate demand (AD) curves determines real output (Y) and the price level (P). In the money market, the supply and demand for money determines the nominal interest rate (*i*). The link or bridge between the goods and money market is the IE curve.

The authorities may use fiscal policy and monetary policy to influence real output and the price level.

In the upper right-hand diagram in Figure 10.8, the economy is at potential real output Y*, on the long-run aggregate supply (LRAS) curve. Let us suppose the authorities mistakenly believe that output can be increased and unemployment reduced and they implement an expansionary monetary policy to achieve this. Figure 10.8 illustrates the effect of an increase in the money supply. In the lower diagram on the left, the central bank increases the money supply from M^s_1 to M^s_2. The nominal interest rate falls from i_1 to i_2.

This fall in the nominal interest rate also leads to a fall in the real interest rate via the Fisher equation. In the bottom diagram on the right, the fall in the real interest rate leads to an increase in interest-sensitive expenditure, IE.

In the top diagram, the increase in IE shifts the aggregate demand schedule upwards to the right and the economy moves from E to F. In the short run, output, Y, increases from Y_1 to Y_2 and the price level from P_1 to P_2. This increase in real output also leads to lower unemployment.

In the short run the sequence of events is:

$$\uparrow M^s \rightarrow \downarrow i \rightarrow \downarrow r \rightarrow \uparrow IE \rightarrow \uparrow AD \rightarrow \uparrow Y \rightarrow \downarrow U \text{ and } \uparrow P$$

NOTE: Fiscal policy is much more direct in its effects than monetary policy: an increase in G increases aggregate demand directly, whereas an increase in M^s operates indirectly through its effect on the rate of interest.

FIGURE 10.8 Expansionary monetary policy

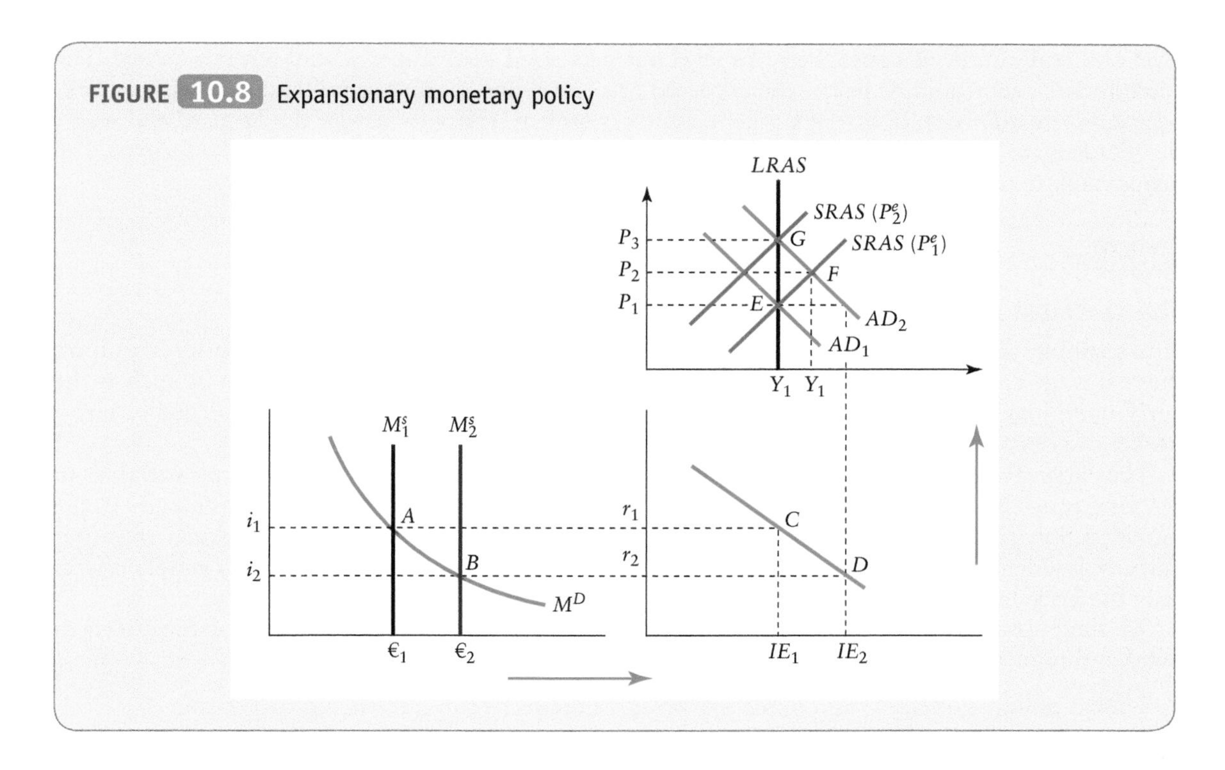

However, that is not the end of the process. At point F in the upper diagram, the actual price level is greater than what was expected. As a result, real wages have fallen below what was anticipated and the economy is over-heating. (The price level has increased while nominal wages are unchanged.) Workers will now increase their wage demands in line with the rise in the expected price level in an attempt to restore the original real wage. As price expectations change, the SRAS curve moves up to the left and the economy reverts back to the LRAS curve to point G. At the end of the process, the increase in the money supply is exactly equal to the rise in the price level and real output and unemployment are unchanged. (This is the quantity theory prediction discussed in Chapter 19.)

NOTE: A qualification is necessary at this point. The increase in investment (brought about by the fall in the interest rate) will also increase the capital stock (roads, factories, equipment and technology). This, in turn, will increase the level of potential output, Y*. Hence, the increase in investment can be expected to shift both the SRAS and the LRAS out to the right. However, there is a lag between the initial investment and when the resultant capital stock becomes available to produce goods and services. It takes time to build the factories, set up the production process and produce and market the product. To simplify the analysis we ignore the effect of a change in investment on Y*. A change in personal consumption expenditure or net exports will have no effect on potential real output and the over-heating situation depicted in Figure 10.8 will emerge.

A restrictive monetary policy

Conversely, if the central bank were to introduce a restrictive monetary policy, it would reduce the money supply and the M^s curve would shift left. (The reader is urged to re-draw Figure 10.8 to verify the following sequence of events.) Nominal and real interest rates would increase and IE fall. Because of the fall in IE, the AD curve would shift down to the left, resulting in a fall in the price level and real output. Because the price level has decreased, real wages would have increased. The actual price level would be below the expected price level and workers would adjust their price expectations downwards. If workers accept a cut in nominal wages to restore the original real wage, the SRAS curve would shift down to the right and the economy revert back to the LRAS curve. The proportionate fall in the price level would exactly equal the fall in the money supply.

10.8 Monetary Policy and the Keynesian/Classical Debate

The classical dichotomy

Real variables are measured in physical units, quantities or relative prices – the quantity of output, the real wage and the real interest rate. Nominal variables are measured in money units such as the euro – nominal wages, the nominal interest rate and the price level (how much is needed to buy a basket of goods).

The classical dichotomy refers to the belief that nominal variables do not affect real variables in the long run. This is at the core of the classical model. An example is the belief that changes in the money supply (a nominal variable) do not affect the long-run levels of real variables such as output and employment. This point is illustrated in Figure 10.8. The expansion of the money supply affects only the price level in the long run.

We shall now discuss the differences between Keynes and the classicists concerning the effects of fiscal and monetary policy on the economy. The extreme Keynesian position is that:

- fiscal policy is effective and monetary policy is ineffective in influencing real output.

In contrast, neoclassical economists and monetarists argue that:

- fiscal policy is ineffective and monetary policy has a significant effect on the price level and little or no impact on real output.

The disagreement between Keynesian and neoclassical economists essentially revolves about two relationships, namely, those between:

- the interest rate and the demand for money – this is referred to as the interest elasticity of the demand for money and the existence of the liquidity trap
- the interest rate and interest-sensitive expenditure.

The Keynesian position

Keynesians argue that:

- The demand for money curve is relatively elastic. This means that an increase in the money supply leads to a small decrease in the interest rate and that the zero lower bound problem we discussed above places a floor below which central banks cannot push interest rates.
- On the other hand, the IE curve is relatively inelastic. Changes in the interest rate have a weak effect on expenditure. With regard to the effect of the interest rate on investment, Keynes emphasised factors such as changes in the level of business confidence, uncertainty and expectations about the future. He wrote about 'Dark forces of time and ignorance which envelop our times' (Keynes 1936). For Keynes, the problem was to examine 'the economic behaviour of the present under the influence of changing ideas of the future' (Keynes 1936).

The effect of these two assumptions is that monetary policy has a weak effect on real output and unemployment. A given increase in the money supply leads to a small change in the nominal and real interest rates. This, in turn, will have a weak effect on expenditure. Overall, the AD curve will not move very much to the right and there will be little or no change in real output and the price level. (Again we suggest that the reader experiments with Figure 10.8 in order to verify that this is the case.) In this case, monetary policy is akin to pushing on a rope: it is very ineffective.

NOTE: If the demand for money curve is horizontal at low interest rates or if interest rates hit the zero lower bound, it is no longer possible to stimulate the economy via conventional monetary policy. This is the *liquidity trap*. Some commentators fear that this is the situation we now face in Europe and America. The central banks have pushed interest rates to historically low levels – virtually to zero – but banks have absorbed the extra liquidity instead of lending more money to businesses.

The classical position

Neoclassical economists argue that:

- The demand for money curve is steep (inelastic). An increase in the money supply will lead to a large fall in the nominal interest rate.
- The IE curve is relatively flat (or elastic). Changes in the interest rate have a strong effect on expenditure (aggregate demand).

Taking these two assumptions together, an expansionary monetary policy leads to a significant fall in interest rates, which in turn provokes a large rise in aggregate demand as C, I and NX respond. However, as demonstrated in Figure 10.8, given that the LRAS curve is vertical at potential real output Y*, the result is that the expansionary monetary policy leads to a proportionate increase in the price level and has no effect on real output and unemployment.

Neoclassical economists also believe that fiscal policy has little or no effect on real output. At first sight this appears rather odd. After all, an increase in G boosts aggregate demand and real output and must influence Y. Neoclassical economists, however, point to crowding-out as a reason why fiscal policy is ineffective. We discuss this in the following section.

10.9 Crowding-out

An expansionary fiscal policy, such as increases in G or cuts in taxation, shifts the AD curve to the right and both Y and P increase. However, neoclassical economists dispute this conclusion by pointing to the possibility of 'crowding-out'.

$$\text{Nominal Y} = \text{AD: C} + \text{I} + \text{G} + \text{X} - \text{M} \qquad (8)$$

An expansionary fiscal policy such as an increase in G will increase aggregate demand and nominal output.

$$\uparrow \text{G} \rightarrow \uparrow \text{AD} \rightarrow \uparrow \text{nominal output}$$

However, the increase in nominal output increases the demand for money (M^d) due to higher transactions demand. If there is no increase in the money supply, this will push up interest rates. The rise in interest rates will, in turn, lower IE. In terms of equation (8), the G element is going up and the C, I and NX components are going down. The initial increase in government spending leads to a reduction in IE. In other words, investment, along with consumer spending and net exports, has been crowded-out by government spending.

$$\uparrow \text{nominal output} \rightarrow \uparrow \text{M}^d \rightarrow \uparrow i \rightarrow \uparrow \text{r} \rightarrow \downarrow \text{IE}$$

If $\uparrow$ G = $\downarrow$ IE, there is 100 per cent crowding-out. In this case, AD and nominal output revert back to their original level and fiscal policy is completely ineffective. This is the extreme neoclassical position.

FIGURE 10.9 The crowding-out effect

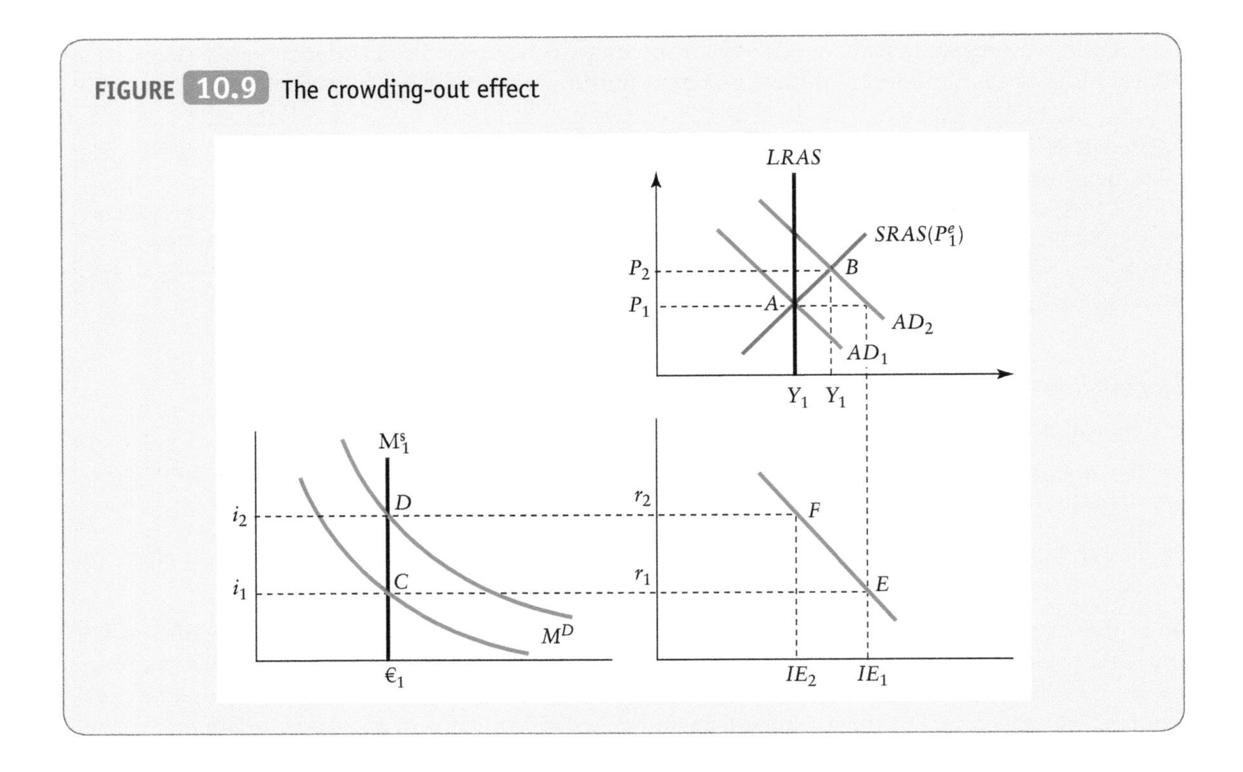

Figure 10.9 illustrates the crowding-out effect. Starting on the LRAS curve at A, the expansionary fiscal policy shifts the AD up to the right. Both the price level (P) and real output (Y) increase. However, in the lower left-hand diagram, the increase in nominal output shifts the demand for money curve upwards from M^d_1 to M^d_2. The nominal interest rate rises from i_1 to i_2 along the vertical axis. In the lower right-hand diagram, this is reflected in an increase in the real interest rate and IE falls along the horizontal axis. The fall in IE shifts the AD curve back from B to A. In terms of the components of aggregate demand, the fall in IE offsets the initial increase in government spending and AD reverts back to its initial level.

The elasticity of the IE schedule is what determines the degree of crowding-out. The neoclassical contention that the IE being flat (elastic) at the current interest rate means that a small increase in the interest rate will have a relatively large effect on IE. If this is the case, crowding-out will be important. If, however, as the Keynesians argue, the IE curve is steep (inelastic), crowding-out will not be important, as changes in interest rates have little or no effect on expenditure.

It could be argued that under the Agreement between Ireland and the ECB–EU–IMF Troika a form of 'reverse crowding-out' or 'crowding-in' should occur. This would happen if the lower budget deficits led to a reduction in interest rates and boosted investor confidence. The interest-sensitive expenditure would increase. However, the interest rate set by the ECB has been reduced to 0.75 per cent and this has not led to increased bank lending in Ireland.

The issue in Ireland is the inability/reluctance of the Irish banks to lend money. Following the implosion of 2008, the Irish banking system now comprises what have been called 'zombie banks'. The phrase was first coined in the 1980s by Ed Kane, an economics professor at Boston College, to refer to non-functioning banks propped up by bail-outs and subsidies. It applies to the Irish banks today because their brush with insolvency has left them trying to shrink their balance sheets by 'deleveraging' – selling off loans and advances and using any retained earnings they have to increase their Tier I capital ratio (see Chapter 9). The last thing the banks want to do now is to accommodate new business or individuals who come looking for new lines of credit. It does not matter how low the ECB pushes its interest rates, the Irish banking system will for the foreseeable future concentrate on strengthening its balance sheet by shedding rather than advancing loans.

However, crowding-in could occur if the reduction in the budget deficit reduced the perceived risk of sovereign default and narrowed the yield differential between Irish and German government bonds. This would reduce the cost of borrowing to the Irish Exchequer and allow more headroom in future budgets.

10.10 Government Monetary Financing

It is important to note that the crowding-out effect only occurs when the money supply remains unchanged in the face of a fiscal expansion. If the money supply increases as the demand for money rises, the interest rate need not rise and crowding-out need not occur.

In this context, the method of financing spending and deficits is important. In the past, a government could finance a deficit by borrowing from four sources:

1. abroad
2. the central bank
3. the commercial banks
4. the domestic non-bank public.

Borrowing from the first three sources increases the money supply and constitutes *monetary financing*. This is because this type of borrowing affects high-powered money (see Chapter 9). Borrowing from the domestic non-bank public does not affect the money supply.

Prior to joining the EMU, Irish government borrowing relied from time to time on monetary financing by borrowing from the Central Bank of Ireland. Consequently, increases in government spending tended to be accompanied by increases in the money supply and interest rates were not unduly affected. Moreover, in a small open economy such as Ireland, higher interest rates tend to attract capital inflows from the rest of the world. Both these considerations reduce the risks of crowding-out.

All this changed in the new environment of the EMU. One of the rules of the new system is that neither national central banks nor the ECB can indulge in monetary financing of fiscal deficits. (However, we saw above that these rules are now being interpreted more flexibly to allow the purchase of government bonds in certain circumstances, in particular through the programme of OMTs.)

A separate issue arises from the fact that in 2010 the Irish government issued €31 billion in promissory notes to the Irish Bank Resolution Corporation (IBRC), formerly Anglo Irish Bank, to cover the cost of rescuing Anglo Irish Bank and Irish Nationwide Building Society. These notes were government IOUs to the Central Bank. The IBRC used them as collateral to obtain a loan from the Central Bank. The Central Bank created money that was deposited with the IBRC.

This was a way of side-stepping the ban on government and national central banks creating money. However, the ECB has insisted that the Irish government make annual payments to the Central Bank of Ireland over the next ten years to extinguish the debt that this mechanism created. The government renegotiated the arrangement made in 2010 by obtaining a longer repayment time on the outstanding loans and at a lower interest rate. This means the government has secured a deferral of the €3.06 billion cash sum that was due in 2012, equivalent to some two per cent of GDP. The government agreed with the ECB to replace promissory notes with long-term bonds in January 2013.

10.11 Key Terms and Concepts

In this chapter we have extended our basic macroeconomic model by incorporating a money market. The extended model consists of a goods market and a money market and the authorities can influence the economy through fiscal policy or monetary policy. The key points covered in this chapter included:

- the demand for money: changes in nominal output and interest rates affect the demand for money
- the interaction of the supply and demand for money determine the nominal rate of interest
- the Fisher equation, which distinguishes between nominal and real interest rates
- the link between interest rates and interest-sensitive expenditure is known as the IE schedule
- monetary policy: changes in the money supply affect aggregate demand and output via the real rate of interest and its influence on expenditure
- open market operations, quantitative easing and outright monetary transactions
- the differences between Keynes and the classicists with regard to fiscal and monetary policy and the concept of crowding-out
- government monetary financing.

Appendix 10.1 Net present value

The concept of net present value (NPV) is used to demonstrate the effect of a change in the interest rate on the profitability of an investment project. The NPV technique is now routinely used in the evaluation of investment projects by firms, banks and governments.

The significance of the 'net' in NPV is that the income stream is net of costs. We are calculating the net income or profit from the investment project.

To illustrate its use, let us suppose that you have the opportunity of investing in a project that is forecast to generate profits over a three-year period. For simplicity, we assume that no assets remain at the end of the three-year project. We also ignore inflation, so that the above income flows are given in constant (year 1) prices.

How much would you be prepared to pay to buy into such a project? To answer this, we must discount the projected profit stream to calculate its NPV. Discounting is the inverse of the more familiar concept of compounding, according to which a sum of money, €x, invested today at r per cent is worth €x(1 + r) at the end of the year. Hence, €1,000 invested at 10 per cent generates a total return of €1,100: (€1,000(1 + 0.1) = €1,100).

Discounting inverts this process and asks: how much is €x to be paid at the end of a year worth today? What is its present value? The answer is €x/(1 + r). Extending this logic, a sum paid at the end of two years has a present value of $€x/(1+r)^2$. Similarly, a sum of money paid at the end of three years has a NPV of $€x/(1+r)^3$.

Assuming a real interest rate of 5 per cent (r = 0.05), Table 10.2 shows how the NPV of a hypothetical profit stream is calculated. (Note that what matters for investment projects in the real, not the nominal, rate of interest.)

These calculations tell us that while this project yields an undiscounted profit stream of €315,000, the NPV of this profit stream is €285,714, given an interest rate of five per cent.

Table 10.3 shows how the NPV of the hypothetical investment project falls as the interest rate increases. As, for example, the interest rate rises from five to 10 per cent, the NPV falls from €285,714 to €260,706. The higher the rate of interest, therefore, the lower the value of the project to

TABLE 10.2 Calculating net present value using a 5% discount rate

Year	Net profit at end of year €	Discount factor €	Net present value €
	1	2	3 = 1 × 2
1	100,000	$1/(1.05) = 0.9524$	95,238
2	110,000	$1/(1.05)^2 = 0.9070$	99,773
3	105,000	$1/(1.05)^3 = 0.8638$	90,703
Total	315,000		285,714

TABLE 10.3 NPV and the interest rate

Interest rate %	NPV €
0	315,000
2.5	299,763
5	285,714
7.5	272,731
10	260,706

a prospective investor. As a consequence, a rise in the interest rate can make a previously profitable project unprofitable. A fall in the interest rate can make an unprofitable project profitable. This explains the inverse relationship between interest rates and investment.

Note that the interest rate has a greater effect on the NPV of projects that are long lived: some very capital-intensive investments that have a very long life, such as electricity-generating projects, can only be profitable at low rates of interest.

CHAPTER 11

The IS-LM Model

11.1 Introduction

In this chapter we outline a standard macroeconomic model that is often referred to as the *IS-LM model*. This depicts the economy as an interaction between the goods and money markets. The 'I' in IS stands for investment and 'S' for savings. The 'L' in LM denotes liquidity preference (demand for money) and 'M' the money supply. The Nobel prize-winning English economist John Hicks (1904–1989) developed the IS-LM framework very shortly after the publication of Keynes's *General Theory* (Hicks 1937).

An important assumption of this model is that the price level is fixed in the short run and so the short-run aggregate supply (SRAS) curve is horizontal. However, we relax this assumption towards the end of the chapter and we explain how, over the medium term, the money supply is the key mechanism in adjusting back to potential output following an economic shock. In the course of the chapter we will explain how the Keynesian cross diagram underlies the IS curve and Keynes's theory of liquidity preference underlies the LM curve. The complete IS-LM model then provides the theory underling the aggregate demand (AD) curve.

We focus on the closed economy case. The open economy version is covered in Chapter 16. In the concluding sections of this chapter we use the IS-LM model to discuss the issues of 'crowding-out', the relative effectiveness of fiscal and monetary policy and how the economy adjusts back to its potential output level following an economic shock. Finally, the IS-LM model is applied to analysing the Irish economic crisis of 2008.

11.2 Equilibrium in the Goods Market: The IS Curve

The IS curve describes the combination of real interest rate (r) and output (Y) that establishes equilibrium in the market for goods and services. Equilibrium in this market requires that the value of the goods and services produced (Y) equals total spending or aggregate demand (AD). Aggregate demand, in turn, is identically equal to the sum of consumer expenditure (C), investment (I) and government current consumption (G). There are no net exports as we are considering the closed economy case. That is:

$$Y = AD \equiv C + I + G \qquad (1)$$

We assume here that government spending (G) and taxation (T) are exogenous. The consumption function we discussed in Chapter 6 states that consumer expenditure is a function of income. As income and output are closely related we can write the consumption function as:

$$C = a + cY \qquad (2)$$

The intercept term a represents autonomous consumer expenditure, that is, expenditure not influenced by changes in income. The coefficient c indicates what proportion of extra income is consumed and is referred to as the marginal propensity to consume (MPC).

We now introduce the relationship between the (real) interest rate (r) and aggregate demand. (Since the price level is assumed constant the nominal and real interest rates move in tandem.) In Chapter 10 we pointed out that changes in the real interest rate affect consumer expenditure, investment and net exports. This type of expenditure is called interest-sensitive expenditure (IE). To simplify the analysis we assume here that the interest rate does not affect consumer expenditure and, as we are dealing with a closed economy, we ignore net exports. Hence, an increase in the interest rate only influences investment. At higher interest rates, the demand for investment funds falls and, conversely, at lower interest rates it rises. The relationship can be written:

$$\mathrm{I} = d - b\mathrm{r} \tag{3}$$

The intercept term d indicates autonomous investment, that is, investment not influenced by changes in the interest rate. The coefficient b indicates how investment reacts to changes in the interest rate (r). Substituting (2) and (3) into (1) we have:

$$\mathrm{Y} = a + c\mathrm{Y} + d - b\mathrm{r} + \mathrm{G} \tag{4}$$

Rearranging:

$$\mathrm{Y}(1 - c) = (a + d + \mathrm{G}) - b\mathrm{r} \tag{5}$$

Let total autonomous expenditure $(a + d + \mathrm{G}) = \mathrm{Z}$, then:

$$\mathrm{Y} = \left[\frac{1}{(1 - c)}\right](\mathrm{Z} - b\mathrm{r}) \tag{6}$$

It can be seen from (6) that there is a negative relationship between Y and r. Basically, what happens is that an increase in the interest rate lowers the level of investment, which in turn reduces aggregate demand and ultimately real output (Y), and vice versa. In short:

$$\uparrow \mathrm{r} \rightarrow \downarrow \mathrm{I} \rightarrow \downarrow \mathrm{AD} \rightarrow \downarrow \mathrm{Y}$$

Underlying the IS curve is the 'Keynesian cross' diagram. In this closed economy model, output is determined by expenditure. We assume that consumers, firms and government have a planned level of spending (PE):

$$\mathrm{PE} = \mathrm{C} + \mathrm{I} + \mathrm{G}$$

On the other hand, real output Y equals actual expenditure. The equilibrium condition is where planned expenditure equals actual expenditure.

$$\mathrm{Y} = \mathrm{PE}$$

Figure 11.1 shows planned expenditure along the vertical axis and income or output along the horizontal axis. At all points along the 45-degree line the equilibrium condition is established as PE is equal to Y.

Consider now the planned expenditure line in Figure 11.1. The planned expenditure line is positively sloped as an increase in Y along the horizontal axis will increase planned expenditure via the consumption function.

$$\uparrow \mathrm{Y} \rightarrow \uparrow \mathrm{C} \text{ (via the consumption function)} \rightarrow \uparrow \mathrm{PE}$$

The slope of the PE line is the marginal propensity to consume (MPC or c in equation (2)). The larger the MPC, the steeper the PE line and vice versa. At point A in the diagram, planned expenditure cuts the 45 degree line and therefore PE equals Y and the goods and services market is in equilibrium.

Consider now the effect of an increase in government spending. In Figure 11.2, an increase in government spending (G) shifts the PE line upwards. At an income or output level of Y_1, planned expenditure now exceeds actual output and firms find that there is an unplanned fall in stocks or

FIGURE 11.1 The Keynesian cross

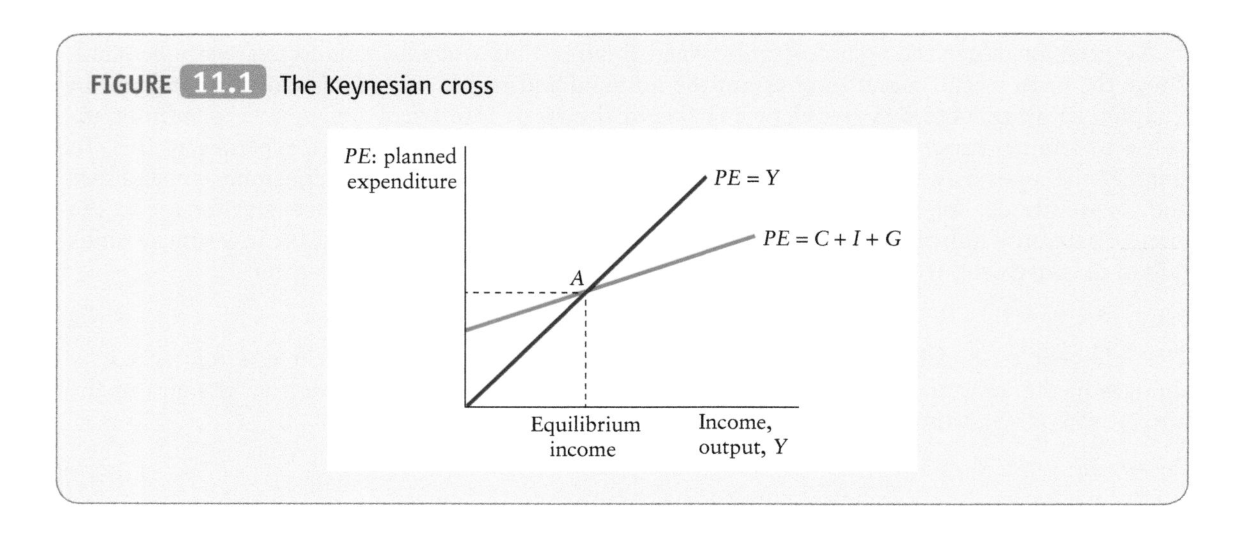

FIGURE 11.2 An increase in government purchases

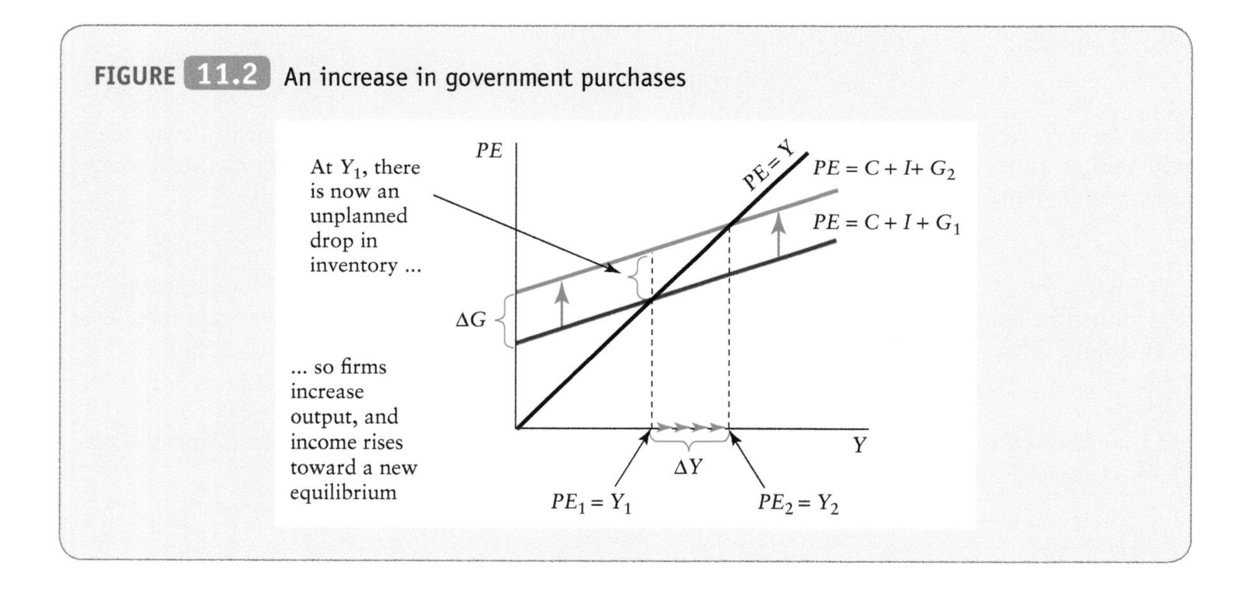

inventories (the role of stocks was discussed in Chapter 5). This fall in stocks sends a signal to firms to increase output from Y_1 to Y_2. Hence, although the level of stocks is small as a proportion of GNP or output, it does play an important role in the adjustment process. At an output level of Y_2, planned expenditure again equals actual output and the goods and services market is in equilibrium.

Note that the increase in output along the horizontal axis is greater than the initial increase in G on the vertical axis. This is the multiplier effect discussed in Chapter 6. The initial increase in G leads to an increase in Y but this, in turn, leads to a further increase in consumer spending (C) which leads to further increase in Y and so on. The final impact on Y is much bigger than the initial increase in G. In this simple model the size of the multiplier is determined by the MPC.

$$\uparrow G \rightarrow \uparrow Y \rightarrow \text{(via the consumption function)} \rightarrow \uparrow C \rightarrow \uparrow Y \ldots$$

Deriving the IS curve

Figure 11.3 illustrates how the Keynesian cross diagram can be used to derive the IS curve. A decrease in the real interest rate (r) increases investment (I) and, in the upper diagram, the planned expenditure line shifts upwards. Actual output now increases from Y_1 to Y_2 in order to restore equilibrium in the goods and services market. A new equilibrium is established at point B.

In the lower diagram, point C represents the initial combination of r and Y, which is one point on the IS curve. Point D represents the second point on the IS curve as it shows the r_2, Y_2 combination. By changing the interest rate and thereby shifting the PE line upwards and downwards we can trace out each equilibrium interest rate, output combination, and construct the complete IS curve. The IS curve is downward sloping and represents equilibrium in the goods and services market.

FIGURE 11.3 Deriving the IS curve

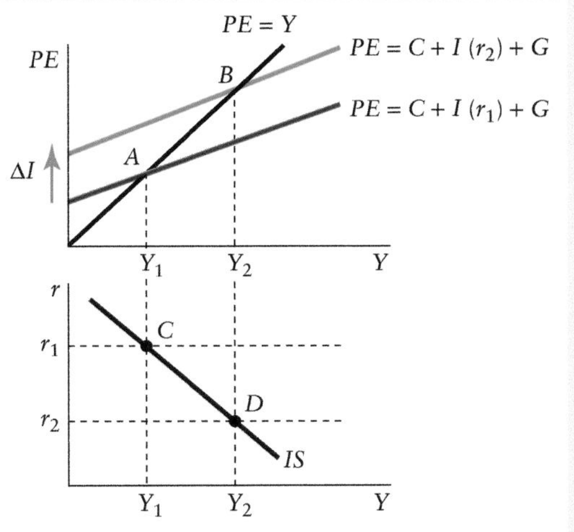

The slope of the IS curve

The slope of the IS curve indicates how a change in the interest rate affects Y. It can be seen from equation (6) that the interest rate affects Y via the b coefficient and the $1/(1-c)$ term. A curve relating the real interest rate to the level of investment is called the marginal efficiency of investment (MIE) curve.

Hence the slope of the IS curve depends on:

- the b coefficient, which represents the link between the interest rate and investment (the MEI curve)
- the $1/(1-c)$ term, which reflects the link between investment and Y (the multiplier).

It follows therefore that:

- the IS curve will be flat (elastic) and a given change in the interest rate will have a large effect on investment if b is large (elastic MEI curve) and/or $1/(1-c)$ (the multiplier) is large.

Conversely,

- the IS curve will be steep (inelastic) if b is small and/or the multiplier $1/(1-c)$ is small.

NOTE: To keep the analysis as simple as possible we have ignored the marginal propensity to tax (MPT) and the marginal propensity to import (MPM) in deriving the multiplier. These two coefficients also influence the slope of the IS curve.

The location of the IS curve

Consider now the factors that determine the location of the IS curve. In the upper diagram in Figure 11.4 an increase in government spending shifts the PE line upwards and output increases along the horizontal axis to restore equilibrium. This is an example of a change in autonomous expenditure, that is, an increase in PE not brought about by a change in the interest rate.

In the bottom diagram, point C represents the initial r_1, Y_1 combination. The increase in autonomous expenditure has increased output from Y_1 to Y_2. If the IS curve is shifted out to the right this enables us to examine the relationship between the initial interest rate r_1 and the new, higher level of output, Y_2. Point D, for example, on the new IS curve represents the original interest rate, r_1, and the new, higher level of output, Y_2. It follows from this that a change in any of the components of autonomous expenditure – C, I, G (or NX in the open economy model) – will affect the location of the IS curve. Thus an expansionary fiscal policy will shift the IS curve to the right and a deflationary fiscal policy will shift it to the left. Changes in the interest rate, on the other hand, cause movements along the IS curve.

FIGURE 11.4 Shifting the IS curve

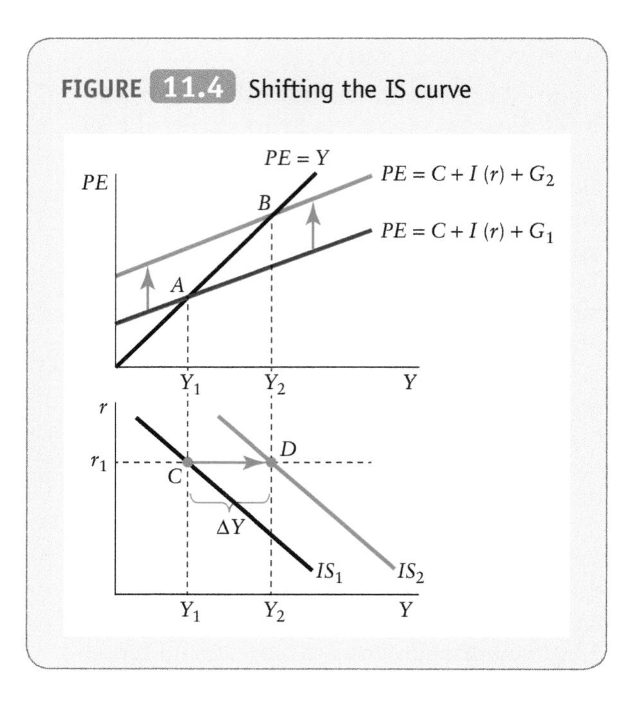

11.3 Equilibrium in the Money Market: The LM Curve

Consider now the relationship between the interest rate and real output as reflected in the money market. The level of output (Y) and the interest rate determine the demand for money.

$$M^d = eY - fr \tag{7}$$

As explained in Chapter 10, there is a positive relationship between Y and M^d due to the transaction and precautionary motives for holding money. The coefficient e indicates how a change in Y influences the demand for money and is referred to as the income elasticity of the demand for money. The larger the coefficient e, the greater the effect Y has on M^d.

The interest rate reflects the speculative demand for money. There is an inverse relationship between r and M^d. The coefficient f shows how changes in the interest rate affect the demand for money and is referred to as the interest elasticity of the demand for money.

NOTE: In this chapter, the demand for money is a function of the real interest rate, r, whereas in Chapter 8 we related it to the nominal interest rate, *i*. Given that the price level is assumed to be constant there is no inconsistency between these two treatments.

It is assumed that the central bank controls the money supply (M^s). Hence the equilibrium condition in the money market is:

$$M^s = M^d \tag{8}$$

Substitute equation (7) into (8) to obtain:

$$M^s = eY - fr \tag{9}$$

Solving equation (9) for the interest rate, we have:

$$r = (1/f)(eY - M^s) \tag{10}$$

FIGURE 11.5 Deriving the LM curve

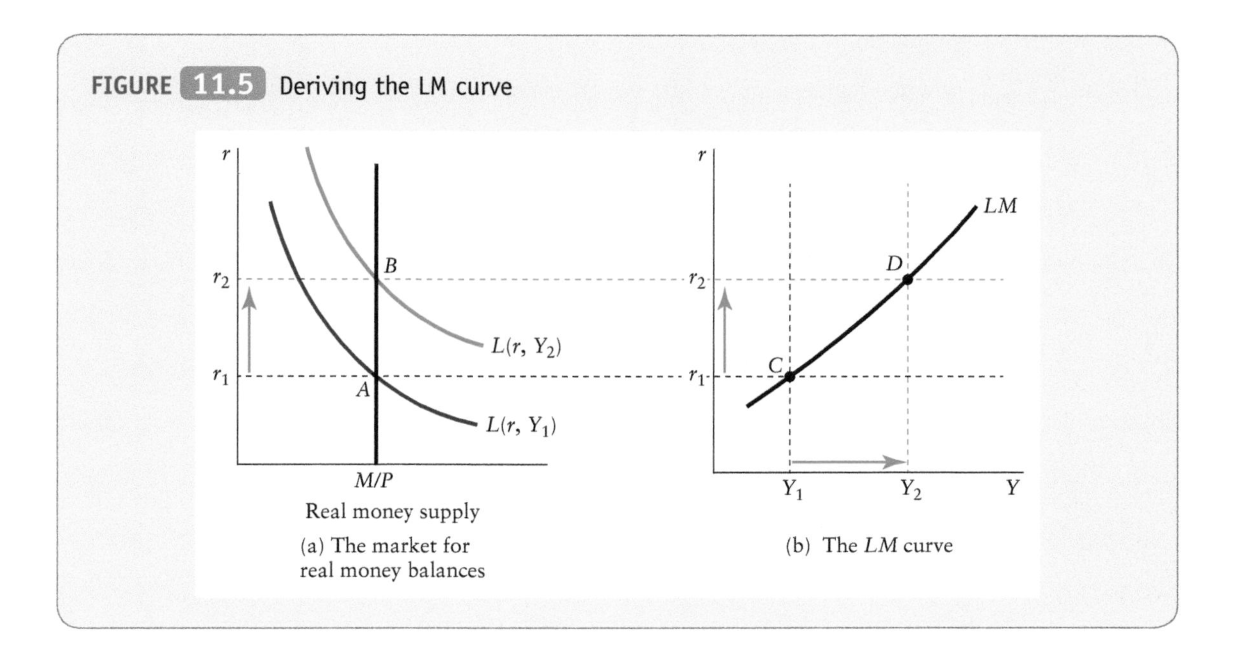

(a) The market for real money balances

(b) The *LM* curve

Equation (10) shows that there is a positive relationship between Y and the interest rate in the money market. The LM curve, which shows the r, Y combinations consistent with equilibrium in the money market, is therefore upward sloping.

Figure 11.5 illustrates why this positive relationship exists. The left-hand diagram shows equilibrium in the money market. The supply and demand for money interact to determine the interest rate on the vertical axis. Initially, we are at point A in the money market. Suppose Y now increases from Y_1 to Y_2. The M^d curve shifts upwards and the money market moves to point B, with the interest rate increasing to r_2 along the vertical axis. This is because the money supply is fixed and the excess demand for money causes the interest rate to rise.

Hence, in the money market there is a positive relationship between the level of Y and the interest rate that is consistent with equilibrium. This is represented in the right-hand diagram as an upward-sloping curve labelled LM. In short:

$$\uparrow Y \rightarrow \uparrow M^d \rightarrow \uparrow r$$

In the right-hand diagram point C represents the initial r_1, Y_1 combination. This is one point on the LM curve. Point D, in turn, indicates the new r_2, Y_2 combination and is another point on the LM curve. By shifting the M^d curve in the money market we can trace out the various r, Y combinations consistent with equilibrium in the money market. These points lie on the LM curve.

The slope of the LM curve

Consider now the factors that determine the slope of the LM curve. A steep LM curve means that a given change in Y has a large effect on the interest rate and vice versa. An examination of equation (10) indicates that the effect of changes in Y on the interest rate depends on the coefficients *e* and *f*. Hence:

- The LM curve will be steep (inelastic) if *e* (income elasticity of the demand for money) is large and/or *f* (interest elasticity of the demand for money) is small.
- The LM curve will be flat (elastic) if *e* is small and/or the coefficient *f* is large.

FIGURE 11.6 How the money supply shifts the LM curve

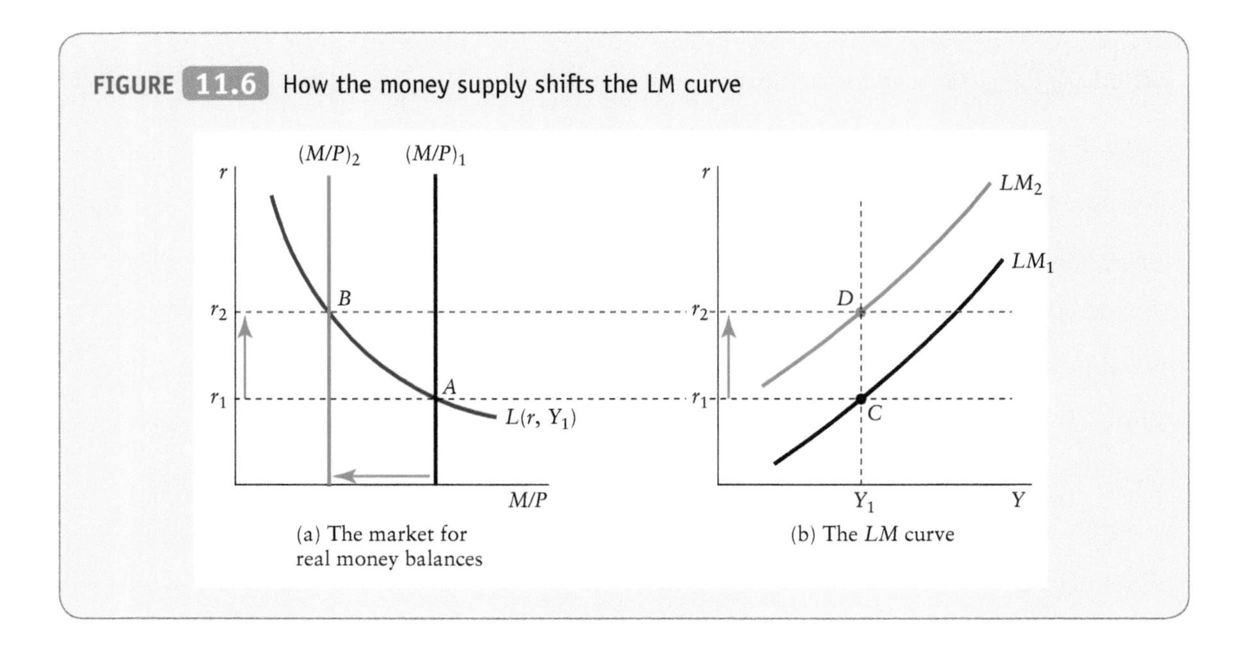

The location of the LM curve

The location of the LM curve depends on the level of the (real) money supply. A decrease in the money supply shifts the LM curve upwards and an increase downwards. For example, in the left-hand diagram in Figure 11.6 the money market is initially in equilibrium at point A. This equilibrium point corresponds to r_1 and Y_1. Holding Y constant, a decrease in the money supply (M/P) shifts the money supply line from $(M/P)_1$ to $(M/P)_2$ and the interest rate rises from r_1 to r_2. The excess demand for money causes the interest rate to rise.

In the right-hand diagram point C corresponds to the initial r_1, Y_1 combination. By shifting the LM curve upwards, we can examine the relationship between Y_1 and the new higher interest rate, r_2. For example, point D corresponds to the new r_2, Y_1 combination. Conversely, an increase in the money supply will shift the LM curve downwards. By moving the money supply line back and forth, we can trace out different combinations of r and Y that correspond to equilibrium in the money market. These lie on the LM curve.

11.4 Equilibrium in the Goods and Money Markets

Figure 11.7 amalgamates the IS and an LM curves. Recall that points on the IS curve are consistent with equilibrium in the goods market and points on the LM curve are consistent with equilibrium in the money market. Hence, at point A, where the two curves intersect, there is equilibrium in both the goods market and the money market. At this point, and only here, aggregate demand equals planned production and the stock of money equals the desired holdings of cash balances by the public.

If disequilibrium should arise, either because r or Y is too high or too low, then it can be shown that the economy will adjust back to equilibrium. In Figure 11.8 point A corresponds to r_1 and Y_1 and, as we are on the IS curve, the goods market is in equilibrium. Suppose, however, that output is to the left of the IS curve. Since Y is lower than what is necessary for equilibrium, there must be an excess demand for goods and services. That is, $Y < AD$ and there is excess demand. Hence:

- all points to the left of the IS curve are associated with an excess demand for goods and services
- all points to the right of the IS curve are associated with an excess supply of goods and services.

FIGURE 11.7 The short-run equilibrium

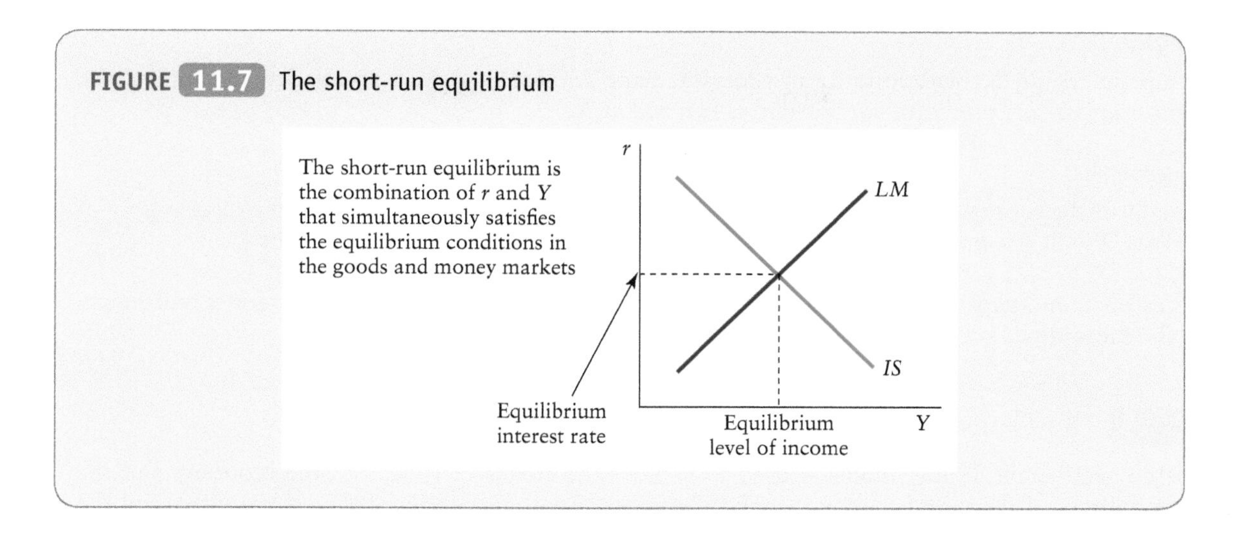

Consider now the LM curve in Figure 11.8. The combination of r_1 and Y_1 represent the interest rate and the level of output consistent with money market equilibrium as this is a point on the LM curve. If, however, output is less than Y_1, there is an excess supply of money. The reason is that Y and therefore the demand for money is lower than that necessary for equilibrium. That is, $M^D < M^S$ and there is an excess supply of money. It follows, therefore, that:

- points to the left of the LM curve represent an excess supply of money
- points to the right of the LM curve are associated with an excess demand for money.

FIGURE 11.8 Establishing equilibrium

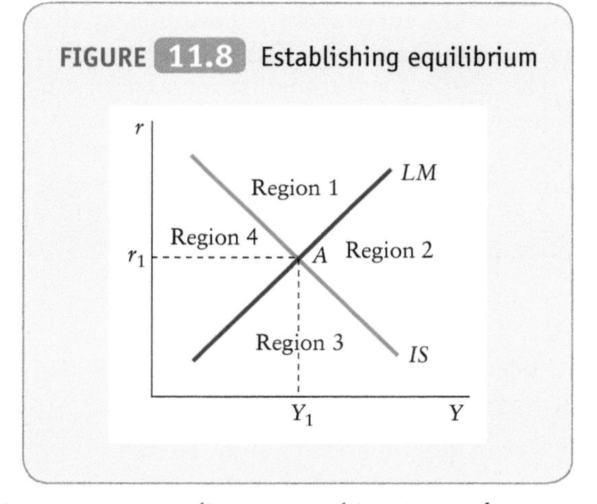

We can divide the area in Figure 11.8 into four regions, corresponding to combinations of excess supply and demand in the goods and money markets. The economy will adjust towards equilibrium (represented by point A) because:

- output rises whenever there is an excess demand for goods and vice versa
- the interest rate rises when there is an excess demand for money and vice versa.

Region 1

Points in region 1 correspond to an excess supply of goods and an excess supply of money. If the economy were in this region, the excess supplies in both the goods and money markets would interact in such a way as to drive r and Y to an equilibrium point such as A.

Region 2

Points in region 2 correspond to an excess supply of goods but an excess demand for money. In this situation, the interest rate will rise and Y will fall until equilibrium is reached at point A.

Region 3

Points in region 3 correspond to an excess demand for goods and an excess demand for money. Both r and Y will rise until equilibrium is reached at A.

Region 4

Finally, if the economy is in region 4, there is an excess demand for goods and an excess supply of money. Y will rise and the interest rate would fall until equilibrium is re-established.

Thus the combination r_1 and Y_1 represents a stable equilibrium to which the economy will return if the economy is subjected to a shock.

11.5 The Crowding-out Effect

In this section the IS-LM model is used to explore the effects of shocks to the economy and the effectiveness of fiscal and monetary policy. Suppose that there are unemployed resources and the government embarks on an expansionary fiscal policy. This is shown in Figure 11.9 as the IS curve shifting outwards from IS_1 to IS_2. If we ignored the monetary sector, the economy would move from point A to point B and real output would increase to Y_2. However, when we take account of the possible repercussions of the fiscal expansion on the money market, we see that the economy moves up along the LM curve and equilibrium is established at point C. Output increases only to Y_3, which is lower than the level, Y_2, that would have been reached if there had been no monetary repercussions.

The reason for the smaller increase in output is the crowding-out effect. The rise in Y leads to an increase in the demand for money. Given a constant supply of money, this pushes up the interest rate (along the vertical axis in Figure 11.9) and this, in turn, reduces investment expenditure. Hence, increased government expenditure is partly offset by a reduction in investment and the impact of fiscal policy on Y is reduced. The crowding-out effect reduces the effectiveness of fiscal policy. In short:

$$\uparrow G \rightarrow \uparrow Y \rightarrow \uparrow M^d \rightarrow \uparrow r \rightarrow \downarrow I \rightarrow \downarrow Y$$

An accommodating monetary policy

The crowding-out effect may be reduced if the government implements an accommodating monetary policy simultaneously with an expansionary fiscal policy. This was the case after the economic collapse of 2008 when the Federal Reserve undertook a major monetary expansion, using not only conventional open markets operations (OMOs) but also quantitative easing (QE). This accommodated the rapid increase in the government deficit under the various 'stimulus packages' launched by the Obama administration. If, instead of assuming that the money supply is held constant, we assume that the expansionary fiscal

FIGURE 11.9 An increase in government purchases

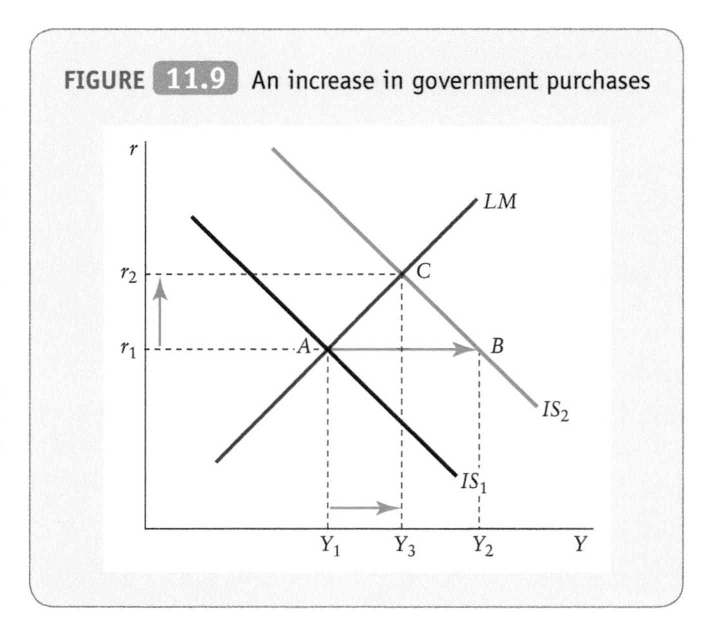

policy is accompanied by an increase in the money supply, the crowding-out effect is averted. This is shown in Figure 11.10 where an increase in the money supply shifts the LM curve downwards from LM_1 to LM_2. The economy moves to point B, Y increases to Y_2, and because there is no increase in the interest rate along the vertical axis, investment expenditure is not crowded-out.

FIGURE 11.10 Accommodating monetary policy

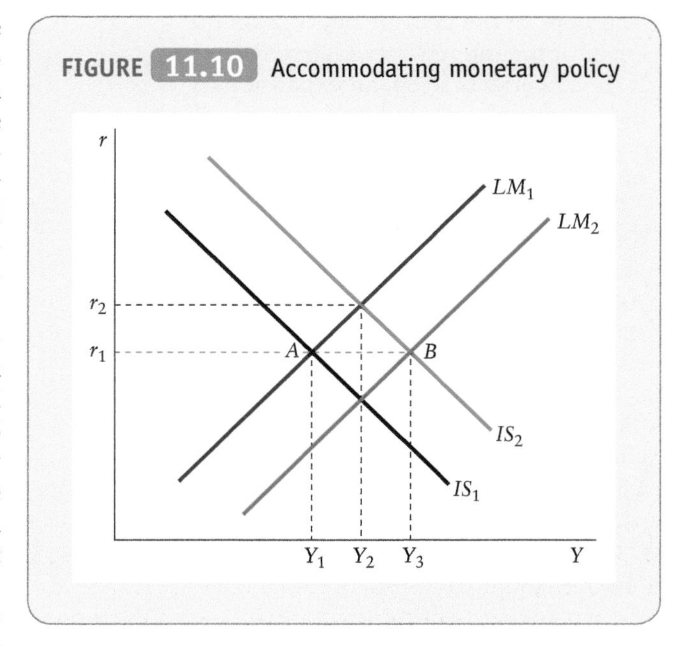

It should be noted that the effectiveness of fiscal policy also depends on the slope of the LM curve. If the LM curve is relatively flat, a shift of the IS curve to the right leads to a relatively large increase in Y. This is because there is a small increase in the interest rate on the vertical axis and the crowding-out effect is insignificant.

On the other hand, if the LM curve is relatively steep, a similar shift of the IS curve has a small effect on Y. This is because with a steep LM curve, there will be a large increase in the interest rate and the crowding-out effect will be significant.

Implications for EMU countries

This analysis is relevant to the euro area. If the large countries were to embark on a co-ordinated fiscal expansion, it is likely that euro area interest rates would rise and private sector investment would be crowded-out (assuming no accommodating action by the ECB). If the LM curve is steep the crowding-out effect would be significant.

However, the LM curve is likely to be horizontal for a small euro area country, like Ireland, operating in isolation. Ireland's fiscal budget is too small to have an impact on euro area interest rates. In this case, there would be little or no crowding-out. Fiscal policy would be effective, provided it did not provoke investor fears about the country's solvency, which would lead to a rise in interest rates.

During the early years of EMU, before the current euro crisis led to soaring interest rates on the sovereign bonds of the peripheral countries, a small euro area country could be a free rider, enjoying the reputation of the core countries (like Germany) for monetary stability. As long as they obeyed the Maastricht Treaty rules and avoided 'excessive deficits', they were able to conduct an independent fiscal policy knowing that it would not drive up interest rates. This all came to an end after 2007. Since then the fiscal policies of countries like Greece, Portugal, Ireland, Spain and even Italy have been carefully watched by the markets and any evidence of increasing deficits is punished by rising yields on their bonds.

11.6 The Relative Effectiveness of Fiscal and Monetary Policy in the IS-LM Model

Figure 11.11 examines the case of an expansionary monetary policy (shift of the LM curve to the right). The increase in the money supply reduces the interest rate and this increases investment, aggregate demand and output (Y). In short:

$$\uparrow M^s \rightarrow \downarrow r \rightarrow \uparrow I \rightarrow \uparrow Y$$

The slope of the IS curve depends on the effect of the interest rate on investment. If the IS curve is steep, an expansionary monetary policy has a relatively small effect on Y. The reason is that investment is not very sensitive to interest rate changes and, as a result, the decrease in the interest rate on the vertical axis has an unimportant effect on investment. As a result, monetary policy has only a small effect on the level of output and employment.

However, if the IS curve is relatively flat because investment is sensitive to changes in the interest rate, a shift of the LM curve to the right has a large effect on Y. As a consequence, a change in the money supply has a relatively large effect on Y.

FIGURE 11.11 Expansionary monetary policy

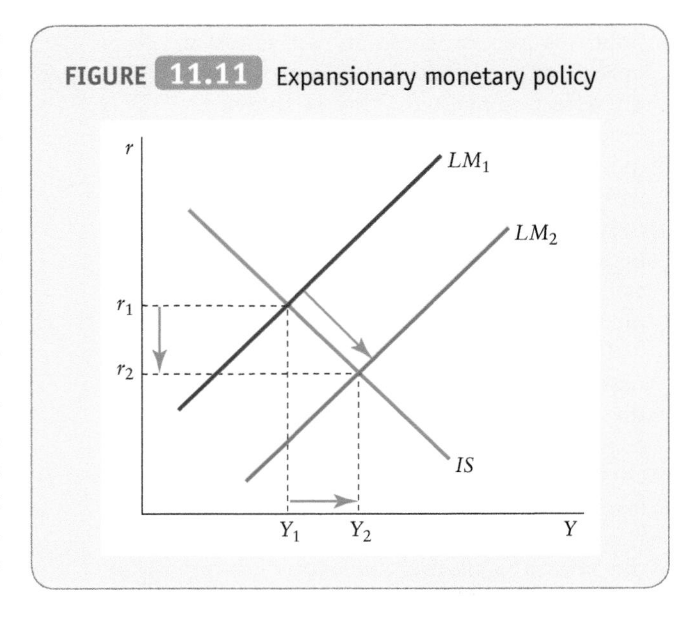

What is the best mix of fiscal and monetary policy?

When there are unemployed resources in the economy, the government should consider which mix of fiscal and monetary policies is best to increase output and reduce unemployment. If the government implements an expansionary fiscal policy the IS curve will shift outwards to the right. Both output and the interest rate will increase. This implies some crowding-out of private sector spending.

If, alternatively, the government or central bank pursues an expansionary monetary policy, the LM curve shifts down to the right. Now the increase in output is accompanied by a reduction in the interest rate and this causes private sector investment to increase. It might appear that this outcome is preferable.

The choice between an expansionary fiscal or monetary policy is clearly, in part, a political one. Conservative politicians tend to prefer tax cuts to increases in public expenditure. They would also worry about the longer-run inflationary implications of an expansionary monetary policy. Left-wing politicians, on the other hand, generally favour increases in public expenditure over tax cuts and tend not to be as worried about inflation as are conservatives. The choice also depends on the relationship between the country's central bank and the government. We saw that, in principle, the central banks of the major industrialised countries are independent of their governments. If a central bank fears that the government's fiscal policy is too expansionary and will in the long term lead to high inflation, it will not accommodate it through a monetary easing.

The Keynesian/classical debate

We can use the IS-LM model to summarise the debate between the Keynesian and classical schools of macroeconomics. Recall from Chapter 5 that the Keynesian recipe for ending a recession is a fiscal expansion. For this to be effective crowding-out must be minimal. This will be the case if there is a flat LM curve and a steep IS curve. We illustrate this in the left-hand diagram in Figure 11.12.

The reader can experiment by shifting the IS or LM curves. Fiscal policy has a significant effect on Y (large increase along the horizontal axis) and monetary policy has little or no effect on Y (small effect on the horizontal axis). An extreme Keynesian position is the concept of a liquidity trap when the LM curve is horizontal. Under this condition, there is no crowding-out of investment and fiscal policy is very effective.

FIGURE 11.12 Keynes versus the classical school

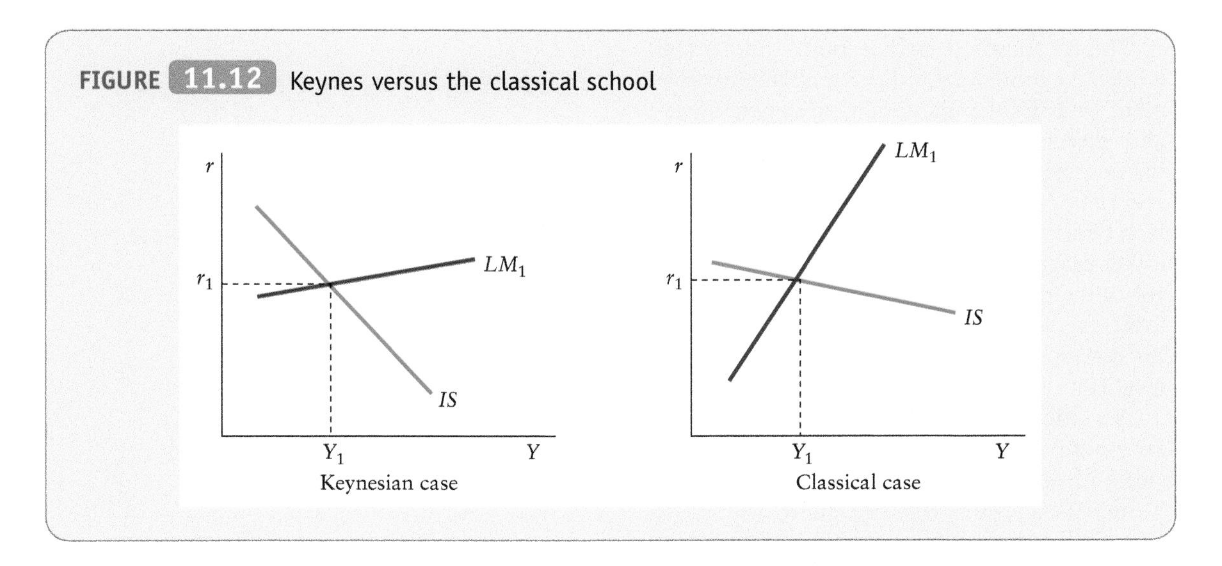

The classical view is just the opposite, namely that fiscal policy is ineffective and that crowding-out is significant. It will be recalled that the classical school argue that fiscal policy is ineffective and that instead governments should rely on flexible wages and prices to restore the economy to its optimum position. This will be the case if the LM curve is steep and the IS curve is flat. We illustrate this case in the right-hand diagram in Figure 11.12.

In this case, government spending crowds-out private sector investment and fiscal policy is ineffective. In contrast, changes in the money supply have an important effect on the level of Y. The extreme classical case is that the LM curve is vertical and an expansionary fiscal policy has no effect on output. With a vertical LM curve there is 100 per cent crowding-out.

A compromise suggests that the truth lies between the extremes represented by the Keynesian and classical views. When interest rates are low, for example, an increase in interest rates may not crowd-out investment and the Keynesian view that fiscal policy is effective may be valid. On the other hand, when interest rates are relatively high any further rise in interest rates may lead to significant crowding-out of investment. In this case, the classical view that fiscal policy is ineffective may be valid. However, it is clear that the relationship between the interest rate and interest-sensitive expenditure (in this case, investment) is of crucial importance in assessing policy prescriptions. Over seventy years after Keynes wrote the *General Theory* the economics profession has still not reached a consensus on the controversies it provoked.

11.7 The IS-LM Model and Aggregate Demand

Up to this point we have assumed that the price level is constant and the short-run aggregate supply (SRAS) curve is horizontal. However, the location of the LM curve is determined by the real money supply (M/P) and this means that a change in the price level (P) will shift the LM curve. A fall in P increases (M/P) and the LM curve shifts to the right. Figure 11.13 illustrates the case of a rise in the price level. In the upper diagram, the LM curve shifts up to the left, the interest rate (r) rises along the vertical axis and output (Y) decreases along the horizontal axis. The sequence is:

$$\uparrow P \rightarrow \downarrow (M/P) \rightarrow \uparrow r \rightarrow \downarrow I \rightarrow \downarrow Y$$

In the lower diagram, the inverse relationship between P and Y is shown as a movement along the aggregate demand (AD) curve. We can vary P and observe the change in Y and trace out the complete AD curve. This illustrates that the IS-LM model underlines the AD curve.

The implication is that both the central bank (via monetary policy) and the government (via fiscal policy) can influence aggregate demand. For example, in Figure 11.14 the central bank increases the money supply and the LM curve shifts to the right. The interest rate falls and output increases. In the lower diagram, the price level is constant and we move the AD curve to the right. This allows us to examine the relationship between the new, higher level of Y and the initial price level (P).

A similar situation holds in the case of an expansionary fiscal policy. The IS curve shifts upwards (not shown) and both r and Y increase. Again, the AD curve is moved out to the right and the relationship between the initial P and the new, higher Y can be examined.

The long-run aggregate supply (LRAS) or potential real output schedule is vertical above Y* in Figure 11.15. The short-run aggregate supply SRAS curve is upward sloping and its location is determined by the expected price level. Starting from point A in the upper diagram, suppose the economy is subject to a demand-side shock that shifts the IS curve down to the left (a decrease in investment, for example). Output (Y) falls along the horizontal axis.

In the lower diagram, the AD curve shifts down and both the price level and output decrease. The economy moves into recession to the left of the LRAS curve and unemployment increases. Point B, in this lower diagram, is not, however, a long-run equilibrium point as the economy is operating below potential. The fall in the price level will lead to a revision downwards in price expectations.

Figure 11.16 shows the transition back to the LRAS curve. In the lower diagram, as price expectations are revised downwards, the SRAS curve moves down along the AD_2 curve. But what causes aggregate demand (AD) to increase? In the upper diagram, the fall in the price level increases the real money supply and the LM curve shifts down to the right. It is the expansion of the real money supply that creates the demand impetus. This process continues until the economy reverts

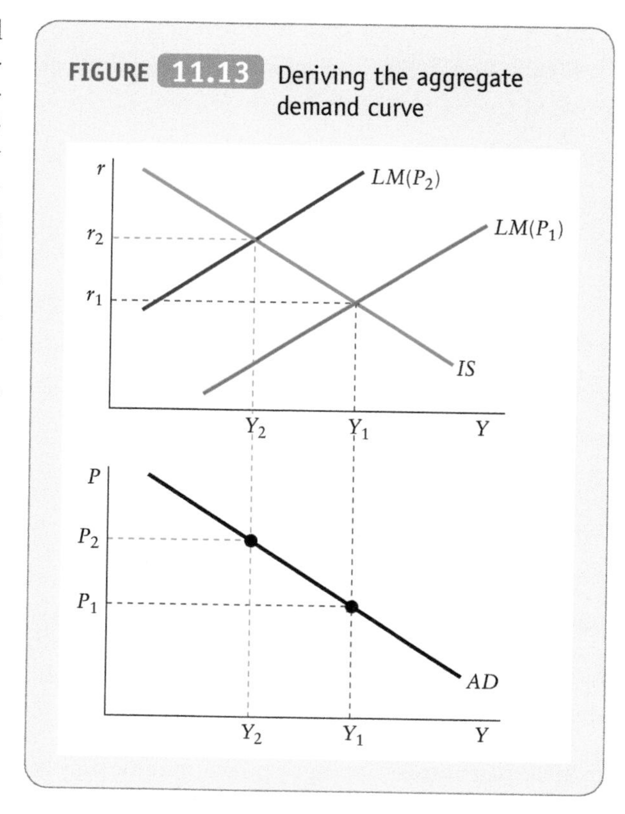

FIGURE 11.13 Deriving the aggregate demand curve

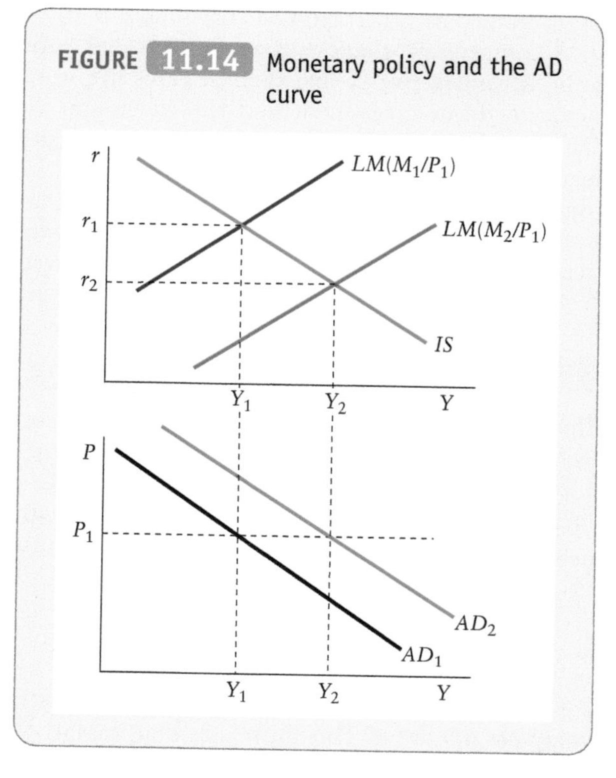

FIGURE 11.14 Monetary policy and the AD curve

to the LRAS curve at point C. (Note that in Figure 11.14, the increase in the money supply shifted the location of the AD curve. Here the fall in the price level causes the economy to move along the AD curve.)

This process is similar to the analysis in Chapter 5 in that the adjustment back to potential output depends crucially on the flexibility of prices in a downward direction. However, the difference is that here the fall in P increases the real money supply whereas in Chapter 5 we had not yet introduced the money market.

Note that at point B in Figure 11.15, the real wage increased. Therefore, as part of the adjustment process, we are still relying on a fall in the nominal wage to restore equilibrium. Keynes described this in the *General Theory* as 'monetary management by trade unions', as the decrease in prices and wages leads to an increase in the real money supply.

The reader is encouraged to try the opposite case of an expansionary demand-side shock (not shown). Starting from equilibrium on the LRAS curve, the IS curve shifts upwards to the right. Output (Y) increases and the economy is now over-heating. In the lower diagram, the AD curve shifts upwards. This causes the price level to rise and the SRAS curve shifts upwards over time. The rise in the price level also reduces the real money supply and the LM curve shifts upwards to the left. Eventually an equilibrium is achieved on the LRAS curve.

FIGURE 11.15 The short- and long-run effects of an IS shock

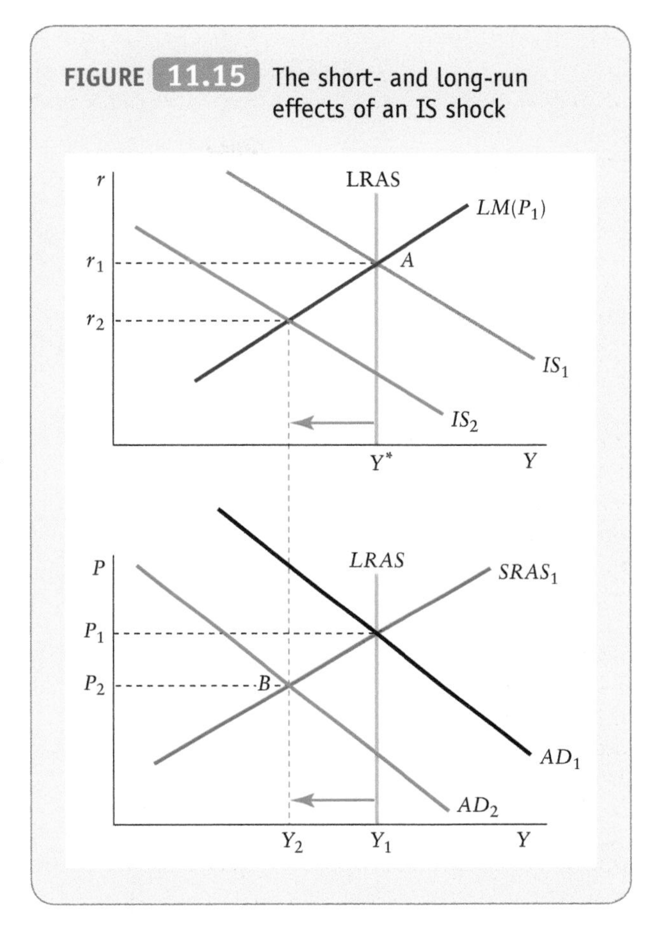

11.8 The IS-LM Model and the Economic Crisis of 2008

We can use the IS-LM model to describe what happened during the post-2007 economic crisis in Ireland.

In Chapter 5 we saw that the contraction of the economy was due to a collapse in aggregate demand, especially the domestic components of AD (C, G, and I). This corresponds to a large leftward shift in the IS curve as shown in Figures 11.15 and 11.16.

In 2008 the 'automatic stabilisers' kicked in as tax revenue slumped and social welfare spending soared, widening the fiscal deficit. However, discretionary increases in government spending and/or tax cuts were ruled out because the budget deficit was already spiralling out of control and Ireland was no longer able to borrow at sustainable rates on the bond market. Far from falling in the face of an inward shift in the IS curve, the interest rates relevant to investment in Ireland actually rose as banks restricted credit and applied more stringent conditions to the limited number of new loans they were prepared to extend. This is part of the reason why the fall in real output was more pronounced in Ireland than it was in most other euro area economies.

FIGURE 11.16 The transition back to the LRAS curve

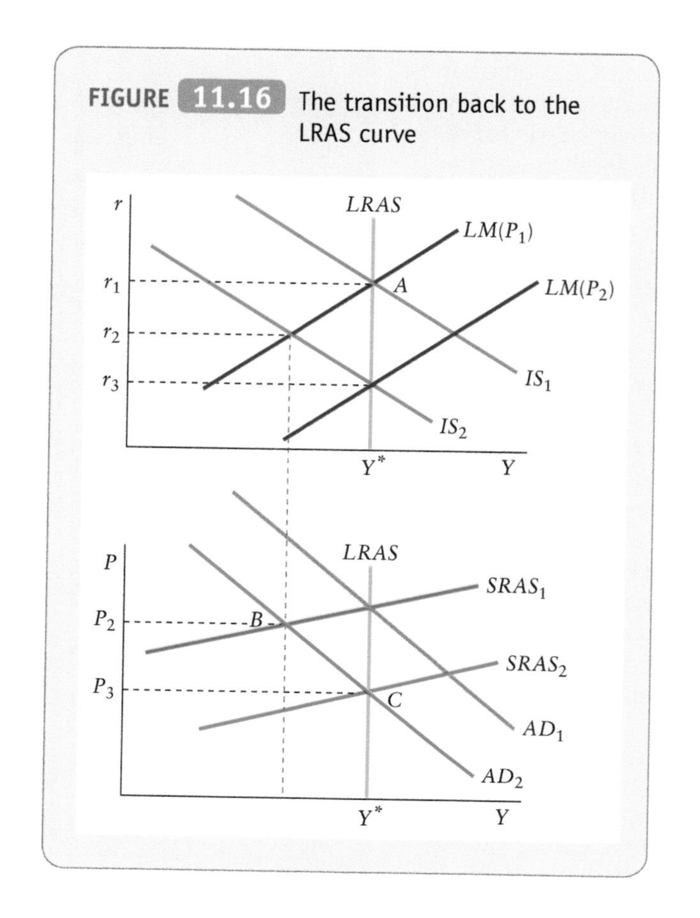

Our model predicts that in a recession the SRAS curve should move down to the right as the rise in unemployment leads to lower prices and wages. We reviewed the evidence on this adjustment process in Chapter 5. We saw some evidence of price and wage flexibility, but noted that the adjustment has been slow and incomplete. Moreover, the problems facing Ireland have been compounded by a renewed weakness in the European and US economies in 2012. One of the few bright spots for Ireland after 2007 was the strong performance of exports, but the markets into which we export are now weakening and this is not helping the recovery process. This could be modelled as a further leftward shift in the IS curve.

Falling prices, combined with the massive expansion of liquidity through the ECB's monetary operations, should have eased conditions in credit markets. This would be illustrated as a rightward shift in the LM curve. But we have drawn attention to the peculiar conditions prevailing in the Irish banking system, which is still in intensive care following the collapse of 2008. The urgency of complying with the new stricter Basel conditions means that, as outstanding loans are paid off, the cash inflow is being added to capital reserves rather than being re-loaned. The additional liquidity that has been made available through the ECB's bond-buying programme is also effectively being hoarded by the banks. Despite the massive state aid to the banks, which was supposed to get them to resume 'normal business', this has not happened. The prospects are for a slow return to the economy's potential level of output.

11.9 Key Terms and Concepts

The key points covered in this chapter include the following.

- The Keynesian cross diagram.
- The IS curve shows the combinations of the interest rate and output that give an equilibrium in the market for goods and services.
- The LM curve shows the combination of the interest rate and output that give equilibrium in the money market.
- The intersection of the IS and LM curves represents a simultaneous equilibrium in both the goods and money markets.
- The Keynesian case is represented by a flat (elastic) LM curve and a steep (inelastic) IS curve.
- The classical case is represented by a steep (inelastic) LM curve and a flat (elastic) IS curve.
- The crowding-out effect.
- Expansionary fiscal and monetary policies have different implications for interest rates.
- The relationship between the IS-LM model and the aggregate demand curve.
- A discussion of the Irish economic crisis of 2008 using the IS-LM model.

CHAPTER 12

The Phillips Curve and the Inflation–Unemployment Trade-off

12.1 Introduction

In this chapter we examine the relationship between inflation and unemployment. The New Zealand economist A. W. H. Phillips (1914–1975), working at the London School of Economics (LSE) in the 1950s, presented evidence that showed an inverse relationship between the percentage change in wages and the rate of unemployment. A curve depicting this inverse relationship has come to be known as the Phillips curve.

We begin this chapter by discussing the original version of the Phillips curve and its implications for economic policy. This is followed by a discussion of subsequent modifications and critiques of the Phillips curve. We use this theory to discuss the costs associated with implementing a deflationary or anti-inflationary economic policy. We conclude the chapter by demonstrating the relationship between the Phillips curve and the short-run aggregate supply (SRAS) curve and by discussing recent developments relating to the Phillips curve.

12.2 The Original Phillips Curve

Phillips noted that between 1861 and 1957 in Britain there was a tendency for periods of low unemployment to coincide with periods of rising wage rates. Conversely, during periods of high unemployment, the rate of increase in wages moderated. Phillips drew a diagram depicting this inverse relationship (Phillips 1958). Variants of it have appeared in macroeconomic textbooks ever since.

An early extension of the idea was to replace the rate of increase in nominal wages by the increase in prices or the inflation rate. This assumes that prices are set as a mark-up over wages. If wages rise, so too will the price of output, and vice versa. Expressed in terms of price inflation, the Phillips curve can be written as:

$$\pi = F(\mathrm{U}) \quad F_1 < 0 \tag{1}$$

where π is the rate of inflation and U the unemployment rate and $F_1 < 0$ indicates that we expect an increase in unemployment to lead to a fall in the rate of inflation and vice versa.

Phillips suggested that the best fit to the historical data was a non-linear one, as shown in Figure 12.1, which has unemployment on the horizontal axis and inflation on the vertical axis. A low level of unemployment is associated with a high rate of inflation. Conversely, a high level of unemployment is associated with a low level of inflation. Note that at some stage, the Phillips curve cuts through the horizontal axis. This suggests that high levels of unemployment are associated with deflation.

NOTE: Phillips actually obtained his curve using data over the sub-period 1861–1913, not the entire period 1861–1957. He then applied the curve to the sub-periods 1913–1948 and 1948–1957 and discussed the appropriateness of the fit. What he found was that the data moved in loops around the curve. It is of interest to note that in obtaining the curve for the 1861–1913 period, Phillips did not appear to use any statistical technique but actually drew the curve freehand to obtain the best fit.

NOTE: In 1949 Phillips built in a garage in Croydon the first MONIAC (Monetary National Income Analogue Computer) or 'Phillips Machine'. The machine is a hydraulic version of the IS-LM model. It was, in effect, one of the first computers used in economics. It was, for a number of years, used for teaching purposes at the LSE.

Policy implications

The thinking behind the Phillips curve was enormously influential in the 1960s. It led macroeconomic policy-makers to believe, in a phrase used by Paul Samuelson and Robert Solow (both Nobel Prize laureates teaching at Massachusetts Institute of Technology) in 1960, that there exists a 'menu for policy choice'; that is, a trade-off between the two evils of inflation and unemployment. It is not possible to enjoy a low rate of inflation and a low rate of unemployment at the same time, but it is possible to have less of one if more of the other is tolerated. Countries and policy-makers have to decide how much extra inflation they are prepared to tolerate in order to achieve a reduction in unemployment. For example, suppose the economy is initially at point A in Figure 12.1, where an inflation rate of two per cent is combined with an unemployment rate of four per cent. If the government now uses fiscal or monetary policy to move the economy to point B, unemployment is reduced to two per cent, but inflation rises to six per cent. The gain in terms of lower unemployment has been paid for in terms of a higher rate of inflation.

The choice between these two evils is essentially a political one. Conservatives might prefer low inflation and ignore the high unemployment that this entails, whereas Labour or left-wing parties might tend to opt for low unemployment and accept the consequences for inflation.

FIGURE 12.1 The Phillips curve

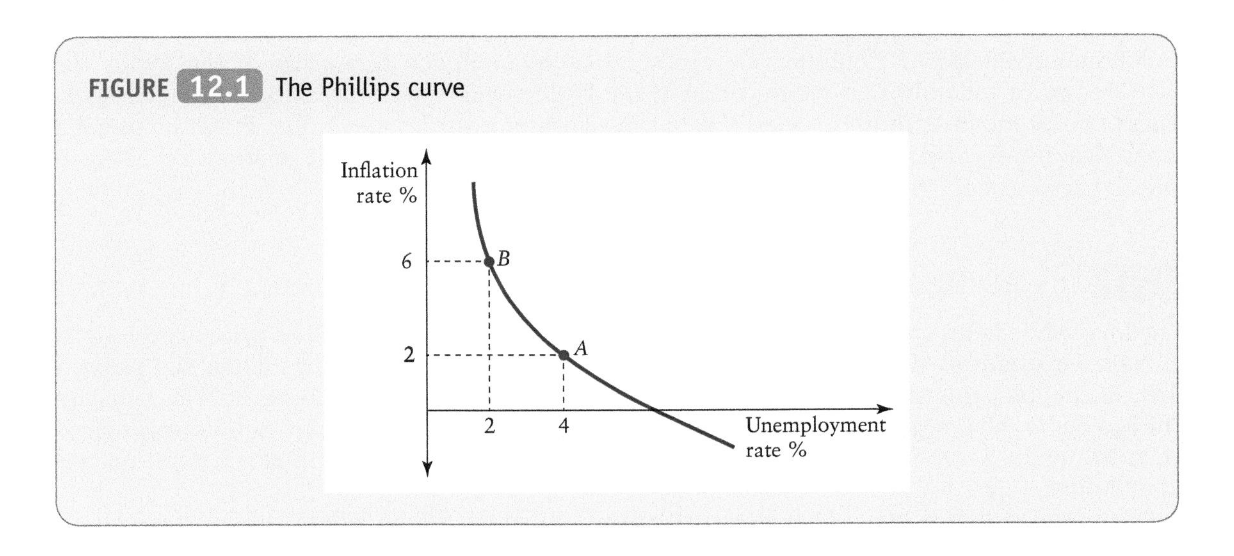

Various attempts were suggested in the 1960s to improve the trade-off. For example, a freezing of prices and wages could be used to try to contain inflation and fiscal or monetary policy used to lower unemployment. The result would be to shift the Phillips curve down to the left and improve the trade-off. The British Prime Minister Ted Heath tried such a policy in the early 1970s with disastrous results. The price and incomes policy led to a pent-up demand for higher wages and caused major industrial strife.

FIGURE 12.2 Stagflation

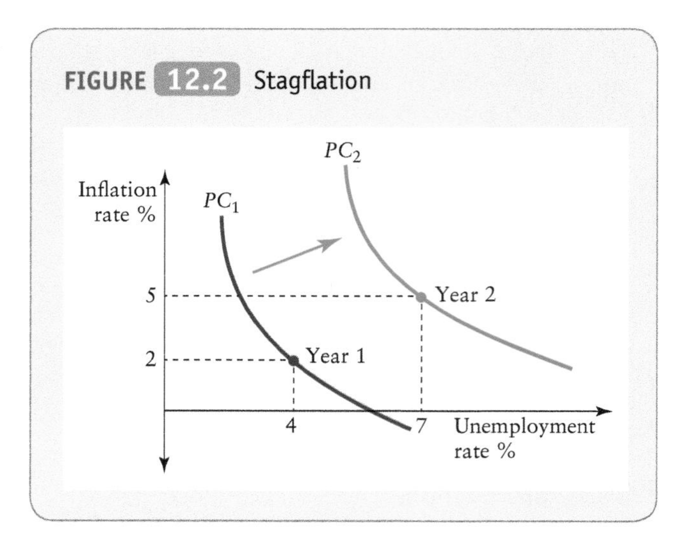

Breakdown of the Phillips curve relationship

Attempts to exploit the trade-off between unemployment and inflation led to increasing disillusionment. The emphasis during the 1960s was on keeping the rate of unemployment low and a fair degree of success was achieved in this regard. However, in many countries it became evident that the rate of inflation associated with what was considered full employment was rising. Even worse was the experience of the mid-1970s, when the rate of inflation began to increase at a time of rising unemployment. This became known as *stagflation*. It appeared that the policies designed to move the economy up the Phillips curve were, in fact, causing the curve to shift upwards to the right. That is, as shown in Figure 12.2, a higher level of unemployment was associated with a higher level of inflation. The inflation/unemployment relationship, which apparently had been stable for over a hundred years, appeared to be breaking down.

There was much discussion of possible explanations for this: increased trade union militancy; a growing mismatch between the skills of job seekers and the requirements of employers; a more generous social welfare system; and so on.

However, none of these explanations seemed to go to the heart of the matter and explain what was happening. It seemed that a fundamental reformulation of the Phillips curve idea was required. In this regard, two economists, Milton Friedman of the University of Chicago and Edmund Phelps of Columbia University, deserve credit for foreseeing in the 1960s the acceleration of inflation that would occur if the Phillips curve were used for policy purposes. These two economists (both of whom were subsequently awarded the Nobel Prize) provided a theoretical framework that significantly advanced our understanding of the relationship between inflation and unemployment.

12.3 The Revised Phillips Curve

Friedman and Phelps argued that the original Phillips curve ignored the role of price expectations in wage negotiations. They incorporated price expectations into the Phillips curve and showed that, in the long run, there is no trade-off between inflation and unemployment. The long-run Phillips curve is vertical at the natural rate of unemployment. Any attempt to hold unemployment below the natural rate would result, not just in higher inflation, but in an accelerating rate of inflation.

They argued that a vertical Phillips curve would intersect the horizontal axis at the natural rate of unemployment. This 'natural' rate is also known as the non-accelerating inflation rate of unemployment or NAIRU. (The phrase NAIRU was introduced by James Tobin, of Yale University. It has the merit of avoiding the moralistic overtones of the 'natural' rate. We continue, however, to use the term 'natural rate' in the remainder of this chapter.)

NOTE: Economists and journalists sometimes mistakenly refer to a *rising* inflation rate as *accelerating* inflation. An inflation rate that goes from two to four to six per cent is rising. Only when the inflation rate is rising at an increasing pace – from two to four to eight to 16 per cent – is it accelerating.

The role of expectations

We need to reformulate the Phillips curve in terms of how workers bargain for wage increases. Here it is essential to distinguish between the change in nominal wages (ΔW) and the change in real wages (ΔRW). The real wage is the nominal wage adjusted for inflation (π). That is:

$$\Delta RW = \Delta W - \pi \tag{2}$$

The next point to note is that wage bargaining is forward looking and incorporates an anticipated or *ex ante* rate of inflation. That is, because wage contracts last into the future, workers will try to anticipate the rate of inflation in order to protect their real wages for the duration of the contract. For example, if inflation is expected to be 10 per cent over the coming year, workers will demand at least a 10 per cent increase in nominal wages to compensate for anticipated inflation and maintain real wages at the present level. Hence the variable that matters in wage bargaining may be defined as:

$$\Delta RW^e = \Delta W - \pi^e \tag{3}$$

where π^e is expected price inflation and ΔRW^e is the expected real wage.

Given that prices are set as a mark-up over wages, it follows that an increase in inflationary expectations will increase wage demands, which will in turn increase the inflation rate. In short:

$$\uparrow \pi^e \rightarrow \uparrow \Delta W \rightarrow \uparrow \pi$$

It follows from this that it is in the best interest of the policy-maker to maintain a low inflation environment. If workers anticipate low inflation they will set their wage demands accordingly.

The natural rate of unemployment

The second main strand in the Phelps–Friedman theory is to incorporate the natural rate of unemployment into the analysis. This is the level of unemployment that exists when the economy is growing at the potential real growth rate. It is a normal feature of any dynamic economy that some minimal 'natural unemployment' remains even when the economy is growing at its potential rate (see Chapter 4).

However, as we emphasised in Chapter 4, the natural rate of unemployment can vary over time. This makes the policy-maker's task more difficult as he is, in effect, aiming at a moving target. In this chapter, in order to facilitate the analysis, we assume that the natural rate remains constant.

On this basis, Friedman and Phelps argue that inflation depends on the gap between the actual unemployment rate (U) and the natural rate (U_n). That is, inflation is influenced by ($U - U_n$), rather than U. If U is greater than U_n, there is downward pressure on inflation. This is because in times of high unemployment, the trade unions' bargaining position is weak and they settle for lower wage demands. Conversely, if U is less than U_n, there is upward pressure on inflation. This is because in boom times, there are bottlenecks and labour shortages and the unions are in a strong position and can demand higher wages. No inflationary pressures emanate from the labour market when U is equal to U_n.

The expectations-augmented Phillips curve

Taking the above two adjustments together, the accelerationist or expectations-augmented Phillips curve may be written:

$$\pi_t = \pi_t^e - \alpha(U - U_n) \qquad (4)$$

Equation (4) states that the inflation rate in time t depends on the expected rate of inflation (π_t^e) plus an adjustment based on the difference between the actual rate of unemployment and the natural rate. The coefficient α indicates how the rate of inflation reacts to the difference between the unemployment rate and the natural rate of unemployment ($U - U_n$). A high coefficient would indicate that inflation is very sensitive to the unemployment gap and a low coefficient indicates that inflation is not very responsive to the unemployment gap.

How are expectations formed?

In the simplest model, workers use *adaptive expectations* to forecast inflation. It is assumed that this year's inflation rate will recur next year; that is, $\pi_t^e = \pi_{t-1}$, where the subscript t indicates the year. This means that if inflation is three per cent in 2012, it is expected to be three per cent in 2013 also. This is a backward-looking approach to formulating expectations and in periods of volatile inflation it is likely to lead to systematic errors in the inflation forecast. Inserting this formulation of expectations into equation (4), we have:

$$\pi_t = \pi_{t-1} - \alpha(U - U_n) \qquad (5)$$

Equation (5) states that the inflation rate in time t depends on inflation in the previous year plus an adjustment based on the unemployment gap. Later in this chapter we discuss the more sophisticated model of '*rational expectations*'.

12.4 The Accelerationist Theory of Inflation

The expectations-augmented Phillips curve is illustrated in Figure 12.3. The Phillips curve is again downward sloping, indicating an inverse relationship between inflation and unemployment. The vertical line is labelled the long-run Phillips curve, which is located at the natural rate of unemployment, shown here as six per cent.

Suppose now that the economy is at the point A in Figure 12.3. At this point, expected inflation (π^e) equals zero and the actual unemployment rate equals the natural rate of six per cent. It can be seen from equation (5) that under these circumstance, the actual inflation rate will also be zero. Hence, at point A, zero inflation is combined with a six per cent unemployment rate. Note that the relevant short-run Phillips curve is labelled SRPC ($\pi^e = 0$) to indicate that it corresponds to zero expected inflation.

Perhaps a government with an election approaching wants to drive the unemployment rate below six per cent. If the government uses monetary or fiscal policy to reduce unemployment the economy moves up along the Phillips curve to the point B. At B, inflation increases to four per cent and unemployment falls to two per cent.

The movement from A to B in Figure 12.3 is a satisfactory outcome from the government's point of view. An expansionary macroeconomic policy has lowered unemployment to two per cent at the cost of a four per cent increase in inflation. Perhaps it helps them to win the election.

FIGURE 12.3 The accelerationist theory of inflation

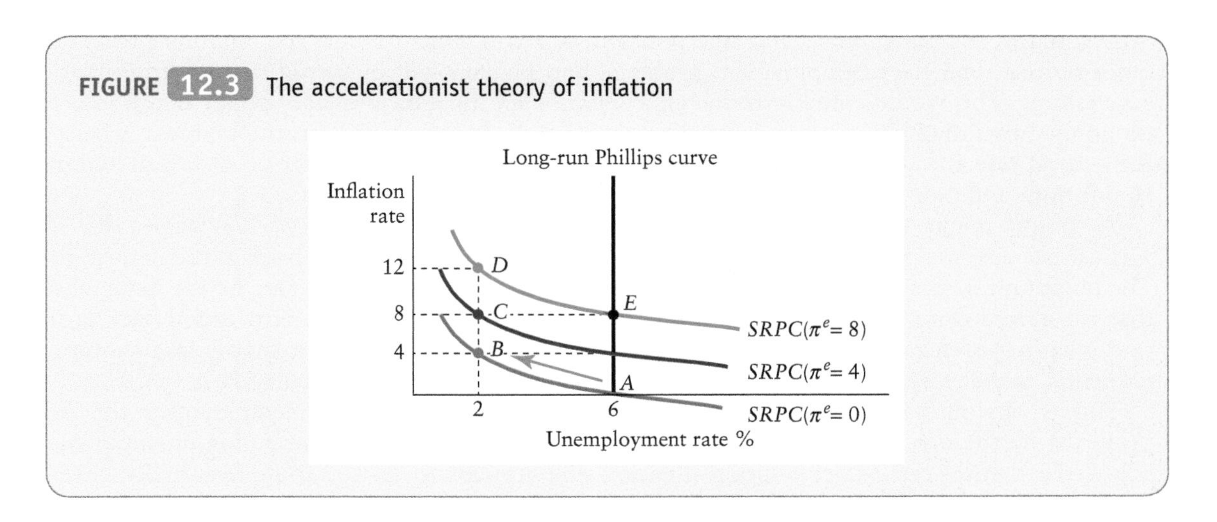

However, the point B is not a long-run equilibrium point. Inflation has increased from zero per cent to four per cent, but workers were expecting it to be zero. In the next round of wage negotiations, workers will revise their inflation expectations upwards from zero to four per cent. In the diagram the short-run Phillips curve shifts upwards from SRPC ($\pi^e = 0$) to SRPC ($\pi^e = 4$).

NOTE: When unemployment equals the natural rate, actual inflation is determined by expected inflation. In other words, the short-run Phillips curve intersects the long-run Phillips curve at the point corresponding to the expected rate of inflation. The long-run Phillips curve is the locus of points on short-run Phillips curves where actual inflation equals expected inflation.

If the policy-makers persist in trying to maintain the rate of unemployment at two per cent, the economy will move, in the next round of wage negotiations, to C on SRPC($\pi^e = 4$). At this point, two per cent unemployment is combined with an inflation rate of eight per cent. Why has the inflation rate increased from four per cent to eight per cent? The answer is that the revision in price expectations from zero per cent to four per cent resulted in an increase in wage demands. This increase in wages (via the mark-up model) added a further four per cent to the inflation rate, bringing the new rate to eight per cent. At the point C, the trade-off between unemployment and inflation is becoming less favourable.

However, the economy is not in long-run equilibrium at C. Workers were expecting an inflation rate of four per cent, but the actual inflation rate turns out to be eight per cent. In the next round of wage negotiations, workers will again revise their inflation expectations upwards from four per cent to eight per cent. This is reflected in Figure 12.3 as the Phillips curve shifting upwards from SRPC($\pi^e = 4$) to SRPC($\pi^e = 8$). The economy now moves to the point D, where two per cent unemployment is combined with a twelve per cent inflation rate.

The crucial point that emerges from this analysis is that as long as policy is dedicated to maintaining the rate of unemployment below its natural rate, the economy will not be in a steady equilibrium. Inflation will go on accelerating as workers continually revise price expectations upwards.

The consequences of trying to maintain the rate of unemployment below its natural rate are now very unsatisfactory. The cost of the reduction in unemployment is a continuously rising rate of inflation. The expansionary macroeconomic policy has not just caused a once-off increase in inflation but has led to an accelerating rate of inflation.

Eventually, the public and hence the policy-maker will come to view the inflation problem as more serious than the unemployment problem, and policies will be introduced to stop inflation accelerating. This would entail introducing a deflationary fiscal or monetary policy that moves the economy down the Phillips curve from the point D to E. At the point E, unemployment is back to the natural rate and workers' price expectations prove to be correct and the point E is in long-run equilibrium. Inflation is, however, higher than it was before the expansion.

By joining points such as A and E, we obtain the long-run Phillips curve. We can see that it is vertical because we started at the natural rate and, ultimately, we end up back at the natural rate. The inflation rate may differ, but the unemployment rate will, in the long run, be the same. Given that we started from the natural rate of unemployment and that we have now ended back at this rate, what has been gained by the expansionary macroeconomic policy? The answer is: a temporary reduction in the rate of unemployment and a permanent increase in the rate of inflation.

This is obviously less attractive than the permanent reduction in unemployment that was promised by the original version of the Phillips curve. If the cost of maintaining unemployment below the natural rate is accelerating inflation, the attempt to do so would eventually have to be abandoned in order to prevent the breakdown of economic life. Accelerating inflation would lead to hyperinflation of the sort experienced in central Europe after World War I and in many east European countries in the 1990s. Such inflation is so disruptive that it undermines normal economic processes and leads to a sharp decline in living standards.

On the basis of their critique of the earlier Phillips curve analysis, therefore, Phelps and Friedman rejected the notion that in the long run unemployment could be reduced by accepting a higher rate of inflation. They left little or no room for expansionary macroeconomic policy as an instrument for lowering the rate of unemployment.

An alternative explanation

The above analysis could also be conducted in terms of equation (5) above. Recall that:

$$\pi_t = \pi_{t-1} - \alpha(U - U_n)$$

The expansionary monetary policy reduced U below the natural rate of unemployment and this added four per cent to π_t in the first year. In the second year this increase in inflation feeds back into the π_{t-1} term and this pushes the actual inflation rate to eight per cent. In the third year the increase in inflation again feeds back into the π_{t-1} term and inflation again rises, and so on. Eventually, the policy-maker decides that the rise in inflation is no longer acceptable and introduces policies to move the economy back to the natural rate of unemployment.

12.5 Inflation and Unemployment in Ireland

The Phillips curve was originally applied mainly to large and relatively closed economies. Its relevance to a small open economy such as Ireland, on the other hand, might be questioned. With such a high proportion of our consumer and investment goods imported, external influences are obviously a far more important factor in Irish inflation than would be the case in the USA or the UK. These external factors are mediated through the exchange rate.

In the period when we had a fixed exchange rate with sterling it became widely accepted that Irish inflation would track British inflation very closely and the evidence supported this. One of the motivations for adopting the euro was the belief that, in a currency union, our inflation rate would converge on the lower euro area inflation rate, which in turn would reflect the low German rate.

This view of Irish inflation relegates the domestic unemployment rate to a secondary role as a determinant of Irish inflation. Figure 12.4 shows that there has been no stable unemployment–inflation trade-off in Ireland over the decades. Note that the natural rate of unemployment is given as 8.7 per cent. This calculation is explained in Section 12.7 below.

FIGURE 12.4 Inflation and unemployment, Ireland 1960–2010

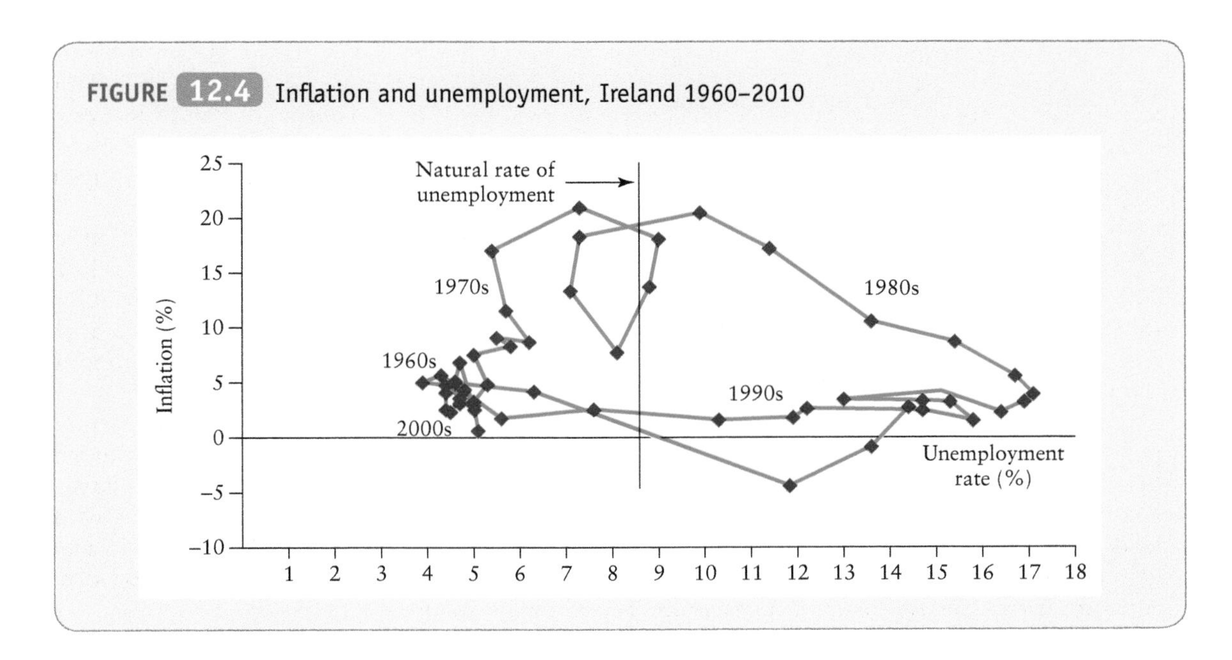

However, the period of disinflation during the 1980s did correspond to the traditional Phillips curve prediction that as unemployment rose, inflation fell. Of course this was a period of global disinflation and to some extent the Irish inflation experience just mirrored the international experience.

Similarly, in Ireland during the late 1960s and early years of the 1970s, falling unemployment coincided with rising inflation, but again this also mirrored the external situation.

The really striking feature of Figure 12.4 is the long series of points that run parallel to the horizontal axis. These are the combinations of inflation and unemployment over the period after 1986, when the unemployment rate fell from over 17 per cent to between four and five per cent early in the present century, but inflation remained close to or under four per cent in all but one year (2000).

The traditional Phillips curve analysis would seem to be largely irrelevant to the study of this period, especially when it is borne in mind that in the 1980s plenty of reasons were advanced to back assertions that the 'natural' rate of unemployment was very high in Ireland due to the intractable nature of the structural unemployment left in the wake of the recession.

12.6 Deflation, Expectations and Credibility

So far we have concentrated on the hypothesis that accepting a higher inflation rate may be a price that has to be paid for a low unemployment rate. But what of the opposite case, where a government is willing to accept higher unemployment in order to bring down inflation? This was the view of those who supported the 'monetarist' policies introduced by Mrs Thatcher in Britain in 1979 (which led to a year-long strike by the miners in 1984). In the USA, Paul Volcker, chairman of the Federal Reserve Board, addressed the high rate of inflation with a contractionary monetary policy. This led to high unemployment, but is credited with restoring stability to the world's largest currency. These deflationary policies are the reverse of the expansionary policy discussed in the previous section.

Figure 12.5 depicts an economy that is initially at the natural rate of unemployment. Suppose also that inflation is 20 per cent and that this is unacceptable to the government. To reduce inflation the government introduces a deflationary fiscal or monetary policy. As a result, the economy moves from the point A to the point B along the Phillips curve labelled SCPC($\pi^e = 20$). This Phillips curve is associated with inflation expectations of 20 per cent.

FIGURE 12.5 Deflationary economic policy

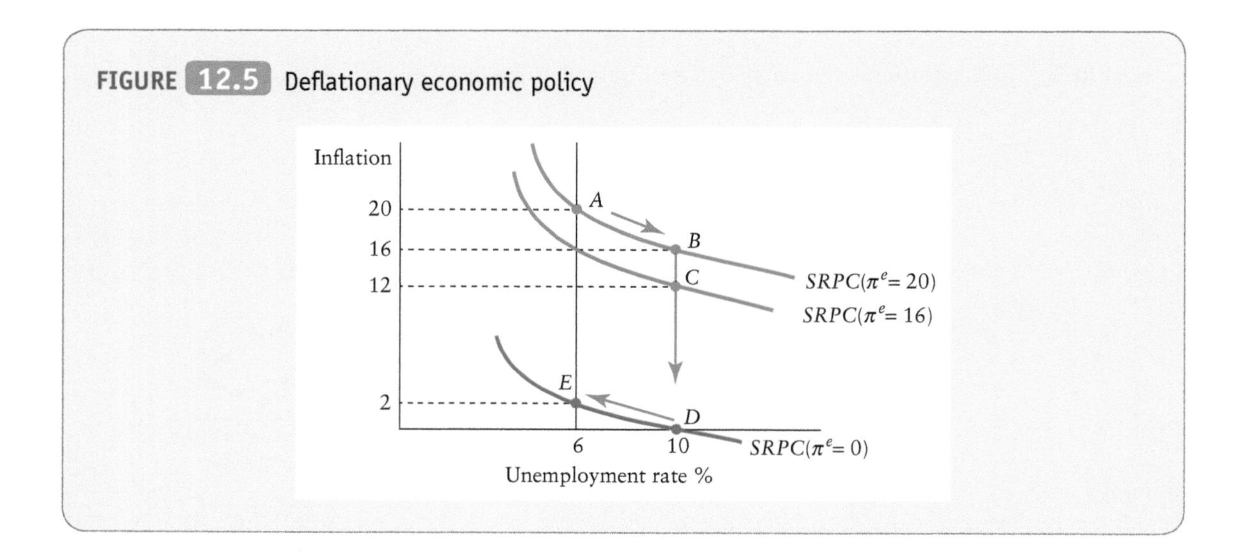

At the point B unemployment has risen from six to 10 per cent but actual inflation has fallen to 16 per cent. (Note that the decrease in inflation depends on how far the economy moves down the Phillips curve.) At the point B the economy is said to be experiencing an inflationary recession.

In the next round of wage negotiations, workers realise that inflation is lower than expected and they revise inflation expectations from 20 to 16 per cent. This is reflected in a shift downwards in the Phillips curve. As workers' inflation expectations fall, wage demands are moderated and the actual inflation rate in the following year falls to 12 per cent.

Over time, the Phillips curve will gradually drift down as price expectations are revised downwards. Eventually the economy will move to a point such as D. At this point, a low rate of inflation is combined with a 10 per cent unemployment rate. The government may now decide to introduce an expansionary fiscal policy to move the economy up the Phillips curve from the point D to E. The economy reverts back to the natural rate of unemployment and inflation increases to two per cent.

The sacrifice ratio

The cost of reducing inflation is the lost output and the rise in unemployment associated with the policy-induced recession. The sacrifice ratio is one measure of this cost. It indicates how much unemployment has to be increased in order to reduce inflation. To explain this sacrifice ratio, we first define a point-year of excess unemployment as being the difference between actual unemployment and the natural rate multiplied by the number of years. For example, suppose actual unemployment is 10 per cent for two years and the natural rate is six per cent. This is equivalent to eight point-years of excess unemployment.

$$\text{Point-year of excess unemployment} = 4 \text{ per cent excess unemployment} \times 2 \text{ years} = 8 \text{ points}$$

The sacrifice ratio is now defined as the point-year of excess unemployment divided by the decrease in inflation. That is:

$$\text{Sacrifice ratio} = \text{Point-year of excess unemployment/decrease in inflation}$$

Hence if it takes eight point-years of excess unemployment to reduce inflation by two per cent, the sacrifice ratio is four (8/2).

Equation (5) above can be used to throw light on the potential size of the sacrifice ratio. By taking the π_{t-1} term to the left-hand side we have:

$$\pi_t - \pi_{t-1} = -\alpha(U - U_n) \quad (6)$$

or

$$\Delta\pi = -\alpha(U - U_n) \quad (7)$$

Suppose that the natural rate of unemployment is 6 per cent and that the α coefficient is estimated to be equal to one. If the policy-maker wishes to reduce inflation by five per cent, equation (7) suggests that actual unemployment will have to be increased to 11 per cent for one year.

$$-5\% = -1(11 - 6)$$

Inserting this information into the definition of the sacrifice ratio above, we calculate that the sacrifice ratio is one. (Five point-years of excess unemployment divided by a five per cent reduction in inflation.)

Alternatively, the policy-maker could increase actual unemployment to 8.5 per cent for two years to achieve the same five per cent reduction in inflation. Again the sacrifice ratio is one.

However, if the α coefficient is instead equal to, say, 0.5, the sacrifice ratio would be twice as high. For example, the policy-maker would have to increase actual unemployment to 16 per cent to bring about a 5 per cent reduction in inflation in one year.

$$-5\% = -0.5(16 - 6)$$

Alternatively, the policy-maker could opt for an actual unemployment rate of 11 per cent for two years to bring about a similar result. The sacrifice ratio depends on the α coefficient. The higher the α coefficient the lower the sacrifice ratio and vice versa. We present some empirical evidence on the α coefficient later in this chapter.

The sacrifice ratio also depends on how rapidly inflationary expectations are revised. If inflation expectations are quickly revised downwards, the adjustment costs will be relatively small. Conversely, if inflation expectations are slow to change, the adjustment costs will be relatively high. Equation (7) does not throw any light on this issue as we have assumed adaptive expectations. That is, we have assumed that this year's inflation rate is the best indicator of next year's inflation rate. This assumption is 'built in' to the equation and hence cannot be empirically evaluated.

'Gradualist' or 'cold turkey'

As mentioned above, the α coefficient, in part, determines the sacrifice ratio. However, there is some international evidence which shows that the sacrifice ratio tends to be lower, the quicker the disinflation. This raises the question of whether the policy-maker should introduce a 'gradualist' or 'cold turkey' approach in deflating the economy. That is, should the policy-maker slowly deflate the economy and move gently towards a low inflation rate?

Alternatively, should the policy-maker introduce a once-off deflationary policy that hits the economy so hard that market participants cannot but recognise the government's intention and therefore revise their expectations? In this case, the movement to a low inflation rate should happen very quickly and unemployment would not remain above the natural rate for very long.

The problem with the 'cold turkey' approach is that it can lead to a severe recession that leads to civil unrest and political instability. Also it will impact disproportionately on vulnerable sectors of the labour market such as the unskilled and the young. The headline 'Sachs cuts dog's tail off at neck' that appeared in a Polish newspaper was a reference to the American economist Jeffrey Sachs who was responsible for introducing economic reforms in Poland during the late 1980s. Obviously, the media felt he had overdone the 'cold turkey' approach! A more recent example is the austerity measures being imposed on Ireland and Greece following the economic crash of 2008. However, the intention here is not to reduce inflation, which is already low, but to restore order to the public finances.

Rational expectations

The theory of rational expectations assumes that people and firms base their inflation expectations on all available information, including information on current and possible future policies. Economists such as Robert Lucas of Chicago University argue that if rational expectations are the norm, the sacrifice ratio may be small. If the central bank announces that it will do whatever is necessary to reduce inflation and the announcement is credible, people will reduce their inflation expectations and inflation will fall without any increase in unemployment. This implies 'talking-down' inflation expectations with a minimal increase in unemployment. This is very different from the case depicted in Figure 12.5. There, it is the increase in unemployment that drives inflation down and this, in turn, leads to a revision downwards in inflation expectations.

However, the evidence does not support the belief that inflation can be reduced at such a minimal cost in terms of higher unemployment. In the UK, Mrs Thatcher's monetarist experiment resulted in a painful transition. Inflation fell from 18 per cent in 1980 to four per cent in 1983, but absolute GDP fell by three per cent between 1981 and 1983, and unemployment increased from 1.1 million in 1979 to 3 million in 1984.

Similarly, in the USA, Paul Volcker's deflationary monetary policy reduced US inflation from 21.5 per cent in 1979 to four per cent in 1983. However, the real growth rate averaged only –0.3 per cent from 1980 to 1982 and unemployment increased from 5.5 per cent in 1979 to 10 per cent in 1983. It took several years for inflation to fall to the 5.5 per cent level. Clearly, these disinflationary episodes were painful, but they did contribute to restoring price stability and confidence to the two economies. It is difficult to say what alternative policy would have achieved this and whether it would have been at a lower cost.

Policy credibility

Another factor impacting on inflation expectations is the credibility of the commitment to the measures needed to bring about the required adjustment. It is argued that if the policy is credible, economic agents (firms and workers) will quickly adjust prices and wages to take account of the new policy. However, if the government lacks credibility and is viewed as likely to waver under pressure, adjustment will be prolonged and the costs will be high. Factors influencing credibility include:

- actions taken to reduce budget deficits;
- effective public communication of the rationale for the policy;
- a willingness to soldier through the unpopularity that inevitably attaches to increases in unemployment.

If policy-makers are above politics and do not have to pander to the electorate they can pursue hard-nosed economic policies more freely than politicians who face period elections. For that reason, it is argued that if monetary policy is placed in the hands of an independent central bank, such as the US Federal Reserve, the Bank of England and the ECB, it is likely that the public will believe their commitment to squeezing inflation out of the system.

If, on the other hand, the central bank is ultimately controlled by politicians, as is the case in many Latin American countries, and in European countries such as Italy before the launch of EMU, for example, the public will expect the politicians to instruct the bankers to ease up on disinflation as unemployment rises – especially if an election is in the offing.

An approach that has been widely used by small economies to gain credibility is to peg the currency to a hard currency such as the euro or the US dollar, and then to implement appropriate fiscal, monetary and incomes policies to back up the peg. Ultimately this approach implies the abandonment of an independent national monetary policy. In the case of joining the EMU in 1999, responsibility for domestic inflation was removed from the national central bank and transferred to the ECB in Frankfurt. Ireland took this decision in 1998.

12.7 The Augmented Phillips Curve: Evidence from the Euro Area

It would be informative if we could estimate equation (7) above, as this would give an indication of the sacrifice ratio for any particular country. However, estimating equation (7) is problematic because the natural rate of unemployment is unknown. An alternative to equation (7) is to estimate the following equation:

$$\Delta\pi_t = \beta - \alpha U \tag{8}$$

This equation examines the relationship between the change in the inflation rate and the unemployment rate. The β term is the intercept, which may reflect how firms mark up prices over wages and other rigidities in the system such as national wage agreements and so on. The α term shows how the change in inflation reacts to the unemployment rate. This is the same coefficient as in equation (7) and can be used to estimate the sacrifice ratio. Box 12.1 demonstrates that equation (8) is consistent with equation (7). Equation (8) can easily be estimated without having to make any assumptions about the natural rate of unemployment.

Box 12.1 Deriving the Phillips curve

Equation (8) in the main text states that:

$$\Delta\pi_t = \beta - \alpha U \tag{9}$$

We start with a definition. The natural rate of unemployment is the level of unemployment that prevails when actual inflation equals expected inflation. That is, when $\Delta\pi_t = 0$. Setting equation (9) equal to zero and substituting the natural rate of unemployment for the actual rate, we have:

$$0 = \beta - \alpha U_n \tag{10}$$

Rearranging:

$$\alpha U_n = \beta \tag{11}$$

Return now to equation (9) above. This equation can be rewritten as:

$$\pi_t = \pi_{t-1} + \beta - \alpha U \tag{12}$$

Substitute equation (11) into (12) to obtain:

$$\pi_t = \pi_{t-1} + \alpha U_n - \alpha U \tag{13}$$

Rearranging:

$$\pi_t = \pi_{t-1} - \alpha(U - U_n) \tag{14}$$

which is equation (7) in the main text. Hence equations (7) and (8) are equivalent.

Table 12.1 shows the results of estimating equation (8) for the main euro area countries. Recall that the higher the α coefficient, the lower the sacrifice ratio and vice versa. The results in Table 12.1 indicate significant differences in the α coefficient across the euro area countries; from a low of –0.03 in Finland to a high of –0.32 in Greece. The euro area was subject to a common shock in the form of the financial crisis of 2008. The results in Table 12.1 suggest that the transition back to the natural rate of unemployment would be very uneven across the euro area. Even after 10 years of monetary union, the countries of the euro area differ markedly in how their economies adjust to shocks.

Estimates of the natural rate of unemployment

The empirical results in Table 12.1 can also be used to get an indication of the natural rate of unemployment. From equation (11) in Box 12.1, we can write:

$$U_n = \beta/\alpha$$

Using the estimates of β and α, the natural rate of unemployment for each of the euro area countries is given in column three in Table 12.1. Again there appears to be some considerable variance in the natural rate: from a high of 11.7 in Spain to a low of 2.8 in Austria. In countries like Spain, Ireland and Italy the natural rate of unemployment seems to be relatively high. In contrast, in countries like Luxembourg, Finland and Germany the natural rate is lower.

These differences may be due to many factors. It is possible that, despite the use of a common definition of unemployment, based on active job search, these concepts are interpreted differently in different countries. It is likely that differences in social welfare systems affect the natural rate of unemployment, which will tend to be lower in countries with low 'replacement ratios' (see Chapter 4) and stricter enforcement of the social welfare codes. Finally, the interaction between

TABLE 12.1 Estimates of the augmented Phillips curve for the euro area countries, 1961–2010

	β	α	Natural rate of unemployment
Austria	0.59	−0.21	2.8
Belgium	0.82	−0.12	6.8
Finland	0.11	−0.03	3.7
France	0.73	−0.11	6.6
Germany	0.16	−0.05	3.2
Greece	2.12	−0.32	6.6
Ireland	0.96	−0.11	8.7
Italy	1.79	−0.24	7.5
Luxembourg	0.46	−0.16	2.9
Netherlands	0.6	−0.14	4.3
Portugal	1.69	−0.31	5.5
Spain	1.17	−0.1	11.7

Source: Authors' estimates

the housing market and the labour market may affect the natural rate of unemployment. An unemployed worker is not likely to sell up (or relinquish a council house) in the north of England and move to the London area, where jobs are available, because of the difficulty of obtaining comparable housing there.

Hysteresis

A worrying possibility is that the natural rate of unemployment can vary from one period to another. That is, the natural rate tends to rise during recessions and fall during boom periods. Economists use the concept of hysteresis to describe this phenomenon. Hysteresis refers to a situation in which the natural rate of unemployment depends on the actual level of unemployment. This means that the natural rate of unemployment increases during recession (mid-1980s) and falls in boom periods (1990s).

One reason for hysteresis is that workers' skills and work ethic deteriorate as a spell of unemployment becomes prolonged. This makes them less employable as time goes by. Another possible explanation is that unemployed workers lose their influence on the wage bargaining process. Employed workers then negotiate higher wages for themselves and this leads to structural unemployment and a higher natural rate of unemployment. The employed 'insiders' price the unemployed 'outsiders' out of employment.

The German and Spanish experience

It is interesting to compare the unemployment/inflation record of two other euro area countries with the Irish record. Figures 12.6 and 12.7 show the combination of price inflation and the unemployment rate in Germany and Spain respectively from 1961 to 2010. We have inserted into each diagram a line indicating the natural rate of unemployment based on the estimates in Table 12.1. Generally, the inflation/unemployment combinations for each country seem to oscillate around the natural rate of unemployment. (This is of course a simple reflection of the way the 'natural' rate was estimated.)

FIGURE 12.6 Inflation and unemployment in Germany, 1961–2010

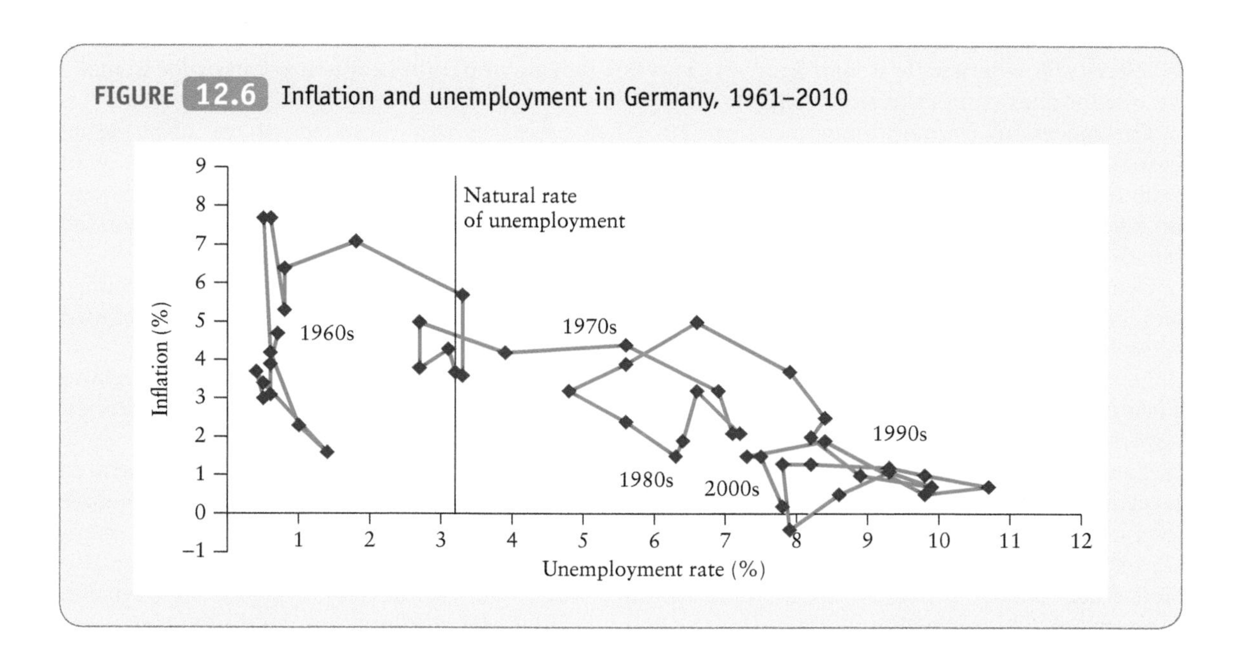

FIGURE 12.7 Inflation and unemployment in Spain, 1961–2010

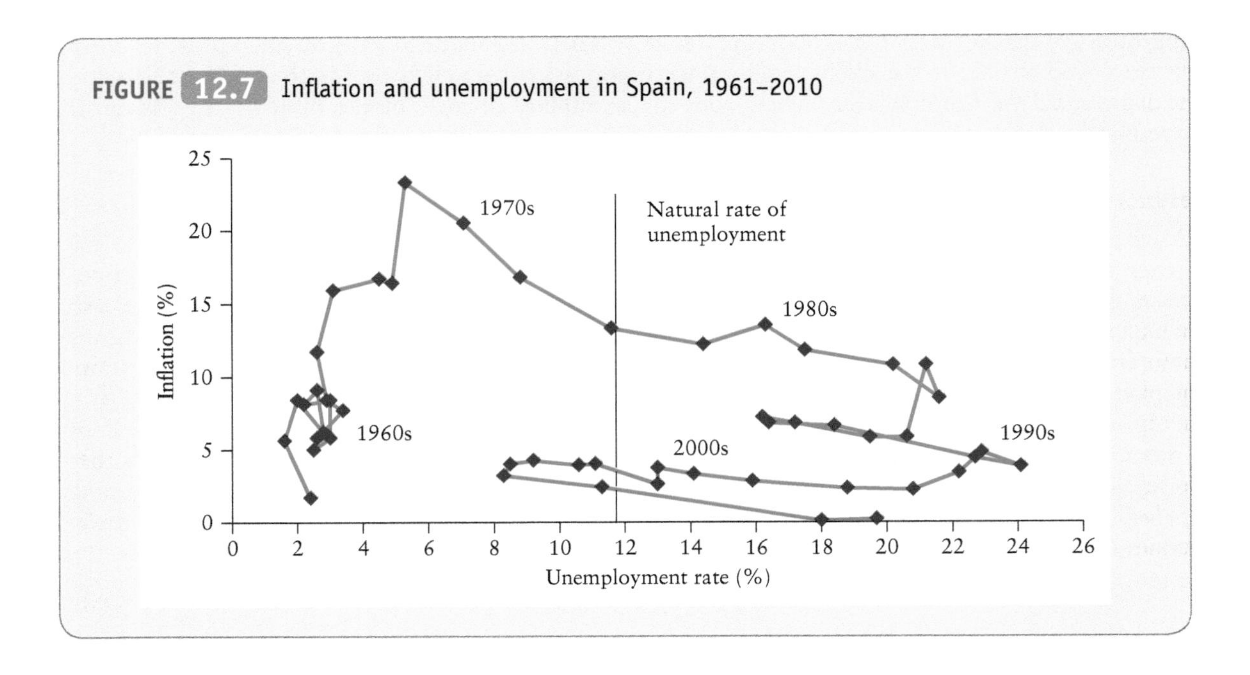

In the 1980s high unemployment was associated with a high, but falling, inflation rate. The short-run Phillips curves moved downwards from right to left. In the 1990s and early 2000s, Spain appears to have made the perfect touch-down, arriving at its natural rate which was, however, high. Germany, following reunification in the early 1990s, entered a prolonged recession and became the 'sick' economy of the euro area. However, over the years after 2002 Germans accepted major sacrifices in the form of higher taxes and stagnant nominal wages and gradually regained competitiveness. It is this experience that has made many Germans in 2012 unsympathetic to the reluctance of the Greeks, Portuguese, Irish and Spanish to go through a comparable adjustment in order to make their economies competitive once again.

The successful German adjustment pre-2007 helps explain why the effect of the 2008 global financial crisis was very pronounced in the case of Ireland and Spain but less so in Germany. In Ireland, there is a significant shift down to the right of the Phillips curve and high unemployment has been combined with deflation. Spain experienced a rise in unemployment, but so far has avoided deflation.

Generally, the German and Spanish experiences conform more to the predictions of the Phillips curve analysis than does the Irish case. This is perhaps not surprising as the theory was developed to explain inflation in large and relatively closed economies.

As we pointed out above, the relevance of the theory to a small open economy such as Ireland is less obvious. This is because inflation in small open economies is strongly influenced by external factors. In Ireland, it is possible that insider–outsider considerations have insulated the wage bargaining process from the effects of high unemployment. Job losses were heavily concentrated in certain sectors (construction, manufacturing). Other sectors, especially the public services, have been insulated. While some wage cuts have occurred (see Chapter 5), the Croke Park Agreement has insulated public sector workers from any further wage cuts. Income tax increases have also been ruled out. A previous cut in the minimum wage was restored by the present coalition government. These developments buffer the local Irish labour market from the downward wage pressures exerted by high unemployment.

12.8 Recent Developments

The augmented Phillips curve is:

$$\pi_t = \pi^e - \alpha(U - U_n)$$

Rearranging, we can write:

$$\Delta\pi^e = -\alpha(U - U_n)$$

This equation states that deviations of current actual inflation from the expected inflation rate are explained by deviations of unemployment from its natural rate. The implication is that if the unemployment gap could be eliminated, inflation would equal its expected rate. However, it is not plausible to explain the deviations of actual inflation from the expected rate entirely on the unemployment gap. Clearly, other factors are important (Gordon 2011).

Since the mid-1970s the Phillips curve literature has moved in two distinct paths. These paths are the new-Keynesian Phillips curve (NKPC) and the triangle Phillips curve (TPC) models.

The TPC model extends the Friedman–Phelps model in two ways. First, it allows for inertia and, second, for supply-side shocks. The model can be written as:

$$\pi_t = \beta_1\pi_t^e - \beta_2(U_t - U_n) + \beta_3 z_t \tag{15}$$

The 'triangle' comes from using three explanatory variables representing the role of inertia, demand and supply-side shocks. The inertia or persistence effect arises because of the time it takes for changes in raw and intermediate good prices to be reflected in the final output price. It also arises because of the effect of fixed-duration wage and price contracts between suppliers and producers of final goods. This effect is captured by the π_t^e variable (expected inflation in time t), which is derived by using a long series of lagged inflation rates and not simply a one-year adaptive expectation measure.

Demand shocks are represented by the traditional unemployment gap $(U_t - U_n)$ but can also be proxied by an output gap. Supply-shock variables are represented by the z_t term. This variable can include, for example, changes in the relative prices of food and energy and the growth rate of productivity. The inclusion of the z_t term represents a departure from earlier Phillips curve representations as supply shocks can now have a direct influence on inflation. The coefficients β_1, β_2 and β_3 show the response of inflation to each of the three explanatory variables.

The NKPC formulation specifies that the inflation rate (π_t) depends on expected *future* inflation (π^e_{t+1}) and the unemployment (or output) gap:

$$\pi_t = \beta_1\pi_{t+1}^e - \beta_2(U_t - U_n) \tag{16}$$

There are two essential differences between this model and the TPC model. First, there is no explicit treatment of supply shocks and, second, expectations are explicitly forward-looking. In the TPC model, expectations can be either forward-looking or backward-looking, or both. Because inflation expectations are strictly forward-looking in the NKPC model, there is no role for the inertia effect.

12.9 The Phillips Curve and the AD-AS Model

The economic rationale underlying the Phillips curve can be explained in terms of movements of the aggregate demand (AD) curve along the short-run aggregate supply (SRAS) curve. For example, referring back to the AD/SRAS model of Chapter 5, shifts of the AD curve to the right lead to increases in both the price level and real output. The increase in real output or GNP is, in turn, reflected in a fall in unemployment. This is akin to a movement up the Phillips curve. Lower unemployment is associated with a higher price level. Conversely, a shift of the AD curve to the left would reduce the price level and real output and increase unemployment. This is equivalent to a movement down the Phillips curve as a lower price level is associated with higher unemployment.

The slope of the Phillips curve is determined by the slope of the SRAS curve. At very low levels of unemployment, the SRAS curve tends to become steep and the price level increases more rapidly. Conversely, at high levels of unemployment, the SRAS curve is relatively flat and there is a small increase in the price level.

Note that prior to the publication of the Phillips article, economists tended to view the SRAS curve as being shaped like an inverted L. That is, the SRAS curve is horizontal when unemployment is high and vertical when full employment is reached. This meant that as the AD curve shifts to the right, the economy went from a position of constant prices and variable unemployment to a position of constant unemployment and variable prices. The implication was that there is no trade-off between inflation and unemployment.

Earlier in Chapter 5, equation (13), we derived the equation for the SRAS curve. It can be shown how this equation relates to the augmented Phillips curve derived in this chapter.

$$Y = Y^* + \delta(P - P^e) \tag{17}$$

where P is the actual price level, P^e is the expected price level, Y is actual output, Y^* is the potential rate of output and δ is a coefficient which shows how sensitive Y is to the difference between the actual and expected price level.

Multiply through:

$$Y = Y^* + \delta P - \delta P^e \tag{18}$$

and

$$\delta P = Y - Y^* + \delta P^e \tag{19}$$

Divide both sides by δ:

$$P = P^e + (1/\delta)(Y - Y^*) \tag{20}$$

Subtract the price level in the previous period (P_{-1}) from both sides:

$$(P - P_{-1}) = (P^e - P_{-1}) + (1/\delta)(Y - Y^*) \tag{21}$$

That is:

$$\pi_t = \pi^e + (1/\delta)(Y - Y^*) \tag{22}$$

According to Okun's law the output gap is directly linked to the unemployment gap:

$$-\alpha(U - U_n) = (1/\delta)(Y - Y^*) \tag{23}$$

Substituting into equation (22):

$$\pi_t = \pi^e - \alpha(U - U_n) \tag{24}$$

The SRAS curve is therefore consistent with the Phillips curve. The SRAS curve shows that real output is related to unexpected changes in the price level. The Phillips curve, on the other hand, shows that inflation is related to deviations of unemployment from the natural rate.

12.10 Key Terms and Concepts

In this chapter we have discussed how inflation and unemployment are inter-related. The main topics discussed were:

- the Phillips curve
- the demise of the original Phillips curve in the early 1970s and the advent of stagflation

- the Phelps–Friedman critique of the Phillips curve analysis
- the long-run Phillips curve, which is vertical at the natural rate of unemployment: holding the rate of unemployment below this rate will lead not just to higher inflation, but to accelerating inflation
- the costs of deflation and the importance of credible policies
- the sacrifice ratio
- the unemployment–inflation trade-off in Ireland, Spain and Germany
- recent developments relating to the Phillips curve
- the relationship between the expectations-augmented Phillips curve and the short-run aggregate supply (SRAS) curve.

CHAPTER 13

The Balance of Payments and the Exchange Rate

13.1 Introduction

In this chapter we focus explicitly on open economy macroeconomics. We go into some detail on the structure of the balance of payments, discussing how the Irish tables are presented and how they relate to the economy. We pay particular attention to the effects on the trade statistics of the multinational companies operating in Ireland. We then describe the foreign exchange market and the history of Irish exchange rate arrangements. We give an overview of the value of the Irish currency and euro relative to the US dollar and the pound sterling.

13.2 The Balance of Payments

The balance of payments is a record of a country's monetary transactions with the rest of the world. When a country has its own national currency, this tracks all transactions that involve the exchange of domestic for foreign currencies, and vice versa. When a country is part of a monetary union, as Ireland now is, it involves tracking all transactions between residents and non-residents, some of which will be in foreign currencies and some of which will be in the currency of the monetary union (the euro in the Irish case).

It is also possible to construct the balance of payments between regions within countries. Scottish nationalists use the Scottish balance of payments surplus (due to its oil exports) to support the case for Scottish independence from the UK. Irish regional economists are interested in estimating the balance of payments between regions like the Border–Midlands–West region and the rest of the country.

The basic rules for drawing up the balance of payments accounts are:

- Items such as exports that involve receipts by residents of the country or region from non-residents are credit entries or inflows.
- Items such as imports that involve payments by residents of the country or region to non-residents are debit entries or outflows.

In Table 13.1 we summarise the way the Irish balance of payments is presented by the Central Statistics Office (CSO). The three main sub-accounts of the balance of payments are:

- the current account (CA)
- the capital account (CPA)
- the financial account (FA).

TABLE 13.1 Summary layout of Irish balance of payments with estimates for 2011 (net balances)

				€ billions
Current account (CA)				
	Merchandise trade			36.6
	Invisibles	Services		−1.8
		Income	Compensation of employees	−0.2
			Investment income	−31.6
		Current transfers		−1.2
		Total		34.8
	Balance on CA			1.8
Capital account (CPA)	Mainly capital transfers			−0.3
Financial account (FA)	Direct investment			11.3
	Portfolio investment			27.5
	Other investment			−33.1
	Reserve assets			0.3
	Balance on FA			6.1
Net errors and omissions (NEO)				−7.6
CA + CPA + FA + NEO				0

Note: The figures in this table are net balances. The detailed tables present gross flows (credits and debits) for many of these rows.

Source: CSO, Balance of International Payments 2012 Q1, July 2012.

Because it is not possible to keep exact track of all the myriad transactions between countries there is always another entry in the accounts called 'net errors and omissions' (NEO). This is derived as a residual and ensures that the sum of all the credits equals the sum of all the debits and the overall balance of payments balances.

In 1999 the exchange rates between the Irish pound and the currencies of the other countries that entered the new EMU were fixed 'irrevocably'. In 2002 the old 'legacy currencies', including the Irish pound, ceased to exist. Since then Ireland has not had a separate national currency. It is using the euro along with the other 16 euro area countries. The Irish balance of payments is, therefore, not an account of the receipts and expenditures in any national currency and it does not have much significance for the foreign exchange markets, but it is still very important because, as we explain below, it measures changes in the country's net external indebtedness.

We now consider the Irish balance of payments and its sub-accounts in some detail, using the estimates for 2011 published by the CSO in July 2012. Many of these estimates are preliminary and will be revised in later years as more information becomes available.

The current account (CA)

The CA is comprised of two major sub-accounts, namely:

- merchandise trade; and
- invisibles, which is further sub-divided into:
  - services
  - income
  - current transfers.

The merchandise trade account tracks exports and imports of goods – everything from cattle and cars to computer chips and books. Estimates are published monthly and always attract considerable attention in the media.

For many years, the value of Irish merchandise exports has been much greater than that of its merchandise imports. In 2011 the surplus of exports over imports was €36.6 billion. This is almost twice the level recorded in 2007 and reflects the very strong export performance of Irish manufacturing industry in recent years.

Branches of multinational companies account for over 90 per cent of Irish merchandise exports by value. In some sectors, such as chemicals, the multinationals are almost completely dominant. The gross export values are misleading because of the very high import content of many multinational firms. For example, while subsidiaries of big pharmaceutical firms such as Pfizer and GlaxoSmithKline export billions of euro worth of drugs and drug ingredients from Ireland, the value added in Ireland is much smaller than suggested by the gross export figures. Embodied in the price charged for these exports are expensive patent fees and royalties that have to be paid to parent companies.

Typically up to half the profits on inwards foreign direct investment are remitted abroad. To keep the current and financial accounts in balance, the reinvested profits are also shown with opposite sign under 'direct investment' in the financial account. From an economic perspective this treatment reflects the increase in the value of the direct investment enterprise because of reinvested profits.

The merchandise exports of multinationals, therefore, give rise to large outflows in other parts of the balance of payments, such as payments for royalties, licences and business services. This means that their net contribution to the Irish balance of payments is much smaller than is suggested by the gross export figures. On the other hand, some of the exports of agribusiness firms such as the Kerry Group and Avonmore have high domestic value added and make a more significant contribution to the balance of payments than appears from the crude export data. The net contribution to the economy of a euro of exports from companies like Coca-Cola is smaller than that of a euro of exports of Irish whiskey.

The services sub-account of the invisibles account of the CA records imports and exports of services such as tourism and travel, software, insurance, a range of business, financial and computer services and the payment of royalties and licences. In 2011, the largest credit items in this account were receipts from exports of computer software (€31.8 billion) and business services (€22.8 billion), while the largest outflows were due to payments of licences and royalties (€29.2 billion) and business services (€34.6 billion). It is striking how these relatively new sectors now dwarf traditional sectors like travel and tourism, which used to account for our largest exports of services. In 2011, tourism and travel accounted for an inflow of only €3.3 billion. There was an outflow of €5.0 billion under this heading due to Irish residents' spending on foreign travel.

The figures for 'exports of goods and services' and 'imports of goods and services' included in the national income accounts, NIE (which we labelled X and M in Chapter 5) correspond fairly closely to the sum of the gross credit and debt items recorded in the merchandise trade and services sub-accounts of the CA.

The exceptional openness of the Irish economy can be demonstrated by considering that in 2011 exports of goods and services amounted to €166.8 billion, while imports of goods and services amounted to €131.9 billion. A frequently used measure of an economy's openness is the ratio of the sum of its imports and exports to GDP, that is (X + M)/GDP. In Ireland in 2011 this ratio was (166.3 + 131.5)/159 or 187 per cent. In fact it may be seen that the value of our exports exceeds our GDP. Students may find this puzzling, but they should bear in mind that it is the difference between exports and imports, or net exports (NX) = X − M, that constitutes a component of expenditure on GDP. In 2011 this amounted to €166.3 billion *minus* €131.5 billion, or €34.8 billion – equal to 22 per cent of GDP, which is still very large by international standards.

By contrast with Ireland's small economy, the large US economy is much less open, with exports plus imports amounting to just 31 per cent of GDP. For the euro area as a whole, exports plus imports amount to 88 per cent of GDP, so it lies in the middle of the range between Ireland and the USA in terms of openness.

As its name implies, the income sub-account of the CA records the flows of income into and out of the country. These are almost entirely due to flows arising from investments, which are further broken down into direct investment income, portfolio investment income, and other.

Direct investment income is the largest sub-category of income outflows. It records dividends, distributed profits and reinvested earnings flowing into and out of the country. There have been large net outflows under this heading in recent years, reaching €26.5 billion in 2011, mainly due to the profits of multinationals. This too should be borne in mind when gauging their net contribution to the economy.

Portfolio investment income arises from dividends and interest receivable on foreign financial assets held by Irish residents and payable on Irish financial assets held by non-residents. The interest on Irish government debt securities held outside the country is a debit item in this sub-account. There was a net outflow of €7.4 billion from portfolio investment income in 2011. Interest payable on government loans (e.g. interest payable on the borrowings from the IMF, EU and European Financial Stability Facility (EFSF) under the Stability Framework) are included under other investment income.

Box 13.1 Transfer pricing

Transfer pricing occurs when multinational firms avail of differences in national rates of corporation profits tax (CPT) to maximise their global profits in locations with lower CPT rates. Ireland's 12.5 per cent CPT is low relative to that charged in other countries (see Table 22.1 in Chapter 22). In the USA the CPT rate is estimated to be 40 per cent when both federal and state taxes are taken into account.

While controversy surrounds how these taxes are calculated and levied, there is no doubt that many US firms find it advantageous to pay profit taxes in Ireland rather than in other jurisdictions. To avail of this attraction, an American Big Pharma company, for example, can sell inputs to its Irish subsidiary at low book cost. When the subsidiary exports the manufactured product at its high market value the profits attributed to the Irish subsidiary are boosted. When these are taxed at our low CPT more after-tax profits are available to be remitted to anywhere the company desires. Note that if the profits are remitted to the USA, the difference between the Irish and US CPT will have to be paid to US Revenue. There is a strong incentive, therefore, not to remit the profits to the US if at all possible.

This practice is undoubtedly significant and gives rise to some extraordinary statistics for multinational firms operating in Ireland. For example, Pfizer forecast profits of €1.35 billion for 2012 based on revenue of €11.6 billion. The company employs almost 5,000 people across 11 locations in Ireland.

The scale of transfer pricing among multinational companies operating out of Ireland has attracted adverse comment from politicians and economists in other countries, notably France and Germany, in recent years.

When summed up, all the flows recorded on the income sub-account gave rise to a net outflow of €31.8 billion in 2011. This is the figure on which the estimate of net factor income from the rest of the world (F) in the NIE is based.

Under the sub-account for current transfers there was a net negative entry of €1.2 billion in 2011. This represents the difference between an inflow of €5.4 billion (largely subsidies and current transfers received from the EU, much of them arising from the operation of the Common Agricultural Policy) and an outflow of €6.6 billion, which includes taxes paid by Ireland to the EU, our contribution to Third World aid programmes and some amounts related to insurance transfers.

Remittances by emigrants to their families living in Ireland used to form a significant component in the balance of payments and were included under this heading. It is a sign of the times that there is no longer any mention of these remittances in the balance of payments tables! In countries such as Turkey, the Philippines and Mexico, net inflows under this heading are very significant relative to GDP.

Adding the balance on merchandise trade and on invisibles, we obtain a net surplus of €1.8 billion on the CA in 2011.

13.3 The Significance of the Current Account Balance

Figure 13.1 shows the CA balance as a percentage of GDP from 1960 to 2011. Very large deficits were recorded during the 1970s and 1980s. A surplus was recorded during the boom years and early in this century. But between 2005 and 2009 a large deficit emerged. In 2010 and 2011 the CA returned to surplus.

FIGURE 13.1 The current account of the balance of payments as a percentage of GDP, 1960–2011

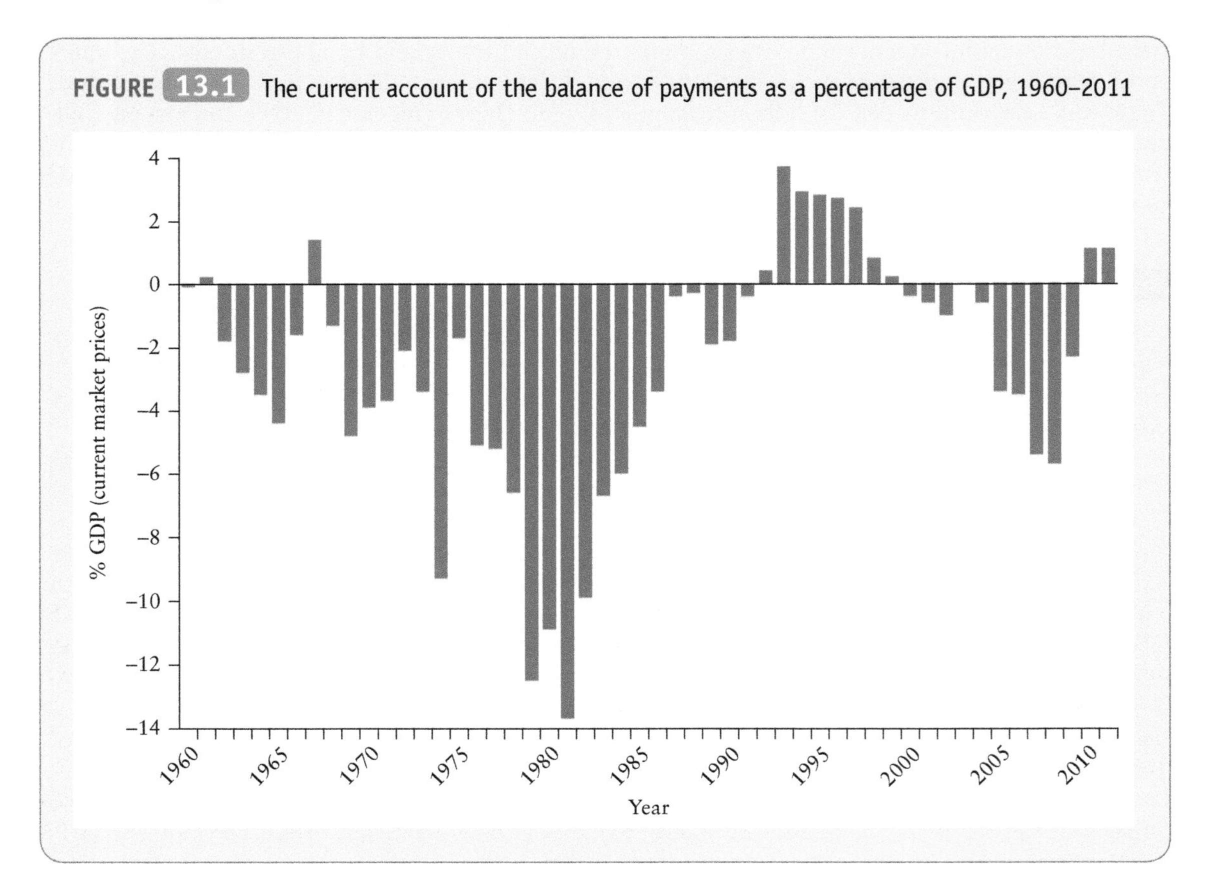

We have emphasised that Ireland's CA is no longer a measure of the balance between the supply and demand of a currency on the foreign exchange markets, as it was when we had an independent Irish pound. Between 1979 and 1999, when the Irish pound was either pegged or floating on the foreign exchange markets, the CA balance was significant for the exchange rate between the Irish pound and foreign currencies. Today, to get a measure of the excess supply or demand for the euro on world foreign exchange markets we would have to look at the CA for the euro area as a whole, of which the Irish CA accounts for less than two per cent. (The relationship between the CA balance and the foreign exchange market is examined later in this chapter.)

However, the CA balance equals the difference between national savings and national investment and measures changes in the country's net foreign indebtedness. A country with a CA deficit is spending more than its income and borrowing from the rest of the world. On the other hand, a country with a CA surplus is spending less than its income and lending to the rest of the world. (This issue is explained in more detail in Chapter 20.) China has for many years run massive CA surpluses while the USA has run large deficits. This has made China a major investor in the rest of the world, while the USA has become progressively more indebted to the rest of the world.

Commentators tend to focus on the balance on current account (CA) in discussions of 'the balance of payments'. The fact that the current account of the Irish balance of payments moved back into surplus in 2010 was widely welcomed.

There are dangers, however, in thinking of a current account surplus as a good thing and a deficit as a bad thing. The 'mercantilist fallacy' is the name economists give to the notion that a country should maximise its exports. It derives from the views of seventeenth-century, mainly British and Dutch economists who believed that a country grew powerful by amassing the gold or bullion obtained from running balance of trade surpluses.

While there is an element of truth in this – as the present-day example of China demonstrates – we should bear in mind that exports are ultimately only valuable because they allow us to purchase imports. The people of China would enjoy a much higher standard of living if they spent more of their vast exports receipts importing more from the rest of the world, boosting the population's consumption and lowering its savings rate. The USA has enjoyed a higher standard of living than its income justified by running large current account deficits. Foreign investors are lending the country the money to finance these deficits and allowing it to 'live beyond its means'. This is fine as long as the rest of the world has confidence in the US dollar and the country's ability to service its growing external debt service obligations.

Time may be running out on this confidence. Sooner or later foreign exchange markets tend to take a dim view of a country that consistently runs current account deficits. There were currency crises in Mexico in 1994–95 and in Malaysia, Thailand and several other South Asian countries in 1997 due to panics over their ability to continue to borrow abroad to finance balance of payments deficits.

13.4 The Capital and Financial Accounts

The capital and financial accounts of the balance of payments are much more technical and less familiar to the public than the current account. The main item in the capital account (CPA) is capital transfers – money received under the EU Regional Development Fund and the Cohesion Fund. It also covers estimates of transfers of various intangible assets such as patents and copyrights. As the CSO points out in its notes on the balance of payments, 'these transactions tend to occur only infrequently but the amounts involved can vary substantially. Because of certain data limitations only the net flows are recorded.' Between 1998 and 2008 a small positive net balance was recorded on the capital account, but in 2009 a net outflow was recorded. In 2011 this account was almost exactly balanced.

In the financial account (FA) the CSO distinguishes four sub-accounts:

- direct investment
- portfolio investment
- other investment
- reserve assets.

These are transactions in financial assets (claims on non-residents) and liabilities (obligations to non-residents). Note that the flow of income associated with the stock of these assets is accounted for in the income sub-heading of the CA.

Direct investment refers to long-term investment in plant and equipment and other assets in Ireland by foreign companies and individuals (on the credit side) and comparable investments by Irish residents abroad, including investment in residential and commercial property (on the debit side). The accounting procedures used to measure these flows are very technical because of the complexities involved in keeping track of the flows of equity capital, reinvested earnings and debt capital into and out of the country. Surprisingly, there were substantial net outflows under the direct investment heading between 2004 and 2006, implying that the acquisition of assets abroad by Irish residents exceeded the acquisition of assets by non-residents in Ireland. However, this was reversed in 2010. In 2011 a net inflow of €11.3 billion was recorded under this heading.

Portfolio investment covers the buying and selling of equity and debt (stocks and shares and bonds). In recent years there were very large net inflows under this heading (€86.0 billion in 2010 and €27.5 billion in 2011). Because of the vast scale of the gross transactions on the financial account, it is very hard to say much about categories such as portfolio investment. The biggest component of these inflows in 2010 and 2011 was due to inflows into investment funds located in Ireland classified as portfolio investment equity.

'Other investment' refers to loans, currency and deposits, trade credits, and other dealings in financial assets. Borrowings from the IMF, EU and EFSF are part of other investment. The net entry here turned sharply negative in 2009 and reached −€94.1 billion in 2010, falling back to −€33.1 billion in 2011. This reflects the massive outflow of deposits from the Irish banking system due to the downgrading of the main banks by the credit agencies and the international loss of confidence in the Irish economy and the euro.

Changes in reserve assets

Finally, the FA also includes a sub-account for changes in reserve assets. This records movements in the reserves of the Central Bank of Ireland. Since the introduction of the euro in 1999, these have been defined by the ECB as the Central Bank of Ireland's holdings of non-euro currency (mainly dollars, sterling and yen) and some other highly liquid and marketable claims on non-euro area residents, as well as gold, special drawing rights (SDRs) and the country's reserve position with the IMF.

Before 1999, when we had a separate national currency, the level of reserve assets held by the Central Bank was very important because these reserves were the backing for our currency. If the sum of the net balances on all the other accounts of the balance of payments was negative the reserves would tend to fall. A substantial outflow of reserves would have been regarded as a sign that the currency was 'under pressure', and in danger of depreciating or being devalued.

Now that we are members of the euro area the reserves held by the national central bank do not have this significance. What matters for the euro is the level of reserves held by the ECB on behalf of the euro area as a whole, of which the Irish reserves are a very small part. In recent years the net figures for this sub-account have been small, indicating very little movement in these assets.

When the four sub-accounts of the FA are summed, the net total was an inflow equal to €7.3 billion in 2010 and €6.1 billion in 2011. It is perhaps surprising to note that despite the gravity of our current financial crisis, there should be a net inflow on the financial account of the balance of payments. However, this is largely due to the large net inflows under the direct and portfolio investment headings. Other investment includes the inflows associated with the large borrowings by Irish banks from the ECB.

13.5 Making the Balance of Payments Balance

Like any double-entry accounting statement the balance of payments should sum to zero. To every purchase there is a corresponding sale, and increases in claims by residents on non-residents must be matched by increases in obligations by non-residents to residents. As we noted above, if we in Ireland are buying more from the rest of the world than we are selling to it (a negative balance on the CA), we are becoming more indebted to the rest of the world. This, in effect, means that we are borrowing from the rest of the world. This borrowing gives rise to a net inflow on the CPA and FA that must match the outflow due to the deficit on the CA (see Chapter 20).

Conversely, if we are selling more to the rest of the world than it is buying from us, the net inflow of money to the country caused by the CA surplus will be offset by our net purchases of foreign assets. As we lend money to the rest of the world, this entails an outflow on CPA and FA. Hence, in principle:

$$\text{CA} = -(\text{CPA} + \text{FA}) = 0$$

or

$$\text{CA} + \text{CPA} + \text{FA} = 0 \tag{1}$$

However, collecting accurate figures for all the items included in the balance of payments is a daunting task. Surveys are used to collect data on services, assets and liabilities and related income. The accounts are then constructed from the survey data and from other data sources, such as trade and tourism statistics, administrative data on transfers, and Central Bank returns on financial flows and the level of reserves.

Numerous difficulties and complications arise in compiling balance of payments data. For instance, revisions regularly arise due to restructuring of multinational enterprises. Then there are the problems associated with illicit money laundering and drug dealing. In addition to this type of problem, the measurement of financial flows is unusually complicated due to the size of our International Financial Services Centre (IFSC).

The IFSC employs over 14,000 people and houses banks and investment funds, law and accountancy firms and taxation advisers, providing services mainly to non-residents. The gross flows into and out of the financial institutions in the IFSC are massive relative to the size of the Irish economy. Keeping track of them, and segregating their overseas activities from those that are part of the domestic economy, is very difficult.

It is to be expected, therefore, that the estimates of three accounts (CA, CPA, and FA) do not in practice sum to zero as they should in theory. In 2011, for example, the CSO's estimates show the following net flows under the three accounts (€ billion):

$$\text{CA} = +1.8$$
$$\text{CPA} = -0.3$$
$$\text{FA} = +6.1$$

Summing these, we obtain a total of +€7.6 billion, not zero. To make the balance of payments balance, a 'net errors and omissions' (NEO) entry is added to these three accounts. By entering a figure of *minus* €7.6 billion for NEO we obtain a balance of payments that sums to zero:

$$CA + CPA + FA + NEO = €1.8 \text{ bn} - €0.3 \text{ bn} + €6.1 \text{ bn} - €7.6 \text{ bn} = 0$$

The 2011 figure for NEO item is large (equal to almost five per cent of GDP) and it fluctuates considerably from year to year. It is also subject to major revisions as more data become available for the other accounts. In the 2010 issue of the balance of payments, the NEO for 2010 was estimated at −€12.5 billion. A year later this was revised down to −€8.4 billion, primarily due to a major revision in the FA.

However, statisticians point out that the relevant comparison is between the size of the NEO item and the combined value of all the credit and debt transactions in the three accounts of the balance of payments. Viewed in this light, a figure of €7.6 billion is relatively small because the gross flows in the separate accounts are so enormous. We can also take comfort from the fact that the NEO entries over the past 10 years fluctuate between positive and negative totals. There has been no tendency for large positive or negative estimates to accumulate, which would suggest the presence of systematic errors.

13.6 Ireland's Merchandise Trade Patterns

In Table 13.2 we show the main countries from which Ireland's merchandise imports come and to which our exports go. What stands out from the Table is the importance of the US and the UK in our trade. In 2010 the UK accounted for 30 per of our imports and 14 per cent of our exports went to the UK. The large share of the UK in our imports would not surprise anyone who shops in Ireland and checks the proportion of ordinary consumer goods sold here made in the UK.

TABLE 13.2 Ireland's main trading partners, 2010

	Merchandise	
	Exports	Imports
	%	
USA	23.2	14.1
UK	13.9	29.9
Euro area countries, of which:	36.7	23.3
Belgium	14.3	2.4
Germany	8.1	7.7
France	5.0	4.0
Netherlands	3.5	4.9
Italy	3.0	1.7
China, Hong Kong & Macau	3.1	5.5
Other countries	23.1	27.2
Value of total trade	€89.4 bn	€45.5 bn

Source: CSO Trade Statistics

The USA is our largest single export market. It accounts for 23 per cent of our exports and 14 per cent of our imports. The large share of the USA in our exports reflects the role of American-owned firms, particularly in the pharmaceuticals sector, who manufacture for the US market in Ireland. It is surprising that Belgium is our second largest export market, but this too is related to the pharmaceuticals sector, as Belgium is a major hub for re-exporting drugs round the world.

Surprisingly, perhaps, our trade with China is fairly balanced, with imports of €2.7 billion matched by exports of €2.5 billion. Proportionately, though, China is more important to us as a source of imports than as a destination for exports. However, it might surprise many people that only five per cent of our imports originate there.

The dominance of the USA and UK – and, indeed, China – in our trade is of great significance from the perspective of our membership of the EMU. These three countries, which are not members of the euro area, account for 50 per cent of our total imports and 40 per cent of our total exports. In fact the euro area accounts for only 23.3 per cent of our imports and 36.7 per cent of our exports, or 32.2 per cent of our total merchandise trade. Even more surprising is that these proportions have not changed greatly since we broke the link with sterling in 1979 or since we joined the EMU in 1999. It is highly unusual for a country as dependent on trade as Ireland to share a common currency with a group of countries that account for less than a third of its trade. This is relevant to our discussion of the costs and benefits of our membership of the EMU in later chapters.

Table 13.3 contains a summary of the distribution of our trade by broad category or commodity group in 2011. If there is one striking statistic in this table it is surely the dominance of 'chemicals and related products' in our exports. The value of these exports came to €56 billion in 2011 – equivalent to 35 per cent of GDP.

This amazing figure reflects, of course, the role of multinational pharmaceutical companies in our economy – 'organic chemicals' and 'medicinal and pharmaceutical products' accounted for €44 billion of these exports. Earlier in this chapter we drew attention to the caveats attached to the interpretation of these statistics. The net contribution of these exports to the Irish economy is much smaller than is suggested by these numbers.

Exports of 'machinery and transport equipment' include €4.5 billion of 'office machinery and automatic data processing equipment' and over €2.7 billion of 'electrical machinery'. These are products that are largely produced by multinational companies in Ireland.

TABLE 13.3 Ireland's merchandise trade by commodity group, 2011

	Imports	Exports	Imports	Exports
	€ billion		%	
Food and live animals	5.0	7.9	10.4	8.5
Beverages and tobacco	0.8	1.2	1.7	1.3
Mineral fuels, lubricants, etc.	6.8	1.4	14.1	1.5
Chemicals and related products	10.5	56.0	21.8	60.3
Other manufactured goods	9.7	12.7	20.1	13.7
Machinery and transport equipment	12.5	11.2	25.9	12.0
All other commodities and transactions	2.9	2.5	6.0	2.7
Total	48.2	92.9	100.0	100.0

13.7 The Foreign Exchange Market

Our discussion of Ireland's balance of payments has already drawn attention to how we must distinguish between countries like Mexico and China that have their own national currencies and countries like Ireland and Scotland that do not because they are members of currency unions. The foreign exchange market is the market where currencies are bought and sold. This market is essential for trade between countries that use different currencies. Consider, for example, an Irish firm sending a shipment of computers to the USA. If the US importer pays the Irish exporter in dollars, the Irish exporter will exchange these dollars for euro on the foreign exchange market. This completes the transfer of purchasing power from the US importer to the Irish firm.

The foreign exchange market spans the globe by means of telephones, computers and telex machines, and is open 24 hours a day. It is possible to sell, for example, dollars for euro in Tokyo and buy sterling for euro in Dublin. The main markets are in Sydney, Tokyo, Hong Kong, Singapore, Bahrain, Frankfurt, London, New York, Chicago and San Francisco. The opening hours of these markets overlap, so it is possible to buy or sell currencies at any time of the day or night.

Exchange rates

The exchange rate is the price of one currency in terms of another. In Ireland, the exchange rate is defined as the foreign price per unit of the domestic currency. This is referred to as an *indirect quote*. At end 2012, the euro exchange rate was $1.32/€1, Stg£0.81/€1 and ¥111.0/€1. Those were the foreign currency prices of the euro. This way of quoting exchange rates is the British convention, used in Ireland, the UK, Australia and New Zealand. The alternative (American and European) convention is known as a *direct quote*. This expresses the domestic currency (the euro) in terms of the foreign currency. Following this convention, the euro exchange rate at end-2012 was €0.76/$1, €1.22/Stg£ and €0.009/¥1.

> **NOTE:** The reason why Ireland and the UK use indirect quotes is that it was awkward to express the price of foreign currencies in the old pounds, shillings and pence (£ s d) used until the early 1970s in Ireland and the UK.

A currency is said to depreciate when it falls in value relative to other currencies and to appreciate when it rises. For example, the dollar/euro rate moved from $1.334/€1 in 2011 to $1.22/€1 by August 2012. This was a depreciation of the euro. Irish residents had to pay almost 10 per cent more for each dollar they bought than previously. An advantage of the British convention is that when a currency appreciates, its exchange rate rises; when it depreciates, its exchange rate falls. This is more natural than what happens under the American convention, where depreciation is a rise in the rate and appreciation is a fall. We follow the British convention in this book.

Two other related terms are *revaluation* and *devaluation*. The difference between devaluation and depreciation, and revaluation and appreciation, arises from the type of exchange rate regime in operation. Depreciation and appreciation occur under floating exchange rate systems; devaluations and revaluations in fixed exchange rate systems.

Bid and offer exchange rates

Bureaux de change and banks charge hefty commissions for small transactions in foreign currencies. As a result, converting small amounts of currency is expensive. In addition to commission charges, banks earn a profit by quoting different exchange rates for buying and selling foreign currency. These rates are known as the *bid rate* (the rate at which banks will buy euro or sell foreign currency) and the *offer rate* (the rate at which banks sell euro or buy foreign currency). The difference between the bid and offer rates is known as the *spread*. The spread decreases as more money is exchanged. For transactions less than €1,000 the spread is relatively large and for transactions in excess of €100,000 it is relatively small.

For example, in August 2012 banks bought €1,000 for $1,200 ($1.20/€1 bid rate). Later the bank will sell €1,000 to another customer for $1,240 ($1.24/€1 offer rate). The profit to the bank from this transaction is $40.

In most cases, the dealers are content to act as brokers between people buying and selling currency, but they take speculative positions that can result in heavy profits or losses. As in the previous example, a dealer buys €1,000 for $1,200 at an exchange rate of $1.20/€1. She holds the €1,000 in the hope that the euro exchange rate appreciates. If the euro goes to $1.30, the dealer sells the €1,000 for $1,300 and makes a profit of $100 for every €1,000 transaction (ignoring the bid-offer spread). If, however, the exchange rate falls below $1.20, the dealer incurs a loss. Exchange rates can react in a very fickle way to breaking news. We have seen this during the current protracted euro area crisis. The morning after each emergency summit over the period 2008–2012 (there were over 20 up to June 2012) the euro exchange rate tended to bounce up on the announcement of some new initiative to solve the crisis. Almost invariably this bounce proved short-lived and, by the end of the week, the euro's value on international exchanges had fallen below where it was before the summit.

13.8 The Rise and Fall of the Irish Foreign Exchange Market

Up to the early 1970s there was virtually no foreign exchange market in Ireland. The sterling/Irish pound exchange rate was fixed at a one-to-one parity; a very large proportion of Irish trade was with the UK; and the commercial banks held their reserves in sterling in London. The Irish demand for currencies such as dollars and francs was easily dealt with on the London foreign exchange market.

In 1969, the Money Market Committee set up by the Central Bank of Ireland, under the chairmanship of Professor W. J. L. Ryan, recommended that the Central Bank of Ireland (CBI) should encourage the development of a foreign exchange market. In line with this recommendation, in the early 1970s the commercial banks reserves were transferred from London to the CBI and the banks were requested to conduct their foreign exchange business directly with the CBI. In 1976 the CBI quoted for small amounts of foreign exchange. This encouraged the banks to hire and train dealers and to conduct more of their business directly between themselves and on world foreign exchange markets.

Until 1979 the exchange rate of the Irish pound was pegged to sterling on a one-to-one basis. On 13 March 1979, Ireland entered the exchange rate mechanism (ERM) of the European Monetary System (EMS) but the pound sterling did not. The potential now existed for a breaking of the sterling link and the birth of a new currency – the Irish pound. The *Irish Times* economics correspondent tells the story.

> *Finally, the day came. On March 29th [1979], sterling went on a strong run ... and things were happening. After the close (of business) that day, the pound was trading outside the EMS limits and I called a New York bank several times for rates of sterling against the DM [Deutsche mark]. It was the makings of a scoop. None of the other papers had been on to the story to the same degree – and I hoped that they were not on to the goings on that night. Finally, at about 7.30 p.m. I rang the governor of the Central Bank (Charles Murray) at home and reported on the latest rates from New York. I didn't need to. What would happen if the same rates applied in the morning? Without any equivocation he said: 'we'll break the link', and I had my story. We had the scoop on the front page the next morning – and within hours of the paper appearing, history had been made.* (O'Brien 1989)

On the morning of 30 March 1979 the sterling exchange rate fell and for a time the one-to-one exchange rate held. However, sterling then rose to a level that was incompatible with holding the Irish pound in the EMS band and soon afterwards the link was broken. The first deal was done at 10.15 a.m., when Stg£500,000 was purchased at an exchange rate of Stg£0.9975/IR£. With the termination of the sterling link, Irish foreign exchange dealers moved from being 'price-takers' to being 'price-makers'. Many firms with large sterling debt lost heavily as the Irish pound unexpectedly depreciated against sterling. However, the banks coped very well with the new arrangements.

Over the next two decades the Irish foreign exchange market grew at a significant pace. By the late 1990s, the daily turnover was in excess of £2.5 billion. About 80 per cent of the deals involved exchanging one foreign currency for another rather than Irish pounds for foreign currencies. The reason for the scale of transactions in foreign currencies is the relative size of Irish trade with the USA and, in particular, Britain. Thus if an Irish firm was selling into the USA and obtaining dollar receipts and buying its raw materials in the UK, paid for in sterling, it would want to exchange dollars for sterling without converting any money into or out of Irish pounds.

EMU was launched in January 1999, and the exchange rates between the 11 participating countries were 'irrevocably fixed'. However, it was not until early in 2002 that the national currencies of the 12 countries (Greece was added to the original 11) participating in EMU ceased to exist and were replaced by the euro. New euro notes and coins were put into circulation and the old national currencies withdrawn.

Between 2007 and 2011 five additional countries joined. In 2012 the euro area comprised Austria, Belgium, Cyprus, Estonia, Finland, France, Germany, Greece, Ireland, Italy, Luxembourg, Malta, the Netherlands, Portugal, Slovakia, Slovenia and Spain. Note that Ireland's largest trade partner, the UK, is not in the euro area.

The foreign exchange dealers in Ireland have again become price-takers when they quote exchange rates for the euro. The introduction of the euro entailed a considerable loss of business for the banks and the numbers employed in foreign currency dealing fell. On the other hand, there was a significant gain for people trading with other euro area countries (and tourists coming from and going to Europe) as they no longer had to incur the costs of converting Irish pounds into foreign currencies. This was one of the benefits of joining the EMU but, as we discuss in Chapter 17, there were offsetting costs.

13.9 The Exchange Rate of the Irish Pound and the Euro

Figures 13.2 and 13.3 show the exchange rate between the Irish pound and the dollar and sterling over the periods 1966–2000 (US dollar) and 1976–2001 (pound sterling). These were the most important bilateral rates of the Irish pound. As already mentioned, up to March 1979, the sterling/IR£ rate was fixed on a one-to-one basis. Between 1979 and 1999 this exchange rate moved fairly widely in both directions, but it did not drift far from the original parity. The following paragraphs describe some of the main trends in the value of the Irish pound since 1979.

Following the break in the link with sterling, the Irish pound depreciated sharply, falling as low as Stg£0.72 in 1981. In the latter half of the 1980s it gained relative to sterling, culminating in the crisis of 1992, when sterling depreciated sharply against the EMS currencies and the Irish pound rose to Stg£1.10. Following the 10 per cent devaluation of January 1993 the Irish pound traded at lower levels, depreciating sharply as sterling strengthened in 1997–98.

The US$/IR£ exchange rate has fluctuated widely, reflecting the movement of the dollar against the European currencies, as well as the fluctuations of the Irish pound relative to the latter. The dollar was weak in 1980 but climbed to a peak in 1985 (when for a brief period the IR£1 was worth less than $1), but in the latter half of the 1980s it weakened considerably. The dollar strengthened in the mid-1990s. Over these years, the exchange rate followed a fairly random path, lacking a clear trend. At the end of 2012 the euro/sterling exchange rate was equivalent to an Irish pound/sterling rate of 1.04.

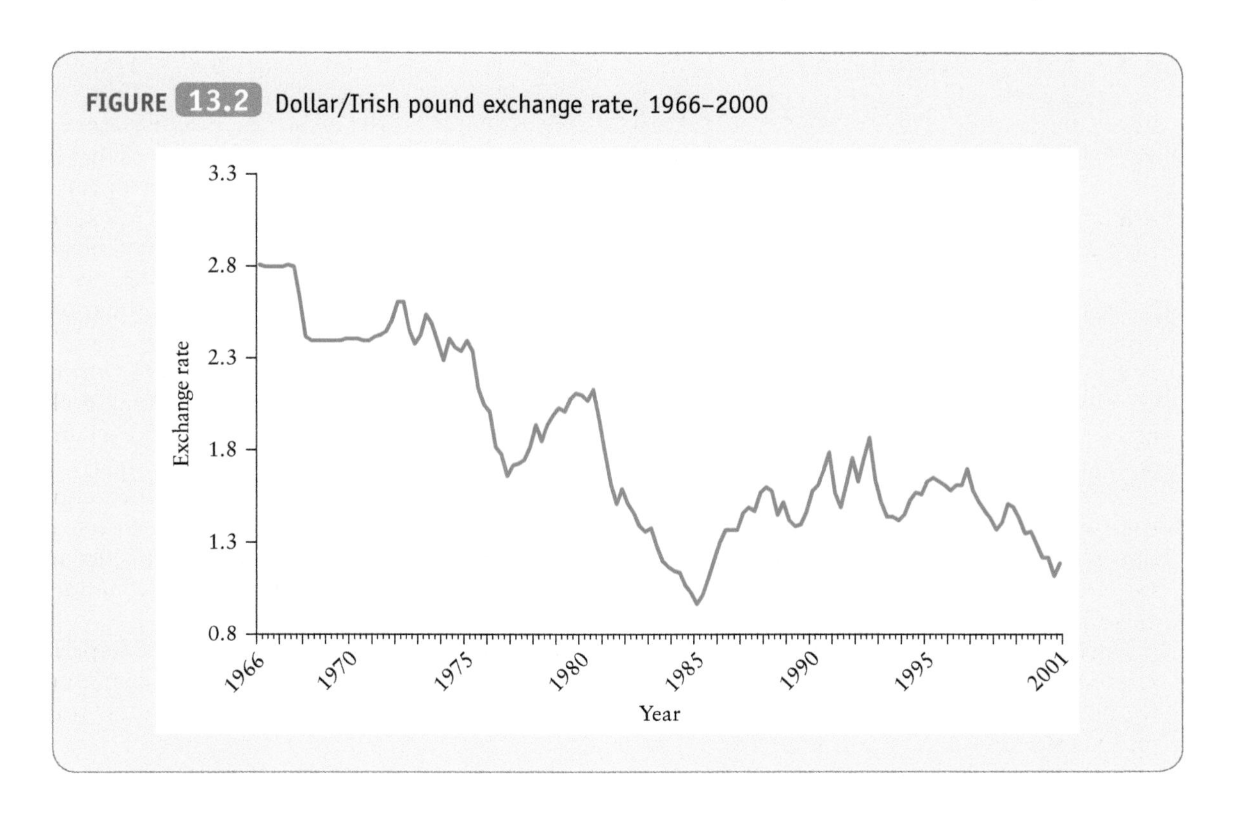

FIGURE 13.2 Dollar/Irish pound exchange rate, 1966–2000

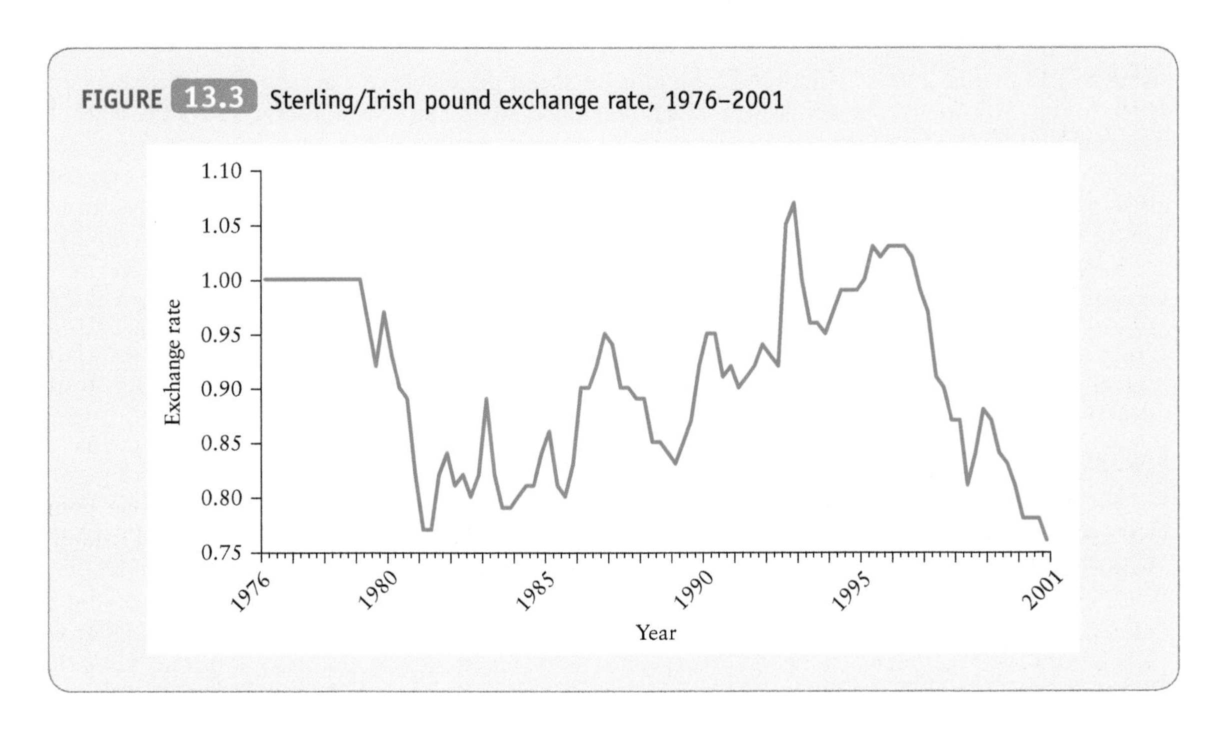

FIGURE 13.3 Sterling/Irish pound exchange rate, 1976–2001

FIGURE 13.4 Dollar/euro and pound/euro exchange rates, 1999–2012

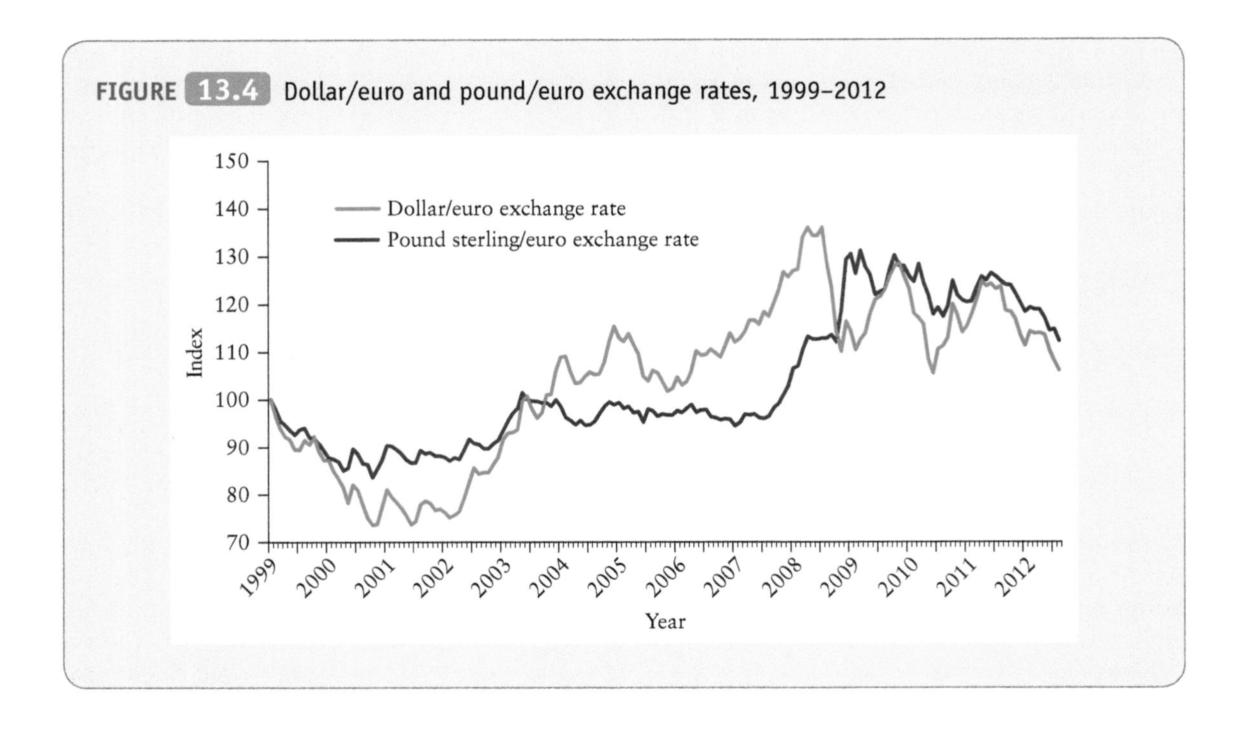

Figure 13.4 shows the exchange rate of the euro to dollar and sterling measured as an index with the start date, January 1999, set equal to 100. It can be seen that both the sterling and dollar exchange rates have moved generally in line and that there has been considerable variation since the introduction of the euro. The dollar/euro exchange rate fell to an index of 75 in mid-2000 before rising to 136 in mid-2008. By mid-2012, amid fears about the future of the euro area, the euro had fallen to the lowest level reached against the dollar since 2010, but it was still far above the level at the launch of EMU. The euro has proved to be a strong currency.

The exchange rate is the most important price facing any country because it affects the price of all its exports and imports. A change in the exchange rate affects a country's competitive position. This in turn affects the aggregate demand curve and therefore the price level, output and unemployment. A misaligned exchange rate is economically damaging. At least over the short run, an overvalued currency adversely affects a number of key macroeconomic variables, while an undervalued currency will have some beneficial effects. Over-valuation leads to a loss of competitiveness and makes it difficult to export, while imports become more attractive. This is like an adverse demand-side shock.

Exchange rate hedging

Buying and selling goods and services across international borders involves exchange rate risk. Consider, for example, the case of an Irish exporter selling goods into the US market. Suppose the exporter expects to receive $1 million in one month's time and anticipates that the exchange rate will be $1.3/€1. At this exchange rate, euro receipts will be:

$$€769{,}230.8 = (\$1 \text{ million}/1.3)$$

Suppose, however, that the euro unexpectedly appreciates to $1.4. The exporter's receipts will fall to:

$$€714{,}285.7 = (\$1 \text{ million}/1.4)$$

This is €54,945 less than was anticipated (for every $1 million transaction) and will impact negatively on the company's profits. Hence, even small changes in the exchange rate can result in large profits or losses. Note that when exporters lose, importers gain. The importer has to pay less in euro for US goods and services. We should also bear in mind that if the company imports raw materials from the USA there will be a gain from exchange rate depreciation.

Traders naturally wish to minimise this type of risk. In an appendix to this chapter we outline a number of different hedging techniques that have been developed for this purpose. However, these hedging techniques offer only short-term protection against exchange rate risk. In the longer term the firm will have to accept the consequences of exchange rate movements.

13.10 Exchange Rate Determination

Why, for example, is a euro worth somewhere in the region of US$1.30 and not, for example, US$1 or US$2? As discussed in section 13.2 above, a sale by an Irish resident of goods or services to someone outside the euro area is an export and gives rise to a receipt of foreign currency and a demand for euro. The person who receives foreign currency will exchange it in a bank for euro.

Conversely, a purchase by an Irish resident of goods or services from someone outside the euro area is an import and gives rise to a supply of euro and a demand for foreign currency. The importer must exchange euro for a foreign currency to pay for the import.

A graphical representation of the supply and demand for euro is given in Figure 13.5. The exchange rate, e, is expressed as the foreign currency price of a euro (for example, $/€) on the vertical axis and the number of euro supplied/demanded is shown on the horizontal axis. The demand curve is downward sloping and the supply curve is upward sloping. Consider first the demand curve.

The demand for euro

A downward-sloping demand schedule implies that a depreciation increases the demand for euro. This is because, when the euro depreciates relative to the dollar, Irish exporters can reduce their prices in the USA. Irish exports to the USA become more competitive and, as a result, more goods and services are demanded. The demand for euro, therefore, increases. Start from an exchange rate of $1.2 = €1. Ignoring transport costs, taxes and other factors, if the price of a sweater is €40 in Dublin, at this exchange rate the price in New York would be $48. If the euro depreciates to $1/€1, and Irish prices and costs do not change in the short run, the sweater will still cost €40 in Dublin,

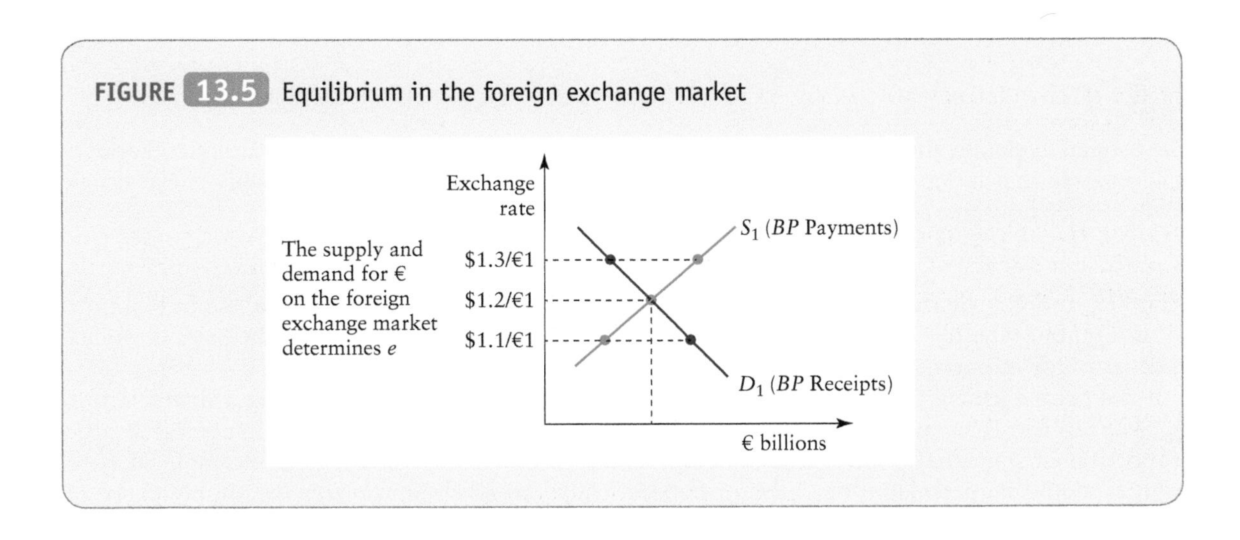

FIGURE 13.5 Equilibrium in the foreign exchange market

but the exporter could afford to lower the New York price from $48 to $40. At the lower price in New York more sweaters are sold and as a result the demand for euro increases.

Alternatively, the exporter could decide to leave the New York price at $48 and allow her profits to benefit in full from the depreciation. Assuming no change in the number of sweaters sold, the demand for euro would still increase because the euro equivalent of $48 would rise from €40 to €48. Thus a fall in a currency's exchange rate must increase the value of exports denominated in its currency. This is why the demand curve for the home currency slopes downwards.

The supply of euro

An upward-sloping supply curve for euro indicates that a depreciation reduces the supply of euro on the foreign exchange market and an appreciation increases it. The logic behind this is that a depreciation makes imports more expensive and consequently less are sold. For example, at an exchange rate of $1.2/€1, a pair of jeans selling for $30 in New York would sell in Dublin for €25. If the euro depreciates to $0.95, the Dublin price would rise to €31.58 unless some of the depreciation were absorbed as lower profits by the US exporter. As the price increases, the quantity of imports demanded falls. Provided the demand for imports is price elastic, the euro value of imports will fall, leading to a reduction in the supply of euro on the foreign exchange market.

Equilibrium in the foreign exchange market

The equilibrium exchange rate is determined by the intersection of the supply and demand schedules. In Figure 13.5, at a rate of $1.2/€1 the supply and demand for euro are equal. At an exchange rate higher than this, say $1.3/€1, there is an excess supply of euro. This is equivalent to a balance of payments deficit on the combined current and capital accounts. The value of payments is greater than that of receipts. The excess supply will cause the exchange rate to depreciate. This, in turn, increases demand along the demand curve and reduces supply along the supply curve until equilibrium is established.

At a lower exchange rate, say $1.1/€1, there is an excess demand for euro which, under a floating exchange rate regime, leads to an appreciation. This reduces demand along the demand curve and increases supply along the supply curve until equilibrium is established.

The crucial point is that the foreign exchange market must clear, as it takes two to make a transaction. When there is an excess demand for a currency, its value rises (the exchange rate appreciates) and when there is an excess supply, its value falls (the exchange rate depreciates). Appreciation or depreciation continues until supply equals demand. Hence under a floating exchange rate system the current and private capital accounts of the balance of payments must sum to zero.

13.11 The J Curve

The foreign exchange market does not always adjust in the well-behaved manner described above. It is possible that a depreciation increases the euro value of imports and the supply curve slopes down. To see how this could happen, note that:

$$\text{Value of imports} = P_m \times Q_m$$

where P_m and Q_m are the price and quantity of imports. A depreciation leads to a rise in P_m and a fall in Q_m, but whether the value of imports (in euro) rises or falls depends on the price elasticity of demand for imports.

If the price elasticity is less than one (inelastic), then as P_m increases following a depreciation, Q_m will fall less than proportionately and ($P_m \times Q_m$), will increase. This could happen if a large proportion of imported goods have no domestically produced substitutes. An example of such imports would be petroleum products in Ireland. Under these circumstances the supply curve of euro is downward sloping and the foreign exchange market is unstable. This is illustrated in Figure 13.6. The market is initially in equilibrium at an exchange rate of \$1.2/€1. If the exchange rate fell to \$1.1/€1 there would be an excess supply of euro, leading to further depreciation. The exchange rate would move away from equilibrium.

FIGURE 13.6 An unstable foreign exchange market

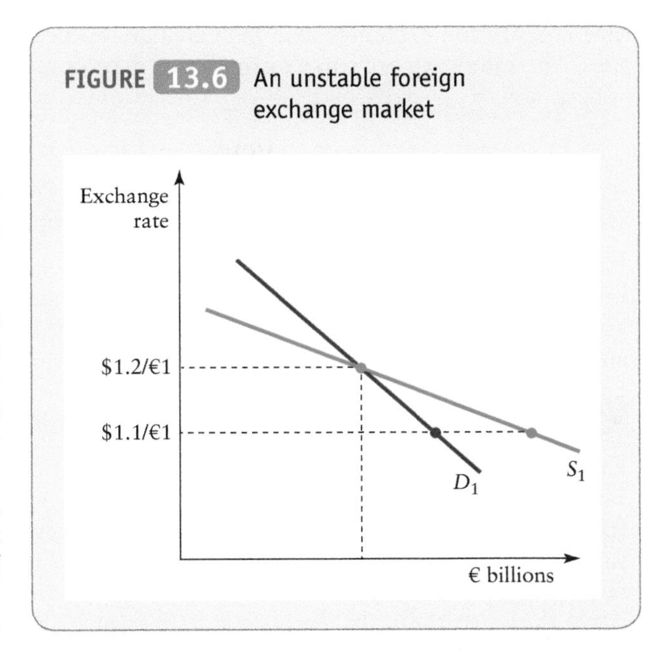

The slope of the supply curve for the domestic currency has implications for the effect of a depreciation on the current account of the balance of payments. If there is a downward-sloping supply curve for the home currency, as in Figure 13.6, a depreciation will lead to a deterioration, rather than an improvement, in the current account (that is, it becomes less instead of more positive).

Suppose that the country is experiencing a current account deficit and the government decides to devalue the currency in order to correct this (how they do this is explained in Chapter 14). If the supply curve of domestic currency is downward sloping, the depreciation initially leads to a deterioration in the current account. In due course, however, the price effects work in the correct direction (the long-run elasticity of demand for imports is greater than one), so there is eventually an improvement in the current account. In Figure 13.7 the current account balance is shown along the vertical axis and time along the horizontal axis. Along the line labelled CA = 0, the current account is zero or in balance. Points above are associated with a CA surplus and points below with a deficit. Starting from a position of a CA deficit, the curve that maps out how the current account changes over time following a depreciation is known as the J curve. The curve shows how the current account, measured on the vertical axis, initially worsens and, over time, begins to improve, mapping out a J-curve effect.

FIGURE 13.7 The J curve

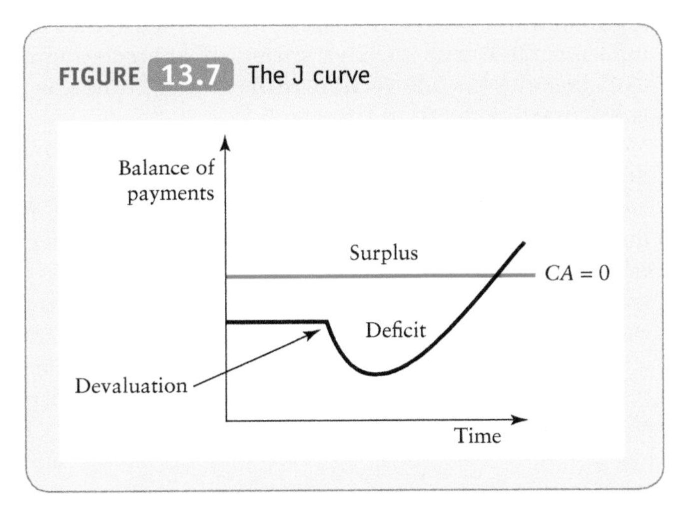

13.12 Shifts in Supply and Demand for Foreign Exchange

Any transaction that occurs through the balance of payments will affect either the demand or supply curves (or both) and therefore the exchange rate (e). The process is as follows:

↑Exports → ↑receipts → demand for euro → curve shifts right (vice versa)

↓Imports → ↓payments → supply of euro → curve shifts left (vice versa)

The equilibrium exchange rate then changes according to shifts in the demand and supply schedules. The following are some examples of developments that would shift these schedules:

- Recession in UK → ↓ Irish exports → demand curve shifts left → ↓ e.
- Increase in US tourism to Ireland → ↑ Irish exports → demand curve shifts right → ↑ e.
- Foot and mouth epidemic in 2001 → ↓ Irish exports → demand curve shifts left → ↓ e.
- Recession in Ireland → ↓ Irish imports → supply curve shifts left → ↑ e.

In reality, Ireland is too small an economy to have any significant bearing on the euro exchange rate. Hence, the examples given above relate primarily to large economies or small economies with an independent exchange rate. But, in principle, any transaction through the balance of payments should have some impact on the exchange rate.

13.13 Factors Influencing Exchange Rates in the Medium Term

Factors influencing exchange rates in the medium term include inflation, speculation, interest rates and growth rates. (We examine the speculation case in the following section.) A rise in Irish inflation relative to that in other countries will lead to a loss of competitiveness. As a result, exports will tend to decline and imports to increase. In the foreign exchange market, the fall in exports shifts the demand curve down to the left and the rise in imports shifts the supply curve down to the right. As shown in Figure 13.8, the result is a depreciation of the exchange rate (assuming equal movement of both curves). The implication is that countries with relatively high inflation rates tend to have weak or depreciating currencies, while those with relatively low inflation rates tend to have strong or appreciating currencies. The link between inflation and exchange rates is one version of the theory known as purchasing power parity (PPP). This theory is discussed in detail in Chapter 15.

Governments or central banks frequently use interest rates to influence capital inflows or outflows from a country and thereby attempt to influence the exchange rate. High interest rates in the euro area compared with the USA could lead to a capital inflow as investors take advantage of the higher returns. The inflow of funds would shift the demand curve up to the right and the exchange rate would tend to appreciate. Conversely, relatively lower interest rates in the euro area would lead to a capital outflow as investors move funds into the USA. This outflow of capital would shift the supply curve down to the right and the exchange rate would fall. Central banks can raise interest rates to try to prevent their currency from depreciating.

FIGURE 13.8 An increase in (relative) inflation

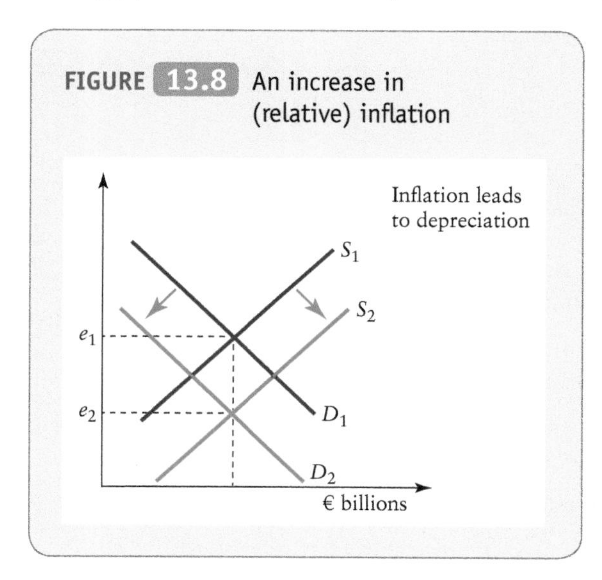

Furthermore, countries with relatively high inflation rates tend to have relatively high nominal interest rates (the Fisher effect). This is the price that investors extract to be persuaded to hold currencies that look weak.

The real growth rate has two effects on the balance of payments. First, a rapid rate of economic growth increases the demand for imports (via the marginal propensity to import) and this leads to a trade deficit. Second, a rapid rate of economic growth may be reflected in high company profits, a rising stock market and high share dividends. This could lead to a capital inflow as investors attempt to take advantage of the profit opportunities offered by the boom. The result will be a capital account surplus.

As long as the capital account surplus rises by more than the current account deficit, the exchange rate will appreciate. This was the situation in the USA in the 1990s and into the twenty-first century. Despite massive current account deficits, the dollar appreciated against most other currencies due to a capital account surplus. In contrast, Ireland during the 1990s enjoyed both a high growth rate and a balance of payments surplus due to the rapid increase in net exports that underpinned the boom.

13.14 Speculation

When discussing the balance of payments in section 13.2, we assumed that the demand and supply of foreign exchange arise because people wish to import and export goods and services or to deal in assets such as stocks and shares across national boundaries. However, the reality of foreign exchange markets today is that, in the short run, they are dominated by speculative flows: that is, individuals and institutions trying to make money by dealing in currencies. This can be done by correctly anticipating movements in exchange rates.

Speculators can shift vast amounts of money from one currency to another in the course of a few minutes. A speculator tries to buy a currency cheap and sell it dear. The profit is derived from correctly anticipating an exchange rate movement. A simplified example would be if a speculator believed today's exchange rate of $1.3/€1 is high. He expects the dollar to appreciate and the euro to depreciate. If he buys €1 million worth of dollars at $1.3 he obtains $1.3 million. If the euro depreciates to $1.2 he can sell these dollars and obtain €1,083,333 ($1.3 million/1.2) – a profit of €83,333. Not all of this will be pure profit, however, because the speculator probably had to borrow the money used in this deal. The net profit depends on the interest rate paid on the loan, the interest rate earned on the dollars, and the length of time the speculator had to wait for the anticipated devaluation to materialise. Of course, if the devaluation did not materialise he would have made a loss due to the cost of the borrowed funds.

Selling short

Real-world speculators frequently sell a currency short: that is, they sell the currency on the forward market (for delivery some time in the future) and hope to be able to complete the contract by buying the currency at a lower price when the time comes. We discuss the forward foreign exchange market in the appendix to this chapter.

Speculative attacks developed on the currencies of the EMS during the crisis of 1992–93. Speculators took the view that the value of sterling was too high and began to sell it short in anticipation of making a profit when it was devalued.

In September 1992, the Hungarian-born financier George Soros, among others, became convinced that the British government would not be able to maintain sterling at its level in the EMS. He speculated that the pound would be devalued and is estimated to have made a profit of £1 billion on 'Black Wednesday', when sterling withdrew from the system and fell sharply on the foreign exchanges. There is a sense in which speculators can create a self-fulfilling prophecy – by heavy selling of a currency they help force its depreciation. However, it does not always work that way. Mr Soros speculated against the French franc during the currency crisis, but eventually became convinced that concerted action by France and Germany would be sufficient to maintain the parity set in 1987 and this turned out to be the case.

NOTE: During the East Asian currency crisis of 1997, politicians blamed Mr Soros, among others, for undermining confidence in the currencies' fixed exchange rates.

Speculation may make exchange rates volatile. Following the outbreak of the Gulf War in January 1991, the US dollar rose on the foreign exchange markets. Dealers, suddenly expert in military matters, read the results of the first day's air strikes as an indication that Saddam Hussein's forces could not put up any real resistance. As the week went on and the battlefield situation became less clear, the dollar lost all its gains. Later in the month, as the military defeat of Iraq became inevitable, the dollar began to appreciate again. Speculators respond almost instantaneously to any news that is likely to affect the long-run value of a currency.

Leading and lagging

Countries sometimes introduce exchange controls to try to prevent speculative inflows or outflows. Since 1992 this is no longer permissible between EU states. Moreover, speculation is very difficult to stop. It can take many forms. Leading and lagging by companies has been an important type of speculation in Ireland. It works as follows: if an exporter to the UK expects the euro to depreciate relative to sterling in the near future, he will delay (lag) converting his sterling receipts into euro because they will be worth more after the depreciation has taken place. Similarly, an importer may speed up (lead) payments to his UK supplier in order to avoid paying more after the depreciation. In the past, before the introduction of the euro, because of the size of Ireland's trade in relation to GNP, leads and lags in payments and receipts put tremendous pressure on the exchange rate.

Should speculation be curbed?

Speculators must base their expectations on the underlying 'fundamentals' – they have reasons for believing a currency is over- or under-valued. When they act to correct a misalignment of a currency – that is, to force down a currency that is over-valued or to force up an under-valued currency – speculation is beneficial. If, however, speculation is uninformed it can destabilise a currency, increasing volatility and uncertainty in the market. This is undesirable. Some economists, including Nobel Prize-winner James Tobin, have proposed that taxes be imposed on speculative gains to curb the level of speculation. He described his idea as 'throwing some sand in the works' to slow down the wheels of speculation. Most economists reject the notion of a 'Tobin tax' as unworkable, because it would be impossible to distinguish between 'speculative' and 'non-speculative' deals. The tax may also be unnecessary; there is no agreement that speculation is harmful to any significant degree. The type of speculation that provoked the loudest outcry in the 1990s was against currencies that were pegged at fixed exchange rates. This type of speculation can be avoided by allowing currencies to float, which deprives speculators of a target to attack.

However, the Tobin tax proposal has enjoyed renewed popularity during the prolonged financial instability in the euro area since 2008. French politicians like Nicolas Sarkozy and his successor François Hollande like to blame the crisis, at least in part, on speculation by 'Anglo-Saxon' (British and American) speculators. To dampen down this speculation they have proposed the introduction of a Tobin tax on short-term currencies dealing. Needless to say, the Anglo-Saxons in the City of London are strongly opposed to this proposal. It would not be in Ireland's interest either, given the importance of our IFSC, in which a fair amount of 'Anglo-Saxon speculation' takes place.

13.15 Exchange Rate Regimes

There are different ways in which countries can organise their foreign exchange systems. The dominant arrangement, which currently applies to the world's main currencies, is that each nation state – or certainly the larger ones – have separate national currencies and the exchange rates between these currencies are floating. This means that currencies are free to move up or down on the foreign exchange markets in response to shifts in the supply of and demand for currencies.

When the exchange rate is floating, governments and central banks should not in principle intervene to influence the value of their currencies. As a consequence, exchange rates may be volatile. In practice it is difficult to find a situation where exchange rates are allowed to float completely free of central bank intervention. Central banks buy and sell foreign exchange in order to stabilise the market and keep currencies in informal target ranges. Even when there is no formal target range, central bankers and ministers for finance may believe that their currencies are 'too high' or 'too low' and try to nudge the rate up or down by intervening. This is known as dirty floating.

The alternative to floating is a fixed exchange rate regime. Under this arrangement the values of currencies are fixed or pegged relative to each other. Governments and central banks are committed to maintaining the declared parities. The Gold Standard and the post-war Bretton Woods system were examples of such a regime. We explore the various possible exchange rate arrangements in more detail in Chapter 14.

13.16 Key Terms and Concepts

In this chapter we discussed a number of topics relating to the balance of payments and the determination of exchange rates. The main issues and concepts covered included:

- the balance of payments – a record of a country's economic transactions with the rest of the world. Apart from errors in measurement, the current, capital, and official external reserves accounts must sum to zero
- the foreign exchange market
- how supply and demand for foreign exchange determine the nominal exchange rate
- the trend in the exchange rate of the dollar and sterling relative to the Irish pound
- the trend in the euro exchange rate
- how inflation, real growth rate, interest rates and speculation influence exchange rates
- hedging against exchange rate risk.

Appendix 13.1 Hedging against exchange rate risk

Buying and selling across international borders between countries that use different currencies involves exchange rate risk. This continues to be a problem for Irish exporters and importers even after the introduction of the euro in 1999. Trade between Ireland and the UK, the USA, Japan and other countries outside the EMU still involves exchange rates. Even if a firm's sales are entirely in euro, it may still be exposed to exchange rate risk if it imports some of its inputs from outside the euro area.

Because of its importance to a country like Ireland, in this appendix we provide a brief survey of some technical aspects of foreign exchange markets. We describe the various techniques that have been developed to hedge against exchange rate risk.

INTERNAL HEDGING TECHNIQUES

In this section we outline some of the more common *internal* hedging techniques. These techniques are less costly than *external* hedging techniques, but can achieve the same objective.

Use euro area suppliers

One way of eliminating exchange rate risk is to switch from a foreign to a domestic supplier. This was not very feasible prior to the introduction of the euro because many of the raw materials imported into Ireland had no domestic substitutes. However, with the introduction of the euro, the possibility of finding a supplier in the euro area has increased significantly. If it remains the case that no supplier can be found in the euro area, a supplier operating out of a weak currency country is preferable to a strong currency country supplier. If the foreign currency depreciates, imports will cost less in euro.

Invoice in euro

If a company can invoice in euro, then exchange rate risk is eliminated. In effect, the exchange rate exposure is transferred to the other party in the transaction. Whether or not this is possible will probably depend on the relative strength of the parties to the deal. For example, a large buyer may be able to pressurise a small supplier into accepting the exchange rate risk. On occasions, both parties may agree to trade on the basis of a mutually acceptable hard currency such as the US dollar.

Match assets (liabilities) against liabilities (assets) in the same currency

Consider the case of an Irish firm with foreign assets, such as a subsidiary company in Britain. All of the assets and liabilities of the company in Britain will have to be translated from sterling to euro in order to prepare the balance sheet of the parent company in Ireland. If the euro appreciates on the foreign exchange market, the euro value of the British subsidiary will fall and this will lower the value of the parent company. This type of exchange risk is referred to as *translation exposure*. One way to avoid or minimise it is to match overseas assets with liabilities in the same currency by, for example, borrowing in sterling. Then if the euro appreciates, the value of both the sterling assets and liabilities will fall. However, there is some debate as to the importance of translation costs and gains in determining a firm's stock price. Modern security analysis should disclose translation gains and losses in income statements and, as such, should not unduly influence prospective buyers of the firm's stock.

Foreign currency accounts

Another way of reducing exchange rate exposure is to match foreign currency receipts (from the sale of output) against foreign currency payments to suppliers. That way a loss on receipts will be matched by a reduction in payments. This technique will not, however, be possible unless the firm has a reasonable two-way flow in the same foreign currency.

To use this technique a firm will normally operate a foreign currency account. This is an account denominated in a currency other than euro. These accounts allow the trader to match inflows and outflows in the same currency.

Another technique relates to a trader who has payments in one foreign currency (dollars) and receipts in another foreign currency (sterling). It is possible to convert from sterling to dollars using the cross exchange rate and thereby reduce conversion charges. Normally, the trader would convert his sterling receipts to euro and then use the euro to obtain dollars. However, the greater the number of conversions, the higher the charges and the lower the revenue to the trader.

Borrowing foreign currency

Consider the case of an exporter who expects to receive a certain amount of sterling in one month's time. She could borrow the sterling now and convert it into euro at the current spot exchange rate. The foreign borrowing is subsequently repaid by the proceeds from the exports. By using this technique the exporter avoids exposure to exchange rate risk for the period she is waiting to be paid.

Leading and lagging of payments or receipts

As mentioned in the main chapter, importers and exporters can minimise exchange rate losses through leading (importers paying before time) and lagging (exporters delaying receipts for as long as possible). If, for example, the euro were expected to depreciate, importers would pay their bills as soon as possible and exporters would delay converting their foreign currency receipts into euro. In the past, the very high exports/GNP and imports/GNP ratios in Ireland ensured that leading and lagging had a very significant impact on the level of Irish external reserves.

Transfer pricing

Transfer pricing is concerned with setting intra-firm prices so as to minimise tax burdens. It is also possible to use transfer pricing to reduce exchange rate exposure. For example, suppose a company has two subsidiaries, one in a strong currency country and the other in a country whose currency is expected to depreciate. If the subsidiary in the weak currency country sells at cost to the other subsidiary, profits are maximised in the hard currency country and minimised in the weak currency country. The company will then gain if currencies move in the expected direction. (See also Box 13.1.)

External hedging techniques: the forward market

In this section we describe one of the most widely used external hedging techniques, the use of the forward exchange rate. A forward exchange contract consists of an agreement between a bank and a customer to buy or sell a specified amount of foreign currency for delivery some time in the future at an exchange rate agreed today. Payment and delivery are not required until the maturity date.

Consider the example of an Irish firm importing cars from the USA. The cars will arrive in three months' time and the Irish importer will be required to pay, say, $2,500,000 at that time. If the current (spot) exchange rate is $1.2/€1, the importer's bill will be €2,083,333 million. The importer, however, may be worried that over the next three months the euro could depreciate against the dollar and might not be prepared to take the exchange rate risk. (If the euro fell to $1.1/€1, the importer's bill would increase to €2,272,727 or by €189,394.)

To remove this uncertainty the importer could enter into a contract that provides forward cover and removes the exposure to exchange rate risk. For example, he could arrange today to have $2,500,000 delivered in three months' time at an exchange rate (the three-month forward rate) agreed today. (Forward exchange rates are quoted for one, two, three, six and 12 months, and contracts can be arranged for longer periods. The rates are available from the banks and are published in the financial newspapers.)

The forward exchange rate is normally at a premium or a discount relative to the spot exchange rate. Using indirect quotes (i.e. £/€), which is the convention in Ireland, if the forward exchange rate is lower than the spot rate, the euro is said to be at a discount relative to the foreign currency. Conversely, if the forward rate is higher than the spot rate, the euro is said to be at a premium relative to the foreign currency. If the spot and forward rates are exactly the same, the forward price is said to be flat.

CHAPTER 14

Fixed Exchange Rate Systems

14.1 Introduction

In the last chapter we discussed the exchange rate and pointed out that exchange rates in most countries are floating; that is, free to move up and down on the currency markets. However, this is not the only possible exchange rate arrangement. At the other end of the spectrum are fixed exchange rate systems. Proponents of fixed exchange rates believe that freely floating rates create uncertainty and discourage international trade and investment. It is claimed that speculative flows may drive exchange rates significantly above or below their equilibrium levels, distorting the pattern of trade and investment between countries. When exchange rates are fixed, so the argument goes, uncertainty is reduced and trade and investment are promoted. This, in turn, should increase output and employment. These arguments have been very influential as justifications for establishing a single currency in the euro area.

In this chapter we first explain how a fixed exchange rate system works. We then examine some important case histories of such systems: the Gold Standard; the Bretton Woods system; the Snake system; and the European Monetary System (EMS). We conclude by discussing the advantages and disadvantages of fixed and floating exchange rates.

14.2 How a Fixed Exchange Rate System Works

When exchange rates are allowed to float, the foreign exchange market is just like any other market. The price (exchange rate) adjusts automatically to equate supply and demand. There is no need for central banks or governments to become involved. Fixed exchange rate systems, on the other hand, require countries to observe elaborate 'rules of the game'.

Fixed exchange rate systems generally involve central banks agreeing on central exchange rates and on upper and lower limits within which the market rate should be maintained. The Exchange Rate Mechanism (ERM) of the EMS was such a system.

A fixed exchange rate system entails central banks intervening on the foreign exchange markets to support a currency. The official external reserves play a key role in central bank intervention.

The official foreign exchange reserves or 'reserve assets' are a central bank's holdings of foreign currencies and other external monetary assets. The external reserves are primarily made up of currencies other than the euro, for example dollars, sterling and yen.

In addition to foreign currencies and gold, the reserves assets also consist of assets created by international agencies like the IMF. Special Drawing Rights (SDRs), sometimes referred to as 'paper gold', are reserve assets created by the IMF in order to supplement the world's monetary reserves. SDRs were first issued in 1970 to member countries in return for subscriptions in their own currencies. The SDR is a basket of the currencies of five of the main industrial nations.

Figure 14.1 illustrates the principles underlying central bank intervention to stabilise an exchange rate. Participating central banks agree on a central exchange rate and on upper and lower limits within which the exchange rate should be maintained. We can illustrate this

FIGURE 14.1 A fixed exchange rate system

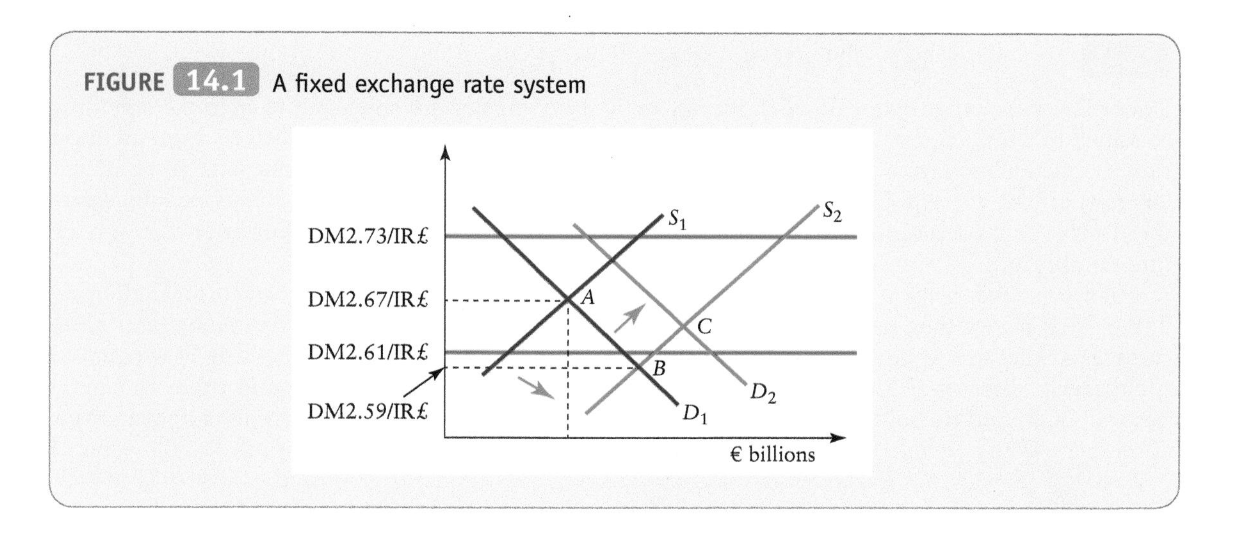

using the narrow band exchange rate mechanism (ERM) of the EMS that operated between 1979 and 1993. In 1992 the central rate of the Irish pound against the German mark was DM2.67. The permissible fluctuation margin was a range of ± 2.25 per cent around this rate. The upper limit to this band would be DM2.73 = IR£1 and the lower limit DM2.61 = IR£1. The Irish and German Central Banks were committed to intervene if these limits were about to be breached.

In Figure 14.1 the market is in equilibrium at DM2.67 = IR£1. Suppose now there is an increase in imports that shifts the supply schedule for Irish pounds to the right (S_1 to S_2). At the new equilibrium, point B, the Irish pound has depreciated to DM2.59 = IR£1. This exchange rate is below the agreed lower limit of DM2.61. To prevent the pound falling outside the target zone, the Central Bank of Ireland (CBI) and the Bundesbank must buy Irish pounds and sell German marks on the foreign exchange market. In effect, they create an artificial demand for Irish pounds and an artificial supply of German marks. The CBI must use up some of its external reserves for this purpose, whereas the Bundesbank acquires additional reserves in the form of Irish pounds. The purchase of Irish pounds would have the effect of shifting the demand curve for Irish pounds to the right (D_1 to D_2). The new equilibrium would be at C and the exchange rate would have been kept within the agreed band.

Conversely, central banks can keep the exchange rate from rising above the upper limit of the agreed band by selling pounds and buying marks. The CBI sells Irish pounds and the Bundesbank buys them. This will keep the exchange rate within the band.

When a currency is depreciating, a central bank's ability to support it is limited by its holdings of reserves of foreign exchange. Were reserves to fall below the minimum level believed to be prudent (often expressed as a multiple of the country's monthly import bill), the bank would be unable to continue to support the exchange rate. More damaging is the fact that central banks will also raise interest rates to encourage speculators to hold the currency and to compensate them for potential losses due to further depreciation.

The combination of falling reserves and penal interest rates have, time after time, forced the abandonment of the target exchange rate. What normally happens is that a new, lower central rate is agreed and the upper and lower banks are determined relative to this central rate. The currency has been devalued and this should improve competitiveness. The system starts anew.

14.3 The Monetary Adjustment Mechanism

Under fixed exchange rates, flows of money between countries are supposed to help the economy to adjust to changing circumstances. Consider the case of a country with a relatively high inflation rate. Because its inflation rate is high, its goods become expensive on world markets and a deficit emerges on the current account of its balance of payments. If it adheres to a fixed exchange rate there is, in theory, a mechanism that will reduce its inflation rate and move its current account back into equilibrium.

High-powered money (H) is defined as the sum of the central bank's assets or liabilities. Table 14.1 shows that on the liability side, H is equal to currency (CU) plus commercial bank reserves at the central bank (RE) plus government deposits (GD). On the assets side H is equal to the external reserves (R), plus central bank credit to the government (CCG) and the commercial banks, (CCB) and its holdings of government securities (GS). Hence on the liability side we have:

$$H \equiv R + CCB + CCG + GS \qquad (1)$$

In Chapter 9, we showed that high-powered money affects the money supply (M^s) via the money multiplier (m).

$$M^s = mH \qquad (2)$$

It follows from these two equations that changes in external reserves affect high-powered money, which in turn causes a change in the money supply.

$$\Delta R \rightarrow H \rightarrow \Delta M^s$$

For example, if the central bank buys €1 billion and pays for this out of its external reserves, in Table 14.1 R falls on the asset side and RE on the liability side. (People and firms who sell euro to the central bank take the money from their deposit accounts in the commercial banks.) The fall in R leads to a fall in H and, via the multiplier, a decrease in the money supply.

Conversely, if the central bank sells domestic currency to the foreign exchange market to avert an appreciation, R increases on the asset side and RE on the liability side. As H increases, the money supply expands. A key conclusion from this is: when a country adheres to a fixed exchange rate it loses control over its money supply. Hence it is not possible to participate in a fixed exchange rate and simultaneously follow a monetary policy of controlling the money supply.

Taking the analysis one stage further, recall from Chapter 10 that changes in the money supply affect nominal GNP and, in particular, the price level. Consider the case of a country with relatively high inflation and an associated current account deficit. How does that economy adjust back towards equilibrium? (Under flexible exchange rates, the balance of payments deficit would result in depreciation.)

TABLE 14.1 Changes in central bank balance sheet (hypothetical data) € billions

Assets		Liabilities	
External reserves (R)	−1	Currency (CU)	
Loans:		Commercial bank reserves (RE)	−1
Banks			
Government		Government deposits	
Government securities (GS)			
Total (H)	−1	Total (H)	−1

Under a fixed exchange rate, the central bank intervenes by buying its currency on the foreign exchange market and the external reserves fall. This leads to a fall in H and M^s, which, in turn, leads to an increase in both the nominal and real interest rate. The higher real interest rate leads to a fall in aggregate demand (AD) and the price level (we ignore the effect on real output, Y).

$$\text{Current account deficit} \rightarrow \downarrow R \rightarrow \downarrow H \rightarrow \downarrow M^s \rightarrow \uparrow i \rightarrow \uparrow r \rightarrow \downarrow IE \rightarrow \downarrow AD \rightarrow \downarrow P$$

where i and r are the nominal and real interest rate, IE is interest-sensitive expenditure, AD is aggregate demand and P is the price level. The decline in the price level improves the country's competitive position, exports increase and imports fall, leading to the elimination of the current account deficit.

A country with a current account surplus sees its external reserves and money supply rise. This increases the price level, making the country less competitive. Exports fall, imports rise and the current account surplus is eliminated.

$$\text{Current account surplus} \rightarrow \uparrow R \rightarrow \uparrow H \rightarrow \uparrow M^s \rightarrow \downarrow i \rightarrow \downarrow r \rightarrow \uparrow IE \rightarrow \uparrow AD \rightarrow \uparrow P$$

This adjustment mechanism is a key feature of fixed exchange rate systems.

14.4 Sterilisation

Central banks, even if they are participating in a fixed exchange rate system, are often unwilling to surrender control over the money supply and the price level. Sterilisation is a way of breaking the link between changes in the external reserves to the money supply. To see how sterilisation works, consider again the central bank's balance sheet in Table 14.2.

Suppose the central bank is intervening in the foreign exchange market to prevent its exchange rate depreciating. This intervention will lead to a fall in the external reserves (R) on the asset side and a fall in commercial bank reserves (RE) on the liability side. This, in turn, will reduce high-powered money (H) and, via the multiplier, the money supply (M^s).

The sterilisation strategy involves trying to keep H constant. This can be done by buying government securities (GS) and by paying for them by issuing new currency (CU). Hence on the asset side of the balance sheet, GS rises; and on the liability side, CU rises. If the rise in GS is exactly equal to the fall in R, the monetary base or high-powered money remains constant. The central bank has broken the link from changes in R through to M^s.

NOTE: In September 2012 the ECB announced a programme of 'Outright Monetary Transactions' under which it will purchase bonds issued by euro area countries that have signed up to a fiscal adjustment programme. To allay German fears that this will result in an expansion of the ECB's balance sheet and of high-powered money, it also announced that these bond purchases will be sterilised.

TABLE 14.2 Changes in central bank balance sheet (hypothetical data) € billions

Assets		Liabilities	
External reserves (R)	−1	Currency (CU)	1
Loans:		Commercial bank reserves (RE)	−1
Banks			
Government		Government deposits	
Government securities (GS)	1		
Total (H)	0	Total (H)	0

One difficulty is that when the central bank buys bonds, it tends to drive their price up. But this implies lower interest rates, which will encourage an outflow of funds. This could lead to a capital outflow, which on top of the current account deficit will put even more pressure on the central bank.

Consider now the case of a country that is experiencing an inflow of foreign exchange that threatens to increase the domestic money supply and eventually increase the price level. R increases on the asset side and RE on the liability side of the central bank's balance sheet. If the central bank now sells bonds, both GS and CU will fall. If the rise in R is equal to the fall in GS, H will remain unchanged and the sterilisation policy will be complete.

Selling bonds to the public could mean a fall in their price. This implies that interest rates would have to rise and higher interest rates would tend to attract a capital inflow from abroad that would augment the current account surplus. Given that higher interest rates would also be harmful to the domestic economy, the central bank would sooner or later find it more attractive to allow its exchange rate to rise rather than to continue with its sterilisation policy.

History shows that sterilisation is of limited effectiveness. It is usually abandoned after a short trial period. A good example is the Bundesbank's unsuccessful attempt to sterilise the inflow of dollars when the Bretton Woods system was breaking down in the early 1970s.

14.5 Why Fixed Exchange Rate Systems Do Not Endure

In Chapter 13 we discussed the determinants of exchange rates and we pointed out that there are many factors that impinge on a country's exchange rate, for example differences in growth rates and adverse economic shocks such as an increase in the price of oil or the foot and mouth disease in 2001. Inflation rate differentials, in particular, have a very important impact on exchange rates. (We explain why this is so when we discuss the theory of purchasing power parity in Chapter 15.) Countries with relatively high inflation rates will tend to have weak or depreciating exchange rates and visa versa.

Hence, for a fixed exchange rate system to succeed, the participating countries must have similar inflation and growth rates. Divergence of inflation and/or growth rates will give rise to a fundamental misalignment that will force a change in the agreed exchange rates. An appreciating exchange rate is a normal consequence of rapid economic growth; a depreciating rate is a normal consequence of relatively high inflation. Under a fixed exchange rate system, these adjustments are closed off.

Lack of policy co-ordination

Going one stage further, it is also essential that the participating countries pursue similar macroeconomic (fiscal, monetary and incomes) policies so as to achieve similar inflation and growth rates. If the currencies are misaligned to start with, or divergent policies create misalignments with the passage of time, persistent balance of payments current account deficits and surpluses will arise. These symptoms of disequilibrium will eventually lead to realignments and the possible breakdown of the fixed exchange rate system.

The lesson to be learned is that fixed exchange rate systems can only reduce exchange rate uncertainty if macroeconomic policies in the individual states are consistent. This can be achieved by explicit or implicit policy co-ordination. It is unlikely that large, independent countries would pursue consistent fiscal and monetary policies over long periods. This is a basic reason why in the past fixed exchange rate systems have tended to break down.

Speculation – a one-way bet under fixed exchange rates?

A problem with fixed exchange rates is that they offer speculators opportunities for making a killing. If foreign exchange dealers became convinced that a particular currency is over-valued, each dealer (or speculator, if you prefer) would have an incentive to speculate against the currency.

As explained in Chapter 13, speculators generally borrow the money with which to speculate. For example, the speculator borrows £1 billion at an interest rate of 10 per cent. He then sells the sterling for dollars and deposits the proceeds at an interest rate of two per cent. As soon as the devaluation occurs he will switch back to sterling and close out both accounts. In the meantime the cost of the speculation is the interest rate differential. The longer the devaluation fails to materialise, the larger will be the losses on the interest rate spread.

A central bank – committed to the fixed exchange rate – will increase interest rates in an attempt to persuade investors to hold the domestic currency and discourage them from dumping it on the foreign exchange market. The process of defending the exchange rate can become very painful for the domestic economy, as Ireland found out in 1992.

The level of official external reserves sets a limit to how long a central bank can continue to intervene to support its currency. However, the rise in interest rates and the adverse affect on consumer and investor confidence tends to break governments' resolve to support fixed exchange rates. In Ireland and Britain, high interest rates are particularly unpopular because so many households hold variable rate mortgages. Politicians quickly decide that the possible benefits of a fixed exchange rate do not merit the unpopularity and economic costs of the measures needed to defend it. Speculators are aware of this weakness in the commitment to the exchange rate target and are encouraged to continue to sell the currency in order to make a speculative profit.

All this suggests that fixing exchange rates between countries is unwise unless we can be sure that the countries are similar in terms of macroeconomic conditions, have a roughly synchronised business cycle, are growing at similar rates, and pursuing broadly similar fiscal, income and monetary policies. Some pairs of countries do meet these conditions. For a long time the Netherlands successfully hitched its exchange rate to the German mark. The close links between the two countries and their structural similarities, as well as the willingness of the Dutch Central Bank (the Nederlandsche Bank) to follow the policy lead set by the German Central Bank (the Bundesbank), allowed this to work. Similarly, long before the launch of EMU, Belgium and Luxembourg were in a currency union.

There is also the extreme ultimate alternative of abolishing the national currency and adopting a common currency such as the euro or the US dollar. Many very small countries take this approach. For example, Panama and some Caribbean islands use the US dollar and in Zimbabwe the US dollar and the South African rand replaced the domestic currency in an effort to end hyperinflation. This implies completely abandoning an independent monetary and exchange rate policy.

14.6 Which Exchange Rate Regime is Best?

In principle, countries have a choice between fixed and floating exchange rate systems, or various compromises between these two systems. Orthodox economic opinion has varied as to the relative merits of the alternatives. In this section we examine the arguments on both sides of this debate.

Advantages of floating exchange rates

The basic argument in favour of floating is that the foreign exchange market should be allowed to function free of government intervention and find its own equilibrium through the interaction of the forces of supply and demand. Attempts by governments to set targets and peg exchange rates are, according to this view, as misguided in this market as they would be in the market for apples or shoes. How do governments know what the 'correct' exchange rate is? How can they distinguish a temporary fluctuation in the supply and demand for foreign exchange (which should be smoothed out) from a fundamental adjustment (which should not be resisted)? How can they avoid handing speculators sure bets by merely delaying a devaluation or revaluation?

Even if governments are successful in maintaining a fixed exchange rate, the result can be a misalignment. This gives rise to problems of adjustment. If, for example, the exchange rate is over-valued, but the government is committed to a fixed exchange rate, measures will have to be taken to reduce domestic costs and prices. This approach is called trying to achieve an 'internal devaluation' – a reduction in the real exchange rate without an adjustment in the nominal exchange rate. The required deflationary policies will have an adverse effect on output, employment and unemployment, in the short run at least, and are politically difficult to implement. Furthermore, it is difficult to get employees and trade unions to understand that they should accept cuts in nominal wages so as to restore the country's international competitiveness. We discuss the Irish experience with internal devaluation during the current economic crisis at various stages in this book.

Disadvantages of floating exchange rates

The most frequently made argument against allowing currencies to float freely is that left to its own devices the foreign exchange market tends to be dominated by speculative flows. In principle, this should not be a problem if speculators base their actions on the 'fundamentals' that ultimately determine the relative value of currencies. However, at times speculators' expectations appear to lack an anchor. In the short run, currencies can gyrate widely in response to all sorts of news and rumours. As a consequence many small countries, although proclaiming that their currencies are floating, in fact intervene in the foreign exchange markets and try to maintain fairly stable exchange rates. This has been referred to as a 'fear of floating'.

An argument in favour of fixed exchange rates is that they avoid the uncertainty and volatility that occur when currencies are allowed to float freely. However, there is surprisingly little evidence that this volatility actually reduces the level of international trade and investment.

A further potential disadvantage of flexible exchange rates is that depreciation may provoke a depreciation-inflation spiral. This occurs when an initial depreciation increases domestic costs and prices and generates pressure for further depreciation, and so on. Why do we have such high inflation? Because the exchange rate is depreciating. And why is the exchange rate depreciating? Because we have high inflation. The experience of a number of South American countries illustrates how difficult it can be to stop this spiral.

There is no consensus as to which exchange rate regime is the best. In fact, it is unlikely that any one regime is ideal in all circumstances. The UK experience after 1992 showed that a floating currency combined with disciplined domestic policies could deliver relatively high growth and low inflation. Countries with a history of high inflation can use a peg to a strong currency such as the dollar or the euro to win the fight against inflation, but only if the peg is supported by tight fiscal and monetary policies. The more inflation-prone euro area countries – Italy, Ireland, Greece, Spain and Portugal – had to achieve low inflation and fiscal discipline in order to be allowed into the EMU and adopt the euro in 1999. But we shall see that since 2008 these countries, in particular, have been the focus of a debate about the viability of currency union.

The Argentine case is instructive. In 1991 a new Argentine peso was launched and rigidly pegged to the US dollar at 1:1 through a currency board that could only issue currency that was fully backed by dollars. Note that the country preserved its national currency and did not adopt the US dollar as its currency. This is a key difference from, for example, Greece abandoning the drachma and adopting the euro in 2002.

During the 1990s Argentina enjoyed a sharp fall in inflation and a resumption of economic growth. But by 2001 the contradictions between the currency peg and the lack of domestic economic discipline led to a collapse of the exchange rate peg and the peso was allowed to float. By mid-2002 the peso had fallen to almost 4:1 and the country was plunged in a dire economic crisis. In 2012 a dollar is worth 4.7 Argentine nuevo pesos.

Before the launch of EMU, some economists made extravagant claims regarding the potential benefits of adopting a common currency. One author, for example, claimed that the historical evidence showed that (otherwise similar) countries that adopted a common currency experienced a trebling of their trade (Rose 2000).

This implausible claim has since been debunked. It has been argued that if the use of a common currency greatly increases trade between countries, abandoning the link would be expected to reduce it. A study of the effects of breaking the sterling link showed that it had little effect on the development of trade between Britain and Ireland (Thom and Walsh 2002).

Others claimed that the use of a common currency would lead to rapid synchronisation of the business cycle across participating countries, reducing the risk of misalignments. However, this too proved over-optimistic. In Chapter 4 we drew attention to the divergence in the business cycle (as reflected in unemployment rates) between the core and periphery of the euro area since 2007.

Excessive enthusiasm with respect to the effects of a common currency led many to fail to perceive the flaws in the design of the euro area during the 1990s.

14.7 The Gold Standard

The most famous example of a system of fixed exchange rates is the Gold Standard, which was in full force from 1870 to the outbreak of World War I in 1914. Over this period the values of the world's major currencies were fixed in terms of gold. This determined their value relative to each other. For example, a US dollar was worth 23.22 grains of gold and a pound sterling 113 grains, so the parity between the pound and the dollar was £1 = 113/23.22 = $4.8665 or roughly 1:5. The pound was devalued against the dollar in 1940 to £1 = $4.03, so a dollar was now worth five shillings or a crown. That is why a 'half crown' in old money (2s 6d) was colloquially known as 'half a dollar'.

NOTE: Sir Isaac Newton, as Master of the Mint, set the price of gold at £3 17s 10d (£3.89) per troy ounce in 1717. The more familiar (avoirdupois) ounce is almost 10 per cent heavier than a troy ounce, so the price of gold was £4.25. The exchange rate of £1 = $4.86 in the 1930s was still very close to this.

While this example is now remote in time, the rise and fall of the Gold Standard contains instructive lessons for the creation of a currency union in Europe in 1999.

The Gold Standard relied on the automatic adjustment mechanism to correct current account balance of payments surpluses and deficits. If a country was experiencing a current account deficit, gold would flow out of the country. This reduction in the money supply (gold) would put downward pressure on the price level. Lower prices, in turn, improved competitiveness, increased exports and reduced imports. The incipient current account deficit would be automatically eliminated by this redistribution of the world's gold supply. Similarly, a country with a current account surplus would experience an increase in its money supply and rising prices. The loss in competitiveness would choke off the current account surplus. The monetary authorities in these countries should not intervene to prevent these flows or their effects on the price level: this was an essential part of the 'rules of the game'.

In addition to the gold flows, labour and capital were also expected to flow from deficit to surplus countries. This is what happens today between the regions of a country. With the decline of the coal industry, many areas in the north of England went into recession, a deficit emerged on the regional balance of payments, and resources flowed out to the booming south east. On the other hand, the discovery of oil and gas in the North Sea led to a current account surplus in northeastern Scotland and money and resources flowed into the region around Aberdeen. A similar adjustment mechanism is supposed to operate throughout the euro area following the introduction of the euro, with resources flowing from depressed to booming regions. However, as we saw in Chapter 4, high unemployment in Ireland prompts Irish people to emigrate outside the euro area, not to other European regions. The lack of integration of European labour markets calls into question the wisdom of forming a common currency area between the present 17 members of the EMU.

The strains of war and mobilisation often forced countries to abandon fixed exchange rates, for example Britain during the Napoleonic Wars and America during the Civil War. At the outbreak of World War I Britain suspended convertibility of the pound into gold and bank notes became legal tender. France also suspended convertibility of the franc. In Germany the gold mark was abandoned in August 1914 and the paper mark introduced. Although the USA maintained limited convertibility of the dollar, the full-blown Gold Standard had died. This was the first real test of the Gold Standard and in the words of one British economist it failed the test 'utterly' (Lipsey 1975:683–702).

However, at the time the suspension of convertibility to gold was regarded as temporary, like the suspension of gold payments during the Napoleonic Wars, and a major aim of British post-war policy was to return to the Gold Standard at the pre-war value of sterling. In 1925 Winston Churchill, then Chancellor of the Exchequer, put the pound back on the Gold Standard at the pre-war parity. Orthodox financial opinion in Britain was gratified at the thought that the pound was once again worth $4.8665. However, since 1914 Britain had experienced considerably more inflation than the USA and sterling was seriously over-valued at the old exchange rate.

The adjustment to this mistake was slow and painful. It provides an important historical example of how difficult it is to achieve a meaningful 'internal devaluation' when shackled with a fixed nominal exchange rate, which requires price and wage cuts. Unemployment and cuts in wages in England in the late 1920s led to riots and widespread social unrest. We discuss the relevance of this to the current Irish situation in section 14.13 below.

The main reasons the Gold Standard broke up was the differences in inflation rates across member states. In contrast to Britain, France went back on the Gold Standard in 1928 but at a realistic, lower exchange rate that more than compensated for the inflation that had occurred since 1914. Britain was obsessed with returning to the old parity with gold, despite the high inflation it had experienced during the war. There were, however, other fundamental problems with the Gold Standard.

- As international trade increased there was an associated increase in the demand for gold to act as reserve backing for currencies; that is, for money to act as a medium of exchange. Increases in the gold supply, however, depended on new discoveries and these occurred erratically in the course of the nineteenth century, in California, South Africa and Australia. Consequently there was a tendency for periodic shortages of international liquidity to develop.
- Governments were not willing to abide by the 'rules of the game', which were the equivalent of the automatic monetary mechanism we described earlier. For example, the USA had a surplus on its balance of payments and this led to an inflow of gold. However, the Federal Reserve System, created in 1913, prevented these inflows from increasing the US money supply because of the risk of inflation. It operated a sterilisation policy, which thwarted the automatic adjustment mechanism on which the Gold Standard rested.

The Great Depression

Germany went into recession in 1928 and America in 1929. The crisis quickly spread across the world. The restoration of the Gold Standard in the 1920s was one of the reasons for the rapid transmission of the recession and why the recession intensified into the Great Depression. The interlocking of national banking systems and the free movement of reserves from one crisis-stricken country to another transmitted shocks internationally. The financial panics and bank failures that followed in the wake of the stock market crash of 1929 led to the collapse of the already weakened Gold Standard.

Britain suspended sterling convertibility to gold in 1931 and in 1933 dollar convertibility was suspended, to be restored in 1934 at the higher gold price of $35 an ounce. Most other countries abandoned the Gold Standard completely.

John Maynard Keynes regarded the financial world's obsession with gold as a 'barbarous relic'. He thought Churchill's decision to re-establish the pre-war gold value of sterling in 1925 was a quixotic blunder that imposed a severe deflation on the British economy. When Britain abandoned the Gold Standard Keynes wrote:

> *There are few Englishmen who do not rejoice at the breaking of our gold fetters. We feel that we have at last a free hand to do what is sensible. The romantic phase is over, and we can begin to discuss what policy is for the best.* (Keynes 1952)

NOTE: Keynes was visiting Ireland to give the Finlay Lecture in University College, Dublin, in March 1933 when the news arrived that the dollar's convertibility had been suspended. The lecture was followed by a dinner and some of the best-known wits of Dublin were invited. The dinner was a total failure. Keynes was called to the telephone in the middle of the meal. When he came back, he said: 'You may be interested to know that the United States has just left gold.' The short silence that was felt appropriate was broken by Oliver St John Gogarty: 'Does that matter?' (Meenan 1980:171).

As the recession of 1929 intensified into the Great Depression, governments abandoned the commitment to fixed exchange rates, adopting instead a policy of 'beggar thy neighbour' devaluations. They devalued in order to secure a competitive gain over their rivals in trade, but the countries that were adversely affected retaliated by devaluing in turn. The result was that no country gained a lasting advantage. The instability of the floating exchange rate system during the 1930s caused policy-makers to attach a high priority to re-establishing a fixed exchange rate system after World War II.

14.8 The Bretton Woods System, 1945–1971

In Bretton Woods, a mountain resort town in New Hampshire, USA, representatives of 44 nations met in July 1944 (three weeks after D-Day) to discuss the arrangements for the post-war world monetary system. They hoped that when the war ended there would be no going back to the chaotic international financial system that had prevailed after the Gold Standard broke down in the 1930s. They believed that only a system of fixed exchange rates could provide the stable framework required for economic reconstruction.

By 1945, the USA held most of the western world's gold reserves. Consequently it was natural that the dollar should assume the role of the new reserve currency for the western world. The agreement was that the dollar would remain fixed at its 1934 value of $35 per ounce of gold and that all other countries would keep their exchange rates within a one per cent band of an agreed parity with the dollar. Central banks would buy or sell currencies as appropriate to keep exchange rates within the agreed band. This dollar exchange standard was, therefore, an attenuated form of the old Gold Standard.

The principal architects of the new system were J. M. Keynes and an American economist, Harry Dexter White. Mr White may or may not have been a Soviet spy, but it seems that every night he informed the Soviet Embassy of the details of the negotiations!

> *There is no question of treachery, in the accepted sense of betraying one's country's secrets to an enemy. But there can be no doubt that, in passing classified information to the Soviets, White knew he was betraying his trust, even if he did not thereby think he was betraying his country.* (Skidelsky 2000:263)

This was Keynes's last major contribution to public affairs before his death on Easter Sunday, 1946.

The International Monetary Fund and the World Bank

The International Monetary Fund (IMF) was set up to assist countries experiencing balance of payments difficulties and to help maintain fixed exchange rates. The International Bank for Reconstruction and Development (IBRD), better known as the World Bank, was set up to help finance post-war reconstruction. (The IMF and World Bank are still known as the 'Bretton Woods institutions'.) Central banks could borrow foreign exchange from the IMF and use it to support their currency on the markets. If, however, a country was experiencing a 'fundamental disequilibrium' in its balance of payments it could devalue. The IMF could not veto a devaluation if it was less than 10 per cent, but its permission was required for devaluation in excess of 10 per cent.

NOTE: Both the IMF and the World Bank are based in Washington, DC. The IMF makes loans to financially troubled countries and has a staff of 2,500 people including 800 economists. The institution has lending capital of US$395 billion and currently has programmes in 26 countries.

A 10 per cent devaluation of the pound, relative to the dollar, would work as follows. If the initial central rate against the dollar had been $2.8/£1, given the ± 1 per cent band, the ceiling rate was now $2.828 and the floor rate $2.772. Following the 10 per cent devaluation, the new central rate would be $2.52 and the ceiling and floor rates $2.5452 and $2.4948 respectively. This devaluation should remove Britain's balance of payments deficit and permit a return to a fixed exchange rate.

The provision for devaluation marked a crucial difference between the Bretton Woods system and the old Gold Standard. No longer did countries have to suffer the protracted deflation of the automatic adjustment mechanism in order to correct a balance of payments problem. Instead they could obtain international agreement on devaluation.

The demise of the Bretton Woods system

The Bretton Woods System worked well during the 1950s and into the 1960s. The major currencies held to fixed exchange rates for long periods of time. For example, between 1949 and 1967, sterling was worth $2.80 (and because the Irish pound was fixed at one-to-one parity with sterling it too was worth $2.80). For 18 years this was a fact of economic life and no one bothered to look up the newspapers to see if there had been any change. Trade and investment between the nations of the western world expanded rapidly under the fixed exchange rate regime.

However, strains began to be felt in the late 1960s. The United States began running huge fiscal budget deficits to fight a war on poverty at home and a war on communism in Southeast Asia. This, in turn, led to massive US current account deficits and undermined confidence in the dollar. The increase in government spending also increased US inflation.

The other main industrial countries were unwilling to revalue their currencies to help eliminate the US deficit. For a while, central banks were glad of additional dollars to augment their reserves, but the continued loose US monetary and fiscal policies soon created an excess supply of the currency.

By 1970 the German and Japanese central banks held so many dollars that if they had been allowed to obtain gold in exchange for them, American gold reserves would have been completely depleted. In 1969 the German money supply grew by 25 per cent in a week due to the inflow of dollars and the Bundesbank proved powerless to offset this through sterilisation. There was growing reluctance to continue to absorb the dollars flooding on to world foreign exchange markets. The dollar exchange standard was breaking down.

The definitive end of the Gold Standard came in August 1971 when President Richard Nixon officially terminated the convertibility of the dollar into gold. This was called the 'Nixon shock' because it was done without consulting with members of the international monetary community.

In December 1971, the Smithsonian Agreement (which was concluded at the Smithsonian Institution, a museum in Washington, DC), entailed raising the price of gold from $35 to $38 an ounce, which in effect devalued the dollar by almost eight per cent. Most of the other major currencies also devalued in terms of gold. This final attempt to patch up the Bretton Woods system did not succeed. There was a further devaluation of the dollar in February 1973 (which raised the price of gold to $42.22 an ounce), but instead of restoring confidence in the system, this encouraged the countries of Europe to terminate their links with the dollar and to float their currencies.

On the free market the price of gold quickly shot up. It reached $161 per ounce in 1975. By 1976 all the world's major currencies were floating and the price of gold continued to climb. By 2012 an ounce of gold had reached $1,740 – almost 50 times its dollar price in the 1930s.

The decline of the dollar relative to gold paved the way for one of the most significant periods of inflation in the history of the world. As the dollar fell in value, the Organisation of Petroleum Exporting Countries (OPEC) decided to quadruple the dollar price of oil when the opportunity presented itself during the Arab–Israeli War late in 1973.

The rise in oil prices, in turn, fuelled the massive global inflation that occurred between 1973 and 1985. It is understandable, in the light of this chain of events, that governments yearned for a return to some form of backing for their currencies that would prevent a recurrence of this experience.

14.9 The European Snake, 1972–1974

Instability in the foreign exchange markets was unsettling for the European Economic Community (EEC), as it then was. It made it very difficult to operate the Common Agricultural Policy, whose goal was to establish a common price for agricultural products throughout the Community. How could this be done if the currencies of Europe were fluctuating wildly on the foreign exchange markets? But it also undermined the long-standing aim of the Community to establish a common European currency and a single European market for goods and services.

In 1972 the EEC central banks agreed to intervene in the foreign exchange markets to minimise fluctuations. Countries were expected to hold their currencies in a band $\pm$ 1.125 per cent around a central rate (the 'snake'). They also had to maintain their exchange rates in a $\pm$ 2.25 per cent band against the dollar (the 'tunnel'). This system became known as the 'snake in the tunnel' because the European currencies slid up and down within the 'tunnel' as they followed the movements of the dollar.

In March 1973, the European currencies decided to float against the dollar and the 'tunnel' part of the system came to an end. The remaining snake had a short life. The UK joined at the start, but left after two months because it proved impossible to maintain the value of sterling at the target level. (The Irish pound entered and left the snake along with sterling.) France left and rejoined as the franc rose and fell against the DM. By the mid-1970s the snake was dead.

The main reason for the failure of the snake was the same as that which led to the downfall of the Gold Standard and the Bretton Woods system, namely, the lack of economic policy co-ordination between the participating countries and differences in inflation rates. If countries do not have similar monetary policies, leading to similar rates of inflation, they cannot hope to maintain their balance of payments in equilibrium under a system of fixed exchange rates. During the 1970s France and the UK pursued much more expansionary fiscal and monetary policies than Germany. As result they tended to run chronic current account deficits, while Germany ran surpluses. These imbalances eventually forced exchange rate changes and killed off the snake.

The renewed currency instability increased the awareness of the need for a system that would stabilise exchange rates in Europe and led to the initiatives that culminated in the launch of the EMS in 1979.

Exchange rate co-ordination

Following the collapse of the Bretton Woods system in the 1970s, the USA proclaimed that it was committed to allowing the dollar to float. An important change in US policy took place in September 1985, however, when the world's five main industrialised nations (known as the G5) met in the Plaza Hotel in New York City to co-ordinate a depreciation of the dollar against the other currencies. This approach can restore stability to the foreign exchange markets for a while, but does not remove the potential for further tensions. Because of its importance in world trade and because it is the most widely held reserve currency, the dollar always occupies centre stage.

There are big advantages to the USA in occupying this position. In the first place, the vast amount of dollars held overseas increases the country's gains from seigniorage (see Chapter 9). Secondly, the USA can set its monetary policies without regard to the repercussions for other countries and without considering the repercussions of other countries' policies on it. The pre-eminence of the dollar as a world currency and store of value, although not fully merited in light of its current inability to take decisive action to address its fiscal imbalances, allows America to sell its bonds to foreigners and the demand for these bonds has driven US interest rates to historic lows.

The French have long resented what Charles de Gaulle's finance minister Valéry Giscard d'Estaing called America's 'exorbitant privilege' in this area. It was hoped that the creation of the euro would reduce the dollar's prominence in the world financial system, but despite growth in the use of the euro, the dollar continues to rule the roost as the reserve currency.

14.10 The European Monetary System, 1979–1998

Despite the failure of the snake, during the second half of the 1970s the European Commission pressed ahead with plans for a European monetary union. The interim goal was to create a 'zone of monetary stability' in Europe. Following an initiative by the then President of the European Union, Roy Jenkins, an agreement was reached in 1978 between the French president, who was now Valéry Giscard D'Estaing, and the German chancellor, Helmut Schmidt, to fix exchange rates and eventually push for a common currency in Europe. After long and difficult negotiations the EMS was launched on 13 March 1979.

At the heart of the EMS was a system of quasi-fixed exchange rates, known as the Exchange Rate Mechanism (ERM). The ERM was based on the European Currency Unit (ECU), a basket of currencies. (The écu was a medieval French coin, and there was ambiguity as to whether 'ECU' refers to this or is simply an acronym of European Currency Unit.) The Irish pound accounted for only 1.1 per cent of the value of an ECU.

At the start of the EMS, each participating currency declared a central rate against the ECU. These rates were then used to calculate the *parity grid*, the ceiling and the floor relative to the central rate. The idea was that a central bank would not intervene to influence a particular exchange rate while it remained inside the band. The central bank will only intervene if an exchange rate threatens to go through the ceiling or fall through the floor of the system.

There were two important features of the EMS that gave a degree of flexibility to the system. The first was that realignments were permitted. A realignment was an adjustment of a currency's central rates against the other ERM currencies. Thus if circumstances warranted it, the parity grid was altered. Between 1979 and 1998 there were 21 changes in the ERM central rates. The dominant trend was for the German mark and the Dutch guilder to be revalued upwards, and the French franc, Italian lira and the other smaller currencies to be devalued. The Irish pound was devalued by 10 per cent in January 1993 – the largest devaluation during the operation of the system. On the other hand, the Irish pound was revalued by three per cent against all the other currencies, including the German mark, in March 1998.

The second source of flexibility in the EMS was the margin of fluctuation around the central rates. Until August 1993 the maximum permissible deviation of the strongest and weakest currencies in the ERM from their central rates was ± 2.25 per cent. (The Spanish peseta, the Portuguese escudo and the pound sterling were allowed a ± 6 per cent fluctuation margin.) The combination of periodic realignments and the margin of fluctuation round the central rate meant that the EMS was a compromise between a rigidly fixed exchange rate system, such as the Gold Standard or the Bretton Woods system, and free floating.

Although it was recognised that stable exchange rates could not be maintained unless all the countries participating in the system pursued similar economic policies, there was no mechanism to co-ordinate or harmonise their fiscal or monetary policies and this quickly led to strains within the system.

In the early years of the EMS, countries like Germany pursued a tight monetary policy, whereas France under President Mitterrand implemented expansionary socialist measures. The result was that realignments were frequent – two in every year from 1979 to 1983. Italy, for example, devalued the lira eight times between 1979 and 1987. If realignments had continued at this frequency the EMS would have been undermined. A major change occurred in 1983 when the Mitterrand administration abandoned its attempt at domestic expansion in favour of a programme of austerity and stabilisation. Between 1983 and 1986 the system became more stable and transformed into a more rigidly fixed exchange rate system.

Between 1987 and 1992 there were no major realignments and the margin of fluctuation between the main currencies narrowed to a de facto ± 1 per cent. Spain, Portugal, and Britain entered the ERM, and Italy moved from the broad to the narrow band.

14.11 The Currency Crisis of 1992–1993

The apparent stability of the EMS in 1992 was deceptive. A number of factors were soon causing serious tensions and would lead to the eventual breakdown of the system.

In the autumn of 1989, the Berlin Wall came down. In July 1990, after more than 40 years of separation, the economically strong Federal Republic of Germany (West) was united with the economically weak German Democratic Republic (East) in an economic, monetary and social union. In October 1990 German economic integration was made irreversible by political unification.

The immediate effect of reunification was a significant increase in the government's fiscal deficit. The old East mark was converted to the West German DM at a one-to-one parity, which benefited consumers and savers in the East but crippled their old and inefficient industries. Investment in East Germany's infrastructure and its ailing industries, social welfare payments to the unemployed and subsidies to loss-making and inefficient firms ensured a massive increase in government expenditure. On the other hand, the government did not raise taxes to any significant degree to finance this expenditure. Higher taxes would have made it more difficult to sell the reunification policy to the electorate.

The effect of the expansionary fiscal policy was to increase economic growth and inflation in the West. In response to this over-heating, the German central bank, the Bundesbank, tightened monetary policy in order to reduce the inflationary pressures. The combination of an expansionary fiscal policy and a tight monetary policy resulted in a three percentage point increase in German interest rates to 9.7 per cent.

Furthermore, European and US monetary policy became markedly out of sync in the early 1990s. To stimulate the US economy, the Federal Reserve Bank lowered short-term interest rates in 1992 to their lowest levels for 29 years. In Germany, on the other hand, interest rates were rising in the wake of reunification. The combination of lower interest rates in America and higher rates in Germany caused a capital outflow from the dollar into the German mark, leading to an appreciation of the DM.

NOTE: A recurrent problem with the EMS was the fact that when money flowed into Europe from the rest of the world, European currencies – even those participating in the EMS – were not regarded as perfect substitutes. The German mark was favoured over other currencies, putting upward pressure on it and generating strain in the ERM. This is similar to the situation in 2012. When fears of a collapse of the euro area grow, investors sell the bonds of 'peripheral' countries and purchase German bonds. As a result, yields on German bonds fall and those on bonds issued by other euro area countries rise. In mid-2012 German 10-year bonds were yielding 1.255 per cent, Spanish bonds 6.651 per cent, and Irish bonds 8.207 per cent.

The reunification episode illustrates that the Bundesbank's commitment to EMS parities was secondary to its concern for Germany's domestic economy. In other words, the Bundesbank was prepared to implement policies to deal with domestic problems even if these policies were wholly inappropriate for Europe as a whole.

Britain's exchange rate policy was always a major concern for Irish policy-makers. Between 1986 and 1989 the chancellor of the exchequer in the UK, Nigel Lawson, adopted the policy of sterling 'shadowing' the DM. Sterling was pegged unofficially in the range STG£1 = DM2.94 to DM3.00. According to Mrs Thatcher's autobiography, this policy was pursued without her knowledge: apparently it was not until Treasury officials highlighted the stability of the sterling/DM exchange rate that she confronted Lawson about this policy.

This exchange rate eventually proved unsustainable due to the excessive monetary expansion that Lawson had permitted, and by December 1989 sterling had fallen to DM2.80. This depreciation led to pressure for sterling to formally join the ERM. Thatcher remained entrenched in her view, and stated at the Madrid Summit in June 1989 that sterling would participate 'only when the time is right'. In this she was supported by her unofficial economic adviser, Professor Alan Walters (once described by *The Economist* as a 'transport economist'). Disagreement on this issue eventually led to Lawson's resignation in October 1989.

Thatcher finally brought sterling into the ERM, albeit only into the wide (± 6 per cent) band, on 8 October 1990. She argued that this would add credibility to the fight against inflation and she urged unions to accept modest wage increases in order to maintain UK price competitiveness. This proved to be one of her last important decisions as prime minister. She resigned on 22 November 1990.

Between 1990 and 1992 the British experience in the ERM was reasonably favourable. Inflation fell from 10.8 per cent in October 1990 to 4.3 per cent in August 1992, and short-term interest rates fell from 15 per cent to 10.2 per cent. However, the real growth rate remained low and by 1992 the economy was in recession.

Because of the commitment to fixed exchange rates, higher German interest rates were transmitted to the other EMS countries. Rising interest rates and appreciating exchange rates were painful for countries such as Italy, the UK and Spain, which were in recession. What these countries needed was lower interest rates and currency depreciation to kick-start their economies.

The conflict between the tight German monetary policy and the needs of the rest of Europe caused tension in the ERM. The lira, sterling and the peseta were vulnerable to a speculative attack in the early 1990s.

In 1992, despite massive intervention by central banks, a number of currencies quickly fell below their permitted ERM floors. Early in September, the Finnish markaa abandoned its unofficial peg to the German mark. Despite the Bank of Italy raising short-term interest rates to defend its currency, the lira was devalued by seven per cent on 12 September.

Speculators noticed that Britain, in particular, appeared to have entered the ERM at too high an exchange rate. In late summer 1992 the conviction grew that the sterling/DM central rate was unsustainable. Massive amounts of sterling were dumped on the foreign exchanges. On 16 September,

'Black Wednesday', the Bank of England spent an estimated £10 billion supporting sterling and the Bank of France and the Bundesbank bought sterling heavily. British interest rates were raised from 10 to 15 per cent.

Matters were not helped by an apparent personality clash between the prime minister, John Major, and the chancellor of the exchequer, Norman Lamont. At one stage during the crisis, Lamont arrived at 10 Downing Street to discuss with Major the option of devaluating sterling. However, Major refused to leave an unimportant meeting with a delegation of local authority councillors from northern England to talk to Lamont. The chancellor was forced to leave Downing Street without any clear instruction or mandate from his prime minister.

Lamont took the decision to suspend sterling's membership of the ERM on 16 September. Sterling depreciated by 15 per cent and interest rates in London fell from 15 per cent to eight per cent. Despite the large-scale intervention, the speculators had clearly won out. The Hungarian-born financier George Soros is estimated to have made a profit of £1 billion on 'Black Wednesday' and was dubbed 'the man who broke the Bank of England'. Soon afterwards, Lamont resigned as chancellor of the exchequer.

On the following day the Italian government withdrew the lira, and the Spanish peseta was devalued by five per cent. Pressure then switched to the French franc, the Danish krone, the Irish pound, the Portuguese escudo and the Spanish peseta. The Banque de France raised short-term interest rates to 13 per cent and, with the help of the German authorities, fought off the attack on the franc. The successful defence of the franc was the only achievement of central bank intervention during the crisis, but it was an important one because it preserved the commitment of France and Germany to continue to peg their currencies.

Pressure in the system gradually lessened in late 1992, especially after the peseta and the escudo were devalued in November and the Swedish krone (which had been informally pegged to the German mark) was floated.

In the UK, lower interest rates and the competitive gain from the devaluation were instrumental in making the UK economy's recovery from recession more rapid than that of the continental European countries. The Bank of England was allowed to pursue a 2.5 per cent inflation rate target free from political interference. (The independence of the bank was formalised by Tony Blair's new Labour government in 1999.) Since 1992, Britain's experience with a floating exchange rate has been favourable. On the tenth anniversary of 'Black Wednesday' commentators were wondering if 'White Wednesday' would not be a better label. The speculators, it seems, had given the British establishment a lesson in macroeconomics.

By early 1993 virtually all the currencies of the ERM had been devalued relative to the German mark. After a long and painful period of turbulence, the result was much the same as would have followed from a unilateral revaluation of the German currency in 1992. It is believed that the German authorities offered to revalue the mark in mid-1992, but the French and British authorities resisted this because they did not wish to see their currencies devalued. If this was the case, then this is another example of irrational pride in the nominal value of currencies overriding sound economic policy.

NOTE: The way speculators moved from one currency to another during the crisis of 1992–1993 is an interesting example of 'contagion'. Having profited from the vulnerability of one currency to an attack, speculators were quick to realise that other currencies were also vulnerable.

There was a period of stability in the first half of 1993 when the ERM appeared to have weathered the storm and settled back into a stable parity grid. But by the end of the summer, renewed speculative pressures emerged as markets came to view the Spanish peseta and French franc as over-valued. The EU finance ministers finally threw in the towel in August 1993 and announced that the ERM fluctuation margins were being widened to ± 15 per cent. To all intents and purposes the ERM was dismantled. It is important to note, however, that the French franc survived the crisis without devaluation and with its peg to the German mark intact. Although the franc came under heavy selling pressure on several occasions during the 1992–1993 crisis the central rate remained DM1 = FF3.35, the level that had been adopted at the beginning of 1987. The market rate between these currencies at times dipped below the intervention level but, by and large, remained within the ± 2.25 per cent fluctuation margin. Thus since 1987, the two key currencies in the ERM were kept within a target zone.

14.12 The Irish Pound and the Crisis of 1992–1993

Sterling's membership of the ERM was suspended on 16 September 1992 and the currency depreciated by 15 per cent on the foreign exchange markets. This development had a profound effect on Irish money markets.

From the decision to join the EMS in 1979, the sterling exchange rate had been the Achilles heel of Ireland's commitment to the ERM. In March 1983 the weakness of sterling prompted a three per cent devaluation of the Irish pound. A similar situation occurred in August 1986, when the Irish pound was devalued by eight per cent (the largest devaluation of any currency in the ERM up to then). These devaluations were reluctantly undertaken by the Irish authorities as a means of reconciling our ERM membership with our economic dependence on the UK market.

Not surprisingly, the foreign exchange markets formed the view that the Irish pound was likely to be devalued when sterling was weak. Hence, when sterling devalued in September 1992, funds flowed out of Ireland in anticipation of a devaluation of the Irish pound. Figure 14.2 shows that the Irish pound rose from Stg£0.94 to well over parity. (It hit Stg£1.105 on 6 October 1992 – the highest rate ever recorded.) Despite this severe misalignment, the government decided to resist devaluation.

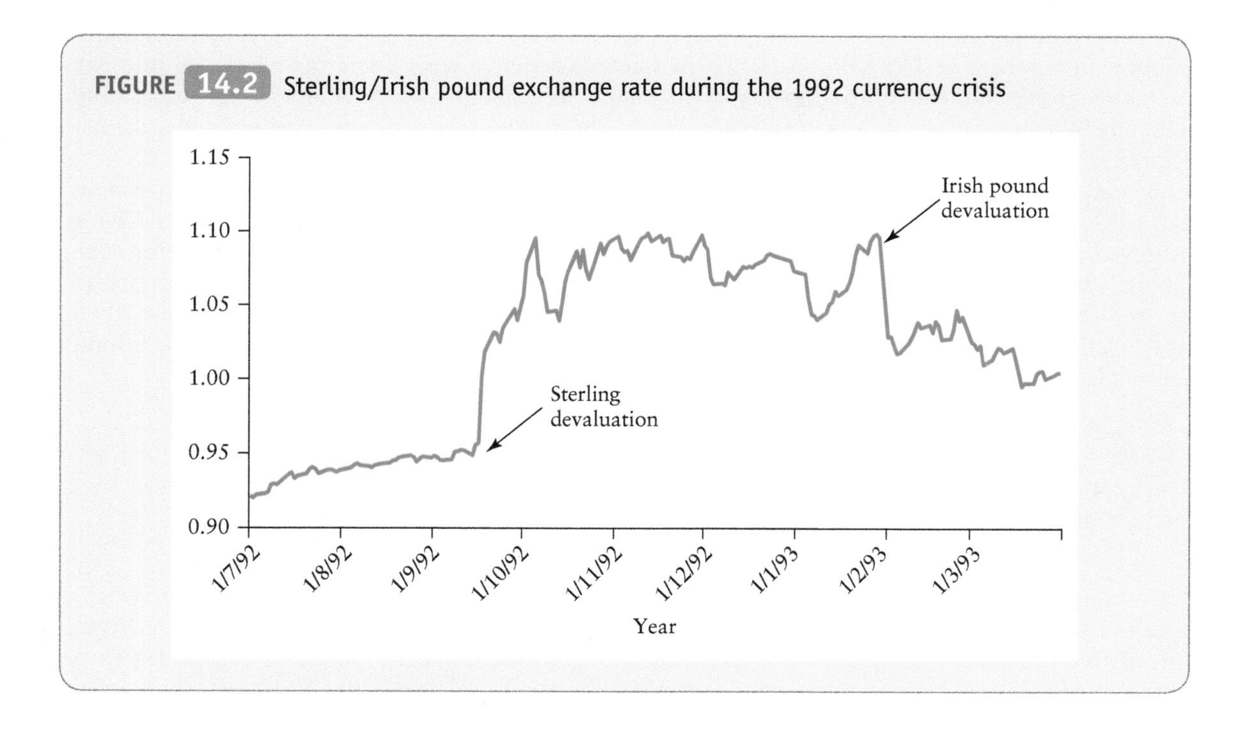

FIGURE 14.2 Sterling/Irish pound exchange rate during the 1992 currency crisis

NOTE: The so-called 'currency crisis war cabinet' comprised: Maurice O'Connell, Department of Finance; Maurice Doyle, Governor of the Central Bank; Adrian Kearns, National Treasury Management Agency (NTMA); Bertie Ahern, Minister for Finance; and Michael Somers, Chief Executive, NTMA.

It is estimated that well over a billion pounds flowed out of Irish financial markets in a few days in September 1992. This outflow of funds had the following effects.

- The Central Bank's external reserves fell from £3.05 billion at the end of August to £1.07 billion at the end of September, despite significant foreign borrowing.
- Short-term interest rates were raised to unprecedented heights to defend the currency from speculative attacks. Figure 14.3 shows that one-month inter-bank interest rates peaked at 57 per cent on 12 January 1993. However, the government was able to break the link between inter-bank rates and mortgage and commercial lending rates. As a result, mortgage and bank commercial interest rates increased by only three per cent. This separation of inter-bank and commercial lending rates was not sustainable in the medium term.
- Overnight interest rates on the euro–Irish pound market rose to 1,000 per cent. Central Bank lending to the money market increased from £74 million at the end of August to £1.8 billion at the end of September. Without this support, interest rates would have been much higher.
- The Central Bank was required to enforce exchange controls to prevent further speculation.

The combination of an overvalued currency and penal interest rates was seriously damaging the Irish economy. In a statement issued in January 1993, on the weekend before the devaluation, the government gave a long list of mostly spurious arguments against a devaluation:

- There was no guarantee that the devaluation would be accepted by the markets. In this case, there would be no significant inflow of funds and interest rates would not fall.

FIGURE 14.3 Nominal interest rates in Ireland during the 1992–1993 currency crisis

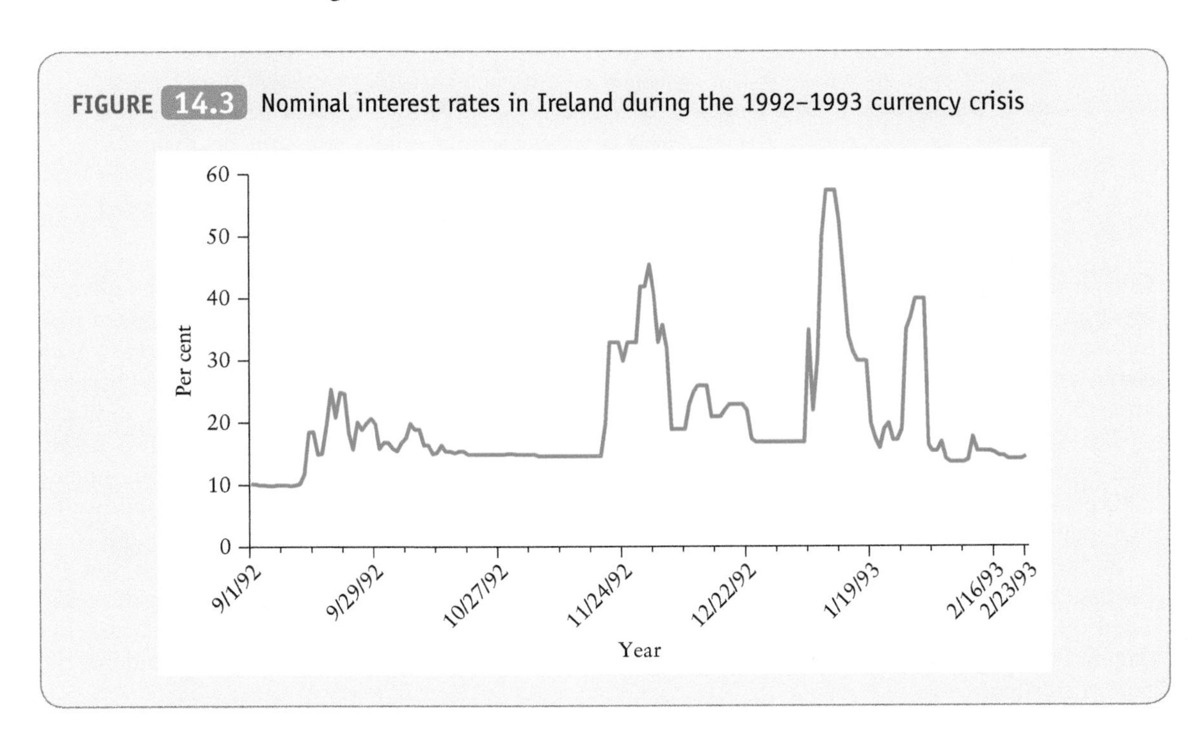

- The currency was not over-valued. As evidence of this the government pointed to the surplus on the trade account of the balance of payments.
- Speculators could not be allowed to destroy the ERM, which was regarded as the stepping-stone to EMU.
- The government wanted to break our dependence on the UK and become a hard-core EMS country.
- Devaluation was ineffective as it resulted in higher prices and only a short-term competitive gain.
- The rise in prices could lead to higher wage demands, resulting in a wage–price spiral. This would erode competitiveness over the medium term and have an adverse effect on growth and employment.
- The foreign debt would increase by £100 million for each one per cent the Irish pound was devalued. This would also increase the debt/GNP ratio and make it more difficult to achieve the Maastricht criteria for participation in EMU.
- The cost of servicing the foreign debt would increase by £8.5 million for each one per cent the Irish pound was devalued.
- The significant foreign debt of the state agencies would also increase. The higher cost of servicing this debt would lead to higher charges and price increases for the consumer.

To compensate for the loss of competitiveness caused by the sharp appreciation relative to sterling after September 1992, a 'Market Development Fund' was launched which paid £50 per job per week to firms affected by the devaluation of sterling.

The government received support for its policy from many quarters. The Irish Congress of Trade Unions, for example, presented the minister for finance with a list of names of banks and stockbrokers believed to be engaging in speculation, and referred to their actions as sabotage and unpatriotic.

Bishops joined in the denunciation of the speculators. Editorial writers warmed to the theme:

> *It is the duty of a sovereign government to defend its currency as it would its national territory. It is the final determinant of a nation's wealth. It represents the accumulated value of its industry, its productiveness, its labour. It is a statement of a country's worth, its reliability, its intrinsic economic soundness. . . . The long-term consequences of devaluation would be little short of catastrophic for the economy. Ireland would be consigned to the outer ring of monetary union, its currency most likely linked to the anaemic pound sterling. High inflation would be introduced once again. And none of this would guarantee even the short-term palliative of lower interest rates.* (*Irish Times*, 9 January 1993)

During the last weekend of January 1993, following a renewed weakness of sterling, the government announced that it was not prepared to guarantee the exchange rate risk on a proposed plan to borrow £1.1 billion of foreign currency. The plan was to channel this money to the building societies and to business to help alleviate the crisis. If the exchange rate were devalued by 10 per cent after the money was borrowed, this would have cost the government an immediate £100 million.

The government requested an emergency meeting of the EC monetary committee in Brussels. The committee met on Saturday 30 January, and at 7 p.m. a press release was issued announcing a 10 per cent devaluation of the Irish pound. This was the largest ever unilateral devaluation of a currency in the ERM.

In the aftermath of the devaluation, Irish politicians blamed our European partners, and the German authorities in particular, for their half-hearted support for the Irish pound during the crisis. The Bundesbank could have intervened on a scale that would have beaten off the speculators, but they did not regard the level of the Irish pound in the ERM as sustainable in view of the depreciation of sterling.

As can be seen from Figure 14.3, in the months after the devaluation the decline in Irish interest rates was dramatic. The fear that we would suffer a long-lasting penalty, in the form of a risk premium due to the possibility of further devaluations, proved unfounded. The size of the devaluation was sufficient to restore our competitive position vis-à-vis the UK and convince the markets that the Irish pound might appreciate in the medium term. Money flowed back into the country and confidence in the economy was restored. There was no resurgence in inflation, and for several years after the event we enjoyed a competitive gain.

It is estimated that the Central Bank of Ireland purchased £8,000 million Irish pounds during the defence of the exchange rate. This entailed using up the external reserves and engaging in foreign borrowing. It is estimated that the cost of intervening in the foreign exchange market during the crisis was between £350 million and £500 million.

Students may wonder why so much space has been devoted to these events of almost a generation ago. The answer is that, apart from historical interest, they provide important insights into the instability of the EU's first attempt to form a 'zone of monetary stability' by linking exchange rates between member states.

The experiment ended in tears. It contributed to the evolution of a two-tier EU, as Britain is now firmly committed to staying aloof from any further attempts at monetary union. It showed that a system of fixed exchange rates in the absence of strict enforcement of policy co-ordination does not work and that monetary union without fiscal union is impossible.

14.13 Lessons for Today

In Ireland after 2008, a fall in the real exchange rate, that is, the nominal exchange rate adjusted for relative prices, was urgently required to restore the loss of competitiveness that had occurred during the boom and to help us out of the recession. But as we no longer had an independent Irish pound, the real exchange rate adjustment required a fall in the Irish wage and price level relative to that of our trading partners. In this we resembled Great Britain in the 1920s, pegged to the Gold Standard at a rate that made the country uncompetitive and called for a reduction in its price level.

For a period early in the current recession the Irish price level and the Irish nominal wages rate did fall. From a peak of 108 in 2008 the Irish Consumer Price Index fell to a low of 100 in January 2010. But by mid-2012 it was back up to 105. The fall in the Harmonised Index of Consumer Prices was even less impressive – from a peak of 110 to a low of 105 and back to 109 by mid-2012.

Because the national price level is influenced by indirect taxes and includes many non-traded services and regulated or administered prices, wages are more important than prices as an index of competitiveness. The index of hourly earnings in manufacturing peaked around 106 at the end of 2009 (2008 = 100) and was stable at 102 in 2011. Even in the construction sector, where employment has collapsed in the wake of the building bust, wage rates declined only by a little over six per cent between 2008 and 2011. The signs are that in 2012 wage rates are stable or even rising again.

While Ireland's modest deflation occurred at a time when prices and wages in other European countries were still rising, the 'internal devaluation' was not very dramatic, despite the crisis level of unemployment. Moreover, it appears to have stalled since the end of 2011, despite the fact that the unemployment rate is still climbing. In fact, Ireland is now (mid-2012) enjoying a more significant gain in competitiveness vis-à-vis the USA and the UK, due to the sharp fall of the euro relative to sterling and the dollar, than it enjoyed on foot of the domestic deflation. This sheds light on the relative ease of adjustment under fixed and floating exchange rate arrangements.

14.14 Key Terms and Concepts

In this chapter we discussed:

- the operation of a fixed exchange rate system
- the official external reserves and their composition
- the automatic adjustment mechanism and sterilisation
- the importance of policy co-ordination
- the limitations to central bank intervention on foreign exchange markets
- the question of the best exchange rate regime
- the Gold Standard
- the Bretton Woods system
- the European snake
- the EMS experience and the currency crisis of 1992–1993
- lessons for today from our experience with a pegged exchange rate.

CHAPTER 15

Inflation and Interest Rates in Open Economies

15.1 Introduction

In this chapter we discuss the interactions between inflation, interest rates and exchange rates. We begin by outlining the theory of purchasing power parity (PPP). This leads into a discussion of real exchange rates and other indicators of international competitiveness. We then explain the relevance of PPP theory under both fixed and flexible exchange rates. This is followed by a discussion of the links between interest rates and exchange rates.

15.2 Purchasing Power Parity (PPP)

The theory of PPP is based on the idea that the prices of similar goods, expressed in a common currency, should be the same in all countries. PPP means equal value for money for goods and services in different countries. Using the euro area (EA) and the USA for the purpose of illustration, the strong version of PPP, referred to as *absolute* PPP, can be stated as:

$$P_{EA} \times e = P_{US} \tag{1}$$

where P_{EA} and P_{US} are the EA and US price levels, respectively, and e is the nominal exchange rate (expressed as the dollar price of a euro). This states that euro area prices equal US prices when converted using the current exchange rate. Put another way, if PPP holds, prices in the EA and USA, converted at the market exchange rate, are equal.

The reason why EA and US price levels, expressed in a common currency, should be equal is based on the *law of one price*. This refers to the tendency for arbitrage to ensure that the same price will prevail for a good everywhere in the world. This tendency depends on the arbitrage of internationally traded goods, which occurs when people take advantage of the opportunity of making a profit by buying cheap in one market and selling dear in another.

Suppose, for example, a pair of Levi jeans costs \$30 in New York and €30 in Dublin. If the exchange rate were €1 = \$1, PPP holds and a person would be indifferent between buying in Dublin or New York. If, however, the exchange rate were €1 = \$1.5, the New York price is much lower when converted to euro. In this case, traders could make a profit by buying in New York and selling in Dublin. The increased demand would drive up the price in New York and the increased supply would drive the Dublin price down. This mechanism should ensure that the prices in the two cities converge.

An illustration of how the prices of internationally traded goods tend to equalise is provided by the Irish experience in the 1980s. Due to movements in the exchange rate and higher rates of indirect taxation in the Republic, a whole range of goods, including petrol, alcohol and electrical appliances, became cheaper (in Irish pounds) in Northern Ireland than south of the border. Excursions were organised throughout the Republic for shoppers to go to Newry and Belfast in search of bargains. Similarly, people living in border areas bought all their petrol and drink in the North. Garages and supermarkets in the Republic, unable to cut their prices because of high taxes, went out of business and those in the North expanded. The Irish minister for finance was forced to reduce indirect taxes on selected items in the Republic.

This was an example of arbitrage forcing prices to converge. It simply was not possible for major price discrepancies to persist north and south of the border. There are, however, many factors that impede the operation of the law of one price and ensure absolute PPP does not hold. These include:

- *Differences in income levels.* Differences in the standard of living, and changes in the standard of living, as measured by national income or GDP, play an important role in explaining why price differences persist. The explanation for this is known as the Balassa–Samuelson effect (discussed in section 15.6 below).
- *Macroeconomic policy.* Different macroeconomic policies can result in countries being in different phases of the business cycle. This, in turn, can influence relative prices over the short run.
- *Transportation costs.* It takes time and money to shop across national borders and to transport goods. In the euro area these costs should decrease over time due to euro credit cards and virtual shopping on the internet. One of the reasons for introducing the euro was to increase price transparency within the euro area.
- *Differences in national preferences.* Market conditions and prices may also be affected by cultural and linguistic preferences. The price of certain types of food will be higher in countries where they are rare and considered a delicacy than in countries where they are part of the ordinary person's diet. Someone once quipped that international marketing consists of persuading yuppies in one country to consume ordinary products from a far-away country – at a high price, of course.
- *Trade restrictions.* Tariffs and quotas drive a wedge between prices in different countries. Even under the European Single Market, it is still that case that when you import wine or beer into Ireland from the Continent you must demonstrate to the customs that it is for personal consumption and not for re-sale.
- *Indirect tax differences.* If you import a car into Ireland you must pay a vehicle registration tax (VRT) of over 20 per cent of the Irish retail price. But since the retail price already contains value added tax (VAT), the VRT is a tax on a tax and it makes the retail price of Irish cars among the highest in Europe, even though the net-of-tax price is one of the lowest.
- *Exchange rate fluctuations.* Firms do not immediately adjust prices as exchange rates fluctuate. This is no longer a factor for countries participating in the euro area.
- *Differences in market structures.* Generally, perfectly competitive markets are perceived to be the most efficient as they result in optimal prices. However, in most cases, manufacturers have some form of control over the market and can influence local prices. Firms can influence the market through product differentiation (a VW car sold in Germany is somewhat different from the model sold in Ireland), after-sales service, regulating distribution networks and market entry, strategic price setting and collusive behaviour, to mention a few.

Traded and non-traded goods

PPP is only expected to operate for traded goods. An increasing proportion of consumer expenditure is on non-traded services, such as personal services – hotel rooms, restaurants – and health care. It is quite possible for prices in non-traded items and indeed traded goods to differ between countries and even between regions of a country.

15.3 The PPP Exchange Rate

While PPP theory can be traced back to the sixteenth century – to studies at the University of Salamanca in Spain – the term 'purchasing power parity' was first coined by the Swedish economist Gustav Cassel (1866–1945) and popularised by Keynes. Cassel wrote that the exchange rate 'between two countries is represented by the ... purchasing power of money in one country and the other. I propose to call this parity "The Purchasing Power Parity".'

As we discussed in Chapter 14, between 1870 and World War I, the world's major currencies had been fixed to gold and therefore to each other. At the start of the war the Gold Standard broke down. In the aftermath of the war many countries attempted to re-establish the system. Given that prices had risen very unevenly in different countries during the war years, the issue that concerned Cassel was to calculate the appropriate exchange rate on which to re-establish the Gold Standard. Cassel proposed using PPP theory to derive the correct exchange rates. This involved calculating the exchange rate that equated prices in the various countries. For example, rearranging equation (1) above, we can define the *PPP exchange rate* as:

$$e_{PPP} = \frac{P_{US}}{P_{EA}} \qquad (2)$$

If the US price level were twice the euro area level, one euro should be worth \$2. This is the exchange rate that ensures that PPP holds.

When Britain went back on the Gold Standard in 1925, Winston Churchill considered it a matter of national pride that sterling should re-establish the old pre-war parity with gold. However, since Britain had experienced much more inflation than the USA since 1914, sterling was over-valued and trying to adjust to an over-valued currency contributed to recession in the UK.

Big Mac parities

Since 1986 *The Economist* magazine has had fun publishing what it calls the 'Big Mac Index'. This is based simply on a comparison of what it costs to buy a Big Mac in various cities round the world. The calculation involves converting local prices into dollars at the prevailing market exchange rate. As an example of how to derive the Big Mac Index, consider the following data for September 2012:

- market exchange rate: €1 = \$1.29
- Dublin price of a Big Mac = €3.80
- New York price of a Big Mac = \$4.33

Convert the Dublin price to dollars at the market exchange rate:

$$€3.80 \times \$1.29 = \$4.90$$

This shows that Big Macs are 13.2 per cent more expensive in Dublin than in USA at the market exchange rate:

$$\frac{(4.90 - 4.33)}{4.33} \times 100 = 13.2$$

The exchange rate implied by the Big Mac PPP is:

$$e_{PPP} = \frac{4.33}{3.80} = 1.14$$

PPP would hold if €1 was worth \$1.14.

The difference between actual and Big Mac PPP exchange rates is:

$$\frac{(1.29 - 1.14)}{1.14} \times 100 = 13.2 \text{ per cent}$$

This calculation leads us to conclude that, with reference to the Irish price level, the euro is over-valued by 13.2 per cent relative to the dollar.

NOTE: To get up-to-date measures of the Big Mac Index, go to: www.economist.com/blogs/graphicdetail/2012/07/daily-chart-17

Since it was first published by *The Economist* in 1986 the Big Mac Index has received a lot of attention. The rationale for the index is that McDonald's offers a fast food service that has a high labour content and incurs a range of local costs, such as rents, electricity and waste management. As a result, local prices should reflect local wages and other costs fairly sensitively. Converting the prices to a common currency (the dollar) allows us to see whether the market exchange rate is aligned with relative costs and prices. The Big Mac Index has stood up well to criticism and earned grudging respect from academics. Currencies that appear over-valued according to the Big Mac Index seem to revert to their PPP level over time.

15.4 PPP and the Real Exchange Rate

The *real exchange rate* (ε) is the ratio of domestic and foreign prices expressed in a common currency. If in equation (1) above, the US price level is brought over to the left-hand side, we can write:

$$\varepsilon = \frac{(P_{EA} \times e)}{P_{US}} \tag{3}$$

The real exchange rate is the nominal exchange rate adjusted for relative prices. The level of the real exchange rate is less important than its movement over time, which provides a measure of whether a country is becoming more or less price competitive relative to its trading partners.

- A rise in the real exchange rate implies a loss of competitiveness because either the domestic price has risen relative to foreign price and/or the nominal exchange rate has appreciated.
- Conversely, a fall in the real exchange rate implies a gain in competitiveness, which could be due to a fall in the domestic price relative to foreign price level and/or a depreciation of the nominal exchange rate.

The real exchange rate is normally expressed as an index set equal to 100 in the base year. If PPP holds over time the real exchange rate will be constant. Increases in the euro area price level will be offset by equal falls in the euro exchange rate and PPP will continue to hold.

Evidence from the Irish economy

We begin by presenting calculations for the Irish real exchange rate up to 2012. Figure 15.1 shows Ireland's real exchange rates relative to the sterling and the dollar from 1991 to 2012. Up to 1999 we use the sterling/Irish pound and dollar/Irish pound exchange rates; after that date we use the euro exchange rate to derive the Irish pound exchange rates.

Between 1992 and 2000 both real exchange rate indexes fell, suggesting an improvement in Ireland's competitive position. During this period the Irish economy grew rapidly. The balance of payments current account was in surplus from 1993 to 1998 (see Chapter 13).

However, after 2000 both real exchange rate indexes increased, showing a deterioration in Ireland's competitive position. Between October 2000 and April 2008, the sterling index rose 55 per cent and the dollar index 97 per cent. This was due to the appreciation of the nominal euro exchange rate and the rise in the relative price level in Ireland. While rapid growth continued, the current account surpluses disappeared and after 2005 large deficits were recorded. Following the economic crash in 2008, both indexes fell due to deflation in Ireland and a weaker euro.

Despite much short-term volatility, the real exchange rate between Ireland and the USA was almost exactly the same in 2012 as it had been in 1991. The relative stability of the real exchange rate over the long run supports the PPP hypothesis – the nominal exchange rate has moved in line

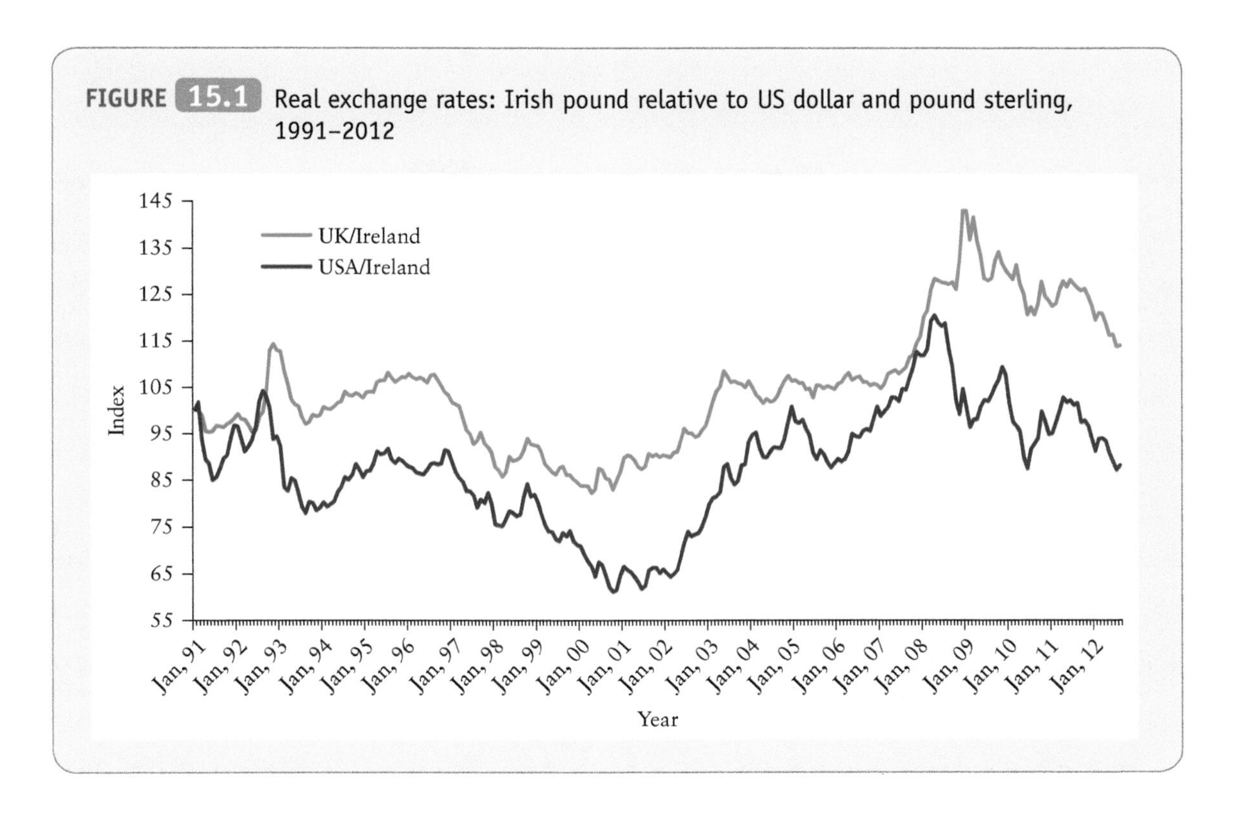

FIGURE 15.1 Real exchange rates: Irish pound relative to US dollar and pound sterling, 1991–2012

with relative prices and the real exchange rate has tended to revert to a stable long-run average. This is called the property of *mean reversion* and it is an implication of PPP. But the Irish experience also shows that there can be significant deviations from absolute PPP in the short run.

NOTE: A real exchange rate index only monitors movements in competitiveness relative to the base year. Its level at a point in time has no significance. The index can be set equal to 100 in any year. The series in Figure 15.1 is based on 1991 = 100, but this does not imply that Ireland and the USA or Ireland and Britain were exactly competitive in that year. We could easily rebase the series to another year. This would not affect the way the graphs move over time.

The real exchange rate does not bring out the dynamics underlying changes in competitiveness. We cannot tell if changes in the real exchange rate are due to movements in the nominal exchange rate or relative prices. An alternative presentation, which gets around this problem, is to graph the nominal exchange rate against relative prices. For example, consider again the absolute PPP relationship (equation (1) above):

$$P_{EA} \times e = P_{US}$$

Taking P_{EA} over to the left-hand side we have the PPP exchange rate:

$$e = \frac{P_{US}}{P_{EA}}$$

If, over time, the trend in the exchange rate is similar to the trend in relative prices, the real exchange rate will be constant. If the graph of the exchange rate rises above the graph of relative prices, this indicates a loss of competitiveness from an Irish perspective. Conversely, if the

FIGURE 15.2 Exchange rate and relative prices: Ireland and the USA

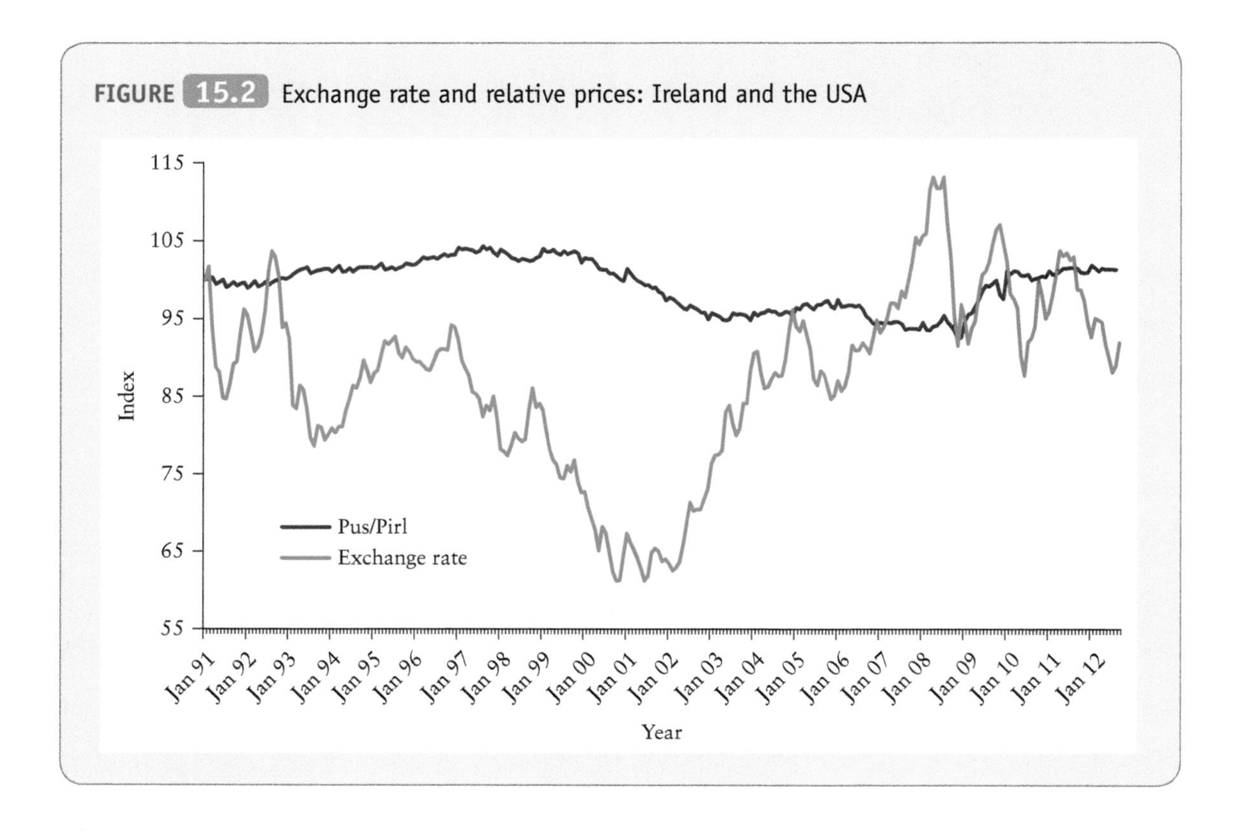

graph of the exchange rate line falls below the relative price graph, this indicates a gain in Irish competitiveness.

Figure 15.2 illustrates the Irish experience relative to the USA from 1991 to 2012. It can be seen that the nominal exchange rate is much more volatile than the relative price series. Up to 2000, the Irish price fell relative to US price, and Ireland experienced a gain in competitiveness. However, due to the appreciation of the euro, all this gain was removed by 2005. In general, movements in the real exchange rate are primarily driven by movements in the nominal exchange rate.

The Irish experience suggests that absolute PPP is a poor guide to the behaviour of exchange rates in the short run. This is not surprising. Persistent deviations from PPP have been documented in studies of the major industrial countries. One study concluded after a review of the literature that the hypothesis that arbitrage quickly equates goods prices internationally has probably been rejected more decisively by empirical evidence than any other hypothesis in the history of economics.

However, this does not detract from the force of the theory as a theory of exchange rates in the longer run. To be convinced of this, just ask yourself what would happen if the exchange rate between the US dollar and the euro were roughly 10:1 instead of 1:1 and the price levels in the two regions remained as they are.

15.5 Harmonised Competitiveness Indicators

It would be useful to have a single statistic that summarises a currency's external value. The summary statistic that used to be most widely used for this purpose is the *trade-weighted exchange rate index* (TWERI), also referred to as the *effective exchange rate index*. This is an

TABLE 15.1 Trade-weighted exchange rate index (hypothetical data)

Country	Trade weight	Bilateral exchange rate index		Trade-weighted exchange rate index	
		2012	2013	2012	2013
	1	2	3	4 = 1 × 2	5 = 1 × 3
USA	0.23	100.0	90.0	23.2	20.9
UK	0.14	100.0	95.0	13.9	13.2
Euro area	0.37	100.0	100.0	36.7	36.7
China	0.03	100.0	90.0	3.1	2.8
Rest of world	0.23	100.0	96.0	23.1	22.2
Total	1.00			100.1	95.8

Note: When calculating the HCI (see text) a geometric average is taken, not an arithmetic average as shown in this illustration.

index of the average value of the euro in terms of the other main international currencies. Each of the currencies in the calculation is weighted by its importance in Irish international trade ('trade-weighted').

In Table 15.1 we show how the trade-weighted exchange rate index is calculated. We use approximate weights based on the pattern of trade shown in Chapter 13 (Table 13.2). The first step in calculating this index is to express bilateral exchange rates as indices. The exchange rates are set equal to 100 in a base year (2012) and the index for subsequent years is calculated with reference to this base. For example, if the $/€ exchange rate went from $1.25 in 2012 to $1.125 in 2013, the exchange rate index would fall from 100 to 90, reflecting the fact that the euro had become cheaper in dollars. Hypothetical exchange rates for 2013 are given for each country or region in column 3 of Table 15.1.

The Irish trade-weighted exchange rate index is calculated by multiplying each exchange rate index by its trade-weight and summing over all countries. Note that the euro exchange rate against the euro area cannot change. On the bottom line in column 5 we see that the trade-weighted exchange rate index fell to 95.8 in 2013. This indicates that the trade-weighted average value of the 'Irish euro' depreciated by 4.2 per cent over the year. (By 'Irish euro' we mean the value of the euro from an Irish trade perspective.)

A new set of indices called the *harmonised competitiveness indicators* (HCI) is now published by the ECB (in collaboration with the Central Bank of Ireland) for all euro area countries. This series goes back to 1995 and includes 57 or 37 trading partners (depending on the index), whereas the old trade-weighted competitiveness indicator had only 10 trading partners. Four versions (one nominal and three real) of the HCI are published quarterly or monthly.

Figure 15.3 shows the nominal and two of the real HCIs for Ireland from 1995 to 2012. The nominal HCI only takes into account bilateral nominal exchange rates. No adjustment is made for movements in relative prices or costs. Two measures of the real HCI are shown. The first is calculated by adjusting the nominal exchange rates for movements in relative prices as measured by the Consumer Price Index (CPI). The second real HCI adjusts nominal exchange rates by movements in producer prices (based on a narrower range of countries). While producer prices are closer than consumer prices to traded prices, they suffer from the limitation that they completely exclude services. Again, a rise in the HCI indicates a loss of competitiveness and a fall indicates a gain (O'Brien 2010).

These measures of competitiveness showed that Ireland's competitiveness improved up to 2001, followed by a significant loss between 2001 and mid-2008, confirming the trends shown in Figure 15.1 above. Since then there has been a significant competitive gain.

FIGURE 15.3 Nominal and real harmonised competitiveness indicators, 1995–2012

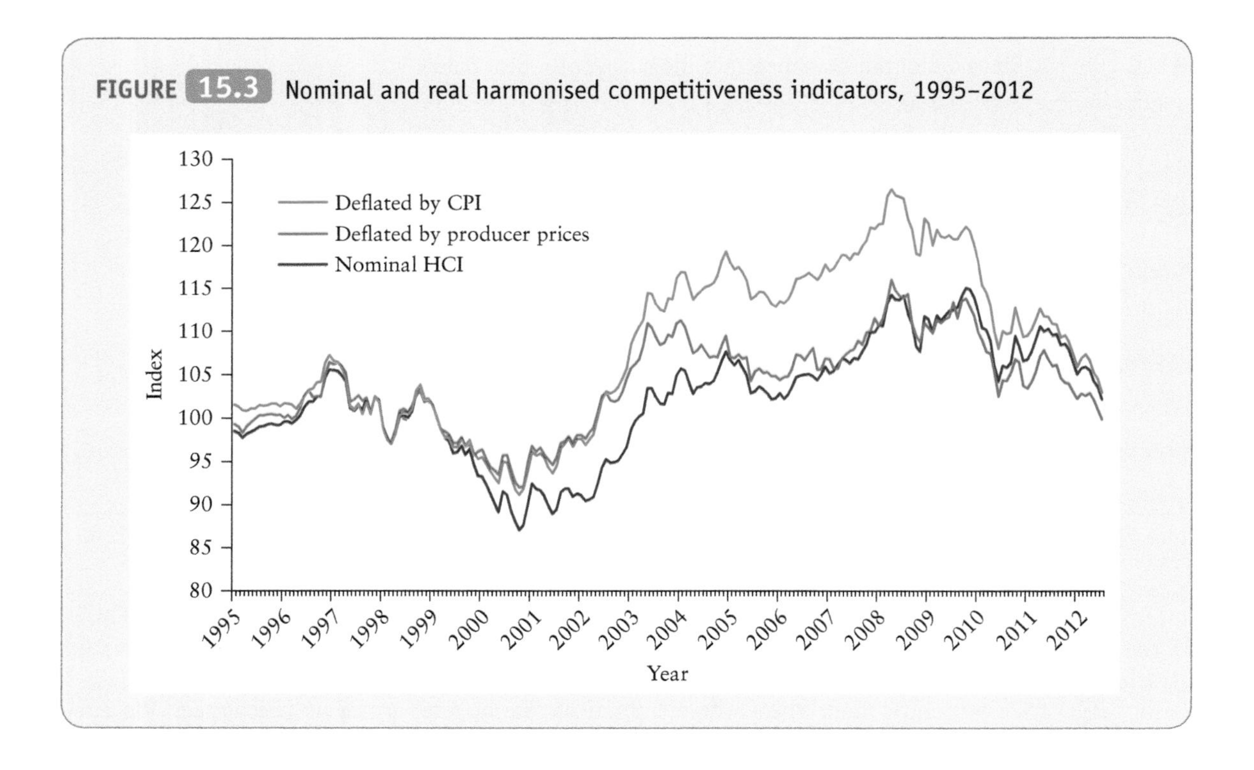

The two real HCIs display the same long-run trends. Between 1995 and 2003 and from 2006 to 2012 they moved closely in sync. However, between 2003 and 2005 the index based on consumer prices rose more rapidly than that based on producer prices. This suggests that there was relatively high inflation in some component of the Irish CPI, perhaps service prices, that was not reflected in producer prices. After 2005 the two real HCIs converge and move closely in sync.

A very important point to note is the close correlation between the real HCI based on producer prices and the nominal HCI. Recall that the nominal HCI is simply a weighted average of the nominal exchange rate between the euro and the currencies of the countries outside the euro area with which we trade. Changes in this index are totally determined by the movement of the euro against other currencies – what is known as the *external value of the euro.*

The message from Figure 15.3 is that Ireland's competitiveness depends heavily on the value of its currency (which is now the euro) relative to other currencies. The weights in Table 15.1 highlight the importance of dollar/euro and sterling/euro exchange rates for Irish international competitiveness. The improvement in our competitiveness from mid-2008 to mid-2012 owed a lot to the weakness of the euro on world currency markets and relatively little to lower inflation in Ireland. This point has immense importance for the costs and benefits that accrue to us as members of the EMU currency union.

A third real HCI, which is published every quarter, deflates the nominal exchange rates by *relative unit labour costs*. This measures the labour cost of producing a unit of output in Ireland relative to its trading partners. This allows for the trend in relative wages and the trend in labour productivity as well as movements in the nominal exchange rate. By taking all these factors into account, this real HCI provides an indication of the competitiveness of the Irish labour force. This is shown in Figure 15.4. It is reassuring to note that much the same picture of the trends in competitiveness emerge from all three real HCIs.

FIGURE 15.4 Real harmonised competitiveness indicator deflated by whole economy unit labour costs

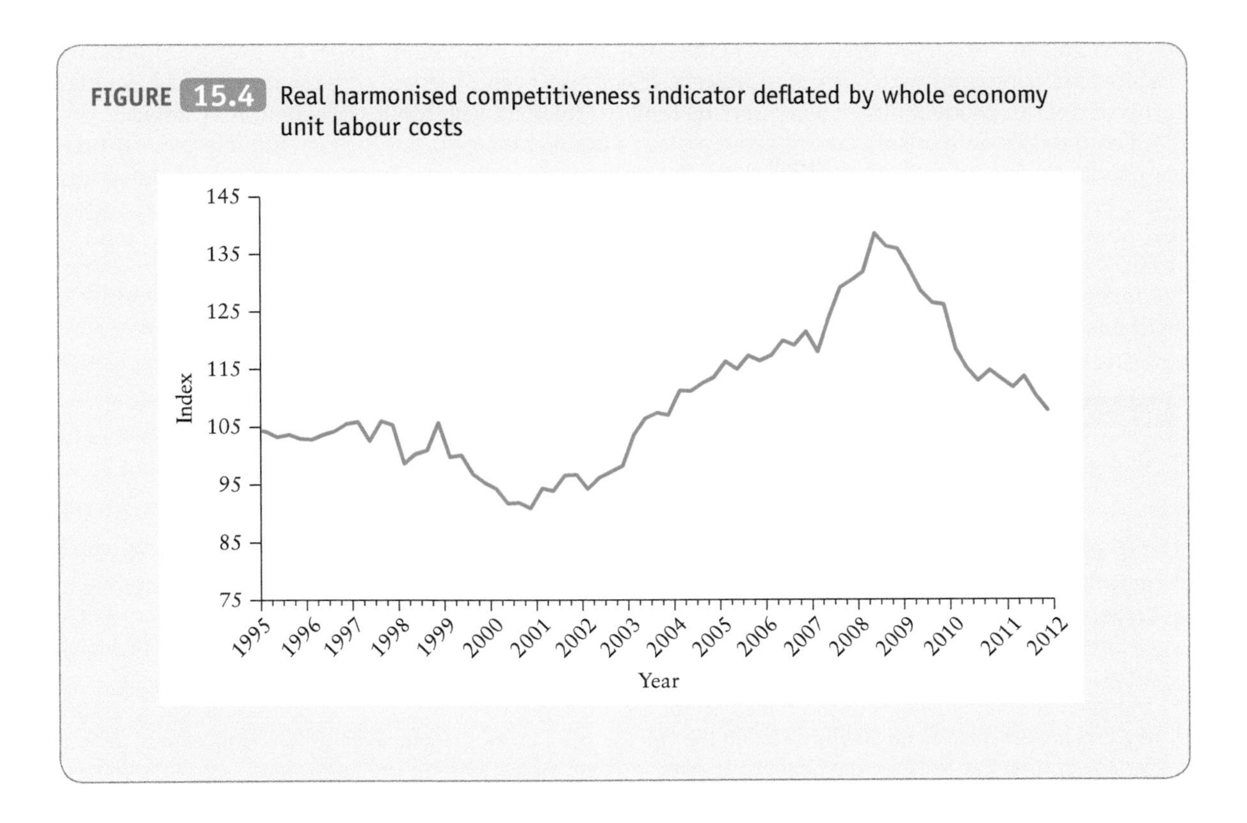

15.6 Relative PPP

Absolute PPP is often referred to as the hard version of PPP because, for the reasons mentioned earlier, prices are unlikely to be the same in different countries at any particular time. An alternative version of PPP is *relative PPP*. This weaker version of PPP expresses equation (1) in terms of percentage rates of change. That is, differentiating equation (1) above gives:

$$\pi_{EA} + \Delta e = \pi_{US} \tag{4}$$

where π_{EA} and π_{US} are the rates of inflation in the euro area and the USA respectively and Δe is the percentage change in the nominal exchange rate. Equation (4) allows for the possibility that prices in different countries may not be at the same level in any particular period, but it assumes that the rate of change in price levels, adjusted for exchange rate changes, should be similar over time.

However, there are reasons why even this weaker version of PPP may not hold. First, due to different macroeconomic policies and other factors, countries may be in different phases of the business cycle. At the end of the 1990s the Irish economy was booming while the German economy was in recession. As a consequence, inflation was relatively high in Ireland, but because we shared a common currency with the rest of the euro area there was no exchange rate depreciation to offset this.

We turn now to discuss an important theory according to which PPP may not hold even over the longer run.

The Balassa–Samuelson effect

It has been observed that prices are much lower in poorer or less developed countries than in rich countries. Labour-intensive services are much cheaper in rural Turkey than in the centre of London. Prices of services can differ even between two cities that are only a few miles apart, for example Bratislava in Slovakia compared with Vienna in Austria. It has also been observed that countries that have high growth rates in productivity in some sectors tend to experience high rates of inflation in services.

The Balassa–Samuelson theory attempts to explain these two findings by linking growth rates in productivity to non-traded prices. Bela Balassa was a Hungarian-born economist at Johns Hopkins University and Paul Samuelson was a Nobel Prize-winner at MIT. Working separately, these economists found that countries with high productivity growth in the traded goods sector tend to experience relatively high inflation rates. If two countries experienced different rates of growth of productivity, these countries would have different inflation rates and the relative PPP hypothesis will not hold. Box 15.1 gives a more detailed explanation of the Balassa–Samuelson effect.

Box 15.1 The Balassa–Samuelson effect

On the basis of a few straightforward assumptions it can be shown that:

$$\pi_{NT} - \pi_T = \Delta PROD_T - \Delta PROD_{NT} \qquad (5)$$

The equation states that if the growth in productivity in the traded sector ($\Delta PROD_T$) is greater than the growth of productivity in the non-traded sector ($\Delta PROD_{NT}$), non-traded inflation (π_{NT}) will rise relative to traded inflation (π_T).

Briefly, the argument is that the growth in productivity in the traded goods sector results in higher wages. However, because the higher wages are offset by the rise in productivity, traded prices remain unchanged. The higher wages in the traded sector are, however, transmitted to the non-traded goods sector. Workers are assumed to be mobile between the two sectors and, as a result, wage differentials cannot get too far out of line. But because the opportunities to increase productivity in the non-traded sector are limited, the higher wages are passed on in higher non-traded prices.

By definition, the overall inflation rate is the sum of the inflation rates in the traded and non-traded sectors:

$$\pi = \alpha\pi_T - (1 - \alpha)\pi_{NT} \qquad (6)$$

where π is the overall consumer price inflation and α is the weight showing the contribution of traded and non-traded inflation to overall inflation. From this equation, it is clear that the rise in non-traded inflation results in an increase in the overall inflation rate.

By adding and subtracting π_T to equation (6) and rearranging, we can rewrite the equation as:

$$\pi = \pi_T - (1 - \alpha)(\pi_{NT} - \pi_T) \qquad (7)$$

Substituting in equation (5) above we have:

$$\pi = \pi_T - (1 - \alpha)(\Delta PROD_T - \Delta PROD_{NT}) \qquad (8)$$

A similar calculation can be done for country B.

$$\pi^B = \pi^B{}_T - (1 - \alpha)(\Delta PROD^B{}_T - \Delta PROD^B{}_{NT}) \qquad (9)$$

Subtracting equation (9) from (8) we obtain the following equation:

$$\pi - \pi^B = (1 - \alpha)(\Delta PROD_T - \Delta PROD^B{}_T) \qquad (10)$$

This equation states that the inflation differential between two countries will depend on the difference in the growth in productivity in the traded goods sectors. High relative productivity results in high relative inflation. Pulling the strands of the theory together, the high productivity in the traded goods sector results in higher wages and higher prices in the non-traded sector. This results in a higher overall inflation rate. Hence, differences in productivity are reflected in different rates of inflation between countries.

There is some evidence to suggest that this type of effect has been in operation in Ireland in recent years as more and more multinational companies established here. An example would be where a hi-tech multinational like Intel, using the latest technology, achieves a high level of labour productivity (the number of computer chips produced per day and the power of these chips). Accordingly workers at Intel command high rates of pay. If, say, a dentist decides that his or her pay should rise in line with what is happening at Intel, dental charges will have to be raised because the dentist can see only so many patients per day and so the opportunity to increase productivity is very limited. The increase in the dental charges will feed through to the overall CPI. Services like dentistry or haircutting do not benefit from the rate of productivity growth that can be achieved in modern manufacturing plants. Hence, if dentists and barbers are to enjoy the same rate of increase in their living standards as workers in manufacturing, they will have to raise their prices more rapidly than the prices of manufacturing goods are rising.

15.7 PPP Under Flexible Exchange Rates

Rearranging equation (4) above we can write:

$$\Delta e = \pi_{US} - \pi_{EA} \tag{11}$$

Equation (11) states that changes in the nominal exchange rate will be offset by differentials in inflation rates between countries. If, for example, the rate of inflation in the euro area exceeds the US rate, the euro should depreciate.

$$\pi_{US} < \pi_{EA} \Rightarrow \downarrow \Delta e$$

Conversely, if euro area inflation is less than US inflation, the euro should appreciate:

$$\pi_{US} > \pi_{EA} \Rightarrow \uparrow \Delta e$$

Hence, PPP theory implies that price or inflation differentials are the most important determinant of exchange rates. Countries with low inflation, such as the USA, will generally have strong, appreciating currencies. Conversely, countries with high inflation rates will have weak or depreciating currencies.

History shows that relative PPP is a good general guide to the behaviour of exchange rates. When exchange rates are free to adjust, it is invariably true that high inflation currencies tend to depreciate sharply relative to low inflation currencies.

To take some extreme examples, in 1921 the dollar/German mark exchange rate was $1 = Reichsmark 270, but by October 1922 the mark had depreciated to $1 = Reichsmark 25,000 million, reflecting the hyperinflation in Germany. In the early 1990s, hyperinflation in Russia and many of the former socialist economies, such as Yugoslavia and Ukraine, rendered their currencies worthless on foreign exchanges. At the beginning of 1992 there were 300 roubles to the dollar; by the end of 1998 there were 6,000. This reflected high inflation in Russia relative to the USA. The same is true of the Latin American countries that have experienced hyperinflation: their currencies have become worthless on the foreign exchange markets.

15.8 PPP Under Fixed Exchange Rates

Fixed exchange rate systems were discussed in Chapter 14. For a small economy with a fixed exchange rate, PPP becomes a theory of inflation. Suppose that instead of comparing the euro area with the USA, we instead compare the Czech Republic with the euro area. Rearranging equation (11) so that the Czech Republic plays the role of the small country 'price taker' we can write:

$$\pi_{CZ} = \pi_{EA} - \Delta e \tag{12}$$

where π_{CZ} is the inflation rate in the Czech Republic and Δe is the percentage change in the crown/euro exchange rate. If the exchange rate is constant ($\Delta e = 0$), Czech inflation should equal euro area inflation. Because of the smallness of the Czech economy relative to the euro area, Czech firms are in general price-takers with little or no market power. Hence, the causation must run from euro area to Czech inflation. This view of inflation is very important in small open economies all around the world.

The theory is also very relevant for those countries participating in EMU. When the national exchange rates were irrevocably fixed at the start of 1999, the Δe term in equation (12) went to zero between all the countries that joined. If relative PPP held, the inflation rates across all the euro area countries should have converged. This was perceived as being one of the important benefits to emanate from EMU membership.

Inflation in the euro area

Adopting the euro should allow formerly inflation-prone countries to enjoy a degree of price stability that they were unable to attain on their own. According to relative PPP theory, the inflation rate in the smaller euro area countries should converge to the rate in the larger countries or the average of the euro area.

The magnitude of this gain depends on how successful the ECB and national governments are in controlling inflation. It is argued that relying on the strength and anti-inflation reputation of the ECB is more beneficial for smaller countries than relying on their own national central banks to maintain low inflation.

Figure 15.5 shows the inflation rate in each of the euro area countries from 1979 to 2010 and Figure 15.6 shows the mean and standard deviation of these rates. Back in the early 1980s, at the commencement of the EMS, inflation rates were both high and divergent. European countries

FIGURE 15.5 Inflation rates in the euro area

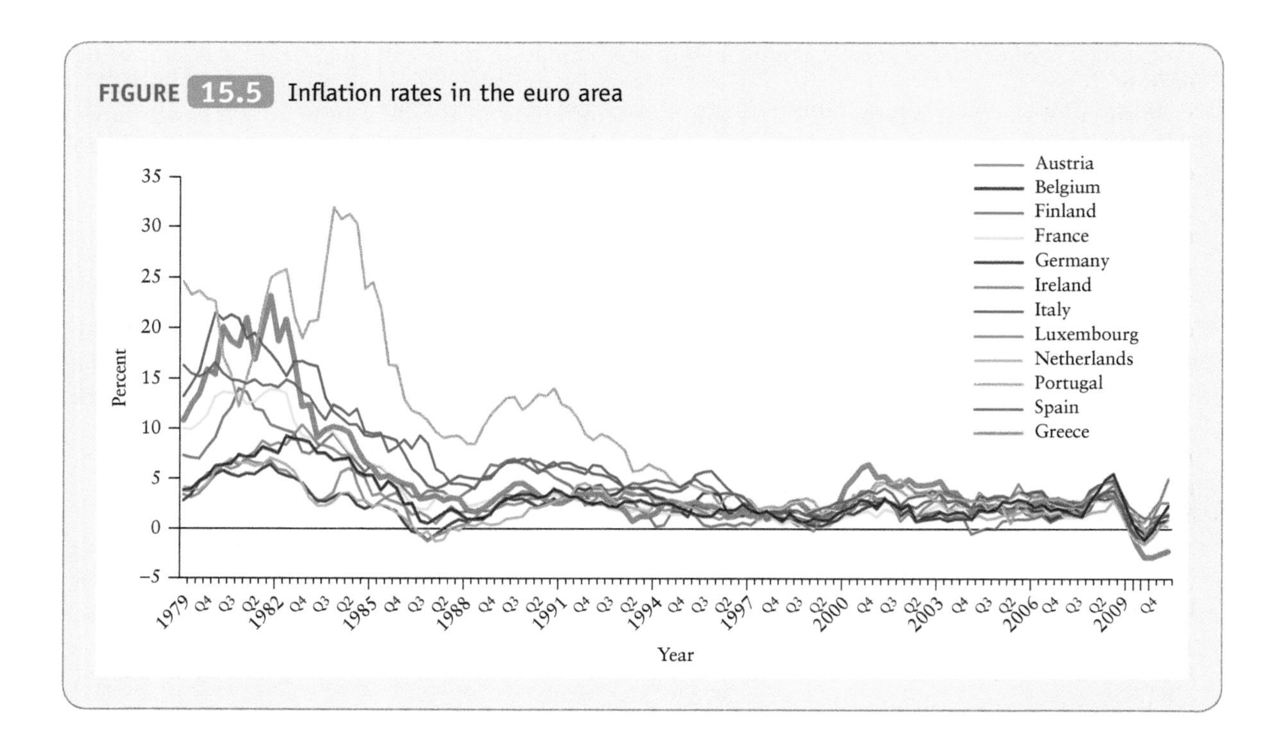

FIGURE 15.6 Mean and standard deviation of inflation rates across euro area countries

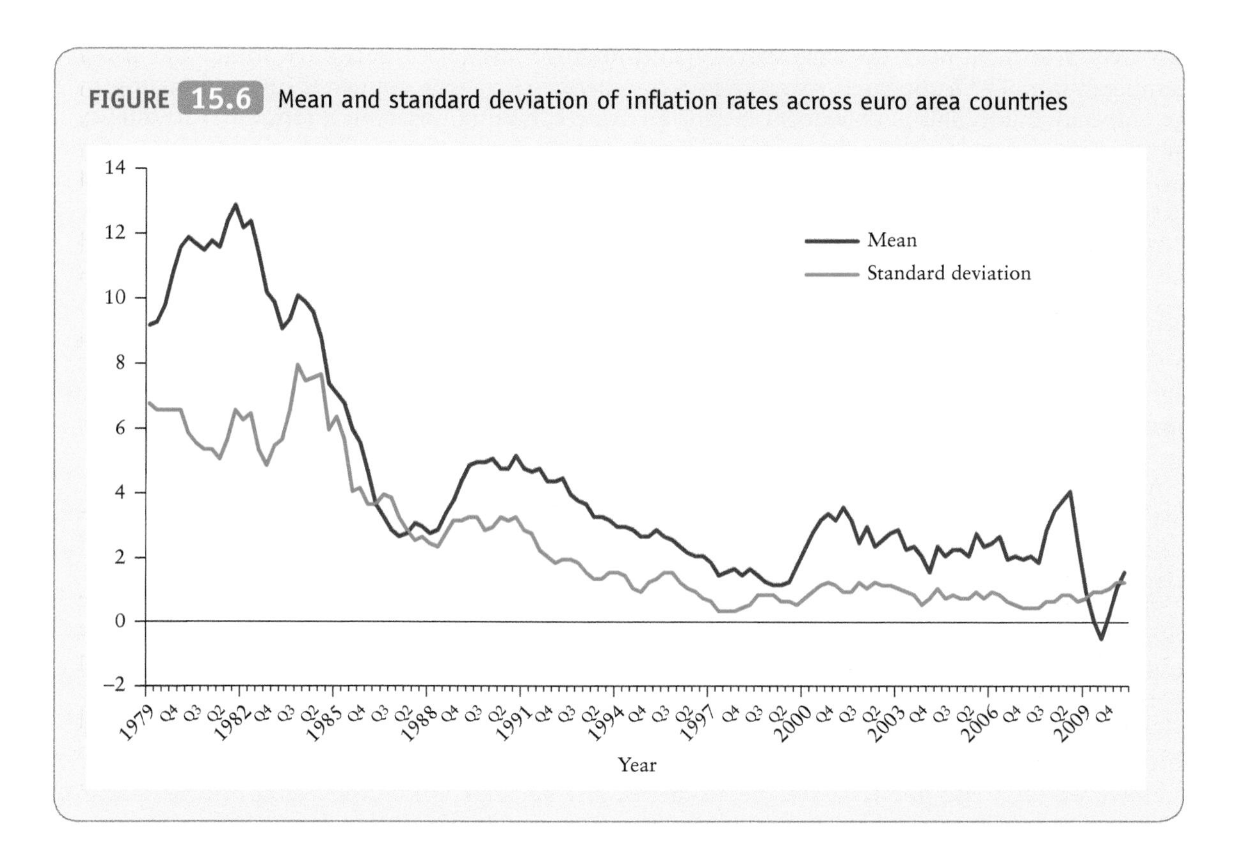

shared in the global deflation of the 1980s and rates fell and converged, but in the early 1990s the average was still over five per cent and the standard deviation over three.

However, inflation rates both declined and converged ahead of the deadline for meeting the Maastricht criteria for entry into EMU in 1997. (The inflation criterion was to bring the country's inflation down 'no more than 1.5 percentage points higher than the average of the three best performing member states of the EU'). Between the early 1990s and 1998 the average rate of inflation fell from 5.2 to 1.2 per cent and the standard deviation fell from 3.3 to 0.4. This showed that it is possible for independent central banks – firmed up by the goal of meeting the Maastricht criteria – to deliver price stability. However, the UK experience after it left the EMS in 1992 also shows that an independent national central bank could deliver low inflation from outside and without aiming to join the euro area.

Over the period from 2002 to 2007 euro area inflation rates remained close to the ECB's target of two per cent, and the spread between countries was very low, as shown by the standard deviation. In 2008, however, booming commodity and energy prices as well as over-heating economies pushed the average inflation to four per cent. With the economic collapse in 2008, inflation also collapsed and a brief period of falling prices was experienced.

Various factors have contributed to relatively high inflation in Ireland in 2002 and 2003. Because of the pattern of our trade the weakness of the euro against sterling and the dollar had a larger inflationary impact on Ireland than on the other euro area countries. The low real interest rates experienced in Ireland since 1999 contributed to an unsustainable real growth rate (10.4 per cent in 2000). This rate of growth contributed to an upsurge in the inflation rate, as would be predicted by the Phillips curve theory discussed in Chapter 12.

It may also have been the case that the anti-inflation discipline necessary to achieve EMU membership in 1997 appeared to wane in a number of euro area countries once admission to the currency union had been won. It is as if an athlete, having observed a strict diet to qualify for an event, reverts to a less demanding lifestyle once the event is over. With hindsight we now realise that adopting the euro did not guarantee uniform inflation across member countries and there is no automatic mechanism that prevents national rates from diverging, at least in the short run.

Relative PPP: a graphical representation

In Figure 15.7, the Irish inflation rate is measured on the vertical axis and the foreign (US) inflation rate adjusted for exchange rate movements along the horizontal axis, that is, $\pi_{US} - \Delta e$ on the horizontal axis. A 45-degree line is then inserted into the diagram. At all points on the 45-degree line relative PPP holds. This is because $\pi_{Irl} = (\pi_{US} - \Delta e)$.

At all points above the relative PPP line, the Irish economy experiences a loss of competitiveness. The Irish inflation rate is higher than that consistent with relative PPP and there is a loss of competitiveness. Below the relative PPP line the Irish inflation rate is lower than that consistent with relative PPP and there is a gain in competitiveness from an Irish perspective.

Figure 15.7 shows the Irish experience relative to the USA over the period 1994 to 2010. Each point in the diagram corresponds to the π_{Irl}, $(\pi_{US} - \Delta e)$ combination for that year. If relative PPP holds, then a trend line through the data would be very similar to the 45-degree line. It can be seen that, while the trend line does not coincide exactly with the 45-degree line, it does have the expected positive slope. Given the volatility of the euro/dollar exchange rate over the period, the observed difference between the two lines is, perhaps, not surprising.

However, the trend line is above the 45-degree line and this, once more, indicates the loss in competitiveness experienced by the Irish economy relative to the USA in the first decade of the new century.

FIGURE 15.7 Relative PPP: Ireland and the USA, 1994–2011

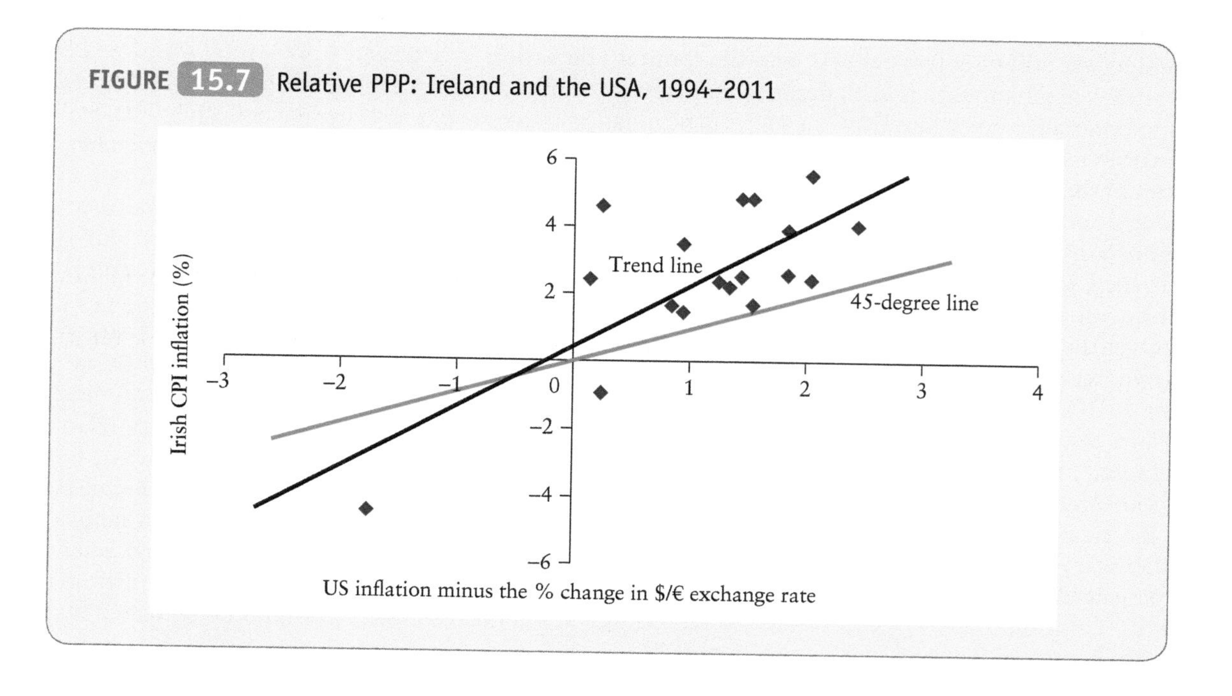

15.9 Uncovered Interest Rate Parity (UIP)

In this section we switch the emphasis away from inflation to nominal interest rates. In a later section we shall combine the two analyses. The theory of uncovered interest rate parity (UIP) is concerned with how interest rate differentials between countries give an indication of how exchange rates will vary in the future.

Consider the case of an investor who is trying to decide whether to invest in the euro area or the USA. The starting point might be a straightforward comparison of nominal interest rates in the two areas. But it would be naive to adopt the rule of thumb of placing your money in the country that offered the highest nominal return over a year. The investor has to take into account expected changes in the exchange rate. To see why, compare the return from an investment in government bonds in the euro area to a similar investment in the USA.

The return from the euro area investment is:

$$(1 + i_{EA})$$

If the interest rate on one-year euro government bond i_{EA} is five per cent, an investment of €1,000 will be worth €1,050 at the end of a year.

$$€1{,}000(1 + 0.05) = €1{,}050$$

The return from the US investment is more complicated. The steps involved are as follows. First we must convert euro into dollars using today's spot exchange rate. Then we must calculate what the investment will be worth in dollars at the end of the year and then convert this dollar amount back into euro using the expected spot exchange rate at the end of the investment period. (We have to use the expected exchange rate as we have no way of knowing the future spot exchange rate.)

We now illustrate this calculation for a sum of €1,000 that could be invested either in the euro area or in the USA. If the spot exchange (dollars per euro) on 31 December 2012 is $e_t = 1.29$, €1,000 will translate into $1,290.

If the interest rate on US Treasury Bills, i_{US}, is 0.25 per cent, the interest paid over a year on the investment will be only $3.25. (Short-term interest rates are extremely low in the USA at present.) The investor will get back $1,293.25 (principal *plus* interest).

If over the year 2013 the dollar strengthens against the euro and on 31 December 2013 the spot exchange rate turns out to be $1.10, the investor will get back €1,176 (that is, 1,293.25/1.1). This is a return of 17.6 per cent on the investment, despite the fact that the bond yield in the USA was only 0.25 per cent. The bulk of the gain was due to the appreciation of the dollar against the euro. Overall, e_t represents the conversion of € to $, $(1 + i_{US})$ the interest earned and $(1/e^e_{t+1})$ the conversion back from $ to € at the end of the year.

Arbitrage

The basis of UIP is that investors will move money between countries so as to obtain the best total return. The total return takes account of the interest received and movements in the exchange rate. If this is the case the return to each euro invested in the euro area $(1 + i_{EA})$ should equal the return to the same euro invested in the USA, $(1 + i_{US})e_t/e^e_{t+1}$

$$(1 + i_{EA}) = \frac{(1 + i_{US})e_t}{e^e_{t+1}}$$

Bring e^e_{t+1} and e_t over to the left-hand side.

$$(e^e_{t+1}/e_t) \times (1 + i_{EA}) = (1 + i_{US})$$

Now bring $(1 + i_{EA})$ over to the right-hand side.

$$(e^e_{t+1}/e_t) = \frac{(1 + i_{US})}{(1 + i_{EA})}$$

Subtract 1 from both sides and rearrange to obtain:

$$\frac{(e^{e}_{t+1} - e_t)}{e_t} = \frac{(i_{US} - i_{EA})}{(1 + i_{EA})} \tag{13}$$

This is the equation underlying *uncovered interest parity* (UIP). This condition is readily interpretable. The equation implies that if the US interest rate exceeds the euro area rate, $i_{US} > i_{EA}$, the market expects the dollar to depreciate, $e^{e}_{t+1} > e_t$. Conversely, if the euro area interest rate is less than the US interest rate the market expects the euro to appreciate. The important implication resulting from equation (13) is that interest rate differentials give an indication of how the market expects the exchange rate to move in the future. This is a handy way of seeing how the market expects exchange rates to change.

Consider now the case where equation (13) does not hold. Suppose, for example, that the USA offered the best rate of return on an investment. In terms of equation (13):

$$(e^{e}_{t+1} - e_t) < (i_{US} - i_{EA})$$

This would set the forces of arbitrage in motion. Investors would withdraw their funds from the euro area and rush to invest in New York. This would tend to drive down interest rates in the USA and to raise them in the euro area. Hence, the term on the right would fall. Second, the increased demand for dollars would drive down the spot exchange rate. The term on the left-hand side will increase. With the right-hand side term decreasing and the left-hand side term increasing, interest rate parity will be quickly re-established. Only the fast movers would benefit as the arbitrage forces will equalise the returns in Europe and New York.

There are two qualifications to the above analysis. The first and more important one is very salient for today's nervous bond markets. It relates to risk. Our example assumed that the two bonds being considered were 'risk free'. That is, the investor was not worried about the possibility that either the US government or the government of the euro area country that issued the bond was likely to renege or default on their debt. This used to be the normal assumption when buying bonds of sovereign governments of advanced countries.

However, since the financial panics of 2008 and after, and the deep crisis in the euro area, this can no longer be assumed. Greece partially defaulted on some of its debt in 2012, and fears that their governments would be unable to honour their outstanding debts drove bond yields in Portugal, Ireland, Spain and even Italy to very high levels in the course of 2011 and 2012. These high interest rates were necessary to compensate investors for the perceived risk of default. Even when the yield on Irish two-year bonds was over 10 per cent in late 2011, few investors were prepared to buy them.

The other, less important, refinement that our analysis ignored is that if interest rates move up or down over the period the investor will suffer a capital loss or gain on the principal. People who invested in Irish government bonds in 2011 gained on two fronts: they enjoyed a high rate of interest on the initial investment; and they enjoyed a sizeable capital gain as the situation for the Irish bond market improved towards the end of 2012 and bond prices rose.

NOTE: If you had bought a 2025 Irish government bond in January 2012 and sold it in September you would have made a 15 per cent capital gain and received a 5.4 per cent coupon in March. That is better than a 20 per cent return in nine months – equivalent to about a 28 per cent annual return.

Speculation

The interest rate parity theorem is very relevant to the phenomenon of speculative attacks. If a speculator expects a currency to depreciate, he or she will only hold it if the interest rate earned is high enough to compensate for the currency's expected loss of value. If a currency comes under speculative attack, the central bank can try to fend off this attack by raising interest rates above those prevailing abroad. While this is unpopular at home, it may persuade speculators to hold the currency and abandon their attack on it. However, this strategy failed repeatedly in the history of the EMS.

Covered and uncovered interest parity

We used the word 'uncovered' to describe the situation in equation (13) because the investor is exposed to exchange rate risk. He or she does not know with certainty what the future exchange rate will be. An investor can hedge against exchange rate risk by entering into a *forward rate agreement*. A forward rate agreement is a contract to buy or sell foreign currency at a specified date in the future but at an exchange rate agreed today (see the appendix to Chapter 13).

The investor is now 'covered' in the sense that she is no longer exposed to unexpected movements in the exchange rate. If the forward exchange rate (f_t) is inserted into equation (13) in place of the expected exchange rate, we have an alternative version of the theory, which is called *covered* interest rate parity (CIPT) theory.

$$(f_t - e_t) = (i_{US} - i_{EA})$$

This raises the question of how the forward exchange rate is formulated. The previous equation suggests that the forward exchange rate is derived from the interest rate differential. This means that either the interest differential or the forward rate can be used to get the market's perspective on the future spot exchange rate.

15.10 Irish and UK Interest Rates

Between 1826 and 1927, Ireland was in a monetary union with the UK and between 1927 and 1979 the Irish pound was rigidly fixed to sterling on a one-to-one, no margins basis. There was no possibility of this sterling link being terminated and the expectation was: no change in the sterling/Irish pound exchange rate. In fact, it was not until the Central Bank Act of 1971 that the government possessed the legal authority to break the sterling link.

Given the size of the UK money market relative to the Irish market, Irish interest rates were dictated by UK rates. In terms of equation (13) above, if the term on the left-hand side is zero (the expected change in the exchange rate is zero), the two interest rates must be equal.

An illustration of this emerged in 1955 when the Irish banks were prevailed on by political pressure not to follow an increase in London interest rates. A gap opened up between interest rates in the two countries. The net external assets of the Irish banking system fell by about eight per cent of GNP during the year, as capital flowed out of the country in response to the higher returns available in London. This led to panic among the Irish authorities and forced them to take corrective action, which contributed to the recession that followed.

Figure 15.8 shows the trend in one-month inter-bank interest rates in Ireland and the UK between 1971 and 2010. Irish and UK interest rates were more or less the same up to 1979, but following Ireland's entry into the EMS and the termination of the sterling link in 1979, exchange rate uncertainty became an extremely important consideration for an investor comparing returns in Dublin and London. The difference between Irish and UK interest rates now reflected exchange rate expectations. After 1979, Irish rates were higher than British rates as there was an expectation that the Irish pound would depreciate relative to sterling. On the three occasions – in 1983, 1986 and 1992 – when the Irish pound appreciated relative to sterling, speculators took the view that the Irish pound exchange rate could not be maintained and would be devalued.

On the first two occasions – in 1983 and 1986 – the Irish authorities reacted quickly and devalued the Irish pound in the EMS. Confidence was restored in the ability of the Irish pound to

FIGURE 15.8 One-month inter-bank interest rates in Ireland and the UK, 1971–2010

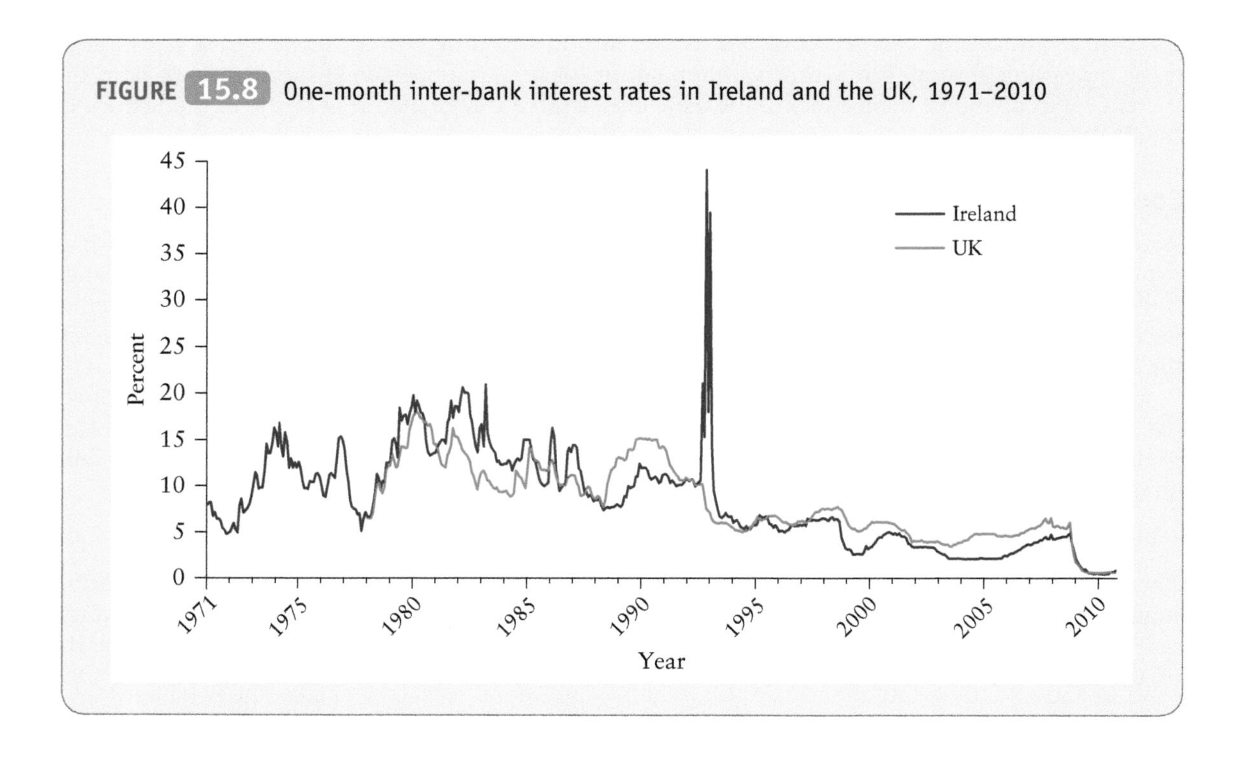

maintain the new lower exchange rate. In 1992, however, the Irish government resisted devaluing the Irish pound for a period of four months. Interest rates in the Dublin money market were raised to unprecedented levels; in November 1992 and January 1993 the Central Bank raised the overnight rate to 100 per cent. The one-month rate peaked at 44 per cent.

Despite these drastic measures, it was clear that the Irish currency was over-valued and that devaluation was inevitable. Eventually the Irish pound was devalued by 10 per cent in January 1993 and this restored confidence in the Irish currency. Money flowed back to Dublin and the Irish–German interest rate differential narrowed.

Now that the Irish pound has been replaced by the euro, movements in the sterling exchange cannot result in speculative flows against the Irish pound exchange rate. It is still the case, however, that swings in the sterling exchange rate can have serious implications for the Irish economy.

15.11 Interest Rates in the Euro Area

With the introduction of the euro in virtual form in January 1999 and in physical form in January 2002, there was no longer an exchange rate between the countries of the euro area. The term on the left-hand side of equation (13) could be set at zero. Ignoring sovereign risk, which emerged as a huge factor after the financial crisis of 2010, there should have been a uniform interest rate across the euro area. Just as there are no significant interest rate differentials for borrowers of equal quality within a country, so too, the theory went, interest rates should have converged across the euro area. This convergence was reinforced by the convergence of inflation rates, which we discussed above.

Figure 15.9 shows the interest rates in the euro area countries from 1979 to 2010. In the early 1980s the divergence between national interest rates was large. However, as the date for the introduction of the euro came closer, rates started to converge and after 1999 there was little or no

FIGURE 15.9 Interest rates in the euro area (official lending rates)

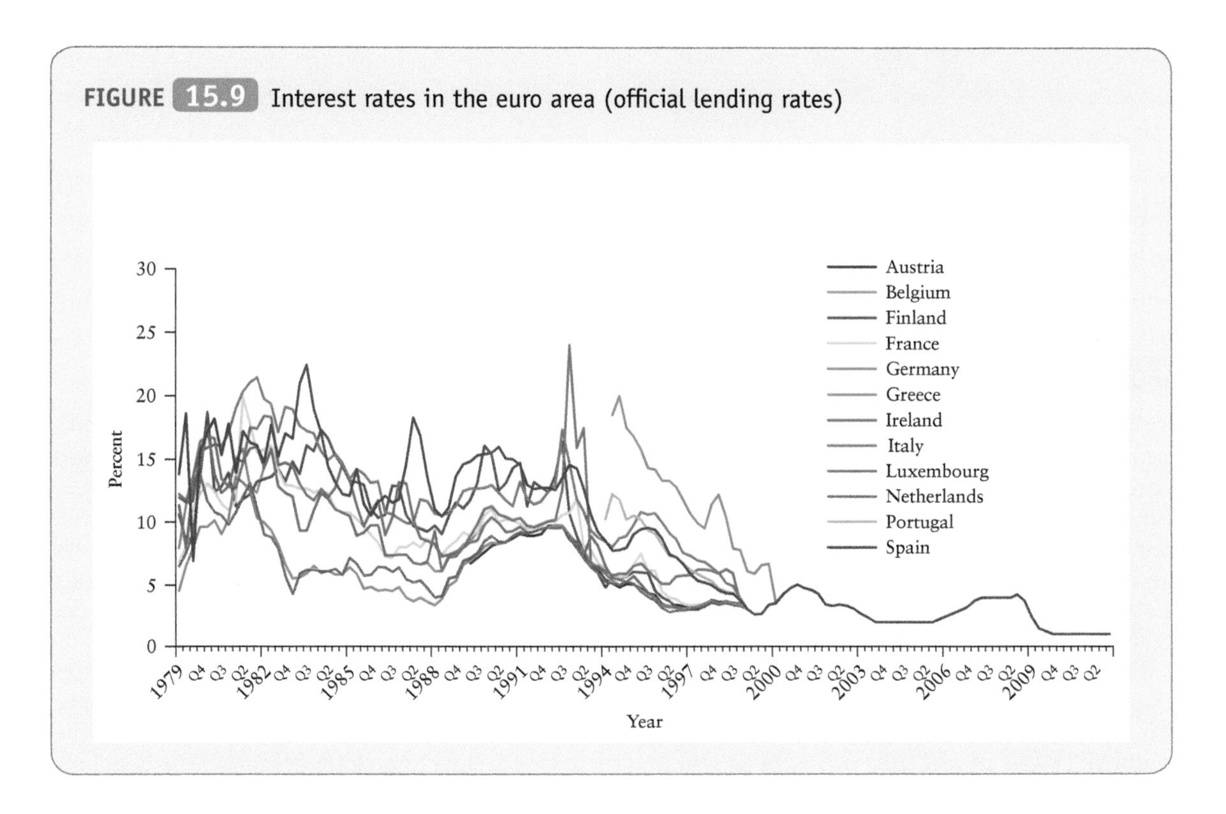

difference. The rate in all euro area countries was close to the ECB's Main Refinancing Interest Rate (MRIR). In Ireland, for example, banks and building societies launched 'tracker mortgages' on which the rate is equal to the MRIR plus one per cent.

This represented a significant change for traditionally high-inflation/high-interest rate countries such as Ireland, Portugal, Spain, Finland and Italy. In Ireland the low nominal interest rate, combined with relatively high inflation, drove the real interest rate below zero in some years. This reinforced inflationary pressures and contributed to the asset price bubble.

15.12 Key Terms and Concepts

In this chapter we have discussed a number of topics relating to the determination of inflation and interest rates in open economies. The main issues and concepts covered included:

- the theory of absolute and relative purchasing power parity
- reasons why the PPP theory may not hold
- nominal and real harmonised competitiveness indicators
- Irish and euro area inflation
- the operation of PPP theory under both fixed and flexible exchange rates
- an exchange rate peg as an anti-inflation commitment
- the theory of uncovered interest rate parity
- Irish and euro area interest rates.

CHAPTER 16

The Mundell–Fleming Model

16.1 Introduction

In this chapter we extend the Keynes–Hicks IS-LM model we discussed in Chapter 11 by making it applicable to open economies. This extension was developed by John Fleming, an Oxford economist, and Robert Mundell, a Nobel Prize-winning Canadian economist teaching at Columbia University in New York. We then use the Mundell–Fleming model to explore the effects of fiscal, monetary and exchange rate policies on output and employment. The model is also used to assess the impact of exchange rate and sovereign risk on output and employment. This builds on our analysis in previous chapters of the open economy and broadens our understanding of the impact on the economy of exchange rate movements.

The concluding section explains how the Mundell–Fleming model provides a theory of the aggregate demand curve. Hence, the Keynesian cross model provides us with a theory of the IS curve and the theory of liquidity preference a theory of the LM curve. The open economy version of the complete IS-LM model then provides us with the theory underling aggregate demand. The concluding section applies the model to the recession in Ireland after 2008.

16.2 Internal and External Balance

In an open economy a key issue is how the policy-maker can achieve simultaneously both full employment and low inflation (internal balance) and balance of payments equilibrium (external balance). To start, we need to extend the IS-LM framework we introduced in Chapter 11 to account for external balance. Recall that the IS line shows the combinations of output (measured using GNP and denoted as (Y)) and the real interest rate (r) consistent with equilibrium in the goods market. The LM line shows the combinations of Y and r consistent with equilibrium in the money market. At the point A in Figure 16.1 the two lines intersect and there is, simultaneously, equilibrium in both the goods and money markets.

A change in any of the components of aggregate demand (C, I, G or NX) shifts the IS schedule. An expansionary fiscal policy, for example, would shift the IS curve to the right. Also an increase in NX will shift the IS curve out to the right, and vice versa. On the other hand, a change in the money supply (monetary policy) will shift the LM schedule.

NOTE: A key assumption underlining the Mundell–Fleming model is that the price level is fixed. In Figure 16.1 we show the nominal (i), and not the real interest rate (r), on the vertical axis. The substitution of the nominal for the real interest rate does not affect the analysis because, with prices fixed, a change in the real interest rate will be completely reflected in a change in the nominal interest rate. The reason for making this substitution is to incorporate into the analysis capital flows through the balance of payments. These capital account flows are responsive to changes in nominal interest rates.

External balance

In Chapter 13 we pointed out that under flexible exchange rates the balance of payments always balances in the sense that the current account surplus (deficit) is always offset by an equal deficit (surplus) on the capital account. If the exchange rate is fixed these surpluses (deficits) will be reflected in an increase (decrease) in the official reserves of foreign exchange held by the central bank. External balance can be said to exist when the central bank does not have to intervene in the foreign exchange market to stabilise the exchange rate. This implies that the sum of the current account and private capital flows is zero. This happens even if there is a large current account deficit, provided it is financed by a private capital inflow.

FIGURE 16.1 The IS-LM model

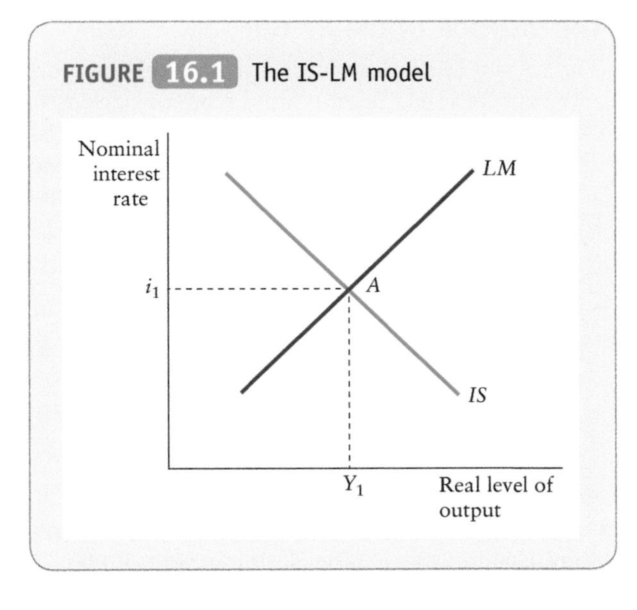

In Figure 16.2 we draw a reference line BP = 0, which shows the combinations of Y and i that result in the overall balance of payments being zero. That is, at all points on the BP = 0 line, the overall balance of payments is zero. The (BP = 0) line slopes upwards because increases in Y and i have opposing effects on the balance of payments. Consider first the effect of an increase in the interest rate. If the exchange rate is fixed, an increase in the domestic interest rate relative to the world rate leads to a capital inflow as investors move funds to the country that offers the highest return.

- $\uparrow i$ (relative to the interest rate in the rest of the world) $\rightarrow \uparrow$ capital inflows $\rightarrow$ surplus on the capital account of the balance of payments.

On the other hand, an increase in Y leads to an increase in imports (M) via the marginal propensity to import (MPM) and a fall in net exports; that is, a rise in the deficit on current account.

- $\uparrow Y \rightarrow \uparrow M \rightarrow$ rise in current account deficit

The BP = 0 line is drawn so that the positive effect of higher interest rates offsets the negative Y effect and the overall balance of payments remains in equilibrium. In Figure 16.2, as the economy moves from A to B the interest rate increases from i_1 to i_2 and this leads to a capital account surplus. On the other hand, the increase in Y from Y_1 to Y_2 leads to a current account deficit.

If the economy is above the BP = 0 line, at a point such as C in the diagram, there is a balance of payments surplus. This is because the interest rate is higher than that necessary for equilibrium. If it is below the BP = 0 line, at D for example, there is a balance of payments deficit. The interest rate is lower than that required for equilibrium.

FIGURE 16.2 Balance of payments equilibrium

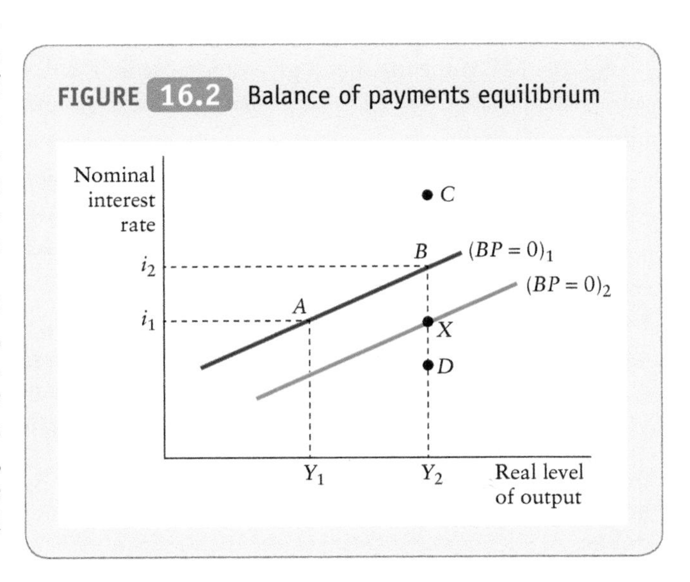

The location of the BP line

The BP = 0 line is drawn for a given level of exports and imports, world interest rates and exchange rate expectations. (Bear in mind from our discussion of interest rate parity in Chapter 15 that if the exchange rate is expected to depreciate, the interest rate will be higher than the world interest rate.) The position of the line changes if any of these variables change.

An increase in exports or a fall in imports (not brought about by a change in Y) will shift the BP = 0 line downwards to the right. To see why, suppose that the economy is initially at the point A and interest rates are kept constant at i_1. Suppose now that there is an increase in the demand for the country's exports. By shifting the BP = 0 line to the right we can again achieve BP equilibrium. The point X, for example, in Figure 16.2 is on the lower $(BP = 0)_2$ line. At X the rise in Y from Y_1 to Y_2 has increased imports sufficiently to offset the increase in exports and the balance of payments returns to equilibrium.

Similarly, an expected exchange rate depreciation would require a higher interest rate and shift the BP = 0 line up. A fall in world interest rates would facilitate a fall in domestic interest rates. By shifting the BP line downwards we can examine the relationship between the new lower interest rate and the initial level of Y.

A fall in exports, a rise in imports (not due to changes in Y), an increase in world interest rates or an exchange rate depreciation would shift the BP = 0 line upwards to the left.

The slope of the BP line

The slope of the BP = 0 line depends on (a) the degree of capital mobility, and (b) the marginal propensity to import (MPM). If capital flows are very sensitive to interest differentials, the BP line will be relatively flat. Only a small change in the interest rate (relative to the world rate) is necessary to attract sufficient capital to compensate for the increased imports due to a given increase in Y and maintain the balance of payments in equilibrium. If there is perfect capital mobility and a stable default risk premium the BP = 0 line will be horizontal. A small change in the domestic interest rate would lead to unlimited capital inflows or outflows. In this case, only the world interest rate, i^*, is consistent with balance of payments equilibrium whatever the level of Y. Changes in exports, imports and the exchange rate will not shift the BP = 0 line because enough capital will always flow in to finance the current account deficit.

On the other hand, if capital flows are restricted by exchange controls (particularly on inflows), the BP = 0 line will be relatively steep. A large change in interest rates would be needed to attract the capital inflows to finance the current account deficit due to a given increase in Y.

A large MPM means that a given increase in Y will lead to a relatively large increase in imports, and interest rates will have to increase accordingly to compensate; hence the BP = 0 line will be steep. In general:

- If there is a high degree of capital mobility and the MPM is small, the BP line will be relatively flat.
- If there is a low degree of capital mobility and the MPM is large, the BP line will be relatively steep.

Exchange rate risk

There are two reasons why the domestic interest rate may differ from the world interest rate. First, if the exchange rate is expected to depreciate lenders will demand a premium to compensate for their prospective losses on the foreign exchange market. Exchange rate risk does not now apply between Ireland and the other euro area countries, but it applies in the case of countries outside the euro area because the euro is floating relative to non-euro currencies. An American investor in bonds issued by a euro area country is exposed to the risk that the euro will depreciate against the dollar.

Second, there is the issue of sovereign or corporate risk. This is the risk that the country's borrowers (government, banks or corporations) will default due to political or economic turmoil. Lenders have to be compensated for the possibility of this risk materialising. During the economic crisis after 2008, the yield on Irish and Spanish government bonds was over eight percentage points higher than the yield on German bonds. This 'spread' is now very familiar to investors and is reported daily on the financial pages of the world's press.

Since the euro crisis broke, it is no longer the case that interest rates are equal across euro area countries. In mid-2012, for example, the yield on Irish 10-year bonds was 8.0 per cent compared to 1.26 per cent on German bonds. However, to illustrate the basic Mundell–Fleming model we initially assume a horizontal BP = 0 line. This implies a very high degree of capital mobility between Ireland and our main trading partners. Any deviation of domestic interest rates and the EMU inter-bank rates is assumed to provoke massive capital flows. In Section 16.6 below we incorporate sovereign risk into the Mundell–Fleming model.

While it is true that the Irish MPM is relatively large, any increase in imports as a result of increases in Y is likely to be dominated by the effect of an incipient rise in interest rates on the capital account.

NOTE: On a historical level the BP = 0 line was horizontal in Ireland up to 1979 when the Irish pound was pegged to sterling and capital flowed freely between Ireland and the UK. Between December 1978 and December 1988 exchange controls restricted capital movements between Ireland and other countries. It is possible that during this period the BP = 0 line sloped upwards, allowing the Irish interest rate to deviate from that in the rest of the world. However, with the complete abolition of exchange controls in 1992 and the introduction of the euro in 1999 it is likely the BP line was virtually horizontal. However, all this changed with the crisis of 2008 and the perceived risk of sovereign default.

16.3 Introduction to the Mundell–Fleming Model

We can now extend our IS-LM analysis to include the effect of changes in the level of economic activity on interest rates and the balance of payments. The Mundell–Fleming model was developed for this purpose (Fleming 1962; Mundell 1962).

The model is based on several assumptions.

1. It assumes that the price levels in the domestic country and the rest of the world are constant. This is obviously a strong assumption because as we have seen, even with the introduction of the euro, inflation across the euro area countries has not been uniform. This assumption will be relaxed towards the end of this chapter.
2. The model assumes that the economy is not supply constrained.
3. Crowding-out is less than complete and, as a result, fiscal policy is an effective policy instrument.

These three assumptions imply that the aggregate supply curve is perfectly horizontal and that changes in real output and employment are determined only by changes in aggregate demand.

4. We assume that an expansionary fiscal policy is financed in a non-monetary way and does not result in an increase in the money supply.
5. Finally, we assume perfect capital mobility and a stable default risk premium so that the BP = 0 line is horizontal. The analysis below, however, does allow for imperfect capital mobility and shows how this alters the conclusions of the model.

Figure 16.3 incorporates these assumptions. A horizontal BP = 0 reference line is amalgamated with the IS-LM model. At the point A, the IS and LM curves intersect with the BP = 0 line. At this point the goods and money markets and the balance of payments are all in equilibrium.

In the next section we use the Mundell–Fleming model to analyse the effects of fiscal and monetary policy on output and the balance of payments when the exchange rate is both fixed and flexible. In what follows, it is important to bear in mind that, under fixed exchange rates, the central bank intervenes in the foreign exchange market to stabilise the exchange rate. As a result, balance of payments deficits or surpluses are reflected in changes in the external reserves, which in turn affect the domestic money supply and shifts the LM curve.

FIGURE 16.3 The Mundell–Fleming model

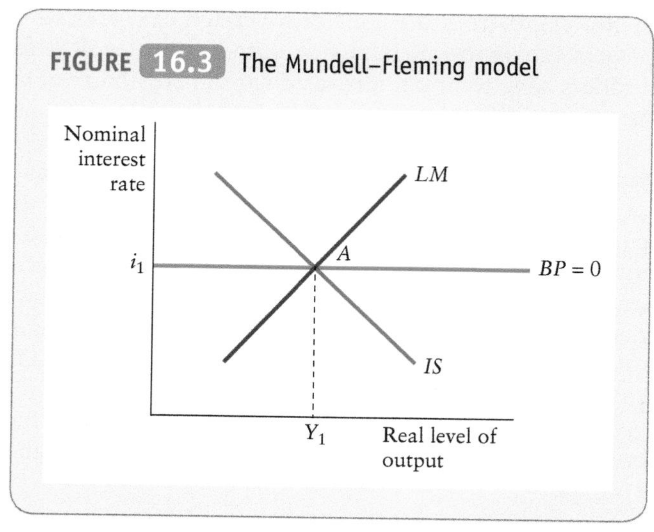

If the exchange rate were floating, the central bank would not intervene in the foreign exchange market and balance of payments surpluses or deficits would result in an appreciation or depreciation of the currency. As we shall see, the effect of fiscal and monetary policy on output and employment is very different, depending on whether the exchange rate is fixed or floating.

16.4 The Model Under Fixed Exchange Rates

Fiscal policy

In Figure 16.4 we show the effect of an increase in government expenditure on output when the exchange rate is fixed. This analysis is relevant in, for example, the case of the USA and China as the Chinese authorities have, for some time, pursued a fixed exchange rate policy relative to the US dollar.

An increase in government expenditure in China shifts the IS curve outwards from IS_1 to IS_2 and the economy moves from A to B. At B, real output, Y, has increased and there is a balance of payments surplus as the economy is above the BP = 0 reference line.

An expansionary fiscal policy results in a balance of payments surplus because:

- The increase in Y leads to an increase in imports via the marginal propensity to import and this results in a deficit in the current account of the balance of payments.
- The increase in Y increases the demand for money and therefore

FIGURE 16.4 Expansionary fiscal policy: fixed exchange rates

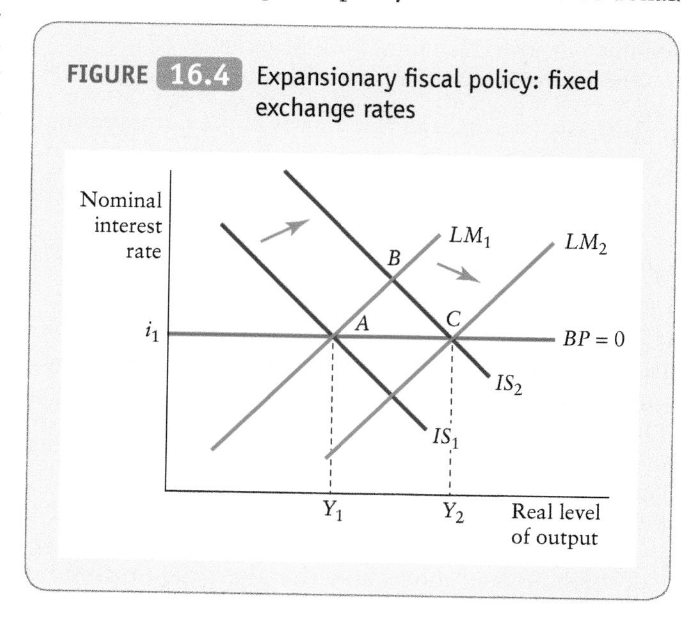

the domestic interest rate. This results in a capital inflow and a surplus on the capital account of the balance of payments.

$$\uparrow Y \rightarrow \uparrow M^d \rightarrow \uparrow i \rightarrow \text{capital inflow}$$

Given perfect capital mobility and a stable default risk premium, the second effect dominates the first, with the result that there is an overall balance of payments surplus: the deficit in the current account is more than offset by the surplus on the capital account.

Point B in Figure 16.4 is not a final equilibrium. Because the exchange rate is fixed, the central bank must intervene in the foreign exchange market to stabilise it following the emergence of a balance of payments surplus. In the case of China, this intervention takes the form of the People's Bank of China selling renminbi and accumulating dollars, which are added to the external reserves. The rise in the external reserves, in turn, increases high-powered money and has a multiplier effect on the overall money supply. The LM curve now shifts outwards from LM_1 to LM_2. The economy moves from B to C.

NOTE: When the exchange rate is fixed or pegged, a surplus (deficit) in the balance of payments will cause the external reserves to rise (fall) and shift the LM curve. Thus in an open economy, with a fixed exchange rate, the country's central bank loses control over the money supply. If, however, the central bank engages in *sterilisation*, it can try to offset this effect. We assume here that the central bank does not engage in sterilisation, which in any event tends to work only in the short run.

At C the domestic interest rate is again equal to the world rate and the overall balance of payments is zero. The current account is in deficit, but this is offset by the capital account surplus. The level of Y has risen as a result of the fiscal expansion. The main conclusion is that fiscal policy is very effective when the exchange rate is fixed and capital is perfectly mobile and the default risk premium is stable (which it will not be if a small country indulges in excessive fiscal expansion). The magnitude of the impact of fiscal policy on output depends on the slopes of the IS-LM curves. Bear in mind, however, that the current account deficit means that foreigners now have a monetary claim on the economy's resources.

Unfortunately, the opposite is also true. A deflationary fiscal policy has a significant impact on the economy. Hence the austerity package imposed on Ireland by the Troika (EU, IMF and ECB) can be expected to have a very severe impact on the economy. In the concluding section to this chapter we illustrate how the economy could adjust back to the potential level of output in the Mundell–Fleming model.

Imperfect capital mobility

If there is imperfect capital mobility between China and the USA, the BP = 0 line will slope upwards. This would occur if China imposed exchange controls on capital flows. In the vast majority of cases, the outcome will be as in the case of a horizontal BP line except that the increase in Y will be smaller and *i* will rise.

One extreme case is where the degree of capital mobility is such that the BP = 0 line is steeper than the LM curve; the reader can verify that an expansionary fiscal policy will result in an overall balance of payments deficit (not shown). The LM curve will then shift back to the left, reflecting a fall in the central bank's external reserves. The increase in Y will be smaller than when there was perfect capital mobility and a stable default risk premium. This suggests that the greater the degree of capital mobility, the more effective is fiscal policy.

Monetary policy

Figure 16.5 shows the effect of an expansionary monetary policy when the exchange rate is fixed. We reiterate the point that this analysis is relevant in the case of China and the USA.

The increase in the money supply in China shifts the LM curve from LM_1 to LM_2 and the economy moves from A to B. At B, Y has increased, but the economy is below the BP = 0 line, indicating that there is a balance of payments deficit.

The balance of payments deficit arises for two reasons:

FIGURE 16.5 Expansionary monetary policy: fixed exchange rates

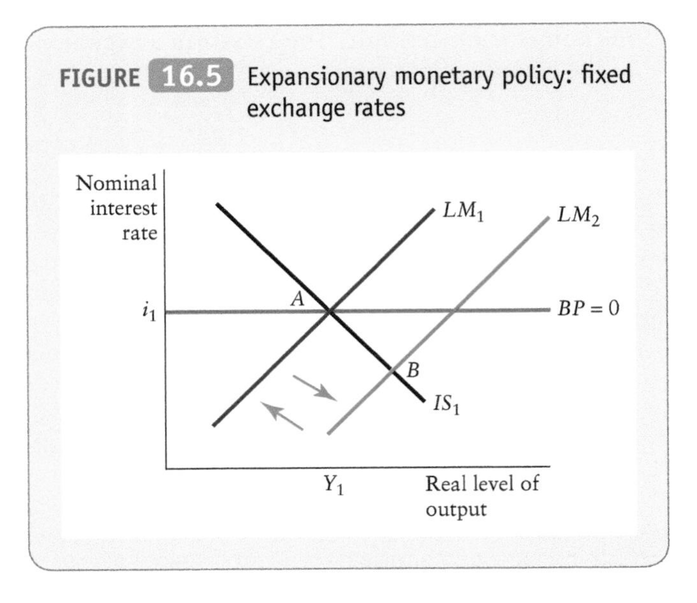

1. The increase in the money supply leads to a fall in the domestic interest rate relative to the world interest rate, and this results in a capital outflow and a deficit on the capital account of the balance of payments.

$$\uparrow M^s \rightarrow \downarrow i \text{ (relative to the world rate)} \rightarrow \text{capital outflow}$$

2. The increase in Y leads to an increase in imports (via the marginal propensity to import) and a current account deficit.

$$\uparrow Y \rightarrow \uparrow M \rightarrow \text{current account deficit}$$

An expansionary monetary policy therefore results in a deficit in both the current and capital accounts of the balance of payments, giving rise to an overall balance of payments deficit.

The economy will not remain at B. Because the exchange rate is fixed, the central bank must intervene in the foreign exchange market to offset the balance of payments deficit. The People's Bank of China does this by buying renminbi with US dollars from the official external reserves. The fall in the reserves results in a contraction in the money supply. This is shown by the backward shift in the LM curve, which continues until the economy returns to its original position at A. At this point, the domestic interest rate is again equal to the world rate and Y has returned to its initial level. From this sequence of events we see that:

- when the exchange rate is fixed, the domestic money supply is no longer controlled by the central bank.

Because capital is perfectly mobile, the fall in the interest rate leads to an immediate capital outflow and the money supply and the interest rate quickly return to their original levels. Given the speed with which capital flows out of the country, the interest rate does not remain below the world rate long enough to have any effect on the level of domestic economic activity. Monetary policy is therefore ineffective when the exchange rate is fixed and capital is perfectly mobile.

Imperfect capital mobility

The degree of capital mobility does not change the result that monetary policy is ineffective when the exchange rate is fixed. The reader can verify that even if the BP = 0 line is upward sloping, an expansionary monetary policy will again result in a balance of payments deficit and the economy will eventually return to the initial level of output. The more imperfect is capital mobility, the longer it takes to revert to point A.

16.5 The Model Under Floating Exchange Rates

Fiscal policy

The analysis in this section is particularly relevant in the case of the euro and the dollar or the euro and sterling. This is because the respective central banks do not intervene in the foreign exchange market to influence exchange rates.

In Figure 16.6 an expansionary fiscal policy shifts the IS curve outwards from IS_1 to IS_2 and the economy moves from A to B. At B, Y has increased and there is an overall balance of payments surplus because the capital account surplus (brought about by higher interest rates) dominates the current account deficit (due to the increase in Y).

FIGURE 16.6 Expansionary fiscal policy: flexible exchange rates

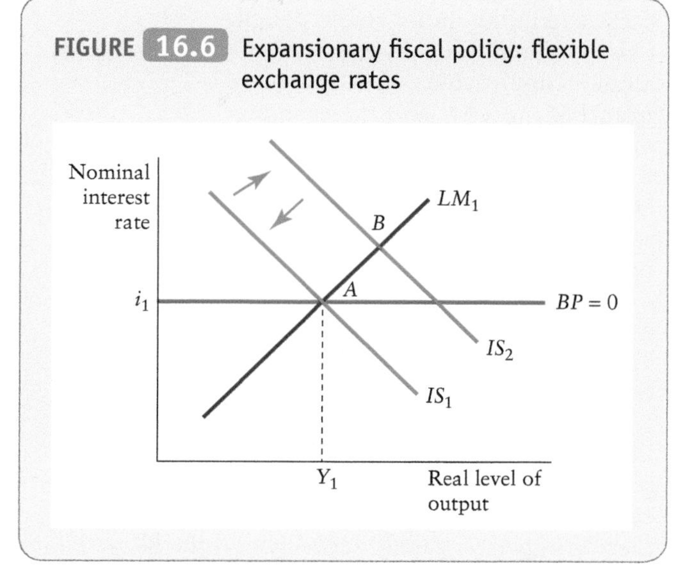

However, if the exchange rate is floating and the central bank does not intervene in the foreign exchange market, the balance of payments surplus will result in exchange rate appreciation. The external reserves and the money supply remain unchanged. The LM curve is therefore not affected.

But the rise in the exchange rate reduces exports and increases imports, and the IS curve shifts backwards to the left. The *real* exchange rate (ε) is defined as:

$$\varepsilon = (e \times P)/P_f$$

where P and P_f are domestic and foreign prices respectively and *e* is the nominal exchange rate. This real exchange rate is one determinant of net exports (NX), that is, exports minus imports. It follows, therefore, that changes in the real exchange rate (brought about by nominal exchange rate appreciation) affect the position of the IS curve in an open economy.

This process will continue until the economy reverts to point A. The increase in Y was, therefore, only temporary. In effect, under floating exchange rates, an expansionary fiscal policy crowds-out NX through exchange rate appreciation. Fiscal policy is therefore ineffective when the exchange rate is floating, even if there is perfect capital mobility and a stable default risk premium.

Imperfect capital mobility

As long as the BP line is below the LM line the outcome will be as in the previous analysis. If we consider the extreme case where the BP = 0 line is steeper than the LM curve due to imperfect capital mobility and a stable default risk premium, an expansionary fiscal policy will result in an increase in Y and a balance of payments deficit. In this case, the exchange rate depreciates and this results in a further increase in Y. The reader can verify that under these circumstances fiscal policy will have a greater effect on output and employment than in the case of fixed exchange rate and perfect capital mobility. Note, however, that we are assuming that there are no supply-side constraints and that no domestic inflation follows from the exchange rate depreciation.

Monetary policy

Figure 16.7 illustrates the case of an expansionary monetary policy under floating exchange rates with perfect capital mobility and a stable default risk premium. The increase in the money supply shifts the LM curve from LM_1 to LM_2 and the economy moves from point A to point B. At B, Y has increased and a deficit has emerged on both the current and capital accounts of the balance of payments.

The exchange rate now depreciates and this increases net exports. The IS curve shifts outwards from IS_1 to IS_2 and the economy moves from B to C. Y again increases and equilibrium is restored to the balance of payments. This implies that monetary policy is very effective when exchange rates are floating, capital is perfectly mobile, and there are no supply-side constraints. This result is not changed if there is imperfect capital mobility and the BP = 0 line is upward sloping.

FIGURE 16.7 Expansionary monetary policy: flexible exchange rates

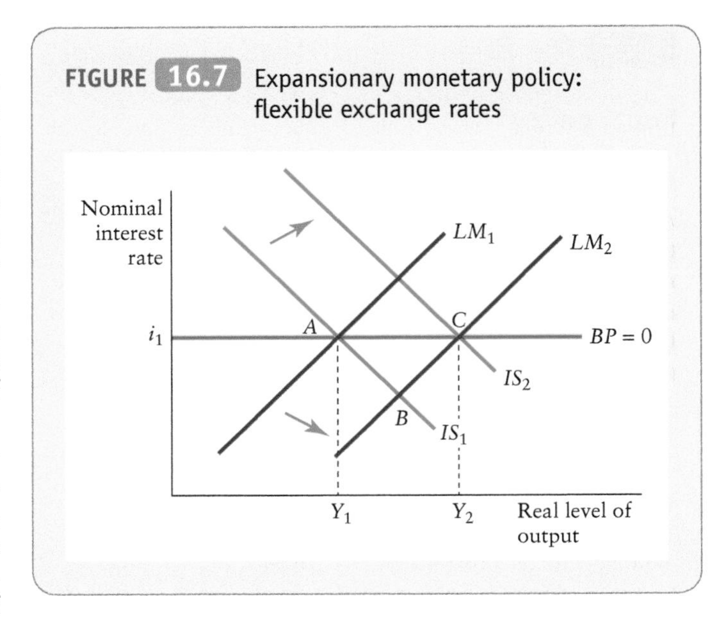

Summary

Table 16.1 summarises our conclusions for fixed and floating exchange rate cases. Monetary policy is ineffective (in terms of achieving increases in output and employment) when the exchange rate is fixed but is very effective when the exchange rate is flexible. This is the case regardless of the degree of capital mobility.

Fiscal policy, on the other hand, is effective under fixed exchange rates and ineffective under floating exchange rates when there is perfect capital mobility and a stable default risk premium. However, this finding tends to get reversed as capital becomes more immobile and if the default risk premium tends to rise in response to a fiscal expansion (which, of course, it would).

Overall, the choice of exchange rate regime and the degree of capital mobility play an important role in determining the effectiveness of fiscal and monetary policy.

TABLE 16.1 The effect of expansionary fiscal and monetary policy on output (Y), the exchange rate (e) and net exports

	Exchange rate fixed			Exchange rate floating		
	Effect on					
	Y	*e*	NX	Y	*e*	NX
Fiscal policy	↑	0	0	0	↑	↓
Monetary policy	0	0	0	↑	↓	↑

16.6 The Exchange Rate and Country Risk

The assumption of perfect capital mobility and a stable default risk premium ensures that the domestic interest rate (i) cannot differ from the world rate (i^*).

$$i = i^*$$

As the price level is fixed, we can work with either nominal (i) or real (r) interest rates. As mentioned earlier, there are two reasons why i may differ from i^*: the first is country and/or sovereign risk (borrowers, government or corporation, may default on their loan repayments); the second is exchange rate risk (if a country's exchange rate is expected to depreciate, lenders will demand a higher interest rate to compensate for this depreciation). If we use Φ to denote the *risk premium* (made up of both exchange rate and sovereign risk), then:

$$i = i^* + \Phi$$

The condition underlying goods market equilibrium (the IS curve) is:

$$Y = C + I(i^*) + G + NX(e)$$

That is, output equals total expenditure. Investment expenditure is determined by the domestic or world interest rate and net exports by the exchange rate (e). This equation can be extended to include the risk premium.

$$Y = C + I(i^* + \Phi) + G + NX(e)$$

An increase in Φ will reduce investment and output and shift the IS curve down to the left. A reduction in Φ will increase both investment and output and shift the IS curve out to the right.

The condition underlining money market equilibrium (the LM curve) is:

$$M/P = L(i^*, Y)$$

This equation states that the real money supply equals the demand for money. Incorporating the risk premium into this equation, we have:

$$M/P = L(i^* + \Phi, Y)$$

An increase in the risk premium will now reduce the demand for money. Because the LM curve is upward sloping, Y must rise to restore equilibrium in the money market. With the nominal interest rate on the vertical axis, the LM curve shifts out to the right. Similarly, a reduction in Φ will shift the LM curve to the left.

Figure 16.8 illustrates the case of an increase in the risk premium under flexible exchange rates. Starting from the point A, an increase in Φ will shift the IS curve down to the left (the higher risk premium reduces investment and therefore output). However, the rise in Φ shifts the LM curve out to the right (the higher risk premium reduces the demand for money and,

FIGURE 16.8 An increase in the risk premium: flexible exchange rates

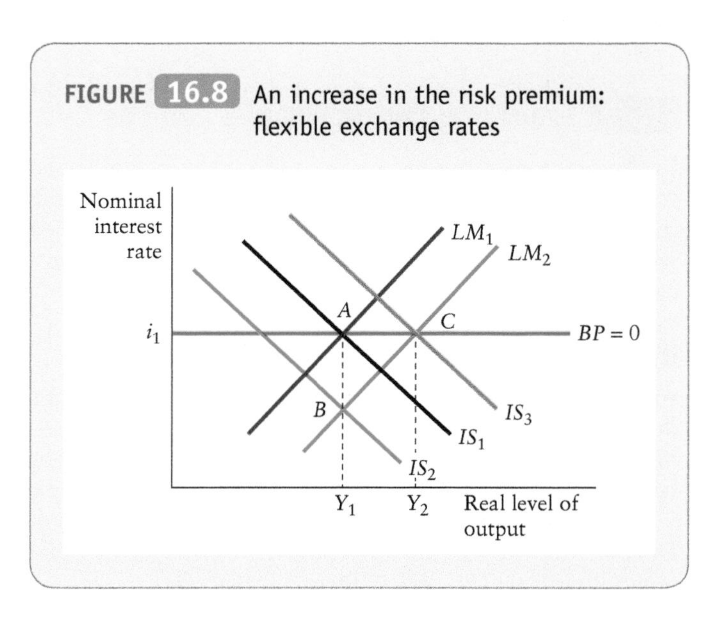

for a given money supply, output must rise to restore equilibrium). The economy moves to the point B and there is a balance of payments deficit.

The economy will not remain at the point B. The balance of payments deficit leads to exchange rate depreciation and this increases net exports. The IS curve now shifts up to the right and equilibrium is eventually achieved at the point C. Overall, the increase in Φ leads to exchange rate depreciation and an increase in output (Y).

FIGURE 16.9 An increase in the risk premium: fixed exchange rate

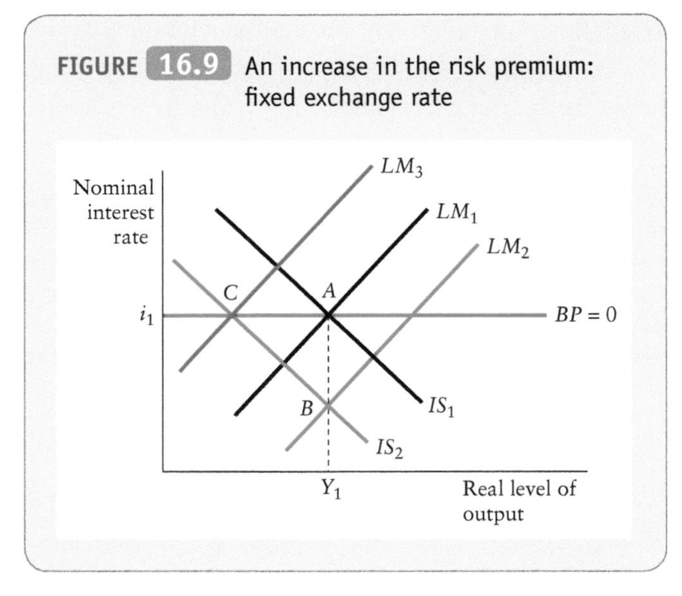

The latter result may seem a little paradoxical: an increase in Φ leads to a fall in investment and yet Y increases. What happens is that the exchange rate depreciation increases net exports (NX) and this more than compensates for the fall in investment. Overall, Y increases. However, it should be borne in mind that the depreciation might increase the price level (due to higher import prices) and this would reduce the real money supply. Also consumers might respond to the increased risk by holding more money. For both of these reasons, the real money supply is reduced and the LM curve would shift to the left.

Figure 16.9 shows the case of an increase in the risk premium in China relative to the USA when the exchange rate is fixed. As in the flexible exchange rate case, the IS curve shifts down to the left and the LM curve shifts down to the right. The economy moves from point A to B and a balance of payments deficit emerges. However, the Chinese central bank will now act to prevent a depreciation of the exchange rate by buying the domestic currency (renminbi) using its external reserves. This reduces the money supply and the LM curve shifts up to the left and the economy moves to the point C. At the point C, the exchange rate is unchanged but there is a fall in Y and an increase in unemployment in the background. Hence, the outcome under fixed exchange rates is very different from the flexible case.

16.7 Economic Policy, Output and the Current Account

In the previous sections we focused on the overall balance of payments (current plus capital accounts). There we saw that as long as a current account deficit is offset by a capital account surplus, the overall balance of payments is in equilibrium and external balance is achieved. In this section we focus on the current (trade in goods and services) account only and examine how this account can influence the design of economic policy.

Devaluation and the current balance

An expansionary fiscal or monetary policy increases Y, but in doing so creates a trade deficit (or reduces a trade surplus). This happens because the increase in Y leads to an increase in imports via the marginal propensity to import (MPM). In certain circumstances, therefore, a policy dilemma can exist because fiscal and monetary policy, while increasing employment, also results in a trade deficit.

Devaluation, on the other hand, increases Y through an improvement in the current balance. Devaluation is therefore a particularly useful policy instrument if there is a current deficit and high unemployment. The policy dilemma that can exist between achieving a current balance (recall that a current deficit leads to external indebtness) and full employment can be resolved by devaluation. We emphasise that devaluation is not an option for any of the countries participating in EMU. It could be an option, however, for the euro area as a whole.

NOTE: An improvement in the home current balance resulting from exchange rate devaluation has to be matched by an increase in some other country's current deficit. Hence the gain in output and employment at home must be at the expense of a reduction in output and employment in some other country. This gives rise to the accusation that devaluation is a 'beggar thy neighbour' policy in that the devaluing country is attempting to 'export its unemployment' to other countries.

The current account

In Figure 16.10 we elaborate on this point by developing a net export, NX = 0 reference line. The analysis is the same as it would be for the BP = 0 line, with zero capital mobility. Note that the current account is interchangeable with the trade account if the other sub-accounts are assumed to be independent of changes in Y. One reason for focusing on the current account is that the capital account does not enter into aggregate demand.

With Y on the horizontal axis and exports and imports on the vertical axis, the import schedule is shown as sloping upwards. This reflects the fact that imports increase as Y rises. The slope of this line is determined by the MPM. The larger the MPM, the steeper the import schedule. The export schedule is shown as a horizontal line, indicating that changes in Y do not affect the level of exports. Exports are determined by the exchange rate and by aggregate demand in our main trading partners. At Y_1, exports equal imports and the current account is balanced. We draw a vertical NX = 0 reference line to indicate this level of Y. To the right of the NX = 0 line there is a trade deficit (imports exceed exports), and to the left there is a trade surplus.

A devaluation will reduce imports and the import schedule will shift down to the right. Equally, a devaluation will increase exports and the export schedule shifts to the right (not shown). The NX = 0 line shifts to the right and the equilibrium level of Y (that level of Y where exports equal imports) will move to the right along the horizontal axis.

Figure 16.11 shows an NX = 0 line that corresponds to a trade balance at Y_1 and a potential real output reference line denoted by Y*. To the right of Y*, the economy is over-heating and there is 'over full' employment. That is, unemployment is below its natural rate. To the left of Y*, the economy is in recession and unemployment is above its natural rate. As drawn, the NX = 0 line is situated to the left of the Y* (other combinations are possible). The economy can be in area 1, 2 or 3. These areas are characterised as follows:

- Area 1 – current account surplus and unemployment.
- Area 2 – current account deficit and unemployment.
- Area 3 – current account deficit and over-employment.

FIGURE 16.10 The trade balance

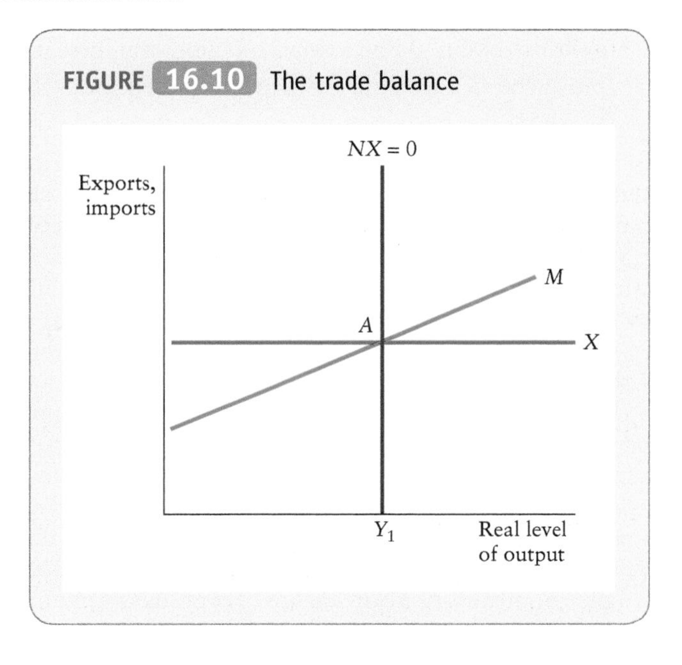

To illustrate the various areas, in the early 1980s the Irish economy was clearly in area 2: the current account deficit was about 15 per cent of GNP and unemployment was high and rising. In the late 1990s, with a current account surplus and a relatively high unemployment, the Irish economy was in area 1.

If the economy is in area 1 or 3 there is no policy dilemma in using fiscal or monetary policy to achieve a current account balance and full employment. For example, if the economy is in area 1, an expansionary fiscal or monetary policy can be used to reduce unemployment and reduce the current account surplus. Similarly, if the economy is in area 3, a deflationary fiscal or monetary policy can be implemented to reduce over-heating and reduce the current account deficit.

FIGURE 16.11 Potential real output and the trade balance

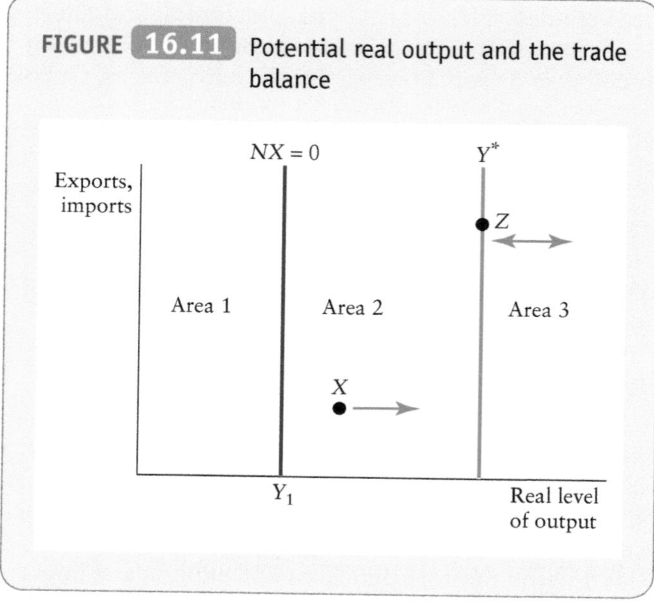

A dilemma does, however, arise if the economy is in area 2. An expansionary fiscal or monetary policy would reduce unemployment but aggravate the current account deficit. In contrast, a contractionary fiscal or monetary policy would aggravate the problem of unemployment while improving the current account deficit.

The policy mix

The dilemma between the internal and external policy objectives that exists when the economy is in area 2 can be resolved by resorting to devaluation. For example, suppose the economy is at the point X in Figure 16.11. A devaluation would:

- shift the NX = 0 line towards Y^* (exports increase and imports fall); and
- move the IS curve out to the right (recall that a devaluation increases NX and therefore the IS curve).

As a result, the economy would move from X towards the Y^* line. The result is that full employment could be restored while at the same time there should be an improvement in the current account. Devaluation resolves the policy dilemma between internal and external balance.

Suppose, however, the economy is at a point such as Z in Figure 16.11, which corresponds to potential real output and a current account deficit. A devaluation would move the NX = 0 line towards Y^*, but because of the shift to the right of the IS curve, the economy moves to the right of Y^*. As the economy moves to the right of Y^*, the current account deficit improves but the economy is now over-heating.

In this situation a deflationary fiscal or monetary policy is required to move either the IS or LM curve back to Y^*. The fall in Y will further improve the current account deficit. This example shows that if the economy is close to potential real output, devaluation will have to be accompanied by an expenditure-reducing policy if the objectives of internal and external balance are to be achieved simultaneously. Put another way, if the objective of devaluation is simply to improve the current account without increasing output and employment, an expenditure-reducing policy will have to accompany it.

These applications illustrate how economists can analyse the appropriate policy mix for an open economy.

16.8 The Aggregate Demand Curve

Up to this point we have assumed the price level (P) to be fixed. If we now drop this assumption we can examine the effect of a change in P in the Mundell–Fleming model and derive the aggregate demand (AD) curve. Note that because P is no longer fixed, the real interest rate (r) determines investment (I) and the real exchange rate (ε) determines net exports (NX).

In Figure 16.12, we start on the lower diagram at the point A, which shows a combination of P_1 and Y_1. This is one point on the AD curve. If there is an increase in P, this reduces the real money supply (M/P) and, in the upper diagram, the LM curve shifts back to the left from LM_1 to LM_2. At B in the upper diagram, there is a balance of payments surplus and the real exchange rate appreciates. The increase in ε reduces NX and the IS curve shifts down to the left from IS_1 to IS_2. Output (Y) falls along the horizontal axis. In the lower diagram, the combination of P_2 and Y_2 is a new point on the AD curve. By varying P we can trace out the complete AD curve, which is downward sloping. In short, the sequence is:

$$\uparrow P \rightarrow \downarrow (M/P) \rightarrow \uparrow \varepsilon \rightarrow \downarrow NX \rightarrow \downarrow Y$$

Figure 16.13 illustrates how the money supply determines the location of the AD curve. Starting from A in the lower diagram and the P_1, Y_1 combination, in the upper diagram, an expansionary monetary policy shifts the LM curve down to the right from LM_1 to LM_2. At B, there is a balance of payments deficit and this causes the real exchange rate, ε, to depreciate. This, in turn, increases NX and the IS curve shifts upwards to the right from IS_1 to IS_2. Output increases along the horizontal axis from Y_1 to Y_2. If we now shift the AD curve out to the right, we can examine the relationship between the initial price level, P_1, and the new higher output level Y_2. The increase in the money supply has shifted the AD to the right. Conversely, a decrease in the money supply will move the AD curve to the left.

FIGURE 16.12 Deriving the aggregate demand curve

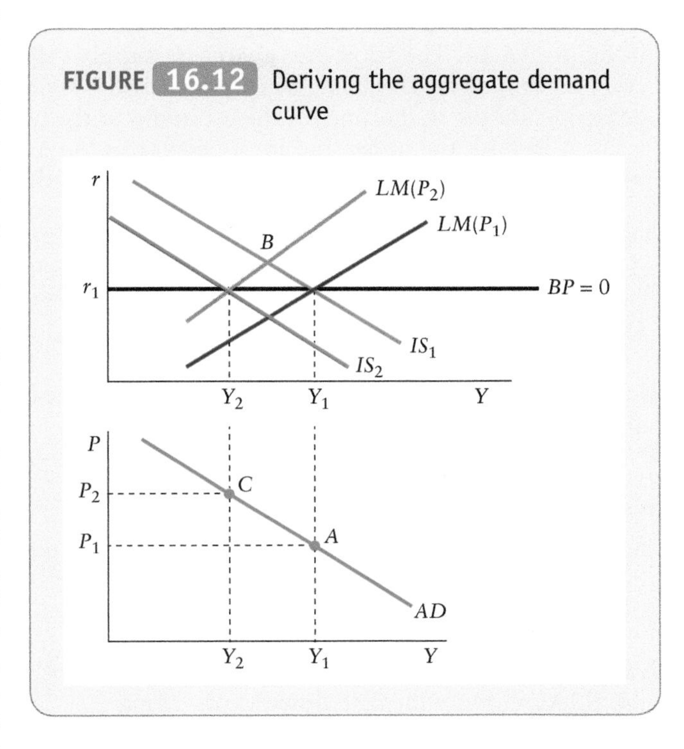

FIGURE 16.13 Monetary policy and the AD curve

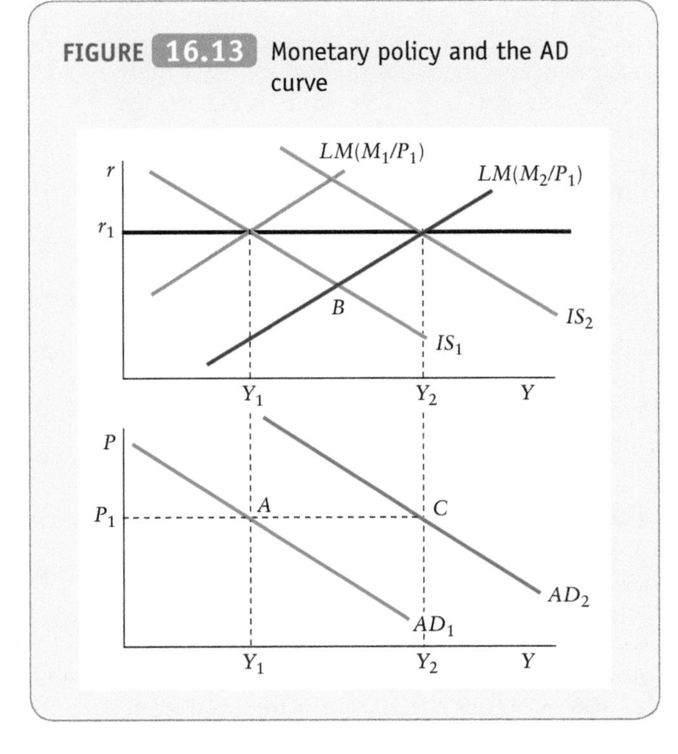

Restoring full employment

Let us now re-introduce into the analysis the potential level of output, Y*. This level of output is represented by the long-run aggregate supply (LRAS) curve. This is given as the vertical line in Figure 16.14. The short-run aggregate supply (SRAS) curve is upward sloping, reflecting the combination of flexible and sticky prices in the short run. Suppose the economy is subject to a demand-side shock that moves the economy to the left of the LRAS line. The economy moves to point A in both the upper and lower diagrams. At A the economy is below the potential level of output, Y*. How does the economy revert back to the LRAS?

We have already described two separate adjustment mechanisms. In Chapter 5, the adjustment depended crucially on the downward flexibility of prices and nominal wages. We depended on a downward revision in price expectations (P^e) and a fall in the nominal wage to restore the real wage (the initial fall in the price level increased real earnings). This reduced the costs facing firms and the SRAS curve moved to the right.

In the closed economy IS-LM model of Chapter 11, we depended on a fall in the price level to increase the real money supply. This, in turn, reduced the interest rate, which boosted investment and, therefore, output.

$$\downarrow P \rightarrow \uparrow(M/P) \rightarrow \downarrow r \rightarrow \uparrow I \rightarrow \uparrow Y$$

In this open economy IS-LM model the mechanism is similar to that of Chapter 11, except that the real exchange, and not the real interest rate, is the crucial adjustment mechanism. The point A in Figure 16.14 is not a long-run equilibrium point as the economy is operating below potential. Over time, the high unemployment will cause the price level to fall. This, in turn, will lead to a revision downwards in price expectations and the SRAS curve will drift downwards along the AD_1 curve.

But what causes aggregate demand (AD) to increase? In the upper diagram, the fall in the price level increases the real money supply (M/P) and the LM curve shifts down to the right. This creates a balance of payments deficit and the real exchange rate starts to depreciate. This, in turn, increases net exports and the IS curve shifts up to the right. Eventually the economy reverts back to the LRAS line and the output gap is eliminated. In short:

$$\downarrow P \rightarrow \uparrow(M/P) \rightarrow \downarrow \varepsilon \rightarrow \uparrow NX \rightarrow \uparrow Y$$

In this open economy IS-LM model it is the real exchange rate that acts as the adjustment mechanism.

FIGURE 16.14 Adjusting to the potential level of output

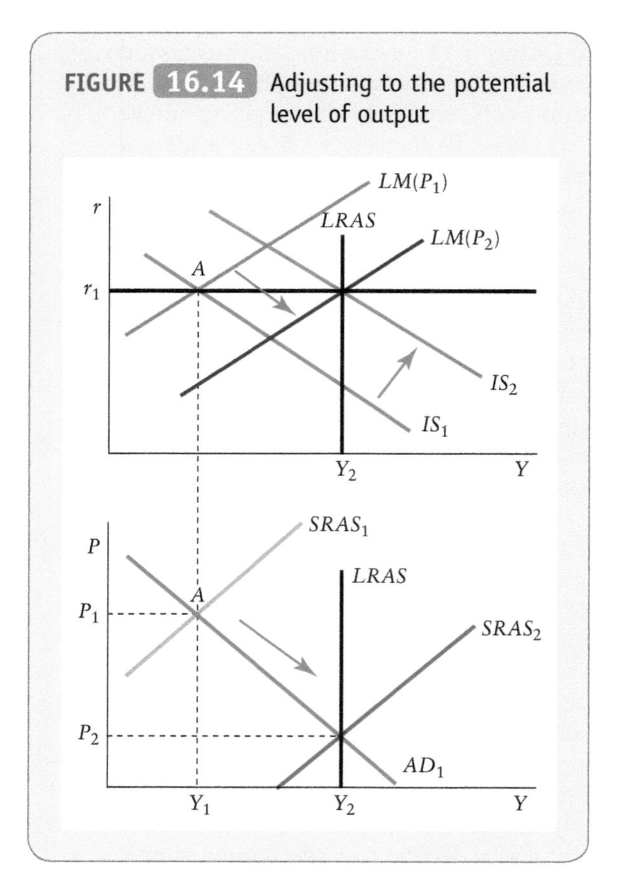

Adjustment in the Irish economy

After the adverse shock of 2007 a number of obstacles prevented the Irish economy from adjusting rapidly. First, the price level was relatively unresponsive to the recession. From a peak of 108 in 2008 the Irish CPI fell to a low of 100 in January 2010, but it then started to rise again and by mid-2012 it was back up to 105. The fall in the internationally more widely used HICP was even less impressive – from a peak of 110 it fell to a low of 105 and rose again above 109. These changes were not much more pronounced that those occurring in several other euro area countries, so the fall in our price level relative to that of some of our competitors was less than the absolute fall in our price level.

Wages are more important than prices as an index of competitiveness because the national price level is influenced by indirect taxes and includes many non-traded services and regulated or administered prices. The index of hourly earnings in manufacturing increased from 100 in 2008 to a peak of 106 at the end of 2009. It then fell to 102 in 2011. Even in the construction sector, where employment collapsed in the wake of the building bust, wage rates declined only by a little over six per cent between 2008 and 2011. Once again the decline in our wage levels relative to those of our competitors was smaller than the decline in the absolute wage level.

The adjustment channel is through the effect of a decrease in the price level increasing the real money supply. As the real money supply rises the LM curve shifts down to the right. In normal circumstances we would expect this increase in the real money supply to be facilitated by the banks extending credit to households and firms. However, as the Irish banks severely curtailed credit after the crash of 2008, this would have hindered the adjustment mechanism.

The third and critical adjustment mechanism is the fall in the real exchange rate that follows from a decrease in the price level. This would boost the NX component of aggregate demand. This also happened in Ireland as the real effective exchange rate fell 13 per cent between 2008 and 2011. The current account of the balance of payments moved from a deficit of 6.6 per cent of GNP in 2008 to a surplus of 0.1 per cent in 2011. However, the nominal euro exchange rate fell for reasons unrelated to conditions in Ireland. As pointed out in Chapter 15, Ireland's real exchange rate is dominated by movements of the nominal euro exchange rate relative to currencies like sterling and the US dollar. An appreciation of the euro exchange rate could reverse this competitive gain very quickly.

A fourth difficulty relates to the fact that competitiveness is a relative concept. It is not possible for all countries to improve their competitiveness at the same time. Many recent pronouncements from Brussels urging all the countries of the euro area to become more competitive seem to miss this point. While the euro area as whole could be more competitive relative to the rest of the world by a fall in the value of the euro or by a spurt of euro area-wide productivity, France and Greece and Ireland cannot all become simultaneously more competitive relative to each other.

Summary

As explained in Chapter 11, the Keynesian cross diagram underlines the IS curve and the theory of liquidity preference underlines the LM curve. The Mundell–Fleming IS-LM model is an open economy version of the closed IS-LM model. This model provides the theory underlining the AD curve. Once the model is expanded to incorporate the LRAS curve, we obtain some insight into how the Irish economy might recover from the recession of 2008.

16.9 Key Terms and Concepts

In this chapter we discussed how the open economy adjusts in the short run when prices are assumed to be constant and there are no supply-side constraints. The main points developed in this chapter were:

- the concepts of internal and external balance
- the BP = 0 line
- the Mundell–Fleming model

- fiscal policy is effective and monetary policy ineffective when the exchange rate is fixed and there is perfect capital mobility and a stable default risk premium
- if the exchange rate is floating and capital perfectly mobile, fiscal policy is ineffective and monetary policy effective
- the impact of exchange rate and sovereign risk on output under fixed and flexible exchange rates
- a policy dilemma can exist when the objective is to achieve a trade balance and full employment
- devaluation must be accompanied by a deflationary fiscal or monetary policy if the economy is close to potential real GNP and the objective is to remove a trade deficit
- the Mundell–Fleming model as an aggregate demand model
- the real exchange rate as an adjustment mechanism to move the economy back to the potential level of output.

CHAPTER 17

The European Monetary Union and the European Central Bank

17.1 Introduction

The European Economic and Monetary Union (EMU) is an experiment without parallel in economic history. Never before has a group of sovereign, independent nations surrendered their currencies and adopted a new common currency. In this chapter we describe the EMU and discuss the costs and benefits of membership. We then discuss the role and policies of the European Central Bank (ECB). We discuss the factors underlying the ECB's policies.

17.2 The History of EMU

The EMU was formally launched in January 1999, but its origins date back to a meeting of the European Council in June 1988 in Hanover, when a committee was given the task of 'studying and proposing concrete stages leading towards [economic and monetary] union'. The committee was chaired by the Commission President Jacques Delors and consisted of the governors of the central banks of the 12 member states (including Ireland's Maurice Doyle), an EU Commission representative and three invited experts. The committee published its report (known as the Delors Report) in April 1989.

We can look at the 'economic' and 'monetary' components of EMU separately. An economic union requires single market within which persons, goods, services, and capital can move freely (the four freedoms). The implementation of the 1987 Single European Act went a considerable way towards achieving this objective. It also established a common competition policy. To establish a 'level playing field' governments are required to eliminate state aids to industry. Following reunification, Germany became one of the main offenders on this front. More recently, Ireland's special 12.5 per cent profit tax rate on industry has come in for criticism, although it is not officially regarded as a state aid to industry.

Finally, economic union presupposes structural and regional convergence. In order to meet this precondition for a successful EMU a Cohesion Fund was established to help peripheral countries in the transition to a single market. Because Ireland lagged behind the average standard of living in the EU in the 1990s, we received considerable subsidies from this Fund.

A monetary union requires the complete liberalisation of capital transactions and full integration of banking and other financial markets. Ultimately, and most radically, it requires the introduction of a single currency.

The idea of a single European currency – or at least irrevocably fixed exchange rates between national currencies – has a long and torturous history. Following the abortive attempts to achieve a 'zone of monetary stability' – the snake and EMS discussed in Chapter 14 – it was decided in the 1990s to press ahead for the adoption of a single European currency. In Madrid in 1995 it was decided that it would be called the euro.

Monetary union and the adoption of a single currency call for monetary policy to be moved from national central banks to the ECB. Participating countries have to be subservient to the ECB's objective of ensuring price stability.

NOTE: The intellectual origins of EMU are in the theory of an Optimum Currency Area (OCA) which was first outlined by the Nobel Prize-winning economist Robert A. Mundell. As its name implies, this theory was developed to assess the optimum size of an area that uses the same currency. Whether the 11 countries that banked together to form the European EMU in 1999 constituted an OCA is very much open to debate.

The framers of the Maastricht Treaty were very conscious of the fact that before full EMU could be launched the participating countries should first have achieved a high degree of 'nominal convergence'. Accordingly they laid down several convergence criteria that would have to be met by any country that wanted to join EMU. These criteria related to inflation and interest rate differentials, the levels of the fiscal deficit, and the national debt in 1997.

The actual criteria proposed were probably framed for the purpose of excluding traditionally inflation-prone countries such as Italy, Spain and Portugal (the 'Club Med') from EMU, but circumstances changed during the 1990s. It became difficult for even France and Germany to meet the convergence criteria. Consequently in May 1998 the criteria were loosely applied and 11 countries were deemed eligible to participate in EMU: Austria, Belgium, France, Finland, Germany, Ireland, Italy, Luxembourg, the Netherlands, Spain and Portugal. Greece initially failed to meet the criteria but was later deemed to have them and allowed to join in January 2001. Sweden, Britain and Denmark opted out for domestic political reasons and because of their misgivings about the soundness of the project.

The steps towards establishing EMU

The Delors Report envisaged Europe evolving towards EMU in three stages. Stages I and II were concerned with completing the internal market and launching the European Monetary Institute (EMI) (the precursor of the ECB). The final stage, Stage III, of EMU ran from January 1999 to March 2002 and involved the following steps.

- May 1998 – the conversion exchange rate from national currencies to the euro was agreed.
- 1 July 1998 – the EMI was replaced by the ECB.
- 1 January 1999 – the euro was introduced in 'virtual' form; that is, exchange rates were irrevocably fixed but the new currency was not yet put into circulation.
- 1 January 2002 – euro notes and coins were introduced. All notes and coins denominated in national currencies were withdrawn by mid-2002. This completed the transition to EMU.

NOTE: There is some awkwardness about what the new currency union should be called. Various labels are used in the press – 'Eurozone', 'monetary union', 'euro area' and so on. When referring to the group of countries that form the EMU we have adhered to the ECB's official label, which is 'the euro area'.

The prospects for EMU

The evidence of history is that systems of fixed exchange rates do not endure. From the Gold Standard to the EMS, previous attempts to stabilise the world's currency markets have eventually collapsed. The most important reason has been that sovereign countries have wished to reassert the right to implement independent economic policies. Sooner or later incompatibilities between national and supranational economic policies have led to strains, speculative attacks, and ultimately the abandonment of fixed exchange rates.

However, the collapse of the EMS in 1993 convinced many that the best way forward was not another 'halfway house' but to abolish national currencies and adopt a single European currency. They argued that only when the commitment to fixed exchange rates was made 'irrevocable' in this manner would the full benefits of a stable international financial system be enjoyed in Europe. Others interpreted the history of the EMS since 1979 as evidence of the dangers inherent in trying to fix exchange rates between sovereign countries. They pointed to the risks involved in the single currency project.

We now turn to an assessment of the cost and benefits of participating in EMU under two broad headings: political and economic.

17.3 The Political Benefits of EMU to Ireland

Some of the most important potential benefits from the adoption of a single European currency are political in nature. This is because it is very possible that EMU is only a prelude to a fully fledged federal EU.

It is argued that if a federal Europe were to emerge this would ensure peace in Europe. The former French President François Mitterrand is quoted as saying 'Nationalism – that is war.' Similarly, the German Chancellor Helmut Kohl stated that EMU would 'free Europe from war in the twenty-first century'. While another war in Europe is inconceivable, it is clear that EMU could lead to a more effective EU foreign policy. It could be expected that Germany would play a key role in the design and implementation of such a policy. In addition, it is claimed that a single currency will increase solidarity between participants and reduce the risks of trade disputes. The EU is frequently compared to a bicycle: it must either move forward or stall, and EMU was the next logical step toward deeper integration.

The political argument that Ireland must be seen to move forward with Europe appears to have been very influential in official circles. Failure to do so, it was claimed, would have serious adverse repercussions such as less favourable treatment in future allocations of Structural Funds and exclusion from key economic decision-making processes.

It was also argued that by participating in EMU from its inception Ireland would have a voice in the formulation of European monetary policy. The governor of the Central Bank of Ireland has a seat on the governing council of the ECB. While European monetary policy clearly is not tailored to Irish problems, our influence has nonetheless been disproportionate to the size of our economy (we have 'boxed above our weight').

17.4 The Economic Benefits of EMU to Ireland

In this section we outline the main economic benefits that are linked to membership of EMU.

Completing the internal market

One economic benefit of adopting the euro is the extent to which it helped complete the single, or internal, European market. There are a number of ways in which the abolition of national currencies deepened economic integration.

First, the use of a common currency increased the transparency of prices and costs across countries. Since all prices are now denominated in euro, price differentials are more obvious and price comparisons easier. This encourages arbitrage, which in turn promotes the convergence of prices across the euro area (see Chapter 15). However, we spend a large and growing proportion of our income on non-traded services. Significant price differentials persist between the cost of educational, medical and personal services around the euro area.

However, a common currency is not a prerequisite for a high level of cross-border shopping: at present Irish subscribers are much more likely to use the internet to purchase from the USA and the UK than from the countries of the euro area. Indirect taxes and red tape are more serious obstacles to price convergence across the euro area than were national currencies, as anyone interested in buying a car in Belgium for use in Ireland will appreciate. Exchange rate transaction costs between euro area countries were estimated to be about one-half of one per cent of GDP. But while they were high for small transactions, such as tourist purchases, they were smaller for larger business deals.

The more important trade with other euro area countries is relative to GDP, the greater the savings in transaction costs from adopting the euro. Ireland is very open to international trade, but a substantial proportion of its international transactions involve sterling and the dollar. Hence, the reductions in overall transaction costs that followed from adopting the euro were not as great as was the case for other euro area countries. On the other hand, the savings on transaction costs within the euro area resulted in a significant fall in foreign exchange earnings in the financial sector.

Reduction in exchange rate uncertainty

Exchange rate fluctuations can result in large profits or losses for importers and exporters. Hedging techniques offer only short-term protection against exchange rate risk. It is argued that doing away with the risk of exchange rate fluctuations will stimulate trade and investment between euro area countries. Uncertainty regarding exchange rate movements is seen as a deterrent to planning long-run investment across international frontiers.

Plausible though this seems, the empirical research has found little evidence that floating exchange rates depress international trade and investment. Trade between Japan and the USA and Europe has grown rapidly even though their exchange rates are not pegged.

It should be recalled that in Ireland exchange rate risk continues to exist in relation to sterling, the dollar and the other currencies outside the euro area. The adoption of the euro did not remove the risk relating to a substantial proportion of Irish international transactions.

Scale economies

Prior to the introduction of the euro, firms had an incentive to spread their factories around Europe to protect their profits or assets from sudden movements in exchange rates. For example, suppose an Irish firm had a plant in Ireland and another in Spain. A depreciation of the peseta/Irish pound exchange rate would have increased the value of the Irish factory and decreased the value of the Spanish one. If the gain offset the loss, the assets of the overall firm would not be adversely affected. If, however, the firm only had a factory in Spain, the assets of the group, measured in Irish pounds, would decline.

Now that the euro has removed the exchange rate risk in the euro area, firms make location decisions on genuine considerations of comparative costs rather than as part of a strategy of hedging against sudden currency movements. That is, firms can locate their plants so as to reap economies of scale, ignoring national boundaries. This should lead to efficiency gains, lower costs and higher company profits.

Lower inflation

Adopting the euro helped formerly inflation-prone countries to enjoy a degree of price stability that they were unable to attain on their own. As we saw in Chapter 15, according to purchasing power parity (PPP) theory, the inflation rate in the smaller euro area countries should converge to the rate in the larger countries or the average of the euro area. The evidence presented in Chapter 15 shows that there was significant convergence during the approach to EMU and after 1999.

Lower interest rates

Under the EMS arrangement that operated from 1979 to 1993 European currencies were pegged but adjustable. For most of the period this did not deliver low interest rates in countries like Ireland, due to the perceived risk that the Irish pound would be devalued sooner or later. There is no exit mechanism from EMU and the commitment to monetary union is strong. Hence, the risk of devaluation is much more remote than under the EMS arrangement. As a consequence, interest rates did converge across the euro area after 1999. (The evidence for this was reviewed in Chapter 15.) However, the 2008 currency crisis shattered the markets' confidence in the permanency of the EMU in its present form and it became common to discuss when or how Greece, for example, would leave or be thrown out (this possibility is now referred to 'Grexit').

In 2010 wide differentials re-emerged between the interest rates or yields on sovereign bonds issued by euro area countries. Yields on the peripheral countries' bonds soared as investors became reluctant to accept the default risk, while the yield on German bonds fell to very low levels as investors flocked to this 'safe haven'. This situation persisted into 2012, but actions taken by the ECB in September 2012 (which we described in Chapter 9) led to an improvement in the situation.

17.5 The Economic Costs of EMU

These gains from membership of EMU did not come at zero cost. We now outline some of the costs of adopting the single currency.

Transition costs

Let us first consider the least important aspect of the changeover – the costs associated with the mechanics of the conversion from national currencies. On 28 February 2002, the transition to the euro was finally completed. As and from that date, national banknotes and coins ceased to be legal tender. Among the currencies made obsolete was the Greek drachma, the world's oldest currency.

> **NOTE:** The drachma was first introduced in the sixth century BC and is mentioned in both the Old and New Testament. It comes from the word *drás-somai*, which means 'to grip', because a drachma was originally equal to a handful of grain. However, during the Greek hyper-inflation in 1945 the exchange rate depreciated to 70 trillion drachmas to one British sovereign.

Once Irish bank notes were withdrawn from the system and were back at the Central Bank of Ireland they were no longer legal tender and were in effect 'old paper'. The Central Bank shredded the paper to make bricks, which were then distributed to poor households in Dublin and burned in fires.

While the euro changeover was described as a great success, considerable costs were involved. It has been estimated that the cost to the banks, government and the non-bank corporate sector of switching to the euro ran into hundreds of millions of euro. The costs include staff training, stationery, marketing and public relations and changes to information technology.

Other costs include adapting both the domestic and international payments system to take account of the euro, storing large volumes of euro prior to their introduction, withdrawing domestic notes and coins and designing euro notes and coins. From the consumer's perspective, the main cost was the price rounding associated with the conversion from national currencies to the euro. In the Irish case, the conversion rate was IR£1 = €1.2697 or €1 = IR£0.787564. At this rate, the euro did not convert exactly into units of the old Irish pound and rounding up or down was required. The Consumers' Association of Ireland, in a nationwide survey, found that this pushed the annual rate of inflation up from 4.2 to 4.9 per cent in January 2002. The survey concluded that the euro was not brought in on the concept of 'new currency – same price'.

It should be borne in mind that these costs were spread across the euro area. A break-up of EMU, on the other hand, would impose high costs on individual countries. There would be a big difference between the cost of reverting to a national currency and the costs involved when Argentina broke the link with the US dollar or Ireland broke with sterling. In those cases the national currency was still in existence. When EMU was launched the old national currencies were abolished: bringing them back to life would be a costly and complicated process that would mainly fall on the weak country leaving the EMU.

Adjusting to an asymmetric shock

A more serious cost associated with EMU membership has been the problem of having to adjust to economic shocks in the absence of a national exchange rate and a national monetary policy.

We live in a dynamic world where the economy is constantly buffeted by different types of shock. These shocks can take many forms, for example increases in oil prices; fluctuations in the sterling, yen or dollar exchange rates; the 11 September terrorist attack; the foot and mouth crisis in 2001; and the 2008 global banking crisis. These shocks can potentially affect all nations, but not equally. A shock that has a disproportionate impact on a particular economy is referred to as a *country-specific* or *asymmetric* shock.

At the time of EMU entry, some economists argued that the risk of an asymmetric shock within the euro area was minimal because the EU economies are highly integrated and structurally similar. A shock to one would be a shock to all. The countries that formed the EMU were not highly specialised in narrow branches of economic activity but more diversified, with increasingly similar industrial structures. A fall in the demand for tourism or automobiles, for example, would affect many European countries about equally seriously.

However, this argument could not be pushed to the point of denying the possibility of region-specific shocks. One of the anticipated benefits of the single market is an increased specialisation across countries. A rationalisation of the car industry is taking place that will concentrate production in fewer plants spread across fewer countries. This makes those countries more vulnerable to an asymmetric shock when there is downturn in the demand for cars.

In the Irish case, there was widespread anxiety that the unusual pattern of our trade, less than one-third of which is with other euro area countries, would make us vulnerable to a sudden strengthening of the sterling/euro exchange rate, which would not have much effect on Italy, for example. However, few anticipated the effect of monetary union on credit markets and the exceptional bubble in Irish property prices that finally burst in 2008. This crash had a disproportionate effect on the Irish economy. The only other euro area country to have experience a comparable boom and bust is Spain.

Adopting the euro meant that an EMU member state could no longer resort to exchange rate devaluation or appreciation as a policy instrument in the face of an asymmetric shock. There is no unanimity among economists on the costs of relinquishing this policy instrument. On one side, it is argued that the exchange rate tends to be less effective as a policy instrument in a very open economy like Ireland. With so many consumer goods and raw materials imported, a devaluation would quickly feed through to higher inflation and the effect on the real exchange rate would be eroded. If this is the case, the costs of relinquishing the exchange rate instrument should be small for Ireland.

The counter-argument is that PPP does not hold in the short run and changes in the exchange rate can result in important competitive gains or losses. For example, the Irish pound devaluations of 1983, 1986 and 1993 were all triggered by a weakening of sterling. If the Irish authorities had not had recourse to the exchange rate option at these times, the economic consequences for the overall economy could have been very serious.

Since the Irish economy entered a very deep recession in 2008 the issue of the value of an independent exchange rate has assumed new prominence. In the absence of an independent currency, the only way to improve price competitiveness is to engineer an 'internal devaluation', that is to cut wages and hope that this leads to lower prices. In Chapter 5 we noted that the downward adjustment of wages has been relatively small and short-lived in Ireland. Four years into the recession, unemployment remains unacceptably high and the price level is rising again. Attempting to improve competitiveness through a fall in domestic prices is made all the more difficult if other euro area countries, such as Spain, Portugal and Italy, are all trying to do the same thing.

So far, our experience with adjusting to a recession as a member of a currency union has been painful and suggests that abandoning control over our currency has been costly. Some of the pain was eased between 2008 and 2012 as the external value of the euro declined, improving Ireland's competitiveness vis à vis the UK and the USA. However, this was due to circumstances beyond our control and could be reversed if market sentiment towards the euro changed.

Normally, a country's exchange rate could be expected to reflect its economic fundamentals. For example, if a country is experiencing a balance of payments deficit or a relatively high inflation rate, the exchange rate could be expected to depreciate. The movement of the exchange rate should help bring the economy back to full employment. However, the Irish economy, which accounts for only about one per cent of euro area GDP, is too small to have any effect on the euro exchange rate or to be taken into account in the monetary policy deliberations of the ECB.

Whether the extra policy instruments an independent currency would have left at our disposal would have produced a better outcome is still an open question.

Without a national currency a country is also deprived of an independent monetary policy. An independent central bank would reduce interest rates in times of recession or increase interest rates when the economy is over-heating. Changes in interest rates would affect consumer expenditure and investment and thereby impact on the demand side of the economy. Ireland has no effect on euro area interest rates except through Ireland's representative on the governing council of the ECB. We discuss Ireland's experience with the ECB's monetary policy later in this chapter.

Constraints on fiscal policy

Keynesian theory recommends an expansionary fiscal policy in times of recession and a deflationary policy in times of over-heating. In principle these options are still open to countries in the euro area. However, we have seen that the Fiscal Compact, which was approved by referendum in Ireland in June 2012, commits government to reduce the budget deficit if the structural deficit reaches 0.5 per cent of GDP. This would impose more austerity on the Irish economy, which would already be in recession.

The absence of a 'transfer union'

In federal political systems a process known as fiscal federalism helps regions to adjust to shocks. After an asymmetric shock the depressed regions pay less in taxes to the central government and receive more in transfer payments from it. Booming regions, on the other hand, pay more in taxes and receive less in transfer payments. These automatic stabilisers help soften the impact of region-specific shocks.

In the USA the federal government absorbs a significant proportion of region-specific shocks. The state of Florida, for example, suffered disproportionately from the 'sub-prime' mortgage crisis, but it is estimated that transfers from the federal government to resolve the banking crisis amounted to 20 per cent of the state's GDP.

When Hurricane Katrina wrought havoc in New Orleans in 2005, the federal government spent billions repairing the damage. In Ireland the Mid-West region has recently suffered more than its share of job losses and increased unemployment, and its residents now pay less in taxes and receive more in unemployment benefit and other transfer payments from central government. These examples illustrate how transfer unions operate.

However, the euro area is not based on a federal political system like the USA. The EU budget is less than two per cent of EU GDP. There are no automatic mechanisms for transferring funds to areas that experience adverse shocks. The money paid from specific funds, the biggest of which is the agricultural fund FEOGA, does not automatically increase in response to downturns in the regions. Although the EU's income – its 'own resources' – is raised as percentages of the customs duties and VAT receipts collected in the member states and of their GDP, they are limited to 1.23 per cent of GDP, so the cyclical variation in them is very small.

However, as the current crisis has deepened, the stronger countries of the euro area, notably Germany, have had to dig ever deeper into their pockets to fund various rescue packages to help the peripheral economies, notably the European Stability Mechanism (ESM). But its contribution has now been capped at a maximum of €190 billion. While this money will be used to fund bail-outs for countries like Greece, Portugal, Ireland and Spain, interest will be paid on the loans and they will have to be repaid.

Nonetheless, the perception in Germany is that their taxpayers are being asked to pay for the profligacy of the peripheral countries. They fear that the EU is moving towards a 'transfer union' in which the richer countries will have to foot the bill for recessions and financial crashes in the weaker countries. They fear that a full-scale banking union, which is now being discussed, would open the door to a fiscal union and large-scale fiscal burden-sharing.

Lack of factor mobility

If Ireland is faced with persistent unemployment it is likely that Irish emigration to Britain and elsewhere will increase – this was an important part of the adjustment mechanism in the 1950s and again in the 1980s. Migration eases labour shortages elsewhere and reduces unemployment in Ireland. However, this channel of adjustment entails personal and social costs for Ireland. In fact, politicians in any country have never welcomed large-scale emigration. However, adopting the euro implied that it would become a more important component of the adjustment process.

While the EU has made considerable progress towards establishing the free movement of labour between member states, it is still far from an integrated single market. Labour mobility is low by comparison with that between the regions of the USA. Differences in language and culture, rigidities in housing markets and ethnic discrimination present significant barriers to the movement of labour between member states.

While immigration into the EU from poorer countries in Eastern Europe, North Africa and further afield is running at a high rate, mobility between the members of the euro area is relatively weak and concentrated among the better educated. It is striking that when the recession began to bite in Ireland in 2008, emigration of Irish people increased, but it was directed mainly outside the euro area – to Britain, the USA, Canada, Australia and New Zealand.

17.6 The European Central Bank

The Treaty on European Union was agreed in December 1991 and signed in Maastricht on 7 February 1992. It entered into force on 1 November 1993. The Maastricht Treaty contains the statutes establishing the ECB and the European System of Central Banks (ESCB). The ESCB consists of the ECB and the national central banks of the euro area countries. On 1 January 1999, the ECB assumed responsibility for monetary policy within the euro area. The countries that joined EMU surrendered to the ECB their powers to make independent monetary policies. Situated on Kaiserstrasse in Frankfurt, some three miles away from the Bundesbank (the German Central Bank), the ECB formulates monetary policy for the euro area as a whole. The ECB is designed to remain a relatively small institution relying on national central banks to perform functions such as bank supervision and regulation at the national level. After the banking crisis of 2008, this came to be regarded as a flaw in the design of EMU. Banks operating across the euro area should not have been left to the 'light touch' regulation of the authorities in countries like Ireland. When they got into spectacular trouble, it was not possible for individual countries to resolve their problems on their own.

In 2011, Mario Draghi, an Italian banker and economist, became president of the ECB, succeeding Jean-Claude Trichet. Draghi was previously the governor of the Bank of Italy and had worked in the USA with Goldman Sachs.

The governing council is the main decision-making body of the ECB. It is responsible for formulating monetary policy for the euro area. This includes decisions relating to monetary objectives, key interest rates, and the supply of reserves in the Eurosystem of banks. It comprises the six members of the executive board, plus the governors of the national central banks of the 17 euro area countries. Decisions are taken by simple majority voting, with the president having a casting vote.

The executive board implements the decisions of the governing council and, when appropriate, sends instructions to the national central banks. It comprises the president and vice-president of the ECB and four other members, appointed by 'common accord' by the heads of the euro area states for an eight-year non-renewable term. Table 17.1 lists the members of the governing council in 2012.

The Maastricht Treaty lays down the responsibilities of the ECB as follows.

- Its primary responsibility is to maintain price stability.
- Without prejudice to price stability, it also supports 'the general economic policies in the Community' so as to contribute to realising the Communitys objectives, which include 'sustainable and non-inflationary growth, a high degree of convergence of economic performance, a high level of employment and social protection, the raising of the standard of living and quality of life, and economic and social cohesion'.
- The ECB is independent of national central banks, national governments and all other bodies in formulating policy: 'Neither the ECB, nor a national central bank, nor any member of their decision-making bodies shall seek or take advice from Community institutions or bodies, from any Government of a Member State or from any other body.'
- The ECB may not lend to any Community institution or government. This is also interpreted to mean that it cannot buy government bonds, but as we saw in Chapter 9 this has recently been interpreted not to stand in the way of a programme of 'Outright Financial Transactions'. This involves buying short-dated government bonds subject to tight conditionality.

Price stability is the ECB's overriding objective. The commitment to promoting the general economic policies of the Community is too vague to be of much significance. There is a contrast here with the US Federal Reserve System (the Fed), which has a much more binding commitment to maintaining full employment under the Full Employment Act of 1946.

TABLE 17.1 The governing council of the ECB, 2012

1	Mario Draghi	President (Italy)
2	Vitor Constâncio	Vice-president (Portugal)
3	Jörg Asmussen	Executive Board (Germany)
4	Peter Praet	Executive Board (Belgium)
5	Benoît Coeuré	Executive Board (France)
6	Yves Mersch	Executive Board (Luxembourg)
7	Luc Coene	Belgium
8	Jens Weidmann	Germany
9	Patrick Honohan	Ireland
10	Georgios Provopoulos	Greece
11	Luis Maria Linde	Spain
12	Christian Noyer	France
13	Ignazio Visco	Italy
14	Panicos Demetriades	Cyprus
15	Gaston Reinesch	Luxembourg
16	Josef Bonnici	Malta
17	Klaas Knot	Netherlands
18	Ewald Nowotny	Austria
19	Carlos Costa	Portugal
20	Marko Kranjec	Slovenia
21	Erkki Liikanen	Finland
22	Jozef Makúch	Slovakia
23	Ardo Hansson	Estonia

The ECB's inflation target

In 2003 the Governing Council of the ECB clarified that 'in the pursuit of price stability, it aims to maintain inflation rates below but close to 2 per cent over the medium term'. Note that this involves not allowing the inflation rate to fall too low as well as preventing it from rising too high. As we discussed in Chapter 3, a negative rate of inflation – deflation – could pose serious problems for a modern economy.

A problem in setting inflation targets is that inflation rates are not uniform across euro area countries. The ECB target is a weighted average of inflation rates measured by the Harmonised Index of Consumer Prices in the euro area and ignores regional differences. However, since the launch of EMU in 1999, there has been marked convergence of inflation rates across countries, so this is not a serious problem.

17.7 ECB Independence

The Maastricht Treaty contains several provisions that make the ECB extremely free from political interference. It is only required to present an annual report on its activities to the European Parliament, the Council of Ministers and the Commission. The Parliament may decide to hold a debate on the report, but it has no powers to sanction the members of the ECB's governing council. This means that the ECB is not directly accountable to elected politicians or to the public. This level of independence is even greater than that of the Bundesbank and the US Federal Reserve Bank. The Bundesbank is ultimately subject to the German parliament and the Fed to the US Congress. However, neither the European Parliament nor the national parliaments can interfere with the ECB. It would require a revision of the Maastricht Treaty – ratified by referendum in all the EU member states – to alter this.

Furthermore, unlike the Bank of England, the ECB does not publish the minutes of governing council meetings. It is argued that this would create a 'false transparency' and force all important decisions to take place 'in the corridor'. This lack of accountability, however, gives rise to the accusation that there is a 'democratic deficit' because a small number of non-elected individuals have control over key macroeconomic policy instruments and are not accountable to parliament or the public. This is part of the reason why the UK, Denmark and Sweden decided not to join EMU.

The reason for giving the ECB such exceptional autonomy is that complete independence from political pressure is seen as essential in achieving low inflation.

The record

Figure 17.1 shows the relationship between central bank independence and inflation for a sample of countries (data derived from Williams and Reid 1997). Measured along the horizontal axis is the average annualised inflation rate for each country over the period 1960–1990. An index of central bank dependence is measured along the vertical axis. This index is compiled by reference to legal provisions relating to:

- appointment and dismissal of the governor
- procedures for the formation of monetary policy
- objectives of the central bank
- limitations on lending by the central bank.

FIGURE 17.1 Central bank independence and the inflation record

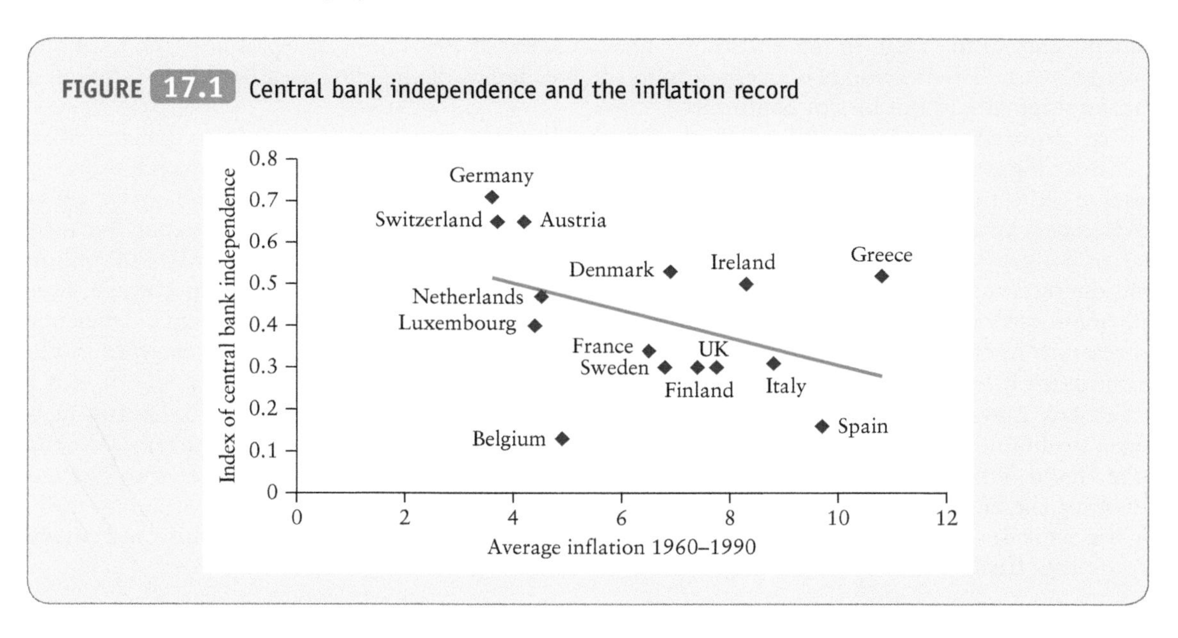

The minimum score of zero indicates no independence and a maximum score of one indicates complete independence.

The line running through the scatter plot shows an inverse relationship indicating that the greater the independence of the central bank, the lower the average inflation rate. The Bundesbank and the Swiss and Austrian central banks were reckoned to be very independent of political influences and to have delivered low inflation. In contrast, the Banco de España was at the other end of the spectrum. The central banks of Belgium and Greece are the most obvious outliers. While there are a number of misgivings about the validity of this type of analysis, particularly in relation to the construction of the 'independence index', the findings tend to confirm that independence is a prerequisite for attaining low inflation.

Related to these arguments for central bank independence is the problem of *inflation bias* and *time inconsistency*. As discussed in the context of the Phillips curve in Chapter 12, the trade-off between unemployment and inflation only exists in the short run. In the longer term, the effect of the increase in the money supply will be a proportionate increase in the price level and no change in real output. This means that monetary policy has no long-run effect on the real economy. In the short run, however, a surprise expansionary monetary policy could be used to boost output and employment at the expense of higher inflation.

The problem is that politicians are (time) inconsistent in their commitment to curbing inflation. On assuming office it makes sense for them to declare that they are committed to price stability, but sooner or later and especially at election time, they will change their mind (*time inconsistency*), opt for lower unemployment and relent on curbing inflation (*inflation bias*). They may be trying to get re-elected by exploiting the movement along the short-run Phillips curve. If policy-makers are subservient to politicians they will be obliged to engineer the desired surprise inflation.

An early example of this occurred in March 1999 when the German finance minister of the day, Oskar Lafontaine, put pressure on the ECB to cut interest rates in order to stimulate the stagnant EU economy. Relations between Lafontaine and the then ECB president Wim Duisenberg became very strained and the episode ended only when Lafontaine was removed from office.

17.8 How Interest Rates are Set in the Euro Area

In Chapter 15 we discussed the convergence of interest rates across the euro area on the main refinancing rate of the ECB. In this section we look at some of the technicalities of how the ECB sets interest rates. (This section is concerned with the mechanics of the euro area banking system and can be skipped without loss of continuity.)

The required reserve ratio is a crucial link in the determination of interest rates in the euro area. Consider Figure 17.2, which shows the variation in the banks' reserves in relation to the required reserve ratio. In 2011, the reserve requirement was set at two per cent of the 'reserve base' (it was revised downwards to one per cent in 2012). Compliance with the reserve base is based on the average of daily balances over a one-month maintenance period. If the reserve base is €10,000 billion and the reserve ratio is two per cent, the banks must keep €200 billion in reserve, on average, over the one-month maintenance period. The diagram shows that collectively the banks had a deficiency in reserves in the earlier part of the month and this requires them to hold excess reserves in the latter part of the month.

A bank may hold excess reserves, but in normal circumstances it will not do so, because it is more profitable to loan out as much as possible while complying with reserve constraint. On the other hand, a bank is not allowed to have a deficiency in reserves. Penalties range from fines to revoking the bank's licence.

If a bank is short of reserves coming towards the end of the maintenance period it can borrow from other banks (inter-bank market) or from the ECB.

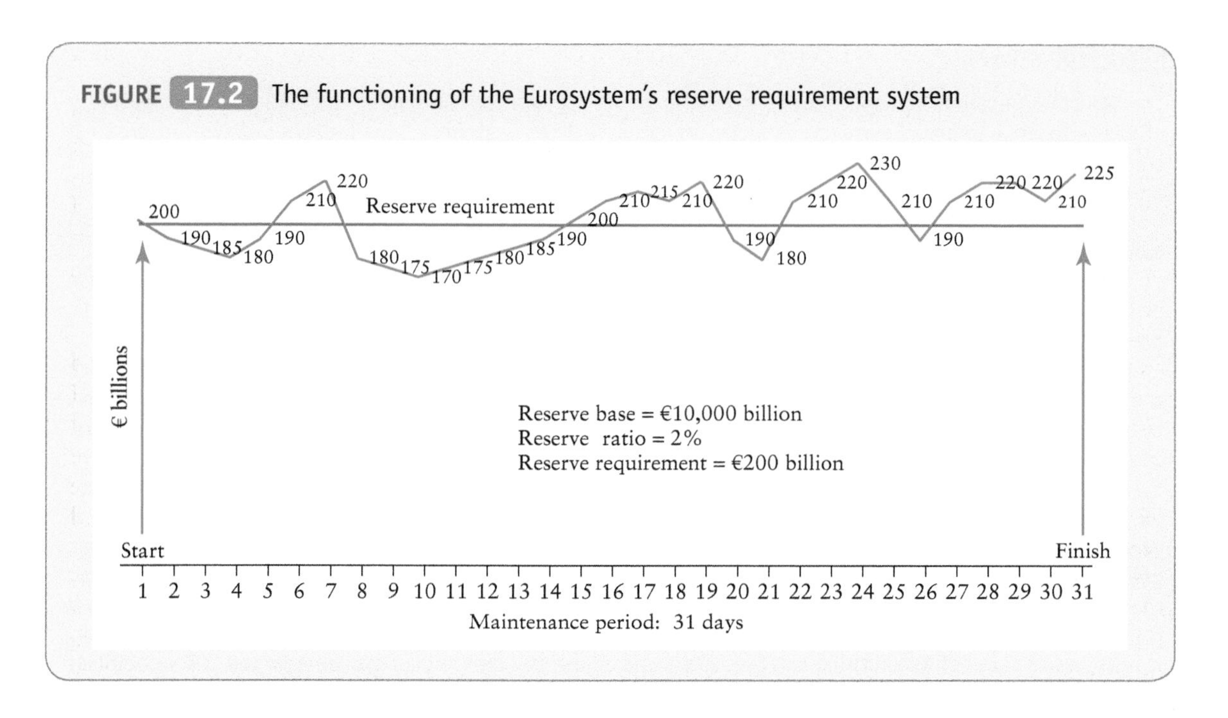

FIGURE 17.2 The functioning of the Eurosystem's reserve requirement system

If a bank borrows from the ECB, the interest rate charged by the ECB is the main refinancing interest rate (MRIR). This is the critical interest rate in the euro area. The ECB also has two other important interest rates called the marginal lending rate (MLR) and the deposit rate. The MLR provides overnight funds at an interest rate higher than MRIR. The commercial institutions, therefore, only use it as a last resort and this acts as an interest rate ceiling.

Commercial institutions can make lodgements with the ECB at the overnight deposit rate. This rate is much lower than MRIR and is used by the commercial institutions only if funds cannot be put to any other use. The deposit interest rate acts as a floor for interest rates.

Consider now the alternative case where a bank with a deficiency in reserves borrows from another commercial bank. The key interest rates in the euro area are EONIA (Euro overnight index average) and the one-, three-, six-, and 12-month EURIBOR (Euro inter-bank offer rates). EONIA is described as a 'weighted average of overnight loans made by a panel of banks most active in the money markets'. These rates are determined on the European inter-bank market. This is a market where banks and other financial institutions lend (supply) and borrow (demand) money from each other for periods ranging from a day to a year. This inter-bank market has no exact location. It is a market conducted through computers, telephones, fax and telex machines. The forces of supply and demand in this market determine the EONIA and EURIBOR interest rates.

NOTE: TARGET stands for Trans-European Automated Real-time Gross settlement Express Transfer. TARGET2, the second version, was introduced in 2007. It is the cross-border payments system on which the euro area banking system depends. It enables payments to be made quickly across member states. Each country has an RTGS (real-time gross settlement) system at its national central bank (NCB). Each national RTGS is then linked through TARGET. The use of the NCBs means that TARGET is a decentralised system, and this minimises the administrative structure at the centre which would be required to manage over 8,000 financial institutions in the euro area. In Box 17.1 we discuss an important issue that has been raised about this system in recent years.

Box 17.1 TARGET2

The TARGET2 system is complex, but it is vital to the continued functioning of the EMU and the credibility of the euro as a common currency. It works as follows: When a student uses a cheque drawn on an Irish commercial bank to pay for her overnight stay in a hotel in Berlin, the hotel will lodge it to its account at a German commercial bank. The cheque then enters the TARGET2 system. This entails deducting the amount from the student's Irish commercial bank's account at the Central Bank of Ireland and crediting the German commercial bank's account with the same amount at the Bundesbank.

The Bundesbank now has an increased liability to the hotel's commercial bank, but also a matching increase in its assets in the form of its deposit with the ECB. The Central Bank of Ireland's liabilities to the student's bank fall as the cheque clears through the TARGET2 system, but so too do its net assets with the ECB.

Countries running large balance of payments deficits will tend to accumulate large negative balances with the TARGET2 system, while the surplus countries accumulate large positive balances. Figure 17.3 shows how in 2012 Germany had accumulated vast positive balances and most other countries large negative balances, of which Ireland's and Spain's were the largest.

Professor Hans-Werner Sinn, a leading conservative German economist, claims that this system is working like a vast 'stealth bail-out' of the peripheral euro area countries by Germany. Professor Karl Whelan of University College Dublin has provided an important rebuttal of this claim (Whelan 2011). (Our account draws heavily on Professor Whelan's piece.) He points out that the Bundesbank does not have any claims against the Central Bank of Ireland as a result of its positive balances in TARGET2. Its claims are against the ECB and it can only lose money if the ECB reneges on its liability. Since the ECB is required by statute to be solvent, it is as near a safe bet as anything can be. At the end of the day the German exposure to the ECB's liabilities is limited to its contribution to the Bank's capital, which is 27 per cent of the total.

If a country's net balances in TARGET2 were to be limited, we could face the situation where a cheque written on an Irish bank would bounce not because the drawer had no money in her account, but because when presented for payment through the system it breached the Irish limit in TARGET2. If she had her money in a German bank account it would have been honoured. This situation would spell the end of the euro as a common currency. In fact anything that undermines the credibility of the TARGET2 system threatens the survival of EMU.

FIGURE 17.3 Net balances with the Eurosystem/TARGET2 balances, 1999–2012

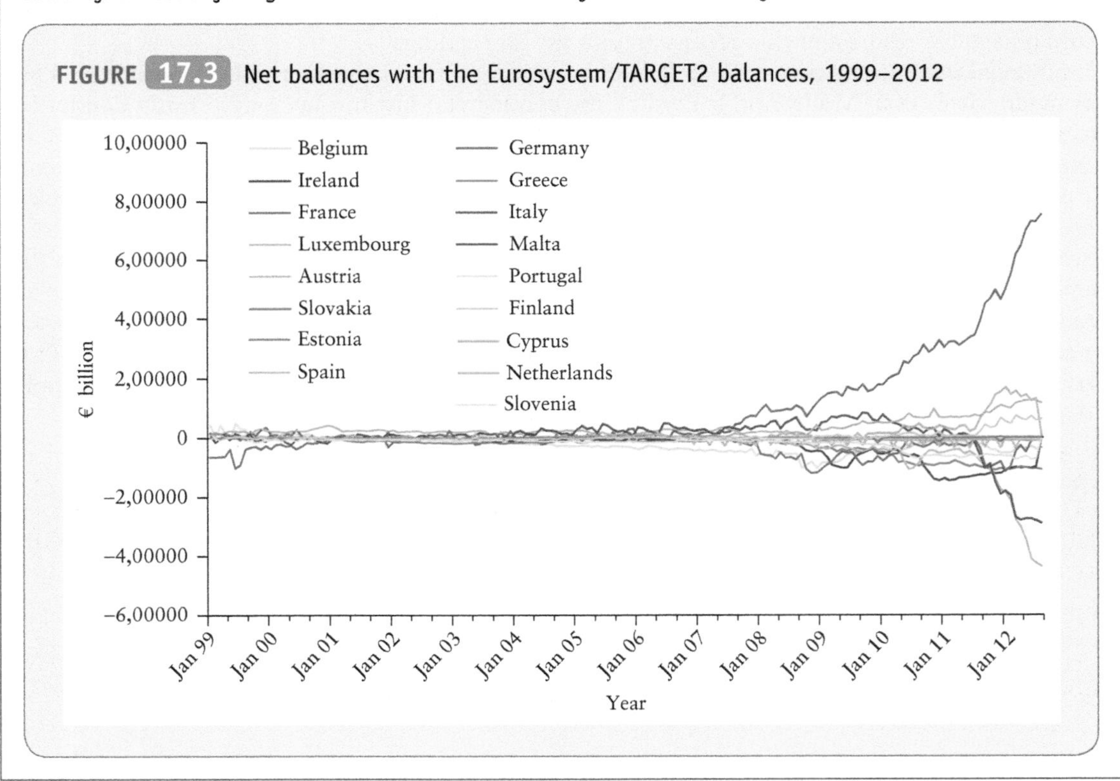

These inter-bank interest rates are crucially important because of their influence on all the other interest rates (deposit and lending rates) in the banking system. When EONIA and EURIBOR change, the commercial banks quickly change their lending and deposit interest rates because they are heavily dependent on the inter-bank market as a source of funds.

The important point is that if a bank has a deficiency of reserves, it will borrow (demand) funds on the inter-bank market. Conversely, a bank with excess reserves will lend (supply) funds to the inter-bank market and earn interest on them. There is therefore a direct link between the adequacy of the banks' reserves (their liquidity) and the supply of and demand for funds on the inter-bank market. If supply exceeds demand, EONIA will fall and, conversely, if supply is less than demand, EONIA will rise. Changes in EONIA will quickly have an impact on the whole spectrum of commercial bank interest rates.

It follows from this that the ECB's interest rate, MRIR, and the inter-bank interest rates, EONIA and EURIBOR, cannot get too far out of line with one another. If the person responsible at a commercial bank for ensuring reserve adequacy has to borrow funds he/she will opt for the lowest rate. Hence:

- if MRIR $>$ EONIA $\rightarrow$ banks borrow in the inter-bank market $\rightarrow \uparrow$ inter-bank interest rates until MRIR = EONIA
- if MRIR $<$ EONIA $\rightarrow$ banks borrow at the ECB $\rightarrow \downarrow$ the demand for funds in the inter-bank market until MRIR = EONIA.

Going one stage further, this means that the ECB can dictate interest rates in the euro area. If the governing council decides to raise MRIR it will back this up with an open market sale of bonds which will absorb funds from the banking system. Conversely, if the governing council decides to lower MRIR it will conduct a purchase of bonds injecting funds or liquidity into the money market. EONIA will quickly fall to the new lower MRIR. Overall, the ECB is able to steer interest rates (EONIA), signal the stance of monetary policy and manage the liquidity position in the money market.

On a technical note, commercial banks' holdings of bonds and foreign exchange are not counted as part of a bank's required reserves. If a bank has foreign exchange (dollars, sterling, yen, etc.) for use at a later date and is short of reserves, the foreign exchange can be temporarily swapped for funds at the ECB. This 'foreign currency swap' can be used both to inject liquidity into the market (the ECB swaps euro for foreign currency) or remove liquidity (the ECB swaps foreign currency for euro).

A repurchase agreement involves the ECB lending money to the commercial banks at a fixed rate of interest for a fixed period. In return, a commercial bank transfers government stock or some private debt instrument to the ECB with an agreement that the banks will buy them back (repurchase) at the end of the period. This provides the banks with temporary additional reserves. This transaction is called a *repurchase agreement*, or REPO, and provides funds for a limited period (usually two weeks). This technique is 'liquidity-providing' only.

Figure 17.4 shows the relationship between the key interest rates using daily data over the period January 1999 to December 2010. It can be seen that the ECB's MRIR and EONIA move closely together. As explained, the reason for this is that the commercial institutions can get funding from either the inter-bank market or the ECB and hence the rates cannot differ very much. It also follows from this that changes in MRIR will impact on EONIA and this, in turn, will affect all the commercial interest rates in the euro area.

The exception to this is the financial crisis period after 2008, when there was a noticeable divergence between MRIR and EONIA. This was because the commercial banks chose to keep excess reserves during the crisis in order to ward against the possibility of deposit flight. There was a 'rush

FIGURE 17.4 Interest rates in the euro area

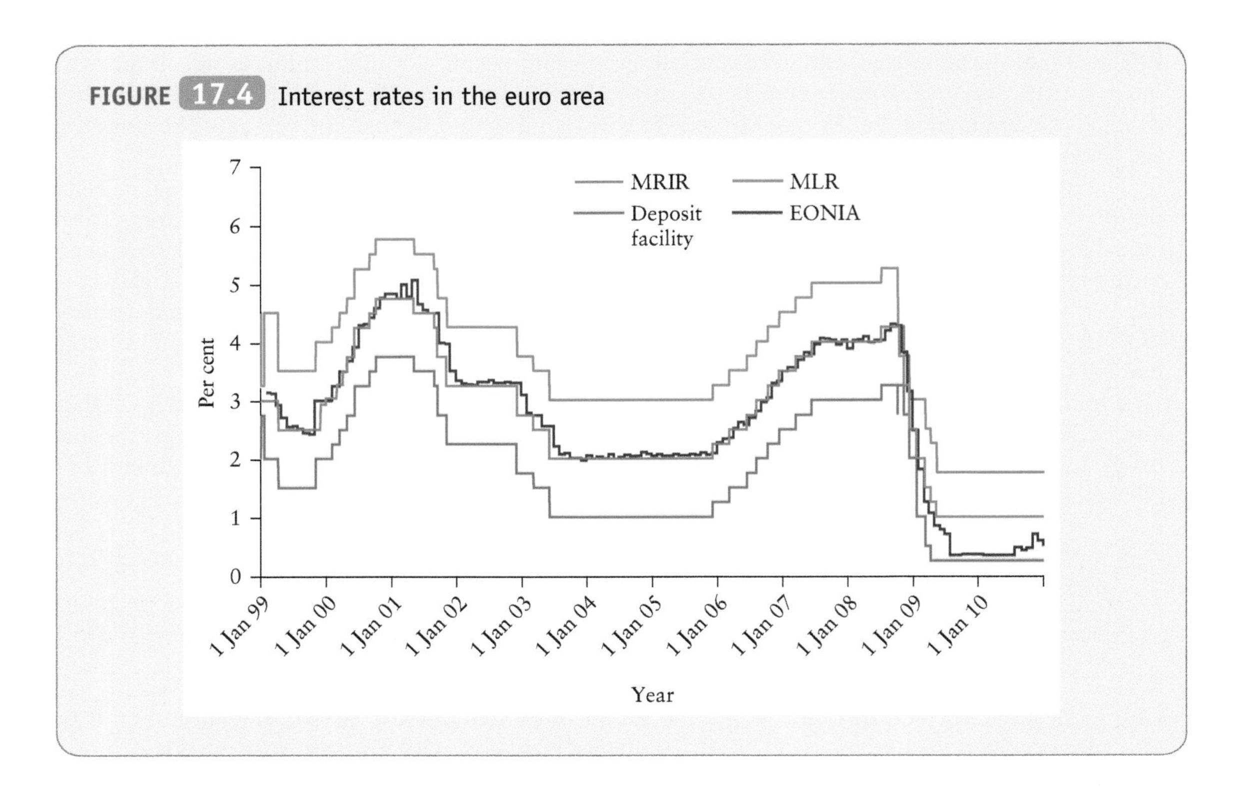

into liquidity' following the financial crisis and the rise in uncertainty. In normal circumstances, however, MRIR and EONIA move closely together.

Jean-Claude Trichet, a former French civil servant, was president of the ECB from 2003 to 2011. He has been criticised for raising interest rates between 2006 and 2008 as the economy plunged into the worst recession since the war. His reputation has been tarnished by these decisions. It has been argued that his actions, and those of the governing council, was 'behind the curve' compared with the policies of the Fed. His successor, Mario Draghi, has been more aggressive in addressing the recession by reducing interest rates and announcing new programmes of liquidity support for the banks and of bond purchases.

17.9 Monetary Policy in EMU

The ECB's monetary policy is referred to as the Eurosystem's Stability-Oriented Monetary Policy Strategy. This policy, described in 1999 by the ECB as a 'new and distinct strategy', involves the interaction between two pillars: the quantity theory of money; and inflation targeting. We defer until Chapter 19 a discussion of the quantity theory (which is a long-run theory) and concentrate in this section on inflation targeting.

Inflation targeting

Although not explicitly mentioned by the ECB, pillar 2 of the ECB's monetary policy is very similar to the 'inflation targeting' approach that has become fashionable in recent years. This approach can be explained by reference to the so-called Taylor rule, after the Stanford University economist

Box 17.2 The US Federal Reserve System and the ECB

There are close parallels between the structure of the US Federal Reserve System (the Fed) and the ECB. The Fed consists of 12 Federal Reserve Districts (each with its own Federal Reserve Bank) and the Federal Reserve Board of Governors in Washington, DC. The president of the United States appoints the seven members of the Board for 14-year terms of office. The chairman of the board, who is appointed for a four-year term, is considered to be the most powerful monetary policy-maker in the world. (The current chairman is Ben Bernanke, a former professor of economics at Princeton University.) The 12-member Federal Open Market Committee (FOMC) comprises five of the 12 presidents of the Federal Reserve District Banks and the seven members of the Federal Reserve Board. This committee has been described as the 'most powerful group of private citizens in America' because it formulates America's monetary policy.

The Employment Act of 1946 specifies that the Federal Reserve shall pursue three objectives: maximum employment; stable prices; and moderate long-term interest rates. This is a wider remit than that of the ECB, which is primarily required to achieve price stability.

The relationship of the national central banks of the euro area to the governing council of the ECB can be compared to that of the Federal Reserve Districts (Boston, New York, Chicago, San Francisco, Philadelphia, Cleveland, St Louis, Kansas City, Atlanta, Richmond, Dallas and Minneapolis) to the Federal Reserve Board and the FOMC. It remains to be seen whether the president of the ECB will come to rival the global influence of the chairman of the Fed. However, in reality the Fed is a much more centralised system, with the real power resting with the New York Fed. It is said that the district banks were set up to gain acceptance of the system and reassure the public outside New York that they retained some control over local banking conditions.

The operation of monetary policy is also similar to that in the euro area. The *federal funds effective rate* is the interest rate commercial banks borrow and lend to each other. The Fed at its meetings decides on the *federal funds target rate* and then implements open market operations to ensure that the effective rate is similar to the target rate. If, for example, there is a shortage of liquidity in the market and the effective rate is above the target rate, the Fed will buy bonds and inject liquidity into the market. This will drive the effective rate back down towards the target rate. As commercial banks deposit and lending rates are determined by the federal funds effective rate, the Fed's interest rate policy is transmitted to the economy as a whole.

John Taylor. Taylor showed that the behaviour of the US Federal Reserve Bank could be closely modelled by the following rule:

$$i_t = \pi_t + \rho + \theta_\pi(\pi_t - \pi^T) + \theta_\psi(Y_t - Y^*) \qquad (1)$$

where:

i_t = nominal interest rate set by the ECB (main refinancing interest rate)
π_t = inflation rate in time t
π^T = ECB's inflation target
ρ = natural rate of interest
Y_t = actual level of output
Y^* = potential level of output
θ_π = a coefficient showing how the ECB changes its interest rate when the actual inflation rate deviates from the target rate
θ_ψ = a coefficient that shows how the ECB changes its interest rate when actual output deviates from the potential level of output. If the economy is overheating the ECB will raise its interest rate.

TABLE 17.2 Illustration of the Taylor rule with inflation target of 2%

Case	Actual inflation rate π_t %	Natural rate of interest ρ %	Inflation gap coefficient θ_π	Inflation gap $(\pi_t - \pi^T)$ %	Output gap coefficient θ_ψ	Output gap (Y−Y*) %	ECB's interest rate i %
A	2	2	0.5	0	0.5	0	4
B	4	2	0.5	2	0.5	0	7
C	4	2	0.5	2	0.5	−5	4.5
D	4	2	0.9	2	0.1	0	7.8
E	1	2	0.9	−1	0.1	0	2.1
F	4	2	0.9	2	0.1	−5	7.3

Table 17.2 illustrates how the ECB would set its interest rate if it used the Taylor rule. Suppose that the two coefficients, θ_π and θ_ψ, are both equal to 0.5. Assume that the natural rate of interest is two per cent and that the inflation target is two per cent. Case A assumes that the actual inflation rate is equal to target and the output gap is zero. Solving the equation, the ECB's interest rate will be four per cent, which is the sum of a two per cent natural real rate of interest and a two per cent inflation rate.

NOTE: The output gap is equal to [Y – Y*]/Y*. It is the percentage by which actual GDP is above or below its potential level.

Case B demonstrates how the ECB responds if the actual inflation rate rises to four per cent (the output gap remains at zero). The ECB's interest rate is raised to seven per cent. This highlights an important point: whereas the inflation rate rose by two per cent, the ECB's interest rate is raised by three percentage points. In other words, the ECB increased the real interest rate by one per cent. This is necessary to deflate the economy and curtail inflation. The coefficients θ_π and θ_ψ are decided by the governing council of the ECB. Because the ECB is primarily concerned with price stability, the output gap may not have an important bearing on its decision to change interest rates. In this case, the θ_ψ coefficient might be expected to be near zero. The more 'hard-nosed' or inflation-adverse the ECB, the larger will be θ_π and the smaller θ_ψ. Case D in Table 17.2 shows the ECB's response when θ_π is equal to 0.9 and θ_ψ is equal to 0.1. When the actual inflation rate rose to 4 per cent, the ECB increases its nominal interest rate to 7.8 per cent, which is a 1.8 percentage point increase in the real interest rate.

Conversely, if inflation falls to below the target rate of two per cent to, say, one per cent, the ECB will cut its rate to 2.1 per cent. This should inject a stimulus into the economy and prevent deflation. (For an application of the Taylor rule to the euro area, see www.economist.com/blogs/freeexchange/2011/06/europes-europe-crisis.)

It is important to note that the emphasis here is very much on the future or forecast inflation rate rather than the current inflation rate. Even if the current inflation rate is very close to the target rate, the ECB may still raise interest rates if it forecasts a rise in inflation in the future. In this sense, the policy is a pre-emptive strike which is designed to prevent deviation from its target rate of inflation.

The inflation-targeting approach has been adopted in the 1990s in Canada, New Zealand, Australia, Israel, Sweden, Finland, Spain and the UK, among other countries. New Zealand pioneered

Swedish Exports

34% of GDP 1963.

38% 1973

94% 2002

Look at graphs

online.

the approach by signing a Policy Targets Agreement in 1990, setting the target inflation rate in the range between zero and three per cent and raising the possibility that the governor of the Central Bank would be fired if this target was not met. (The target was missed during the 1990s. The governor was not dismissed.)

The UK adopted a target of 2.5 ± 1 per cent in 1992. Similar targets were subsequently adopted by the other countries listed above, except for Israel, which set a target range of eight to 11 per cent.

It is intended that this inflation-targeting approach will act as an anchor for the public's inflation expectations. By making the policy clear, understandable and transparent, the ECB is hoping the policy will be credible and the public will adopt it in formulating inflation expectations. If this is the case, the inflation target may be a self-fulfilling prophecy. This would be the case if the inflation target had a strong bearing on wage demands. If the trade unions anticipate a low inflation rate next year, they may settle for a low nominal wage increase. If, on the other hand, a high inflation rate is anticipated, this could lead to high wage demands. It is essential, therefore, that the public believes that the inflation target will be achieved as this will minimise the rise in costs and wages.

Problems with inflation targeting

One of the major problems with the inflation-targeting approach is to accurately forecast inflation. Inflation is very difficult to forecast even over a short-term horizon. Different economic models may result in different forecasts and there is no agreement on which economic model is best. In addition, there is the problem of identifying external shocks and projecting their influence on inflation.

A second problem is that to forecast inflation, the structure of the economy must be stable and easily modelled. EMU, however, represented a regime shift creating behavioural, institutional and structural uncertainties. This means that the old structural relationships may have changed, making forecasting difficult.

The ECB has stated that it uses a 'broad base assessment' in forecasting inflation. This means that it uses 'leading indicators' such as the trend in price indices, labour costs, exchange rates, bond prices, measures of real economic activity, fiscal policy indicators, and business and consumer surveys, as well as actual indices of inflation.

A third problem with the inflation-targeting approach is that changes in interest rates may have a long and variable effect on the inflation rate. Given that the inflation rate itself is changing over time, the ECB is aiming at a moving target. As the late American economist Rudiger Dornbusch commented: 'Shooting at a moving target in the fog is no easy task.' Skill and luck are required if the inflation target is to be achieved. (See the discussion of the relationship between interest rates and interest-sensitive expenditure in Chapter 10.)

17.10 The Euro Area Inflation Record

Figure 17.5 shows the relationship between the ECB's interest rate (MRIR) and the rate of inflation measured by the HICP since the start of the euro area. (See www.ecb.int/stats/monetary/rates/html/index.en.html and www.global-rates.com/interest-rates/central-banks/european-central-bank/ecb-interest-rate.aspx.)

Between 2003 and 2006 the main ECB interest rate was stable at two per cent. However, as concerns about rising inflation grew, the Bank raised its rate in a series of 25 base point increases, until it reached 4.24 per cent in September 2008. (A 'basis point' is one hundredth of one per cent, so 25 basis points is 0.25 per cent.) This meant that as recession loomed in the euro area during 2007 the ECB was implementing a contractionary monetary policy. It feared that the surge in commodity and energy prices triggered by the boom in emerging countries such as China, India and Brazil would continue or even accelerate, triggering inflationary pressures in Europe.

FIGURE 17.5 Inflation and interest rates in the euro area 1999–2012

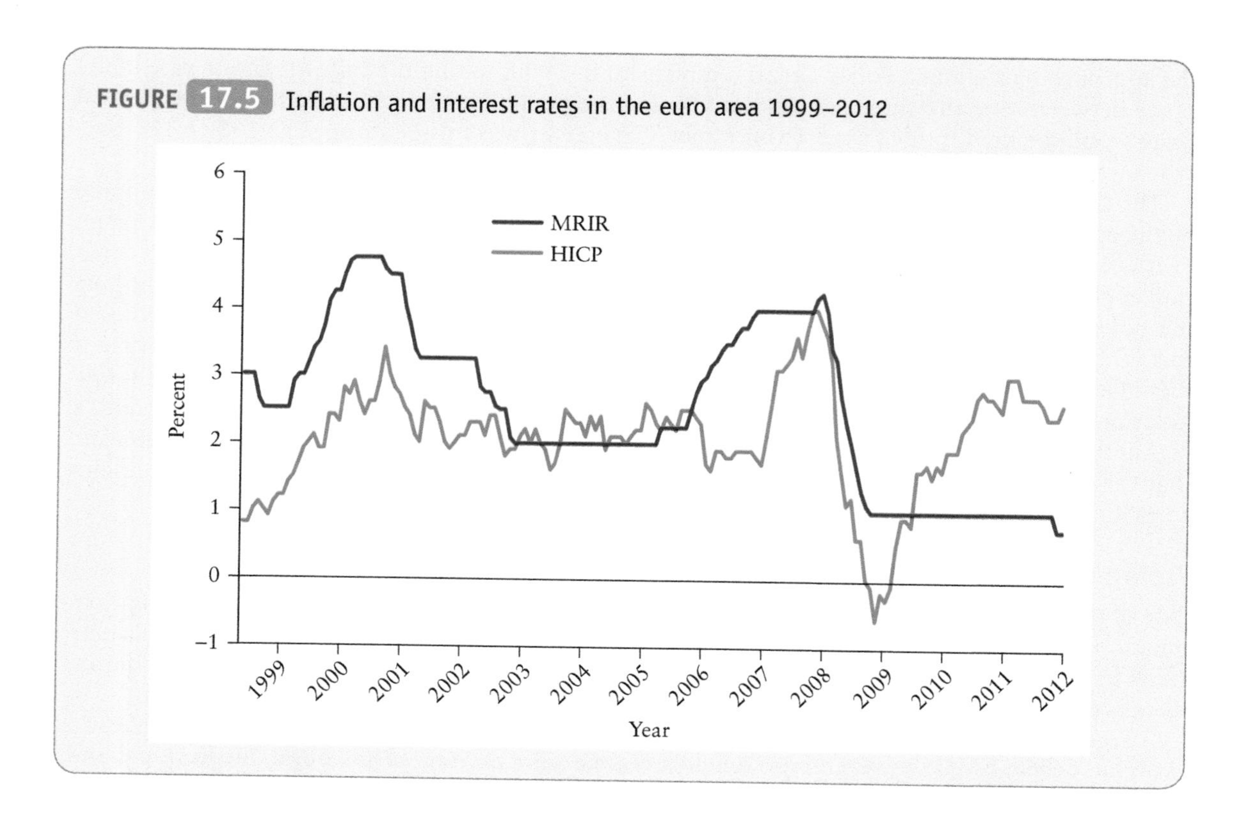

It was not until clear evidence emerged that inflation was falling rapidly in the second half of 2008 and unemployment rising in many euro area countries that the ECB reversed its monetary tightening. The first reduction in interest rates was delayed until 8 October 2008, but by mid-2010 the rate was down to one per cent. Under Mario Draghi's new presidency, the ECB lowered its main interest rate to 0.75 per cent in July 2012.

It has also taken 'non-standard' measures to stimulate the euro area economy. This phrase refers to new ways of providing liquidity to the European banking system by expanding the assets that banks can use as collateral. For example, in March 2012 it launched a Long-Term Refinancing Operation (LTRO). This is a form of quantitative easing (although the term is never used by the ECB). As the *Wall Street Journal* reported in March 2012:

> *The European Central Bank handed out €529.5 billion ($712.81 billion) in cheap, three-year loans to 800 lenders. This is the central bank's latest effort to arrest a financial crisis now entering its third year. Wednesday's loans were on top of the €489.2 billion of similar loans the ECB dispensed to 523 banks in late December. The ECB's goal is to help struggling banks pay off maturing debts and to coax them to lend to strained governments and customers. The take-up of this week's loans was roughly consistent with what bankers, investors and analysts had expected.*

In September 2012 the ECB introduced a new programme of bond purchases called 'Outright Financial Transactions'. As explained in Chapter 9 the aim of this programme is to reduce the differentials on bond yields between the peripheral and core countries of the euro area. In return for a government's commitment to enter a programme of fiscal austerity (such as that imposed on Ireland by the Troika), the ECB will purchase its bonds of up to three years' maturity to ensure that yields remain at sustainable levels rather than the crisis levels reached in 2010.

17.11 One Monetary Policy Fits All?

The transfer of responsibility for monetary policy from national central banks to the ECB implied that the 17 member countries would all be subject to the same monetary policy regardless of the economic conditions in their national economies. There might not be a problem with this if the ECB's monetary policy had the same effect on real output, unemployment and the price level in each country and if the business cycle were fully synchronised across member states. One monetary policy would fit all.

If, however, the business cycle is not synchronised and some countries are growing relatively fast and some relatively slowly, and if the 'interest-sensitivity of aggregate demand' varies from country to country, it is impossible for the ECB to find a monetary policy that suits all. The uniform monetary policy implemented by the ECB will not be appropriate to all members of the euro area and it could even be the case that 'one size fits none'.

The property boom of the early twenty-first century was much stronger in Spain and Ireland than, for example, in Germany and Austria. This may account for the ECB's lack of decisive action to deal with the problems that were brewing in the booming countries. *The Economist* accused the ECB of serious policy mistakes in regard to the property boom:

> *The ECB stood idly by while the periphery over-heated because it was making policy with an eye toward the core nations. Now that the peripheral booms are over ... the central bank is ... continuing to pursue a policy that is most appropriate for the core economies. ... Now perhaps the ECB thinks it is not responsible for managing divergent economic cycles within the euro zone. Indeed, the ECB may well be trying to force core nations to take on this responsibility and move toward closer fiscal union. If the ECB is unsuccessful in winning such progress from core governments, however, we should not be surprised if peripheral economies find euro-zone policy intolerable and eventually drop out of the system entirely.* (*The Economist* 2011)

In Figure 17.6, we show the average real growth rate over the period 1999–2010 along the horizontal axis and average inflation over the same period along the vertical axis. If the ECB's targets

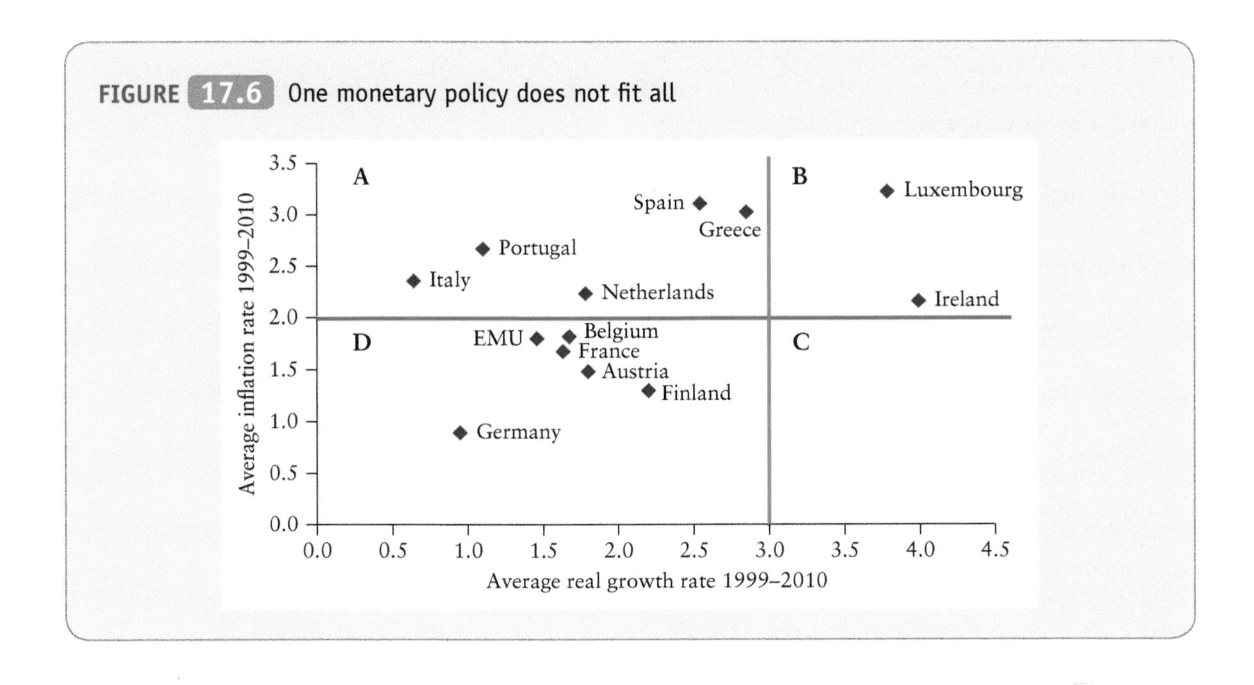

FIGURE 17.6 One monetary policy does not fit all

were a growth rate of three per cent and an inflation rate close to or below two per cent, we can divide the diagram into four quadrants, A, B, C and D.

Countries with relatively low inflation and slow growth, the largest group, fall into quadrant D. Ireland and Luxembourg in quadrant B have relatively rapid real growth rates and high inflation. The second largest group is in quadrant A, with below-target growth and above-target inflation. This group includes Portugal and Italy. There were no countries in quadrant C with low inflation and high growth. This shows how patchy the outcome of EMU membership had been up to 2010. The weighted average of countries falls into zone D, for whom an expansion policy would be appropriate. But this would be inappropriate for countries in zone B.

But even more important is the evidence we presented in Chapter 4 on the divergence of unemployment rates after 2007. Germany and some other countries came through the crisis of 2008 relatively unscathed and with falling unemployment. Other countries, such as Greece, Portugal, Ireland and Spain, experienced deep recession and crisis levels of unemployment. This shows how difficult, if not impossible, it is to implement a monetary policy that would fit the needs of all euro area members.

In its favour it may be said that eventually the ECB recognised the gravity of the problems facing the peripheral countries and put in place an exceptional package of monetary stimulus in the face of strong opposition from the Bundesbank.

There is a tendency to feel that each of the 17 member states of the euro area should be treated as of equal importance. But the ECB is designed to achieve price stability in the whole of the euro area and it is natural that its stance should be strongly influenced by the inflation rates in Germany, France and Italy, whose economies account for over 70 per cent of the euro area's output. Some form of compromise has to be reached, and it is likely to be one that will involve giving concerns of the smaller countries disproportionate weight, to the chagrin of those in the larger countries.

17.12 Key Terms and Concepts

In this chapter we have outlined the implications of economic and monetary union and discussed the main benefits and costs of adopting the euro. We also discussed the framework within which monetary policy is formulated in the euro area. Among the main points discussed were:

- political and economic benefits associated with EMU membership
- the main costs associated with EMU membership
- the constitution and structure of the ECB
- the independence of the ECB from political pressures
- the main objective of the ECB – to maintain price stability
- inflation targeting
- the problem of one monetary policy fitting all the economies of the euro area.

CHAPTER 18

A Dynamic Model of Aggregate Demand and Aggregate Supply

18.1 Introduction

The models developed so far in this book have focused on the level of real output and the price level. In this chapter we outline a macroeconomic model that examines the relationship between inflation and the level of real output. This introduces a new, dynamic aspect into our model and offers a new perspective on how the economy adjusts back to the potential level of real output following a demand- or supply-side shock.

Earlier models developed in this book highlighted key adjustment mechanisms. For example, in the Mundell–Fleming model, recession reduced the price level and this lowered the real exchange rate and improved competitiveness. In the dynamic model developed in this chapter, the central bank plays a key role in the adjustment process. We assume that the central bank follows a Taylor rule policy of targeting inflation (see Chapter 17). The central bank's monetary policy (changing its interest rate to achieve an inflation target) is the key mechanism for ensuring that the economy reverts back to the potential real level of output.

The dynamic model is based on key relationships developed in earlier chapters such as the Phillips curve, the Taylor rule, adaptive expectations and the Fisher equation. We use these equations to derive aggregate demand and aggregate supply and then use this model to examine how the economy adjusts to economic shocks.

18.2 The Dynamic Model of Aggregate Demand and Aggregate Supply

In this section, we outline a macroeconomic model following closely the presentation by N. Gregory Mankiw (2012). The output equation used in this chapter is a variation on equations developed in Chapters 5 and 6 and the closed economy IS equation developed in Chapter 11. It states that actual output is determined by the potential level of output, the difference between the real interest rate (r) and the natural rate of interest (ρ) and exogenous demand-side shocks (ε). The 'natural interest rate' is defined as the rate prevailing when actual output equals potential and expected inflation equals the actual inflation rate.

$$Y_t = Y^* - \alpha(r_t - \rho) + \varepsilon_t$$

If there are no demand-side shocks ($\varepsilon = 0$) and the real interest rate equals the natural interest rate, Y equals Y^*. The main difference between this and the previous output–demand equations is the introduction of the natural real rate of interest. The ε term picks up random effects on aggregate demand.

The next equation in the model is the Fisher equation discussed in Chapter 10.

$$r = i_t - E_t\pi_{t+1}$$

where i_t is the nominal interest rate and $E_t\pi_{t+1}$ is expected inflation in time t + 1 but formulated in time t (E_t).

The third equation is the Phillips curve, which was outlined in Chapter 12.

$$\pi_t = E_{t-1}\pi_t - \lambda(U_t - U_n) + \nu_t$$

π_t is the inflation rate in time t, $E_{t-1}\pi_t$ is expected inflation in time t, formulated in time t − 1, U_t and U_n are the actual and natural rate of unemployment respectively and ν_t is a variable capturing supply-side shocks. The term λ is a coefficient which shows how inflation responds to the unemployment gap. If we assume that the unemployment gap is equivalent to the output gap the Phillips curve can be rewritten:

$$\pi_t = E_{t-1}\pi_t + \phi(Y_t - Y^*) + \nu_t$$

This equation states that inflation in time t depends on expected inflation in time t, the output gap and supply-side shocks. We assume that inflation expectations are formulated using the simplest adaptive expectations model, so that the expected inflation rate in time t is whatever inflation rate was recorded in the previous year (see Chapter 12):

$$E_t\pi_{t+1} = \pi_t$$

Substituting into the Phillips curve equation we have:

$$\pi_t = \pi_{t-1} + \phi(Y_t - Y^*) + \nu_t$$

The final step is to introduce the monetary policy rule (or Taylor rule) from Chapter 17.

$$i_t = \pi_t + \rho + \theta_\pi(\pi_t - \pi^T) + \theta_\psi(Y_t - Y^*)$$

The variables are as previously defined. The variable π^T is the ECB's inflation target, θ_π is a coefficient which shows how the ECB changes its nominal interest rate when actual inflation deviates from the target inflation rate. θ_ψ is also a coefficient which shows how the ECB changes its interest rate when actual output deviates from the potential rate (see Chapter 17 for a detailed explanation).

The endogenous variables (variables determined within the model) in this model are Y_t, π_t, r_t, i_t and $E_{t-1}\pi_t$, Y^*, π^T, ε_t and ν_t are exogenous (determined outside the model). The lagged endogenous variable, π_{t-1} is 'predetermined' – its value is known at the start of period t. The economy's long-run equilibrium occurs when there are no supply- or demand-side shocks and expected inflation equals the target rate of inflation. That is:

$$\varepsilon_t = \nu_t = 0$$
$$\pi_{t-1} = \pi_t$$

In this case, the real rate of interest will equal the natural rate of interest, ($r_t = \rho$) and $\varepsilon_t = 0$. It follows from the output equation that actual output will equal the potential level of output ($Y_t = Y^*$).

18.3 The Dynamic Aggregate Supply (DAS) Curve

The dynamic aggregate supply (DAS) curve shows a positive relationship between inflation and the level of output. This equation comes from the Phillips curve and the assumption of adaptive expectations:

$$\pi_t = \pi_{t-1} + \phi(Y_t - Y^*) + \nu_t$$

Figure 18.1 shows the upward-sloping DAS curve. The DAS curve shifts in response to changes in π_{t-1}, Y^* and ν_t. An increase in any of these variables will shift the DAS curve upwards to the left and vice versa.

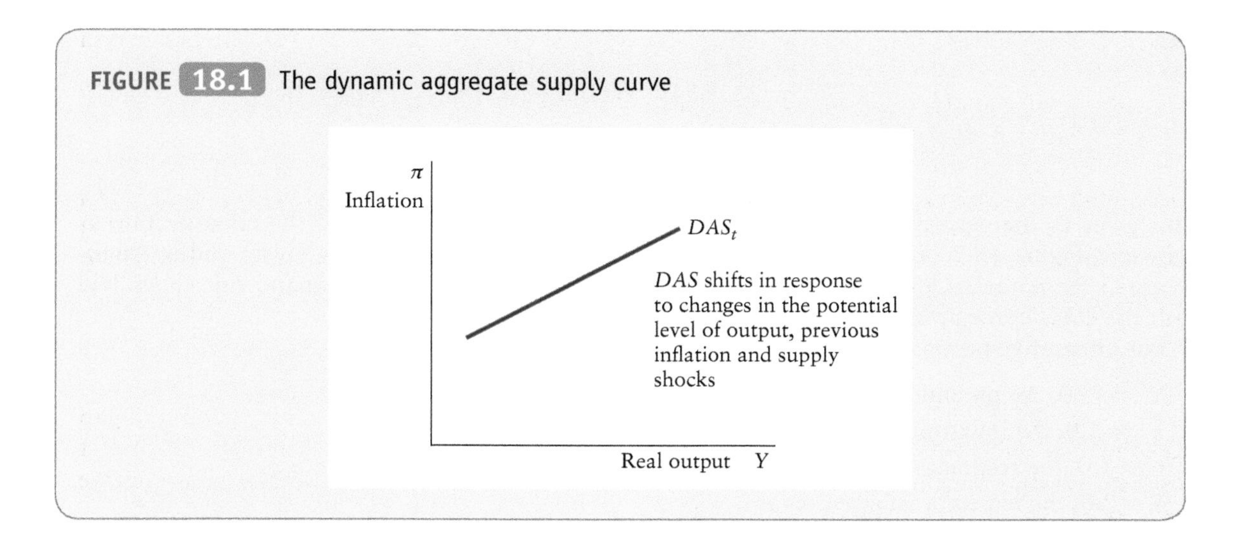
FIGURE 18.1 The dynamic aggregate supply curve
π
Inflation
DAS_t
DAS shifts in response to changes in the potential level of output, previous inflation and supply shocks
Real output Y

18.4 The Dynamic Aggregate Demand (DAD) Curve

The dynamic aggregate demand (DAD) curve is more complex to derive. We need to establish a negative relationship between the level of real output and inflation on the demand-side of the economy. To do this we need to eliminate all the endogenous variables bar Y_t and π_t. We start with the output equation:

$$Y_t = Y^* - \alpha(r_t - \rho) + \varepsilon_t$$

Substitute into this equation the Fisher equation $r = i_t - E_t\pi_{t+1}$

$$Y_t = Y^* - \alpha(i_t - E_t\pi_{t+1} - \rho) + \varepsilon_t$$

Assume that the expected inflation rate is equal to the current inflation rate, that is: $\pi_t = E_t\pi_{t+1}$. Substitute into the output equation:

$$Y_t = Y^* - \alpha(i_t - \pi_t - \rho) + \varepsilon_t$$

Next, we substitute the monetary policy rule, $i_t = \pi_t + \rho + \theta_\pi(\pi_t - \pi^T) + \theta_\psi(Y_t - Y^*)$, into the output equation:

$$Y_t = Y^* - \alpha[\pi_t + \rho + \theta_\pi(\pi_t - \pi^T) + \theta_\psi(Y_t - Y^*) - \pi_t - \rho] + \varepsilon_t$$

Cancelling the π_t and ρ terms we have:

$$Y_t = Y^* - \alpha[\theta_\pi(\pi_t - \pi^T) + \theta_\psi(Y_t - Y^*)] + \varepsilon_t$$

Or:

$$Y_t = Y^* - \alpha\theta_\pi(\pi_t - \pi^T) - \alpha\theta_\psi Y_t + \alpha\theta_\psi Y^* + \varepsilon_t$$

Bring the output variable to the left-hand side:

$$Y_t(1 + \alpha\theta_\psi) = Y^*(1 + \alpha\theta_\psi) - \alpha\theta_\pi(\pi_t - \pi^T) + \varepsilon_t$$

Divide both sides by $(1 + \alpha\theta_\psi)$:

$$Y_t = Y^*[(1 + \alpha\theta_\psi)/(1 + \alpha\theta_\psi)] - [\alpha\theta_\pi/(1 + \alpha\theta_\psi)](\pi_t - \pi^T) + [1/(1 + \alpha\theta_\psi)]\varepsilon_t$$

Or:

$$Y_t = Y^* - [\alpha\theta_\pi /(1 + \alpha\theta_\psi)](\pi_t - \pi^T) + [1/(1 + \alpha\theta_\psi)]\varepsilon_t$$

Let $A = \alpha\theta_\pi /(1 + \alpha\theta_\psi)$ and $B = 1/(1 + \alpha\theta_\psi)$:

$$Y_t = Y^* - A(\pi_t - \pi^T) + B\varepsilon_t$$

This gives us the negative relationship between the level of real output and the inflation rate as shown in Figure 18.2. Aggregate demand changes in response to changes in Y^*, π^T and ε_t. An increase in the potential level of output, the inflation target or a favourable demand-side shock will shift the DAD curve up to the right and vice versa.

For illustrative purposes we assume the following parameter values:

$Y^* = 100$, the potential level of output.
$\pi^T = 2.0$, the inflation target.
$\alpha = 1.0$, the responsiveness of real output to changes in the real interest rate.
$\rho = 2.0$, the natural real interest rate.
$\phi = 0.25$, the responsiveness of inflation to the output gap.
$\theta_\pi = 0.5$, how much the ECB changes its interest rate when inflation deviates from target.
$\theta_\psi = 0.5$, how much the ECB changes its interest rate when actual output deviates from the potential level of output.

Substituting these values into the expression for A and B above, we have:

$$A = \alpha\theta_\pi/(1 + \alpha\theta_\psi) = 0.333$$
$$B = 1/(1 + \alpha\theta_\psi) = 0.67$$

Hence, the DAS and DAD equations can be written:

$$\text{DAS } \pi_t = \pi_{t-1} + 0.25(Y_t - Y^*) + \nu_t$$
$$\text{DAD } Y_t = Y^* - 0.33(\pi_t - \pi^T) + 0.67\varepsilon_t$$

FIGURE 18.2 The dynamic aggregate demand curve

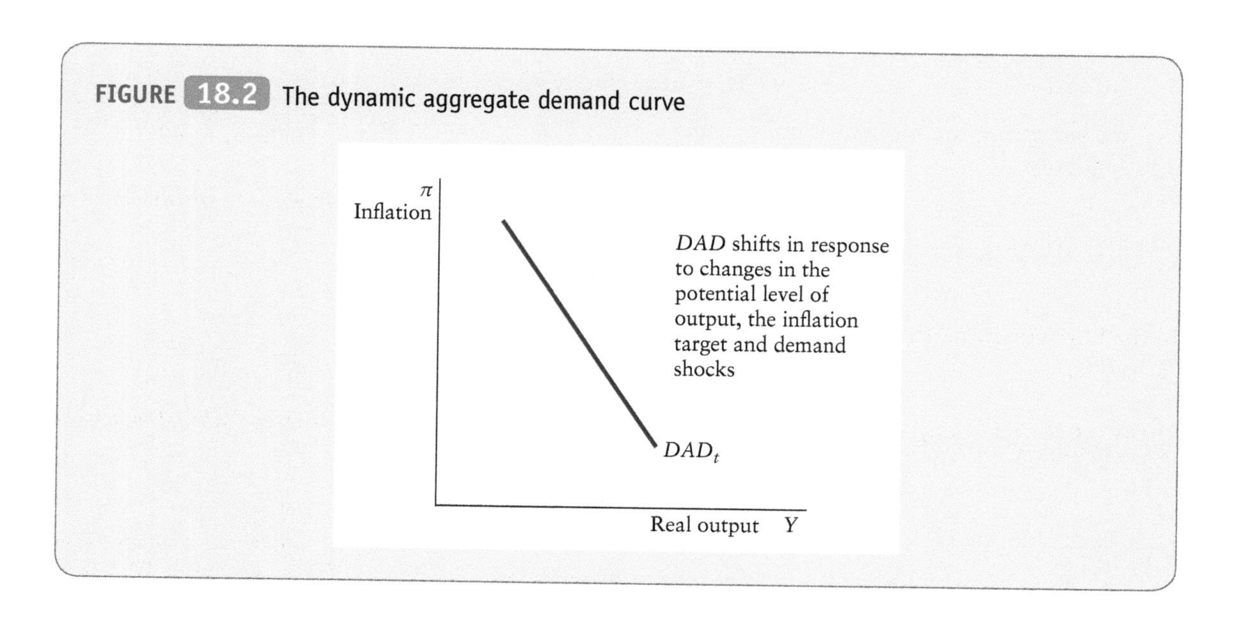
π
Inflation
DAD shifts in response to changes in the potential level of output, the inflation target and demand shocks
DAD$_t$
Real output Y

FIGURE 18.3 The short-run equilibrium

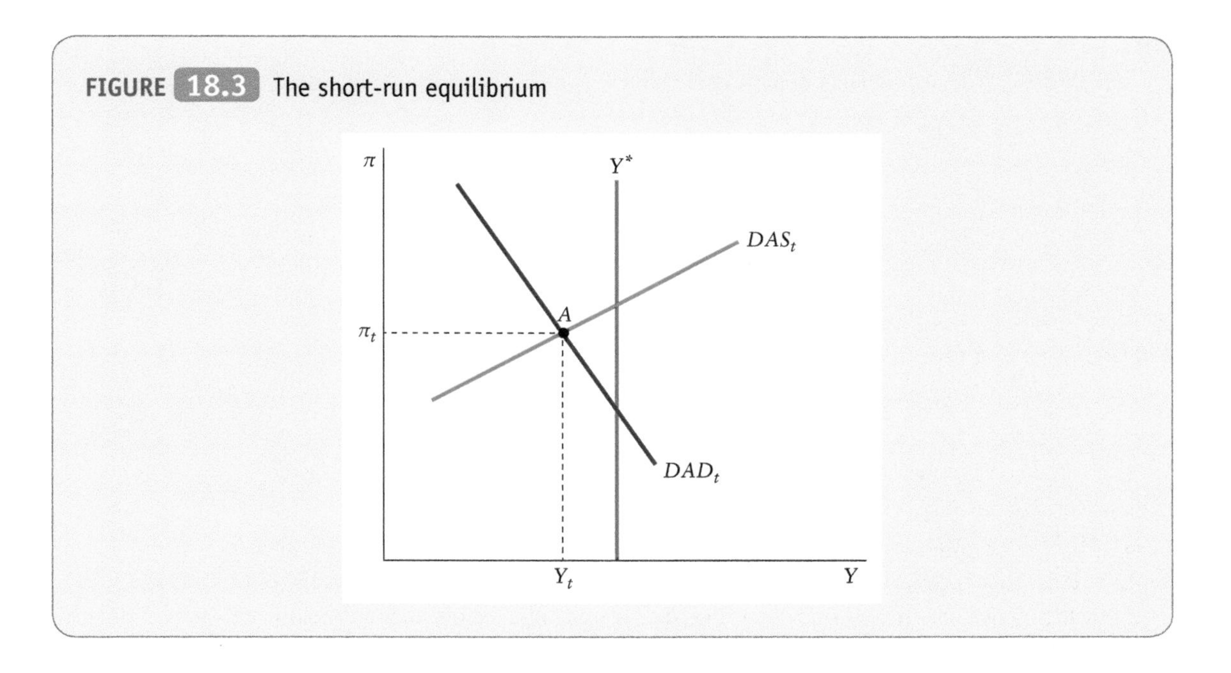

Figure 18.3 shows that the intersection of the DAS and DAD determines the inflation rate and the level of real output. Point A is a short-run equilibrium below the potential level of output.

We now use this model to examine the effects of demand- and supply-side shocks and discuss its usefulness to a small open economy like Ireland participating in a monetary union.

18.5 Deflationary Demand-side Shock

Figure 18.4 and Table 18.1 show how the economy adjusts to a five-period adverse demand-side shock. We assume that Y^* is initially equal to 100 and the parameters are as given in the previous section. Using the DAD and DAS equations we can trace how the economy reacts to the shock.

The economy is in equilibrium in time periods t-3, t-2 and t-1 and, as shown in Table 18.1, Y, π, *i* and r are at their long-run equilibrium values. Then in time t, a five-period adverse demand-side shock shifts the DAD curve down to the left, the economy moves from the point A to B and both inflation and the level of real output fall. From the DAD equation, we can calculate the effect of a one-unit decrease in ε_t on Y:

$$99.3 = 100 - 0.33(2 - 2) - 0.67(1)$$

In the DAS equation, this fall in Y reduces the inflation rate to 1.83.

$$1.83 = 2 + 0.25(99.33 - 100)$$

However, the economy will not remain at the point B. The lower level of inflation feeds back into the DAD equation and increases Y to 99.39:

$$99.39 = 100 - 0.33(1.83 - 2) - 0.67(1)$$

This process continues for the duration of the adverse demand-side shock. Inflation continues to fall and real output slowly begins to recover and, as shown in Figure 18.4 and Table 18.1, the

FIGURE 18.4 An adverse demand-side shock

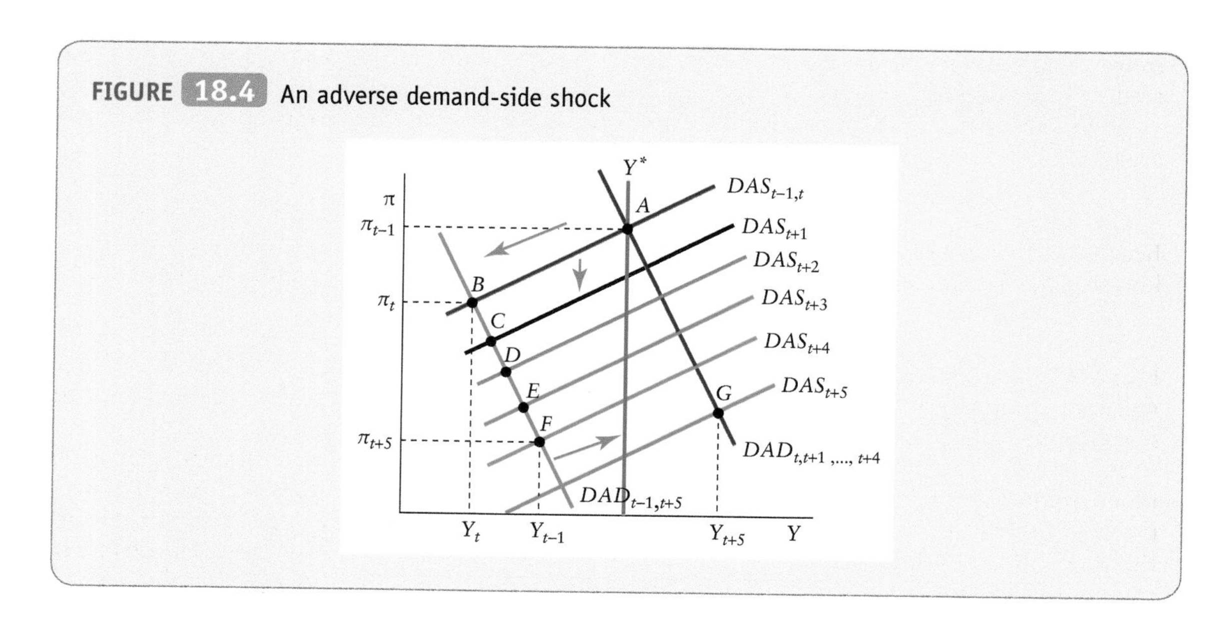

TABLE 18.1 An adverse demand-side shock

	ε	Y	π	r	*i*
t − 3	0	100	2	2.00	4.00
t − 2	0	100	2	2.00	4.00
t − 1	0	100	2	2.00	4.00
t	−1	99.33	1.83	1.58	3.41
t + 1	−1	99.39	1.68	1.53	3.21
t + 2	−1	99.44	1.54	1.49	3.02
t + 3	−1	99.48	1.41	1.45	2.85
t + 4	−1	99.53	1.29	1.41	2.70
t + 5	0	100.23	1.35	1.79	3.14
t + 6	0	100.22	1.40	1.81	3.21
t + 7	0	100.20	1.45	1.82	3.28
t + 8	0	100.18	1.50	1.84	3.34
t + 9	0	100.17	1.54	1.85	3.39
t + 10	0	100.15	1.58	1.86	3.44
t + 11	0	100.14	1.61	1.88	3.49
t + 12	0	100.13	1.64	1.89	3.53

economy moves from B to F. At F, the demand-side shock ends, the level of real output has recovered to 99.53 and inflation has fallen to 1.29.

At this point the DAD curve is back to its original position (the effects of the demand-side shock are over) and real output has increased to 100.23, over-shooting Y^*.

$$100.23 = 100 - 0.25(1.29 - 2)$$

Because inflation is below target, the ECB continually cuts its interest rate, which provides a stimulus to real Y. The increase in real output feeds into the DAS equation and inflation rises to 1.35.

$$1.35 = 1.29 + 0.25(100.23 - 100)$$

Because inflation has started to rise, inflation expectations will be revised upwards. The DAS curve will now gradually drift upwards to the left and the economy reverts back to the point A after several time periods.

Figure 18.5 A–E show the impulse response functions or how real output, inflation, the real and nominal interest rate react to the adverse demand-side shock. (These response charts are based on the hypothetical data in Table 18.1.) As explained above, real output falls and then recovers after the shock. Inflation falls and after a time also reverts to its initial level. The nominal interest rate can be derived from the Taylor rule equation, which shows how the ECB reacts to the deflation. The nominal interest rate is reduced as the inflation rate falls and then gradually rises.

At this stage the central bank's policy response is crucial. We assume that the ECB is pursuing an inflation target of two per cent and changes its policy interest rate to achieve this target. We assume that in response to the deflation the ECB reduces its policy interest rate. As mentioned in the introduction, this adjustment process differs from that in previous models in this book. In the Mundell–Fleming model, recession lowered the price level and the real exchange rate, leading to an improvement in competitiveness and an increase in net exports. The central bank keeps the money

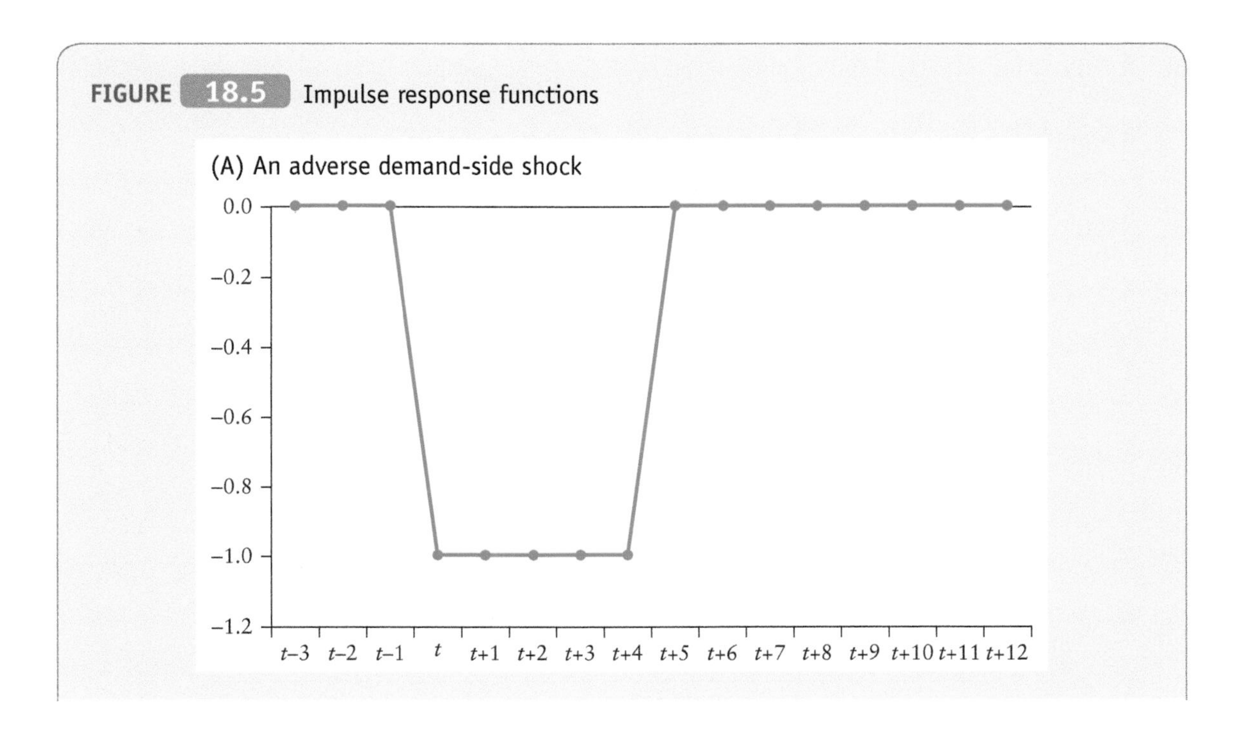

FIGURE 18.5 Impulse response functions

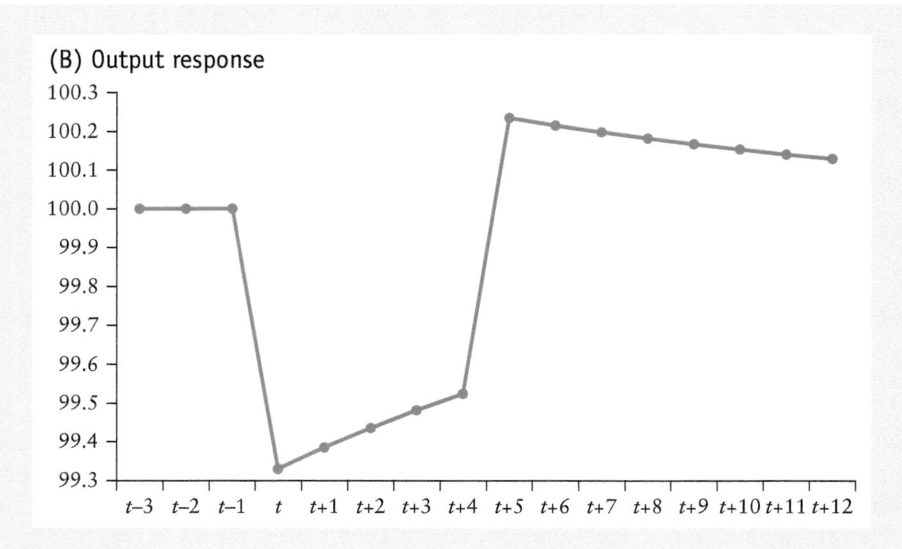
(B) Output response
100.3
100.2
100.1
100.0
99.9
99.8
99.7
99.6
99.5
99.4
99.3
t–3 t–2 t–1 t t+1 t+2 t+3 t+4 t+5 t+6 t+7 t+8 t+9 t+10 t+11 t+12

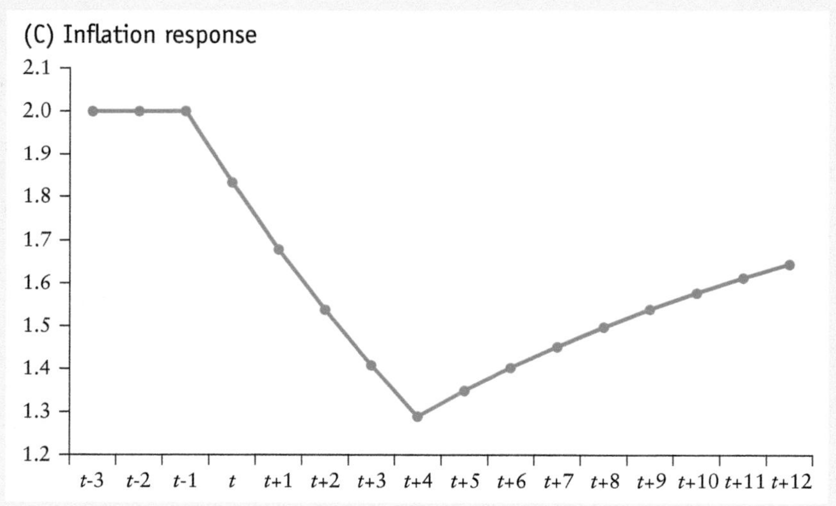
(C) Inflation response
2.1
2.0
1.9
1.8
1.7
1.6
1.5
1.4
1.3
1.2
t-3 t-2 t-1 t t+1 t+2 t+3 t+4 t+5 t+6 t+7 t+8 t+9 t+10 t+11 t+12

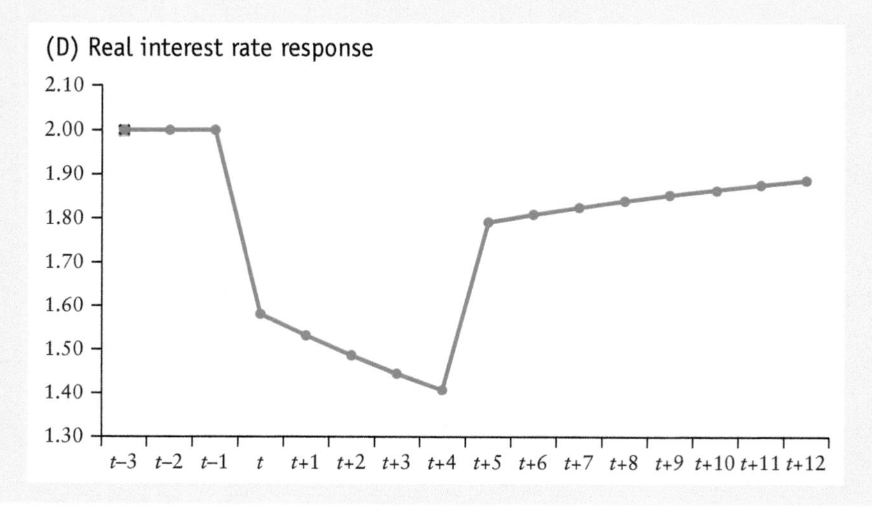
(D) Real interest rate response
2.10
2.00
1.90
1.80
1.70
1.60
1.50
1.40
1.30
t–3 t–2 t–1 t t+1 t+2 t+3 t+4 t+5 t+6 t+7 t+8 t+9 t+10 t+11 t+12

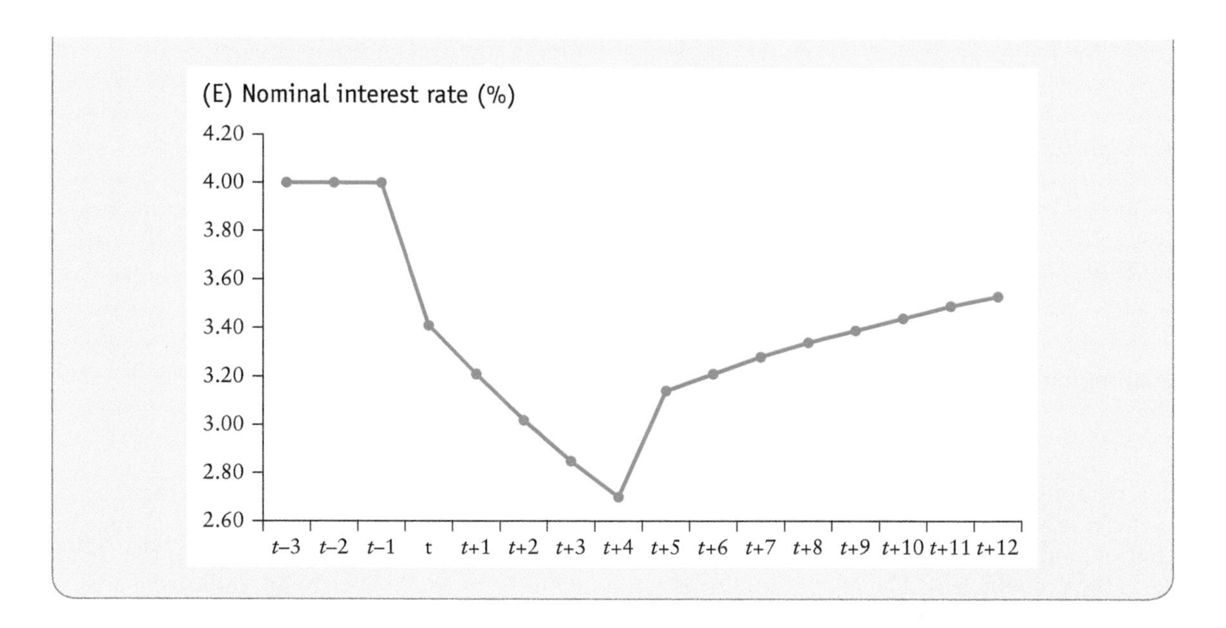

supply constant in the Mundell–Fleming model, but in this dynamic model reacts to the inflation gap by changing the money supply and the interest rate.

A difficulty for a small country such as Ireland that is participating in a monetary union is that Irish inflationary conditions may not reflect the inflation rate in the euro area as a whole. As the ECB is concerned with euro area inflation, it will not lower interest rates in response to a fall in the inflation rate that is confined to Ireland. This, in effect, means that the A coefficient in the DAD equation is zero. As Irish inflation falls below the two per cent inflation target, the ECB does not introduce any stimulus in the form of lower interest rates unless a similar fall occurs in other euro area countries.

If there is no policy response from the ECB the adjustment process is entirely dependent on the responsiveness of inflation to the output gap, which is given by ϕ in the DAS equation. In the following section we present some empirical evidence on the size of the ϕ coefficient. For the moment, given that the ECB does not respond to a fall in Irish inflation, the adjustment mechanism described in the Mundell–Fleming model is perhaps a better explanation as to how the Irish economy might adjust out of recession.

The relationship between inflation and the output gap

In order to establish the empirical relationship between the output gap and inflation we use a technique previously outlined in our discussion of the Phillips curve in Chapter 12. A problem with estimating the DAS equation is that we do not know with certainty the level of Y^*. Hence estimating the equation is problematic. An alternative is to estimate the following equation:

$$\Delta\pi_t = \beta + \phi Y$$

This equation can easily be estimated because Y^* has been substituted out. What we need to demonstrate is that the ϕ coefficient in this equation is the same as the ϕ coefficient in the DAS equation. As explained in Chapter 12, we start with a definition: the potential level of output is the level of output that prevails when actual inflation equals expected inflation and there are no supply-side shocks. That is, when $\Delta\pi_t = 0$ and $Y = Y^*$ and $\nu_t = 0$. Setting the previous equation equal to zero and substituting the potential level of output for the actual rate we have:

$$0 = \beta + \phi Y^*$$

Rearranging:

$$\beta = \phi Y^*$$

The previous inflation equation can be rewritten as:

$$\pi_t = \pi_{t-1} + \beta + \phi Y$$

Substitute for β:

$$\pi_t = \pi_{t-1} - \phi Y^* + \phi Y$$

Rearranging and inserting the supply-side shock variable:

$$\pi_t = \pi_{t-1} + \phi(Y - Y^*) + \nu_t$$

This demonstrates that the inflation equation and DAS equation are equivalent and that the ϕ coefficients are the same. Figure 18.6 shows a scatter plot of the relationship between the change in inflation and the level of real output for Ireland over the period 1961–2008. The slope of the trend line is the ϕ coefficient. The regression line is estimated to be virtually horizontal, indicating a very weak relationship between the output gap and inflation.

This tentative result has important implications because virtually all the automatic adjustment mechanisms outlined in this book are initiated by the output gap changing the price level or the rate of inflation. If the price level does not respond quickly and effectively to output gaps the adjustment process is prolonged and costly in terms of lost output and employment. This suggests that an 'internal devaluation' may not be a reliable way of restoring equilibrium after a demand-side shock.

FIGURE 18.6 Inflation and real output: Ireland 1960–2008

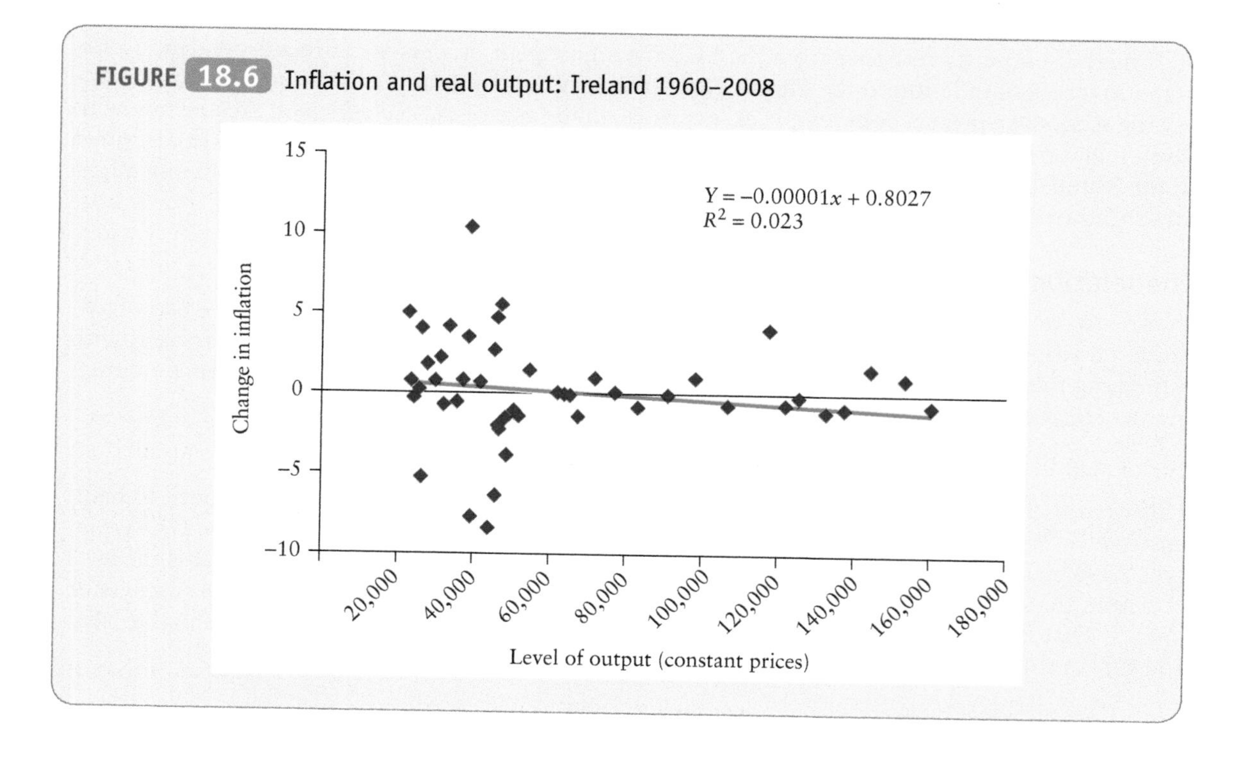

18.6 The Central Bank's Inflation Target

The anti-inflationary stance of the central bank plays a key role in the adjustment process. Recall that the slope of the DAD curve is determined by the A coefficient:

$$A = \alpha\theta_{\pi}/(1 + \alpha\theta_{\psi}) = (1 \times 0.5)/(1 + (1 \times 0.5)) = 0.333$$

If the θ_{π} coefficient (how much the ECB changes its interest rate when inflation deviates from target) is large and the θ_{ψ} coefficient (how much the ECB changes its interest rate when real output deviates from its potential level) is small, the DAD curve will be relatively flat (elastic). For example, if $\theta_{\pi} = 0.9$ and $\theta_{\psi} = 0.1$ (as opposed to 0.5 and 0.5 as previously assumed):

$$A = (1 \times 0.9)/(1 + (1 \times 0.1)) = 0.818$$

This means that small changes in the inflation rate will bring forth large changes in real output. If, for example, inflation falls below target, the central bank aggressively reduces its interest rate and this increases real output.

If the DAD curve is relatively flat or elastic the implication is that, as the DAS curve moves down, the economy will revert back to the potential level of output relatively quickly. However, when the demand-side shock ends, the degree of over-shooting will be larger. In Figure 18.4, the DAD curve is drawn as relatively steep (inelastic) and after five periods of a demand-side shock the economy remains in recession. If the DAD curve was relatively flat the recession would end quickly but the over-heating effect would be amplified.

The effect of changes in the central bank's interest rate on the level of real output played an important role in the adjustment mechanism identified in the closed economy IS-LM model of Chapter 11. The adjustment mechanism was as follows: recession leads to a fall in the price level, which increases the real money supply and reduces the real interest rate. The fall in real interest rate increases interest-sensitive expenditure (IE) such as consumer expenditure, investment and net exports. This, in turn, increases aggregate demand and real output. In short:

$$\text{Recession} \rightarrow \downarrow P \rightarrow \uparrow (M^s/P) \rightarrow \downarrow r \rightarrow \uparrow IE \rightarrow \uparrow AD \rightarrow \uparrow Y$$

This adjustment process is known as the *Keynes effect*. However, it will be recalled that Keynesians believe that there is a weak link between the real interest rate and aggregate demand. Hence, having identified the effect, Keynes dismissed it as having little practical significance. If the price level, and the real interest rate, has only a small impact on real output, this is akin to the DAD curve being relatively steep. Large changes in the inflation rate (or the price level) are necessary to bring forth a given change in real output. On the other hand, if the monetarists are correct and there is instead a strong link between the real interest rate and real output, the DAD curve would be relatively flat.

18.7 An Expansionary Demand-side Shock

Figure 18.7 illustrates the case of a five-period expansionary demand-side shock. Starting from A, the demand shock shifts the DAD curve up to the right. The economy moves to the point B and both real output and the inflation rate increase.

In subsequent periods, the increase in inflation raises inflation expectations and the DAS curve moves up to the left. As the actual inflation rate is above the target rate, the ECB reacts by raising the real interest rate. At the end of the five-period shock the DAD curve reverts to its original position and the economy moves from the point F to G. Inflation starts to fall and there is a significant fall in real output as the economy moves from an over-heating position into recession.

At the point G, inflation has fallen and this leads to a revision downwards of expected inflation. Over time the DAS curve will shift down and the economy reverts to A.

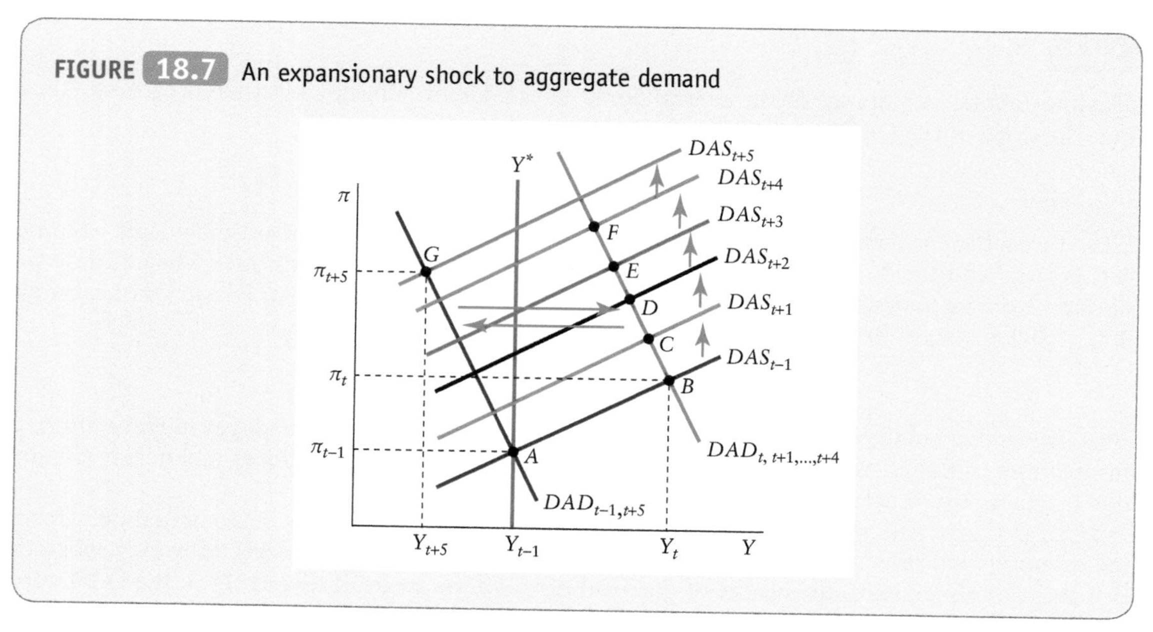

FIGURE 18.7 An expansionary shock to aggregate demand

This sequence is the mirror opposite of the adverse demand-side shock discussed in the previous section. The economy initially moves into an over-heating situation before swinging into recession and back to the initial equilibrium point. The ECB again plays a key role in the adjustment process as it raises the real interest rate to achieve its inflation target.

The ECB cut its policy rate from 4.75 per cent in May 2001 to 3.25 per cent in November 2001 and to two per cent in June 2003, where it remained until December 2005. Irish inflation rose after entry to EMU, peaking at 5.6 per cent in 2000. It fell to 2.1 per cent in 2004. After 2003 the real interest rate was negative and this, along with an abundance of freely available credit, fuelled the property and construction bubble.

18.8 The Labour Market and the Adjustment Process

Although not explicitly specified in the DAS-DAD model, the labour market plays an important part in the adjustment process. When the economy moves from the point A to B in Figure 18.7, both inflation and real output increase. Figure 18.8 shows the impact of this movement on the labour market. (We presented a simple model of the labour market in Chapter 4.) In line with the earlier model, we use the price level instead of the rate of inflation.

NOTE: In the presentation of the labour market in Chapter 4 we showed the real wage along the vertical axis. This reflected the profit maximisation rule: W/P = MPL. A firm's profits are maximised when the real wage rate (W/P) is equal to the marginal product of labour, MPL. The demand for labour can instead be plotted as a function of the nominal wage. Rearranging, the previous equation can be written W = P × MPL. Using this rule, firms hire workers up to the point where the nominal wage equals the value of the output produced by workers. The term P × MPL is the value of workers' output and is referred to as the marginal revenue product (MRP). The location or position of the L^d curve is now determined by the price level (P) and MPL. To reflect this the L^d curve is relabelled L^d(P, MPL).

The increase in the price level shifts the labour demand curve (L^d) curve up to the right, the nominal wage rises on the vertical axis and employment increases along the horizontal axis. The increase in the nominal wages is smaller than the rise in the price level and, as a result, real wages fall.

The labour supply (L^S) curve does not immediately shift because the change in the price level was unexpected. In the DAD-DAS model, the use of adaptive expectations means that workers formulate price expectations by looking at the historical trend in prices. Price expectations are, in effect, backward looking and this gives rise to forecast errors. If the L^S curve does not immediately shift, workers supply more labour in response to higher nominal wages whereas in real terms they are worse off. Workers are under the illusion that the wages they are offered are worth more than is the case in reality. In a sense they have been tricked. This is known as money illusion.

FIGURE 18.8 The labour market

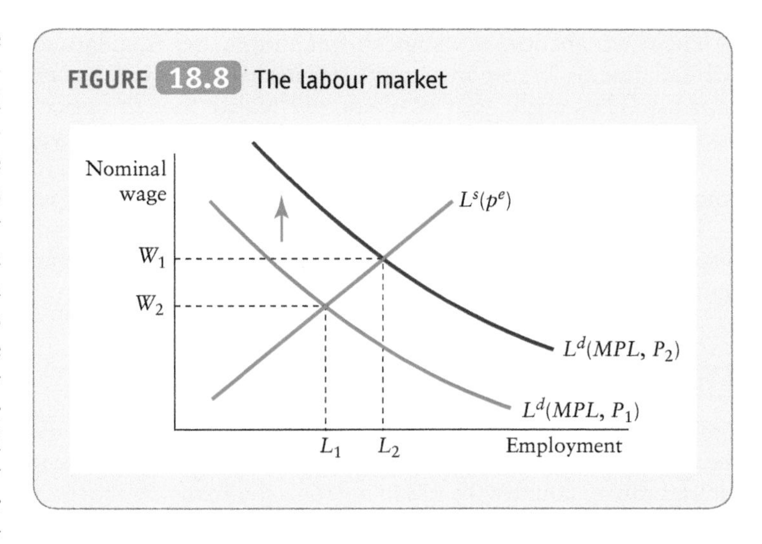

The result is that employment increases in response to a higher nominal wage (but a lower real wage) and the economy moves up along the supply of labour curve. It is this increase in employment from L_1 to L_2 that enables firms (via the production function) to increase real output.

In the longer term workers will recognise the effect of higher prices or inflation on real wages. They will demand an increase in nominal wages to compensate. The increase in price expectations (P^e) shifts the L^s curve up to the left (not shown) and employment and output revert back to their initial levels. The increase in nominal wages, W, will equal the increase in P and the real wage returns to its initial level. Employment, L, reverts back to its original level.

The increase in inflation expectations also shifts the SRAS curve upwards to the left in Figure 18.7. The economy reverts back to potential real output.

If money illusion exists, the steepness of the SRAS curve depends on the slope of the labour supply (L^S) curve. The flatter (more elastic) the L^S curve, the flatter the SRAS curve. To see this point, note that if the SRAS curve is flat, an expansionary demand-side shock will lead to a large increase in real output. As before, the change in the price level will shift the L^d curve to the right. However, if the L^S curve is flat, the shift of the L^d curve will lead to a large increase in employment. It is this increase in employment that enables firms to increase real output in the goods and service market.

Note that the analysis in Figure 18.7 is based on an expansionary demand-side shock and applies to the case of an expansionary fiscal policy. An expansionary fiscal policy can influence the level of output and employment in the short run, but as soon as workers adjust price expectations there is no effect in the long run. This means that there is a trade-off between inflation and real output (and indirectly unemployment) in the short run but not in the longer term. That is, in the longer term the policy-maker cannot reduce unemployment at the cost of higher inflation. Furthermore, the short-run trade-off depends on the degree of money illusion and workers' inability to accurately forecast inflation.

A deflationary demand-side shock

The previous analysis is also relevant to the earlier example of a deflationary demand-side shock (see Figure 18.4). When the economy moves from A to B in Figure 18.4, the inflation rate falls along the vertical axis. The fall in inflation shifts the L^d curve down to the left (not shown) and both the nominal wage and employment decrease. However, the fall in the nominal wages is smaller than the fall in inflation and, as a result, the real wage increases for workers lucky to still have jobs.

Those who believe in a smooth-functioning, self-regulating economy claim that prices and wages will fall quickly in response to the rise in real wages and the emergence of unemployment and spare capacity. They argue that workers will realise that the price level or inflation has fallen and will accept a cut in the nominal wage so as to restore the real wage. This change in price expectations shifts the LS curve down to the right in the labour market (not shown). If the fall in the nominal wage is equal to the fall in the price level, the original real wage is restored.

The flexibility of wages was discussed in Chapters 4 and 5. Keynesian economists argue that wages and prices are inflexible in a downward direction and that as a result the economy could remain in recession for some time.

18.9 An Adverse Supply-side Shock

Figure 18.9 and Table 18.2 show the effect of a one-period adverse supply-side shock. The shock moves the economy up along the DAS line by three percentage points (not shown). If the ECB raises its policy interest rate to counter the rise in inflation the economy moves back down along the DAS line to a level of output equal to 99.7 (not shown). The initial result of the supply-side shock is stagflation.

In the next period, both real output and inflation are lower and this sets in motion a revision downwards of inflation expectations. The DAS curve drifts downwards to the right and real output gradually begins to increase. Eventually the economy reverts back to equilibrium at A.

Throughout the adjustment process the ECB is setting its interest rate to counteract the rise in inflation. Again the 'one monetary policy fits all' is a concern. If the Irish economy is out of sync with the overall euro area economy, the ECB's policy will not be appropriate to our needs.

Figure 18.10 A–E show how real output, inflation and the real and nominal interest rates respond to the one-period supply-side shock. Real output falls sharply in time t and then recovers over many time periods. Inflation rises and then gradually reverts back towards the ECB's target rate. The rise in the nominal interest rate is greater than the increase in inflation and hence the real interest rate also increases. As inflation moves back to the target rate the real interest rate falls towards the natural real interest rate.

FIGURE 18.9 An adverse supply-side shock

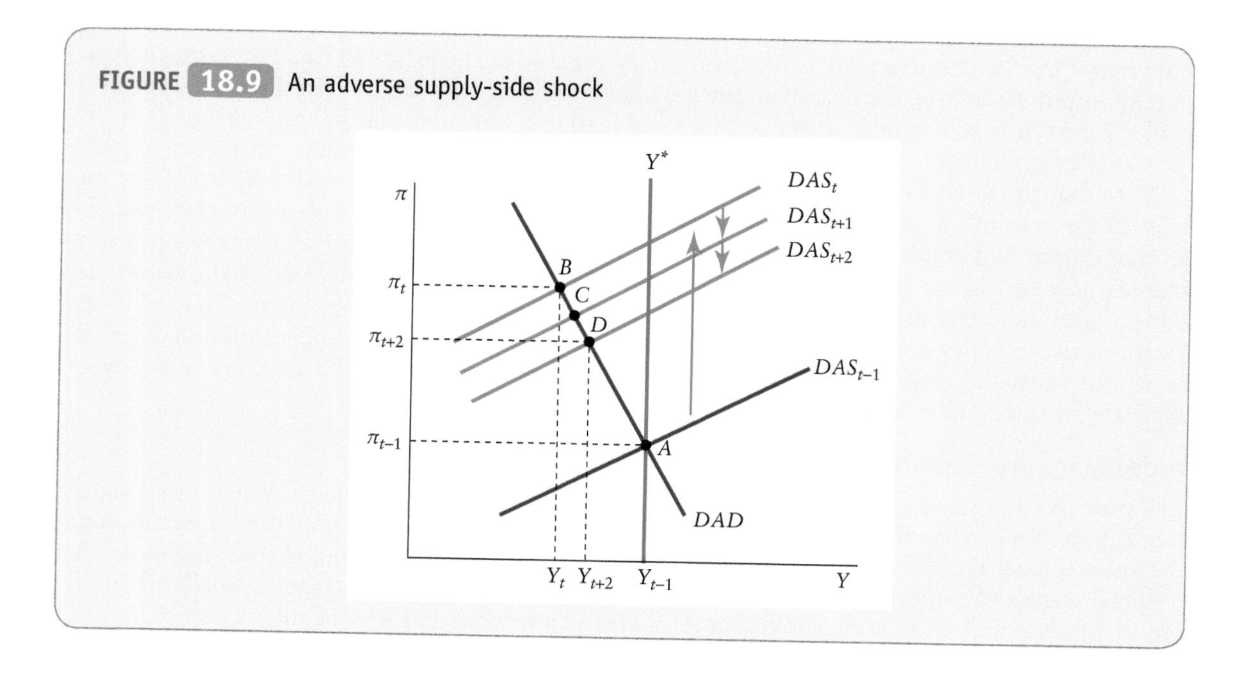

TABLE 18.2 An adverse supply-side shock

	ν	Y	π	r	i
t − 3	0	100.00	2.00	2.00	4.00
t − 2	0	100.00	2.00	2.00	4.00
t − 1	0	100.00	2.00	2.00	4.00
t	1	99.67	3.00	2.34	5.34
t + 1	0	99.70	2.92	2.31	5.22
t + 2	0	99.72	2.84	2.28	5.12
t + 3	0	99.75	2.77	2.26	5.03
t + 4	0	99.77	2.71	2.24	4.95
t + 5	0	99.79	2.65	2.22	4.87
t + 6	0	99.80	2.60	2.20	4.80
t + 7	0	99.82	2.55	2.18	4.73
t + 8	0	99.83	2.50	2.17	4.67
t + 9	0	99.85	2.46	2.15	4.62
t + 10	0	99.86	2.42	2.14	4.56
t + 11	0	99.87	2.39	2.13	4.52
t + 12	0	99.88	2.36	2.12	4.48

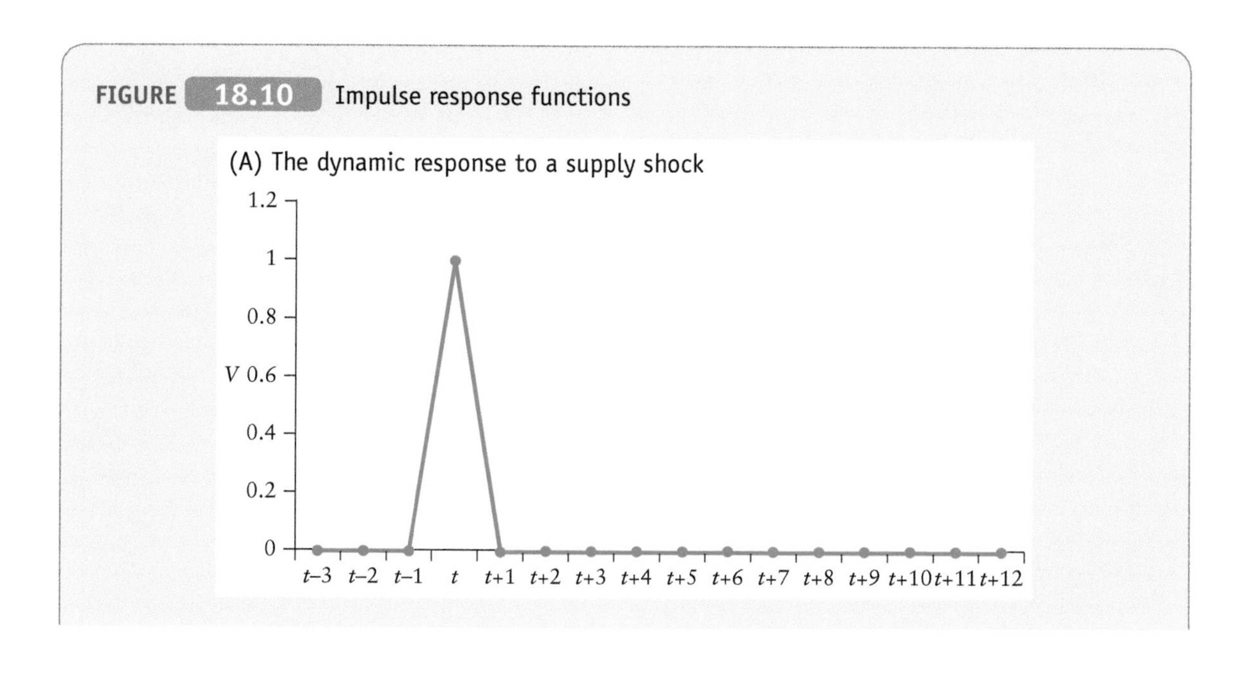

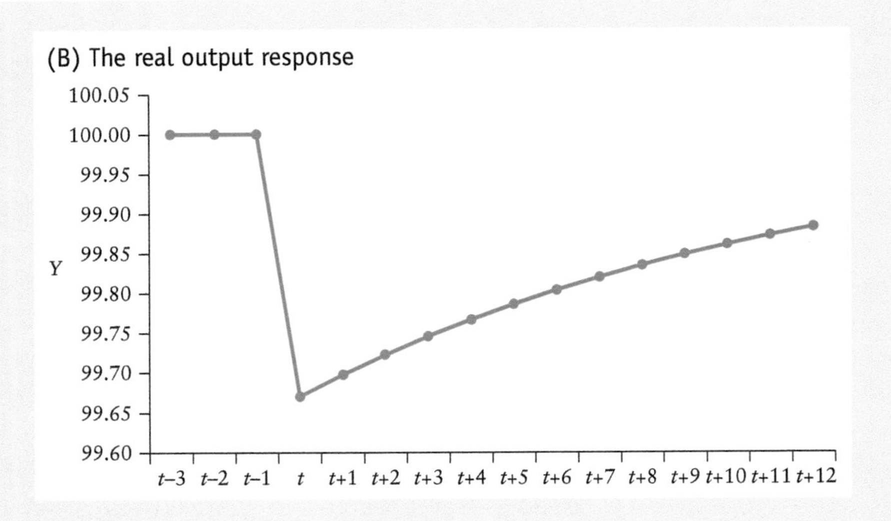
(B) The real output response
Y
100.05
100.00
99.95
99.90
99.85
99.80
99.75
99.70
99.65
99.60
t–3 t–2 t–1 t t+1 t+2 t+3 t+4 t+5 t+6 t+7 t+8 t+9 t+10 t+11 t+12

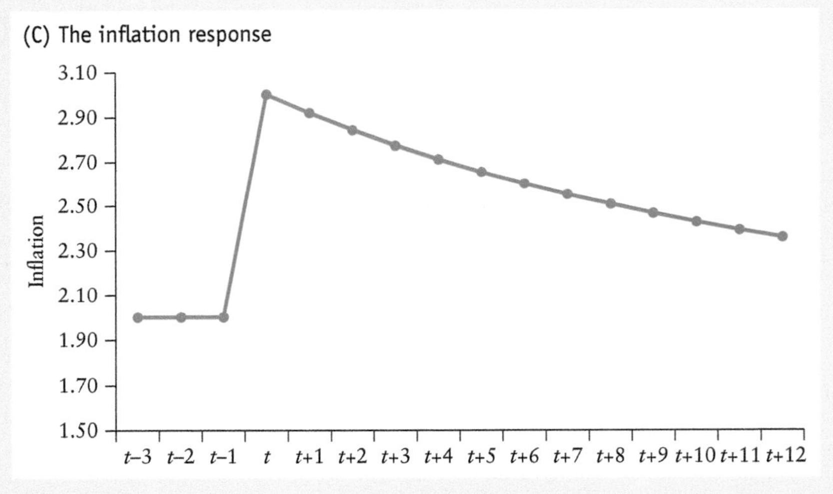
(C) The inflation response
Inflation
3.10
2.90
2.70
2.50
2.30
2.10
1.90
1.70
1.50
t–3 t–2 t–1 t t+1 t+2 t+3 t+4 t+5 t+6 t+7 t+8 t+9 t+10 t+11 t+12

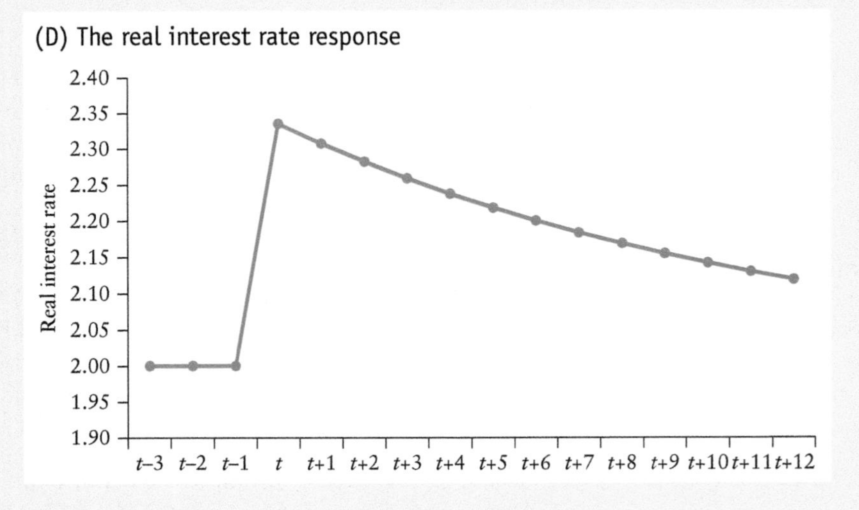
(D) The real interest rate response
Real interest rate
2.40
2.35
2.30
2.25
2.20
2.15
2.10
2.05
2.00
1.95
1.90
t–3 t–2 t–1 t t+1 t+2 t+3 t+4 t+5 t+6 t+7 t+8 t+9 t+10 t+11 t+12

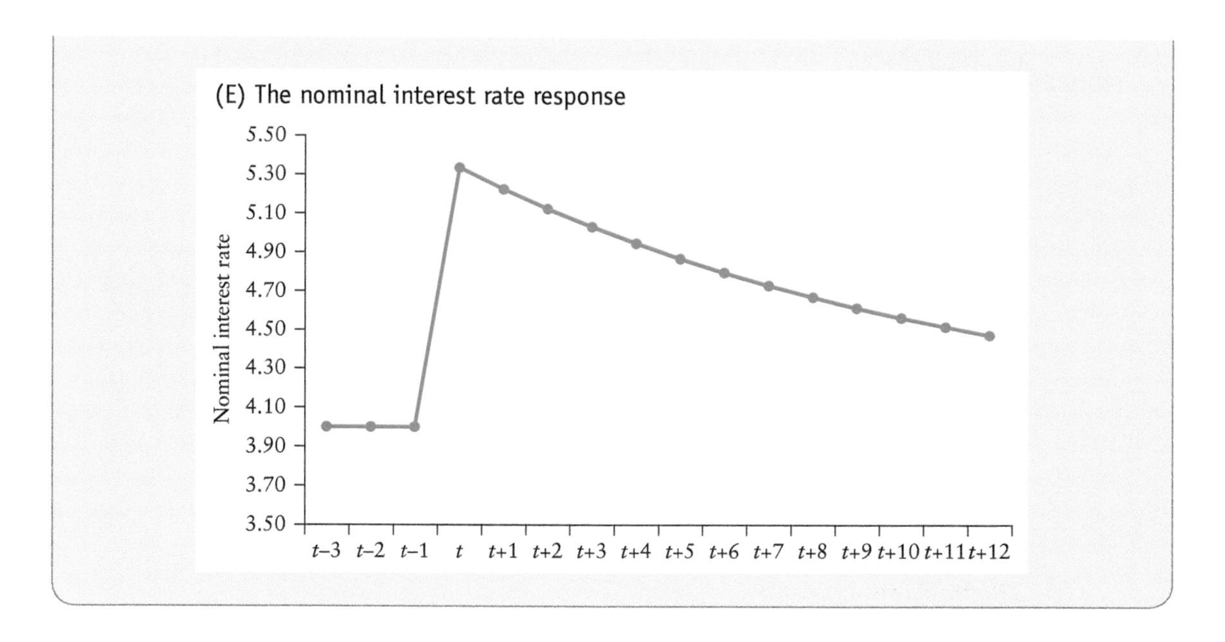

The labour market

Consider now how the adverse supply-side shock (such as an increase in oil prices) impacts on the labour market. In the labour market the increase in the price level or the inflation rate would normally shift the L^d curve out to the right. However, recall from Chapter 5 that a firm's profit is equal to total revenue minus total cost:

$$\text{Profit} = \text{total revenue} - \text{total cost}$$

where total revenue equals the price of output (P_q) multiplied by the volume of output (Q). Total cost equals the price of inputs (P_z) multiplied by the volume of inputs (Z), such as raw materials and labour. Rewriting the profit function:

$$\text{Profit} = (P_q \times Q) - (P_z \times Z)$$

Until now the increase in the price level increased the firm's total revenue and therefore profits. Higher profits, in turn, created the incentive for firms to increase the demand for labour and produce more output (shift the L^d curve to the right). However, in this supply-side analysis, the rise in the price level is due to the rise in costs (higher oil prices). The firm's profits are at best unchanged or, worse, decrease. There is therefore no incentive for the firm to hire more workers or expand output. This means that the L^d curve does not shift to the right. (Note that it is possible for profits to fall, in which case the L^d curve moves to the left. We ignore this possibility here.) In Figure 18.11, we assume that the L^d curve is unchanged.

The second modification relates to workers' expectations. In the DAD-DAS model we assumed that workers do not anticipate the effect on the price level of a demand-side shock. However, it is one thing to assume that workers do not correctly anticipate the consequences of a surprise fall in, say, investment on the price level or inflation rate. But it is quite another thing to assume that workers are not aware of the consequences of a rise in oil prices (which will be loudly broadcast in the media). Hence, in the case of a oil price increase, workers gauge quickly and correctly the effects on the overall or general price level. That is, there is little or no money illusion when it comes to oil price changes. If this is the case, the L^S curve moves up to the left and, in Figure 18.11, we move

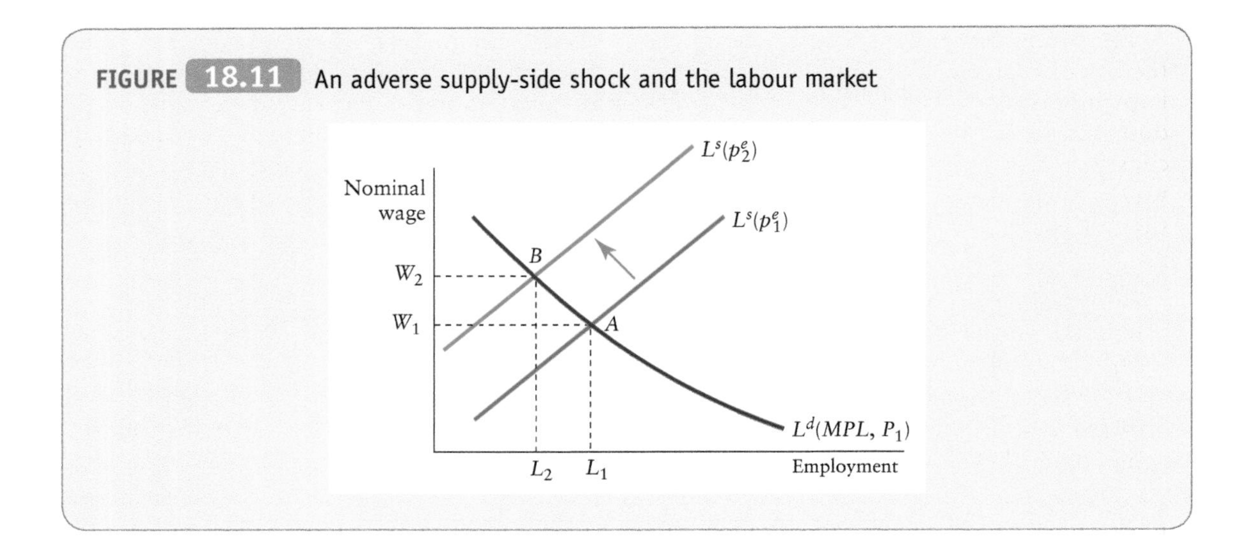

FIGURE 18.11 An adverse supply-side shock and the labour market

from the point A to B. The decrease in employment in the labour market is associated with a fall in real output in the goods market.

At B the real wage (W/P) has decreased. It can be seen from the diagram that the increase in the price level is greater than the rise in nominal wages. Hence, at the point B workers are worse off.

In order for the economy to return to potential real output, it is necessary for the SRAS curve to shift back down to the right. This comes about because the actual inflation rate is above the target rate and the central bank raises the real interest rate. This leads to a fall in the actual inflation rate, which in turn leads to a revision downwards of inflation expectations.

The problem here, however, is that since workers already experienced a fall in real wages in the movement from A to B in Figure 18.11, such a development is likely to be resisted. If a fall in nominal earnings is not forthcoming, it is possible that the economy would remain at B for some time.

After a time, the rise in unemployment and the downwards revision of inflation expectations could be expected to put downward pressure on wages and shift the SRAS curve back down. The economy will revert back to Y*, the potential output level. However, this whole process could take some considerable time and the costs in terms of lost output and employment are likely to be high. This was certainly the case in Ireland after the oil shock of the early 1980s.

18.10 Rational Expectations

There is considerable controversy surrounding the way in which economic agents (firms and workers) form expectations about key variables such as the rate of inflation. In this section we examine the rational expectations model and assess the implications for economic policy.

The traditional view was that economic agents (workers and firms) form their expectations of the price level and the rate of inflation by looking back to the recent past and extrapolating from that to the future. If last year's inflation rate was 4.5 per cent, it is not unreasonable to expect this year's rate also to be in the region of four per cent. This forecast of inflation is based on adaptive expectations. This approach was incorporated into the DAS-DAD model developed in this chapter and the Phillips curve (Chapter 12). This approach is backward-looking and can also lead to systematic forecast errors. In a period of accelerating inflation, for example, the expected rate of inflation will always be less than the actual rate.

Expectations that are formed rationally avoid systematic forecast errors. They are formed on the basis of all available information (including past inflation, and also changes in policy) and a knowledge of how the economy works. This approach does not result in systematic errors. This does not imply that the forecasts will always be accurate – just that there will be no tendency to consistently over- or under-predict inflation. Rational expectations have become a very influential way of thinking about the economy. This approach is associated with Robert Lucas of the University of Chicago, who was awarded the Nobel Prize in economics in 1996.

NOTE: Inflation expectations can influence actual inflation. If workers expect the rate of inflation to increase they will demand increases in nominal wages in compensation. If households anticipate a rise in inflation, they will rush to buy at today's prices. These reactions will of themselves tend to push up the rate of inflation. Feedback from expectations to outcomes is very important in economics. Things are very different in meteorology: unfortunately, a forecast of fine weather is not enough to ensure that the weather will be fine!

Incorporating rational expectations into the DAS-DAD model assumes that workers anticipate or forecast the increase in prices or inflation and they demand an immediate increase in nominal wages in compensation. That is, if a medium-term wage agreement is in force it can be renegotiated. In contrast to the adaptive expectations case, workers do not suffer from money illusion. Because expectations are formed rationally, workers anticipate that prices will change following some demand- or supply-side shock. That is, there is no delay or lagged effect as in the adaptive expectations model.

This means that the labour supply (L^S) curve shifts in response to changes in price expectations. The SRAS curve also shifts much more quickly and there will be little or no trade-off between inflation and unemployment other than in the very short run.

One implication is that the money illusion we discussed earlier in this chapter can only come about through surprise or unanticipated inflation. Policy-makers can only achieve this result by an unannounced change of policy that takes firms and households by surprise or if there is an unexpected demand- or supply-side shock. Hence a surprise fiscal or monetary expansion could lead to an increase in real output in the short run by creating an unanticipated increase in the price level or the rate of inflation.

However, the effects of such a policy surprise will not last, because the public quickly learns from the evidence and adjusts its expectations. This means that only in the very short run do these shocks have any effect on real output.

Neoclassical economists argue that there is no role for a stabilisation policy or for any form of government intervention to offset the instability brought by a shock. They argue that even after the financial market turmoil of 2008 the economy did not need stimulus packages or an aggressive loosening of monetary policy to return to full employment. Because the shock was unanticipated, both the private and the public sector were caught unawares. However, once the shock had occurred, firms and workers understood its implications and adjusted prices and wages accordingly. Expectations, formed rationally, will on average correctly anticipate the consequences of the shock for the price level or the rate of inflation. In the labour market, firms and workers will quickly adjust the supply and demand for labour curves to ensure that the economy reverts to potential real output.

For these reasons, economists who believe in rational expectations are sceptical about governments' ability to 'fine-tune' the economy in response to shocks. As Robert Lucas comments on economists: 'As an advice-giving profession we are in way over our heads.'

However, the slow adjustment of the US economy in the aftermath of 2008 raises doubts about the soundness of these views. Despite massive stimulus packages (expansionary fiscal policy) and an unprecedented monetary expansion, the US unemployment rate has remained close to nine per cent as late as September 2012, four years after the financial upheaval. The automatic adjustment mechanisms in which economists like Lucas place so much trust have been slow to take effect even with the help of active policy interventions.

18.11 Key Terms and Concepts

In this chapter we outlined:

- a standard dynamic aggregate demand and aggregate supply model
- how the model can be used to examine demand-side shocks
- the key role of the central bank in the adjustment process
- the implications of an adverse supply-side shock
- the role of the labour market in the adjustment process
- rational expectations.

CHAPTER 19

Money and Prices in the Long Run

19.1 Introduction

In this chapter and the next we outline a long-run model of the open economy. Recall from Chapter 5 that the distinction between the 'long' and 'short' run is that in the long run prices are completely flexible. In the short run, at least some prices are sticky and other prices are flexible. As a result, the short-run aggregate supply (SRAS) curve slops upwards. However, in the long run all prices have had sufficient time to adjust and the economy remains on the long-run aggregate supply (LRAS). The LRAS curve is vertical at the potential level of real output, Y^*.

In this chapter we outline a long-run theory of the price level and inflation, namely the quantity theory of money. Before doing so, however, we present an overview of the open economy long-run model. A key issue is how the economy adjusts back to potential real output following some form of shock.

The second half of the chapter provides a long-run review of money and banking and monetary policy in Ireland. We begin with a discussion of the development of an Irish currency until its withdrawal in 2002. This is followed by an outline of the Irish banking sector and the evolution of central banking in Ireland.

19.2 Overview of the Open Economy Long-run Model

Figure 19.1 shows a representation of the goods and services in the long run. As is normally the case, the price level is on the vertical axis and real output on the horizontal axis. As discussed in Chapter 4, Y^* is determined by the production function:

$$Y^* = AF(L, K, H, N)$$

- Y^* = potential level of output
- A = available production technology
- L = quantity of labour
- K = quantity of physical capital
- H = quantity of human capital
- N = quantity of natural resources
- *F*( ) is a function that shows how the inputs are combined to product output. The technology variable, A, is multiplied by this function as we do not attribute technology to either capital or labour. That is, technology is attributed equally to all of the factors of production.

In Figure 19.1, Y^* is represented by a vertical line. As labour, capital and the other factors of production increase over time the long-run aggregate supply (LRAS) curve moves to the right. Note that a vertical LRAS curve indicates that the price level on the vertical axis has no bearing on Y^*. Potential real output is determined only by the factors of production.

There is no short-run aggregate supply (SRAS) curve as, in the long run, all prices are flexible and the economy adjusts back to Y* following some disturbance. In Chapter 20 we explain that the loanable funds model underlines the adjustment mechanism. In the closed economy version, the real interest rate is the key adjustment variable. However, in the open economy version of the model, the real exchange rate ensures the economy revers back to Y*.

The level of unemployment underlying potential real output is the natural rate of unemployment. This type of unemployment consists of both frictional and structural unemployment. A discussion of the natural rate of unemployment was presented in Chapter 4. We now turn to the issue of what determines the price level in this model.

FIGURE 19.1 The long-run aggregate supply curve (classical model)

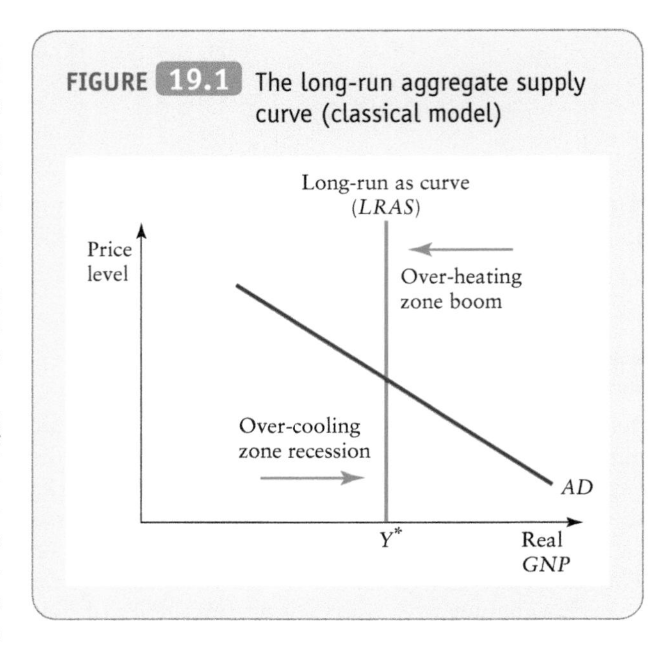

19.3 The Quantity Theory of Money

The quantity theory of money its simplest form states that the larger the quantity of money in the economy, the higher the price level. It also implies that the more rapid the rate of increase in the money supply, the higher the rate of inflation.

NOTE: The discovery of large silver mines in Mexico, Bolivia and Argentina led to a vast increase in the stock of silver coins in circulation in Europe from the sixteenth century onwards. The rise in the price level experienced at the same time was attributed by many observers to the increase in the quantity of money. This is the origin of the modern quantity theory, which can be traced back to Richard Cantillon, who was from County Kerry, in his *Essai Sur la Nature du Commerce en Général* (published in 1755 but written 20 years earlier) and by David Hume in *Political Discourses* (1752). (See Murphy 1986.)

To set out the quantity theory in algebraic terms, we define the velocity of circulation of money (V) as the number of times the average euro coin in Ireland changes hands in a given time period. V is defined as the total number of all transactions (T) divided by the stock of money (M^S):

$$V \equiv T/M^S$$

Measuring total transactions is, however, problematic as billions of transactions take place in the economy every year. We can resolve this problem by using nominal GDP as a proxy for T. GDP is the total amount of final goods and services sold during the course of the year. As T and GDP are highly correlated, we can use GDP as a proxy for total transactions. This is the best available proxy for the value of all transactions. If nominal GDP is equal to €150 billion and the money supply is €100 billion we can calculate V to be 1.5:

$$V \equiv \text{Nominal GDP}/M^s = \frac{€150\text{bn}}{€100\text{bn}} = 1.5$$

Since it takes two parties to make a transaction, output sold is equal to output purchased. Hence, the figure of €150 billion is also the amount of goods and services purchased during the year. Given a money supply of €100 billion, this means that the average monetary unit financed €1.5 worth of expenditure on final goods and services. In other words, the average monetary unit was used one and a half times during the year. This is what is meant by 'velocity'.

As nominal GDP is equal to real GDP multiplied by the price level, the quantity equation can be written:

$$V \equiv \frac{(P \times \text{real GDP})}{M^s}$$

Multiply both sides by M^s and, using the symbol Y for real GDP:

$$M^s \times V \equiv P \times Y$$

This is the equation of exchange. It is an identity or something that holds true by definition. It simply states that the money supply multiplied by velocity must equal nominal GDP (or the price level multiplied by real GDP).

To get from the equation of exchange to the quantity theory, we make two assumptions:

1. V is relatively stable.
2. The economy is at the potential level of real GDP, Y^*. And as mentioned in the previous section, Y^* depends on the production function. The price level does not enter into the determination of Y^*.

Given these assumptions, it is clear that if the money supply, M^s, is increased the brunt of the adjustment must come through an increase in P, the price level. Increases in the money supply lead to higher prices. This quantity theory is a cornerstone of that school of economics that has come to be known as monetarism.

How changes in the money supply determines the price level is not specified. It is, in effect, a 'black box'. One possible explanation is as follows: an increase in the money supply will shift the AD curve up to the right (not shown). In the short run, the effect of the increase in the money supply is to increase both P and Y along the SRAS curve. As P is now higher than expected, price expectations will be revised upwards and the economy will revert back to Y^*. In the longer term, the effect of the increase in the money supply has been a proportionate increase in the price level and no change in the actual level of output Y or in the potential level of output, Y^*.

This gives rise to the so-called classical dichotomy. This relates to the distinction or separation between real and nominal variables. The change in the money supply does not impact on real variables, such as Y and unemployment, but only affects nominal variables such as P. This proposition is also known as the neutrality of money.

Another way of representing the quantity theory is to totally differentiate the equation of exchange to obtain:

$$\Delta M^s + \Delta V = \Delta P + \Delta Y$$

where the symbol Δ is used to signify the percentage rate of change. The percentage change in the money supply plus the percentage change in velocity must equal the inflation rate plus the real growth rate. (Notice that in totally differentiating, the multiplication sign changes to a plus sign.) Assuming that velocity is relatively constant and the economy is at Y^*, the quantity theory predicts a one-for-one relationship between changes in the money supply and the inflation rate. Causation is assumed to run from left to right.

The quantity theory provides the basis for a standard approach to inflation targeting. The ECB's key objective is to keep inflation 'below but close to two per cent'. Assume that economists at the ECB forecast that velocity will remain stable and that the real growth rate will be 2.5 per cent. On this basis the ECB's policy would be to allow the money supply to grow at the rate that is consistent with the two per cent target rate of inflation:

$$\Delta M^s + \Delta V = \Delta P + \Delta Y$$

$$4.5\% + 0\% = 2.5\% + 2\%$$

The money supply should increase at the rate of increase in real output plus the target rate of inflation. Economists who believe that the quantity theory should act as the bedrock of monetary policy are known as monetarists. They believe there should be no discretionary monetary policy: in the long run the authorities should simply maintain the growth in the money supply to achieve the inflation objective and accommodate the real growth rate. If this monetary rule is followed, the actual inflation rate should remain close to the target rate.

Which inflation rate should be targeted?

Inflation is most often measured as the rate of increase in a consumer price index, such as the CPI or the HICP, which we discussed in Chapter 3. An important feature of these indices is that they focus on the prices of goods and services, but exclude the price of assets, such as houses and stocks and shares. House prices affect the Irish CPI only to the extent that they affect rents and mortgage payments. The HICP regards the purchase of an owner-occupied house as an investment and excludes it from the Index.

During the housing and stock market booms of the first decade of this century, the inflation targets used when formulating monetary policy did not reflect the very high inflation in asset prices that was occurring. Yet when these bubbles collapsed enormous damage was inflicted on the real economy. With hindsight, most central bankers now regret not having taken more heed of asset price inflation over these years.

19.4 The Quantity Theory and Economic Policy

As support for the quantity theory, monetarists point to the close correlation between inflation and the growth in the money supply over the long run in different countries and at different periods of time. Milton Friedman's *Monetary History of the United States: 1867–1960*, written with

FIGURE 19.2 The quantity theory of money

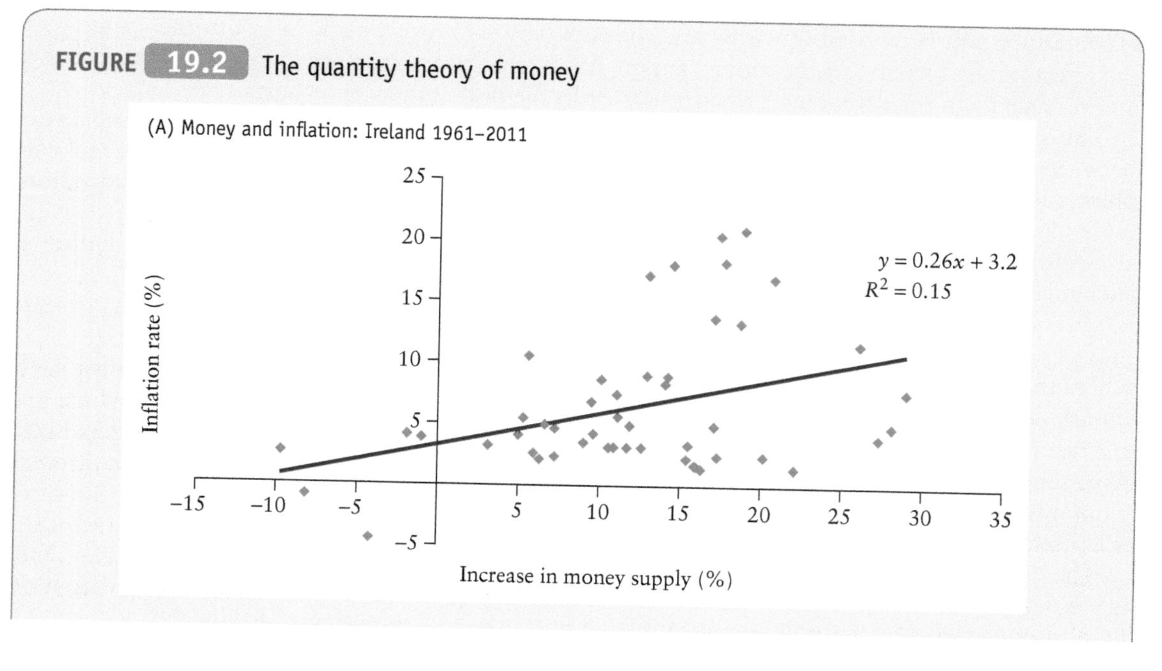

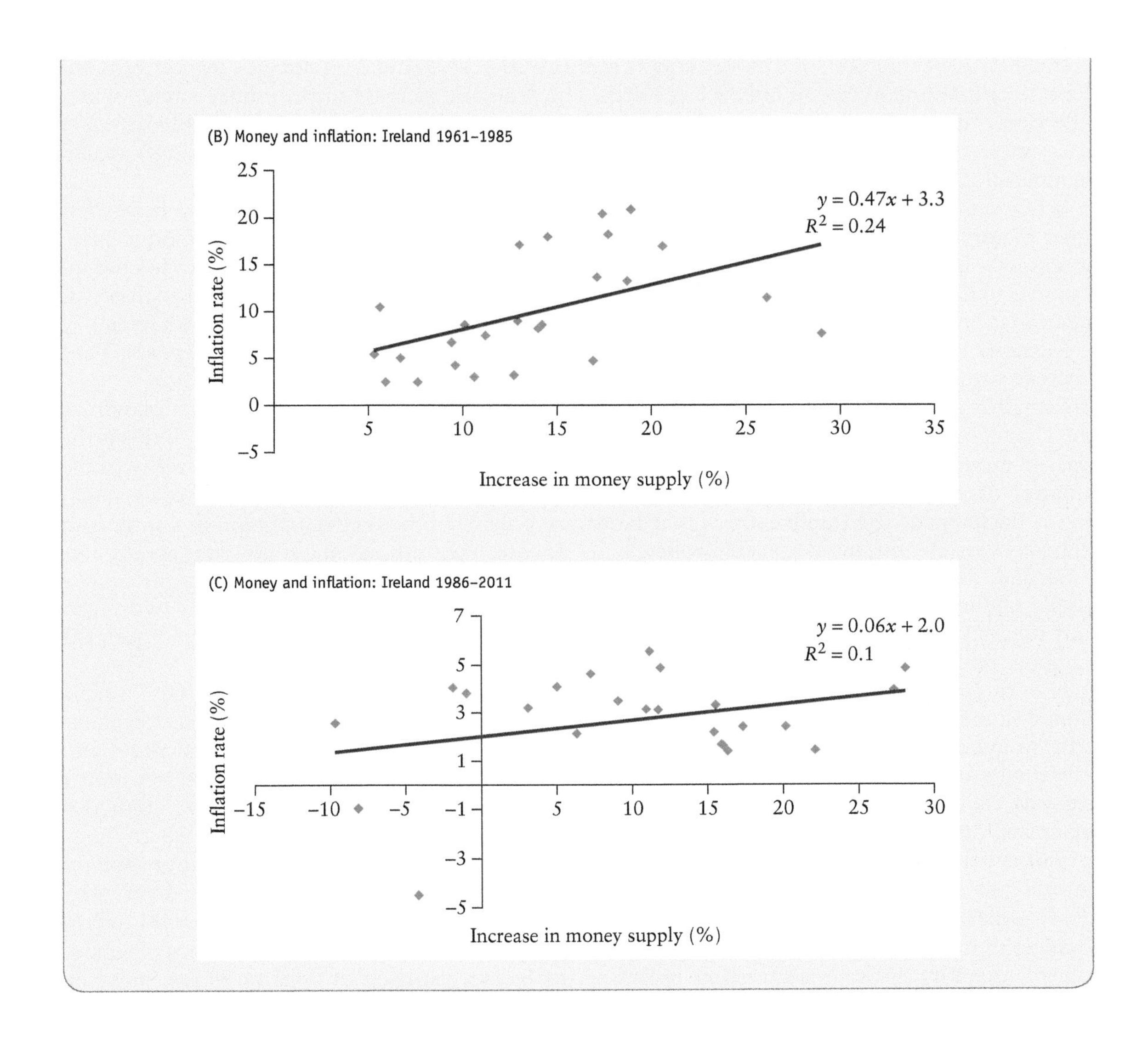

his wife Anna Schwartz, found support for the monetarist point of view in the experience of the United States since the nineteenth century. Friedman also found support for the quantity theory in inflation-prone countries such as Brazil, Bolivia and Israel. These countries have had high growth rates in their money supplies and rapid inflation. This led Friedman to conclude: 'Inflation is always and everywhere a monetary phenomenon.' While this view has been considerably modified in the light of recent evidence, there is still a good deal of truth in the assertion.

Figure 19.2 examines the relationship between the growth rate of the money supply and the rate of inflation in Ireland from 1961 to 2011. The measure of the money supply is M3, which we defined in Chapter 9. Inflation is measured as the rate of change in the CPI. We present three graphs in Figures 19.2A, B and C, the first covering the entire period 1961–2011 and the other two the first and second halves of the period (1961–1985 and 1986–2011).

It is clear from all three graphs that the relationship between the two variables, although positive – as expected – is weak. The regression line fitted through the two series is statistically significant, but not at a high level. It is, however, notable that the relationship is much closer over the first half of the 50-year period than over the second half.

In 2005, 2006 and 2007 the money supply grew by 20.1, 27.9 and 27.4 per cent respectively, but the rate of inflation averaged only 3.8 per cent. The dramatic increase in the money supply was a reflection of the increase in bank credit that fuelled the property and construction bubble. If asset prices were included in our measure of inflation, the relationship between the two variables would be much closer over these years.

While the quantity theory is a long-run theory of inflation, it does not rule out the belief that other factors can trigger inflation, such as oil price increases or more generally commodity price booms like the one that occurred between 2008 and 2011. In small, open economies like Ireland inflation is to a significant degree exogenous and strongly influenced by external factors. Much of our inflation is imported, the exact mechanism depending on the exchange rate regime (see Chapter 15).

Keynesian economists argue that the quantity theory cannot be used for policy purposes. They advance a number of arguments to support this proposition.

First, it is argued that velocity is not constant and is instead inversely related to the money supply. That is, an increase in the money supply will lead to a fall in velocity and vice versa. If this is the case, an increase in the money supply may have little or no effect on nominal output. In terms of the equation of exchange, if the increase in M^s is matched by a fall in V, the right-hand side of the equation is unchanged. The implication is that monetary policy will be ineffective even in a large and relatively closed economy. Monetary policy, is in this case, like pushing on a rope – very ineffective.

Second, Keynesians argue that there is a long and variable lag between changes in the money supply and inflation. Milton Friedman himself admits that this lag could be as long as two years. This suggests that a deflationary monetary policy, intended to curb inflation, may instead push the economy into recession.

A third criticism of the quantity theory is that causation may run from nominal GNP to the money supply and not the other way round. In other words, the money supply may be 'demand-led'. An increase in nominal GDP increases the demand for money for transaction purposes and households and firms take out loans to finance expenditure and investment. That is, as the economy expands, more money is required as a medium of exchange. As the economy grows and more jobs are created, people borrow more from the banks and lending increases.

This is what happened during the property bubble in Ireland. As more and more people bought into the property market, the banks supplied more credit by borrowing from the inter-bank market. In situations like that, the causation in the equation of exchange is running from right to left. Changes in nominal GDP cause an expansion of the money supply and not the other way around.

If the quantity theory is accepted as providing the best explanation of inflation in the long run, from a policy perspective this raises the question of how to control the money supply. The relationship between high-powered money and the overall money supply (see Chapter 9) tends to vary. This makes the central bank's job of regulating the money supply very difficult. Furthermore, the narrow and broad definitions of the money supply do not move in tandem. This raises the question of which definition of the money supply (the narrow or broad definition) the central bank should attempt to control.

19.5 Hyperinflation

Hyperinflation is the label given to extremely high inflation rates, say in excess of 1,000 per cent a year. When annual inflation rates are so high it is easier to state monthly rather than annual inflation rates. In Germany and Austria in 1922–23, the average inflation rate was 322 per cent per month. Under the German Weimar Republic the peak rate of inflation was recorded in October 1923, when the monthly inflation rate touched 29,000 per cent. A good that cost Mark 1 at the beginning of the month cost Mark 290 at the end of the month. This led to a currency reform and the introduction of the Reichsmark (RM) in 1924. The exchange rate between the old and the new currencies was RM1 = Papiermark 10^{12} (1 : 12 billion).

Box 19.1 Change in the price of a newspaper during German hyperinflation

	Marks
1921	
January	0.3
1922	
May	2.0
October	8.0
1923	
February	100
September	1,000
1 October	2,000
15 October	20,000
29 October	1 million
9 November	15 million
17 November	70 million

Box 19.1 shows how the price of a newspaper changed between January 1921 and November 1923.

Although the German and Austrian experience is probably the best known, there are numerous other examples of hyperinflation. In Greece in 1943, inflation reached 365 per cent per month; in Hungary in 1945–46, inflation went to 3,170 per cent per month; in Bolivia in 1985, a monthly inflation rate of over 3,000 per cent was recorded; and in Serbia in 1993 the monthly inflation rate reached 100,000 per cent – it took 6 million dinars (the local currency) to buy one Snickers bar.

Until early 2009, the Reserve Bank of Zimbabwe printed money to finance the government's budget deficit. This led, as predicted by the quantity theory, to hyperinflation. The annual inflation rate rose from 30 per cent in the late 1990s to an official annual rate of 11,200,000 per cent in 2009. The result was that prices doubled in under two days. In early 2009, the domestic currency was abandoned and replaced by the US dollar (dollarisation) and the South African rand. This ended the hyperinflation and restored price stability. Inflation in 2011 was estimated to be five per cent. The problem now in Zimbabwe is that there is little or no US coin in circulation; no cents, dimes or quarters. As a dollar is a lot of money in a poor country like Zimbabwe, change has become a chronic issue.

Hyperinflation in German memory

It is said that the German hyperinflation of the 1920s is so engraved on the minds of German policy-makers today that they dread inflation. As a result, they are extremely averse to policies they believe will give rise to inflation in the future. In September 2012 the president of the Bundesbank, Jens Weidmann, who is *ex officio* a member of the ECB's governing council, voted against the bond-buying proposal we discussed in Chapter 9. He was quoted as saying that the measures were 'too close' to central bank financing of government deficits 'with a printing press'.

Many historical commentaries attribute the rise of National Socialism (the Nazi Party) to the collapse of the savings of the German middle class due to runaway inflation. However, some historians point out that this may be a misreading of German history. The hyperinflation came to an end by 1923 and the Nazis did not come to power until 1933. The worldwide Great Depression and collapse of the stock market brought the German economy to its knees after 1929, and the unemployment rate averaged over 30 per cent in the early 1930s. When Paul von Hindenberg was elected president in 1932 (as the only alternative to Adolf Hitler), the political unrest was so great that he had no option but to appoint Adolf Hitler as his chancellor in January 1933.

The consequences of hyperinflation

There are numerous illustrations of what hyperinflation does to an economy. Here are some examples.

> *Argentines went on a buying spree yesterday in a race against soaring prices. In a whirl of hyperinflation, supermarkets are sometimes marking up prices twice a day while the Argentine currency, the austral, plunges in value. Customers overturned trolleys full of goods at one supermarket after the management announced over loudspeakers that all prices were being immediately raised by 30 per cent.* (*Irish Times*, 26 April 1989)

John Maynard Keynes noted that if you went into a bar in Germany during the hyperinflation of 1922–23, it would be worth your while to buy two pints of beer rather than one. The reason was that the rate of inflation was higher than the rate at which the second pint went flat! Another story goes that a woman went to buy bread with a basket full of money. A mugger snatched the basket from her and ran off, throwing the worthless paper money on the roadside. It has also been pointed out that if you take a taxi ride in a hyperinflation period it is important to pay when you enter the taxi – the fare will be considerably higher by the time you reach your destination.

Countries with high inflation rates inevitably have weak or depreciating exchange rates. For example, in Bolivia the exchange rate fell from Peso500,000/$1 to Peso900,000/$1 in a single day. In Argentina, soaring inflation also undermined the exchange rate of the country's currency. The austral was introduced in 1985, when it was worth $1.25. By mid-1991, there were 10,000 Australs to $1. The government announced plans to replace it with a new currency, which would be called the (nuevo) peso. This was only the most recent in a series of new currencies introduced as inflation undermined the old ones: one new peso would be worth 10,000 billion of the old pesos that were in use in the 1960s.

As inflation soars and the exchange rate depreciates, there is a flight from domestic money. Salaries and wages denominated in the local currency are falling rapidly and people attempt to switch into a stable currency such as the dollar or the euro. This process is called dollarisation.

A nation of 'money-changers' emerges and wages have to be paid several times during the day. Bribes, strikes, stealing and smuggling become the norm. Eventually, the inflation becomes so disruptive that the country's social and political culture becomes undermined.

Causes of hyperinflation

The quantity theory of money comes into its own in explaining hyperinflation. Such high rates of inflation are simply not possible without equally high rates of increase in the money supply, as shown by the example of the Weimar Republic in the 1920s and Zimbabwe in this century. But this, of course, simply pushes the explanation back a stage and provokes the question: Why is the money supply increasing so rapidly?

One of the most common contributing factors to excessive monetary expansion is excessive fiscal deficits. That is, the government's budget deficit lies at the root of the problem. Suppose a government is running a very large deficit, but is unable or unwilling to cover its expenditure through taxation. It has to borrow to balance the books. The public and the foreign banks may refuse to lend to the government, possibly anticipating a default on the loan in the future.

The government is now forced to borrow from its own central bank. Table 19.1 illustrates how this would work on the balance sheet of a central bank. Loans to government increase on the asset side

TABLE 19.1 Central bank balance sheet (€ millions)

Change in assets	Change in liabilities
External reserves	Currency
Loans: Banks	Commercial bank reserves
Government +1	Government deposits +1
Government securities	
Total +1	Total +1

(+€1 million) and government deposits increase on the liability side (+€1 million). The government can now run down its deposits by obtaining currency or by writing a cheque on its account. Either way, the stock of high-powered money (the monetary base) increases and there is a multiple expansion of the money supply. This is the equivalent of printing money and is referred to as debt monetisation.

According to the quantity theory, as the money supply increases the inflation rate will accelerate. However, as inflation takes off, the budget deficit automatically gets worse. This is because:

1. People and firms will delay paying their taxes. Inflation reduces the real value of the domestic currency, so the longer people delay paying taxes the less they have to pay in real terms. Note, however, that some taxes, such as VAT, yield more revenue as inflation rises. Also inflation erodes the values of the income tax bands and allowances, and this pushes up the average income tax rate.
2. Governments adopt 'populist' policies by charging low prices for public services and subsidising staples like bread. This raises the government's deficit.
3. Since the nominal interest rate is equal to the real rate plus the expected rate of inflation (Fisher equation), the nominal interest rate tends to rise in line with inflation and, as a result, the interest payments on the public debt increase.

Overall, with the tax revenue falling and public spending increasing, the budget deficit worsens and this leads to further borrowing from the central bank.

To stop the hyperinflation, the government must stop using the printing presses to finance the budget deficit. But this presupposes a fiscal reform in the shape of cuts in government spending and higher taxes. Hence, ending the hyperinflation requires action on both the fiscal and monetary fronts. The credibility of both the government and the central bank is crucial to the process. What matters is their ability to convince the public of their unwavering commitment to austerity.

Often governments find that it is beyond their power or political will to introduce the necessary measures of their own accord. Instead they resort to calling in the IMF. It is then left to the IMF to shoulder much of the blame and opprobrium that follows when the austerity measures needed to halt inflation are implemented.

19.6 Real and Nominal Interest Rates and Expected Inflation

In the past, unexpected inflation made it easy for governments to raise money in the short run. This is no longer the case in today's more globalised and sophisticated economy. People are no longer prepared to buy bonds issued by profligate and unstable governments. Investors demand guarantees that their money will be repaid and the value of the principal protected against inflation. In response, many governments now issue what are called inflation-indexed or *inflation-linked bonds*.

These guarantee the investor that the real value of her investment will be preserved. The British Treasury was the first to issue modern inflation-linked gilts (linked to the UK Retail Price Index) in 1981. They now amount to about a quarter of the UK total bond market. The USA followed by issuing Treasury Inflation Protected Securities (TIPS) linked to the US Consumer Price Index in the 1990s. In the euro area, the largest and most liquid inflation-linked bond market is for French Treasury OATs (*Obligations Assimilables du Trésor* – tradeable Treasury obligations). The category known as OAT€i is linked to the euro area inflation rate. The Irish government has yet to issue any inflation-linked bonds, so these French bonds are the best available inflation-linked bonds for an Irish investor who wants to avoid currency risk.

Inflation-linked bonds guarantee to preserve the real value of the investor's principal. This is done by linking the amount invested to a price index such as the CPI (usually excluding the price of tobacco products). As the principal rises with inflation, so too do the annual income payments or coupons. To take a very simplified example, suppose an investor buys a €1,000 inflation-linked bond, maturing in a year, that promises to pay a real return of two per cent. If inflation runs at five per cent over the year, at the end of the year she will be repaid €1,050 (principal adjusted for inflation) plus a coupon (dividend) of $21 (two per cent of the inflation-adjusted principal). If this bond had a 10-year maturity and inflation remained at five per cent over the period, the investor would be repaid €1,629 and the final coupon would be €32.58 (two per cent of €1,629).

The demand for inflation-linked bonds has driven their price up and real yield down. For example, in October 2010 investors drove the yield on TIPS (US Treasury Inflation Protected Securities) into negative territory for the first time. They bought €10 billion of four-and-a-half-year TIPS with a 0.5 per cent coupon but they paid an average price of $105.51 for a $100.00 bond. The pricing of the bonds implied that the real yield to maturity was *minus* 0.5 per cent. Investors who bought these securities were expecting to lose a half of one per cent a year on their investment in real terms. In the prevailing climate of uncertainty about currencies and sovereign debt they were willing to pay a penalty to insure against bigger losses.

The same has happened with European inflation-linked bonds. In September 2012 the yield on a French OAT€i maturing in 2020 was 0.0 per cent. The best an investor could do was to ensure that the real value of her principal was maintained.

One approach to forecasting inflation is to compare the difference between the yield on nominal bonds and the yield on inflation-linked bonds. Recall the Fisher equation from Chapter 10:

$$i = \mathrm{r} + \pi^{e}$$

where i is the nominal interest rate, r is the real interest rate and π^e is the expected rate of inflation. Now if an index-linked bond offers a real yield of one per cent and the nominal bond a yield of four per cent, then inflation would have to run at three per cent in order to equalise the two yields. If inflation turns out to be higher than three per cent, the investor who bought the nominal bond would be worse off. On the other hand, if inflation turns out to be lower than three per cent, the nominal bond offers a higher return.

Turning this around, we can derive what is called the 'break-even inflation rate' as:

$$\pi^{e} = i - \mathrm{r}$$

In this example, break-even inflation is equal to four per cent minus one per cent or three per cent.

We can calculate break-even inflation using up-to-date information from the bond market. A 10-year inflation-linked French bond (OAT€i) maturing in 2020 yielded 0.0 per cent in mid-September 2012. The yield on a comparable non-inflation-linked bond (OAT) was 1.3 per cent. This implies that break-even inflation was 1.3 − 0.0 = 1.3 per cent. Very low inflation rates are implied by the yields now available in the European and American bond markets.

19.7 The Development of the Irish Currency

We digress now to provide a brief history of money in Ireland.

Early history

Gold and silver were used as a medium of exchange in Ireland in ancient times, although the units took the form of rings and bracelets rather than coins. Money, however, took many other forms, as the following quote suggests:

> *The Annals of the Four Masters, originating from* AD *106, state that the tribute (Boroimhe meaning literally 'cow-tax') paid by the King of Leinster consisted of 150 cows, 150 pigs, 150 couples of men and women in servitude, 150 girls and 150 cauldrons.* (Einzig 1966:239)

The first coinage in Ireland can be traced to the Norse settlement in Dublin in the 990s. The amount of coinage in circulation was relatively small and largely confined to the main trading towns. The use of coinage increased after the arrival of the Normans in 1169. In 1460 the Irish parliament met in Drogheda and established the first separate Irish currency. This currency was subsequently devalued relative to the English currency. The exchange rate used was 15 Irish pence to 12 English pence (one English shilling). Over the centuries the exchange rate between the Irish and English currencies has varied considerably.

In the sixteenth century the English monarchy allowed the so-called 'Harp coinage' (sometimes referred to as 'white money') to be issued. In doing so, the monarchy acknowledged the existence of a separate Irish currency unit. This was followed in 1601 by an issue of copper coinage by Queen Elizabeth I.

By the 1680s, when banking-type activities first began to emerge, the currency situation in Ireland was unsatisfactory for a number of reasons. First, there was a general shortage of coins and the economy still operated partly on a barter system. So bad was the currency situation that James II melted down cannons to manufacture coins. This became known as 'gun money' and gave rise to the expression 'not worth a brass farthing'.

Generally, the coinage in circulation consisted of a mix of Spanish, French, Portuguese and English coins, which were of different quality and design, and this lack of uniformity impaired its ability to function as a medium of exchange (as predicted by Gresham's law).

In the early 1720s a Mr Wood received a patent to issue coinage (Wood's half-pence) which would have increased the copper coinage in circulation by about a quarter. However, this patent was withdrawn two years later, partly because of the argument used by Jonathan Swift in *The Drapier's Letters* that the increase in currency would raise prices (the quantity theory). A general shortage of coinage continued in Ireland, but as the poorer people in country areas still lived in a subsistence and semi-barter economy, this had little effect on them. Merchants also issued their own coins in order to facilitate trade.

From the eighteenth century to independence

Throughout the eighteenth century, the Irish currency was at a discount of about eight per cent relative to the English currency: 13 Irish pence equaled 12 English pence. In 1797, during the turmoil of the Napoleonic Wars, the convertibility of Irish and British coins to gold was suspended, and in 1803 the Irish currency depreciated sharply. A parliamentary inquiry was established, which issued a report known as the *Irish Currency Report* (1804). This report argued that excessive credit expansion caused the depreciation and that the exchange rate could be stabilised if the growth of credit were controlled.

After 1804 the Irish currency gradually stabilised at a 13/12 exchange rate against sterling. By the time gold convertibility was resumed in 1821, this rate was sufficiently re-established for the

Bank of Ireland (a commercial bank) to accept responsibility for maintaining the Irish currency at this rate. Following the implementation of the monetary provisions of the 1800 Act of Union in 1826, the Irish currency was abolished and full political and monetary union was established between Ireland and Great Britain. Thereafter British coins and notes circulated freely in Ireland.

NOTE: The *Irish Currency Report* influenced thinking in the 'bullionist controversy' in England (1796–1821) and is an important document in the history of monetary economics. The key issue it addressed was whether there could be an 'excessive' growth in the money supply. The report set out what came to be the orthodox view – that an 'excess' increase in the money supply would lead to an increase in the price level and this, in turn, would make exports less competitive and cause the exchange rate to depreciate. This reasoning was influential in the development of the modern quantity theory of money.

Developments since independence

Following the foundation of the Irish Free State in 1922, the Coinage Act of 1926 was passed in order to enable the minister for finance to issue new Irish coins. These coins were used in Ireland until 1971, when a new design was introduced and the coinage decimalised.

NOTE: Until the 1950s the 'silver' coins minted for Ireland in fact contained significant amounts of silver. Some of them became very valuable as the price of silver rose. Two-shilling and half-crown coins from the early 1940s are now worth hundreds of euro, so following Gresham's law they have entirely disappeared from circulation.

A commission was set up in 1926 to advise the government on the establishment of an Irish pound. This was known as the Parker Willis Commission, after its chairman, Professor Henry Parker Willis (1874–1937) of Columbia University, a former secretary of the Federal Reserve Board. The commission's final report was signed in January 1927. It recommended that a new currency unit, the Saorstát pound, be created and that in order to ensure public confidence in the new currency, it should be backed 100 per cent by sterling reserves, British government stock and gold reserves, and be freely convertible into sterling. It was also recommended that the value of the new currency in terms of sterling could not be changed without the introduction of additional legislation. Thus the new currency would, in effect, be sterling with an Irish design. This would ensure that it would be acceptable alongside sterling as a medium of exchange. The Commission also recommended the establishment of a new body, confusingly to be called the Currency Commission, to oversee the issue of the new legal tender notes.

The recommendations of the Parker Willis Commission were incorporated into law in the Currency Act 1927. The Currency Commission was established and remained in existence until 1942, when its powers were transferred to the new Central Bank. Its only chairman was Joseph Brennan (1887–1963), who became the first governor of the Central Bank of Ireland. The first Irish notes were issued in September 1928.

NOTE: Under the new arrangements the commercial banks were allowed to issue a certain number of private banknotes that bore the banks' names. These were called the Consolidated Bank Note issue and the notes were known as 'ploughman notes' because of their design. These notes were finally withdrawn from circulation in 1953.

The share of Irish legal tender notes in the total supply of money in circulation is believed to have reached about two-thirds by the beginning of World War II. This represents another example of the benefits of seigniorage. This arose because in 1928 the Irish public gave their holdings of sterling to the Currency Commission in exchange for an equivalent amount of the new Irish currency. The Commission placed the sterling it had obtained on the London money markets and earned interest. This represented seigniorage profits. It has been estimated that the value of the seigniorage amounted to about 0.2 per cent of national income at the time (Ó Gráda 1994:42).

19.8 The Evolution of Central Banking in Ireland

A key date in Irish banking history is 1783. In that year the Bank of Ireland was founded by royal charter. It performed some of the functions of a central bank; it issued notes and managed the government's account. Because of its size it was able to lend money to banks that were in distress, but it was not always willing or able to provide enough support to avert bank failures. Greater competition in the banking sector following the Bankers' (Ireland) Act of 1845 forced the Bank of Ireland to evolve along commercial lines. This reduced its willingness to help out other banks in times of crisis.

Also following the Act of Union in 1801 and the abolition of the Irish currency in 1826, the Bank of England was given some responsibility for supervising banking in Ireland. The banks at this time were primarily involved in facilitating the trade of agricultural produce. Merchants borrowed from the banks to pay farmers for crops that were sold on the domestic market or exported. With their receipts, the merchants repaid their bank loans. The farmers used the banknotes given to them by the merchants to pay the landowners' rent. The landowners then returned the notes to the private banks in exchange for gold, silver or foreign currency. Hence the private banks facilitated a transfer of resources from tenant farmers to landowners.

Because there was no lender of last resort, the Irish private banks were very vulnerable in times of crisis. In 1820, for example, after the end of the Napoleonic Wars, there was a slump in agricultural prices and widespread bankruptcy among the merchants to whom the banks had loaned money. When depositors got wind of this there was a 'run on the banks'. However, the banks did not have enough cash on hand to meet the demand and could not call in their loans from bankrupt clients. They had to close their doors and call in liquidators. In Munster the 'run' started in Cork city and quickly spread throughout the province. In Limerick, the four private banks (Maunsells' Bank, Furnell and Company, Bruce's Bank and Roche's Limerick Bank) all ceased trading. In one month 30 banks failed in Munster alone and the crisis spread throughout the rest of the country, leaving only 10 banks solvent outside Dublin (O'Kelly 1959). As the banks were private companies, when they failed the partners who owned them lost their capital and frequently had to sell off their town houses and country estates as well. Depositors were lucky if they got back half the money they had lodged with the banks.

The private banks were superseded by joint stock banks following the banking crises of the 1820s. These had at least six major shareholders (who accepted unlimited liability) and they were therefore better able to withstand crises.

The Currency Commission

The question of the appropriate way to regulate the banking system emerged as an issue after independence. It was recognised that a serious conflict of interest would have emerged if the Bank of Ireland were asked to act as the central bank in the Free State. Nonetheless, the minister for finance in the new provisional government asked the Bank of Ireland to continue to manage the government's account. The Banking Commission that reported in 1927 did not intend that the Currency Commission would become a fully fledged central bank. It was not given the power to act as a lender of last resort, nor could it set reserve requirements for commercial banks. It did not gain control over the commercial banks' sterling assets, which continued to be kept in London. Furthermore, the commission did not manage the government's account, nor did it advise the government on monetary matters.

Perhaps the main reason a central bank was not established in the 1920s was that there was little such an institution could usefully do as long as the country remained in a monetary union with Great Britain. There was a fixed exchange rate between the Irish currency and sterling and there was no money market in Ireland. Under these circumstances, a central bank could not control the money supply or have any influence on the price level, output or employment. All that was needed was some type of *currency board*, to issue local currency in exchange for approved assets such as sterling. This function was discharged by the Currency Commission.

Another possible reason why a central bank was not established after independence was:

> *. . . a conviction that central banks were being promoted as antidotes to backward or unduly risk-adverse commercial banking systems. Accordingly, creating an Irish central bank might be seen as both a slight and a threat to the long-established commercial banks.* (Ó Gráda 1994:27)

In the same vein, when government asked the commercial banks to underwrite a flotation of government stock in the 1930s, the banks were reluctant and wanted to know how the government intended to spend the proceeds.

When in September 1931 the UK terminated the Gold Standard and sterling was devalued by 25 per cent against gold, there were misgivings in some quarters in Ireland that the Irish currency was automatically devalued due to the link with sterling. The Fianna Fáil government established a second Banking Commission in 1934 to report on money and banking in Ireland. The new commission included Joseph Brennan (chairman of the Currency Commission), George O'Brien (professor of national economics at University College, Dublin) and the Swedish economist Per Jacobsson, who later became president of the IMF. (John Maynard Keynes was considered but was not invited, possibly because of his criticism of the Irish government's protectionist policies in a lecture in Dublin in the previous year.) A bishop was included, but Dr McNeely was 'unaware of any reasons why he should have been appointed, except to add an atmosphere of respectability to the Conference' (Ó Gráda 1994:42.)

This second Banking Commission deliberated for nearly four years and reported in 1938. As one commentator put it: 'The opinion of the majority report on the system of banking and currency may be summarised as a recommendation to leave things as they were' (Meenan 1970:222.)

The creation of an Irish central bank was not recommended, but it was suggested that the Currency Commission be allowed to engage in open market operations and that its name be suitably altered to 'indicate that the monetary authority envisaged in these recommendations is a central banking organisation'. Thus, the commission tried to steer a course between outright advocacy of a central bank and the status quo. In the days before the start of World War II, the Bank of Ireland approached the Bank of England to see if it would act as a lender of last resort to the Irish banks in an emergency. The Bank of England replied that it was not in a position to provide assistance and suggested that 'as Eire was a separate political entity it should have a central bank of its own' (Ó Gráda 1994:39).

Perhaps in the light of this rebuff the Irish commercial banks, which had been heavily represented on both banking commissions and had staunchly opposed the creation of a central bank, had second thoughts on the issue.

In any event:

> *The government chose to ignore the Report, and used the threat of war to produce central banking legislation. In the end, the Central Bank Act of 1942 was a compromise between, on the one hand, Brennan and the Department of Finance [who did not wish to establish a Bank], and the majority of ministers [who did] on the other.* (Ó Gráda 1994)

The Central Bank Act was passed in 1942 and soon afterwards the Central Bank of Ireland was established, with Joseph Brennan, the former chairman of the Currency Commission, as the first governor.

The Central Bank of Ireland

Since its launch in 1942, there have been nine governors of the Central Bank (see Box 19.2). All but Joseph Brennan and Patrick Honohan had been Secretary in the Department of Finance. The primary function of the new Central Bank was to 'safeguard the integrity of the currency'. Its powers were, however, limited. It could act as lender of last resort and use open market operations to influence liquidity in the money market, but it could not set reserve requirements or act as a banker to either the government or the commercial banks. The government continued to hold its account with the Bank of Ireland and the commercial banks held most of their reserves in the London money markets. Thus, little changed in Irish banking immediately following the establishment of the Central Bank of Ireland.

The 1960s, however, was a period of rapid development in Irish banking. A number of new banks began operations in Ireland and there was a wave of mergers among the established ones. The Bank of Ireland acquired the Hibernian Bank in 1958 and the National Bank in 1965. The Allied Irish Bank group was formed in 1966 with the merger of the Munster and Leinster Bank, the Provincial Bank and the Royal Bank of Ireland.

In 1965, the Central Bank of Ireland first issued 'letters of advice' (or credit guidelines) to the banks, telling them to restrain credit expansion in order to curtail the growing balance of payments deficit. The Central Bank began to promote new markets in foreign exchange, government stocks and money. Because of these developments, it was becoming increasingly clear that the 1942 Central Bank legislation was inadequate. In response the Central Bank Act 1971 was passed. This Act significantly increased the powers of the Central Bank. Its main features were:

- The Central Bank became the licensing authority for banks.
- The government's account was transferred from the Bank of Ireland to the Central Bank.
- The commercial banks were required to keep their reserves with the Central Bank.
- The Central Bank was given the power to issue primary and secondary reserve ratios (these were first issued in August 1972).
- The new legislation made it possible to break the sterling link by government order. This power was exercised in March 1979 following Ireland's entry to the European Monetary System.

Box 19.2 Governors of the Central Bank of Ireland

Joseph Brennan	1943–53
James J. McElligott	1953–60
Maurice Moynihan	1961–69
T. K. Whitaker	1969–76
Charles H. Murray	1976–81
Tomás Ó Cofaigh	1981–87
Maurice F. Doyle	1987–94
Maurice O'Connell	1994–2001
John Hurley	2001–2009
Patrick Honohan	2009–

The Central Bank Act 1989 brought money brokers, financial futures traders and companies associated with the new International Financial Services Centre (IFSC) under the supervision of the Central Bank. In addition, commercial bank charges were brought under its control and, as mentioned earlier, a deposit protection scheme was established to protect the savings of small depositors. Under the Building Society Act 1989 and the Trustee Savings Bank (TSB) Act 1989, the Central Bank gained responsibility for supervising the building societies and the Trustee Savings Banks.

In 1978 the Irish government decided to participate in the European Monetary System (EMS), even as Britain decided to stay out. In the 1990s, the Irish government took the decision to participate in European Monetary Union (EMU) when it commenced in 1999. This involved replacing the Irish currency with the euro and surrendering monetary independence to the ECB. The governing council of the ECB, which includes the governors of the central banks of the participating countries, formulates monetary policy in the euro area.

In effect Ireland had an independent currency for less than 20 years – between breaking the link with sterling in March 1979 and fixing the value of the Irish pound to the euro in January 1999. The Irish pound ceased to exist as a legal currency on 9 February 2002.

In 2003, the Central Bank was divided into two branches responsible for central banking and financial regulation respectively. This move was reversed in 2010 when a new single unitary body – the Central Bank of Ireland – was created.

19.9 Key Terms and Concepts

In this chapter we outlined the quantity theory of money. This theory explains how the price level is determined in a long-run model of the economy. Among the terms and concepts discussed were:

- the velocity of circulation of money
- how the quantity of money determines the price level
- the quantity theory and economic policy
- hyperinflation
- inflation-indexed bonds and expected inflation
- the development of money and banking in Ireland
- the structure of the Irish financial sector
- the evolution of central banking in Ireland.

CHAPTER 20

Savings, Investment and the Balance of Payments

20.1 Introduction

In this chapter we explore the relationships between savings, investment and the balance of payments. We start from a closed economy in which national savings and investment must be equal. We present a loanable funds model in which the real interest rate equates savings and investment. We then consider the more complicated relationship between savings and investment in an open economy. This involves explaining how an excess or deficit of national savings over national investment is reflected by a current account surplus or deficit. We extend the loanable funds model to include the relationship between the real exchange rate and the current account.

The models we use in this chapter are long-run models in the sense that we assume that all prices have sufficient time to adjust and the economy remains on its long-run aggregate supply (LRAS), which is vertical at the potential level of real output. In the course of the chapter we use the data for Ireland to show how savings, investment and the balance of payments have evolved up to 2011.

20.2 Savings and Investment in a Closed Economy

In this long-run model the potential level of real output is determined by the production function and the price level is determined by the quantity theory. The key adjustment variable is the real interest rate.

National savings

We can think of savings as 'loanable funds'. They represent a flow of funds that can be made available to investors. Savings are vital for investment in new capital equipment and innovation, which are essential to drive the economy forward. In a closed economy, national savings would be the only source of such funds. In an open economy, the picture is more complicated.

Savings can be measured gross or net; that is, they can be measured including the provision for depreciation or after this provision has been subtracted. A nation's savings can be disaggregated into public and private sector saving. Public sector saving is the excess of total revenue minus total expenditure. Here we denote total revenue as T as it largely consists of taxes (T). We denote government consumption by the symbol G. We can write:

$$\text{Public savings} = T - G \qquad (1)$$

Note that T here denotes taxes net of government transfers to firms and households, that is net taxes. If $T > G$ there is a budget surplus and if $T < G$ there is a budget deficit. If $T = G$, the government is said to have a balanced budget. The government's budget deficit is also called public sector dissavings.

Private sector saving can be broken down into household or personal saving and company or corporate saving. (The main component of the latter is the retained earnings of the larger corporations.) Ignoring corporate sector savings, private savings is equal to disposable income (gross income (Y) minus taxation (T)) minus consumption (C):

$$\text{Private savings} = (Y - T) - C \tag{2}$$

National savings (S) is the sum of public and private savings:

$$S = (Y - T) - C + (T - G) \tag{3}$$

Or

$$S = Y - C - G \tag{4}$$

Savings is the source or the supply of loanable funds to the market. Households place their savings in bank deposits or buy company shares and government bonds with them. These are ways of making funds available to firms to borrow to finance investment spending. Households save to earn income (interest and dividends), to provide for retirement, to invest in children's education and to finance purchases of consumer durables and their own homes.

In Figure 20.1 we show net national savings as a percentage of GNP from 1970 to 2011. Four distinct phases may be discerned. During the 1970s national savings were reasonably high relative to GNP, but they collapsed during the 1980s, reaching a low point of less than one per cent of GNP in 1984. In that year net savings were so low that the economy was making virtually no provision for the future through investment in new plant and equipment.

National savings did not recover until the early years of the 1990s, but from 1994 to 2007 the savings ratio was over 10 per cent, quite high by international standards. Inevitably, following the

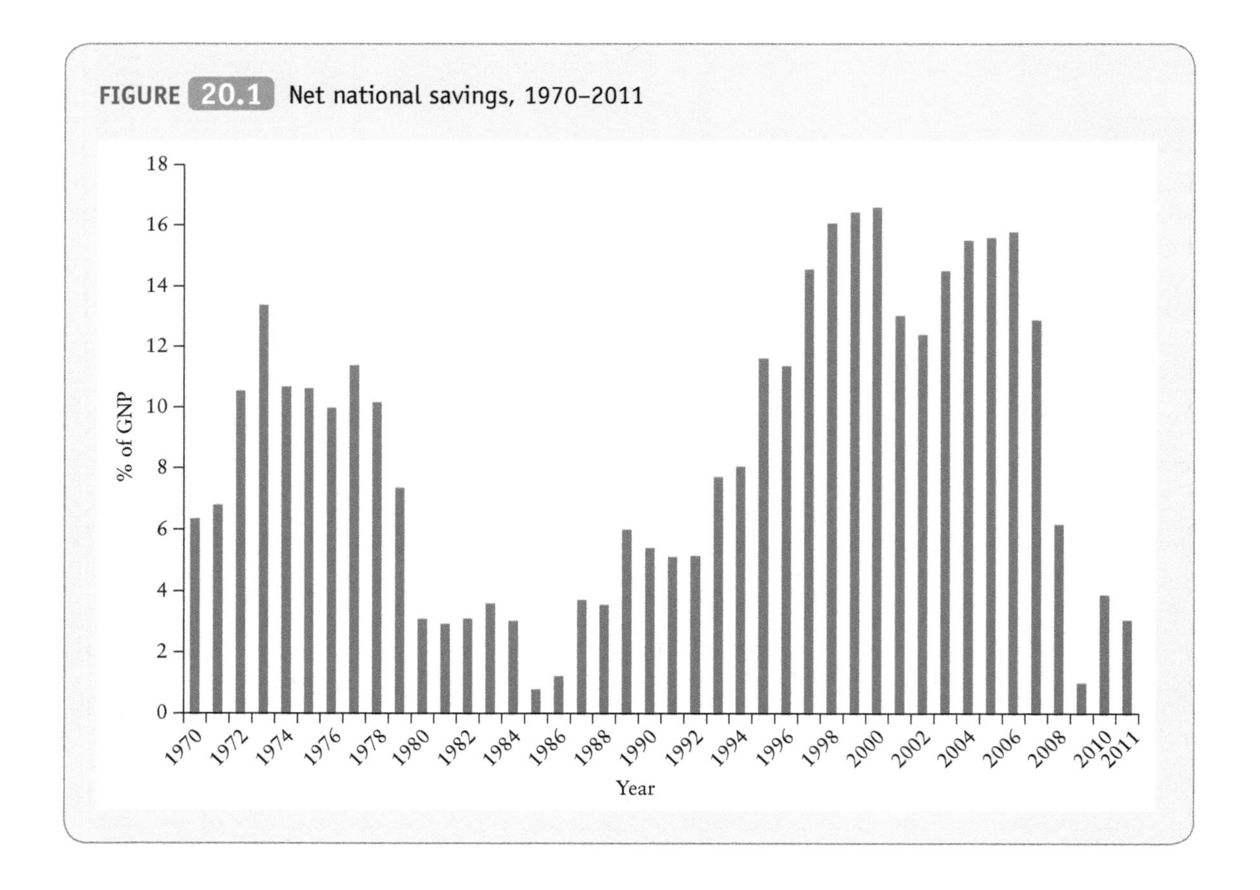

FIGURE 20.1 Net national savings, 1970–2011

FIGURE 20.2 Net national savings by sector, 1970–2011

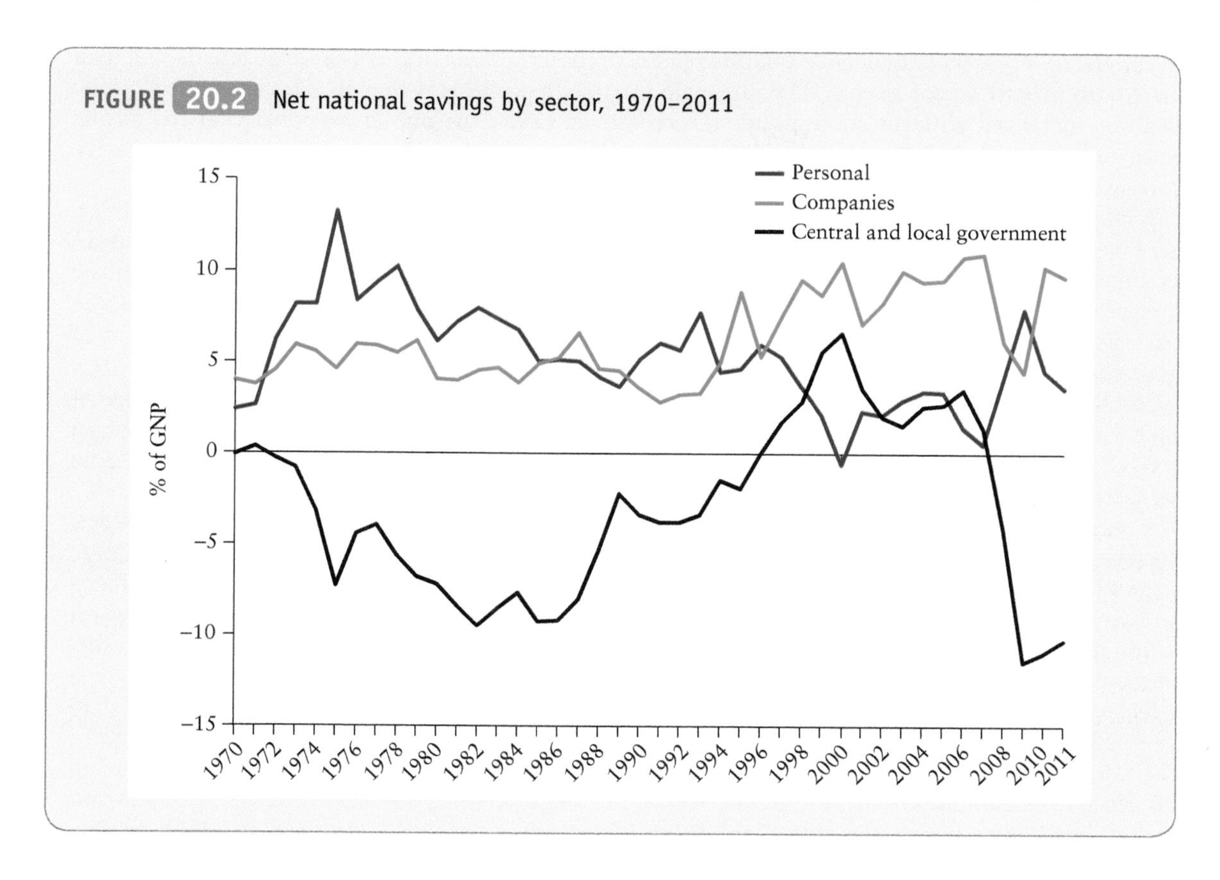

crash of 2008 the savings ratio fell sharply, in 2008 falling to just one per cent of GNP – almost as low as in 1984. There was some recovery in 2010 and 2011.

For more insight into the factors behind these fluctuations in the national savings rate, it is helpful to look at the composition of savings by sector, which is shown in Figure 20.2.

Company or corporate savings have been the most stable component of the total, but they too declined in the 1980s. From lows in the region of four per cent of GNP in the first half of the 1980s, corporate savings climbed to 10 per cent of GNP for most of the period from 1994 to 2007. This reflected the increased profitability of Irish companies. They dipped in 2008 and fell to four per cent of GNP in 2009, but recovered somewhat in 2010 and 2011.

Personal saving reached 13.3 per cent of GNP in 1975. This exceptionally high savings rate reflected the economic uncertainty of that year, with high and rising unemployment and falling incomes. Despite the squeeze on their living standards, households responded by setting aside a higher proportion of their income as savings. At the other extreme, the personal savings ratio fell to an average of just under two per cent of GNP during the boom years from 1999 to 2007. Personal savings were actually negative in 2000, as people borrowed to buy property and finance consumption spending.

The public sector saving rate has been twice as volatile as the corporate savings rate (based on standard deviations). Large negative numbers were recorded almost continuously from 1975 to 1988. This reflected the huge public sector deficits that were incurred over these years (discussed in Chapter 8). However, from 1996 to 2007 public sector savings were positive, reflecting the fiscal surpluses of those years. Since 2008 record-breaking public sector deficits are reflected in a high dissavings rate, which was over 11 per cent of GNP in 2009 and 2010. (As explained in Chapter 8, these figures do not include the money spent on bank recapitalisation.) Ireland is now committed to the target of reducing the public sector deficit to three per cent of GDP by 2015.

The Barro–Ricardo equivalence theorem states that an increase in public sector deficits will lead to a rise in private sector saving. The rationale for this hypothesis is that if taxes are cut or public spending increased without corresponding increases in taxes, the public perceives that the public sector deficit implies higher taxation in the future. The prudent thing to do, therefore, is to save more in anticipation of the leaner times ahead.

While this implies a high level of foresight and forward planning by households and companies, there were some years (such as in the mid-1970s and in 2009 and 2010) when anxiety about future tax burdens may have been part of the motivation for the rise in personal savings, while in the early years of this century the reverse was the case – public sector surpluses may have lured people into a sense of security about the future and contributed to the very low personal savings ratios of those years.

To allow us to examine the correlation between the two categories of savings, Figure 20.3 displays a scatter plot of private (personal plus corporate) and public sector savings as percentages of GNP. It may be seen that there is a weak negative relationship between the two. This could be interpreted as some evidence in favour of the Barro–Ricardo hypothesis.

A feature of the Irish economy since the crash of 2008 has been that all three sectors – companies, households and the public sector – have been trying to reduce their indebtedness. Since 'leveraging' or 'gearing' was the phrase used to describe how firms borrowed money to increase their profits during the boom, 'deleveraging' is the phrase used to describe the process of reversing this and reducing debt. A household's debt can only be reduced if it increases its savings out of current income. An example would be paying off a mortgage more rapidly than originally scheduled.

Deleveraging is evidenced in Ireland today. Households are borrowing less than they did in the boom years and, where possible, they are paying off credit card and mortgage debts ahead of schedule. Similarly, the corporate sector, especially the banks, is anxious to unwind its borrowing and rebuild its capital. Finally, the public sector, no longer able to borrow from the normal bond market, has had to accept the terms laid down in the Agreement with the ECB–EU–IMF Troika,

FIGURE 20.3 Private and public sector savings, 1970–2011

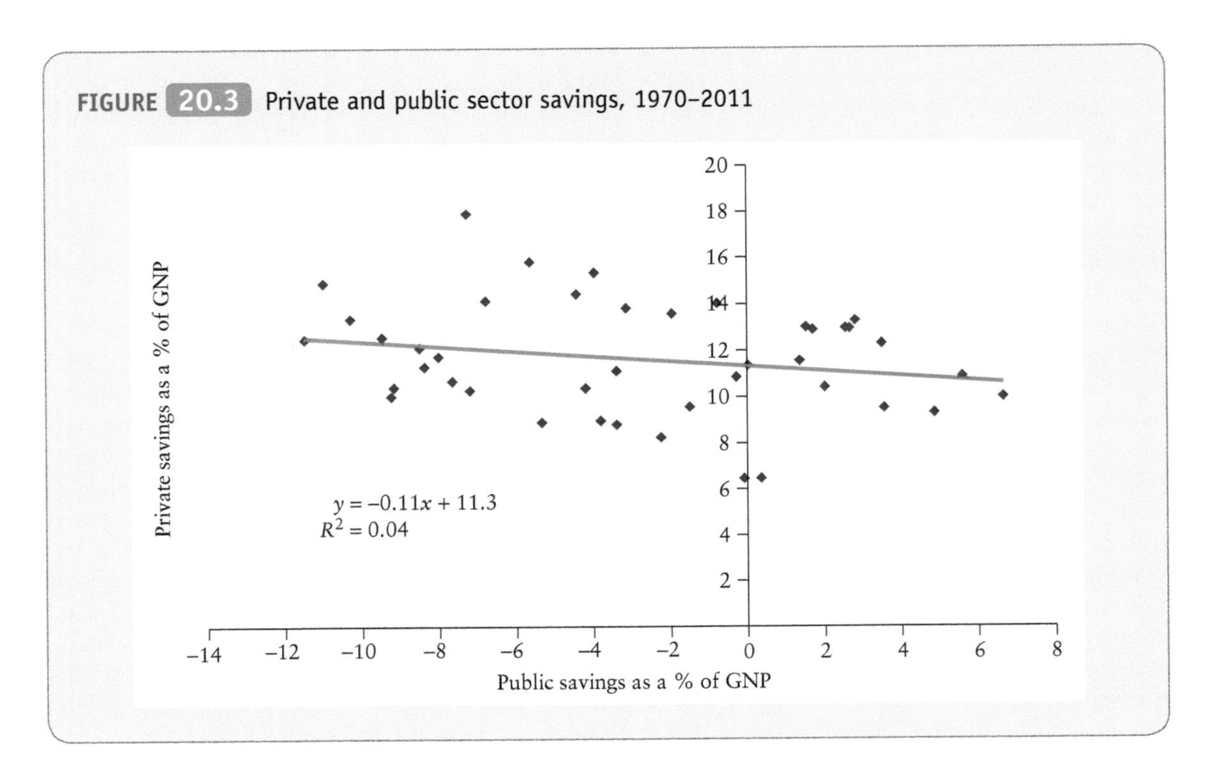

which includes a strict timetable for reducing the public sector borrowing requirement over the next three years.

Thus all three sectors are desperately trying to save more (or borrow less). The result is that the domestic components of aggregate demand, C, G and I, have been falling and are likely to continue to fall over the medium term. This is contributing to the length of the ongoing recession.

Governments often express concern about the low level of national savings, focusing usually on personal savings. We noted that the personal savings rate had fallen to around two per cent of GNP at the start of the twenty-first century when the economy was booming. Minister for Finance Charlie McCreevy introduced a scheme designed to boost personal savings and to rein in the growth in aggregate demand. This was the Special Savings Incentive Account (SSIA) that ran for five years from May 2001 to April 2006. Under the scheme, the government paid a 25 per cent bonus on regular household savings that were maintained over the full period. When the scheme matured in 2006/7 it is estimated that it had added over €14 billion to households' wealth. It is not clear how much of this was genuinely additional savings as opposed to savings that would have been undertaken anyway. Nor is it clear how much of the proceeds of the scheme were channelled into additional investment and how much spent on a consumption spree. The maturing of the scheme at the peak of the construction boom could have contributed to destabilising the economy at that time.

Investment

The demand for loanable funds comes from firms and households who have insufficient resources of their own and need to borrow from the financial markets to invest in new opportunities and to purchase houses and consumer durables such as cars. Firms invest to increase productivity, generate higher profits and create new wealth, while households borrow to smooth out consumption over their lifetimes. Borrowed money has to be repaid with interest over an agreed future time period.

In what follows we first assume that savings is not a function of the real interest rate, r, while investment is inversely related to the real interest rate:

$$S \text{ constant and } I = I(r) \tag{5}$$

In Figure 20.4, the real interest rate is shown along the vertical axis and investment on the horizontal axis. The saving line is vertical, indicating that changes in r have no effect on savings. This

FIGURE 20.4 The loanable funds model in a closed economy

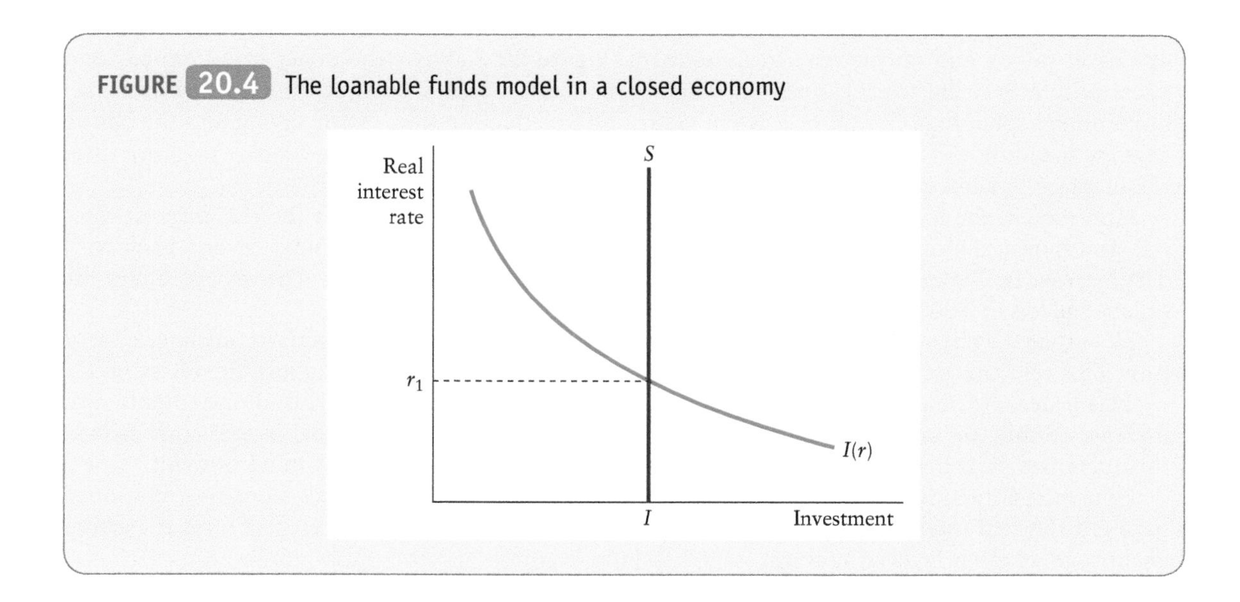

assumption can be relaxed and savings shown as a positive function of r, so that the savings line slopes upwards in the diagram.

The investment schedule is downward sloping as high interest rates discourage households and firms from borrowing. At a real interest rate of r_1, investment equals savings and the demand equals the supply of loanable funds. At rates higher than r_1 there is an excess supply of savings and this leads to a fall in its price, r. If r is lower than the equilibrium rate, there is an excess demand for funds, the interest rate rises and drives up the price of money.

By definition, in a closed economy the goods market is in equilibrium when:

$$Y = C + I + G \tag{6}$$

or

$$Y - C - G = I \tag{7}$$

We defined national saving (equation (4) above) as:

$$Y - C - G = S$$

Hence:

$$S = I \tag{8}$$

It follows from this that when saving equals investment, both the loanable funds market *and* the goods and services market are in equilibrium. The real interest rate adjusts to ensure the loanable funds market is in equilibrium and, as a consequence, the goods and services market clears. The real interest rate plays a key role in this long-run model by ensuring that the actual level of output (Y) remains at its potential rate (Y^*) and the economy remains on the LRAS curve.

If the economy were initially on the Y^* line (not shown) and there is an increase in private savings due to some new government incentive, this would imply a fall in consumer expenditure and a fall in aggregate demand. The economy would enter a recession. In the loanable funds market the increase in savings would lead to a fall in the real interest rate, r. This, in turn, would increase investment. The fall in C is matched by an equal increase in I and the economy reverts back to Y^*. Hence, the real interest, r, is the key adjustment variable.

Policy applications

Still maintaining the assumption of a closed economy, we can examine the effect of an expansionary fiscal policy and an increase in investment. Figure 20.5 shows the effect of an expansionary fiscal policy. Starting from a position where Y equals Y^* and a balanced budget, an increase in government spending (G) and/or a cut in taxation (T) reduces public sector saving and the national savings schedule shifts to the left. The economy now moves into an over-heating position due to the increase in aggregate demand.

However, in the loanable funds market, the reduction in savings causes the real interest rate to rise and investment to fall along the investment curve. Actual output, Y, now reverts back to Y^*. The increase in G must lead to a fall in I in order to maintain Y equal to Y^*. The expansionary fiscal policy has led to 100 per cent crowding-out of investment.

Note that the change in the real interest rate may also affect interest-sensitive consumer expenditure. This reinforces the effect on investment. To simplify the analysis we ignore the effect on C.

This process should also work in reverse. Lower government expenditure and/or higher taxation increases public saving which shifts the S schedule out to the right. The real interest rate falls and this increases investment. In this case, the deflationary fiscal policy crowds-in investment.

Figure 20.6 introduces an upward-sloping savings schedule. This assumes a positive relationship between the real interest rate and saving, to reflect the idea that higher interest rates reward and encourage a higher level of savings.

FIGURE 20.5 An expansionary fiscal policy

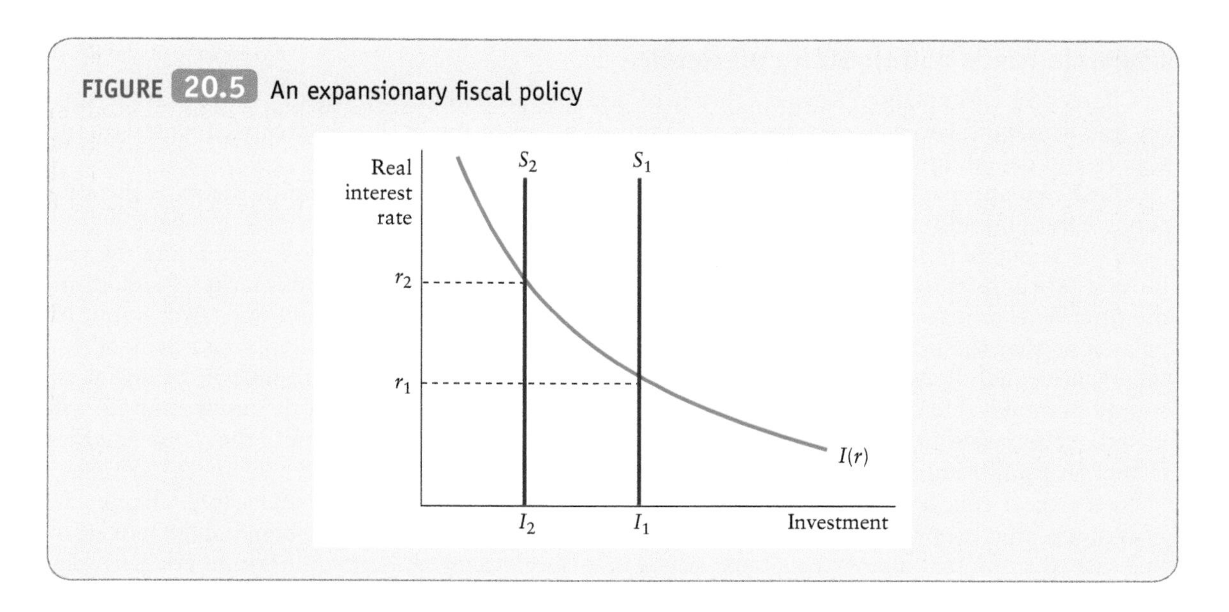

FIGURE 20.6 Increase in investment

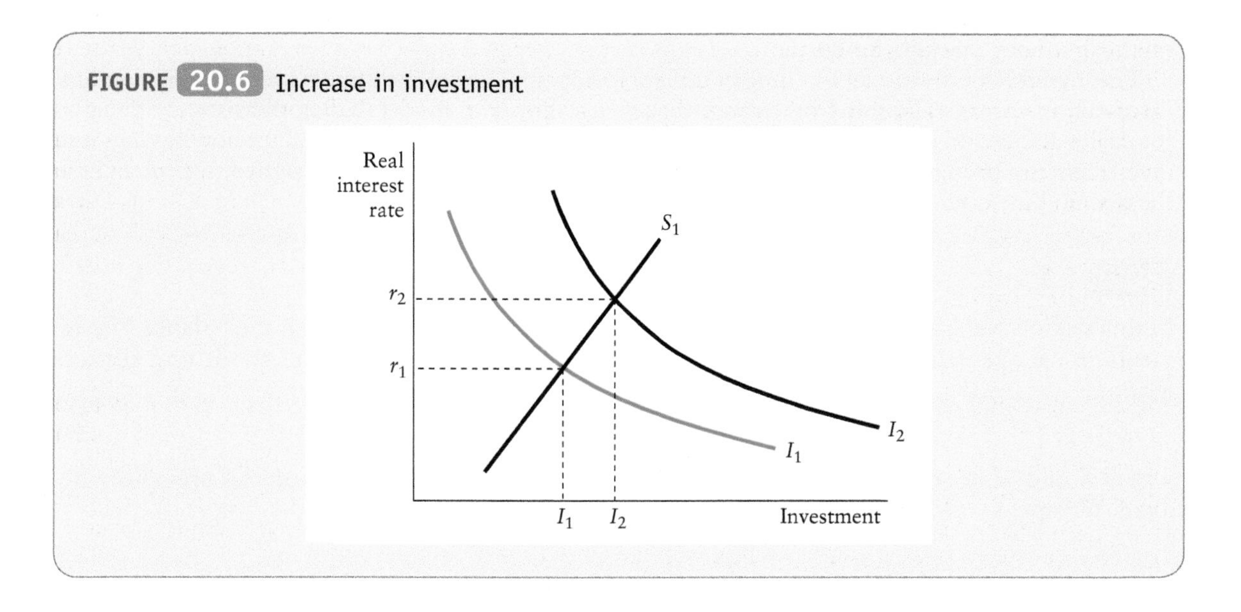

Consider now the effect of a change in investment on the economy. An increase in investment shifts the investment schedule out to the right. The increased demand for investment funds might be due to a technological innovation that raises the profitability of new business projects. Advances in smartphone technology, for example, compels companies who want to keep up with the ever-changing market to invest heavily in research and development and new plant and equipment.

A new investment tax credit would also encourage more investment at each level of the interest rate. The shift in the investment schedule raises the real interest rate, which brings forth additional savings. However, the higher real interest rate moves firms back down along the investment schedule. Overall, savings, investment and the real interest rate all increase.

Loanable funds and liquidity preference

In Chapter 10 we explained Keynes's theory of liquidity preference. This theory states that the supply and demand for money determines the nominal interest rate. In this chapter, we focused on the supply and demand for loanable funds and the real interest rate.

These two approaches are not contradictory. The focus of the loanable funds theory is the long run, whereas liquidity preference is a short-run theory.

In the loanable funds model, real output is determined by the production function and the real interest rate adjusts to ensure that supply equals demand in the loanable funds market. In addition, the price level adjusts to ensure equilibrium in the money market. To explain this latter point, let us assume that the money market is initially in equilibrium and that the supply and demand for money are equal. If the central bank now increases the money supply, the result will be an excess supply of money. However, according to the quantity theory the increase in the money supply will lead to an increase in the price level. This will reduce the real money supply until the money market is back in equilibrium.

In the short run, however, some prices are flexible and other prices are sticky (see Chapter 5). This means that the price level does not adjust fully to equate the supply and demand for money. In this case, the nominal interest rate must adjust to ensure money market equilibrium. For example, if the central bank increases the money supply, the M^S curve moves out to the right (see Figure 10.3 in Chapter 10). The excess supply of money will lead to a fall in the interest rate, which in turn will increase the demand for money (cash balances held by the public). The interest rate will adjust to establish money market equilibrium.

The loanable funds model is a long-run theory that emphasises the importance of saving and investment. In contrast, liquidity preference theory is a short-run model that emphasises the demand for cash balances. In other words, the loanable funds model is designed to explain how savings and investment are brought into equilibrium; the liquidity preference theory is designed to explain how the demand for cash balances is brought into equilibrium.

20.3 Saving, Investment and the Balance of Payments

In this section we analyse the interaction between savings and investment and the balance of payments in an open economy. Starting with the equilibrium condition for the goods and services market:

$$Y = C + I + G + X - M \tag{9}$$

where X and M are exports and imports respectively and the other variables are as previously defined. Writing X − M as net exports, NX, and rearranging:

$$NX = Y - C - G - I \tag{10}$$

But, from equation (4) above:

$$Y - C - G = S$$

Hence:

$$NX = S - I \tag{11}$$

This states that if saving exceeds investment, net exports will be positive.

$$S > I \Rightarrow NX > 0$$

On the other hand, if saving is less than investment, net exports of goods and services will be negative.

$$S < I \Rightarrow NX < 0$$

TABLE 20.1 Savings, investment and the balance of payments

Row			2006	2011
			€ billion	
a		Gross national savings	43.1	19.1
b		Net foreign capital transfers	0.2	−0.3
c		Statistical discrepancy	0.1	−1.0
d = a + b + c	S	Total available for gross domestic investment	43.4	17.8
e	I	Gross domestic fixed capital formation	49.9	16.3
f = d − e		Net foreign investment	−6.4	1.5
g	CA	Current account of balance of payments	−6.6	1.8

Source: CSO, National Income and Expenditure 2011, Tables 11.1 and 30a

This simplified example makes no distinction between GNP and GDP. In Chapter 13 we explained that the current account of the balance of payments (CA) includes not only net exports, NX, which is the trade balance in goods and services, but also F, which is net factor income from the rest of the world, as well some small subsidies and transfers. In Table 20.1 we explain how S, I and CA may be identified in the Irish national income accounts.

Recall from Chapter 13 that when a country runs a current account surplus it must be offset with a capital account deficit. This could take the form of investing abroad – buying foreign bonds, shares, property, industrial assets and so on. Hence, a CA surplus is associated with a capital outflow and a reduction in the country's external indebtedness.

On the other hand, a country that runs a current account deficit must run a capital account surplus. That is, it must sell assets to non-residents, get them to invest in bonds and shares or buy property in the country. This increases the country's external indebtedness.

Overall:

$S > I \Rightarrow$ NX positive and capital outflow $\Rightarrow$ reduction in external indebtedness

$S < I \Rightarrow$ NX negative and reduction in capital outflow $\Rightarrow$ increase in external indebtedness

NOTE: To explain the relationship between NX and capital outflows in more detail, consider the following case. Suppose the current account consists of a single export, say, Tipperary Crystal sold to an American citizen for US$400. The single export means NX is positive or in surplus. Consider now what happens to the $400 received at the Tipperary company's office in return for the shipment of the crystal. The company cannot spend the dollars in Ireland as the euro is the unit of account. The company could buy US government bonds or shares on Wall Street, or even property in the USA. This, however, represents a capital *outflow* and the company is a net saver. In all cases, money is flowing out of Ireland to the USA and the Irish company is increasing saving.

The Tipperary company could, of course, go to the bank and exchange the dollars for euros. But now the bank has to do something with the dollars. Most likely the bank will sell the dollars to a customer who wants to buy US assets. So again there is a capital outflow. Note that if the Tipperary company uses the dollars to buy a US-made good, this represents an offsetting import and a balanced trade situation prevails. Overall: $S > I \Rightarrow$ surplus NX and capital outflow. The opposite happens in the case of an NX deficit.

The most pertinent contemporary examples of these imbalances are the USA and China. Since the early 1980s, the USA has consistently had a current account deficit. This reflects the country's low net saving rate which, in turn, is due to its strong appetite for investment and consumption relative to its income. On the other hand, China, since it entered its spectacular economic boom in the late 1970s, has held consumption in check and achieved a spectacular savings rate. The corollary of this has been a persistent balance of payments CA surplus, which has allowed China to acquire enormous stocks of overseas assets, including US bonds. Foreign governments hold about 46 per cent of all US debt, which now amounts to more than $4.5 trillion. China holds the largest slice of this, about $1.2 trillion in bills, notes and bonds, according to the US Treasury.

On a much smaller scale, New Zealand has had a current account deficit every year since the mid-1970s. The result is that foreigners are accumulating New Zealand dollars, which are a claim on New Zealand resources in the future. If the foreigners decide to buy New Zealand bonds or purchase farms with the money, there is an inflow of money into the country – surplus on the capital account to offset the current account deficit. Needless to say, there is resentment at the idea of foreigners buying land in New Zealand.

We now turn to the Irish experience and use the national income accounts to show how national savings are supplemented or reduced by the current account deficit to finance national investment. Table 20.1 sets out the relevant data for 2006 and 2011.

Starting from gross national savings, which is net savings plus the provision for depreciation, two small adjustments bring us to what is known as the 'total available for gross national investment'. This can be used to invest either in Ireland or abroad. Investment in the country is the familiar 'gross domestic physical capital formation' (I). Investment abroad is known as 'net foreign investment' and (after a minor adjustment) is the current account of the balance of payments (CA). If foreign investment is a negative figure it augments domestic savings.

Table 20.1 shows that in 2011 Ireland ran a small current account surplus, which was available for investment abroad. This could take many forms, including paying down some of our foreign borrowing. In 2006, on the other hand, the country ran a current account deficit. The counterpart of this was an inflow on the capital account as non-residents purchased Irish assets or loaned to Irish banks. Whereas in 2011 S > I and CA > 0, in 2006 S < I and CA < 0.

It is of interest to trace the balance between savings and investment over the years. Figure 20.7 shows S, I and CA as a per cent of GNP from 1995 to 2011. Note that CA is measured on the right-hand axis. (The balance of payments statistics were completely overhauled in the 1990s. These series are not available on a consistent basis prior to 1995.) It tells a similar story to that implied by the graph of the current account in Figure 13.1 in Chapter 13. Savings exceeded investment up to 2001. The surplus was devoted to net foreign investment. Between 2002 and 2004 savings and investment were balanced. Over the following years investment exceeded savings and the gap was made up through a sizeable net foreign disinvestment, especially in 2006, 2007 and 2008. This took the form of a net capital inflow as the private sector engaged in foreign borrowing, much of it to fuel the property bubble.

As we noted in Chapter 13, the significance of the balance of payments changed following entry into the EMU and the demise of the national Irish currency. The balance of payments no longer records the supply and demand for Irish pounds on international markets, as for example, the Danish balance of payments still records the supply and demand of Danish kroner.

The Irish current account balance or net foreign (dis-) investment is still of great significance because of its link to the changes in Ireland's net international indebtedness. It tells by how much the country's net external assets are changing over time. Details from the balance of payments are used to estimate the country's 'international investment position'. This is like a national balance sheet, showing the stocks of Ireland's financial assets and liabilities.

Table 20.2 shows the estimates for March 2012. Overall, foreigners' claims on Ireland exceed our claims on them by €161.5 billion. Two-thirds of this is accounted for by the government's

FIGURE 20.7 Savings, investment and the current account balance 1995–2011

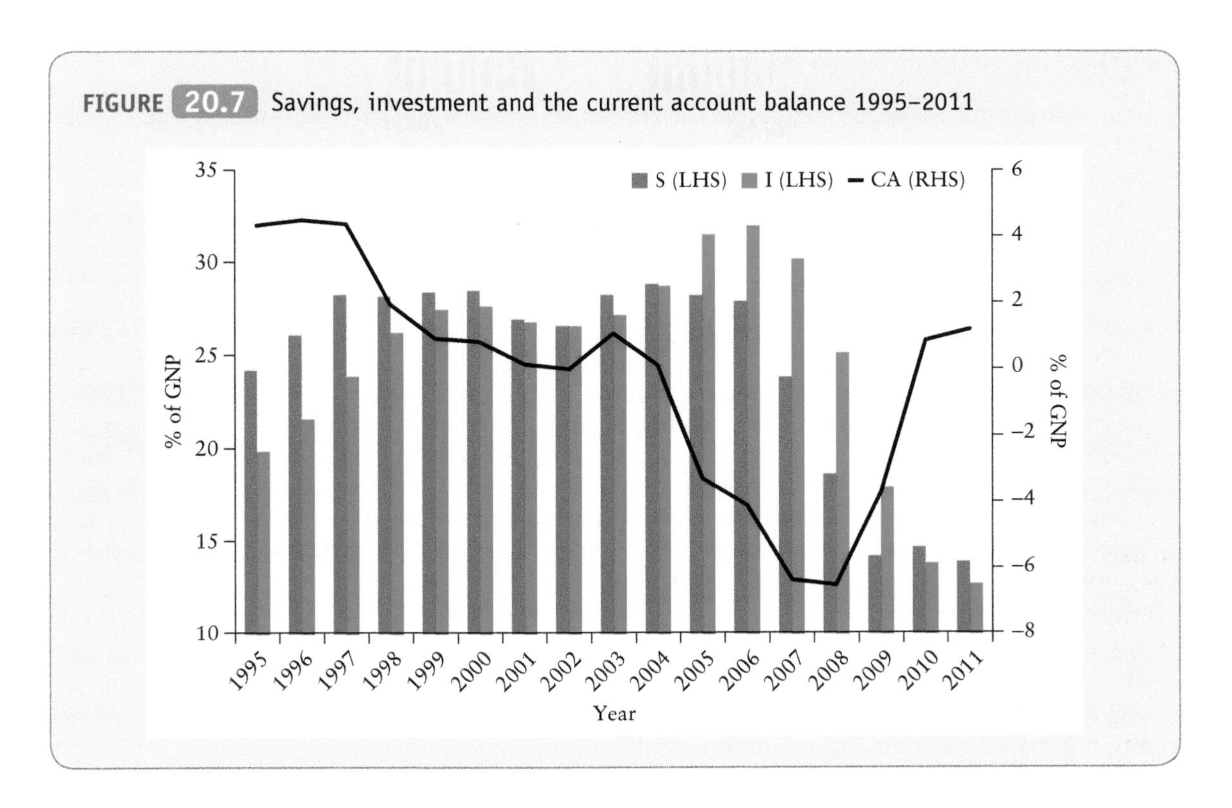

TABLE 20.2 International investment position

	March 2012		
	Assets	Liabilities	Net
		€ billion	
General government	6.1	109.3	−103.2
Monetary authority	19.9	96.0	−76.1
Monetary financial institutions	748.5	715.5	33.0
Other financial intermediaries	1,686.2	1,628.4	57.8
Non-financial companies and households	244.3	317.3	−73.0
Total	2,705.0	2,866.5	−161.5

Source: CSO, 'International Investment Position and External Debt', March 2012.

foreign debt of €103.2 billion and the rest is largely accounted for by the net foreign liabilities of the Central Bank of Ireland (the 'monetary authority'), which are mainly its indebtedness to the ECB. The massive asset and liability figures for 'other financial intermediaries' reflects the scale of the activities of the IFSC in the management of international financial portfolios. The banks ('monetary financial institutions') have both large foreign assets and foreign liabilities. The liabilities are mainly deposits owed to non-residents and foreign equity stakes in Irish banks, while the assets represent their investments in foreign bonds, stocks and money on deposit abroad.

20.4 The Interest Rate and Capital Flows

We now develop a model that explores the relationship between savings, investment and the balance of payments in a small, open economy such as Ireland in the 1990s. The model can be extended to take into account the characteristics of the Irish economy in EMU.

We shall assume:

- that domestic and foreign bonds are perfect substitutes (there is no country or sovereign risk)
- perfect capital mobility (no restrictions on the movement of capital between countries)
- that we are dealing with a small, open economy with an independent currency and exchange rate (i.e. Ireland in the 1990s).

Under these assumptions, the domestic real interest rate (r_{Irl}) will be determined by the exogenous foreign or world real interest rate (r^*). If, for example, $r_{Irl} > r^*$, investors will move money into Ireland as it offers the best return and this will reduce r_{Irl} to r^*. On the other hand, if $r_{Irl} < r^*$, funds will flow out of Ireland to take advantage of the better returns elsewhere and r_{Irl} will increase to r^*.

Figure 20.8 shows a loanable funds model of an open economy. The world real interest rate, r^*, determines the domestic real interest rate, r, and is shown on the vertical axis. The investment schedule is:

$$I = I(r^*) \tag{12}$$

If, as drawn, the world real interest rate (r^*) is higher than the rate that equates savings (S) with investment (I), there will be a CA surplus and a capital outflow. In effect, r^* determines domestic I and the difference between I and S determines net exports and net capital flows. (Note we once more revert to the simplifying assumption that S is independent of r^*.)

On the other hand, if r^* is less than the equilibrium rate there will be a CA deficit and a capital inflow. This is essentially what happened in Ireland after 2002. The ECB lowered its interest rate and this was transmitted to Ireland. The reduction in the interest rate in turn increased investment, particularly in the construction sector. As S was now lower than I, NX went into deficit and there was a capital inflow that fuelled the property bubble.

Note that whereas in a closed economy S must equal I, this is not true in an open economy. A small, open economy can finance some of its investment by borrowing the funds from abroad. Alternatively, if there is a CA surplus, part of national savings will be invested abroad, resulting in a net capital outflow.

FIGURE 20.8 The open economy loanable funds model

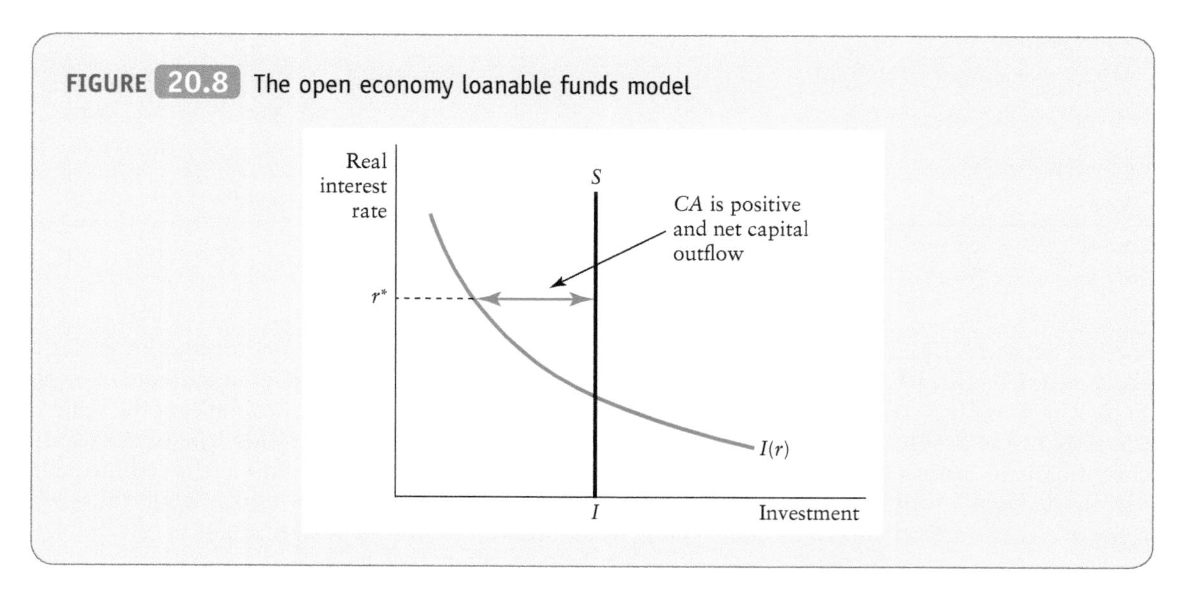

20.5 The Real Exchange Rate and Net Exports

In Chapter 15 we explained the concept of the real effective exchange rate (ε) and how it is measured using the Harmonised Competitiveness Indicator (HCI). The real HCI takes into account movements in the nominal exchange rate and relative prices at home and abroad. It is the most comprehensive indicator of Ireland's price competitiveness. A rise in the index indicates a loss of competitiveness and a fall in the index indicates a gain in competitiveness.

We expect an inverse relationship between net exports and the real exchange rate:

$$NX = NX(\varepsilon) \qquad (13)$$

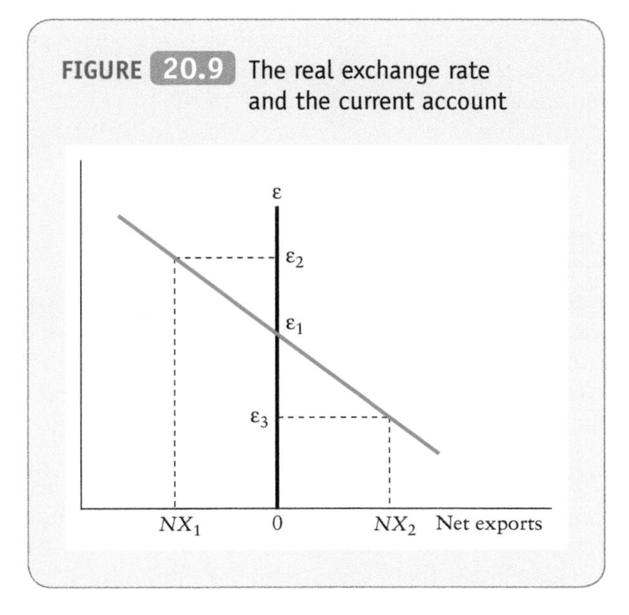

FIGURE 20.9 The real exchange rate and the current account

Equation 13 states that NX is a function of ε. A rise in ε means a loss of price competitiveness and this can be expected to lead to a fall in the NX and vice versa. We use NX as a proxy for the current account because it contains the components of the CA that are most exchange-rate sensitive. Thus we show a downward-sloping NX line in Figure 20.9 with the current account measured along the horizontal axis and ε on the vertical axis. At a real exchange rate of ε_1, the NX line cuts the vertical axis and NX = 0. At a higher real exchange, ε_2, there is a loss of competitiveness, and NX moves into deficit. In contrast, at a lower real exchange rate, ε_3, there is a gain in competitiveness, and NX moves into surplus.

Figure 20.10 shows a scatter plot of the real exchange rate (measured as the real HCI index on the horizontal axis) and NX (as a per cent of GNP on the vertical axis) for the years 1995 to 2011.

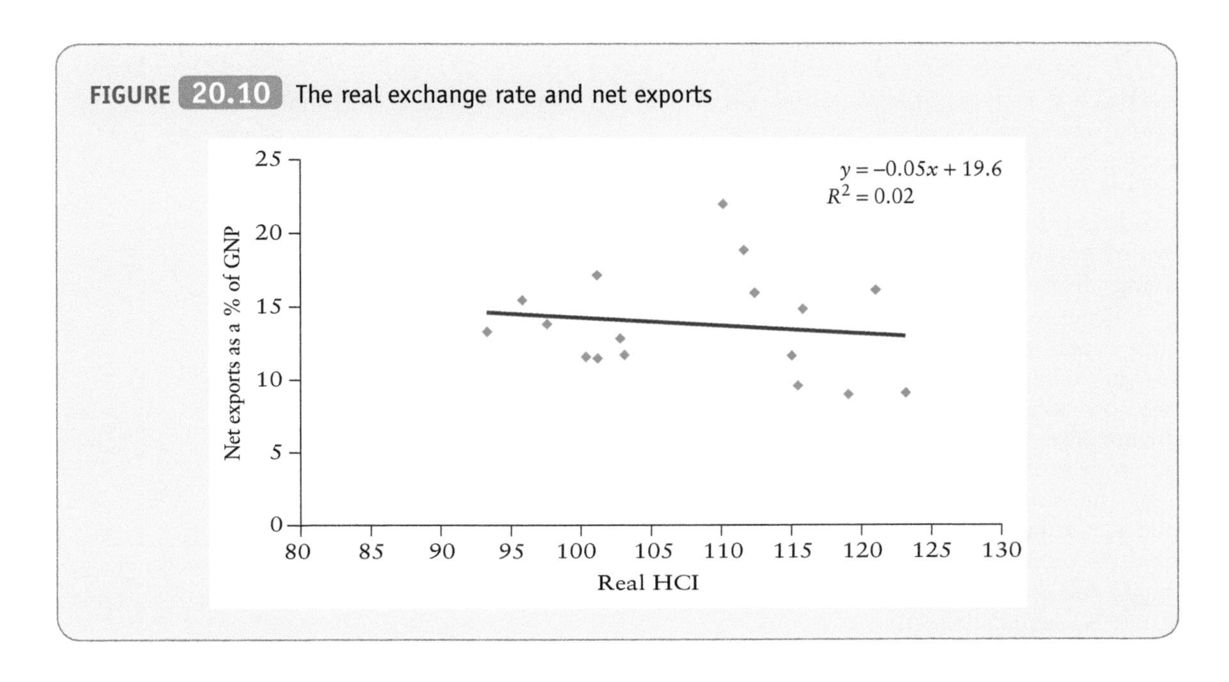

FIGURE 20.10 The real exchange rate and net exports

There appears to be a weak inverse relationship between the two variables over the entire period. The slope of the regression line is −0.05, indicating that NX is not sensitive to changes in ε. However, it is possible to identify sub-periods where an inverse relationship is apparent. For example, between 2002 and 2007 the real exchange rate increased by 33 per cent and net exports as a percentage of GDP fell from 17 to nine per cent of GDP. But over the whole 16-year period the relationship is not significant. Clearly, a lot of factors in addition to the real exchange rate have affected Irish net exports over the years.

20.6 Savings and Investment in the Small, Open Economy

In this section we work with an economy that has an independent currency and a floating exchange rate, as Ireland did in the 1990s. Up to now we are relying on the NIE accounts to ensure NX equals (S − I). However, as explained earlier, (S − I) represents the capital outflow and NX is the current account of the balance of payments. What ensures that the capital and current accounts of the balance of payments are equated?

If we consider the Irish case in the 1990s, (S − I), the capital outflow, represents the net supply of the domestic currency (the Irish pound) on the foreign exchange market. Irish pounds are exchanged (supplied) for some foreign currency such as the dollar. Net exports, on the other hand, represents the net demand for the domestic (Irish pound) currency. The exporter receives dollars and exchanges them (demands) Irish pounds. In short:

- $S > I \rightarrow$ capital outflow $\rightarrow$ supply of Irish pounds
- NX (positive current account balance) $\rightarrow$ demand for Irish pounds

Instead of relying on the NIE accounts, we are now stating that the real exchange rate, ε, adjusts to ensure demand equals supply on the foreign exchange market. That is, NX equals (S − I).

This analysis is very similar to that in Chapter 13. The difference here is that the real exchange rate replaces the nominal exchange rate on the vertical axis, S − I is the supply of Irish pounds and NX the demand for Irish pounds. Note that if the price levels at home and abroad are the same, the nominal and real exchange rate move in tandem.

Figure 20.11 illustrates this addition to the model. The vertical line represents (S − I) and this is the supply of Irish pounds on the foreign exchange market. The downward-sloping NX represents the demand for Irish pounds.

Starting from equilibrium at an exchange rate of ε_1, suppose there is an increase in savings from S_1 to S_2 (Figure 20.11). The (S − I) curve moves to the right and there is an excess supply of Irish pounds on the foreign exchange market. The real exchange rate now falls and this increases NX. Equilibrium is re-established at a new, lower real exchange rate of ε_2.

In the closed economy loanable funds model, r adjusted to ensure S equals I. In the open economy model, S need no longer equal I and the real exchange rate adjusts to ensure NX equals (S − I).

FIGURE 20.11 The determination of the real exchange rate

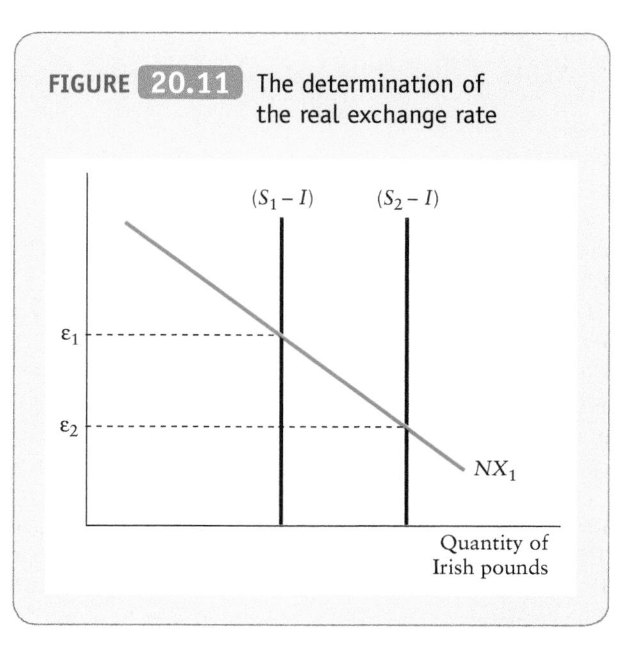

FIGURE 20.12 Long-run model of a small, open economy

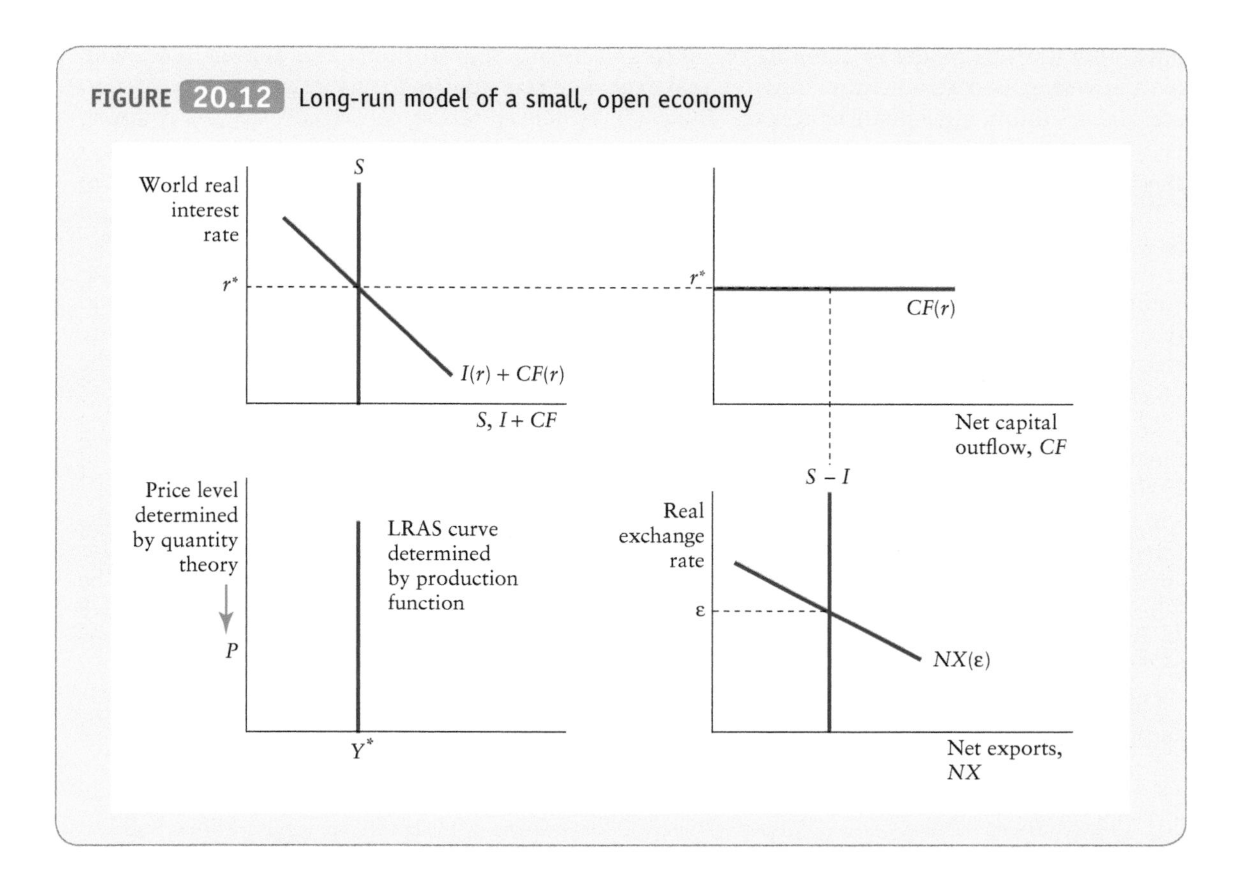

Overview of the model

Figure 20.12 shows a model for a small, open economy outside EMU. The diagram on the bottom left shows that the potential level of real output is determined by the production function and the price level is determined by the quantity theory of money.

The top left-hand corner of Figure 20.12 shows the open economy loanable funds market. The world real interest rate (r^*) determines domestic investment (I). Savings (S) is assumed to be independent of r^*, as shown by the vertical line in the diagram. Given r^*, the difference between I and S determines the capital outflow. As shown, at r^*_1 S equals I and the loanable funds market is in equilibrium. If, however, r^* increases relative to r^*_1, I will fall relative to S and there will be an increase in the capital outflow. If r^* decreases relative to r^*_1, I will rise relative to S and the capital outflow will be reduced.

The diagram in the top right-hand corner shows the relationship between r^* and the capital outflow. This is a bridge diagram between the loanable funds market (top left-hand side) and the foreign exchange market (bottom right-hand side). The CF schedule is horizontal as the Irish economy is too small to influence r^*. Its location is determined by r^*. A decrease in r^* moves the CF downwards and an increase upwards. In the case of a large open economy (USA) the curve would be downward sloping as the USA is big enough to affect world interest rates. We explain this point further below.

The extent of the capital outflow now feeds into the foreign exchange rate market shown in the bottom right-hand corner. The real effective exchange rate (ε) is shown along the vertical axis and the net exports (NX) schedule is shown as downward sloping. As the capital outflow is equal to (S – I) this is shown as the vertical line in the lower right-hand diagram. As mentioned, (S – I) or the capital outflow is determined in the loanable funds market.

We now use this model to examine the effects of fiscal policy at home and abroad. The main point, however, is to demonstrate how the real exchange rate adjusts to ensure actual Y returns to potential Y^* following a disturbance.

20.7 The Effects of Fiscal Policy

Figure 20.13 shows the effects of an expansionary fiscal policy. (Again we emphasise that we are discussing a small, open economy like Ireland in the 1990s.) An increase in government expenditure (G) and/or a cut in taxation (T) will reduce public sector saving and, therefore, national savings. In the top left-hand diagram, the S schedule shifts to the left. The world real interest rate determines investment and this remains unchanged. Starting from a situation where S equals I, the reduction in saving means that $S < I$.

As there are not enough loanable funds available to finance desired investment, this leads to a reduction in the capital outflow. This is reflected in the top right-hand diagram as a reduction in CF along the horizontal axis.

In the foreign exchange market (bottom right), the (S − I) line also moves to the left. This results in an appreciation of the real exchange rate and net exports fall. The overall effect of the expansionary fiscal policy is to crowd-out net exports. There is no increase in real actual output as the increase in G is entirely offset by a fall in NX. Hence, while the expansionary fiscal policy may have created an over-heating economy in the short run ($Y > Y^*$), in the long run the economy reverts to Y^*.

The effects of a deflationary fiscal policy are the opposite to those depicted in Figure 20.13. For example, the austerity measures forced on Ireland by the Troika should lead to recovery as the fall

FIGURE 20.13 Expansionary fiscal policy

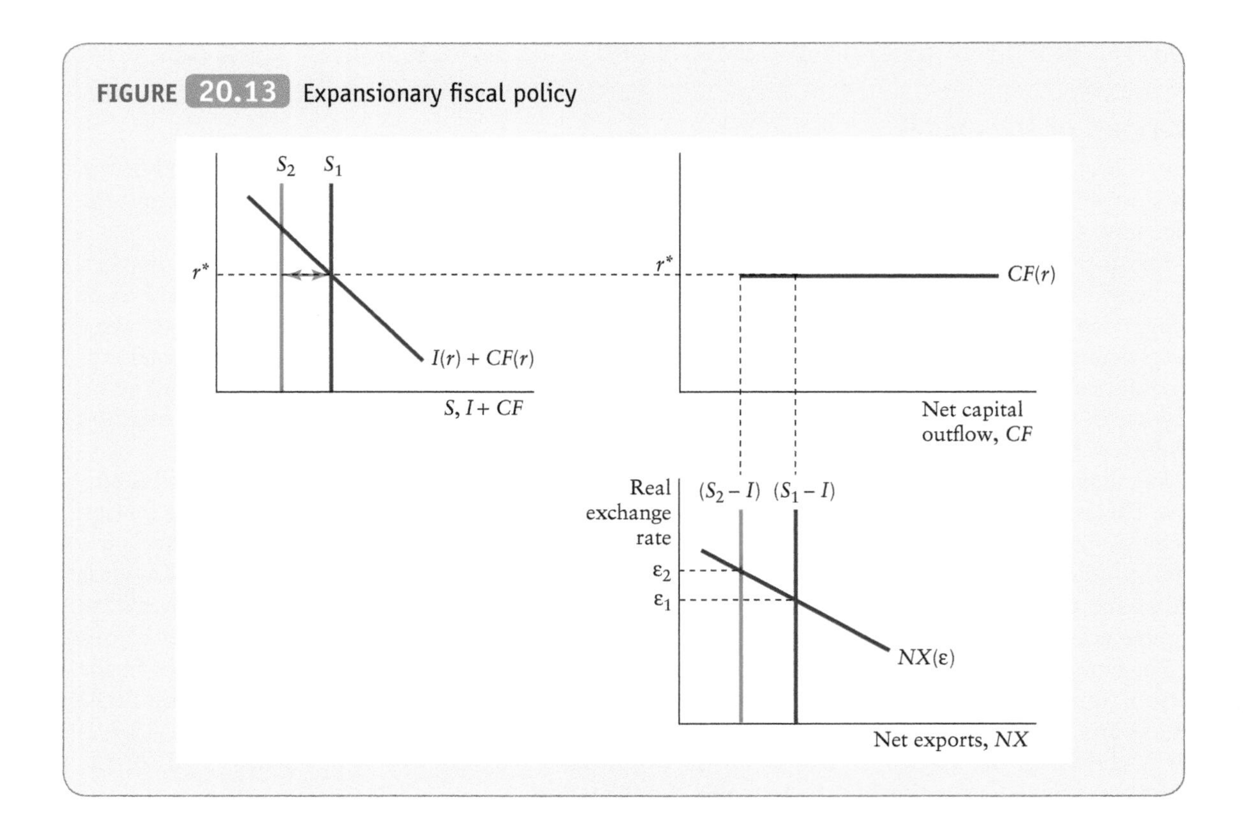

in ε crowds-in NX. Indeed, most models predict that a recession and higher unemployment will lead to a fall in the price level and this, in turn, decreases ε and increases NX. One problem is, of course, that it is impossible for all countries to achieve a simultaneous increase in their NX – one country's exports are the other country's imports.

NOTE: As mentioned, in the case of a large, open economy the CF schedule is downward sloping. A reduction in national savings due to an expansionary fiscal policy now raises the real interest rate. The large, open economy (USA) is big enough to affect the real interest rate. If the horizontal CF schedule in Figure 20.13 is replaced by a downward-sloping schedule (not shown) it can be seen that both investment and net exports decrease. Hence, the fiscal policy crowds-out both I and NX.

Twin deficits

An interesting empirical question is whether there is a relationship between the fiscal deficit and the current account. Is there a tendency for budget deficits to drive the current account into deficit? Since a current account deficit reflects a deficiency of S, relative to I, an increase in the government's budget deficit (a fall in national savings) could, or should, be correlated with balance of payments deficits. This is sometimes referred to as a theory of 'twin deficits'.

Figure 20.14 shows the relationship between the Exchequer balance and the current account of the balance of payments, both as a percentage of GNP, in Ireland between 1972 and 2011. There is a significant positive correlation between the two series. In the 1980s both the fiscal deficit and the current account deficit were large, whereas over the period 1994–2000 both were smaller or even moved into surplus.

This analysis is very relevant in the case of the USA. The expansionary fiscal policy pursued by the Obama administration since 2008 can be expected to lead, in the future, to an increase in both the government budget and balance of payments deficits.

FIGURE 20.14 The twin deficits, 1972–2011

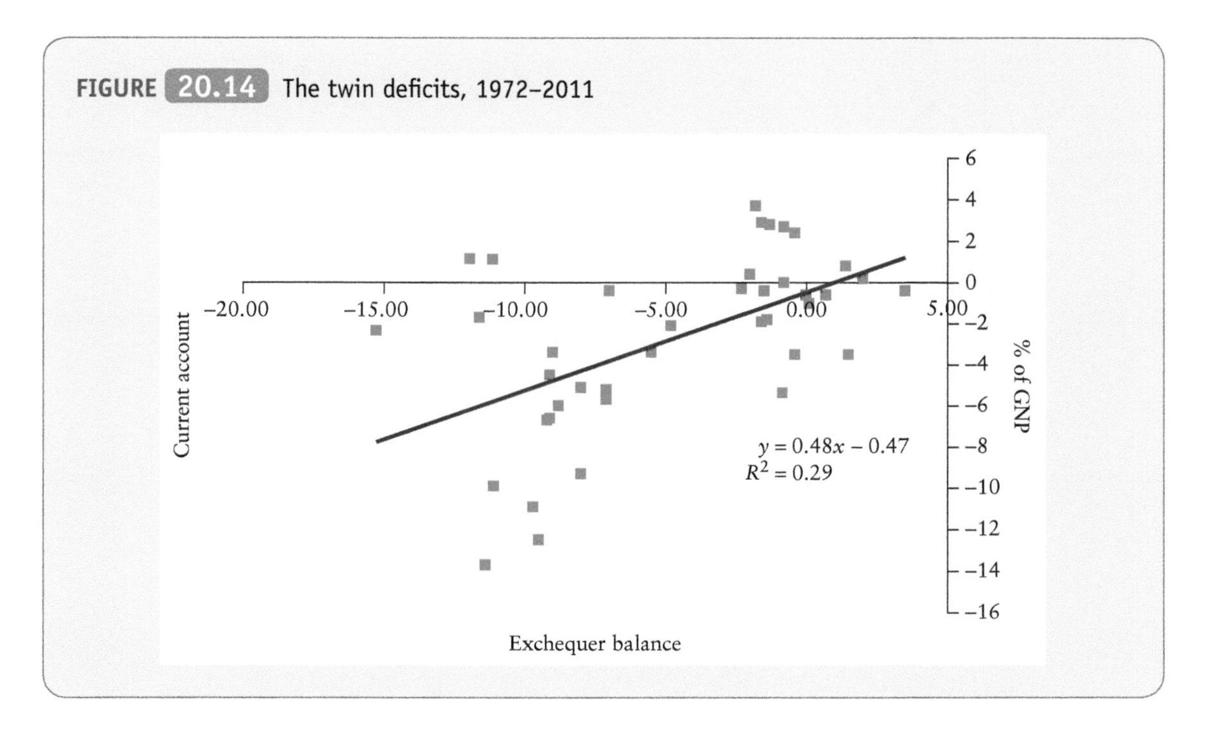

20.8 The Effects of a Change in the World Interest Rate

Again taking the case of Ireland in the 1990s, Figure 20.15 examines the case where there is a cut in the world real interest rate. Starting from a position where S = I, an interest rate cut from r^*_1 to r^*_2 in the loanable funds market leads to a downward movement along the I curve and an increase in domestic investment. As savings is unchanged, S < I and there is an excess demand for loanable funds.

In the top right-hand corner, the CF schedule shifts downwards in line with the fall in r*. Along this new CF schedule, the capital outflow is reduced along the horizontal axis. This is because I has increased relative to S.

In the foreign exchange market (bottom right), the (S − I) line also shifts left due to the increase in I. The real exchange rate appreciates and this reduces NX. The increase in I is completely offset by the fall in NX and the real output reverts to Y^*. Hence, the fall in the real world interest rate increases investment but decreases net exports. Again, this is similar to what happened in Ireland after 2001 when the ECB cut its interest rate.

In contrast, a rise in the world real interest rate will have the opposite effect. A decline in I will be offset by a rise in NX and the level of real output is unchanged.

The fall in the world real interest rate is also equivalent to the case of an increase in the world savings rate or a deflationary world fiscal policy. In both cases, the world savings schedule would shift to the right and the world real interest rate will fall. The impact on the domestic Irish economy in the 1990s will be as outlined in Figure 20.15.

FIGURE 20.15 Decrease in the world's real interest rate

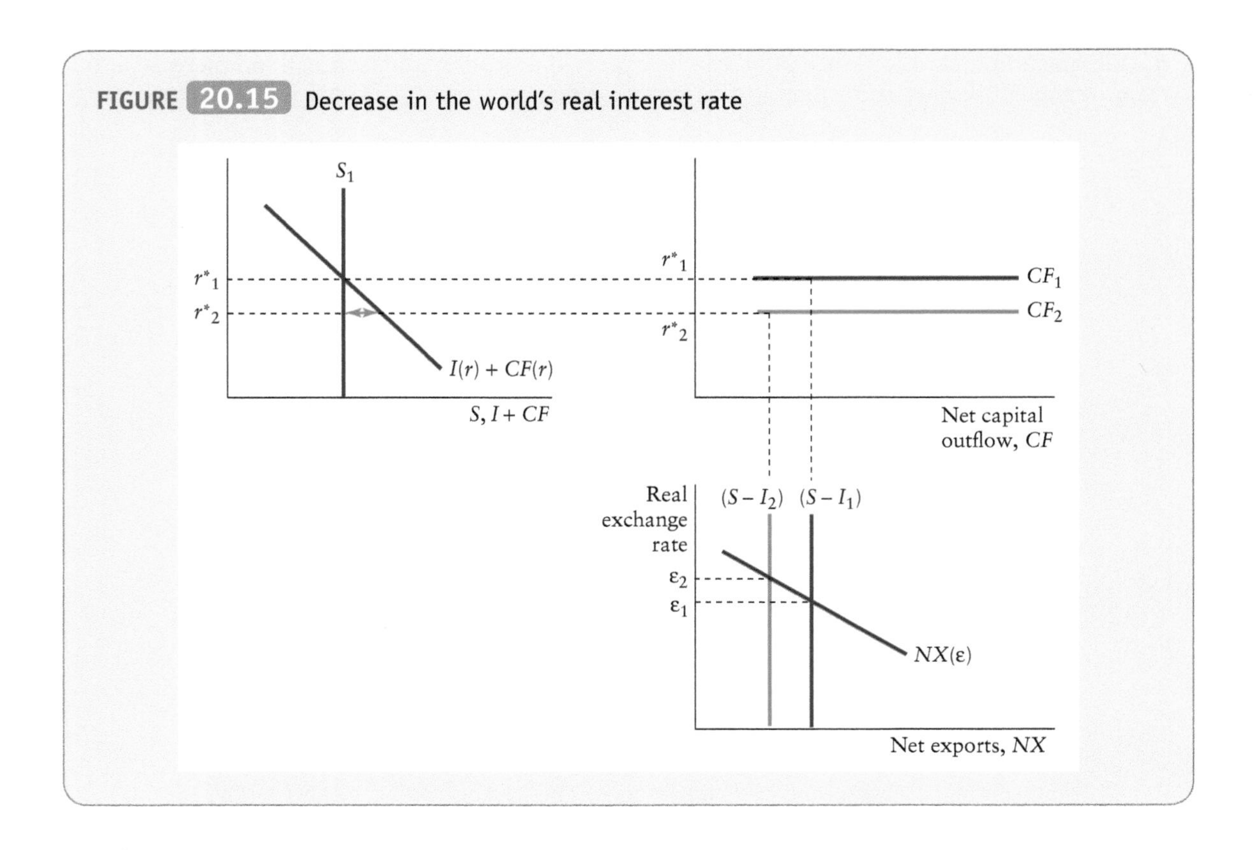

20.9 Applying the Model to the Irish Economy in EMU

A number of adjustments need to be made to the model outlined in previous sections to make it applicable to a small country participating in a monetary union. We continue to assume that the potential level of output is determined by the production function. However, the domestic real interest rate is determined by the euro area real interest rate. We must acknowledge at this point that sovereign risk can result in a divergence in real interest rates. For example, in 2012, in Spain and Italy the nominal interest rate is seven per cent and six per cent respectively and even higher in Greece, Portugal and Ireland. In Germany it is about one per cent. Since inflation in all three countries is much the same, real interest rates have diverged enormously.

A further adjustment needs to be made in relation to the determination of the price level. The quantity theory of money needs to be replaced by either absolute or relative purchasing power parity (PPP) as the main explanation of domestic inflation. PPP theory states that the Irish price level (absolute PPP) or inflation (relative PPP) is, in the long-run, exogenously determined abroad. This alters the model significantly.

Let us first reconsider the case of the Irish economy in the 1990s. If PPP holds in the long run, Ireland's NX schedule will be horizontal (or very elastic). This is shown in the bottom right-hand diagram in Figure 20.16. This means that NX is extremely sensitive to changes in ε. As discussed earlier, a decrease in r* leads to an increase in investment and a decrease in capital outflows (CF). That is, the (S – I) line shifts to the left in the bottom right-hand diagram in Figure 20.16. However, the increase in the supply of Irish pounds leads to only a slight increase in ε. As NX is very responsive to changes in ε, NX decreases and the demand and supply of Irish pounds is equalised. So whereas there will be a very small increase in ε (if at all), there will be a significant fall in NX until equilibrium is re-established in the foreign exchange market.

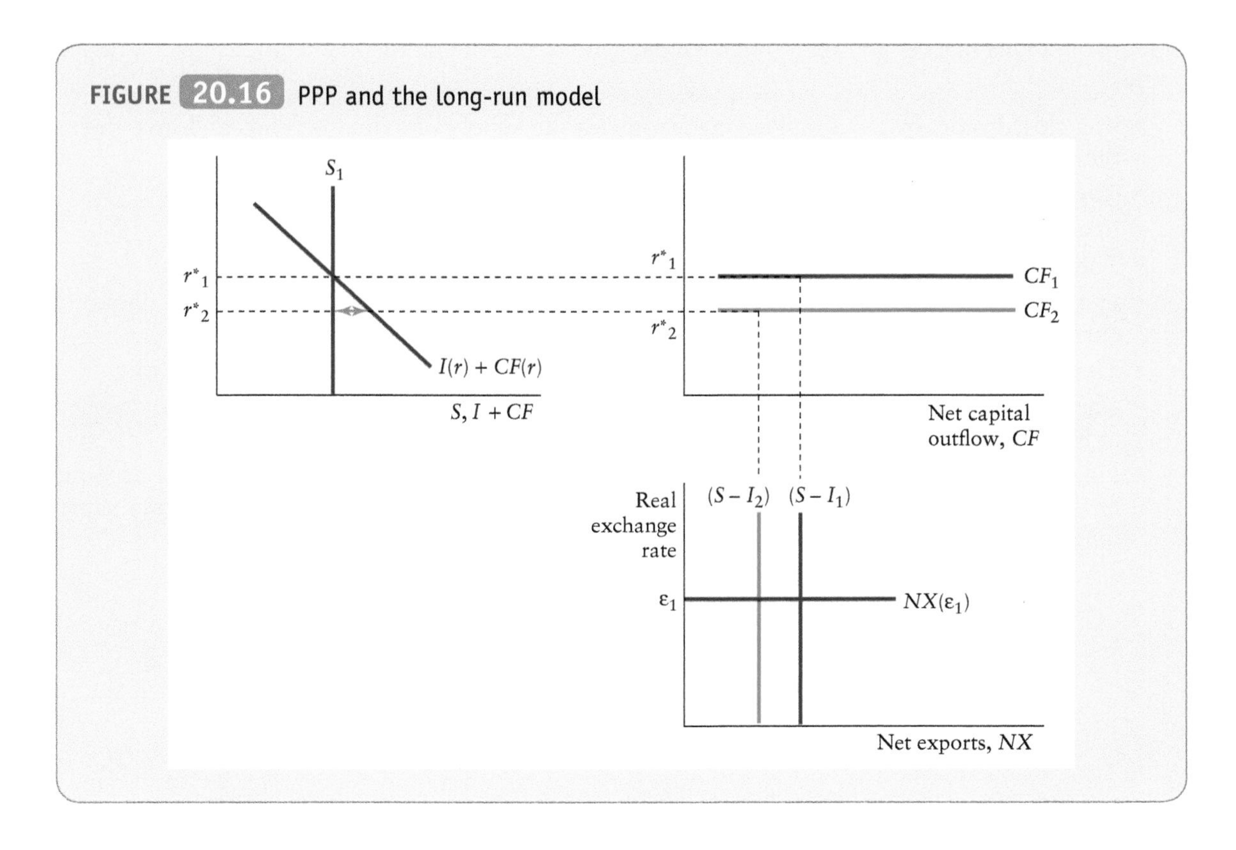

Consider now the case of Ireland in EMU. How realistic is the assumption of a horizontal NX curve? In the Irish context the answer is probably 'not very'. In Chapter 15 we showed that between 2000 and 2008, the real exchange rose 55 and 97 per cent against sterling and the dollar respectively. This outcome is not supportive of the extreme PPP hypothesis.

We can go a stage further and argue that Ireland's real exchange rate is, in large part, exogenously determined. The movement of the real exchange rate is determined by the domestic price relative to the foreign price and the nominal exchange rate. But as the Irish economy is too small to have any impact on the euro exchange rate, the nominal exchange rate is exogenous. As explained in Chapter 15, the nominal exchange rate is, however, the dominant force determining fluctuations in the real exchange rate. It follows, therefore, that the real exchange rate is also largely determined exogenously.

Furthermore, as shown in Figure 20.10, there appears to be a weak relationship between ε and NX. (Note that in Figure 20.10, ε appears on the horizontal axis as the causation is running from ε to NX.) This finding is merely tentative: it would take much more advanced empirical techniques to establish the definitive relationship between the two variables (see for example Chen *et al.* 2012).

Overall, for a small, open economy participating in a monetary union, both the real interest rate and the real exchange rate are exogenous. The experience of the years prior to 2008 illustrates some implications of our membership of EMU. Conditions outside our economy were imposed on us. Without an autonomous central bank we did not have the usual instruments of monetary policy that might have allowed us to achieve better outcomes in the face of the global crisis that broke in 2007.

20.10 Key Terms and Concepts

In this chapter we outlined a long-run model of the open economy. This long-run model consists of a loanable funds market and the foreign exchange market. Among the key relationships discussed were:

- In a closed economy, national savings represent the supply of loanable funds and investment the demand for loanable funds.
- The interaction of savings and investment determine the real interest rate.
- In an open economy, the real interest rate is exogenously determined.
- The interaction of savings and investment determines the net capital outflow.
- In the foreign exchange market, net capital outflows represent the supply of the domestic currency and net exports the demand for the domestic currency.
- The interaction of net capital outflows and net exports determine the real exchange rate.
- The long-run model was used to examine the long-run effects of an expansionary fiscal policy at home and a cut in the world's real interest rate.
- Finally, it was pointed out that the model needs to be significantly modified to take account of the special circumstance of a small, open economy like Ireland participating in a monetary union.

CHAPTER 21

The Irish Crash of 2008 and its Aftermath

21.1 Introduction

In this chapter we discuss the crisis that broke in Ireland in 2008 and its aftermath. We pay particular attention to the causes and consequences of the credit-fuelled property boom that raged in Ireland in the early years of this century. The collapse in 2008 caused enormous damage to the economy which is still continuing four years later. We then examine how the government coped with the crisis and the Troika agreement and conclude with a discussion of policy options.

21.2 The Property Boom

Irish house and commercial property prices behaved unspectacularly over the decades before the turn of the twenty-first century. Prices stagnated during the 1980s, even though consumer price inflation was running high, and then recovered during the 1990s. In real terms they showed little trend, despite the persistent sales pitch of the property industry that 'you can't go wrong investing in bricks and mortar'.

Something unprecedented happened over the 10 years or so from the late 1990s to 2007. House and office prices began to rise at a rate that far outpaced the rate of general inflation and the rate of increase in wages and salaries. Even more significantly, the inflation in property prices far outpaced the rate of increase in rents. The rental return on investing in property fell, so buying property as an investment was only justified if the investor believed that property prices would go on rising. This is one definition of a bubble.

Figure 21.1 shows an index of house prices in Ireland from 1996 to 2010. This index was compiled by the ESRI. It shows that between 1996 and the last quarter of 2006 *nominal* house prices quadrupled. Between the last quarter of 2006 and the end of 2010 they fell by 40 per cent. *Real* house prices rose less spectacularly but fell just as sharply.

In 2011 the CSO began publishing a new series on house prices. This series is shown for the period 2005–2012 in Figure 21.2. Importantly, this series shows the decline in house prices continuing into 2012. By mid-2012 house prices were down almost 50 per cent from their 2007 peak. It is interesting to note that although real house prices (that is, nominal prices adjusted for CPI inflation) rose more slowly before 2008, they too fell by almost exactly 50 per cent between end-2007 and mid-2012.

NOTE: Both the house price indices discussed here are adjusted for the mix of properties being bought and sold. They are what are known as 'hedonic indices'. That is, the indexes are adjusted for characteristics such as size and location that are known to influence house prices.

FIGURE 21.1 House price index, 1996–2010 (ESRI series)

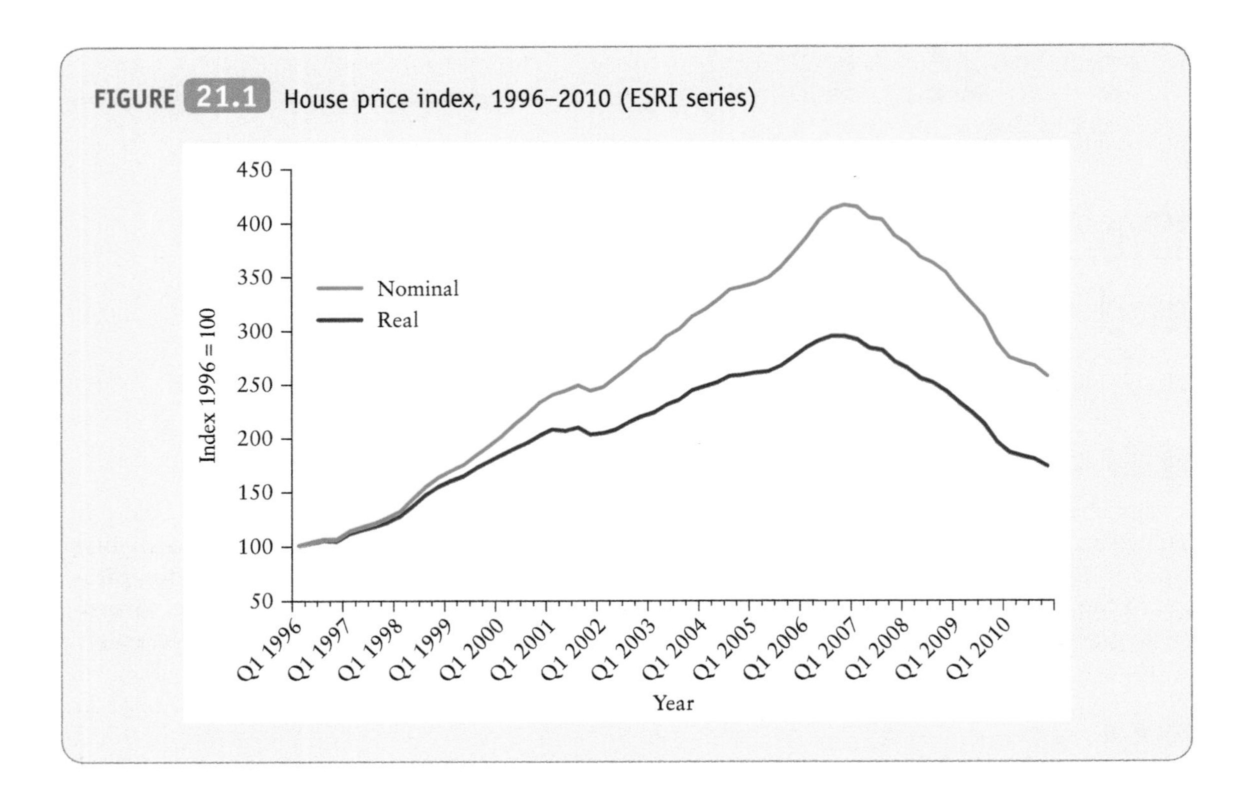

FIGURE 21.2 Index of residential property prices, 2005–2013 (CSO series)

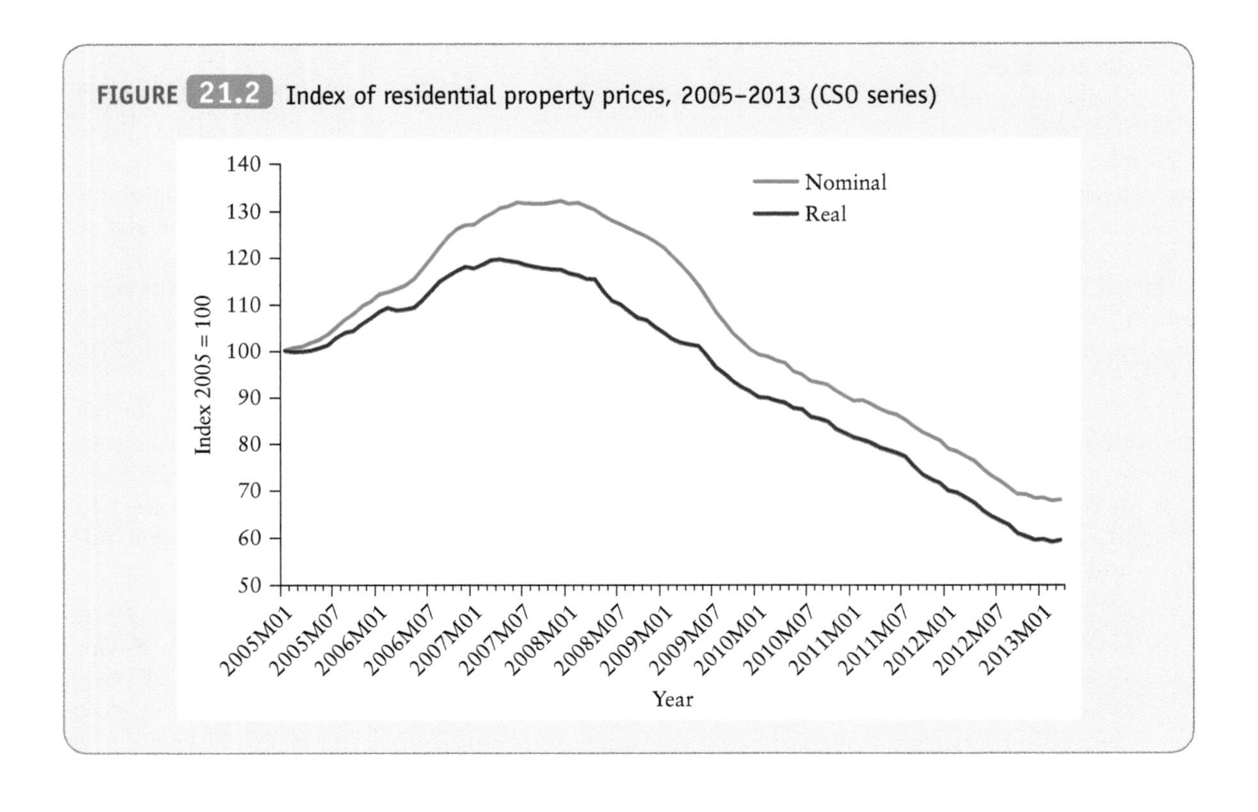

The late Professor Charles Kindleberger (1910–2003) of the Massachusetts Institute of Technology wrote a classic survey of bubbles and busts in 1978 (Kindleberger 1978). He proposed that any bubble can be described in five stages.

We apply these five stages to our account of the Irish property boom and bust.

1 Displacement

The Irish property boom was one of many that occurred in western economies in the early years of the twenty-first century. As is often the case, these booms began with an exogenous shock that raised the profit opportunities in property relative to other sectors. The deregulation of the banking system and increased competition in the mortgage market is usually cited as the 'shock' that triggered the property boom in the USA and other countries. In the Irish case, entry into EMU in 1999 and the fall in the real interest rate in the following years were further important contributing factors.

2 Credit expansion

During the 1990s, facilitated by the removal of capital controls and increased financial integration, international capital flows increased greatly. Ireland's entry into EMU in 1999 increased the ease of access by Irish financial institutions to European financial markets. Borrowing from banks in other euro area countries no longer involved an exchange rate risk and it became cheaper as interest rates in the euro area converged on the low level prevailing in Germany.

It should, however, be noted that some big lenders into the Irish market were from outside the euro area (e.g. Royal Bank of Scotland, through its subsidiary Ulster Bank; and Danske Bank, through its subsidiary Irish National Bank). Moreover, countries outside the euro area, notably Iceland, experienced the same pattern of boom and bust as we did in Ireland.

3 Euphoria

At some stage bankers, property developers and other supposedly sober and rational economic agents get caught up in a group psychology of 'irrational exuberance'. This widely used phrase originates in a speech given by Alan Greenspan, then Chairman of the Federal Reserve Board, in December 1996, in which he said:

> *Clearly, sustained low inflation implies less uncertainty about the future, and lower risk premiums imply higher prices of stocks and other earning assets. We can see that in the inverse relationship exhibited by price/earnings ratios and the rate of inflation in the past. But how do we know when irrational exuberance has unduly escalated asset values, which then become subject to unexpected and prolonged contractions as they have in Japan over the past decade?*

The term was used as the title of a very influential book on the stock market boom by Robert Shiller of Yale University in 2000. The idea that investors get carried away by optimism is an old one: Keynes said that investors were driven by 'animal spirits'.

> *Speculators may do no harm as bubbles on a steady stream of enterprise. But the position is serious when enterprise becomes the bubble on a whirlpool of speculation. When the capital development of a country becomes a by-product of the activities of a casino, the job is likely to be ill done.* (Keynes 1936)

In the upswing, bankers and speculators tend to throw caution to the wind and are seized by the fear of 'missing the boat', 'being left behind' and 'not getting in on the action'. If prices are rising and are going to go on rising, buy now or you will lose the opportunity to get rich quick. God, after all, is not making any more land. Planning permissions are scarce. This leads to 'over-trading' and wild over-estimates of prospective returns. Frank Daly, former Chairman of the Revenue

FIGURE 21.3 Bank lending to households and non-financial firms as a percentage of GDP, 1997 and 2008

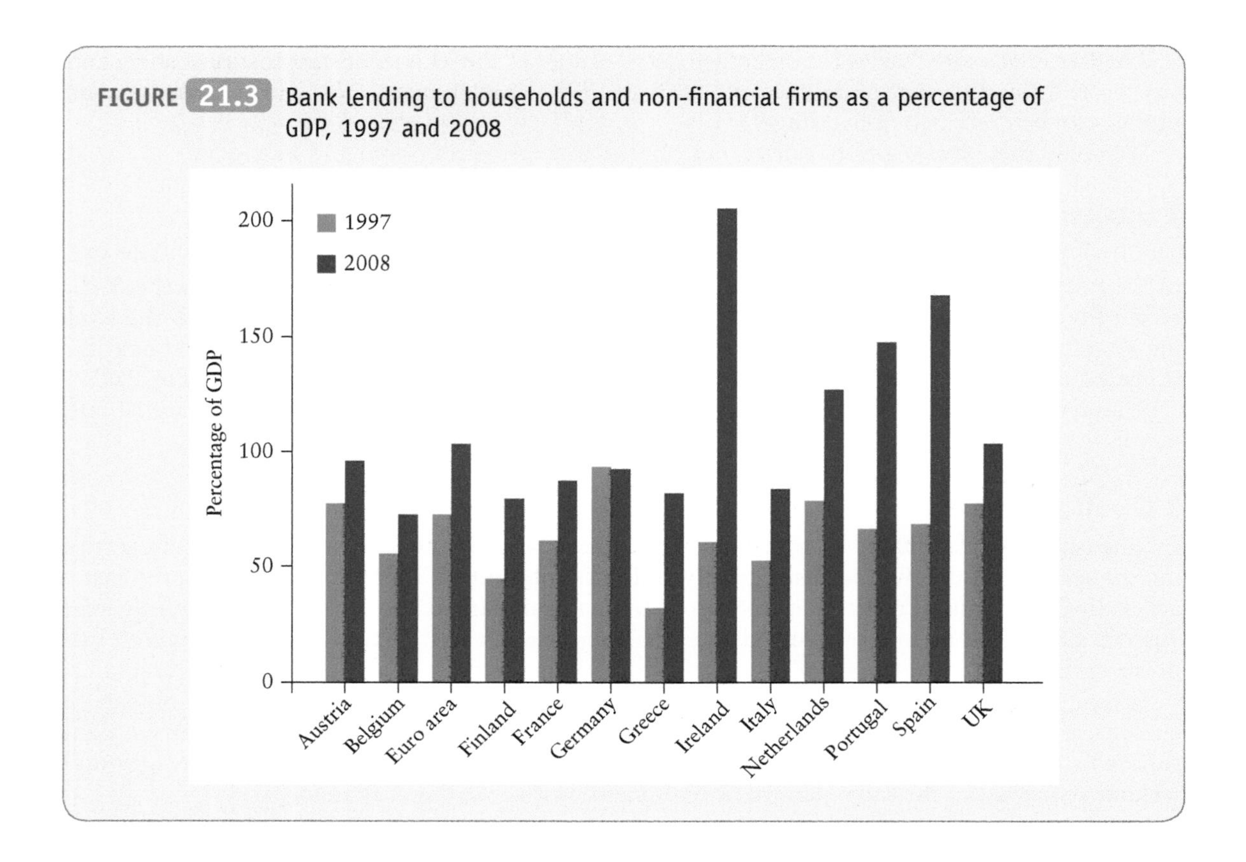

Commissioners, and now Chairman of the National Asset Management Agency (NAMA), whose role we discuss below, described the Irish housing market during the boom as 'a market . . . driven by irresponsible lending, unsustainable prices and inglorious hype'.

Our review of the banking system in Chapter 19 indicated that Irish banks had traditionally been conservative in their approach to lending. But the Irish banking scene was shaken up through the arrival of new, brash players in the 1990s. Anglo Irish Bank, which grew spectacularly in the 1990s through takeovers of small overseas banks, relied on borrowing from the inter-bank market to create an enormous portfolio of loans to property developers. It fundamentally altered that situation with its aggressive approach to lending, growing market share and spectacular profit growth. Anglo boasted 21 years of successive profit growth and a 10-year annual growth rate in profit (before tax) of 39 per cent. Other Irish banks, Allied Irish Bank in particular, came under pressure from their shareholders to emulate Anglo and joined in the lending frenzy.

The Irish mania differed from the US mania in that there were no fancy financial innovations in the Irish mortgage market, such as the securitisation of subprime loans that figured prominently in the US crisis. Ours was an old-fashioned property bubble, driven by easy credit and expectations of continued inflation in asset prices. Bankers and developers substituted crude extrapolations from the past for serious project analysis.

Irish investors' mania for property was not confined to houses and offices in Ireland. Several property developers acquired large and complex foreign property portfolios çat astronomical values, including top hotels and prime sites in London, the USA and Eastern Europe. Smaller players in the market favoured buying foreign holiday developments in sunny climes.

For a while booms are self-reinforcing: rising property prices improve the net wealth of investors and bankers uncritically accept property as collateral for more borrowing, fuelling further credit expansion.

The boom was also fuelled from the public capital programme. Buoyant tax revenues made it easier for the public sector to invest in 'infrastructure' projects, even as these projects became increasingly less justified on cost-benefit criteria. The cost of completing these projects escalated as landowners, contractors, surveyors and all those associated with the construction sector took advantage of the general laxity and lack of cost control that became rampant in public sector procurement.

The inflow of financial capital was complemented by a surge in inward migration when Ireland allowed free labour mobility to the new EU member states, especially Poland. For a few years between 2003 and 2007 we had the highest rate of net in-migration of any country in Europe. Borrowed speculative money was putting immigrants from Eastern Europe to work on projects many of which now lie vacant in the Irish countryside.

4 Financial distress

> *The social objective of skilled investment should be to defeat the dark forces of time and ignorance which envelop our future. The actual, private objective of the most skilled investment to-day is 'to beat the gun', as the Americans so well express it, to outwit the crowd, and to pass the bad, or depreciating, half-crown to the other fellow.* (Keynes 1936)

Reality eventually broke through the fog of irrational exuberance of the Irish property boom, as it did in all others in history. Cracks begin to appear in the fragile edifice on which the boom had been built. As is also often the case, external events triggered the loss of confidence and the change in the psychology of the market. In 2007 and 2008 it was developments in the USA that triggered the crash in Ireland.

The peak of the booming US housing market came in mid-2006. This revealed the weakness of many American financial institutions that had piled into the 'subprime' mortgage market, chasing higher profits by increasingly risky lending. Mortgages had been extended to borrowers who could not produce the usual proof of income and had no track record of loan repayments. (NINJA refers to people with 'No Income, No Job or Assets'.) Professor Harvey S. Rosen of Princeton University defended this type of 'financial innovation': 'The main thing that innovations in the mortgage market have done over the past 30 years is to let in the excluded: the young, the discriminated against, the people without a lot of money in the bank to use for a down payment' (*New York Times*, 29 March 2007).

For a while this apparent generosity was also immensely profitable for the banks. The bad mortgages were cleverly hidden in bundles of securitised mortgages that were sold on to other banks in an elaborate version of a 'pass the parcel' game. Some clever bankers borrowed to buy these and took out relatively cheap insurance that guaranteed them the full value of loans should the borrowers default.

Eventually this elaborate charade became known for what it was. The first to go was Bear Stearns, a New York investment bank that pioneered mortgage securities. In March 2008 the Federal Reserve Bank of New York arranged a deal which allowed J. P. Morgan to buy Bear Stearns shares that had traded as high as $114 for $10 a share. The biggest shock, though, was the collapse of the financial services firm Lehman Brothers, which filed for Chapter 11 bankruptcy protection on 15 September 2008. Its exposure to bad mortgages led to its collapse. Lehman's liabilities were over $600 billion, making it the largest bankruptcy filing in US history.

These events reverberated around the world. On 14 September 2007, Northern Rock, which had been a small building society in the northeast of England, but had expanded vastly on the basis of an online banking model that was innovative at the time, had to seek liquidity support from the Bank of England following problems caused for it by the US subprime mortgage crisis. Queues formed outside its Dublin branch as Irish depositors feared their money would not be available for withdrawal. On 22 February 2008 the bank was nationalised by the UK government.

Iceland experienced a banking collapse in 2008. Like Ireland, it had built its banking boom on external borrowing and a bloated banking system based on property speculation.

The Irish banking system was soon to follow Iceland into crisis and the crisis has rumbled on across Europe ever since. It was not until mid-2012 that the Spanish banking system was finally acknowledged to be largely insolvent, for much the same reasons as the Irish one was in 2008. There were fears that even the German banking system is unsound, due to its heavy lending to banks in the peripheral countries such as Greece, Portugal, Ireland and Spain.

5 Revulsion

This phase is a natural consequence of the collapse of the property values. The banks cease to lend on the collateral of property. Speculators and investors belatedly realise that the market has turned and 'fire sales' become frequent as they try to sell before prices fall any further. The cumulative collapse of prices undermines the solvency of banks, who cry out for 'rescues' or 'banking resolution' plans to be put in place at taxpayers' expense. We discuss the Irish response below.

As the panic spread, banks around the world stopped lending to each other. None of them knew how much risk the others had on their balance sheets. Inter-bank lending dried up.

For a bank like Anglo Irish Bank this was effectively the end of the party. It was borrowing short in the inter-bank market (rolling over its liabilities on a continuous basis) and lending long on the property market. When the inter-bank market froze in 2008, Anglo could no longer roll over its borrowings, but neither could it realise its outstanding loans.

NOTE: Rolling over is the process whereby a bank borrows short term on the inter-bank market to finance long-term loans. The process could start with a bank borrowing €100 million for a month to extend a five-year loan to a developer. At the end of the month, the bank would have to borrow €100 million again to repay the first €100 million loan. Short-term borrowing has to be repeated at the end of each subsequent month until the developer repays (if he has not become bankrupt). If the inter-bank market suddenly shuts down, as it did late in 2008, the banking system faces a crisis.

By 2009 it was clear that the prices of the property for which the loans had been advanced were collapsing and developers were going into liquidation. The valuations on which the banks' property loans had been based looked increasingly fantastical. Depositors, fearful that the banks might become insolvent, rushed to withdraw their money. A nascent run on the Irish banks developed. There was large-scale deposit flight and a full-blown banking crisis was in the offing.

It took some time after the property crash before the scale of the bank losses could be estimated with any precision. Anglo Irish Bank eventually wrote down at least €30 billion in bad debts. The scale of these losses, which were underwritten by the Irish bank guarantee (see below) and hence the Irish taxpayer, prompted the *New York Times* to ask: 'Can one bank bring down a country? Anglo Irish Bank, the midsize Irish lender whose profligacy has come to symbolize the excesses of the real estate bubble here, is doing its best to find out' (31 August 2010).

In his account of the Irish bank crash, Michael Lewis wrote:

> *Even in an era when capitalists went out of their way to destroy capitalism, the Irish bankers set some kind of record for destruction. Theo Phanos, a London hedge-fund manager with interests in Ireland, says that 'Anglo Irish was probably the world's worst bank.'* (*Vanity Fair*, February 2011)

After the collapse it emerged that much of the collateral used to back property loans was not properly secured. Bankers lent money against the personal guarantees of newly wealthy speculators. Not surprisingly, many of these transferred their personal wealth to family members or hid it in foreign tax havens to escape having to surrender it to the banks when things went wrong.

The first people to be jailed as a result of the crash were members of the Seán Quinn family. In the Commercial Court on 25 July 2012 Mr Justice Peter Kelly described as 'mesmerisingly complex' the scheme devised to put their assets beyond the reach of the former Anglo Irish Bank. He said he had presided over the Commercial Court since 2004 and was having to deal more often with cases involving 'national and international fraud, sharp practice, chicanery and dishonesty', but the Quinn scheme was the largest and most devious seen to date.

In 2008 and 2009, Ireland was facing the country's severest economic crisis since World War II. The banking system was teetering on the brink of insolvency and the fiscal deficit was unsustainable. International bonds markets were increasingly reluctant to lend to us on any terms.

21.3 Coping with the Fiscal Crisis

At various points in this book we have discussed how economic models suggest that an economy can adjust to a demand-side shock of the type we experienced in 2007–2008. We have also outlined how the Irish economy has adjusted and was continuing to adjust during 2012. Our emphasis has been on the difficulty of making the necessary adjustments to costs and prices, especially as a member of a currency union, the EMU.

Since 2008 the government's most pressing priority has been to continue to borrow the money needed to cover the government's deficit. We have seen that at the end of November 2010 the international bond market was to all intents and purposes closed to us and, as a result, we sought and obtained a 'bail-out' from the IMF–EU–ECB (the Troika) under an Agreement that laid down a challenging timetable of reforms and budget discipline. These were designed to bring about the country's re-entry to the normal bond markets by 2013 (at the earliest).

Since then Irish budgetary policy has been adhering to a timetable that is being monitored by the Troika on their quarterly visits. In addition, in May 2012 Irish voters approved the Referendum on the Fiscal Compact (formally known as the Treaty on Stability, Co-ordination and Governance in the Economic and Monetary Union), which binds the country to limiting its 'structural' budget deficit to 0.5 per cent of GDP and to several other complicated fiscal rules. The adjustments involve higher taxes and expenditure cuts, which are widely seen as very severe and are politically unpopular. However, the process laid down in the Agreement calls for at least one more austerity budget, in 2013. As in other countries under the surveillance of the Troika, the Irish government is facing a major political challenge to implement the austerity package while keeping a coalition government in place.

Restoring international competitiveness

The measures taken to move towards a sustainable fiscal situation have also contributed to improving Ireland's international competitiveness. Wage cuts, rent reductions and some other cost adjustments (such as lower VAT on selected services) have reduced prices relative to those in other euro area countries, although Ireland remains expensive by comparison with most of them.

We saw in Chapter 15 that Ireland's Real Harmonised Index of Competitiveness indicated a significant loss of competitiveness over the five years before 2008. By mid-2012 the index had fallen by 17 per cent from its peak (on the basis of consumer prices) and by 22 per cent (on the basis of unit labour costs).

Most of this improvement should not, however, be attributed to the austerity measures that have been taken to achieve an 'internal devaluation'. Although there was some reduction in wage levels in 2009 and 2010, the contribution of these to restoring competitiveness has been minor compared with that made by the fall of the euro on the foreign exchanges. In May 2008, the dollar/euro exchange rate briefly reached €1 = $1.60. By August 2012 it had fallen to €1 = $1.21. This was the main force behind Ireland's improved competitiveness. However, by mid-September 2012 the dollar/euro exchange rate had risen back to $1.31. These gyrations illustrate how our price competitiveness relative to the USA and UK is buffeted by external developments that have a bigger and quicker effect than the slow-working process of an 'internal devaluation'.

The fall in the euro does nothing to make members of EMU more competitive relative to one another, but it does make them more competitive relative to non-members. Because a higher proportion of Ireland's trade is with non-members, the beneficial impact of the weak euro is greater for us than for other countries. It is ironic that the Troika should praise Ireland for improving competitiveness when, in fact, this has been largely due to the falling external value of the euro.

21.4 Coping with the Banking Crisis

The initial reaction in Dublin, Brussels and Frankfurt to the financial panic that spread through the banking system in Europe in the wake of the collapse of Lehman Brothers in September 2008 was that the problem was a loss of bank *liquidity*. This could be addressed by providing short-term emergency support to troubled banks. It took a long time for people in authority to realise that the huge property-related losses meant that all the Irish banks were *insolvent* and that this problem could not be solved by short-term liquidity injections. What was required was a way of resolving the balance sheets of banks that had become incapable of covering their liabilities with the assets for which they had advanced loans.

There was no bank resolution protocol in place in the euro area. This had not formed part of the design of the EMU in the 1990s and no progress had been made on it since the adoption of the euro in 1999. The issue of how to deal with insolvent banks that are part of the EMU system of banks had not been resolved when another full-blown banking crisis erupted in the summer of 2012, this time in Spain.

In terms of the Irish banks' balance sheet in 2008, there were two problems: first, and most urgent, what to do to avert deposit flight; and second, how to cleanse the balance sheets of the now virtually worthless property assets against which the banks had advanced billions of depositors' and borrowed money.

Halting deposit flight

In regard to the first issue, a major flaw in the design of the EMU had become apparent. There was no euro area-wide system of deposit insurance comparable to the Federal Deposit Insurance Corporation, whose sticker you see on every bank window in the USA. Given the absence of adequate deposit insurance it was inevitable that the public would lose confidence in the security of their deposits and that panic withdrawals would start, and this could lead to the collapse of the whole system.

In Ireland a Deposit Guarantee Scheme covering up to €20,000 per person of deposits against the risk of bank failure was in place, but this was clearly inadequate to the situation that developed in 2008. The government response in September 2008 was to introduce a guarantee scheme (which became known as the Eligible Liabilities Guarantee Scheme in 2009). This scheme guaranteed *all* the deposits and other liabilities (including bonds) in all Irish banks and building societies. It was subsequently extended to the end of June 2012, after which 'only' €100,000 of deposits per person are guaranteed. This effectively removed the risk of a run on the Irish banks and building societies by ordinary depositors.

Big corporate depositors had withdrawn their deposits long before this. Over the years 2009–2011 various international rating agencies (private companies that offer their opinion on the creditworthiness of banks and other financial institutions) downgraded the Irish banks from AAA to various shades of 'junk' status. This had the effect of requiring most large institutional investors, such as insurance companies and pension funds, to withdraw their deposits from the Irish banks.

Box 21.1 The bank guarantee: dramatis personae

On the evening of 28 September 2008, the CEOs of the two main banks, Eugene Sheehy (AIB) and Brian Goggin (Bank of Ireland), arrived at government buildings with the stark warning that the banks might not open for business the following day.

The following represented the government that evening (we give their university or professional qualifications where available):

Taoiseach Brian Cowen, lawyer
Brian Lenihan, Minister for Finance, lawyer
Paul Gallagher, Attorney General, lawyer
Dermot McCarthy, Secretary to Government, economics
David Doyle, Secretary General, Department of Finance, history
Kevin Cardiff, Deputy, Department of Finance, sociology and anthropology
John Hurley, Governor, Central Bank of Ireland, classics
Patrick Neary, Financial Regulator, classics.

The government agreed to put in place a guarantee arrangement to safeguard all deposits (retail, commercial, institutional and inter-bank), covered bonds, senior debt and dated subordinated debt. Total liabilities covered under the scheme amounted to approximately €485 billion. To put this is context, Irish GNP in 2010 amounted to €132,584 million. In September 2011, the Comptroller and Auditor General estimated that this bail-out of the banking sector would cost the public more than €50 billion. It is not clear whether minutes of this meeting were kept. No official inquiry has yet been published into exactly what transpired and why the guarantee was so extensive.

Critics of the Irish response to the banking crisis pointed out that the Irish bank guarantee scheme was over-inclusive in two ways: first, too wide a range of institutions was covered; and second, too wide a range of bondholders and other creditors was covered. The case for the inclusion of the major deposit-taking banks (Bank of Ireland and Allied Irish Bank) in the guarantee was that they were of systemic importance to the Irish economy. If they had closed their doors chaos would have ensued. However, what was the case for including a casino-type bank like Anglo Irish or the Irish Nationwide Building Society in the scheme? These financial institutions were not of systemic importance to the economy. They had no national branch network and their continued existence was not essential to the continued functioning of the Irish economy.

A case could be made that allowing the failure of *any* monetary institution that was licensed to conduct business in Ireland would have inflicted serious 'reputational damage' on the whole economy and made the country unattractive for foreign businesses. Indeed, it seems to have been argued by the ECB that to allow any bank that was a member of the European System of Banks to fail would have damaged the whole monetary framework of the euro area. If that were true, there was also a case to be made that the ECB should not have required the Irish taxpayer to shoulder the full cost of keeping these institutions afloat.

On the thornier issue of why bondholders were covered by the guarantee, rumours abound that pressure was brought to bear from the ECB in Frankfurt and even from the US Treasury Secretary Tim Geithner to avert the collapse of any deposit-taking institution in the euro area. Whatever the truth of these rumours, the outcome was that the Irish taxpayer was left underwriting a guarantee whose exact magnitude was unknown at the time, but which ultimately added €58.4 billion to the Irish general government debt.

TABLE 21.1 The NAMA haircut

	NAMA value 2010 €bn	Book value €bn	Haircut %
Anglo Irish Bank	13.0	34.0	62
Irish Nationwide Building Society	3.0	8.5	65
Educational Building Society	0.3	0.8	63
Allied Irish Bank	8.5	18.5	54
Bank of Ireland	5.5	9.5	42
Total	30.3	71.3	58

The National Asset Management Agency (NAMA)

Turning to the second issue, what to do with the rotten assets the banks were carrying on their balance sheets? It was decided to remove the bad loans from the banks' balance sheets by parking them in a new 'bad bank' to be known as the National Asset Management Agency (NAMA).

NAMA acquired €71.3 billion of loans from the troubled banks at a cost of €30.3 billion. This implied a discount or 'haircut' of 58 per cent to the banks. (Phrases plucked from the jargon of bond dealers became common parlance in Ireland during the crisis.) Table 21.1 shows how the haircuts applied to the bad loans of each of the banks. Anglo Irish Bank, not unexpectedly, accounted for the largest absolute loss and Irish Nationwide Building Society (INBS) for the largest percentage haircut.

The mechanism used by NAMA to build its 'bad bank' and clean up the balance sheet of the insolvent Irish banks was at follows. First, the Irish government gave bonds to NAMA. These NAMA bonds were then used by NAMA to purchase bad loans from the commercial banks. The commercial banks, in turn, used the NAMA bonds to borrow from the ECB. Whereas the ECB does not accept property as collateral, it did accept NAMA bonds because they were guaranteed by the Irish state. With the newly acquired funds, the Irish banks were able to replenish their Tier I capital and the bad loans had been removed from the banks' balance sheets.

The injection of funds into the Irish banking system by the Irish Central Bank and the ECB totalled €120 billion at September 2011. Without this the Irish banking system would have collapsed. It is ironic to recall that two years previously we had been reassured by bankers at all levels that the Irish banks were well capitalised and would not need any assistance from the state. On 31 January 2008 the governor of the Central Bank of Ireland said that stress-testing of the financial system had shown that 'Irish banks are solidly profitable and well-capitalised and with no major exposures.' A few months later the OECD repeated the same view: 'The Irish banks are well-capitalised and profitable, which provides a cushion to weather the more difficult times ahead.'

The issue of NAMA bonds was treated as part of the government's budget deficit and the NAMA bonds become part of Irish sovereign debt. As a result in 2010 the Irish general government debt rose by €58.4 billion and the general government balance (which includes the money used to recapitalise the banks) soared to 31 per cent of GDP – probably the largest ever recorded in an advanced economy.

A recurrent criticism of the way the bank recapitalisation problem was dealt with by the ECB and EU centres on their refusal to lend directly to the Irish banks. Instead they chose the roundabout mechanism of the Irish government giving NAMA bonds to the banks and then the banks using the bonds as collateral to borrow from the ECB.

While this might seem just a bit of window-dressing, it had the very unfortunate consequence of making the Irish sovereign liable for recapitalisation of its banks. In a 'normal' rescue plan, such as was implemented in the USA, a Bank Resolution Corporation would have issued the debt required to recapitalise the banks and this liability would not have dragged down the sovereign's credit rating.

Spain finally sought external aid (although still refusing to enter a full bail-out programme) in the summer of 2012 to rescue its insolvent banks. The EU–ECB agreed to lend directly to the banks so as to avoid further undermining the already weak Spanish government bonds. Needless to say, this prompted immediate hopes that Ireland would be able to renegotiate its deal with the ECB.

There was much debate about the appropriate size of the haircut to be applied to the toxic assets acquired by NAMA. On the one hand, some people seemed to believe that a large haircut was an appropriate punishment for banks' past recklessness. On the other hand, it was clear that the less they received for these toxic assets the weaker their capital position would become and the larger the required infusion of new capital to be paid for by the taxpayer.

Table 21.2 provides details of the five bail-outs up to March 2011 that cost the exchequer €58.4bn. The extent of the bail-outs caught the government unawares as further hidden losses were revealed by the banks. It was becoming apparent that the government had entered into a guarantee that was open-ended.

In return for the money allocated to bank recapitalisation, the government acquired equity stakes in the banks, which are also shown in Table 21.2. AIB has been largely nationalised, the former Anglo Irish Bank has been closed and replaced by the state-owned National Irish Bank Resolution Corporation and Bank of Ireland is half state-owned.

An AIB share was worth €22 in 2006. At the end of July 2012 it was quoted at €0.05 on the Irish Stock Exchange. Many households had used these so-called 'blue-chip' shares as a savings vehicle

TABLE 21.2 Irish government bank bail-outs

	Bail-out 1 Feb–May 2009	Bail-out 2 Mar 10	Bail-out 3 Sep 10	Bail-out 4 Nov 10	Bailout 5 3 Mar 11	Total per bank
AIB €bn	3.5	3.9	3	5.2	−2.3	13.3
Government stake %	25	18	92	93	93	
Bank of Ireland €bn	3.5			2.2	−0.5	5.2
Government stake %	25			36	50	
Anglo Irish Bank €bn	4.0	18.0	7.0			29.0
Government stake %	100	100	100		Closed	
Irish Nationwide €bn		2.7	2.7			5.4
Government stake %		100	100		Closed	
Educational Building Society		0.875		0.425	0.2	1.5
Government stake %		100		100	Merge with AIB	
Irish Life and Permanent €bn			0.145	0.098	3.757	4
Government stake %			0	0	90+	
Total	11.0	25.5	12.8	7.9	1.2	58.4

FIGURE 21.4 AIB share price, 2003–2012

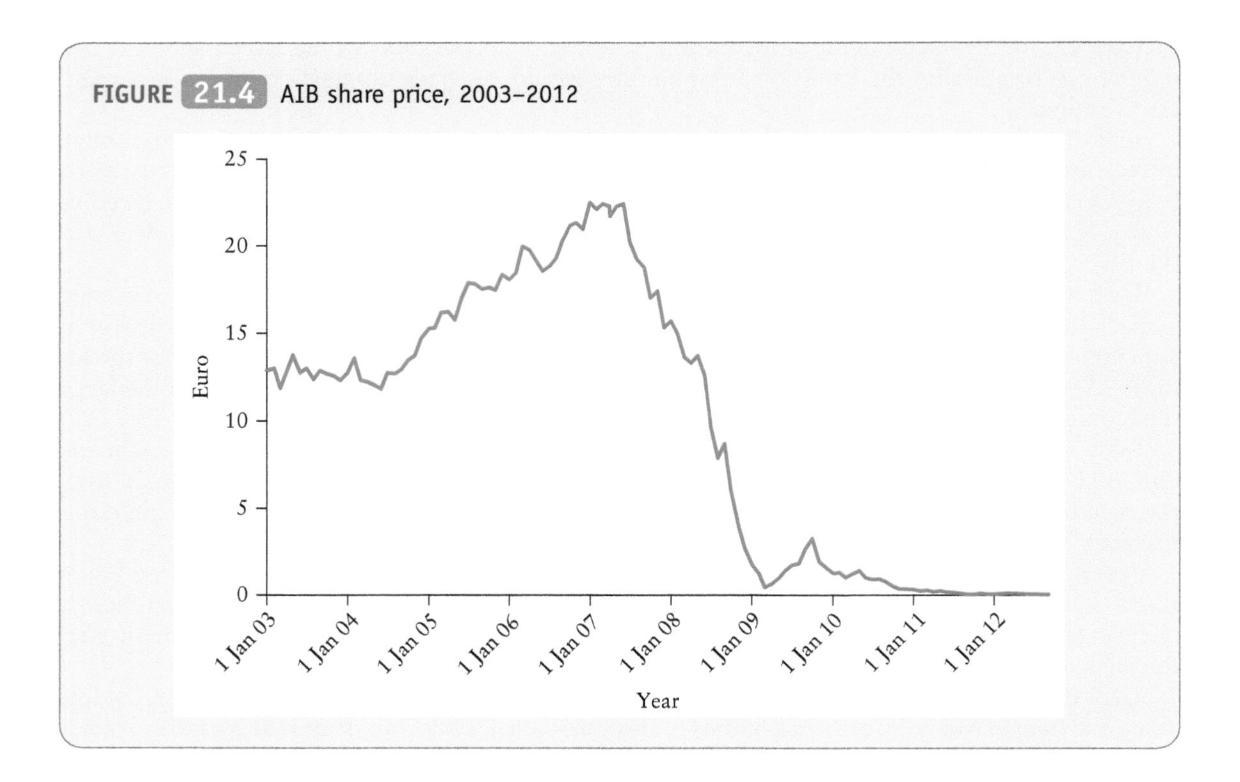

for future expenses like their children's education, health emergencies and so on. Irish pension funds invested heavily in these shares. Through its effect on the value of bank shares the property crash badly affected many people who had not directly invested in the property market.

21.5 The Troika Agreement

In a pattern that was to become familiar, as its fiscal situation steadily deteriorated through 2009 and 2010, the Greek government consistently denied the severity of the crisis and claimed it would be able to survive without external help. (Three years later, at the time of writing, the Spanish government is similarly insisting that it does not require a full bail-out.) However, in May 2010 the Greek government finally applied to the Troika for an agreement to borrow €120 billion. This led the markets to look more and more critically at the situation in Portugal and Ireland. In a process that has been called 'contagion', the heightened risk associated with Greek bonds spilled over to Portugal and Ireland and would eventually spread to Spain and Italy. Public attention is now focused as never before on bond yields, with newspapers in Italy and Spain carrying daily accounts of 'the spread', the gap between the yield on their bonds and on comparable German bonds.

Behind the phenomenon of rising yields on sovereign debt is the spectre of national insolvency, of governments being unable to access at a sustainable price the borrowed funds needed to finance their day-to-day spending. Figure 21.5 shows the yield on long-term (10-year) bonds in Ireland, Germany and Greece between 2008 and 2012. Starting from a situation in 2008 where the gap between the highest and lowest was insignificant, the yields on Greek and Irish bonds rose sharply while German yields actually fell. In July 2011 the Irish yield reached a peak of 12.45 per cent, while the German yield was 2.9 and falling. The Greek yield was 16.7 in mid-2011 and eventually rose to 29 per cent, at which stage no one was willing to lend to the country.

FIGURE 21.5 Long-term interest rates in Ireland, Germany and Greece, 2008–2012

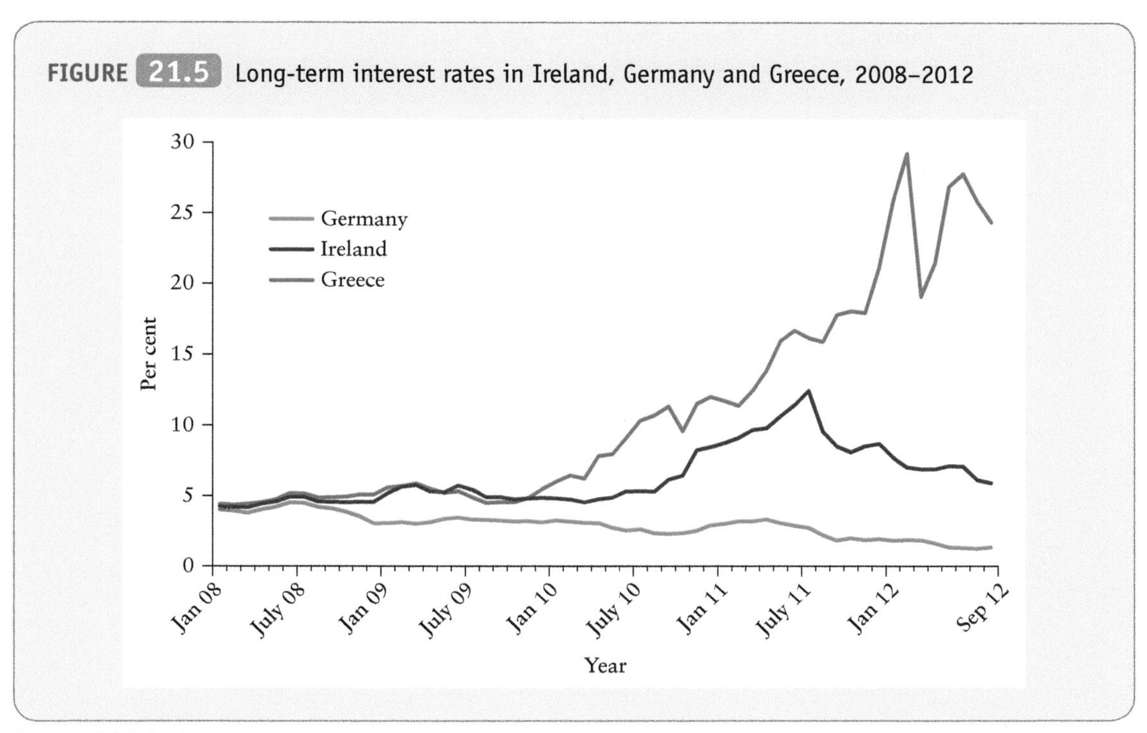

Source: ECB database

Piecemeal actions, such as the fiscal corrections introduced by the Irish government between 2008 and 2010, failed to convince the international bond markets. The price of Irish bonds went on falling and the spread against the German bond increased.

By Autumn 2010, although the government was funded for one year in advance and had no immediate need to borrow funds on the international market, the price of Irish government bonds fell sharply, raising their yields to more than 600 basis points (or six per cent) above the yield on German bonds. Then, unexpectedly, the banks needed a further bail-out arising from yet another 'stress test' that revealed their position to be worse than previously thought (see Table 21.2). As the government was effectively shut out of international credit markets, there was little option but to approach the Troika for a 'bail-out'. In November, after the usual ritual denials that external help was needed, the government announced that it was seeking an agreement with the Troika.

The deal that was eventually done involved a credit of up to €85 billion over the period 2011–2014. As a condition of the loan the Irish government agreed to a schedule for bringing its budget deficit below three per cent of GDP by 2015. Table 21.3 shows the measures that were agreed to achieve this. €17.5 billion of the €85 billion is to come from the National Pension Reserve Fund and cash reserves. The IMF is committing €22.5 billion.

Note that the bail-out was not a 'hand-out'. It was a set of loans that originally carried a relatively high interest rate, although one much below what we would have had to pay on the bond market, if we could have borrowed there at all. Initially a rate of 5.8 per cent was set on the IMF loan and four per cent on the EU loan. However, these rates were subsequently reduced. Changes announced in March 2011, for example, mean that Ireland will pay an average rate of 3.04 per cent on the €22 billion it is borrowing from the IMF.

Table 21.4 shows the budgetary cuts in government expenditure and increases in taxation contained in the Troika agreement. These measures, combined with the earlier 2008–2010 cutbacks,

TABLE 21.3 Ireland's credit from the Troika, 2010

	€bn	€bn
National Pension Reserve Fund	12.5	
Cash reserves	5.0	
Ireland's contribution		17.5
IMF		22.5
European Union	22.5	
European Financial Stability Fund	17.7	
European contribution		40.2
UK	3.8	
Sweden	0.6	
Denmark	0.4	
Total bilateral loans		4.8
Total		85.0
Total less Irish contribution		67.5

TABLE 21.4 Summary of budgetary measures in the Troika agreement 2010

		2011 €m	2012 €m	2013 €m	2014 €m	2011–14 €m
Expenditure measures	a	−3,930	−2,100	−2,000	−2,000	−10,030
Taxation/PRSI measures	b	1,410	1,500	1,100	1,100	5,110
Other	c	660				660
Total fiscal consolidation	d = a − c	−6,000	−3,600	−3,100	−3,100	−15,800

amount to taking €30,400 million out of the economy over the period 2008–2014. These austerity measures are equivalent to withdrawing over three per cent of GDP a year from aggregate demand.

21.6 Is the Irish National Debt Sustainable?

In Chapter 7 we explained the dynamics of debt accumulation. Two key conditions are necessary to stabilise the debt/GDP ratio:

1. The growth rate of nominal GDP must exceed the nominal interest rate.
2. There must be a surplus on the primary (non-interest) budget.

Note that the relevant interest rate is the average interest rate on the outstanding stock of government debt. The interest rates at which Ireland must now borrow make it very difficult to achieve condition (1), which throws more of the adjustment on to condition (2). The Department of Finance estimates that the average interest rate on our debt is 3.8 per cent in 2012, rising to 4.9 per cent by 2015. The aim is to achieve a primary surplus by 2014 and a falling debt/GDP ratio after 2013. (For details of the agreement and the Department of Finance's review of progress towards implementing it, see www.finance.gov.ie/documents/publications/other/spuapr2012.pdf.)

The official view is that the target can be achieved if we adhere to the conditions laid down in the agreement. A sceptical view is that these projections are unlikely to be met. They are based on assumptions about growth that seem optimistic in light of the slow-down in the global economy (some of it induced by the austerity programmes being imposed in so many industrialised countries). They also, and crucially, assume that the Irish government can successfully implement the austerity package agreed with the Troika without completely choking off growth in the domestic economy. With slow growth, unemployment will remain high, tax revenues weak and a primary budget surplus could recede in the future.

21.7 No one Shouted 'Stop'

With hindsight it is easy to say what might have been done better. Nonetheless, even at the time there was widespread agreement that many errors were being made in Ireland by politicians, central bankers and civil servants, as well by their counterparts in the EMU institutions, notably the ECB and the IMF.

Early in the crisis there were attempts, mainly by Irish politicians, to shift the blame by emphasising that Ireland was caught in a global whirlwind and could not have avoided the banking crash that spread from the US subprime crisis and the collapse of Lehman Brothers. These claims are not very convincing.

While it was difficult for any country to survive the global financial crisis unscathed, many components of the Irish crisis were home-made. In particular, the Irish authorities were mainly to blame for allowing the banking system to run amok in property speculation. It is, though, fair to lay some of the blame for the mistakes of this period at the door of the ECB due to its failure to exercise the vigilance over national central banks and commercial banks that should have been expected in an 'economic and monetary union'.

Irish politicians and their advisers were to blame for failing to take corrective action to rein in public spending from levels that were only sustainable as long as the windfall tax revenue from the booming property market continued to flow. The general laxity in public spending, especially the inflation of public sector wages and salaries beyond what could be justified by international comparisons or comparisons with the private sector, was also a home-grown mistake.

The problems facing Ireland and other EMU countries were exacerbated by flaws in the design of EMU reaching back to the 1990s. It is now widely acknowledged that the 11 founding member countries in 1999 did not come close to meeting the conditions for an Optimal Currency Area laid down by Robert Mundell. Indeed, the countries that were admitted in 1998 did not fully comply with the criteria laid down in the Maastricht Treaty, and the admission of Greece in 2000 did not improve matters.

A fundamental issue that was not addressed was whether the ECB should serve as a fully fledged central bank (with the duty to act as lender of last resort in crises). This omission proved very damaging during the crisis. The absence of an EMU-wide banking regulatory regime, of a proper bank resolution mechanism, and of an EMU deposit insurance scheme also proved costly.

EMU is not a deep fiscal union and proper rules for co-ordinating the public finances across the member states are still not in place, although the Fiscal Compact is supposed to remedy that. There is not even rudimentary 'fiscal federalism'. This means that when asymmetric shocks hit the member states, the appropriateness of having surrendered the exchange rate as a policy instrument became crucial.

These weaknesses in the design of EMU were exacerbated in the case of Ireland by the determination to join even when it became apparent that the UK would not. Ireland was an outlier from the start, with an exceptionally low proportion of our trade with the other EMU countries, much higher labour mobility with non-EMU countries than with member countries, and a very different (more 'Anglo Saxon') economic culture. Economists and commentators who warned of the inappropriateness of the EMU for Ireland were regarded as 'anti-European' (perhaps even 'pro-British' for wanting to keep the link with sterling). Irish politicians, in particular, hailed the launch of the new monetary union with enthusiasm, ignoring the warnings that it could end in tears.

NOTE: Two official reports have been published into the banking crisis: 'The Irish Banking Crisis, Regulatory and Financial Stability Policy 2003–2008: A Report to the Minister for Finance by the Governor of the Central Bank' (May 2010); and 'A Preliminary Report on the Sources of Ireland's Banking Crisis' by Klaus Regling and Max Watson. Both are available at www.bankinginquiry.gov.ie.

The official reports that have been issued on the banking crisis (see above) highlight the cosy relationship that had long existed in Ireland between government and sections of the business community, especially the bankers and clients in property speculation. This was another problem that should not be blamed on outside influences. The report by the governor of the Central Bank states that:

> *In the case of Anglo Irish Bank, management was seen by at least FR (Financial Regulator) staff as perhaps 'slick and buccaneering' but not as presenting a large or imminent risk. Although it became quite clear to top FR decision-makers that senior Anglo figures were well-liked in political circles, and it cannot be excluded that this played a part in their subsequent continuation in office for some months after September, there was, until very late in the day, no perceived need to take regulatory action against them. The central management figure in INBS (Irish Nationwide Building Society) was seen as an overly dominating figure that needed to be surrounded by a stronger governance structure.* (Honohan 2010:17)

There was also a failure for those with supervisory roles to issue advance warnings of the looming catastrophe.

- In September 2007 (by which stage Irish bank shares had lost one-third of their peak value), the IMF commended Ireland's 'prudent fiscal policy', mentioning 'Ireland's continued impressive economic performance'.
- In 2007, just before the crash, the Central Bank and Financial Services Authority of Ireland commented: 'The health of the banking system remains robust when measured by the usual indicators and the results of in-house stress testing.'
- The governor of the Central Bank claimed on 31 January 2008, 'Irish banks are solidly profitable and well-capitalised and with no major exposures.'
- After the collapse of Lehman Brothers, the Irish Financial Regulator Patrick Neary commented: 'Irish banks are resilient and have good shock absorption capacity to cope with the current situation.'
- From October 2001 to March 2009 Ireland enjoyed AAA credit rating from Standard and Poor's rating agency.
- In April 2008, the OECD noted, 'The Irish banks are well-capitalised and profitable, which provides a cushion to weather the more difficult times ahead.'

The failures of Irish policy were aided and abetted by failures of international agencies that had a considerable duty of oversight on the Irish economy. These include the ECB and the economic agencies of the EU, as well as advisory agencies like the IMF and the OECD, whose advice was all too often an echo of what they had heard from the people they interviewed on their visits to Dublin.

In summer 2012 a 20-year veteran of the IMF resigned, accusing the organisation of 'incompetence' and 'analytical risk-aversion', specifically in relation to its handling of the euro area crisis. He claimed that this had caused suffering in countries like Greece and had brought the world's second global reserve currency (the euro) to the brink of collapse.

21.8 Specific Policy Failures

Some specific policy failures that contributed to the crisis can be traced a long way back. A first issue was the 'light touch regulation' that became fashionable internationally in the early years of this century and was uncritically endorsed by many Irish politicians. For example, in October 2005 the EU Commissioner for Internal Markets and former Irish Minister for Finance, Charlie McCreevy, gave this advice to the Irish Financial Regulator: 'Don't try to protect everyone from every possible accident. Concentrate on the big things that really matter. And leave industry with the space to breathe and investors with the freedom to learn from their mistakes.'

A second issue relates to the pro-cyclical conduct of Irish fiscal policy, which we discussed in Chapter 8. Neither our politicians nor our senior civil servants were able to restrain expenditure during the good times to a level that was compatible with underlying, sustainable tax-generating capacity of the economy.

A third issue was the over-inclusiveness of the bank guarantee. As we mentioned earlier in this chapter, institutions that were not of systemic importance to the Irish economy (notably Anglo Irish Bank) were covered by the guarantee and the range of bank liabilities covered was too broad. It included even subordinated bondholders, who should have known that they were taking extra risk in return for the higher yields. (Subordinate debt has 'subordinate status' in being repaid relative to 'normal' debt.) Junior bondholders did bear losses, with discounts of 80–90 per cent applied to about €20 billion of junior bank bonds in September 2008.

Why was the Irish taxpayer committed to such a comprehensive guarantee? Brian Cowen, who was Taoiseach at the time the guarantee was issued, gave his reasons in a speech at Georgetown University, Washington, DC on 21 March 2012:

1. *Had we not guaranteed the funding of the banks, we faced the real risk of a run on the banks with devastating consequences for the availability of credit, the payments system, jobs, the economy and people's savings.*
2. *The advice was that the banks were solvent but were experiencing a liquidity problem. It subsequently transpired that the banks were insolvent but that was not known at the time of the guarantee.*
3. *The extent to which losses could be imposed on senior bonds of European banks is limited by the legal framework that requires equal treatment of all senior bank creditors, including senior bondholders and depositors.*
4. *At no stage during the crisis would the European authorities, especially the European Central Bank, have countenanced the dishonouring of senior bank bonds. The euro area policy of 'No bank failures and no burning of senior bank creditors' has been a constant during the crisis.*

Some of this defence is based on counter-factual claims (what would have happened if . . .) that are impossible to refute or confirm. Some of it pushes the blame back to the 'legal framework' and advisers. It will be for history to judge the validity of these pleas.

Perhaps a comment made by the President of Iceland, Olafur R. Grimsson, in 2011 is relevant: 'The difference is that in Iceland we allowed the banks to fail. These were private banks and we didn't pump money into them in order to keep them going; the state did not shoulder the responsibility of the failed private banks.'

NOTE: In November 2006, Anglo Irish Bank issued a bond for $1 billion (€720 million) to US bank Citigroup and Japanese bank Nomura. Risk-taking hedge funds and investors in distressed debt bought this bond in 2011 at a deep discount. The hedge fund then received windfall profits when the debt was repaid in full by the state-owned bank to senior, unsecured, unguaranteed, bondholders at 100 cent in the euro. The hedge fund duly received a 'tombstone' – also known as a 'deal toy' – to mark the closing of this business deal.

The issue of 'burning the bondholders' has been hotly debated in Ireland since 2008. It figured during the general election campaign of 2011. It has been claimed that the IMF were in favour of cutting repayments on €30 billion of unguaranteed bonds by two-thirds on average. However, this burning of the bondholders never materialised.

In modern countries the national central bank – in consultation with international agencies like the IMF – is responsible for restoring stability to the banking system during a crisis. The US Federal Reserve acted promptly and boldly in dealing with the subprime crisis from 2006 onwards. Following massive intervention in the financial markets and the injection of trillions of taxpayers' dollars into the system, by 2011 it could be said that the USA had a functioning banking system once again. The same could not be said for Ireland, despite proportionately larger injections of taxpayers' funds into the banks.

The euro area problem has been made worse by the flawed constitution of the ECB and its lack of clarity regarding how to deal with insolvent banks. Banking crises have been addressed as if all that was needed was some short-term, emergency liquidity. The inherent insolvency of large banks in several countries was denied for as long as possible. Individuals in positions of authority in the Bank cannot be absolved of responsibility for the manner in which the crisis was handled, even within the limitations of the Bank's legal structure.

Throughout the years 2008 to 2012 the policy responses were consistently too little, too late. The rhetoric of saving the euro area was not backed by decisive initiatives on a scale that convinced markets. After each of the innumerable (19 by one count) crisis summits over these years communiqués were issued to try to convince markets that 'this time we are serious', but these provided short-term relief at best. ECB and EU officials were not helped by the ambivalence of politicians and voters in the core euro area countries towards the whole EMU project.

It remains to be seen whether the 'big bazooka' unveiled by Mario Draghi in September 2012 will be a game changer. But just a week after this plan was unveiled the initial market euphoria has given way once again to second thoughts.

The contrast between the situation in the euro area and that in the USA was always striking, but never more so than now. A third wave of Quantitative Easing (QE3) was unveiled by the Federal Reserve Open Market on 13 September 2012. This commits the Bank to purchasing $40 billion worth of mortgage-backed securities a month, rising to $85 billion by the end of the year. (Some people have called this QE∞.)

This expansionary monetary policy was justified in language that is never heard from the ECB:

> *The Committee seeks to foster maximum employment and price stability. The Committee is concerned that, without further policy accommodation, economic growth might not be strong enough to generate sustained improvement in labor market conditions. The Committee will closely monitor incoming information on economic and financial developments in coming months. If the outlook for the labor market does not improve substantially, the Committee will continue its purchases of agency mortgage-backed securities, undertake additional asset purchases, and employ its other policy tools as appropriate until such improvement is achieved in a context of price stability.*

The repeated emphasis on conditions in the labour market contrasts with the absence of such references in ECB statements. This reflects the different mandates the two institutions have been assigned by the lawmakers in the USA and Europe, but it highlights the risks to the euro area inherent in the narrow anti-inflationary focus of the ECB.

21.9 Concluding Thoughts

The economics profession and the political establishment are divided about the prospects for success of the approach being taken by the Troika to help Greece, Portugal, Ireland and Spain through the ongoing crisis. On the one hand is the orthodox 'German' view that these countries landed themselves in the mess they found themselves in from 2008 onwards due to:

- lack of fiscal discipline during the good times
- lax administration of lax laws
- failure to control domestic costs and prices, leading to a progressive loss of competitiveness
- leniency in regard to the growth of the 'welfare state'
- high rates of pay and generous pensions in the public sector
- failure to adequately regulate bank lending, which remained a national responsibility even in the EMU
- failure to take prompt corrective action as the public finances deteriorated
- in some cases, downright dishonesty in reporting the condition of the public finances.

The mood of those who hold these views is nicely caught in the following remarks:

> *Irish taxpayers should take the brunt of the pain from the bailout plan. They should foot the bill as they are the ones who benefited during the pre-crisis boom years. Irish people also elected the governments that regulated the banks as the problems built. If taxpayers have the right to share in decision-making, they must also accept the consequences.* (Lorenzo Bini Smaghi (the ECB board member who had praised Ireland in 2007), April 2011)

At a more popular level some newspapers in Germany like to demonise Greek government workers who can retire and go back to their nice farms in the country to live on generous pensions before they reach age 60. Why should German taxpayers shoulder the burden of bailing out the Greek government when it will not tackle these problems? This view argues that only when order has been restored to the public finances and costs brought under control and structural reforms of the economy completed will growth return to these countries.

The various economic models discussed at different stages in this book suggest how prices, wages, costs and the exchange rate have to adjust to help restore full employment. But they provide no guidance as to how rapidly a particular economy will achieve these adjustments. These are empirical questions on which there is little agreement among economists.

The graphs in Figure 21.6 show that the three domestic components of Irish aggregate demand (C, G, and I) have fallen consistently since 2008. It is evidence like this that leads economists like Paul Krugman and Joseph Stiglitz to argue that austerity packages will destroy the countries they are trying to help.

Krugman has pointed out that there is no example of an austerity programme that was followed by recovery. The exception is where the economy undergoing the austerity measures was a small, open economy next to a larger economy that began to grow rapidly. Ireland in the late 1980s is a possible example, but Ireland in 2012 is not. This is because the countries with which Ireland trades (the euro area, the UK and the USA) are all facing into austerity-induced recessions.

Krugman also likes to point out that 'internal devaluation' or 'wage cuts' will work only if there are rapid wage increases in other countries, which is clearly not the case in Europe today.

Moreover, opponents of austerity point to the political unacceptability of these programmes. Since 2008 governments have fallen in Italy (twice), Ireland, Greece, Portugal, Spain, France,

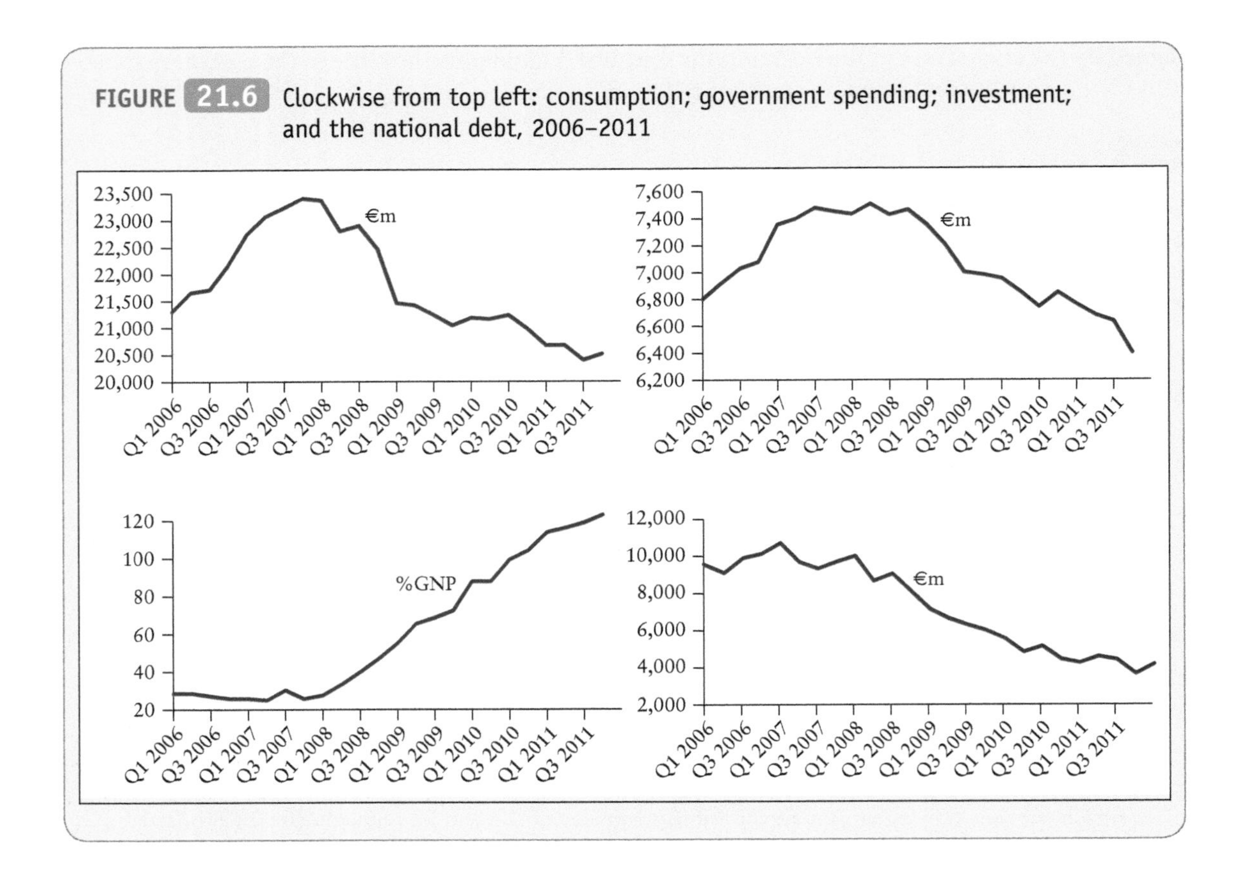

FIGURE 21.6 Clockwise from top left: consumption; government spending; investment; and the national debt, 2006–2011

Denmark, the UK and the Netherlands. Some of the newly elected governments, notably the new French administration, have declared themselves willing to form an 'anti-austerity' axis in Europe. In many countries extremist parties of the left and right gained considerably in recent elections. This bodes ill for the future stability of some of these countries in the face of prolonged austerity. Recent unrest on the streets of Athens and Madrid may be harbingers of wider upheavals.

As this chapter is being written – at the end of 2012 – the future of the EMU and even perhaps of the whole EU is more uncertain than it has been in decades. The European economy is in recession; the currency crisis has gone on longer than World War I. The label 'crisis' now seems to be a misnomer. Greece, Portugal, Ireland and Spain have applied and, to varying degrees, obtained emergency assistance from the Troika. A Greek exit from the currency union is regarded as still a real possibility. The markets remain deeply sceptical about the ability or willingness of the European political and financial classes to tackle the problem in a convincing and decisive manner.

Under the new Presidency of Mario Draghi the ECB has shown greater awareness of what needs to be done and greater alacrity in doing it. Progress has been made on designing a euro area-wide banking regulation in place. Also the ECB is assuming the role of lender of last resort in order to equalise bond yields across the area. There are some discussions about mutualisation of the sovereign debt, so that the perceived risk of default is reduced for the weaker countries. There will probably also be slow but only limited movement towards fiscal burden-sharing.

Whether these steps will be decisive enough to overcome market scepticism and risk aversion remains to be seen. By the time this is being read by students, things will have moved on; but in which direction is impossible to foresee.

21.10 Is Default an Option?

When national debts have once been accumulated to a certain degree, there is scarce, I believe, a single instance of their having been fairly and completely paid. (Smith 1776)

Little has changed in the two and half centuries since Adam Smith wrote this. Debts accumulated during the Napoleonic Wars, the American Civil War and the two World Wars have in general not been 'fairly and completely' repaid. Even post-war Germany defaulted on its war debts before launching itself on the *Wirtschaftswunder* after the currency reform of 1948.

'Default' does not always take the form of crude repudiation of debt. A more subtle way of not repaying debts 'fairly and completely' is to allow inflation to erode the nominal value of the debt, and to repay in devalued currency. The USA emerged from World War II with a huge overhang of debt. In 1946 the US debt/GDP ratio was 109 per cent, but this had fallen to 40 per cent within a decade, mainly because inflation exceeded four per cent a year, while the interest paid on the debt was only 2.5 per cent. In effect high inflation confiscated the purchasing power of those who had put their savings into US bonds during the war.

The claim, used as a threat against states in difficulty due to the burden of their national debt, that 'only pariah states default' is simply unhistorical and untrue. Moreover, the implied moral reproach ignores the fact that some of the blame for excessive borrowing lay with those who extended credit. The lenders who took additional risk in pursuit of higher yields should not be shielded from all the adverse consequences of their appetite for risk.

In 2012 Greece became the most recent example of a sovereign country to default. The world financial markets did not collapse as a result. For the other distressed EMU countries a number of options are being discussed – although not very openly – including various forms of 'restructuring', interest rate concessions, and perhaps linking debt repayments to future growth (which would include an inflationary element). But if defaults, in whatever guise they occur, are not done in an agreed and orderly manner the fear is that distressed countries will lose access to the international credit market and face higher future borrowing costs. There is, therefore, plenty of work to be done to find a way out of the debt dilemma in a manner that is perceived as fair to all the involved parties and inflicts the minimum damage on their economies.

21.11 Key Terms and Concepts

In this chapter we reviewed the economic crash in Ireland in 2008 and the government's response to the crisis. Among the issues examined were:

- the property crash and its implications for the Irish economy
- the banking crisis of 2008
- the government's response to the crisis
- the austerity programme imposed on the Irish economy by the Troika
- a critique of government and EU policies
- the issue of whether Irish debt is sustainable
- the issue of default.

CHAPTER 22

The Long-run Performance of the Irish Economy

Little else is requisite to carry a state to the highest degree of opulence from the lowest barbarism, but peace, easy taxes, and tolerable administration of justice. (Adam Smith)

22.1 Introduction

Economists and historians generally gave low marks to Ireland's economic performance between independence in 1922 and 1960. The years from independence to 1960 saw little economic progress. In the 1960s and 1970s the growth rate rose, but not enough to close the gap in living standards with the richer European countries. In the early 1980s, the Irish economy went through a severe and protracted recession. Unemployment and emigration soared and living standards stagnated. However, these trends were dramatically reversed in the 1990s and into the first decade of the new century. The rapid growth of output and employment during these years led to a convergence of Irish living standards with those of the world's richest nations. This phase ended in a property bubble and a spectacular crash in 2008. Since then, the economy has been mired in recession and is limping along as it adheres to the terms of the Troika's austerity programme.

In this chapter we go back to looking at the business cycle again and try to identify the factors that have influenced our growth rate over the decades. We apply ideas developed in our earlier discussion of macroeconomic theory to gain insight into the Irish experience.

22.2 The Growth of Population

The size of the population is of particular interest in Ireland because of the unique decline in the national population from 1841 to 1961. The first reliable census of population was held in 1841 and there have been 23 censuses since then, mostly at five- or ten-year intervals. The census scheduled for 2016 will be the twenty-fifth in the series.

As we noted in Chapter 4, the change in the population is the sum of the rate of natural increase (that is, the excess of the birth rate over the death rate) and the net migration rate.

Net migration has been strongly influenced by the availability of jobs in Ireland relative to the opportunities abroad. After the Great Famine, throughout the second half of the nineteenth century, and for many years in the twentieth century, the net emigration rate outweighed the rate of natural increase and the population declined. During boom years early in this century, there was very substantial net immigration and the population increased rapidly.

Figure 22.1 shows the population of the 26 counties that now constitute the Republic of Ireland from 1841 to 2011. Figure 22.2 shows the annual average rate of change in population, allowing for the varying intervals between the censuses. What is immediately striking about the graphs is how variable the demographic record has been.

FIGURE 22.1 Population of Ireland (26 counties), 1841–2011

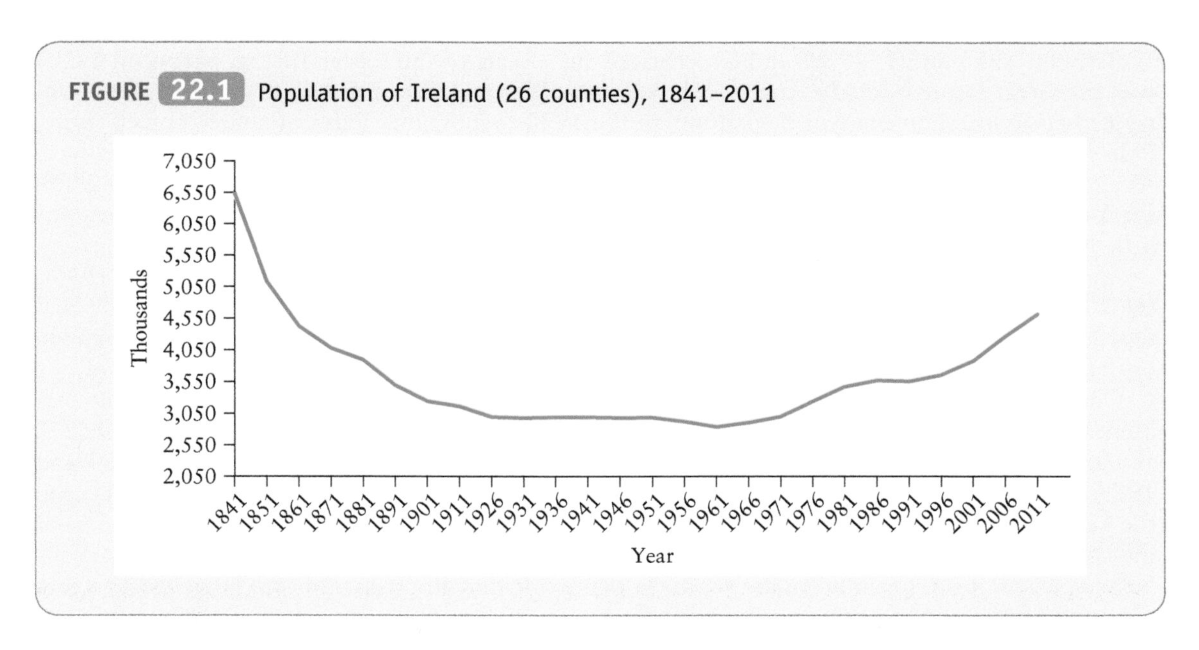

FIGURE 22.2 Population of Ireland (26 counties): annual average rate of change 1841–2011

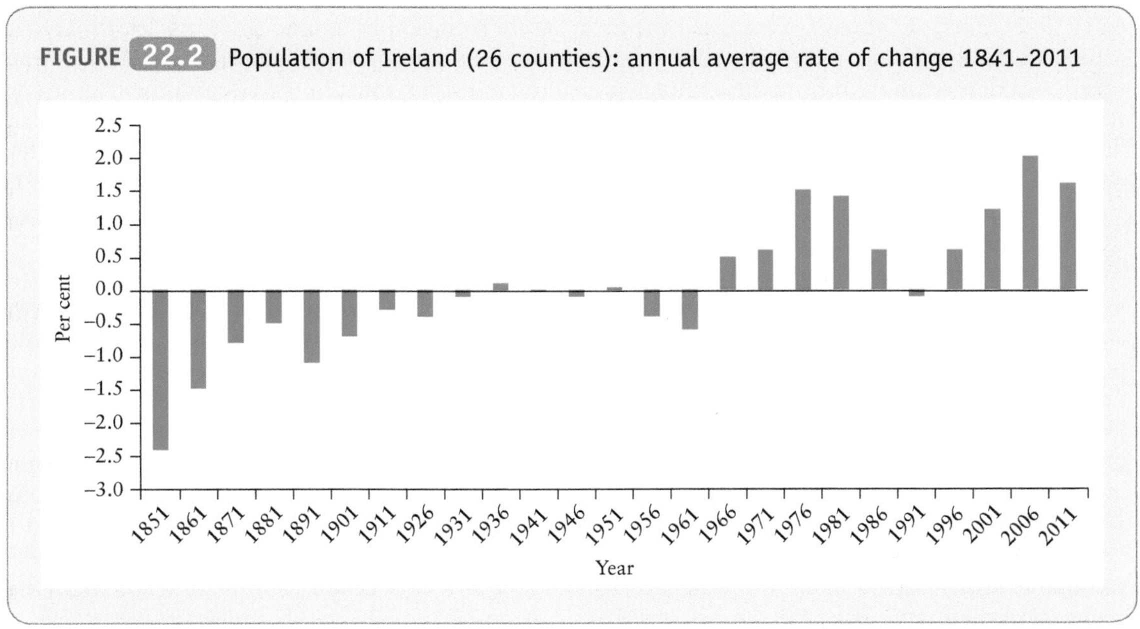

The highest rate of population decline was during and after the Great Famine of the 1840s. The decline continued, but at a slower pace, in the 1850s, 1860s and 1870s. Renewed famine during the 1880s led to a faster rate of decline, which was followed by a lower rate of decline until 1911. There was another increase in the rate of decline in the aftermath of the 1916 Rising and 1921 Treaty. The cumulative result was that between 1841 and 1926 the population fell from 6,528,000 to 2,972,000. This 54 per cent decline in population occurred over a period when the populations of almost all European and New World countries were growing rapidly. The population of England and Wales, for example, grew by 137 per cent from 1841 to 1921. Ireland's population decline was a striking symbol of the weakness of the Irish economy.

Between 1916 and 1945 Ireland experienced the effects of the Easter Rising, partition, a civil war, the Great Depression, the Anglo-Irish Economic War and World War II. In addition, the country turned its back on the world economy in the 1930s, embracing indiscriminate protectionism. Policy remained inward-looking until the 1960s, when a gradual opening up to free trade occurred. As can be seen from Figure 22.1, after 1926 the population stabilised at just under the three million mark until the late 1940s. The available indicators suggest that the average standard of living was little higher in 1945 than it had been in 1914.

The post-war experience was also disappointing. After a spurt of growth in the late 1940s, the 1950s were disastrous. Employment fell, emigration soared and by 1961 the population had dipped to its lowest level: 2,818,300 – 57 per cent below the peak of 1841. With people streaming out of the country, serious concerns were voiced about the viability of an independent Ireland.

One influential study stated: 'It is difficult to avoid the impression that Irish economic performance has been the least impressive in Western Europe, perhaps in all Europe, in the twentieth century' (Lee 1989:521).

However, the country's economic fortunes changed markedly after 1960. Between 1960 and 1979 the annual average growth rate of GDP was four per cent, compared to only one per cent in the 1950s. For the first time in the post-war period Ireland's growth rate was above the average of the OECD countries. The population decline was reversed and modest growth recorded. The 1960s were a period of optimism when the phrase 'a rising tide lifts all boats' indicated that most sectors of society shared in the fruits of economic growth.

However, the era of sustained economic growth came to an end in the early 1980s. The oil crisis of 1979–80 and global recession caused the most severe recession in Ireland since the 1950s. Living standards declined, unemployment rose inexorably and emigration was held in check only by the severity of the recession in Britain and America. Falling unemployment in the UK and the USA in the second half of the decade triggered a resumption of large-scale emigration. (This was the period when illegal emigration by Irish people to the USA became established.) As can be seen from Figures 22.1 and 22.2 the scale of emigration led to a renewed decline in the population between 1986 and 1991.

The resumption of economic growth in Ireland towards the end of the 1980s and the boom from the mid-1990s to 2007 led to unprecedented population growth. Over the two decades from 1991 to 2011 the population increased by 30 per cent. Between 2001 and 2006 the population growth rate averaged two per cent, the highest recorded in the OECD. Surprisingly, population growth continued between 2006 and 2011 despite the resumption of emigration after 2007. By 2011 the population had reached 4.6 million, a level that was last recorded in the 1870s. Over the longer period from 1961 to 2011 the population increased by 63 per cent, proportionately the largest increase recorded in a European country over this period. However, this was still a long way short of the optimistic forecast of Pádraic Pearse made in 1916: '[In a] free Ireland, gracious and useful industries will supplement an improved agriculture, the population will expand in a century to 20 million and it may even in time go up to 30 million' (Meenan 1970).

While Pearse's concern in 1916 with reversing the long decline of the Irish population is understandable, today we are much more concerned with the average standard of living enjoyed by the population than with its size.

22.3 The Standard of Living

Economists use the phrase 'real convergence' to denote the process by which countries with initially low standards of living tend to grow more rapidly than richer countries. This leads to catching up and a narrowing of the gap between rich and poor. In the nineteenth century, latecomers like Germany and Russia industrialised much faster than Britain during its industrial revolution. More recently, formerly very poor countries like Hong Kong, Singapore and South Korea achieved spectacular growth in the 1950s and 1960s. Since the economic reforms of the 1980s, real GDP in China has been growing at almost 10 per cent a year, compared with much lower growth rates in the already-rich countries.

Real convergence is conditional on several preconditions being in place. It is most likely to occur across regions and countries with similar levels of human and physical capital and similar institutional structures. If North Korea were to abandon its protectionist and communist policies it would have access to the new technologies developed elsewhere. Since it shares a culture and values with South Korea it is to be expected that it would quickly catch up with its southern neighbour, as the former East Germany has since German reunification in 1990. Many of the world's poorest countries (especially in Africa) fell behind the emerging economies of Asia in the post-war period due to weak institutions, corruption and unsound economic policies. Recently some have profited from economic reforms and the boom in commodity prices.

Ireland provides a clear-cut example of an economy in recent decades making substantial progress towards closing the gap with the world's richest countries. Figure 22.3 shows the experience of four formerly poor EU countries (Ireland, Spain, Portugal and Greece) from 1960 to 2011. Their standard of living is measured relative to EU15 GDP per person, using PPP exchange rates (market rates adjusted for differences in internal purchasing power).

Back in the 1960s, the standard of living in all four countries was less than two-thirds of the EU average. However, as a result of accelerated growth in the 1990s, Irish living standards by 2007 were 32 percentage points above the EU average. It may be seen that Greece moved up sharply on joining the EU in 1981, but then gradually fell back. Spain made steadier progress, but not as rapid as Ireland. Portugal achieved little catch-up over the period.

It should be borne in mind, however, that these figures are based on GDP per capita, which we have repeatedly emphasised tends to overstate Irish living standards. For this reason we include in Figure 22.3 an estimate for Ireland that adjusts downward by the ratio of national income (NI) to GDP. In the early years, when the gap between GDP and NI was insignificant, the adjustment makes little difference. But as the GDP–NI gap widened, the improvement in Ireland's living standards as measured by NI per capita is less impressive than when GDP per is used. Nonetheless, even after making this adjustment Ireland was still well ahead of the EU15 average and of Spain, Portugal and Greece in 2007.

Figure 22.3 shows that all four countries suffered a decline in living standards relative to the EU15 average after 2007. The scale of the decline is surprisingly uneven, with Ireland suffering a

FIGURE 22.3 Living standards in the EU periphery, 1960–2011 (EU15 average = 100)

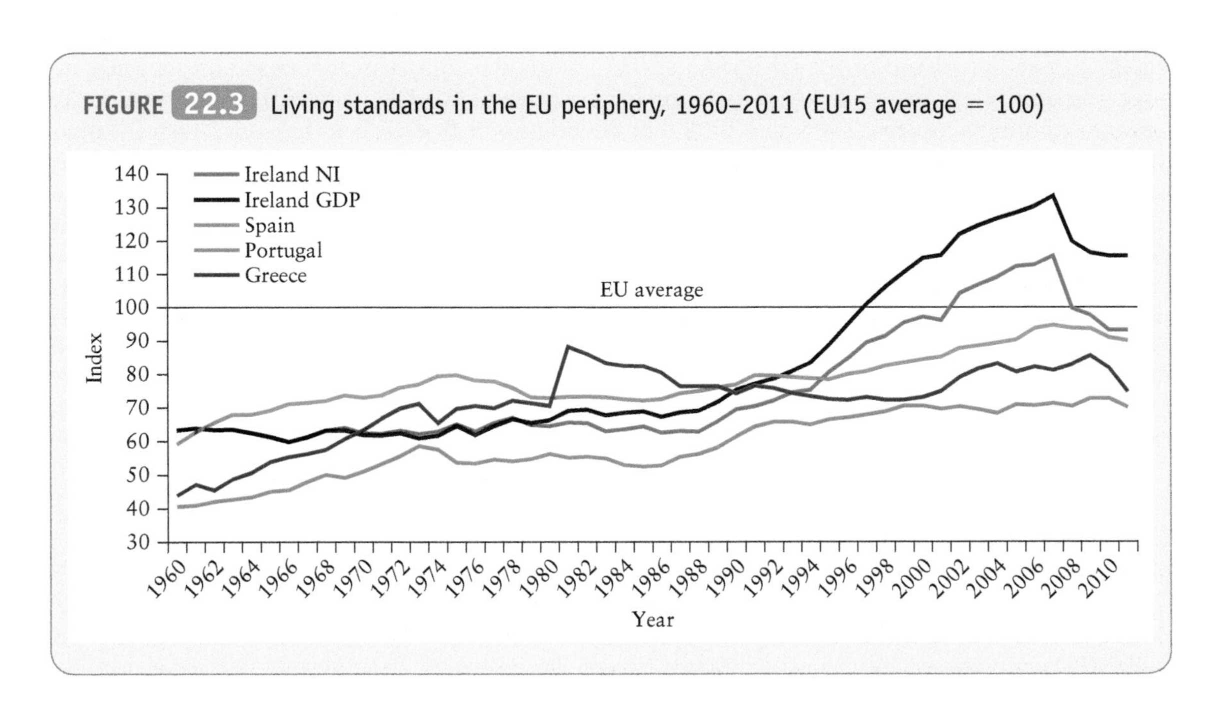

FIGURE 22.4 Irish and UK living standards, 1995–2011 (EU15 average = 100)

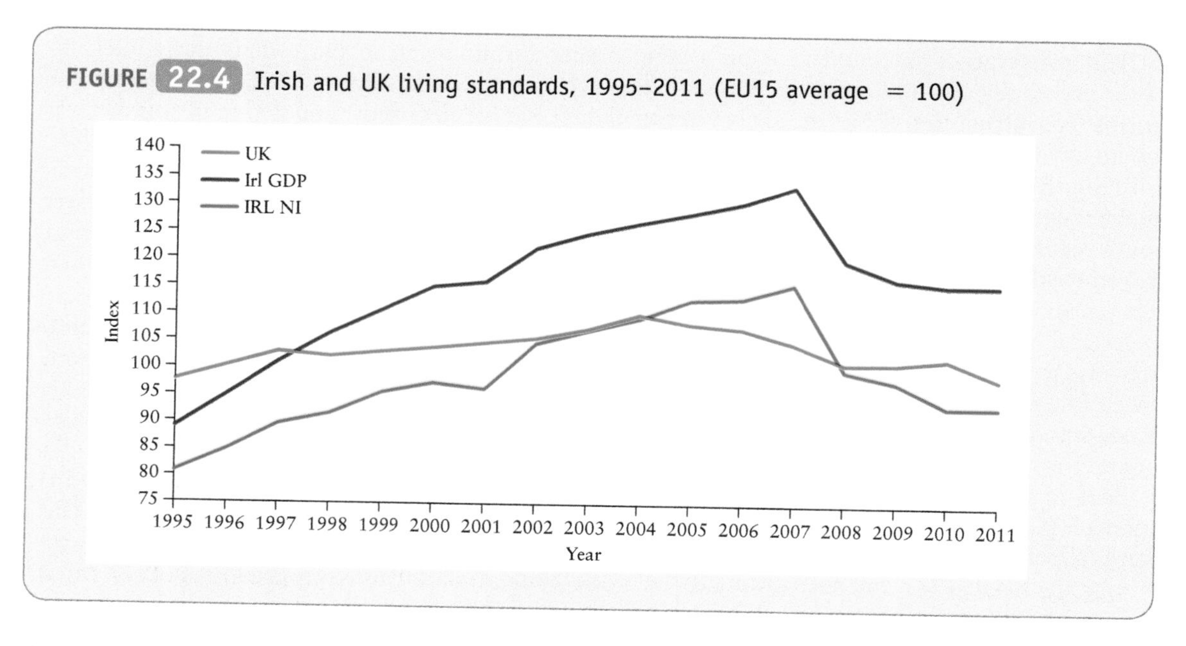

14 per cent drop from 2007 to 2011. The drop in Portugal was only 1.6 per cent, in Spain it was 4.9 per cent and in Greece it was 8.0 per cent. If we focus on the national income measure for Ireland the drop in living standards was almost 20 per cent. This implies that we are now one-fifth worse off relative to the EU15 than we were four years ago. Our standard of living has fallen below the EU15 average for the first time since 2001. However, allowance should be made for the inflation of Ireland's apparent growth by the housing boom.

Comparison with the UK is always of interest to Irish readers, so Figure 22.4 shows living standards in Ireland and the UK based on the same measure that is used in Figure 22.3. When the comparison is based on Irish GDP, it may be seen that Ireland zoomed ahead of the UK between 1998 and 2007. After 2007 the Irish relative position deteriorated somewhat, but we still remained almost 20 per cent ahead of the UK even in 2011. When the comparison is based on national income person (NI), however, the Irish performance relative to the UK is much less impressive. We drew ahead briefly between 2005 and 2008, but are now some five per cent behind. Given the margin of error in these statistics, it is safe to say that Ireland and the UK have been enjoying a similar standard of living over the past 10 years.

Perhaps the real puzzle about Ireland's long-run performance is why it took so long for this convergence process to materialise. Even though Ireland had gained some ground in the 1960s, it slipped behind again in the 1980s, and had a lot of ground to make up at the beginning of the 1990s. With a modern educational system and a favourable business environment in place, the country would have been expected to grow very rapidly once it had resolved the fiscal mess of the 1980s. And indeed this proved to be the case.

In Appendix 22.1 below we discuss catch-up theory in the context of the Solow growth model. The main point is that countries do not all converge to the same income per worker or the same standard of living over time. Savings, population growth and the availability of technology are all important influences on the level of income. Furthermore, 'catching up' is a transitional phenomenon. Once a country has caught up with the leaders and is on the frontier, its growth rate has to fall back to that of the leaders. As a rule of thumb the potential rate of growth of real GDP *per capita* in the US economy is generally seen to be in the region of two to three per cent. It is unrealistic to expect growth in Ireland to be any higher than this over the long run.

22.4 Interpreting the Record: 1922–1961

An important lesson to learn from Irish economic history is that policies matter. We do not attribute Ireland's backwardness and poor economic performance in the early years of independence to the laziness of the population, the isolation of the economy or a lack of natural resources, or even to the disruption suffered during the Rising and civil war, but mainly to bad economic policies.

Post-independence caution

During the first decade of independence, Ireland pursued basically conservative economic policies. In the monetary and financial areas, continuity with the past was maintained and no radical initiatives were launched. The government pursued a balanced budget approach to fiscal policy and the public finances were carefully managed. Although a major state monopoly, the Electricity Supply Board, and a state bank, the Agriculture Credit Corporation, were created in 1927, the role of the state in the economy remained limited. Agriculture, in which half the labour force was still engaged, was viewed as the engine of economic growth. As Kevin O'Higgins, Minister for Justice, remarked, the new government was 'the most conservative revolutionaries in history'.

Tom Garvin, in his widely read book *Preventing the Future: Why was Ireland so Poor for so Long?* (2004) argued that there was a strong anti-growth bias in the mindset of the various elites of post-independence Ireland. The Catholic Church obviously emphasised the importance of spiritual values over mere material progress, and it decried the 'pagan' influences emanating from more prosperous countries like Britain and America.

The Church was the main provider of education, ran the health system, was arbiter of social and cultural affairs and acted as censor of art and literature. It has been argued that a central aim of Church-supported government policy may have been to prevent the spread of education and modernity. Éamon de Valera's St Patrick's Day speech in 1943 gives an indication of the mood:

> *The Ireland that we dreamed of would be the home of a people who valued material wealth only as a basis for right living, of a people who, satisfied with frugal comfort, devoted their leisure to the things of the spirit – a land whose countryside would be bright with cosy homesteads, whose fields and villages would be joyous with the sounds of industry, with the romping of sturdy children, the contest of athletic youths and the laughter of happy maidens, whose firesides would be forums for the wisdom of serene old age. The home, in short, of a people living the life that God desires that men should live.*

In August 1947, under pressure from the Catholic hierarchy, the Fianna Fáil Government considered imposing a ban on the emigration of women under the age of 22 years.

As Garvin points out, even Ireland's socialists were opposed to modern economic growth. The Labour Party, as a member of the 1948–1951 inter-party government, scuppered Fianna Fáil's well-advanced plans to open air links from Shannon to New York. (The planes that had been purchased to serve on the route were sold off to a grateful British Airways, who thus avoided having to pay dollars for them.) Members of that government also opposed building motorways round Dublin on the grounds that they would be no more than 'racetracks for plutocrats'. Not until the twenty-first century did Dublin get its first motorway.

Prolonged inward orientation

From a cautious beginning during the Great Depression and the collapse of the global free trade system in the early 1930s radical and, in the long run, damaging policies were adopted. The Fianna Fáil government took office in 1932 and soon afterwards Éamon de Valera withheld land annuities due to be paid to landowners in the UK. Technically this was a sovereign debt default. It started an economic war with Britain in which both sides boycotted each others' goods. (Jonathan Swift's 1720 slogan, 'Burn everything British except their coal!', became popular again.) Settlement was reached in 1938 and it has been estimated that Ireland came well out of this piece of brinkmanship (Ó Gráda 2011).

> **NOTE:** The land annuities were part of the land purchase scheme that transferred ownership of much of Irish land from landlords to tenants in exchange for bonds. The tenants paid annuities (interest and principal repayments) to a Land Purchase Fund. The money in this fund was transferred by the Irish government to the UK government, which paid it to the bondholders (former owners of Irish estates now resident in the UK). In fact, the Irish Free State partially defaulted on part of our sovereign debt.

Foreign investment was virtually excluded through the Control of Manufactures Acts 1932–34). J. M. Keynes appeared to endorse this protectionist policy at his Finlay Lecture in University College, Dublin in 1933: 'Let goods be homespun wherever it is reasonable and conveniently possible, and, above all, let finance be primarily national.' But note the caveat, which endorsed protectionism only when it is 'reasonable and convenient'. Keynes warned that under Irish circumstances widespread protectionism would severely reduce an already low standard of living. This did not endear him to de Valera, who subsequently vetoed his appointment to the Irish Banking Commission.

High tariffs were imposed on imports to protect anyone willing to manufacture similar products in Ireland. In addition, measures were introduced to encourage the establishment of native Irish industries, as well as a more labour-intensive pattern of farming. The level of protection of Irish industry remained extremely high for the next 40 years. Even as late as 1966 the average rate of 'effective protection' of Irish manufacturing industry was almost 80 per cent, one of the highest in the western world. The hope was that infant Irish industries could grow strong in a protectionist environment and when they had matured sufficiently they would be able to compete on the international stage.

> **NOTE:** 'Effective protection' measures the extent to which a tariff allows an industry to be inefficient relative to international competitive standards and still survive.

The firms that set up behind these high tariffs were Irish owned, but in many cases what happened was that British firms went into joint ventures with Irish residents and formed subsidiaries to cater for their existing Irish markets. Due to the very small scale of this market, separate production facilities proved very inefficient. An extreme example was the car industry, where a British manufacturer in Birmingham would have to dismantle new cars coming off the assembly line, put them in special ('completely knocked-down') kits and ship them to Dublin for re-assembly. A limited number of semi-skilled jobs were created in this manner but at the cost of much higher car prices and very unreliable cars. Within 10 years of the ending of protectionism hardly any of these jobs survived.

The fact that between 1932 and 1966 the Irish economy was one of the most heavily protected in the world is probably the single most important reason for the country's relatively poor economic performance after World War II. Prolonged reliance on generalised protectionism has not proved an effective way of promoting economic development anywhere in the world. Whatever the merits of imposing tariffs on promising 'infant industries' in the early stages of industrialisation, there is no example of a country where indiscriminate protection extending over a generation resulted in a viable industrial sector.

A start was not made on dismantling tariffs until the mid-1960s. The Anglo-Irish Free Trade Area Agreement (1965) led to the elimination of tariffs between Ireland and Britain. The phased elimination of tariffs with European countries was negotiated as part of the terms of our accession to the EEC in 1973. It is hardly a coincidence that the country's relative economic performance improved dramatically as more outward-looking policies were adopted.

Excessive state involvement in the economy

Another factor that has been blamed for Ireland's poor post-independence economic performance was the excessive involvement of the state in the productive sectors of the economy. After 1932 numerous state-sponsored bodies (or 'semi-state companies') were created to fill what were regarded as gaps in the industrial structure left by private enterprise. The areas in which semi-state firms operated included electricity generation and distribution, banking, radio and later TV broadcasting, turf development, air, sea, road and rail transport, hotels, food processing, manufacturing steel and chemical fertilisers – the list is long! Most of the state-owned companies enjoyed significant monopoly power and with the passage of time became overstaffed and inefficient. They were also asked to achieve a variety of political and social objectives, which burdened them with high-cost operations.

NOTE: A sensitive example of the use of state-owned companies to further political goals was the requirement that all transatlantic flights make a stopover in Shannon Airport. This was imposed on Aer Lingus and other carriers with a view to developing the Mid-West region, even though it conflicted with the airline's commercial objectives.

By the 1970s the role of the state in the Irish economy was probably more extensive than in any other country that was not overtly socialist. The result was that private enterprise was deterred from entry to many sectors of the economy and consumers paid a high price for the inefficiencies and low standards that too often characterised state-owned companies. By the 1960s it was clear that the expansion of the role of the state in the economy since the 1930s had not succeeded in its aim of promoting the long-run development of the economy. However, the process of dismantling the state's role in many sectors proved slow and is still not complete.

The recognition of the need for change was also prompted by changes in attitude towards the economic role of the state in Britain and America. It led to the gradual introduction of deregulation and privatisation. Some state companies (Nítrigin Éireann, the Irish Life Assurance Company, Irish Steel, the Industrial Credit Corporation, the Agricultural Credit Corporation, the Irish Sugar Company, Telecom Éireann and parts of the Irish Airlines group) have been privatised. The monopoly privileges of those in areas such as access transport, inter-city bus transport, health insurance, TV and radio broadcasting, and electricity generation have been reduced.

However, despite these changes the state still plays a major role in the productive sectors of the Irish economy. The level of state ownership and regulation of the economy is probably still higher than in many of the former socialist economies of Central and Eastern Europe. We have consistently delayed implementation of EU regulations for liberalisation of civil aviation, insurance and banking. In many areas we have liberalised reluctantly, under pressure from the EU.

The level and structure of investment

In the 1950s Ireland had a relatively low savings rate. A high proportion of the funds available for investment was used by government for social overhead projects such as housing and hospital building. The result was a low rate of investment in productive infrastructure and profitable assets. In the 1970s the rate of investment rose but the government continued to control directly or indirectly an inordinate proportion of it and its productivity was low.

The British connection

Political independence did little to reduce Ireland's heavy economic dependence on Britain. As late as the 1950s, almost 90 per cent of Irish exports went to the UK and almost three-quarters of them consisted of live animals and foodstuffs. Our banking system and financial markets remained integrated with their British counterparts. With such close links to Britain it is hardly surprising that during the 1960s, 1970s and 1980s the growth rate of the Irish economy was closer to that of Britain than of the continental European countries. The relatively slow growth of the UK economy acted as a constraint on Irish economic development.

Emigration

The persistence of high emigration from 1840 to 1961 is often cited not just as a symptom of under-achievement but also as a cause of poor economic performance. As discussed in Chapter 4, this is because emigration and a declining population can have a number of adverse effects on economic development, such as depressing the size of the domestic market and siphoning off the brightest and most entrepreneurial of the young generation.

22.5 The 1960s

The reasons for the marked improvement in Ireland's economic performance after 1960 are largely the reverse of the negative factors that we listed in the previous section.

Opening up the economy

Economists agree that the most important contribution to turning the Irish economy round was the dismantling of protectionism and the return to free trade in the 1960s. By the end of the 1950s it had come to be recognised that inward-looking economic policies offered little hope of averting emigration and raising Irish living standards. The growing momentum towards free trade in Europe and the prospect of eventual entry to the EEC forced Irish policy-makers to think about opening up the economy. After 1960, successive governments were consistent in their commitment to export-led growth. The cover of *Time* magazine on 12 July 1963 showed the protectionist curtains being pulled aside by Seán Lemass and the opening up of the Irish economy to outside trade.

Industrial policy

As tariffs were dismantled in the 1960s an elaborate system of industrial grants and tax incentives was introduced. Instead of giving priority to Irish-owned firms willing to substitute for imported goods, the emphasis of policy was switched to attracting export-oriented foreign direct investment (FDI). The Industrial Development Authority (IDA) and An Forás Tionscal (which had been established in 1949 and 1952 respectively) were given this remit. These two organisations were increasingly successful in attracting foreign firms to Ireland after 1960. Initially, the incentives used to attract foreign investment included fixed asset grants, generous capital allowances and export sales tax relief. These were justified on the grounds of needing to overcome the disadvantages of locating in a 'peripheral' location like Ireland.

In the 1960s a zero rate of tax was applied to profits arising from exports and a 50 per cent corporation profit tax (CPT) on all other domestic industry. During the 1970s several other changes to the CPT laws were introduced to make Ireland more attractive for inward investment. These included a 15-year tax holiday for exporting firms, more generous depreciation allowances and an important provision that allowed total tax relief in respect of royalties and other income from licences patented in Ireland.

However, in 1981 the EU deemed Ireland's preferential treatment of exporting firms discriminatory and it was replaced with a 10 per cent profits tax on all manufacturing firms. This too eventually ran foul of the European authorities. As a response, the Minister for Finance Charlie McCreevy introduced in his 1998 Budget a uniform 12.5 per cent CPT rate. This is credited with a major role in the subsequent boom in FDI in Ireland.

Ireland's 12.5 per cent CPT rate compares favourably with the higher rates prevailing in some European countries, which are shown in Table 22.1. However, some new EU member states now have low corporation tax rates.

There is evidence that in the 1990s 'footloose' capital became more sensitive to tax differentials and more willing to seek out locations that offered higher profitability. This would help explain

TABLE 22.1 Corporation profit tax (CPT) rates, 2012

State	Corporation tax rate (%) 2012
Ireland	12.5
USA	40.0
Australia	30.0
Austria	25.0
Belgium	34.0
Denmark	25.0
Finland	24.5
France	33.3
Germany	29.4
Greece	20.0
Italy	31.4
Luxembourg	28.8
Netherlands	25.5
New Zealand	28.0
Portugal	25.0
Spain	30.0
Sweden	26.3
UK	24.0
Czech Republic	19.0
Cyprus	10.0
Estonia	21.0
Hungary	19.0
Latvia	15.0
Lithuania	15.0
Malta	35.0
Poland	19.0
Slovak Republic	19.0
Slovenia	20.0

Source: http://www.kpmg.com/global/en/whatwedo/tax/tax-tools-and-resources/pages/corporate-tax-rates-table.aspx

why the low tax rate acted as a more powerful magnet in the 1990s than in earlier decades. So successful has Ireland's policy been that it has given rise to complaints of 'unfair tax competition' and pressure to raise the CPT to the average European rate. For example, former President Sarkozy of France stated in a speech at the (loss-making) Airbus plant in Toulouse in January 2011, 'I deeply respect our Irish friends' independence and we have done everything to help them. But they cannot continue to say come and help us while keeping a tax on company profits that is half [that of other countries].'

If Ireland were to lose its low corporation tax rate, the basis on which multinational corporations operate here would be jeopardised. However, using fiscal incentives to attract firms to the country entails risks to the country's reputation. Clever tax accountants in multinational companies exploit the low tax rate in ways that were never intended. Exotic examples have surfaced in recent years. Multinationals such as Facebook, Google, Microsoft and Apple save billions of dollars every year by using a global tax strategy that involves attributing extraordinary proportions of their worldwide profits to their relatively small Irish operations.

An exotic example is known as the 'double Irish'. This uses two Irish companies and subsidiaries in offshore locations such as the Cayman Islands to minimise a company's global tax liability. Companies also shift income through the Netherlands in a technique known as the 'Dutch sandwich' in which the Netherlands acts as a stopover between Ireland and another jurisdiction. Google has reduced the effective tax rate on its global earnings to below three per cent using strategies like this (Drucker 2010).

Using Irish subsidiaries, Microsoft was able to reduce its 2011 US tax bill by $2.43 billion (€1.87 billion). A company called Microsoft Ireland Research (MIR) reported profits of $4.3 billion in 2011. This was approximately $11 million profit per employee. The effective tax rate was 7.2 per cent (*Irish Times* 22 September 2012).

A consequence of these strategies is that the profitability of some sectors of Irish manufacturing is almost literally incredible. Industries like pharmaceuticals, cola concentrates and software reproduction report value added per employee of well over €1 million. Much of the resultant profit flows back out of the country in form of 'repatriated profits' and swells the GDP–GNP gap. However, we should not lose sight of the fact that up to 12.5 per cent of these exaggerated profits are paid as taxes to the Irish exchequer. In Chapter 13 we discussed the very large proportion of our merchandise exports that are accounted for by these companies.

Among the other factors that have been said to contribute to Ireland's attractiveness for foreign investment are the following.

- *The Irish education system* produces a flow of well-educated English-speaking young workers, whose salary expectations are relatively modest. However, while Ireland is the only English-speaking country in the EMU, fluency in English is no longer the preserve of young people in English-speaking countries. Most educated young Dutch people, for example, are fluent in English and Dutch as well as in at least one other major European language. The same is true of young people in many other European countries. Due to our relatively weak performance in teaching modern European languages, we risk falling behind in being able to supply multilingual young people to high-tech and social networking companies that wish to locate in Ireland.
- *Flexible working practices.* Most of the new foreign-owned firms that have located in Ireland are not unionised. They undoubtedly enjoy more flexible working practices than prevail in the highly unionised industries in some European countries. However, inflexibility in the public sector (health and education in particular) does affect the quality and cost of public services, and on this front we have no room for complacency.
- *Ireland is part of the 'Anglo-Saxon' legal and accountancy world.* Our systems are familiar to US investors in particular. We are ahead of the USA but behind Canada and about equal with

Britain on Transparency International's Corruption Perception Index. This is reassuring for firms contemplating locating in Ireland.

- *The IDA acts as a 'one-stop shop' for inward investment.* It enables firms to progress quickly from greenfield site to operational level. Foreign firms do not get bogged down in the morass of Irish planning laws.
- *Success breeds success.* Ireland has established a reputation as a suitable location for new foreign investment. In the microelectronics area, for example, numerous computer companies (Intel, IMB, Digital, Hewlett Packard, Dell) have set up and expanded here – a clear signal to other computer companies looking for a suitable location within the EU. There is now a critical mass of workers with experience in computer-related occupations and the necessary sub-suppliers are in place. The same applies to some extent to sectors such as pharmaceuticals, high-tech food industries, medical equipment, financial services and telemarketing. In fact, success in some areas has led to problems: bottlenecks have emerged in the recruitment of skilled labour, especially in the IT sector; and the education sector has come in for increasing criticism for not producing enough highly numerate graduates capable of filling the posts that have been created by the inflow of high-tech firms in Ireland.

NOTE: The way the IDA targeted leading high-tech companies during the so-called 'Celtic Tiger' period is discussed by a former Minister of Finance (Ray MacSharry) and a former head of the IDA (Padraic White) in their 2000 book, *The Making of the Celtic Tiger Economy.*

An important feature of Irish industrial policy is that it does not involve the state either in direct participation in industry or in explicitly picking winning sectors or firms. There are also no restrictions on firms sending profits out of Ireland. Although sectors such as electronics, pharmaceuticals and medical instrumentation are undoubtedly targeted, the IDA is willing to provide similar assistance to all firms that regard Ireland as a suitable location. This contrasts with, for example, the approach taken in South Korea and Singapore, where the state has been directly involved in guiding the pattern of investment.

NOTE: While it is true that FDI accounts for most of the growth of industrial employment, output and exports, the importance of 'indigenous' Irish industry should not be overlooked. Since the 1960s a core of strong Irish firms have expanded overseas and become multinationals in their own right. Companies such as Smurfit, CRH, Ryanair, Glanbia, Kerry, Greencore and IAWS, among others, derive large and increasing proportions of their profits from their international activities. However, non-Irish investors own significant proportions of their equity and it is becoming increasingly difficult, and less relevant, to distinguish between 'Irish' and 'foreign' industries. Some of the most famous 'Irish' branded products, such as Guinness stout, the main Irish whiskeys, and Baileys Irish Cream, are owned by multinational companies.

External assistance

In 1922 the new Irish Free State was cut off from the financial support that it would eventually have enjoyed as a poorer region of the UK. This loss of support became quite significant as the welfare state was established and various regional policies implemented in the UK after World War II. Despite our neutrality during the war, we benefited from the European Recovery Programme (Marshall Aid) launched by the USA in 1949. Under this programme Ireland received low interest loans amounting to over three per cent of GNP for three years. These funds were used to finance the development of agriculture and forestry, and local authority housing and hospitals.

With the ending of Marshall Aid, however, Ireland had to rely exclusively on its own resources until it entered the EEC in 1973. Since then the country has benefited from high prices for farm products paid for through the Common Agricultural Policy (CAP) and grants from the Regional and Social Funds. During the 1980s the level of aid under the Social and Regional Funds increased significantly and in the 1990s a new Cohesion Fund was established to narrow the gap between rich and poor countries.

EU assistance is often cited as a reason for Ireland's improved economic performance since the early 1970s and, in particular, in the 1990s. Net receipts from the EU reached a peak of 3.9 per cent of GNP in 1990. The money was spent on roads and railways, telecommunications, and aid to industry, agriculture and tourism. The strategy was to strengthen the country's productive capacity by upgrading infrastructure, developing the skills of the population and encouraging local initiatives. It is now generally accepted that EU funding did raise Ireland's growth rate and led to convergence in living standards with the richer EU countries. However, it does not account for the massive growth spurt that was recorded after 1994 and up to 2007.

22.6 The Record since 1971

Figure 22.5 presents the annual growth rate in real GDP over the four decades 1971–2011. The variability of the growth rate is striking and makes it difficult to classify the periods into neat phases. Even a three-year moving average (MA) of the data is still very erratic.

However, it is clear that the Irish economy went through a prolonged and severe recession during the 1980s. Output fell, unemployment soared, inflation rose, large-scale net emigration recurred and the population fell (see Figure 22.2). Table 22.2 shows that between 1981 and 1987, the Irish economy experienced negative real growth, rising unemployment, and inflation (stagflation), a crisis in the public finances and a balance of payments deficit. This led to mass emigration and rising poverty levels. This outcome can be interpreted as largely due to an adverse supply-side shock. In terms of the model used in earlier chapters, the increase in oil prices shifted the short-run

FIGURE 22.5 Real GDP growth rate

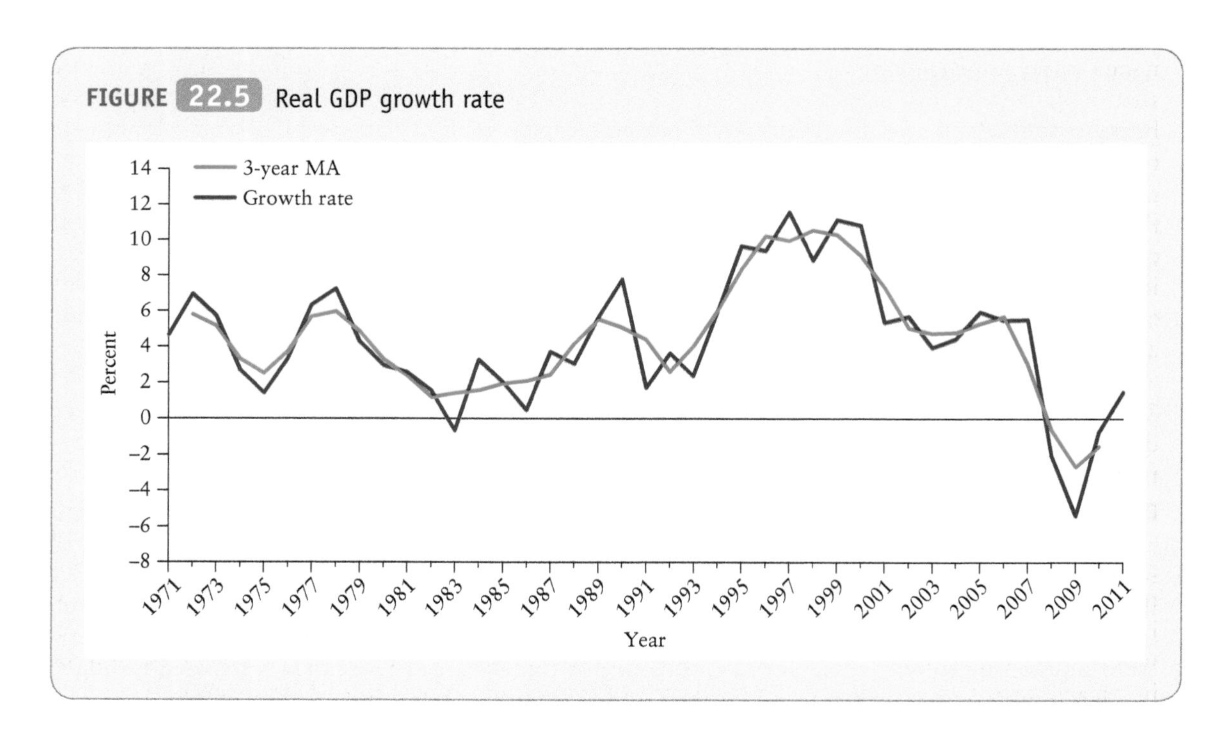

TABLE 22.2 The Irish economy in the 1980s

	1981	1982	1983	1984	1985	1986	1987
Real GDP growth rate %	2.5	1.5	−0.7	3.2	1.9	0.4	3.6
Real GNP growth rate	1.8	−1.3	−1.9	1.1	0.2	0.1	3.7
Employment annual % change	−0.9	0.0	−1.9	−1.9	−2.2	0.2	0.8
Unemployment rate	9.9	11.4	13.6	15.4	16.7	17.1	16.9
CPI inflation rate	21.0	18.9	12.5	10.1	6.2	4.6	3.4
Balance of payments (% of GNP)	−13.7	−9.9	−6.7	−6.0	−4.5	−3.4	−0.4
Current budget deficit (% of GNP)	6.7	7.2	6.9	6.4	7.4	7.3	5.9
National debt (% of GNP)	85.7	84.7	95.8	103.3	106.0	115.1	117.6

aggregate supply (SRAS) curve up to the left, resulting in an increase in inflation, a fall in real output and a balance of payments deficit.

The crisis caused by this shock was more severe and longer-lasting in Ireland than in other Western European countries. Partly to blame for this was the confused policy response. Following a period of political instability in the early 1980s, over the years 1982–1986 the coalition government tried to restore balance to the public finances largely through tax increases. A series of extremely deflationary budgets was introduced by the coalition government between 1982 and 1986, but this approach seemed doomed to failure as the economy shrank under an ever-increasing tax burden.

The Fianna Fáil government that took office in 1987, with Ray MacSharry as Minister for Finance, switched the emphasis of fiscal policy from tax increases to expenditure cuts. Aided by a strong recovery in the British economy (the 'Lawson boom') and the reduction in unemployment brought about by increased emigration from Ireland, the economy began to recover from the protracted recession. This episode is of great interest because it has been cited as an example of how an austerity programme can restore confidence, leading to a rise in investment and consumption and thus to domestic demand-led growth. As we discussed in Chapter 8, the phrase 'expansionary fiscal contraction' (EFC) was applied to this phenomenon and Ireland cited as an important example of its success. However, the evidence we discussed in Chapter 8 is not very supportive of the hypothesis. External factors such as the recovery in world trade and falling oil prices seem to have played a more important role.

As may be seen from Figure 22.5 there was a sharp recovery in economic growth in the late 1980s, with an impressive 7.7 per cent increase recorded in 1990. This was perhaps to be expected during the recovery phase after the prolonged recession of the 1980s. After a couple of years of more modest growth, the economy took off: from 1994 to 2002 the real growth rate was over five per cent a year and from 1995 to 2000 growth averaged an amazing 10.2 per cent.

As Table 22.3 shows, from 1994 to 2000 the Irish economy achieved seven years of spectacular growth, full employment, low inflation and surpluses on both the public finances and the balance of payments. Employment increased by over 46 per cent, from 1,183,100 in 1993 to 1,734,600 in 2000. It can be argued that the real 'miracle' was the extraordinary increase in the numbers at work rather than an increase in average labour productivity. A 46 per cent increase in the numbers in employment over an eight-year period raises the question: Where did all the workers come from?

TABLE 22.3 The 1994–2000 boom

	1994	1995	1996	1997	1998	1999	2000
Real GDP growth rate %	5.9	9.6	9.3	11.5	8.8	11.1	10.7
Real GNP growth rate %	7.4	8.8	7.0	9.4	6.7	7.6	9.3
Employment annual % change	3.2	5.0	3.7	3.8	9.2	6.3	5.2
Unemployment rate	14.7	12.2	11.9	10.3	7.4	5.5	4.2
CPI inflation rate	2.4	2.5	1.6	1.5	2.4	1.6	5.6
Balance of payments (% of GNP)	2.9	2.8	3.3	3.1	0.9	0.4	−0.6
Current budget deficit (% of GNP)	0.0	1.0	−0.7	−1.3	−3.9	−5.7	−7.8
National debt (% of GNP)	89.0	81.6	73.2	65.5	54.7	51.9	40.8

There were three key sources: the fall in unemployment, the increase in the labour force participation rate (LFPR) and the change from net emigration to net immigration.

There is little doubt that the performance of the Irish economy over this period was exceptional. As one economist commented: 'The performance of Irish productivity and Irish employment since the mid-1980s is very impressive. I do not know the rules by which miracles are officially defined, but this seems to come close' (Blanchard 2002).

The image of Ireland abroad changed radically as our economic performance improved. The phase 'Celtic Tiger' was coined in the mid-1990s by Kevin Gardiner in a Morgan Stanley report. He compared Ireland's growth with that of the successful economies of East Asia such as Singapore, Malaysia and Thailand, where tigers do exist outside the zoos! It has been suggested that a more appropriate label for the Irish record would be the 'Irish hare'.

Many factors have been cited to explain the improvement in Irish economic performance after the 1980s. First, as mentioned earlier in this chapter, there was a strong component of 'catch-up' in Ireland's rapid growth over these years. Having lagged behind neighbouring economies for so long, it can be argued that once obstacles were removed and preconditions in place, the economy should almost inevitably have caught up. By the early 1990s, we had removed many of the obstacles to development listed earlier in this chapter to explain why Ireland had performed so badly in the earlier decades of independence. Perhaps most important, the remnants of protectionism disappeared with the completion of the EU internal market. This, combined with the low CPT rate, made Ireland an attractive export platform for US firms seeking to penetrate the large European markets.

Second, while it may not have been the catalyst that believers in the expansionary fiscal contraction give credence to, the painful fiscal correction that halted the upward spiral of debt and taxation of the 1980s did restore confidence in Ireland's economic future.

We have already mentioned the role played by industrial policy in Ireland's long-term performance. The improved performance of the 1990s owes much to the increased success of the IDA in attracting firms in sectors such as information technology and pharmaceuticals to Ireland.

There is less agreement on whether the return to centralised wage bargaining in the late 1980s made a lasting contribution to Ireland's economic performance. The strategy was to get the 'social partners' (employers, trade unions and government) to negotiate a single, centralised agreement setting out guidelines for pay increases over a two- or three-year period.

A feature of these agreements was that in return for moderate nominal wage demands the government held out the prospect of a reduction in income taxation, improvements in social benefits and a variety of other measures that became more inclusive as time went on. There was a dramatic fall in the level of strike activity during the early years of centralised wage bargaining. However, with the passage of time these agreements became less successful in containing cost competitiveness.

It could be argued that the economic measures taken in preparation for membership of EMU contributed to the success of the economy during the period from the end of the 1980s to 1999. The commitment to participate in EMU helped the government's anti-inflation policy stance. However, notwithstanding our success in lowering inflation, immediately prior to joining EMU Ireland lowered the exchange rate of the Irish pound to a level that made the economy very competitive. The convergence of Irish interest rates to the lower level prevailing in Germany following our entry to EMU stimulated the demand side of the economy by increasing investment and consumer expenditure.

However, the impact of EMU membership on Ireland's performance over the long run has been much less benign than it was in the early years. The exaggerated claims about the trade-creating effects of the currency union did not materialise. Our trade remained exceptionally concentrated (by EMU standards) on the UK and the USA. The fears that the 'one size fits all' monetary policy of the euro area would prove damaging to the Irish economy proved not unfounded. The monetary policy of the ECB was too lax for Ireland during the boom years from 1999 to 2007, and since 2008 it has been too restrictive. It is widely believed that the absence of an independent currency and exchange rate policy has made adjustment to the current recession more difficult.

When evaluating Ireland's exceptional growth record in the early years of this century we should bear in mind that the smallness and openness of the economy make it resemble a region within a larger country. Booming regions within larger counties are not an uncommon phenomenon. In the United States the examples of the Dallas–Fort Worth region of Texas and the Silicon Valley region of California can be cited. As in Ireland in the early years of this century, these booming regions provide a favourable climate for business, and draw in capital and educated workers from outside. They can thus grow much faster than the countries of which they form a part.

In the early years of this century, Ireland drew in workers at an exceptional rate from Eastern Europe and capital from the USA, and combined the two to produce some startlingly high growth rates. When the recession hit, the inflow of workers turned into a net outflow, but the inflow of capital and investment has been maintained. It remains to be seen whether the factors we have discussed in this section will in the long run sustain a high growth in Ireland when the current cyclical downturn is over.

To summarise, the list of factors that can be invoked to account for the dramatic improvement in Ireland's economic fortunes since the late 1980s is long. The starting point at the end of a long recession and a decade of underperformance left plenty of resources available to be mobilised for rapid economic growth. A combination of favourable external developments, the stimulus of lower interest rates, and a substantial inflow of capital and labour all combined to lift the growth rate. At least until the early years of the present century the economy enjoyed a combination of rapid growth in living standards, falling unemployment, low inflation and virtuous public finances. This was a unique phase in Irish economic history.

22.7 A Theoretical Framework

Economic data relating to the key macroeconomic variables are given in Table 22.3. In this section we apply the model introduced in Chapter 16 to give a stylised representation of the Irish boom.

The supply side

In Figure 22.6 we show large rightward shifts of both the long-run aggregate supply (LRAS) and the short-run aggregate supply (SRAS) curves. This came about through:

1. An increase in the supply of labour. The two main factors contributing to this were the increase in the labour force participation rate of the working-age population and the change from net emigration to large-scale net immigration.
2. An increase in physical and human capital and in the available technology. The factors behind this were increased investment in education and training and the arrival of several high-tech multinational companies to the country.

FIGURE 22.6 A stylised view of the Irish economy in the 1990s

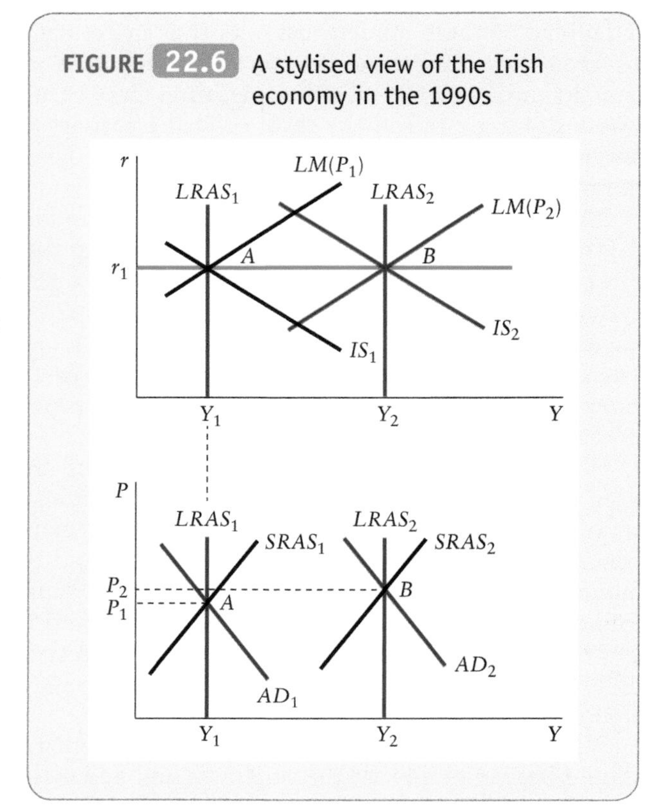

The demand side

The balance of payments current account surplus over much of the 1990s suggests that the accelerated growth was export-led. The factors that contributed to the growth of exports included the exports of the multinational companies, the upturn in the world economy and the Central Bank's competitive exchange rate policy.

In the absence of a significant rise in exports, rapid economic growth would have been accompanied by a deteriorating current account as imports were sucked in to feed a consumption boom.

In Figure 22.6 the rise in net exports is shown as a shift of the I-S curve upwards to the right in the upper quadrant. This leads to a current account surplus.

We can think of the economy as now entering a virtuous circle, as higher growth reduces the government's budget deficit and the debt/GNP ratio. This, in turn, facilitates reductions in tax rates that boost personal consumption spending.

At the end of the 1990s the real interest rate fell due to the anticipated EMU entry. This would be depicted as a downward shift in the horizontal interest rate line in the upper quadrant in Figure 22.6. This increases the level of interest-sensitive spending by businesses and households. The private sector savings ratio fell over the boom period.

The inflation rate remained at or around two per cent until 2000, when it rose to 5.6 per cent. This indicates that by the end of the century, following EMU entry and a switch to a new interest rate and exchange rate regime, the economy was tending to overheat. Capacity constraints were becoming binding in the labour market in particular.

Higher inflation would be expected to reduce the real money supply. We would depict this as shifting the L-M curve to the left in the upper quadrant of Figure 22.6 (not shown). However, by the early years of the new century financial institutions could access virtually unlimited finance from the inter-bank market. The nominal interest rate was determined exogenously and any excess demand for money could be satisfied by borrowing on the inter-bank market. The inflow of money would offset the leftward shift in the LM curve.

Under these assumptions the model fits the facts: large increases in aggregate demand and supply result in a significant increase in the level of real output.

It is possible, therefore, to fit the Irish experience during the boom years into the model discussed in Chapter 16.

22.8 The Property and Construction Bubble: 2001–2007

Table 22.4 shows the economic outcome of the property and construction boom between 2001 and 2007. The Irish economy was hit by several adverse shocks at the start of the new century. These included:

1. a downturn in the US and European economies
2. a fall in world equity markets
3. the local foot and mouth crisis
4. the 11 September terrorist attack (9/11)
5. the bursting of the dot.com bubble
6. higher oil and commodity prices.

As may be seen from Figure 22.5 (above) and Table 22.4, the real growth rate fell from over 10 per cent in 2000 to a low of two per cent in 2002. It can be seen that the downturn of 2001 was relatively short-lived and by 2003 the real growth rate was back to 5.2 per cent. The recovery surprised those who believed that the sharp fall in the growth rate in 2002 was the beginning of a period of lower growth for the economy. In 2004 *The Economist* described the return to higher growth as the 'Luck of the Irish'.

From 2003 to 2007 the growth rate remained in the four to six per cent range – high by European standards. Employment grew rapidly and net immigration reached unprecedented rates. The public finances were in good order with budget surpluses and a declining debt/GNP ratio, which reached a low of 22.3 per cent in 2006. Inflation, which was well above the euro area's average in 2002 and 2003, fell to the average from 2004 to 2008. The current account went from being balanced in 2003 to a deficit of over five per cent of GDP in 2007, but this was not deemed of great significance for a country that was in a currency union.

The nature of the growth after 2002 was fundamentally different from what had gone before. Whereas previously the growth had been led by exports, it became increasingly concentrated in non-traded services and especially in construction. The construction sector's share of total employment grew from just over 10 per cent in 2002 to close to 14 per cent in mid-2007 (Figure 22.7).

TABLE 22.4 The property and construction bubble, 2001–2007

	2001	2002	2003	2004	2005	2006	2007
Real GDP growth rate %	5.3	5.6	3.9	4.4	5.9	5.4	5.4
Real GNP growth rate %	3.1	2.0	4.9	4.0	5.8	6.4	4.2
Employment annual % change	3.0	2.3	1.7	3.7	4.9	4.4	3.6
Unemployment rate	3.9	4.4	4.6	4.5	4.4	4.5	4.6
CPI inflation rate	4.9	4.6	3.5	2.2	2.5	4.0	4.9
Balance of payments (% of GNP)	−1.5	−2.0	0.0	−0.7	−4.1	−4.1	−6.2
Current budget deficit (% of GNP)	−4.8	−5.1	−3.7	−4.4	−4.6	−5.9	−4.3
National debt (% of GNP)	36.9	34.1	31.8	29.9	27.7	23.3	23.1

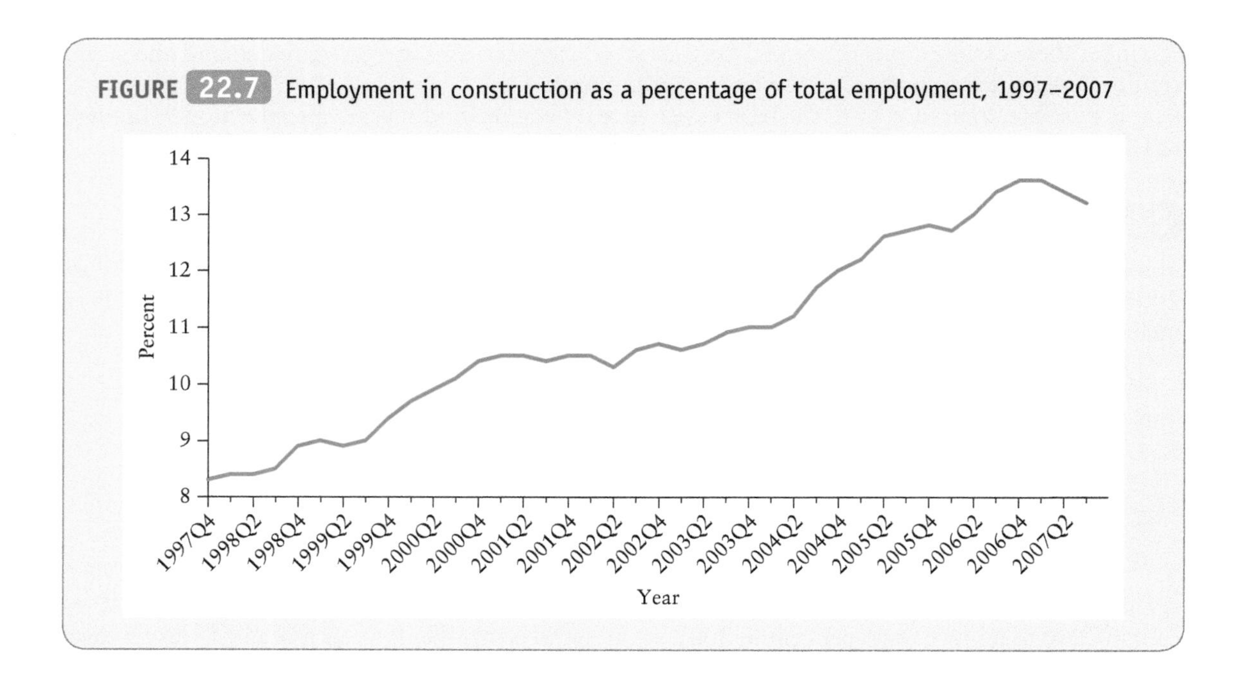

FIGURE 22.7 Employment in construction as a percentage of total employment, 1997–2007

Mainly due to the rise in the euro on the foreign exchange markets between September 2000 and April 2008, Ireland's real exchange rate appreciated 55 per cent against the UK, 97 per cent against the USA and 40 per cent on a real effective exchange rate basis. This undoubtedly contributed to the deterioration in the current account of the balance of payments.

The ECB cut its interest rate from 4.75 per cent in May 2001 to 3.25 per cent in November 2001 to two per cent in June 2003. The rate stayed at this level until it was raised to 2.25 per cent in December 2005. Aided by weak regulation and an unlimited supply of inter-bank credit, the result was negative real interest rates and a property and construction boom. Between 2002 and 2007 the growth rate was increasingly driven by investment in building and construction and the demand for non-traded services. These offset the fall in net exports. The economy looked healthy, with a high growth rate, low unemployment and a balanced budget. However, when the property bubble finally burst in 2008 the economy was exceptionally vulnerable due to a loss of price competitiveness, the bloated construction sector, the seriously flawed banking system and the dependence of government on property-related tax revenues.

22.9 The Great Recession and its Aftermath

The extent of the collapse in the Irish economy after 2007 can be seen from Figure 22.3 and the data in Table 22.5. In 2009 GDP fell by 5.5 per cent, GNP by 8.1. These were the worst figures ever recorded in modern times. By 2011 the unemployment rate was over 14 per cent, where it has remained throughout 2012. The data in Figure 22.3 show that Ireland's living standards declined by almost 20 per cent between 2007 and 2011. Our fiscal crisis is the worst in the euro area. Locked in a monetary union with an exogenous interest rate and exchange rate, and pursuing an unavoidable austerity programme, the outlook is for a slow return to full employment.

The Mundell–Fleming model (Chapter 16) and the savings and investment model (Chapter 20) suggested that recession leads to a fall in the price level, which reduces the real exchange rate and this, in turn, increases net exports. Eventually the economy reverts back to the LRAS line and the output gap is eliminated.

TABLE 22.5 The Great Recession, 2008–2013

	2008	2009	2010	2011	2012F	2013F
Real GDP growth rate	−2.1	−5.5	−0.8	1.4	0.7	1.9
Real GNP growth rate	−2.8	−8.1	0.8	−2.5	−0.3	0.9
Employment annual % change	−1.1	−8.2	−4.2	−2.1	−0.8	0.3
Unemployment rate	6.3	11.8	13.6	14.4	14.7	14.4
CPI inflation rate	4.1	−4.5	−1.0	2.6	0.9	0.4
Balance of payments (% of GNP)	−6.6	−2.8	1.4	1.4	3.3	4.8
Current budget deficit (% of GNP)	2.0	8.7	10.5	9.4	8.1	NA
National debt (% of GNP)	44.2	65.1	92.5	108.2	117.5	120.3

In these open economy models it is the real exchange rate that acts as the key adjustment mechanism. However, since the Irish real exchange is now predominately determined by movements of the nominal euro exchange rate, recovery is in the lap of the gods. A favourable depreciation of the euro exchange rate could facilitate an export-led recovery. But, equally, an appreciation of the euro exchange rate could result in prolonged recession. It may or may not help matters if the Irish government announced targets for inflation and the real effective exchange rate. The stark reality is that Ireland, in EMU, is now even less master of its own economic destiny than it was in the past.

22.10 Key Terms and Concepts

In this chapter we discussed:

- the long-run economic performance of the economy as measured by the trends in population and emigration
- the idea of real economic convergence
- the role of protectionism, state involvement in industry, reliance on the UK economy, and emigration as a brake on economic development up to the 1960s
- the factors that contributed to the improved economic performance after 1960 (the opening up of the economy to international trade and investment, increased investment in education, and fiscal prudence)
- the factors that contributed to exceptional growth in the 1990s and the early twenty-first century
- the Irish property and construction bubble
- the Great Recession after 2007.

Appendix 22.1 Catch-up in the Solow Growth Model

The Solow model starts with the supply side of the economy and the production function (Solow 1956):

$$Y = F(K,L) \tag{1}$$

For simplicity, technological progress, natural resources and other factors of production are omitted. Assuming constant returns to scale, we can divide both output (Y) and inputs, capital (K) and (L) by L:

$$Y/L = F(K/L, 1) \tag{2}$$

Using lower case letters to denote 'per worker':

$$y = f(k) \tag{3}$$

That is, output per worker is a function of capital per worker. In a closed economy model there are no net exports or government sector. This assumption can easily be relaxed and does not affect the main conclusions.

On the demand side of the economy, total expenditure is made up of consumer expenditure and investment. In equilibrium, output equals total expenditure:

$$Y = C + I \tag{4}$$

or, in per worker terms (that is, dividing equation (4) through by L):

$$y = c + i \tag{5}$$

Savings per worker (s) is a function of income per worker (note that 'income' and 'output' are used interchangeably):

$$s = \alpha y \tag{6}$$

where α is a coefficient representing the marginal propensity to save. Consumer spending is equal to income minus savings:

$$c = y - s \tag{7}$$

Substitute (6) into (7) and rearrange:

$$c = (1 - \alpha)y \tag{8}$$

Substitute (8) into (5):

$$y = (1 - \alpha)y + i \tag{9}$$

or:

$$i = \alpha y = s \tag{10}$$

From equation (3) above, $y = f(k)$:

$$i = \alpha f(k) = s = \alpha y \tag{11}$$

That is, investment per worker is a function of capital per worker, which in turn is equal to savings per worker. Savings per worker is also related, via the marginal propensity to save, to income per worker.

In this model, although not explicitly specified, the real interest rate adjusts in the background to ensure that the loanable funds market is always in equilibrium (see Chapter 20). This means that investment always equals savings.

Figures 22.8 and 22.9 illustrate the relationship between k, y, c and i. Figure 22.8 depicts the production function (see Chapter 4 for further discussion). This shows the relationship between the capital stock, k_1, on the horizontal axis and output, y, on the vertical axis. The slope of the curve is determined by the assumption of diminishing returns. As more and more capital is combined with a fixed amount of labour, diminishing returns sets in.

In Figure 22.9, the curve labelled $\alpha f(k)$ represents savings or investment as $i = s = \alpha f(k)$. An increase in savings will shift this curve upwards and a decrease in savings will move the curve downwards. The difference between savings and income equals consumption. In the diagram, k_1 determines y_1 and y_1, in turn, is equal to c_1 plus i_1.

Reverting back to the supply side of the model, a change in the capital stock is equal to investment minus depreciation.

$$\Delta k = i - \text{Depreciation} \qquad (12)$$

Depreciation, in turn, equals δk. That is, if δ equals 10 per cent, the capital stock depreciates by this amount each year. Hence:

$$\Delta k = i - \delta k \qquad (13)$$

Since i equals $\alpha f(k)$, this becomes:

$$\Delta k = \alpha f(k) - \delta k \qquad (14)$$

FIGURE 22.8 Output, consumption and savings

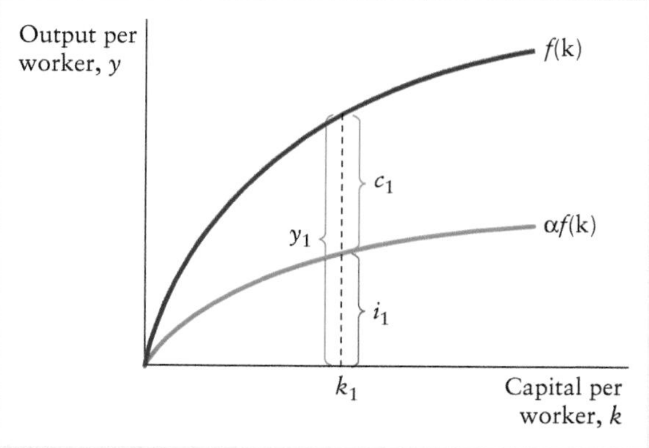

This is the *equation of motion* in the Solow model. This equation determines the behaviour of capital over time. Capital, in turn, determines the behaviour of all the other variables, output and consumption, because they all depend on capital. To see this, recall from above that $y = \alpha f(k)$ and $c = (1 - \alpha)y$ or $c = (1 - \alpha)f(k)$.

The *steady state* is defined as a point when there is no change in the stock of capital. That is, when $\Delta k = 0$. From equation (14) this occurs when investment equals the rate of depreciation. This level of investment is called 'break-even investment'.

$$\Delta k = \alpha f(k) - \delta k = 0 \qquad (15)$$

Or when:

$$\alpha f(k) = \delta k \qquad (16)$$

Alternatively:

$$i = s = \alpha f(k) - \delta k \qquad (17)$$

We now denote k* as the 'steady state' stock of capital, illustrated in Figure 22.9. With both investment and depreciation measured along the vertical axis, the depreciation line is uniform and upward sloping. This is because depreciation is a fixed proportion of capital. On the other hand, the investment schedule reflects the assumption of diminishing returns. Output or income diminishes as more and more capital is applied to a fixed amount of labour and so too do consumption and savings. At the point A in the diagram, investment equals depreciation and k* represents the steady state capital stock.

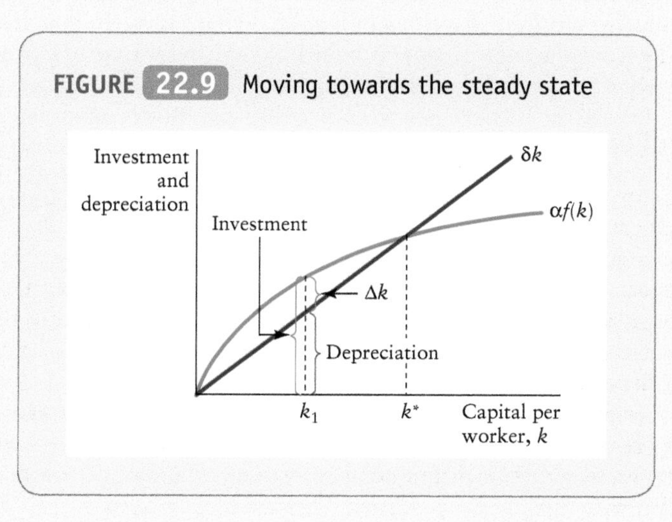

FIGURE 22.9 Moving towards the steady state

The next step is to demonstrate that as long as *actual* k is less than k*, the capital stock will continue to grow until the economy arrives at k*. This is because if k < k*:

$$\alpha f(k) > \delta k$$

and k will increase towards k*. Consider again Figure 22.9 where k_1 is to the left of k*. It is evident from the diagram that investment is greater than depreciation and that Δk is positive. In the next period the stock of capital will increase by Δk and the convergence towards k* commences. Eventually, k equals k*, investment equals depreciation and we arrive at the steady state stock of capital.

Conversely, suppose that actual k is to the right of k*. That is, k > k*. It is again evident from the diagram that depreciation exceeds investment:

$$\alpha f(k) < \delta k$$

The change in actual capital, Δk, is now negative and, in the next period, k will decrease towards k*. Hence there is a natural tendency for the economy to converge to the steady state stock of capital.

This is the basis of catch-up theory. If two economies have the same economic characteristics they should converge to the same steady state. However, note that the location of the investment or savings curve, $\alpha f(k)$, is determined by the level of savings. An increase in the savings rate leads to an increase in investment. This is because the real interest rate adjusts in the loanable funds market to ensure that this is the case. Starting from a steady state stock of capital, k*, in Figure 22.9, the increase in investment shifts the savings curve upwards (not shown). As investment is now greater than depreciation, $i = \alpha f(k) > \delta k$. Δk is positive and k will increase in the next period. A new, higher, steady state will be established at a point where investment equals depreciation and actual k will graduate towards this point.

This means that the savings rate is a key determinant of the steady state capital stock. If two countries have different savings rates they will also have different steady states k*. As previously mentioned, higher k* means also higher income per worker. Hence, we expect to find that countries with relatively high savings and investment also have relatively higher levels of income per worker.

The analysis can be extended to include the public sector. An increase in either private sector or public sector savings will, according to the Solow model, result in higher income per worker. This is clearly another reason why governments should minimise budget deficits.

Other factors affecting the steady state, k*, include population growth and the technology available to workers. Investment can be defined to include investment in human capital (i.e. education). This means that countries could have different steady states, k*, depending on their savings rate, growth in population and technology. The result is that economies do not all converge, or catch up, to the same income per worker over time. But conditional on other factors being equal, economies will tend to converge to a similar level of real income.

References

Barro, Robert (1974) 'Are Government Bonds Net Wealth?', *Journal of Political Economy* 82(6), 1095–117.

— (2010) 'The Folly of Subsidizing Unemployment', *Wall Street Journal* 30 August <http://online.wsj.com/article/SB10001424052748703959704575454431457720188.html>.

Bénétrix, Agustín S. and Lane, Philip R. (2011) 'The Cyclical Conduct of Irish Fiscal Policy', Trinity College, Dublin, IIIS Discussion Paper 374, September.

Blanchard, Olivier (2002) 'Comment on "Catching up with the Leaders: The Irish Hare", by Patrick Honohan and Brendan Walsh', *Brookings Papers on Economic Activity* No. 1, April, 79ff.

Bradley, John and Whelan, Karl (1997) 'The Irish Expansionary Fiscal Contraction: A Tale from One Small European Economy', *Economic Modelling* 14(2), April, 175ff.

Chen, Ruo, Milese-Ferretti, Gian-Maria and Tressel, Thierry (2012) 'External Balances in the Euro Area', IMF Working Paper WP/12/236, September.

Department of the Taoiseach (2008) *Building Ireland's Smart Economy: A Framework for Sustainable Economic Renewal.* Dublin: Stationery Office<www.taoiseach.gov.ie/attached_files/BuildingIrelandsSmartEconomy.pdf>.

Drucker, Jesse (2010) 'Google 2.4% Tax Rate Shows How $60 Billion Lost to Tax Loopholes', Bloomberg.com, 21 October <www.bloomberg.com/news/2010-10-21/google-2-4-rate-shows-how-60-billion-u-s-revenue-lost-to-tax-loopholes.html>.

Easterlin, Richard (1974) 'Does Economic Growth Improve the Human Lot?' in Paul A. David and Melvin W. Reder (eds) *Nations and Households in Economic Growth: Essays in Honor of Moses Abramovitz.* New York: Academic Press.

The Economist (2011) 'One Size Fits None', 14 June <www.economist.com/blogs/freeexchange/2011/06/europes-europe-crisis>.

Einzig, P. (1966) *Primitive Money* (2nd edn). New York: Pergamon.

FitzGerald, John and Kearney, Ide (2011) 'Irish Government Debt and Implied Debt Dynamics: 2011–2015', *Quarterly Economic Commentary*, Autumn.

Fleming, J. M. (1962) 'Domestic Financial Policies under Fixed and Floating Exchange Rates', *IMF Staff Papers* 9.

Friedman, Milton (1957) *A Theory of the Consumption Function.* Princeton University Press.

Friedman, Milton and Schwartz, Anna Jacobson (1963) *A Monetary History of the United States: 1867–1960.* Princeton University Press.

Garvin, Tom (2004) *Preventing the Future: Why was Ireland so Poor for so Long?* Dublin: Gill & Macmillan.

Giavazzi, Francesco and Pagano, Marco (1990) 'Can Severe Fiscal Contractions be Expansionary? Tales of Two Small European Countries', *NBER Macroeconomics Annual* 5, 75–111.

Gordon, Robert J. (2011) 'The History of the Phillips Curve: Consensus and Bifurcation', *Economica,* 78, 10–50.

Hicks, John R. (1937) 'Mr Keynes and the Classics: A Suggested Interpretation', *Econometrica* 6, April.

Honohan, Patrick (1994) 'Currency Board or Central Bank? Lessons from the Irish Pound's Link with Sterling, 1928–79', Centre for Economic Policy Research Discussion Paper 1040.

— (2010) 'The Irish Banking Crisis, Regulatory and Financial Stability Policy 2003–2008: A Report to the Minister for Finance by the Governor of the Central Bank'. Government Publications <www.bankinginquiry.gov.ie/The%20Irish%20Banking%20Crisis%20Regulatory%20and%20Financial%20Stability%20Policy%202003-2008.pdf>.

Humphrey, Thomas M. (1989) 'Lender of Last Resort: The Concept in History', *Federal Reserve Bank of Richmond Economic Review*, March/April, 8–16.

Kearney, Ide (2012) 'Measuring the Fiscal Stance 2009–2012', *Quarterly Economic Commentary*, Autumn <www.esri.ie/UserFiles/publications/QEC2012AUT_SA_Kearney.pdf>.

Kelly, Elish, McGuinness, Seamus and O'Connell, Philip (2008) 'Benchmarking, Social Partnership and Higher Remuneration: Wage Settling Institutions and the Public–Private Sector Wage Gap in Ireland' Economic and Social Research Institute Working Paper 270, December.

Keynes, John Maynard (1919) *The Economic Consequences of the Peace.*

— (1923) *A Tract on Monetary Reform.*

— (1931) 'The End of the Gold Standard' in Rupert Hart-Davis (ed.) *Essays in Persuasion*. London.

— (1933) 'National Self-Sufficiency', the first Finlay Lecture at University College, Dublin, reprinted in *Studies*, June.

— (1936) *The General Theory of Employment, Interest and Money.*

Kindleberger, Charles P. (1978) *Manias, Panics, and Crashes: A History of Financial Crises*. Wiley Investment Classics.

Layard, Richard G., Nickell, Stephen J. and Jackman, Richard A. (1991) *Unemployment: Macroeconomic Performance and the Labour Market.* Oxford University Press.

Lee, J. J. (1989) *Ireland 1912–1985: Politics and Society*. Cambridge University Press.

Lipsey, Richard G. (1975) *An Introduction to Positive Economics* (4th edn). Weidenfeld & Nicolson.

MacSharry, Ray and White, Padraic (2000) *The Making of the Celtic Tiger Economy: The Inside Story of Ireland's Boom Economy*. Cork: Mercier Press.

Mankiw, N. Gregory (2012) *Macroeconomics* (8th edn). New York: Worth Palgrave Macmillan.

Meenan, James (1980) *George O'Brien: A Biographical Memoir*. Dublin: Gill & Macmillan.

Meenan, J. F. (1970) *The Irish Economy since 1922.* Liverpool University Press.

Modigliani, Franco and Brumberg, Richard (1954) 'Utility Analysis and the Consumption Function' in K. Kurihara (ed.) *Post-Keynesian Economics*. New Brunswick, NJ: Rutgers University Press.

Mundell, R. A. (1962) 'The Appropriate Use of Monetary and Fiscal Policy Under Fixed Exchange Rates', *IMF Staff Papers* 9.

Murphy, Anthony and Walsh, Brendan (1996) 'The Incidence of Male Non-employment in Ireland', *Economic and Social Review* 25(5), 467–90.

Murphy, Antoin (1986) *Richard Cantillon: Entrepreneur and Economist* (reprinted 1989). Oxford University Press.

Nolan, Mark C. (2012) 'Keynes's View on Self-sufficiency', letter to the *Irish Times*, 7 August.

O'Brien, Derry (2010) 'Measuring Ireland's Price and Labour Cost Competitiveness', Central Bank of Ireland *Quarterly Bulletin* Q1.

O'Brien, Ken (1989) 'Anatomy of a "Scoop"', *Finance*, March.

Ó Gráda, Cormac (1994) *Ireland 1780–1939: A New Economic History*. Oxford University Press.

— (2011) 'Five Crises'. Central Bank Whitaker Lecture, Royal College of Surgeons, Dublin, 29 June <www.centralbank.ie/press-area/speeches/Pages/AddressbyProfessorCormacO'Gr%C3%A1da,oftheSchoolofEconomics,UCD,totheCentralBankWhitakerLecture,29June,2011.aspx>.

O'Kelly, Eoin (1959) *The Old Private Banks and Bankers of Munster*. Cork University Press.

Phillips, A. W. H. (1958) 'The Relation Between Unemployment and the Rate of Change of Money Wages in the United Kingdom, 1861–1957', *Economica* 25, November.

Regling, Klaus and Watson, Max (2010) 'A Preliminary Report on the Sources of Ireland's Banking Crisis'. Government Publications <http://www.bankinginquiry.gov.ie/Preliminary%20Report%20into%20Ireland%27s%20Banking%20Crisis%2031%20May%202010.pdf>.

Reinhart, Carmen M. and Rogoff, Kenneth S. (2009) *This Time is Different: Eight Centuries of Financial Folly*. Princeton University Press.

Rose, Andrew K. (2000) 'One Money, One Market: Estimating the Effect of Common Currencies on Trade', *Economic Policy* 30, 7–46.

Skidelsky, Robert (2000) *John Maynard Keynes: Fighting for Britain, 1937–1946*. London: Macmillan.

Smith, Adam (1776) *The Wealth of Nations.*

Solow, Robert M. (1956) 'A Contribution to the Theory of Economic Growth', *Quarterly Journal of Economics*, 70 (1), February.

— (1986) 'Unemployment: Getting the Questions Right', *Economica* Supplement S54.

Thom, Rodney and Walsh, Brendan (2002) 'The Effect of a Common Currency on Trade: Ireland Before and After the Sterling Link', *European Economic Review* 46(6), 1111–23.

Walsh, Brendan (2012) 'Adjusting to the Crisis: Well-being and Economic Conditions in Ireland', *International Journal of Happiness and Development* (forthcoming).

Walsh, Brendan and Walsh, Dermot (2011) 'Suicide in Ireland: The Influence of Alcohol and Unemployment', *Economic and Social Review* 42, 27–47.

Whelan, Karl (2011) 'Professor Sinn Misses the Target', *Vox* 9 June www.voxeu.org/article/there-hidden-eurozone-bailout.

Williams, D. and Reid, R. (1997) 'A Central Bank for Europe' in P. Temperton (ed.) *The Euro*. John Wiley & Sons.

Index

Page numbers in ***bold italic*** indicate figures and diagrams, etc.

C

N

O

P

Q

R

S

T

U